The Evolution of International Human Rights

Visions Seen

THIRD EDITION

Paul Gordon Lauren

PENN

University of Pennsylvania Press

Philadelphia

Published by
University of Pennsylvania Press
Philadelphia, Pennsylvania 19104-4012
www.upenn.edu/pennpress

Printed in the United States of America on acid-free paper
10 9 8 7 6 5 4 3 2 1

Library of Congress Cataloging-in-Publication Data

Lauren, Paul Gordon.
  The evolution of international human rights : visions seen / Paul Gordon Lauren.—3rd ed.
    p.   cm.— (Pennsylvania studies in human rights)
  Includes bibliographical references and index.
  ISBN 978-0-8122-2138-1 (hardcover : alk. paper)
  1. Human rights.   I. Title.
JC571.L285   2011
323—dc22   2010017606

to my teachers

Contents

Acknowledgments

One of the most enjoyable pleasures for any author is the opportunity that publication provides to acknowledge the generosity, assistance, and insights shared by others along the way. Many individuals and institutions in many places around the world contributed much to this book, and I am delighted to express my sincere appreciation to:

Herman Burgers, a rare individual of deep conviction and wide experience in the field of international human rights, for first challenging me to write this book and then graciously providing penetrating comments and helpful assistance along the way.

Bert Lockwood, Jr., the insightful, energetic, and creative editor of *Human Rights Quarterly* and the Pennsylvania Studies on Human Rights, for first inviting me to write this book and giving all the encouragement, support, and guidance that anyone could possibly want.

The archivists and staff of the United Nations Archives in New York and Geneva; Archives de la Société des Nations et Collections Historiques, High Commissioner for Refugees, and Archives d'État in Geneva; U.S. National Archives and Manuscript Division of the Library of Congress in Washington, D.C.; British Public Record Office in London; National Archives of New Zealand in Wellington; Hoover Institution Archives at Stanford University; Franklin D. Roosevelt Library at Hyde Park; Ministère des Affaires étrangères and Archives nationales in Paris; Politisches Archiv des Auswärtiges Amts in Bonn; Organization for Security and Cooperation in Europe (OSCE) in Prague; Rare Book and Manuscript Library of Columbia University and Leo Baeck Institute in New York; Council of Europe Archives in Strasbourg; and Diplomatic Record Office of the Japanese Ministry for Foreign Affairs in Tokyo for granting access to rare materials and archival collections.

The librarians at the Maureen and Mike Mansfield Library and the Law Library of the University of Montana, Bibliothèque des Nations Unies at the Palais des Nations in Geneva, Green Library at Stanford University, Hoover Institution Library, Butler

Library at Columbia University, Library of Congress, New York Public Library, Nobel Institute, Dag Hammarskjöld Library at the United Nations, Suzzalo Library at the University of Washington, Alexander Turnbull Library, British Library, Bibliothèque nationale, Yliopiston Kirjasto and Oikeustieteellisen Tiedekunnan Kirjasto of the University of Helsinki, Massey University Library, Bibliothèque Publique et Universitaire de Genève, Library of the European Court of Human Rights, London School of Economics Library, University of Tokyo Library, Toyo University Library, Shanghai International Studies University Library, Columbus Memorial Library of the Organization of American States, and the Musée international de la Croix-Rouge et du Croissant-Rouge, for the use of resources and numerous courtesies.

The Rockefeller Foundation for an appointment as a Humanities Fellow, the Council for International Exchange of Scholars for an appointment as a Senior Fulbright Specialist and in cooperation with the U.S.-New Zealand Educational Foundation and the Fulbright Center of Finland for appointments as a Senior Fulbright Scholar, the Office of Research Administration and Department of History of the University of Montana, and the Tom and Ann Boone and John and Annie Hall endowments, for financial assistance.

Current and former staff members of the Office of the High Commissioner for Human Rights/Centre for Human Rights in Geneva, especially senior advisors Tom McCarthy and Zdzislaw Kedzia, Daniel Atchebro, Andrew Clapham, Fiona Blyth-Kubota, Jakob Moller, Bacre Waly Ndiaye, Anton Nikiforov, Laura Stryker-Cao, and Alfred De Zayas, for giving freely of their time to answer questions and provide invaluable insights about process and substance.

Those who graciously granted interviews, including Martti Ahtisaari, Colin Aikman, Carroll Bogert, Jimmy Carter, Frank Corner, Warren Hewitt, Jaakko Iloniemi, Clement John, the late Martin Luther King, Jr., Irène Kitsou-Milonas, Liu Binyan, J. M. Makatini, the late Mike Mansfield, Jan Mårtenson, Michael Pan, T. C. Ragachari, John Salzberg, Jerome Shestack, the late Clarence Streit, Yvonne Terlingen, Brian Urquart, Sandra Vogelgesang, and several who wish to remain anonymous, for sharing their vast experiences and perspectives on the world of international human rights.

Maurizio Cortiello, Sylvie Carlon-Riera, Anna Rey-Mermier, Jacques Oberson, and Maria del Mar Sanchez Moncho of Registry, Records, and Archives at the United Nations Office in Geneva; Marilla Guptil of the United Nations Archives in New York; Montserrat Canela Garayoa of the Records and Archives of the United Nations High Commissioner for Refugees; and Carol Davies, Salvatore Leggio, Nina Kriz Leneman, Gary Meixner, Pierre Pelou, Werner Simon, and Maggie Wachter of the Bibliothèque des Nations Unies; and Yukiyoshi Asami and Kazuhiro Takahashi of the Diplomatic Record Office of the Japanese Ministry of Foreign Affairs, for assistance in finding documentary needles in haystacks.

Colleagues, friends, and commentators Tunde Adeleke, Reza Afshari, George Andreopoulos, David Aronofsky, Dan Caldwell, Ann Marie Clark, Richard Pierre Claude, the late Gordon A. Craig, Sally Cummings, Richard Drake, Asbjørn Eide, David Emmons, María José Falcón y Tella, Cees Flinterman, David Forsythe, Harry Fritz, the late Alexander George, Robert Greene, Forest Grieves, Kerry Howe, Anya Jabour, Mark Johnson, Darshan Kang, Jan Klabbers, Mehrdad Kia, Peter Koehn, Martti Koskenniemi, Ken Lockridge, James Lopach, J. Paul Martin, Leo Moser, Olatunde Ojo, Yunosuke Okura, Jody Pavilack, Ralph Pettman, Helge Pharo, Henry Sekyi, Tobin Shearer, Frederick Skinner, Anna-Lena Svensson-McCarthy, Ramesh Thakur, Howard Tolley, Richard Tuck, Nobuchika Urata, Philip Veerman, Hanne Hagtvedt Vik, Kyle Volk, Pamela Volkel, John R. Wallach, and Jay Winter, for sharing their expertise.

The Controller of Her Majesty's Stationery Office, the Director and Chief Archivist of the National Archives of New Zealand, and the Director of the Rare Book and Manuscript Library of Columbia University for granting permission to cite materials in their respective collections; and to Patricia Koo Tsien for authorizing the use of papers from her father, Wellington Koo.

Officials of the International Criminal Tribunal for the Former Yugoslavia in The Hague for the opportunity to witness some of the proceedings of the Slobodan Milosevic trial in person.

Nancy Flowers, Mark Fritch, Kirsi Haimi, Judy Horn, Amanda Johnson, Anne Kjelling, Kyu-Young Lee, Kath McChesney-Lape, Elsy Monsalve-Schmidt, Alice Nemcova, Michael Peluso, Diane Rapp, Joyce Rosenblum, the late Tu Baixiong, and Linda Wheeler, for offering various forms of assistance.

The Alaska Humanities Forum, Erik Castrén Institute of International Law and Human Rights, Center for Human Rights Leadership at Claremont McKenna College, Chou University, Columbia University Human Rights Seminar, Columbia University Center for the Study of Human Rights, Helsinki University, Hiroshima University, Hitotsubashi University, Institut Diplomatique of the Ministère des Affairs Étrangères in Algeria, Instituto de Derechos Humanos of Complutense University, Mentouri University, National Endowment for the Humanities and its Institute on Human Rights in Conflict, Nazareth Conference on Children's Rights and Religion at the Crossroads, Netherlands Institute of Human Rights (SIM), Nobel Institute, Pécs University, Penn State University, Pepperdine University, Stanford University, Texas A&M University, UNESCO, the United Nations University, University of Algiers, University of Oran Es-Senia, University of Olso, Urban Morgan Institute for Human Rights, Utrecht University, Washington State University, World Affairs Council, and numerous local, national, and international human rights organizations, for opportunities to publicly address and evaluate issues raised in this book since it first appeared.

The Teaching Company for the opportunity to create one of their Great Courses entitled "The Rights of Man" based upon this book, and thereby reexamine its central ideas and themes.

The many readers, reviewers, students, faculty, officials, activists, and Peter Agree and Alison Anderson of the University of Pennsylvania Press, who through their gracious reactions and insightful comments enabled translations of this book that opened up a much wider global audience and encouraged me to write this third edition.

Sandy and Jeanne, Nick and George, Lauren, Alex, Jacob, Emma, Joshua, Andrew, and especially my wife Susan, for their constant and loving support.

Finally, I am grateful to all those who have taught me so much about human rights in so many different ways in so many different places, and am honored to dedicate this book to them.

What has been accomplished? This: we have kept a vision alive; we have held to a great ideal, we have established a continuity, and some day when unity and cooperation come, the importance of all these early steps will be recognized.

—W. E. B. Du Bois

Human rights were not a free gift. They were only won by long, hard struggle. . . . [R]espect for individual rights, when it passes from theory to practice, entails conflict with certain interests and the abolition of certain privileges. Men and women everywhere should be familiar with the dramatic incidents—well-known and obscure—of a conquest which has been largely achieved through the heroism of the noblest of their fellows.

—UNESCO

Introduction: Visions and Visionaries

> Do not make the mistake of thinking that a small group of thoughtful, committed people cannot change the world; indeed, it is the only thing that ever has.
> —Margaret Mead

There are times when the visions seen of a world of possibilities provide a far better measure of a person's qualities and contributions than the immediate accomplishments of his or her lifetime. Visionary men and women who possess a capacity to see beyond the confines of what is or what has been, and to creatively dream or imagine what might be, sometimes have an impact that far transcends their own time and place. Indeed, visions of prophets, philosophers, and activists seen centuries ago in distant lands are still capable of capturing our imagination, inspiring our thoughts, and influencing our behavior today.

Among all these great visions, perhaps none have had a more profound impact than those of human rights. The reason is that they present something that none of us can ever escape. We cannot escape human rights because they address who we were—and who we are—as human beings. They force us to look at ourselves, at life, and at how we treat each other. They raise universal and controversial questions about the value of individual life, life lived with others, and what it means to be truly human. They make us confront what we believe about the relationship between rights and duties, our responsibilities to those who suffer, and the ultimate value of people different from ourselves. As such, human rights raise some of the most serious, painful, shocking, revolutionary, and hopeful features of the human condition itself, both in the past and in the contemporary world.

Throughout history, thoughtful and insightful visionaries in many different times, places, and circumstances have seen in their mind's eye a world in which they and others might enjoy freedom, dignity, and protection of their fundamental rights against those who would abuse them. Many believed that these rights belonged to all men, women, and children, inherited simply by virtue of being human beings born into the same human family. Nothing more, and most certainly nothing less. With this premise they have envisioned a world without borders that divide people from one another in which we all are entitled to receive just and equal treatment without any prejudice, discrimination, or persecution on the basis of gender, race, caste or class, religion, political opinion, ethnicity, nationality, or any other form of difference.

These visions did not evolve from any single society, political system, culture, geographical region, or manner. Some emerged out of religious belief, compassion, or a sense of duty to care for brothers and sisters suffering in distress. Others grew from philosophical discourse about the nature of humankind itself, natural rights, ethical limits on how we should treat one another, the appropriate powers of government, or the rule of law. Some came not from quiet contemplation or careful reflection, but rather from the heat of outrage generated by a passionate sense of individual or collective conscience over an injustice inflicted upon innocent or defenseless victims. Still others arose out of violence and pain from wars, revolutions, upheavals, or brutal atrocities. Over the centuries these cases have spanned the world, from Asia to Europe, from the Middle East to the Pacific, and from Africa to the Americas, and have involved exploitation, slavery, racial segregation and apartheid, oppression, gender and class discrimination, persecution of minorities, violence in times of war, torture, conquest, and the mass exterminations of genocide or "ethnic cleansing." As one might expect, the responses to such wide-ranging abuses have evolved through time and have varied greatly depending on what was possible within their particular and specific historical contexts, with the result being not just one concept or school of thought, a single definition or mode of expression, or unified vision of human rights—but rather many visions.

Despite their differences of origin, purpose, meaning, applicability, or terminology, however, all these visions of human rights confronted powerful opposition and forces of resistance every step of the way. The reason can be simply stated: they all directly threatened those with power who refused to share it voluntarily, those with vested interests or prevailing prejudice who wanted special privilege, and those government leaders who hid behind the claims of national sovereignty and insisted that they were immune from ever being held accountable for any abuses they might commit. These visions challenged traditional authority and attempted to limit the arbitrary exercise of power. They repudiated ideas of superiority on the basis of gender or the color of skin, refused to accept the proposition that how a state treats its own people is its own business, and rejected the notion that the strong do what they can and the weak do what they must.

As such, these visions of human rights possessed the capacity to challenge, to generate fear, to hold out hope and inspire, and to change the world. This power was understood not only by those who held the visions—but by those who opposed them. Indeed, it is precisely for this reason that the visionaries discussed throughout this book invariably found themselves ridiculed as naive idealists or impractical dreamers, reviled and persecuted as traitors to their own exclusive group or nation, or even tortured and killed as dangerous revolutionaries bent upon destroying the established order.

Although confronted by formidable odds and forces aligned against them, these visions could not be extinguished and the visionaries who saw them refused to be silenced or to remain passive. They saw abuses as wrong, moved into action, and worked to protect victims. Upheavals and revolutions in the eighteenth century and successes against slavery and the slave trade and for the rights of women and workers in the nineteenth century gave them hope. Horrors of the twentieth century gave them determination. The magnitude of suffering, brutality, and genocide during World War II, in particular, created a consciousness about the extremes of cruelty so horrendous, in the words of those who lived through it, as to "outrage the conscience of mankind."[1] This awareness, when coupled with the demands of all those survivors who had been given promises about receiving their rights if they would only join in the crusade of war, created a force of global scale on behalf of international human rights that refused to be denied.

Determined postwar visionaries thus set out to champion the cause of international human rights as never before. They believed that they had a duty to care for their brothers and sisters in need; that respect for human rights would contribute to global security, peace and justice; and that victory in war provided a unique opportunity for action that could not be squandered. They thus established the Charter of the United Nations, announcing to the world that human rights henceforth would be a matter of international responsibility, and then created and proclaimed a bold vision "for all peoples and all nations" known as the Universal Declaration of Human Rights. Since then, a new generation of visionaries has picked up the torch and worked to extend freedom to literally millions of people, to establish universal standards, to create binding treaties with implementation mechanisms, to develop international criminal law and tribunals to hold abusers accountable, to provide access for individual victims to machinery of protection beyond their own borders, and to promote and enhance human rights in innumerable and innovative ways so as to help transform that vision into reality.

In this dynamic and ever-changing process, these visions and those who saw them began to transform the world. They knew when they started that for most people respect for human rights appeared as only a distant vision or remote dream. They knew that the overwhelming majority of all of those who ever lived and ever died in history had suffered under some form of human rights abuse. They knew that kings and emperors demanding obedience from their subjects ruled the earth, that traditional and hierarchical societies prevailed, that women were expected "to know their proper place," and that human bondage and exploitation were regarded as part of "the natural order." They knew that how governments treated their own people was viewed as a matter of exclusive domestic jurisdiction and one of the political and legal prerogatives of national sovereignty. In this setting, they knew that individual victims of abuse could seek no help beyond their own national governments or borders, and thus had always been forced to remain as objects of international pity rather than as subjects of international law, and suffered accordingly. They knew that they faced powerful resistance. They would come to understand that the relationship between history and human rights is complicated and that their efforts would never be uncontested, never follow a straight path or linear line of unbroken progress, and never be fully complete.

But despite all these obstacles, they refused to be deterred. Instead, they imagined a world that might be, and they believed that they could make a difference—and they did. As a result of their remarkable efforts, in the words of one former policy maker, human rights have become "the single most magnetic political idea of the contemporary time."[2] Today they provide the mark by which modern politics and society are defined and play an exceedingly visible and viable role in the lives of individuals at the local grassroots level, the policies of national leaders, and the conduct of international relations. The global community is no longer willing to remain silent over systematic abuses, many victims have a voice and can seek protection, and there is not a government on the face of the earth that can ignore the impact of what is correctly described as "the universal culture of human rights."[3] One perceptive observer writes: "We are scarcely aware of the extent to which our moral imagination has been transformed since 1945 by the growth of a language and practice of moral universalism, expressed above all in a shared human rights culture."[4] Indeed, in the words of one authority, human rights have become "the moral lingua franca of our age."[5] The visions and the visionaries who courageously struggled to make this dramatic and radical transformation possible, and the powerful forces and events against which they fiercely struggled and with which they determinedly worked, provide the subject of this book.

Chapter 1
My Brother's and Sister's Keeper

Visions and the Origins of Human Rights

> Am I my brother's keeper?
> —Genesis 4:9

The historical origins of powerful visions capable of shaping world events and attitudes like those of international human rights are rarely simple. Instead, they emerge in complicated, interrelated, and sometimes paradoxical ways from the influence of many sources, forces, personalities, and conditions in different times and diverse settings. Sometimes together, sometimes overlapping, and sometimes at cross purposes, they each flow like tributaries into ever larger and mightier rivers. At times they flow gently through the calm meadows of religious meditation, prophetic inspiration, poetic expression, philosophic contemplation, or introspection. On other occasions, as we shall see, they smash through human events like torrents through precipitous canyons born of violence and pain from upheaval, enslavement, conquest, revolution, war, torture, and genocide.

Visions of human rights thus are not only complex, but also profound and disturbing. The reason for this is that they tend to strike at our very core and make us confront difficult and discomforting issues. They force us to critically examine ourselves as human beings: to explore our nature, to consider what it means to be fully human, to view both the best and the worst of behavior, to wrestle with how we ought to relate to others in society as a whole, to question the purposes of government and the exercise of power, and especially to assess our own values and deeds in response to those who suffer abuse.

One of the most agonizing issues presented by such visions, for example, is whether we have any responsibilities for other people in need or pain. Thoughtful individuals in many different times and places have pondered whether or not we should possess a concern beyond ourselves that extends to others. If so, they then had to ask further perplexing and age-old questions: who is my "brother" or "sister" and what exactly does it mean to be a "keeper"? That is, just how wide should be the circle of responsibility and what form should concern for others take? A sense of obligation to immediate family members or friends and immediate neighbors might be readily apparent, but what about those beyond the community, the tribe, the clan, the class, the race, the faith, or, particularly in the modern world, the nation? Are these duties merely local or are they universal? Are they individual or collective? Moreover, and equally troubling, are we obliged to simply express words of sympathy or sorrow over the fate of victims of human rights abuse, or do we have a responsibility to take concrete action to actually protect those who suffer?

The historical evolution of visions of international human rights that continues to this day started centuries ago with efforts attempting to address precisely these difficult and universal questions when ideas were communicated by oral traditions, inscribed on clay tablets, or written on papyrus or parchment. It began as soon as men and women abandoned nomadic existence and settled in organized societies, long before anyone had ever heard of the more recent expression, "human rights," or before nation-states negotiated specific international treaties. Moreover, this evolution began not with assertions of entitlements or demands for human rights but instead with discussions of human duties.

Religious Visions: Brothers, Sisters, and Duties Beyond Borders

All the major religions of the world seek in one way or another to speak to the issue of human responsibility to others. Despite their many differences, complex contradictions, internal paradoxes, cultural variations, and susceptibility to conflicting interpretation, reinterpretation, and argumentation, all of the great religious traditions share a universal dissatisfaction with the world as it *is* and a determination to make it *as it ought to be*. They do this by addressing the value and the dignity of human life, and, consequently, the duties toward those who suffer. Each seeks to help us transcend our own self-centeredness and consider the needs of others by behaving toward them as we would have them behave toward us. This is approached through various revelations, narratives, poetry, edicts, laws, and commandments, and stories or parables dealing with right and wrong, moral responsibility, ethical principles of justice, compassion, the essential worth of the human person, and the kinship and common humanity of all.

In Hinduism, the world's oldest living religious tradition, for example, the ancient texts of the Vedas and Upanishads, some written over three thousand years ago in what is now India, stress that divine truth is universal, that life is sacred, and that religious belief must lead to works or paths of action. Although highly diverse, these rich scriptures address good and evil, the virtues of tolerance and compassion, and especially the importance of devout adherence to duty (*dharma*), justice and moral action (*karma*), and good conduct (*sadāchāra*) toward others. They enjoin believers to fulfill faithfully their earthly life journey of moral responsibilities to people beyond the self by practicing selfless concern for their pain, particularly for the hungry, the sick, the homeless, and those who suffer, as discussed in the pivotal text *Manava Dharma Sastra*. All human life, despite the vast differences and stratification between individuals, is considered sacred and a part of a great chain of being that manifests the divine, and thus should be loved, respected, and allowed to enjoy freedom from suffering. For this reason,

Mahatma Gandhi, who in the twentieth century, as we shall see, regarded himself as a deeply orthodox Hindu, emphasized the absolute principle of not harming others. The edict is stated directly and universally: "Noninjury (*ahimsā*) is not causing pain to any living being at any time through the actions of one's mind, speech, or body."[1]

Genesis, the first book of Judaism's Torah written two millennia ago in the Middle East, begins by telling of the shared fatherhood of God to all people. The scriptures teach of God's will being worked out in human history, of the sacredness of life, and of explicitly defined responsibilities of individuals toward each other. The story of two siblings dramatizes the issue of obligation and autonomous individual moral judgment. When Abel cannot be found, Cain is asked about his brother's whereabouts and well-being. Attempting to avoid blame for murder, he denies knowing and then seeks refuge by posing a universal and enduring question: "Am I my brother's keeper?"[2] His question, of course, is completely disingenuous and false. This sets the stage for teachings about ethical behavior, the agony of slavery and release from bondage, mercy and social justice, and instructions that government decrees contrary to divine commands should be disregarded. Further passages address the rights of foreigners in one's own land and the importance of following the law that establishes responsibilities toward others (including six of the Ten Commandments), whether friend or enemy, free or slave, man or woman, young or old, rich or poor.[3] The instructions in Leviticus are clear: "You shall not oppress. You shall do no injustice. You shall love your neighbor as yourself."[4] The prophets spoke out and challenged kings when abuses occurred, as seen in "The Vision of Isaiah" with the charge "to loose the bonds of wickedness, to undo the tongs of the yoke, to let the oppressed go free . . . to share your bread with the hungry, and to bring the homeless poor into your house," and thereby "bring justice to the nations."[5] These commands established a religious tradition that told believers to extend beyond themselves and take action on behalf of others in this world, observes Jewish theologian Martin Buber in *I and Thou*. Such a process, he writes, "is a matter of leavening the human race in all places with genuine We-ness. Man will not persist in existence if he does not learn anew to persist in it as a genuine We."[6]

The principles of Buddhism were established approximately 2,500 years ago in India by Siddhartha Gautama, who gave up his own position of royal privilege and spent the rest of his life teaching about universal human relationships, profound respect for the interconnectedness of the lives of each person, and empathy and compassion to relieve the suffering of fellow human beings. Indeed, he taught that only when we learn to empathize and feel the suffering of others do we become truly and fully human ourselves. He explicitly attacked the entrenched and rigid caste system of his day by opening his order to both men and women, stressing the unique value of all individuals as physical and spiritual beings, and urging his followers to renounce differences "of caste and rank and become the members of one and the same society."[7] The Tripitaka scriptures address the enduring problem of human misery and suffering (*dukkha*) and stress that one's duty is to overcome selfish desires and private fulfillment by practicing charity (*dana*), lovingkindness (*metta*), and compassion (*karunā*) toward others. This ethic forms a part of Buddhism's Ten Duties of Kings and the Noble Eightfold Path instructing believers to practice right thought, right speech, right action, and right effort toward "all beings." It also creates the religious tradition necessary to appreciate the Dalai Lama's more contemporary pronouncement that the world's problems will be solved only by respecting the human rights of all mankind and treating one another "as brothers and sisters."[8]

The founding of Confucianism by Kong Qiu in China at approximately the same time as the emergence of Buddhism brought similar reflections on human nature and responsible behavior. Indeed, Confucian thought articulated in the *Analects*, *Doctrine of the Mean*, and *Great Learning* focused much more on how individuals should live and interact with each other, the perfectability of each individual within the collective, and living an ethical life on earth rather than a divine or spiritual realm beyond. Harmony exists when people overcome their self-interest and egotism, fulfill their responsibility not to harm each other, treat all others as having worth and "moral force," and acknowledge their common humanity and that "within the four seas, all men are brothers."[9] Human nature is viewed as inherently good, and harsh warnings are given about oppressive or despotic governments that rule by force or exploit their people. When the sage was asked whether there existed any single saying that one could act on all day and every day, he answered: "Do not impose on others what you yourself do not desire."[10] The basis of all the teachings can be found by following The Way (*Jen*), etymologically a combination of the character for "man" and for "two" that names the ideal and universal relationship between humans beings. It has been variously translated as goodness, benevolence, love, and human-heartedness. It represents the virtue of all virtues and the condition of being fully human in dealing with others, involving the display of human capacities at their very best and extending far beyond immediate personal or family relationships to include the world as a whole. As the well-known Confucian dictum explains: "If there be righteousness in the heart, there will be beauty in the character. If there is beauty in the character, there will be harmony in the home. If there is harmony in the home, there will be order in the nation. If there be order in the nation, there will be peace in the world."[11]

Christianity extended this theme of responsibility even further. During his ministry two thousand years ago, Jesus taught his followers first to receive God's abiding love and then to let it flow outward toward others. He preached about living a life of love, justice, peace, and compassion by the giving of one's self to others. Jesus thus instructed believers to clothe the naked, to heal the sick, to feed the hungry, to welcome the stranger, to provide hope to the hopeless, and to care for the poor and the oppressed of the world. He challenged the existing order of his day and demonstrated a level of respect for women, children, outcasts, and outsiders that many at the time found completely inappropriate. In this regard, he used one of his best known teaching parables to address one of the most profound and provocative of all possible questions of living life with other people: "Who is my neighbor?" Jesus responded by telling of a man who fell among robbers. They stripped him and beat him, and left him nearly dead. A priest journeying along the same road saw the victim, yet instead of stopping to help the poor man, turned his eyes away and walked on the other side of the road. A passing Levite did the same. But a Samaritan, regarded as an outcast in the community, came upon the man and had compassion. He stopped, bound up his wounds, and carried him to an inn where he paid all the expenses until the victim recovered. Jesus then asked which of these three proved to be the neighbor. The man who asked the initial question replied, "The one who showed mercy on him." But rather than simply stating that this answer was correct, Jesus more forcefully said to him: "Go and *do* like-wise."[12] Lest there be any doubt on this matter, the apostle Paul admonished believers to "clothe yourselves in compassion" and break down all ethnic, class, and gender divisions by recognizing that "there is neither Greek nor Jew, nor slave nor free, nor man nor woman, but we are all one in Christ."[13]

The tenets of Islam, founded five hundred years after the lifetime of Jesus and re-vealed through the writings of Muhammed, also address responsibilities toward others. This begins with that of the duty (*fard*) to practice charity and to protect the weakest members of society. The scripture of the Qur'an speaks to social justice, the sanctity of life, personal safety, mercy, compassion, and respect for all human beings as rooted in the obligations owed by believers to Allah, or God. Moreover, since Muhammed was not only a prophet and teacher, but also a government administrator and statesman, it is hardly surprising that Islam would recognize the connections between religious faith and the political community. In a society riven with class distinctions, oppression, and the tyranny of vested interests, he preached a message of freedom from the various chains that bind, urging the reduction of injustices born of special privilege or race, and insisting that religious believers be treated equally. Muhammed's establishment of the Constitution of Medina and its proclamation that "Jews [and later Christians] who attach themselves to our commonwealth shall be protected . . . they shall have an equal right with our own people . . . and shall practice their religion as freely as the Muslims," for example, has even been described as "the first charter of freedom of conscience in human history."[14]

These many and various religious visions—like all visions—expressed ideals rather than reality. They attempted to address, with various levels of simplicity or sophistica-tion, the best of possible human relationships with compassion and justice instead of the worst. This becomes particularly remarkable when one considers that each emerged historically from traditional, premodern, male-dominated societies char-acterized by enormous disparities, discriminations, hereditary systems of inequality, and hierarchies headed by kings or emperors. Nevertheless, and as we shall soon see, none of these great religious traditions could escape being often overwhelmed by prac-tices of secularization, perversion, compromise, or corruption in one form or another and mobilized in ways that provided a pretext for repression at home and aggression abroad or allowed the powerful to mask their self-interests, ambition, or greed. In reli-gious terms, humans thus often proved themselves to be precisely that—all too human.

It is important to acknowledge these flaws and the many, many abuses often perpe-trated in the name of religion. It is equally important to acknowledge that throughout history there also have been those who, by word or deed, have attempted to faithfully follow the precepts of their visionary teachers and prophets to be keepers of brothers and sisters. For this reason, they would completely agree with the proposition that the very idea of human rights is "ineliminably religious."[15] Some became known as the saints of Christianity, the *murshids* and *pirs* of Sufi Islam, the *sadhus* or holy men of Hinduism, or the *bodhisattvas* of Buddhism, while others remained largely unrecognized and unknown to anyone except those to whom they extended selfless compassion and help as an expression of their faith. They lived in particular historical times and places that conditioned and determined what they could reasonably accomplish. Perseverance did not necessarily require success. Nor did these general religious concepts of responsibility emerging from traditional, hierarchical, and patriarchal societies that far predated the printing press, nation-states, and modern concepts of individual rights contain fully developed political, philosophical, legal, or subtlety nuanced definitions of "rights discourse" of our own day. At this early stage, they simply did not and could not. Instead, they began by developing moral impulses and values, orientations of spirit, and habits of the heart about other people and how they should be treated. All these would evolve through time. If the tenets of helping those who suffered fell short in actual practice or precision, that did not diminish the ultimate value of the ideal as a goal toward which they or subsequent generations would strive.

In so doing, those largely unknown and unassuming men and women who rejected prevailing practices and attempted to follow the precepts of their faith demonstrated that religious beliefs matter—and that for some people they matter greatly. These beliefs left a legacy that eventually made four critical contributions to the evolution of international human rights.

In the first place, they established timeless *visions of ideals and normative standards* in the form of moral codes addressing the worth and dignity of human beings and how they should be treated. These would go on to inspire and sustain many who campaigned for human rights and who looked for a ray of light in times of the darkness of persecution and suffering. They provided hope beyond the world as they knew it to be for a transformed world that might be, stressing that people *could* do what they *should* do.

Secondly, in making sharp contrasts between the world as it *is* and the world as it *ought to be*, these religious visions presented *radical alternatives to the status quo*. Especially when addressing issues of justice, the value of each person, and freedom from oppression, they challenged prevailing power structures, the tyranny of vested interests, injustices born of special privilege or prejudice. This explains why prophets who eventually may have a profound impact are rarely welcomed in their own time.

Thirdly, by developing moral imperatives, these religious visions helped establish an element essential for any and all international human rights: the *concept of responsibility to act on behalf of others*. They called for going beyond one's self, of seeing those not seen by others, and for understanding that it was not enough to simply know or to believe—the key was to transform behavior: to go and do likewise. Assertions for human rights in one place would have remained forever unanswered, isolated, or localized unless there had been people elsewhere in the world who believed that they had larger responsibilities, or "duties beyond borders,"[16] to take action on behalf of common humanity, and protect others regardless of station or location.

Fourthly, by developing concepts of duties, these religious traditions provided a inherent *link between duties and rights*. They were not so much interested in the claims of individuals against governments or others, but in ways of ordering life within the human family collectively so as to ensure dignity and worth for all of its members. In this regard, they saw responsibilities and rights as interrelated and correlative concepts: that a duty is something one owes to someone else, and that that person, in turn, has a right to claim that duty. As Gandhi insightfully observed, "The true source of rights is duty."[17] Thus, ideas about human duties, or what one is due to do, led quite naturally to ideas about human rights, or what is due to one.

Philosophical Visions: Human Nature, Natural Law, and Natural Rights

If religious belief provided one source of tributaries into the ever expanding and evolving river of thought about what would eventually be described as international human rights, moral and political philosophy contributed others. Religion and philosophy have many things in common, not the least of which is their attempt to find answers to some of the same fundamental, universal, and age-old questions about the nature of human beings as individuals and their relationships with each other as members of communitarian society. Like the founders of the world's religions, philosophers from many diverse times and places seriously pondered the value of human life, the universality of fundamental principles, war and peace, moral codes and responsibilities toward brothers and sisters who suffer, whether traditional rules-based societies should be transformed into rights-based societies, how government leaders should exercise their power, and the meaning of justice, liberty, and tolerance. But these philosophers, regardless of their many differences of perspective and cultural tradition, sought understanding through secular inquiry and human reason rather than through the revelation of religious belief.

Nearly twenty-four centuries ago in China, for example, Mo Tze founded the Mohist school of moral philosophy. His writings emphasized the importance of duty, self-sacrifice, and an all-embracing respect toward all others, not confined merely to members of family or clan, but, in his words, "universally throughout the world."[18] Shortly thereafter, the Confucian sage Meng Zi, or Mencius, argued that "all human beings" naturally share a common humanity, moral worth, inherent dignity and goodness, and a compassionate mind capable of empathy "that cannot bear to see the suffering of others." Anyone who saw a child fall into a well, he observed, would take immediate action to save them not because of some calculation about the opportunity to ingratiate themselves with the child's parents or seek commendation from friends, but because they would naturally and instinctively be filled with alarm for the well-being of the child. As he wrote in one of his most celebrated passages:

One who lacks a mind of pity and compassion would not be human. One who lacks a mind that feels shame and aversion would not be human; one who lacks a mind that feels modesty and compliance would not be human; one who lacks a mind that knows right and wrong would not be human.[19]

It is the responsibility of governments, he argued, to nurture these natural qualities through benevolence and proper moral behavior. If rulers failed to do so through oppression, they lost what was called the Mandate of Heaven and thereby forfeited the legitimacy to govern. In this regard, and long before the Enlightenment in Europe, he argued that people possessed the right to overthrow a tyrant. In language recalled with considerable pride by Chinese human rights activists in later centuries, Mencius declared: "The individual is of infinite value, institutions and conventions come next, and the person of the ruler is of least significance."[20] The ancient philosopher Xun Zi asserted the same principle when he wrote emphatically: "In order to relieve anxiety and eradicate strife, nothing is as effective as the institution of corporate life based on a clear recognition of individual rights."[21]

Philosophers from other areas, cultures, and traditions made contributions as well, each in a distinct way. Precepts from ancient Egypt sought to address explicitly issues of social justice and help for the weak by injunctions to "comfort the afflicted. . . . Refrain from unjust punishment. Kill not. . . . Make no distinction between the son of a man of importance and one of humble origin."[22] One pharaoh instructed his viziers to "make sure that all is done according to the law, that custom is observed and the right of each man respected."[23] One of the greatest of these early contributions came from King Hammurabi of Babylon. In approximately 1780 B.C. he instituted the Code of Hammurabi, announcing an extremely important principle: that some laws are so fundamental that they apply to everyone—even the king. The reason why law is so important for the protection of human rights is that it serves as a check against the arbitrary use or abuse of power. "Let the oppressed," he said, "come into the presence of my statue" to seek justice and enjoy certain civil rights such as freedom of speech and particular kinds of protections, including some for women and slaves, some for the weak against the powerful, and some for the poor against the rich.[24] Cyrus the Great, the founder of the Persian Empire, subsequently promulgated the famous Charter of Cyrus around 539 B.C. The text, written in cuneiform on a clay cylinder, is sometimes described as the world's "first charter of human rights" because the word "rights" appears explicitly as it recognizes freedom of movement, religious toleration, and even several economic and social rights.[25] Its impact inspired Sultan Farrukh Hablul Matin to write:

For he, it was who, with supreme insight,
Launched an Empire based not on physical might
But on the vision of a family of nations
Linked by bands of Humanity, truth, and right.[26]

Abu Al-Farabi, an Islamic philosopher of the tenth century, wrote further of a vision of a moral society in which all people were endowed with rights and lived in charity with their neighbors.[27]

Other contributions came from ancient India. Early Sanskrit writings specifically spoke of the responsibility of rulers for the welfare of people by declaring: "No one in his dominion should [be allowed to] suffer . . . either because of poverty or of any deliberate action on the part of others."[28] In the third century B.C., the Indian political philosopher, economist, and prime minister Kautilya argued in his book, *The Arthashastra*, that even kings had an obligation to rule their subjects fairly and benevolently, promoting justice, guaranteeing property rights, and protecting certain kinds of rights for workers.[29] Shortly thereafter, the Indian king Asoka sought to give political expression to his deeply held Buddhist beliefs by issuing edicts carved on stone pillars stressing impartial justice, nonviolence, and benevolence toward others that guaranteed the right of freedom of worship and the right to be free from torture. Others argued for social equality, maintaining, "Just as there is no distinction of classes among the fruits produced by one tree . . . in the form: 'this is a Brāhmana fruit,' 'this is a Ksatriya fruit,' etc., because they are all produced by one tree, even so there is no distinction [of castes] among men because they are all created by one Supreme Being."[30] The Hindu philosopher Chaitanya reinforced this same idea during the sixteenth century, as did others who argued against any distinction that would perpetuate an "untouchable" category of people, asserting simply: "There is only one caste—humanity."[31] Much later, the Sikh leader Guru Gobind Singh also proclaimed the need to create a global society by the universal emancipation of mankind from oppression and the elimination of caste distinctions, instructing his followers to "recognize all the human race as one."[32]

Similar philosophical positions expressing respect for the dignity of each person, ethical behavior toward others, social justice, law or rules above arbitrary power, and rights for all members of the human family can be found in other regions of the world as well. Sometimes simple tribal communities relying on the spoken word rather than written language produced concepts that contributed ultimately to discussions about human rights. Native American oral tradition, for example, has long held that the Iroquois Confederacy developed a Great Binding Law containing passages collectively known as "Rights of the Peoples of the Five Nations."[33] A number of traditional African societies similarly developed a variety of ideas about distributive justice, human dignity, freedom, and protection from the abuse of political authority.[34] Some created sayings to express these beliefs, such as that from the Akan tribe of Ghana warning, "One should not oppress with one's size or might." A Burundi proverb stressing non-discrimination declared, "Imana [God] creates men and draws no distinction between them." Asserted an old Djerma-Songhai adage: "You should not [have to] solicit what is yours by right."[35]

Early ideas about general human rights thus did not originate exclusively in one location like the West or even with any particular form of government like liberal democracy, but were shared throughout the ages by visionaries from many intellectually rich cultures in many lands who expressed themselves in different ways. Although it is necessary to guard against the shallow and unhistorical view that all societies somehow have always subscribed to the same basic beliefs and values, it is also essential to recognize that the moral worth of each person is a belief that no single civilization, or people, or nation, or geographical area, or even century can claim as uniquely its own. The issue of human rights addresses age-old and universal questions about the relationship between individuals and their larger society, and thus is one that has been raised across time, across places, and across cultures. Indeed, as one insightful authority writes: "The struggle for human rights is as old as [world] history itself, because it concerns the need to protect the individual against the abuse of power by the monarch, the tyrant, or the state."[36] What the West did provide, however, was not a monopoly of ideas on the subject but rather much greater opportunities for visions such as these to receive fuller consideration, articulation, public declaration, and eventual implementation.

At approximately the same time as Mencius, but a continent away, several classical Greek philosophers began to argue that a universal law of nature pervaded all creation. This law, they claimed, was eternal and universal, and thus placed well above and beyond the narrow and self-serving dictates of a particular state, the customs or rules of a specific society, or the will of a single lawmaker. It governed every aspect of the universe and provided a framework for rights. Human conduct should thus be brought into harmony with this law of nature and judged according to it.[37] In the *Republic*, Plato served as the voice of his teacher Socrates and argued that a universal standard of moral justice exists that transcends immediate circumstances and allows people in different political systems to recognize that some actions are clearly just and others unjust. Zeno of Citium also spoke extensively of a universal law that binds all together. Aristotle followed in *Politics* by claiming that human nature and virtue can best be perfected when people are actively engaged in the world as good citizens in a good political order and that what is "just by nature" is not necessarily just by the laws of men. This theme is perhaps best represented by the character of Antigone from Greek literature who, on being reproached by the king for refusing his command not to bury her slain brother, asserts: "I did not think your orders were so strong that you, a mortal man, could over-run the gods' unwritten and unfailing laws. Not now, nor yesterday's, they always live, and no one knows their origin in time."[38]

Roman Stoic philosophers extended these ideas by contending that these laws of nature provided rational and egalitarian principles governing the entire universe. They entailed not only physical rules such as the succession of the seasons or the alternation between day and night but also ethical rules such as the obligation to respect one another as moral equals. The great statesman, orator, and philosopher Marcus Tullius Cicero, to illustrate, argued in one of his most famous statements that this natural law, founded "ages before any written law existed or any state had been established," provided the source of knowing one's responsibilities toward all people:

True law is right reason in agreement with nature; it is of universal application, unchanging and everlasting; it summons to duty by its commands, and averts from wrongdoing by its prohibitions. . . . It is a sin to try to alter this law . . . and it is impossible to abolish it entirely. We cannot be freed from its obligations by senate or people. . . . And there will not be different laws at Rome and at Athens, or different laws now and in the future, but one eternal and unchangeable law will be valid for all nations and all times.[39]

The key element to this law, he insisted, was a sense of justice rooted "in nature" and in the fact that we—as human beings—have a 'natural inclination" to be concerned about others."[40] The *Institutes* of Justinian stressed exactly the same point, declaring: "Justice is an unswerving and perpetual determination to acknowledge all men's rights."[41] With this in mind, jurists continued to develop a remarkable body of law known as the *jus gentium*, or law of nations, often described as Rome's greatest contribution to history. They claimed that this law derived from nature rather than man-made governments, and therefore established certain universal duties and rights that extended to all human beings as members of the world community as a whole.

For centuries most of these early philosophical theories of natural law—just like those of religious doctrine—focused on universal moral responsibilities and duties rather than what are now described as legal rights. But modifications of theories and then the transformations of theory into policy, as we shall see constantly, always have been tied to particular political, economic, social, scientific, and intellectual upheavals throughout history. For concepts of natural rights to come to the fore, major changes in beliefs and practices needed to take place. In this regard, monumental movements extending over a period of five hundred years began to occur, particularly in Europe. The gradual decline of feudalism and its monopolistic economy, for instance, eventually would lead to the free markets of capitalism based on the concept of the individual's right to private property, thereby providing greater individual autonomy and opportunities for the beneficiaries to transform their newfound economic power into political power. The wealthy barons of England, for example, claimed that their ruler, King John, had failed to meet his obligations under natural law and forced him to sign the Magna Carta in 1215. This helped establish that royal government had limits, that certain liberties and due process must be guaranteed, and that even kings must respect the rights of others. "To no one," read the text, " . . . will we deny or delay right and justice."[42] The Magnus Lagaboters Landslov issued by King Magnus of Norway in 1275 went further by acknowledging equality before the law.

Movement also occurred in the realm of ideas where interests in rights followed in the wake of a growing consciousness of humanity. During the thirteenth century Christian philosopher Saint Thomas Aquinas redefined natural law as being divinely willed. He believed that justice toward others represented a living out of the love of the divine, and thus posited the radical concept that if laws were not just then people had the right to disobey them. Given his belief in the dignity of all, this made natural law theory support the important principle that every person is an individual apart from their membership in a particular state. The Renaissance of the fourteenth and fifteenth centuries reinforced this concept by opening up new paths for personal expression and freedom.[43] Michelango's famous unfinished statues known as "The Prisoners," for example, visually convey the passion to break away the marble encasing each figure in order to set them free to realize their potential as individual human beings. At the same time the French writer and courageous champion for justice Christine de Pizan dared to argue that any discussions about natural law must include women as well as men.[44] These ideas slowly began to spread by the technological invention of the printing press[45] and received further elaboration by those who drew both on religious precepts of duty as well as principles of moral philosophy. "I would ask you to love one another," said the Czech professor Jan Hus just before he was burned at the stake, "not to let the good be suppressed by force and to give every person his rights."[46]

Still other contributions to the discourse on rights came in the midst of the Reformation of the sixteenth century. Protestants protested (hence their name) existing clerical authorities and the practices and the states they supported. They placed an emphasis on personal spiritual emancipation, individual conscience, and the freedom of religious belief. Humanist philosophers such as Erasmus of Rotterdam further stressed the relationship between this kind of faith and political, economic, and social reform that promoted ethical behavior and human dignity. "The doctrine of Christ," he wrote, "casts aside no age, no sex, no fortune, or position in life. It keeps no one at a distance."[47] All of this contributed to a considerable expansion of interest in justice, equality, and individual freedom, and thus to a corresponding shift from duties to rights.

An enormous transformation in this process of viewing natural law as entailing natural rights occurred during the seventeenth century. The scientific revolution that expanded knowledge to previously unimagined levels created a secular intellectual milieu encouraging a belief that reason could discover rational and universal laws. If laws of physics, biology, medicine, and mathematics could be discerned in nature, then why not laws of government and human behavior as well? Thus, Hugo Grotius, the great Dutch jurist and diplomat who founded modern international law, argued in *The Rights of War and Peace* (1625) that natural law, both physical and moral, existed independently of any political authority. This law, he declared, stood above all human-created governments and served as a measuring rod against which any regime could be judged and provided all humans with certain "natural rights" of protection and just and equal treatment that they ought to enjoy without regard to any religious or civil status.[48] Interestingly enough, similar ideas were being considered during exactly the same century by the Chinese philosopher Huang Zongxi who wrote (in a book banned almost immediately) that attention needed to be shifted from the exclusive rights of rulers to the rights of people.[49]

Political forces unleashed by upheaval also heavily contributed to this growing opinion that human beings were endowed with natural rights. This is not at all surprising. Indeed, as we shall see throughout this book, times of war, revolution, and individual and collective stress always have forced people to think seriously about things that really matter: survival, the power of government over the lives of people, the nature of human beings, and the protection of basic rights. This explains why the Peasants' War in German-speaking lands produced the Twelve Articles of the Black Forest in 1525 delineating a new relationship between peasants and lords and why rebellions in France and Spain challenged deeply rooted prerogatives of unlimited sovereignty by championing the right to resist abusive, absolutist governments. As the Dutch declared in their revolution for independence against the Spanish king: "God did not create the subjects for the benefit of the Prince, to do his bidding in all things, whether godly or ungodly, right or wrong, and to serve him as slaves, but the Prince for the benefit of the subjects . . . to govern them with justice and reason."[50] Upheavals in England resulted in the Petition of Right of 1628 which spoke of "diverse Rights and Liberties" directly challenging the absolutist claims of the monarch. More than forty years of English civil war, revolution, and turmoil, complete with the beheading of a king and the rise of a parliamentary dictator, produced even further changes. One of these was the rise of a group known as the "Levellers" whose program of action entitled "Agreement of the People" called for guarantees of the "native rights" to life, property, equal protection under the law, the election of representatives, freedom of religion, and freedom from conscription.[51] In 1679 Parliament passed the Habeas Corpus Act establishing the right to be brought before a court of law in person in order that their case might be examined. They followed with the 1689 Bill of Rights, a monumental landmark in the history of civil and political rights that spoke explicitly about limited monarchy, security of property, free elections and representative government, freedom of speech, religious toleration, trial by jury, right to petition, and prohibitions against cruel and unusual punishment—all in the name of "ancient" and "undoubted" natural rights and all designed to protect people "from the violation of their rights."[52]

These tumultuous developments also witnessed the emergence of the pivotal philosopher John Locke. Beginning with his strong religious belief in "our duty to God and our fellow creatures," he sought to explain the relationship among responsibilities, natural law, and natural rights.[53] First with his *Letter Concerning Toleration* (1689) and its forceful argument on behalf of freedom of religion and conscience, and then with his masterful *Second Treatise of Government* (1690), one of the most influential political treatises of all time, he stressed that every individual person possessed certain "natural rights" prior to the existence of any organized societies. This concept applied, importantly, not just to those in Europe, but to "common humanity" and "governments all through the world." People are born, Locke declared, in a "state of perfect equality, where naturally there is no superiority or jurisdiction of one over another." All humans, irrespective of the particular socioeconomic, cultural, or political conditions under which they live, he wrote, thus possess "a title to perfect freedom and uncontrolled enjoyment of all the rights and privileges of the law of nature equally with any other man or number of men in the world and have by nature a power not only to preserve his property—that is his life, liberty, and estate—against the injuries and attempts of other men, but to judge and punish the breaches of that law in others."[54] From this premise it followed that people had formed societies and set up governments in order to protect those rights—not to surrender them. Governments thus derived their authority from the consent of the governed. If government leaders failed in fulfilling this responsibility and broke their side of the contract, said Locke, they thereby absolved people from any further obedience and gave them a right to resist. Such a vision of individual rights possessed enormous power. This explains why Locke's ideas went on to influence so many who followed him and why his legacy will live on as long as there are people challenging entrenched privilege and abuse and struggling on behalf of human rights.

Inspired by these provocative theories of Locke, and encouraged by the dynamic temper of the time, leading intellectuals of the eighteenth century known as the *philosophes* sought to free the individual from traditional dogma, authority, privilege, and oppression. The Swiss-French philosopher and visionary Jean-Jacques Rousseau wrote explicitly of the "rights of man" in his *Contrat social, ou Principes du droit politique* (1762), famously crying: "Man is born free, but everywhere he is in chains."[55] He and others such as Jean-Jacques Burlamaqui, Montesquieu, Voltaire, David Hume, and Condorcet all participated in a movement called the Enlightenment, or what they described as the dawning of a new age of knowledge and freedom. Their ideas (increasingly spread through books and newspapers made possible by the printing press) focused not so much on abstract system-building but instead on how a transcendent God, Nature, and/or Reason made it possible for them to actually be keepers of brothers and sisters by applying science and specific reforms to long-festering human problems of economic exploitation, social suppression, political despotism, torture, superstition, and intolerance. They envisioned the spread of liberty, freedom of expression, religious toleration, the rule of law, limited constitutional government, the right to life and property, justice, and peace.

For the great Prussian philosopher Immanuel Kant, the reason to pursue rights could be found in the duty to protect the intrinsic worth and dignity of each person in order that they never be treated as means, but always as ends in themselves.[56] The universal nature and scope of this ethical responsibility led him to write one of his most celebrated statements, cited many times over in subsequent centuries by international human rights activists: "Because a . . . community widely prevails among the Earth's peoples, a transgression of rights in *one* place in the world is felt *everywhere*."[57] Scottish philosopher Francis Hutcheson in his *System of Moral Philosophy* (1755) similarly declared that benevolence, a moral sense of obligation for the welfare of others, and the application of "a right to do, posses, or demand" those things that would enhance the general good of all represented the height of personal and civic virtue.[58] The argument was thus made that human effort could bring about progress, rationality, and greater liberty for all "without distinction of race or sect, towards perfection and happiness."[59]

Other philosophers of the Enlightenment sought to make this connection between natural law and rights even more explicit. In this regard, they were aided by the fact that in French the word *droit* covers both meanings: *law* and *right*. In the entry on "Natural Law" in his *Encyclopédie* (1755) that the authorities attempted to censor, for example, Denis Diderot wrote that the laws of nature provide the most basic foundation for human society by defining what is naturally and universally just for all human beings without any reference to kings, aristocracy, popes or bishops, class, country, or time period. Using the language of equal, individual human rights for all, he challenged existing authority and asserted, "Tell yourself often: I am a man, and I have no other true, inalienable *natural rights* than those of humanity."[60] Shortly thereafter, Voltaire wrote his *Treatise on Toleration* (1763), arguing that natural law established the right of all people to freely practice their religion without fear of persecution. Italian criminologist Cesare Beccaria followed immediately with his hard-hitting *On Crimes and Punishments* (1764), attacking the then-common practices of prisoner abuse, brutal torture, and the death penalty, and writing what subsequently became the credo of many human rights activists:

If, in the course of upholding the rights of men and invincible truth, I should contribute to saving an unhappy victim of tyranny or of equally pernicious ignorance from suffering and the anguish of death, then the blessings and tears of that one person overcome with joy would console me from the contempt of all humanity.[61]

Abbé Guillaume Raynal then used his *Philosophical and Political History* (1770) to denounce the odious practice of slavery as a travesty against natural law and a gross violation of the natural rights of its suffering human victims.

There are times in history when visions and ideas possess enormous power in influencing human events. The second half of the eighteenth century was one of those times. The great philosophers of the Enlightenment had taken ideas about natural law and natural rights that had evolved over the course of many centuries, built upon them, and then shaped them to achieve particular political purposes. These ideas came to be invoked by those who believed that their rights were being denied and who sought protection against arbitrary power and justification for resistance to oppression. In fact, the abject failure of despotic European monarchs and a hereditary elite to modify their privileged positions, and thereby respect the principles of freedom and equality inherent in natural law and natural rights philosophy, provoked the challenges in the first place. As one leading scholar writes, "absolutism prompted man to claim rights precisely because it denied them."[62]

The impact of these challenges became clear when the American colonists revolted against the British by firing those shots "heard around the world" due to their vast implications. The tenets of the Enlightenment increasingly separated many in the colonies philosophically from absolutist monarchies and hereditary class privileges, while at the same time the Atlantic Ocean separated them geographically from the threat of immediate government coercion. Together, these factors afforded an opportunity, perhaps unique in history, for considerations of greater freedoms for the individual. Indeed, even prior to the revolution, the First Continental Congress enacted its own Bill of Rights in 1774, invoking entitlement to "life, liberty, and property" for all men. Lest such rights be restricted, and the expression "men" not refer to all people, Abigail Adams warned her husband to "Remember the ladies."[63]

Explosions of discontent into violence and then war produced further elaboration on human nature, natural law, and natural rights. Carefully schooled in the philosophy and political theory of the Enlightenment, for example, Thomas Jefferson had no trouble in asserting that his countrymen were a free people "claiming their rights as derived from the laws of nature and not as the gift of their Chief Magistrate."[64] The Virginia Declaration of Rights, written by his principled friend George Mason, argued that not just Virginians or even Americans, but "all men are by nature equally free and independent, and have certain inherent rights."[65] This universalist language was followed by one of the most eloquent statements of protest and vision of human rights to ever emerge. Writing with his goose-quilled pen, Jefferson gave expression to the philosophy of the time in the Declaration of Independence on the 4th of July 1776 by referring to "the laws of Nature and Nature's God." He stated his case with these dramatic words:

We hold these truths to be self-evident, that all men are created equal, that they are endowed by their Creator with certain unalienable rights, that among these are life, liberty and the pursuit of happiness. That to secure these rights, governments are instituted among men, deriving their just powers from the consent of the governed. That whenever any form of government becomes destructive of those ends, it is the right of the people to alter or to abolish it, and to institute new government[66]

This declaration was the most radical document Americans had yet produced—radical in its willingness to confront the power of the mighty British Empire, radical in its declaration of an independent existence, and radical in the natural rights it asserted for all.[67] It also was a call to revolution, not only in the New World, but in the Old as well; for as Jefferson would go on to write: "a bill of rights is what the people are entitled to against every government on earth."[68]

Whatever eloquence and inspiration this language might possess, words alone rarely create an immediate reality. In the case of the American colonists, it took several years of warfare against the British to actually secure their independence. When victory finally came, the task at hand was no longer to fight and destroy, but to debate and create. The result was the U.S. Constitution of 1787, establishing the world's first modern democratic republic based upon the consent of the governed, a separation of powers with checks and balances upon the federal government, and a recognition of the political rights to vote and hold public office.

Encouraged by this successful American Revolution, and pressed to the breaking point by its own internal problems and pressures, France also exploded into violent upheaval in 1789. The resulting French Revolution not only destroyed a despotic monarch and the hereditary elite of privilege and power of the *ancien régime* in France, but through its actions and its ideology proved to be one of the most significant revolutions in history. Even before the fall of the infamous Bastille prison, revolutionary leaders sought to proclaim a declaration of rights not just for themselves, but for the world. Inspired by their own *philosophes* and by the American Declaration of Independence, men like Abbé Sieyès and the Marquis de Lafayette, who had participated in the American Revolutionary War and who knew Jefferson well, spoke forcefully for the need to declare publicly the "natural rights" of all people. As their colleague Mathieu de Montmorency asserted in one speech that caused a sensation, "The rights of man are invariable like justice, eternal like reason; they apply to all times and all countries. . . . Let us follow the example of the United States: they have set a great example in the new hemisphere; let us give one to the universe."[69]

The force and inspiration of their argument when combined with the upheaval of revolution led deputies in the National Assembly to proclaim their Declaration of the Rights of Man and Citizen. Here they forcefully asserted that all men "are born and remain free and equal in rights," that these rights were universal and "natural and imprescriptible," and that they included "liberty, property, security, and resistance to oppression."[70] The Declaration of 1789 sought to give more precise definition to these concepts by delineating the political right to vote and several very specific civil rights: equality before the law, protection against arbitrary arrest or punishment, the presumption of innocence until proven guilty, freedom of personal opinions and religious beliefs, freedom of expression, and the right to possess property. By making this declaration an integral part of their new constitution, the deputies transformed their vision of natural rights into the positive law of the land. They established that the legitimacy of government no longer derived from the will of the monarch and a traditional order based upon privilege and hierarchy, but instead from the guarantee of individual rights. The impact of this sweeping declaration on France and on other countries and peoples in the world struggling against oppression would be profound, leading

Figure 1. More Powerful Than Libraries and Armies: The Declaration of the Rights of Man and Citizen, 1789. United Nations Photo.

the historian Lord Acton to describe it as "a single confused page . . . that outweighed libraries and was stronger than all of the armies of Napoleon."[71] Indeed, according to one authority, it "remains to this day the classic formulation of the inviolable rights of the individual vis-à-vis the state."[72]

The Declaration of the Rights of Man and Citizen immediately inspired further visions and efforts, for it demonstrated a level of success and attention that others sought to emulate.[73] The impact could be seen in the one single, extraordinary year of 1791. New articles of the French constitution, for example, specified protection by law of civil and political rights, including those of freedom of thought and worship, to Protestants and Jews who had been persecuted under the old regime, and abolished slavery within the borders of France. Additional provisions mandated public relief for the poor and free public education, items completely unknown in other constitutions of the time and ones that would inspire what eventually would be called economic and social rights. A self-educated butcher's daughter, Olympe de Gouges, issued her own Declaration of the Rights of Woman and Citizen, a pioneering document in the revolutionary struggle for women's rights. Here she insisted that "woman is born free and remains equal to man in her rights," passionately shouting:

Women, wake up; the tocsin of reason sounds throughout the universe; recognize your rights . . . ! Women, when will you cease to be blind? . . . Whatever the barriers set up against you, it is in your power to overcome them; you only have to want it![74]

At the same time black slaves in Saint Domingue (now Haiti) also demanded equal rights and launched a massive and bloody revolt against their white masters in order to obtain them.

This was also the year when the efforts of many citizens throughout the new United States who believed that the founding documents said far too little about protecting individual rights successfully added the first ten amendments to the Constitution, calling them The Bill of Rights.[75] Together, they offered protection under the law of the civil rights of individual citizens against threats from two particularly likely sources: the excessive power of the state and—importantly, and uniquely for the time—the tyranny of the majority, or as James Madison so aptly observed, the "impulse of passion, or of interest, adverse to the rights of other citizens."[76] These rights included freedom of religion and freedom of speech, the right to petition and peacefully assemble, freedom from unreasonable searches and seizures, equal protections under the law and a speedy and public trial by jury, and freedom from cruel and unusual punishments, among others. Together, these provisions would become the very foundation, bulwark, and symbol of rights in America. They also would reside at the very core of some of the most critical and controversial of all issues ever raised in subsequent American history and politics.

Moreover, in 1791 the impassioned and visionary pamphleteer Thomas Paine published in England the first part of his sensational and provocative *Rights of Man*. Drawing on the theory of natural law and natural rights, as well as his own personal involvement in both the American and the French revolutions, he spoke explicitly of political, civil, and economic human rights. In this classic statement of resistance to authority and abuse, he gave credit to religious traditions for observing the unity and equality of all humankind, and then argued that universal natural rights for individuals provided the original source of all subsequent rights for members of society. "Man did not enter into society to become *worse* than he was before, nor to have fewer rights than he had before," claimed Paine, "but to have those rights better secured." Moreover, he returned to the earlier theme of responsibility for being a "keeper" of others by explicitly and importantly responding to the French Declaration in these terms: "A Declaration of Rights is, by reciprocity, a Declaration of Duties also. Whatever is my right as a man is also the right of another; and it becomes my duty to guarantee as well as to possess."[77]

By the end of the eighteenth century, therefore, any number of diverse philosophical visions addressed rights in one form or another. The language and expressions varied between "natural rights," "rights of man," "rights of mankind," "rights of humanity," and "human rights."[78] These were not always equivalent expressions or defined in exactly the same way, and sometimes raised more questions than they answered. At this stage they represented fragments, embryonic attempts to articulate ideas and feelings about rights and duties, not completely crafted doctrines about interdependence and indivisibility. These would evolve, expand and become more sophisticated only through time and within their own historical contexts. But they all stressed the relationship between human nature, natural law, and natural rights, and became both partial cause and effect of revolutions themselves. Some became embodied in positive national law that emphasized secular and democratic values and sought to provide protection for individuals in the exercise of political rights for voting and holding public office and civil rights such as freedom of speech, press, religion, and assembly. Others waited for more than two centuries to be realized in practice, if even then. Nevertheless, these visions collectively established an essential principle of international human rights: if natural law established certain universal principles of justice and natural birthright rights for *all* people—simply as a result of being human—and irrespective of the particular governments or cultures under which they lived, then all people were entitled to claim them.

Most important, these early philosophical and secular visions of human rights also shared several fundamental features with the religious visions that preceded them. They revealed that ideas matter in history—and that for some people they matter greatly. Like all visions, they spoke to an ideal rather than a reality. Abstract theories, as we shall see next, did not always become actual practice. But by raising visions of the best rather than the worst in human nature they, like their religious counterparts, contributed essential elements to the transformative evolution of international human rights. They helped to build ideals that inspired the creation of normative standards and actions in the centuries that followed by envisioning a world that ought to be and in arguing that we are able to do what we should do. They presented serious challenges to traditional authority and structures of power known for their prejudice and abuse by proposing radical alternatives. They greatly enhanced a universal sense about the essential unity of humankind and the larger moral responsibilities to be keepers of brothers and sisters elsewhere. Finally, these visions added the force of their considerable influence to the realization, articulated so well by Thomas Paine, that rights and duties are inextricably linked.

Traditional Practices and Ideas of a Very Different Sort

All societies and cultures possess diverse and countervailing forces. Some of these do everything that they can to support human rights, while others do whatever they can to oppose them. In this regard, the visions of rights that we have explored thus far did not go unchallenged. In fact, their claims and their dreams were vehemently contested by traditional practices and ideas that provided the arsenal of dominant counter forces. Instead of seeing the possibilities for the best in human nature, they often saw the worst. Rather than the universal, or what people share in common, they stressed the particular, or what divides them. In place of rights, they demanded obedience. Instead of justice, they wanted privilege. Rather than change, they pressed for tradition and continuity. In place of equality, they insisted on hierarchies. Instead of inclusive human unity, they sought exclusive identity in terms of distinctions based on gender, race, class or caste, belief, ethnicity, or place of origin in attempts to *dehumanize* others. Instead of being a keeper of all brothers and sisters, they frequently looked no further than themselves or their own narrowly defined group. And, of particular significance to international human rights, rather than acknowledging the sovereignty of the individual or the existence of a broader human family, they emphasized the sovereignty and the authority of the nation-state alone.

On New Year's Day 1792, to illustrate, an enraged mob dragged an effigy of Thomas Paine through the streets of Coventry, England. A sign pinned to its chest revealed the real source of their contempt. It read simply: "Rights of Man." Upon reaching the square the crowd quickly strung the effigy from a gibbet, a gallows from which the bodies of criminals already hung were exposed in death for further scorn, and prepared a roaring fire. For effect, they let the likeness of Paine dangle for a while, twisting in the wind, and then watched as it erupted into flames. The spectators burst into cheers, and as the arms, legs, and face of the effigy were consumed by fire, joined in a loud and energetic rendition of the song, "God Save the King!"[79]

The publication of Thomas Paine's *Rights of Man* provoked not only this spectacle but many others as well. Royal authorities sponsored further hangings of such effigies in public squares, anti-Paine meetings, smear campaigns, book burnings, censorship, the prosecution of bookshops who dared to sell his work, and then arrested him on charges of producing "wicked," "seditious," and "treasonous" writings representing "the total subversion of the established form of government."[80] All these repeated the earlier reactions to the writings of Rousseau, who, charged with inciting rebellion, had been forced into exile to save his life. Although the *Rights of Man* became the biggest best-seller in English history after the Bible and spoke to the needs and the hopes of humankind to such an extent that James Madison praised its author Paine as the "great friend of human rights,"[81] its vision nevertheless directly and unquestionably challenged powerful vested interests, privilege, prejudice, and tradition.

Moreover, the *Rights of Man* was a specific and direct assault on the thought of Edmund Burke, the founder of modern conservatism and author of the influential *Reflections on the Revolution in France* published in 1790. In this classic work, Burke attacked the French Revolution's destruction of established tradition, hierarchy, inherited privilege and property, and historical continuity. He criticized those responsible for this "great departure from the ancient course," argued that liberty could emerge only gradually, and described the Declaration of the Rights of Man and Citizen as "a mine that will blow up, at one grand explosion, all examples of antiquity, all precedents, charters, and acts of parliament." Burke warned that the authors of this declaration had become carried away with extremism and "so taken up with their theories about the rights of man, that they have totally forgotten his nature." He considered humanity seriously flawed, weak, and only intermittently rational. "History consists, for the greater part," wrote Burke, "of the miseries brought upon the world by pride, ambition, avarice, revenge, lust, sedition, hypocrisy, [and] ungoverned zeal," and warned that their nature was such that if people were given too many rights they then would "want everything."[82]

Critics also used this occasion to attack the theories of natural rights as they had evolved up to that point. For example, although he believed in natural law, Edmund Burke nonetheless rejected the notion that so-called rights of man could be derived from it. He denounced the Declaration of the Rights of Man and Citizen as so much "prattling about the rights of men" and those who wrote it as "wantonly" creating "metaphysical abstractions" that produced the "monstrous fiction" of human equality. Such notions, he argued, only served to inspire "false ideas and vain expectations in men destined to travel in the obscure walk of laborious life."[83] He feared that any public affirmation of natural rights would destroy aristocracy and lead to social and political upheaval. Interestingly enough, from the other side of the philosophical spectrum, liberal Jeremy Bentham was no less scornful. He worried that abstract declarations and proclamations of natural rights might easily replace positive law and specific legislation. "Rights," he wrote contemptuously, "is the child of law; from real law come real rights; but from imaginary laws, from 'law of nature,' come imaginary rights. . . . Natural rights is simple nonsense."[84]

Declarations of rights and the visions of authors like Paine were challenged not only by many of his contemporaries but, perhaps more significantly, by both practices and ideas about the nature of human beings and of government that had developed over many centuries. Thomas Hobbes's *Leviathan* (1651), one of the fundamental works of Western political theory, written in England, echoed far earlier writings of some philosophers in Asia, for instance, who also saw in humanity "a perpetual and restless desire of power after power." He wrote pessimistically that without a strong government to protect them, people would turn on themselves, creating "a war of every man against every man" where life would be "solitary, poor, nasty, brutish, and short."[85] To prevent such chaos and gain security, Hobbes argued that people surrendered their "state of nature" rights to a strong ruler. Even the illustration on the book's title page conveyed this messsage, for it symbolically showed to those who could read (and the many more at the time who could not) a multitude of tiny and insignificant individuals surrendering themselves completely into the huge body of the omnipotent monarch and state.

People possessed no rights at all to change the form of government, to protest, or to accuse the ruler of injustice. The monarch alone, insisted Hobbes, determined what truths would be taught, enforced rules, granted rewards, inflicted punishments, and made policy "as he shall think most fit." Consequently, "none of his subjects . . . can be freed from his subjection."[86] This argument was seized immediately by those like Robert Filmer, the author of *Patriarcha: Or the Natural Power of Kings* (1680), and others who insisted that kings possessed absolute authority and governed by divine right. These were the ones who could obviously sing "God Save the King!" with gusto.

These ideas of divinely sanctioned, hereditary rulers born of royal families and governing unquestioning, obedient subjects, of course, extended back in time far beyond Hobbes and his contemporaries. The pharaohs of ancient Egypt, the caesars of Rome, the emperors of Byzantium, the caliphs of the Islamic world, the kings of Cambodia, the jarlar of Scandinavia, the khans of the Mongols, the emperors of China and Japan, the sultans and princes of the Indian subcontinent, the tsars of Russia, the kings of African tribes, the rajas of Java and Sumatra, and the emperors of the Aztecs and Incas, among many others and despite their considerable differences, all ruled traditional and highly stratified hierarchical societies. They drew sharp distinctions between the rulers and the ruled, and subjects were expected to respect and fear authority. The few governed the many, the rich and powerful dominated the poor and weak, and those with influence clearly sought to shape the prevailing culture by explaining this condition was part and parcel of "the natural order" of things to reinforce their interests. Severe class and caste divisions predominated, and human bondage in slavery and serfdom existed in most places on earth. Educational opportunities existed only for the most privileged, the vast majority of people in the world could neither read nor write, and censorship and heavy taxes on printed material controlled the spread of new (and radical) ideas like those of human rights. Torture as a means of punishment, extracting confessions, deterrence, or even entertainment through grisly public spectacle was judicially approved and an accepted part of ordinary criminal procedure. Social stability and conformity overwhelmed individual freedom and self-realization, and most certainly insisted on duties over rights. In fact, all these practices prevailed, and hierarchical and authoritarian governments dominated the world as it had evolved up to that time.

Some of the most vehement challenges to visions of human rights—and ones that would influence the fate of international human rights for centuries—came from those who emphasized the importance of differences between people rather than similarities. For them it was not just that they saw different kinds of humans in the world. Instead, it was that they fundamentally saw different *degrees* of humans in the world. That is, for one reason or another, some people were not regarded as being fully human. If they were severely "inferior," "unfit," or "imperfect" and thus not fully human, the argument went, then they did not deserve rights like others. Rights might apply to some—but most certainly not to everyone.

The criteria for determining who was fully human and thus deserved rights varied greatly. Some argued that the distinctions should be based on education, language, or age, with abuse common against that segment of any society always least able to protect itself—children. For others, they should be based on possession of property, class, or caste. The Indian *varnashramadharma* system provided one of the most extreme examples with its strict divisions between castes and its essential assumption that there are fundamental and unchangeable differences in people that prevent any uniform or universal standard from being even considered, let alone applied. For some, depending on location, important distinctions should be based on associations with family, tribe, clan, village, walled city, province, country, empire, or continent. For others, the most critical factor distinguishing people from each other should be religious belief, with sharp distinctions separating, for instance, Hindus of the orthodox Vedic tradition from Buddhists, Christians from Jews and "heathens," those of the Islamic faith from "infidels," Catholics from Protestants, or Sunnis from Shiites. The Spanish Inquisition, centuries of anti-Semitism, the Tokugawa shogunate's persecution of Christians in Japan, Hindu repression of Buddhists, and forced conversions all bear tragic but ample testimony to long traditions of extreme religious bigotry and discrimination.

Powerful and influential religious leaders more committed to the existing secular order than the precepts of their faith concerning being keepers of brothers and sisters also resisted any visions of human rights. Monarchs and emperors around the world, of course, always had found it possible to perpetuate their claims of divine right to rule over their subjects by securing support from popes, archbishops, patriarchs, clergy, rabbis, *ulema*, Brahmin priests, and others. They could be found to justify hierarchy, bigotry, violence, the subordination of women, slavery, military conquest, genocide, or torture. This is particularly evident among governments that claimed to adopt one religion or another, and then proceeded to rule in secular ways that had little or nothing to do with the original vision. Through time, spirituality and ethical values of simple human charity and unadorned empathy for the sufferings of others often succumbed to cleverly devised theological arguments or laws that attempted to provide rationalizations for elaborate rituals and the trappings of wealth and power concentrated in the hands of a few. The ideals of compassion for all those who suffered gave way on many occasions to particularism and distinctions with "others," expressions of exclusivity and special "chosen people," armed invasions against others in the name of the "Prince of Peace," persecution of "outcasts" or "untouchables," or "holy wars" of slaughter against "infidels." The principles of justice for all frequently yielded to plush privilege for some, exclusion for others, intolerance, forced conversion, conquest, enslavement, exploitation, or discrimination based on notions of superiority in belief, gender, race, caste, class, tribe, clan, or some other criterion of difference.

With the emergence of explicit assertions for human rights, this phenomenon became even more apparent. Clerical authorities in France readily banned Voltaire's writings arguing on behalf of the right to freely practice one's religion. Pope Pius VI strongly condemned the provisions on religious toleration and freedom of opinion contained in the French Declaration of the Rights of Man and Citizen. In the Islamic world, members of the fundamentalist clergy denounced notions of civil and political rights as blasphemous and against the teachings of the Qur'an and Shari'a law developed by medieval jurists. Many Hindu religious leaders similarly continued to urge their followers to resist visions of equal rights that threatened what they claimed to be the divinely sanctioned natural order of caste divisions with "untouchables."

Among all the elements of traditional difference that profoundly challenged larger visions of human rights and equality for all, gender stands out in striking clarity. The subordination of women to men in both the public and private realms represented the well-entrenched norm rather than the exception, and ideas of being a "brother's keeper" often applied literally only to brothers. Throughout most of history, customs and laws governing bodily integrity and rape, marriage and divorce, inheritance and primogeniture, employment, prohibitions about public behavior and appearance, and exclusion from education and the political process, among other matters, resulted in what has been called the systematic and discriminatory creation of "assigned separate spheres" and "gendering of power" against women across the globe.[87] Daughters almost always received far less favorable treatment than sons from the time of birth, and then forced throughout their lives to endure hearing themselves described as members of the "weaker" or "lesser" sex, as no more than "heir providers," as "inferior" and "imperfect" beings, and as "sub-human." If they were not fully human, it was argued, they did not deserve to have equal rights. In Asia, Confucius pronounced that "women . . . are of a lower state than men and can never attain full equality with them."[88] In a popular book in the West entitled *Malleus Maleficarum* (1486), for example, Jacob Sprenger declared that women were "feebler in mind and body," "a defect" of creation, and nothing more than "an imperfect animal."[89] Others viewed them as dangerous threats, and misogyny, or hatred against women, manifested itself in a kind of patriarchal rage that considered females not as loving wives, caring mothers, or equals, but rather as lustful whores or the embodiment of evil. It will never be known how many young women were seriously abused, forced into marriages against their will, or executed as witches, crying out in anguish, "Better it would be for me and better it would have been had I not been born . . . in this joyless world."[90] Some were considered as property to be bought and sold in what Westerners revealingly called the "white slave trade," and confined against their will to households, harems, or brothels. Even during the height of discussion about human rights during the French Revolution, the price that Olympe de Gouges paid for advocating women's rights was death—by beheading. Stated as directly as possible in order that the magnitude might be more fully appreciated: this prejudice and its resulting discrimination, exploitation, repression, and abuse applied to no less than one half of the human race.

In terms of its specific impact on international relations, perhaps no factor of difference confronted basic principles of human rights more directly than that of race. For centuries men and women ranging from Japan to the Islamic world and from the Indian subcontinent to Europe and then the Americas discriminated against those of "backward races" whom they regarded as inferior. Indeed, many traditions from around the world clearly demonstrate what has been called "the impulse to inequality" wherein skin color served to greater or lesser degrees as the badge of master and subject, of the free and enslaved, and of the dominators and dominated.[91] Among the many cases of racial prejudice, however, none came even close to eclipsing that of the white, Western world. From the early ideas expressed by Greek philosophers such as

Aristotle and historians such as Herodotus and Tacitus to geographers and chroniclers writing in the famous sixteenth century *Cosmographie universelle,* Europeans increasingly came to see nonwhites as being not fully human and, hence, treated them very differently.[92]

Widespread territorial empire and exploitation provided but one manifestation of this racial prejudice. In fact, the sufferings and massacres inflicted against helpless indigenous peoples became so horrifying that they provoked moral outrage. The noted Dominican jurist of the sixteenth century Francisco de Vitoria courageously spoke out in condemning the Spanish government's brutal conquest of the Aztecs and Incas, and called for a new international law among nations with universal validity that would include rights and duties for all peoples. Shortly thereafter, a priest by the name of Bartholomé de Las Casas wrote an account of shocking brutality entitled *In Defense of the Indians,* articulating the relationship between natural law and natural rights and pleading: "The Indians are our brothers [and sisters] and Christ has given his life for them. Why, then, do we persecute them with such inhuman savagery?"[93] Although his personal example of courageously challenging one of the most powerful governments in the world eventually would go on to serve as an inspiration for generations of Latin American human rights activists, during his own time he was reviled by most of his countrymen. "To insist with Las Casas that Indians should be won over by persuasion only," writes one historian, "was to abandon all future conquests and admit the injustice of past ones. The full implications of either theory were more than any self-respecting government of the time could stomach."[94]

Theories of the inferiority and superiority of one race over another gained even wider acceptance in the context of slavery. Indeed, the concomitance of racial prejudice and the power to enslave blacks suggests a strong mutual relationship between the two. Both were, after all, twin aspects of the debasement of black men and women from people into property.[95] Slavery, of course, reflected an ancient tradition extending over thousands of years and spread across Asia, Africa, Europe, the Middle East, islands of the Pacific, and the Americas. It was neither invented by Europeans nor confined exclusively to black Africans; and, in fact, whites themselves had known enslavement on the shores of the Mediterranean and Black seas, in Eastern Europe and Russia, in European colonies, and in Africa and Asia.[96] But what emerged by the sixteenth, seventeenth, and eighteenth centuries dramatically transformed slave patterns of the past. In terms of the total numbers of millions of human beings, lucrative financial rewards, impact on several continents, magnitude of extreme brutality, exploitation, and creation of an ideology extolling racial superiority, the transatlantic black slavery simply had no parallel in history.

European slave traders and slave owners in the New World, for example, desperately sought to establish clear hierarchies and to keep the races segregated from each other. The Spanish Crown, for example, promulgated specific laws to "prohibit contact and communication between Indians and Mulattoes, Negroes, and similar races."[97] Portuguese settlers distanced themselves from what they called the *racas infectas* or "contaminated races" and created a caste system based on white supremacy and the institutionalized inferiority of colored slaves.[98] French slave laws, known as the *code noir,* also stressed the need for segregation and keeping the races apart, as did those of the Dutch. British colonists in North America acted in much the same way, constructing legal means to make black men and women slaves "for life," prohibiting interracial marriages, and granting any owner "absolute power and authority over his Negro slaves."[99]

According to their defenders and beneficiaries, these various traditional practices and ideas, and the regimes that flourished with them, had produced societies of remarkable stability. Here, to use Burke's phrase, people knew "their proper place!" To maintain this long continuity and its benefits, he argued, "the body of the people must not find the principles of natural subordination . . . rooted out of their minds" by some misguided and inflammatory visions of human rights.[100] He and others believed that such dangerous ideas and revolutionary notions about liberty and equality for all people would raise unwarranted expectations, encourage challenges to authority of all kinds, disrupt the rich continuity of history and custom, and thereby seriously threaten enviable conditions of law and order and private property that had proven themselves again and again over time and location throughout the world.

Burke's mention of property in this context is of great importance, for it revealed that visions and the language of rights could also present double-edged swords. That is, not all people shared the same vision, and the claimed rights of some could easily challenge the asserted rights of others or create difficult inconsistencies. This was particularly evident in the case of those who argued on behalf of private ownership.[101] Property rights had made a powerful appeal for many centuries to the minds of people by encouraging them to consider ownership as the rightful reward for the sweat of their brows or the intelligence of their minds. John Locke himself helped to elevate these long-held notions of property rights to a higher philosophical plane by declaring that they were an integral part of "natural rights" and essential to the pursuit of happiness. Indeed, he argued that "the great and chief end" of forming governments in the first place was "the preservation of their property."[102] Rousseau joined in by describing this as "the most sacred of all the rights of citizenship" and "even more important in some respects than liberty itself."[103] Hutcheson, Hume, Burke, Bentham, Jefferson, and Alexander Hamilton all added their voices to this chorus as well, as did others from non-Western countries.[104] It thus did not take much effort to use these arguments as a defense for the great holdings of the few rich against the poverty of the many poor, and to do so when definitions of private property at times included living human beings—slaves, serfs, women, and children.

One other element directly and powerfully confronted any and all notions of international human rights: the doctrine of sovereignty. Indeed, from the time it first emerged to the present, no doctrine has served to thwart international human rights more severely than this one. Virtually all governments in the world regarded that how they advanced their own interests was a matter exclusively within their own domestic jurisdiction. Emperors, pharaohs, caesars, khans, sultans, kings, tsars, dictators, and eventually prime ministers and presidents all argued that they and the territory they ruled were completely independent and sovereign. Thus, how they treated their own people or those under their control was their business and most certainly not subject to any outside international standards, scrutiny, or interference.

With the emergence of nation-states, this proposition was not only given more articulate expression but actually confirmed and codified in international law. French political philosopher Jean Bodin began by enunciating the principle of national sovereignty in his book *Les six livres de la République* (1576). States, he asserted, possessed the unique feature of sovereignty, which he dramatically and defiantly defined as "power absolute and perpetual," "supreme," and "subject to no law." Indeed, claimed Bodin, such sovereign power provided "the distinguishing mark of a state." It alone possessed the power to decide how it would behave in the world and how it would treat its own people within its own borders and those under its control elsewhere. Bodin described this power as "absolute authority over all the rest without exception" and "without the consent of any superior, equal, or inferior being necessary."[105] This came to be interpreted that if a government desired to treat its subjects well and acknowledge that they might have rights, it could. If it wanted to exploit them or torture them, it could. If it wanted to persecute them or segregate them, it could. If it wanted to forcibly convert them or enslave them, it could do that as well. The precise nature of the treatment, however, was considered to be a matter of exclusive domestic jurisdiction.

This doctrine of national sovereignty, and its corollary of domestic jurisdiction, received reinforcement in a number of ways. The two treaties comprising the Peace of Westphalia signed in 1648 sought to replace discussions about the "law of nature" with the practice of the "law of nations" by insisting on the power and authority of sovereign, independent states. Only these states could be considered subjects of international law and no international jurisdiction existed to hold government leaders personally or criminally responsible for abuses that they conducted within their own borders. They recognized no universal moral authority of natural law on behalf of individual rights from above, no claims of an emperor or a pope, and no petitions from feudal barons or subjects from below. The publication of *Leviathan* almost immediately thereafter provided even further theoretical justification for the doctrine, particularly when Thomas Hobbes addressed what he described as "the essence of sovereignty." Here he left no doubt that the sovereign powers of the state and the absolute monarch that acted in its name must rule without challenge, doing "whatsoever he shall think necessary to be done."[106] Such was the force of this doctrine, writes one noted authority on international politics, that with the span of a century it "became unchallengeable either from within the territory or from without. In other words, it had become supreme."[107] Theories, of course, are never absolute in practice, but when the doctrine of sovereignty was both asserted and accepted by governments, victims of human rights abuses were forced to suffer alone and made to understand that they could not look for help or protection from beyond the borders of their own state. For them, there was nowhere to run and nowhere to hide. Victims remained objects of international pity rather than subjects of international law.[108] As such, government leaders understood for centuries that they could act in the name of their state largely as they wished or were able, safe in the knowledge that this widespread culture of impunity shielded them from being held internationally accountable.

Further obstacles were presented by those whose only considerations resided in the exercise of sheer, raw, physical power. Religious belief of any kind, let alone that of compassion or responsibilities toward others, left them cold. Philosophical thought, let alone that concerning freedom, or dignity, or justice, failed to move them. Faith in visions of what might be, the power of moral force, or even law, elicited only contempt. Their credo appeared time and time again throughout the ages, bluntly expressed in the famous Melian Dialogue: "You know as well as we do that right, as the world goes, is only in question between equals in power, while the strong do what they can and the weak suffer what they must."[109]

It can thus be seen why, in the vast history of the world, most people experienced not human rights but abuses. Indeed, the extent and duration of this brutal legacy weighed so heavily upon the famous sociologist William Graham Sumner that when he looked back upon the whole of the human experience he felt compelled to conclude: "All history is only one long story to this effect: men have struggled for power over their fellow men in order that they might win the joys of earth at the expense of others, and might shift the burdens of life from their own shoulders upon those of others."[110] The Scottish philosopher Adam Smith reached the same conclusion when he observed that "Slavery . . . has hardly any possibility of being abolished . . . [since it] has been universal in the beginning of society, and the love of dominion and authority over others will probably make it perpetual."[111] No place on earth—West, East, North, or South—by the end of the eighteenth century possibly could claim that human rights for all were somehow broadly based or solidly grounded in their cultures. They simply were not. In fact, it is for precisely this reason that those with powerful and entrenched interests in hierarchy, privilege, prejudice, and sovereignty viewed those who advocated rights, like Thomas Paine burned so vigorously in effigy, as heretics and revolutionaries who threatened to overturn their long-standing exercise of power. They believed that the future should reproduce the past and that continuity should prevail over change. Those of this persuasion consequently vowed that they would do whatever they had to do to oppose dangerous visions of human rights forever, to the end of time.

Visions—and Reality

The interplay between these ideas and traditions that stood opposed to human rights and the religious and philosophical visions that supported human rights, and the various interests they represented, would move the course of much of the history that would follow into our own day. Despite all of the visions of rights that had emerged, the reality at the end of the eighteenth century was that most individuals in the world still found themselves confronting hierarchical societies and imperial or authoritarian regimes in which differences mattered. Whether they lived in Western Europe, the shores of the Mediterranean or the Baltic, the mountains or the plains of Asia, the Indian subcontinent, the Near and Middle East, Africa, North America, Central and South America, or islands of the Pacific, patterns of dominance and discrimination prevailed. Sharp distinctions were made, depending upon particular circumstances of power and privilege, on the basis of gender, race, class or caste, age, education, religion, ethnicity, language, and tribe or clan, among other factors of difference used either individually or in combination. Here, theories such as those of the divine right of rulers or racial superiority and entrenched customs, often ancient in origins, served to support oppresive practices. As such, great contrasts and even chasms emerged between theory and practice, between professed values and conduct—or between the visions and reality—of human rights.

One of the most striking of these contrasts could be seen in the glaring differences between religious principles of compassion and care and the secular desires for power and privilege. Some of those governments and peoples in the West who so vocally claimed to follow the precepts of Christianity and the message to be keepers of brothers and sisters, for example, came to be known internationally as among the most rapacious and the worst offenders against the well-being and rights of others in the world. They persecuted Jews and Muslims, tortured those who held different religious and political beliefs, discriminated against women and children, conquered others, exploited peasants and laborers, and enslaved those whom they came to regard as racially inferior.

In the case of slavery and the slave trade they had no desire to be left out of this enterprise and thus deny themselves either the profits and the power that flowed from it. Indeed, some of the most successful businesses of all time profited enormously from treating human beings as property, including the Royal African Company, Brandenburg Company, and Dutch West India Company. The Board of Trade in London accurately reflected the opinion of investors in many other capitals when it concluded that it was "absolutely necessary that a trade so beneficial to the kingdom should be carried on to the greatest advantage."[112] Official state policy, often enhanced by investments from the royal families of Europe, guaranteed even further financial successes and the growth of commercial capitalism. This explains why at the end of the eighteenth century the bulk of people carried by the British across the Atlantic were not eager white immigrants seeking a better life in the New World (as we are inclined to imagine), but rather black Africans shipped across the ocean against their will who outnumbered white Europeans three to one.[113] As one leading authority on historical slave patterns observes, "black slavery was an intrinsic part of 'the rise of the West'" and for nation-states to refrain from participating in it "was almost as unthinkable as spurning nuclear technology is in the world of today."[114]

What was thinkable and unthinkable was also seen in the attitudes of several Western *philosophes* themselves. Ironically enough, some of the greatest minds of the Enlightenment who espoused the democratic principles of liberation, equality, toleration, natural rights, and respect for the dignity of individuals and who challenged notions that a privileged few should rule over the vast majority of the population, at the same time revealed that they believed that these principles should be applied to their own gender and their own race alone. Rousseau, for example, could wax eloquently about freedom and justice, but at the same time insist that it was part of the order of nature for woman to obey men. "Women do wrong to complain of the inequality of man-made laws," he wrote, and claimed that "when she tries to usurp our rights, she is our inferior."[115] Montesquieu, the articulate exponent of individual worth, simultaneously claimed that black-skinned Africans were "savage and barbarian" and bereft of normal human traits.[116] Voltaire held financial interests in the Compagnie des Indes, the fortunes of which came in part from the slave trade, and wrote that blacks possessed only "a few more ideas than animals" and that "Negroes are thus slaves of other men."[117] Wrote the noted British philosopher David Hume, "I am apt to suspect the Negroes and in general all the other species . . . to be naturally inferior to the whites."[118] Even the distinguished anthropologist Johann Friedrich Blumenbach argued that in comparing races, "the white color holds the first place" while the others of black, yellow, brown, and red skin color were merely degenerates from the original.[119] Such ideas, increasingly presented with the authority of science, easily could be seized on to explain why those of different races—again—should not be regarded as fully human. The ideas consequently were used to justify racial segregation, imperial conquests, exploitation, and especially the capture and sale of living human beings into life-long bondage via the slave trade.

These glaring gaps between visions and reality increasingly began to raise two of the most critical, challenging, and contentious of all questions in the entire subject of international human rights from early history to our own day: *who* should enjoy these rights, and *what* rights should be included? In attempting to answer the question of rights for whom,[120] for example, it became clear that there was not one vision but many. Some held out visions of breadth and depth, as historian Lynn Hunt insightfully demonstrates, arguing that human rights possessed three interlocking qualities: they must be *natural* (inherent in human beings), they must be *equal* (the same for everyone), and they must be *universal* (applicable everywhere).[121] They insisted that for rights to truly be human rights, all people must possess them because of the fact that they are human beings. Condorcet captured the essence of this vision in one sentence:

Either no individual in mankind has true rights, or all have the same ones; and whoever votes against the right of another, whatever his religion, his color, or his sex, has from that moment adjured his own rights.[122]

But others did not agree with this proposition at all and fiercely opposed it. They might consider rights as natural, but most certainly not equal or universal. Whatever human rights existed, in their minds, should not be enjoyed by all but restricted to a select few.

The reality of such serious disagreements over the meaning, the context, and the application of rights could be seen immediately. Given the long history of abuses, expectations were high among activists that the upheavals in America and France during the so-called Age of Democratic Revolutions would mark a dramatic transformation. In many ways they did, particularly as they sought to give political expression to natural rights theory by establishing that sovereignty no longer resided in absolutist monarchs but in the people, by proclaiming that governments were justified only insofar as they guaranteed the rights of their people, and by giving definition to this first generation of human rights focusing on civil and political rights. To see this in perspective, it is important to remember that even in Britain nineteen out of twenty men could not vote, and no women at all. Nevertheless, even revolutions, wars, and violence could not change everything at once. Tensions arose immediately between ideal visions and practical reality, for resistance to any broad-based extension of human rights for all remained determined and strong. As Thomas Paine himself so perceptively observed: "Tyranny, like hell, is not easily conquered."[123]

Despite the remarkable creation of the new United States, its expressed theories of natural law and inalienable rights, and the ringing words "We the people" in the Constitution's preamble, for example, many of the leaders who had launched a revolution in the name of freedom and rights were unwilling to make the principles applicable to all. Equal rights were actually denied to a majority of the population comprising women, slaves, domestic or indentured servants, laborers without property, indigenous peoples, and children. The Constitution itself provided official sanction for the practice of slavery. This was done by establishing that slaves were not to be regarded as fully human when counting the number of residents in apportioning Congressional districts, by prohibiting Congress from taking action to eliminate the slave trade for twenty years, and by insisting that fugitive slaves must be regarded as articles of commerce (rather than people) and returned to their owners. Property rights, in other words, took precedence over human rights. Many prominent leaders, including George Washington, Thomas Jefferson, and judges on the Supreme Court actually owned slaves themselves. In some states black slaves outnumbered free whites. Similarly, women in America would not be guaranteed their right to vote for more than a century. In addition to gender, every state in the new nation restricted voting on the basis of age, race, and property or wealth, and thus denied the political right to vote and effective representation to the majority of people.[124] Nor did these new documents or laws give protection to Native Americans. Washington and Benjamin Franklin described them as "ignorant savages" and "beasts," while Jefferson himself argued that his country had no choice but to pursue them "to extinction."[125] For these disenfranchised and dispossessed, and despite the official rhetoric of rights, neither the Constitution nor its Bill of Rights with their language of "shall" instead of "ought" or "should" provided any immediate protection whatsoever.

Revolutionary France experienced similar difficulties in the distance between vision and reality concerning human rights. Initially swept up in the excitement of radical change, leaders of the National Assembly decreed the abolition of the feudal regime of the past, freed remaining serfs, eliminated special privileges in matters of taxation and public office, issued the Declaration on the Rights of Man and Citizen, and then took the highly unusual steps of extending citizenship to those of color, decriminalizing private homosexual activities, emancipating Jews, legalizing divorce, providing that women could receive inheritance, and abolishing slavery in the colonies. Very quickly, however, the excesses of the Terror descended into the persecution and execution of tens of thousands, egregiously violating many of the proclaimed rights and thereby stimulating counter-revolutionary forces of resistance. Within only months, to illustrate, the Assembly rescinded its decision about equal rights for blacks. French troops were sent to overseas colonies to punish those slaves who had rebelled and to restore slavery itself, and few advocated any extension of human rights to the millions of indigenous peoples subjugated under the French Empire.[126] The political rights of voting and holding public office also possessed restrictions in practice. At first, only white men who passed a test of wealth, known as "active citizens," could exercise the franchise or hold office, as compared to those "passive citizens" of servants, the propertyless, and poor who could not. Women were theoretically citizens, but could not vote, fully participate in the political process, or receive equal protection under the law.[127] Revolutionary leaders here, as in America, understood that the extension in practice of fully equal rights across the lines of race, gender, or class would entail vast social and political consequences—and these they were simply unwilling to accept.

In this regard, it is extremely important to recognize that the Declaration of Independence, the Constitution, and the Bill of Rights in the United States, as well as the Declaration of the Rights of Man and Citizen in France, reflected far more vision than reality. None of these documents were "deeply rooted" in either the practices of the West or even of these two countries, as others wishing to denigrate human rights within their own countries by distorting historical origins eventually would claim.[128] They emerged not out of long tradition or wide-spread experience or inclusive election, but rather out of war and revolution and had to be nurtured in the face of overwhelming opposition. In this context of the late eighteenth century when "democracy" and individual rights were regarded by many as synonymous with anarchy and subversion, they were statements of ideals and aspirations toward which two nations pledged themselves to struggle in the future, but not to guarantee at the moment.

The accuracy of this judgment can be seen in part by the number of outspoken critics who vowed that they would not rest as long as such glaring disparities between visions and realities in human rights existed in these countries. Some women, for example, viewed their exclusion from the extension of rights as a blatant betrayal of the promises of democracy. They wrote petitions, published tracts, and organized clubs to demand more participation. In the new American republic, Abigail Adams accused men of being "naturally tyrannical," and placed them on notice: "If particular care and attention is not paid to the ladies we are determined to foment a rebellion, and will not hold ourselves bound by any laws in which we have no voice or representation."[129] In revolutionary France, men such as Condorcet and Pierre Guyomar and women such as Olympe de Gouges and Etta Palm d'Aelders courageously spoke out on behalf of the rights of women, sometimes sacrificing their very lives for the vision in which they believed. During 1792 Mary Wollstonecraft published her impassioned book in England entitled *A Vindication of the Rights of Woman*, scathingly attacking gender oppression, pressing for equal educational opportunities, and demanding "JUSTICE!" and "rights of humanity" for all.[130] Still others pushed to extend the boundaries even further, such as Thomas Spence with his pamphlet *The Rights of Infants*.[131]

These many discussions about rights in theory similarly challenged the practice of denying rights to other colonists or indigenous peoples who populated the vast European colonial empires sprawled across the world. Although the loss of the American colonies as a result of military defeat forced any number of British citizens into a crisis of conscience that questioned their moral self-worth in the light of conquest and its denial of human rights as never before,[132] it did not lead them to rush into jettisoning any other imperial holdings. In fact, a general and an admiral issued a joint message sternly commanding their officers "to prevent a circulation in the British Colonies of the wild and pernicious Doctrines of Liberty and Equality."[133] The same pattern occurred in virtually all other empires at the time. Even in the wake of evocative revolutionary statements in France about liberty, equality, and fraternity, no national leader rushed to surrender their overseas possessions. Here the contrast between rhetoric and action was so great, in fact, that in a pamphlet entitled "Emancipate Your Colonies!" the French people were pointedly asked: "You choose your own government, why are not other people to choose theirs? Do you seriously mean to govern the world, and do you call that *liberty*? What is become of the rights of men? Are you the only men who have rights?"[134]

But nothing marked the vast distance between vision and reality more starkly than the hypocrisy among those very people who demanded liberty for themselves while they enslaved others. Thomas Paine lashed out early with his *African Slavery in America* (1775), asking how political revolutionaries and Christians could possibly justify treating people as property. Patrick Henry, an American revolutionary himself, posed the same question: "Is it not amazing that at a time when the rights of humanity are defined and understood with precision, in a country, above all others, fond of liberty, that in such a country we find men . . . adopting a principle as repugnant to humanity as it is inconsistent with the Bible, and destructive to liberty?"[135]

This combination of both political persuasion and religious belief by Paine and Henry is particularly instructive and revealing. Those who worked so hard to abolish slavery and the slave trade very often intertwined these two motives and saw them not as conflicting but rather as profoundly complementary to one another. Particularly from within the religious community of reformist evangelical Anglicans and anti-establishment, "dissenting" churches like the Baptists, Congregationalists, Methodists, Presbyterians, and especially the Quakers, came insistent and determined cries that the practice of slavery presented an absolutely intolerable obstacle to any political concept of rights and a violent offense against the Christian principle of being responsible keepers of all brothers and sisters. At a time of religious revival known as the "Great Awakening," articulate and impassioned Protestant spokesmen like John Woolman and Anthony Benezet in North America and James Ramsay, Granville Sharp, Benjamin Rush, and John Wesley in Britain fused the language of rights with that of scripture. With explicit references to "the rights of man" and the "inherent rights of mankind," they argued that the emancipation of slaves was also fundamental to the message of love and compassion, the need to live out the message of the Good Samaritan, the power of redemption, and their responsibility to follow the Biblical injunction "to proclaim freedom to the captives."[136] They found encouragement from the 1772 *Somerset* case in a London courtroom that appeared to make slavery illegal within Britain itself, but realized that there was much more to be done. For them, the struggle against slavery presented an opportunity for their religious visions to become progressive forces in history and posed a decisive test for the strength of their convictions.[137] It was in this spirit that Benezet declared: "At a time when the general rights and liberties of mankind . . . are become so much the subjects of universal consideration; can it be an inquiry indifferent to any, how many of those who distinguish

Figure 2. Brothers and Sisters: A Famous Emancipation Society Image. Library of Congress.

themselves as the Advocates of Liberty, remain insensible and inattentive to the treatment of thousands and tens of thousands of our fellow-men who . . . are at this very time kept in the most deplorable state of slavery?"[138] One group of Quakers pressed this point by writing:

We conjure you, as you love Liberty, to extend its influence, and investigate its import; examine your Declaration of Rights, and see if you can find in it a *term* which conveys the idea of *human* merchandise; examine your hearts, and see if you can find a spark of brotherhood for men who *deal* in men. To defend your own liberties is noble, but to befriend the friendless is Godlike; complete then your Revolution by demanding Commerce to be just, that Africa may bless you as well as Europe.[139]

If human bondage in slavery be "excusable, or pardonable," wrote James Beattie bluntly in his *Elements of Moral Science*, "it is vain to talk any longer of the eternal distinctions of right and wrong, truth and falsehood, good and evil."[140]

Many of these activist opponents of slavery not only drew conviction and determination from their religious faith, they also found inspiration and hope. They believed that they no longer had to accept these traditional practices as they were, that eyes could be opened, that hearts could be changed, and thus that abuses could be ended. This belief found expression in sermons, in print, and even in music. One of the most moving hymns of all time was composed during precisely this period by a former slave trading ship captain named John Newton. His lyrics and melody gave such hope to the hopeless that it eventually would be sung by generations who struggled on behalf of human rights, from those who worked to abolish slavery to those who would later march in the civil rights movement in the Untied States and those who would gather when Nelson Mandela was released from prison more than two centuries later. The title of the hymn was "Amazing Grace" and it began with these words:

Amazing grace! How sweet the sound
That saved a wretch like me!
I once was lost, but now am found,
Was blind, but now I see.

With reference to slavery, the depth of that blindness and the extent of the distance between vision and reality was given dramatic public exposure during the infamous *Zong* trial held in 1783. The case took its name from a slave ship that had been bound from Africa to Jamaica loaded with nearly 450 slaves tightly jammed into the vessel's hold. Due to terrible weather conditions and an inexperienced captain, the voyage took more than twice its normal length. After three months at sea, more than sixty had died, and many of the rest were on the verge of death. The captain thus became increasingly worried—not for the slaves as human victims, but because he realized that dead slaves would bring him no profit. He knew that since the shipping business regarded the slaves as cargo rather than as people, they were insured against "perils of the sea." If slaves were lost because of such "perils," maritime insurance would cover the property loss. With this calculation in his mind, he ordered his crew to throw more than 130 of the sickest slaves overboard while still alive to drown. When the shipping company went to trial in London to collect insurance, the deliberations revolved not around the cold-bloodied murder of human beings, but rather about whether the financial claims should be paid. When the lawyer for the ship owners thought that someone in the courtroom might attempt to bring on a criminal prosecution for homicide, he declared that "*it would be madness: the Blacks were property.*" The presiding judge agreed, insisting that murder was not the issue because, in his revealing words: it was "just as if horses were killed."[141]

The moral outrage provoked by such statements and the continued existence of slavery, when combined with the hope that such blindness could be transformed into sight, soon led to a new element that eventually would prove to be of enormous significance to the evolution of international human rights: the creation of the first human rights nongovernmental organizations (NGOs). Following in the steps of the Society for the Relief of Free Negroes Unlawfully Held in Bondage, the Pennsylvania Society for Promoting the Abolition of Slavery was formed in 1784. Then, three years later, a group of twelve determined men all deeply dedicated to their religious faith, including a twenty-five-year-old Thomas Clarkson who would devote the rest of his life to the cause, gathered together in a London bookstore and print shop. Here they created the Society for Effecting the Abolition of the Slave Trade to pursue a vision of a seemingly impossible task: to end this practice in the largest slave-trading empire on the face of the earth, where powerful economic and political interests guaranteed fierce opposition and where the overwhelming majority viewed slavery as an unalterable fact of life and part of the "natural order." They vowed that they would not quit until they accomplished their goal. In the words of Adam Hochschild, "In all of human experience, there was no precedent for such a campaign."[142]

Actual victims of slavery added their voices to this vision as well. Some of these came from slaves who boldly petitioned for their freedom in the name "of justice, humanity, and the rights of mankind."[143] Another emerged from a remarkable former slave by the name of Olaudah Equiano. In addition to helping to found a group that called itself the "Sons of Africa" to draw public attention to the slave trade, he boldly wrote a book in 1789 entitled *Interesting Narrative*. It was a fascinating and best-selling autobiographical account that gave a name, a voice, and a human face to millions of black Africans who suffered from the horrors inflicted by slavery. Through moving descriptions of his own personal sufferings, Equiano wanted his tens of thousands of readers who enjoyed at least some rights to view the world from the perspective of slaves who possessed none. By such means he hoped that those who once were blind would now see—see that others (including black slaves) were fully human and therefore deserving of their rights. Toward this end, he posed a question that he knew would force his readers into self-reflection: "Can any man be a Christian who asserts that one part of the human race were ordained to be in perpetual bondage to another?" He argued with considerable insight that slavery destroys the humanity of not only the slave, but the slave trader and the slave owner as well, and forcefully condemned those who engaged in treating people as property as the "destroyers of human rights."[144] At the same time, visual images were created to convey the same message. One of the most famous of these shows a black man and a black woman on bended knees. Their wrists and ankles are chained, their hands held together in prayer. They ask simply but pointedly: "Am I Not a Man and a Brother? Am I Not a Woman and a Sister?"

Such images and personal accounts of suffering possessed a capacity to evoke what would become an extremely powerful element in the evolution of international human rights: *empathy*. Religious visions based on belief and philosophical visions based on reason established the foundations sufficient to motivate many people into supporting and protecting rights. But others needed something more deeply emotional, a personal or vicarious experience that would enable them to see or to imagine and then to viscerally feel the inner sense of danger, the outrage, the anger, and the pain of those who suffered. This is precisely what Equiano meant when he wrote about the indispensability of finding men and women "of feeling" who could empathize with slaves not as property—but as real people.[145] Through books, illustrations, sermons, plays like *Slaves in Algiers; or, A Struggle for Freedom*, poems, hymns, and the increasing number of newspapers and popular novels of the period, individuals were given greater means to grow emotionally not only in awareness of others, but, as a consequence, in awareness of self.[146] Thus, when looking one way or another into the face of shackled slaves, of abused women, of exploited workers, of tortured prisoners, or of conquered indigenous peoples, among others, they could begin to identify with them and see something of themselves. As they moved from apathy to empathy they then could reach a profound realization: that could easily be me! Once this crucial emotional threshold was crossed, they could see victims as truly human moral beings—brothers and sisters—who were entitled to rights like themselves.

Sometimes the capacity to see visions is a function of imagination and mental attitude, but sometimes it is a function of concrete information. In this regard, champions of international human rights who attempted to bring visions into reality historically suffered from a very serious practical problem of accurate and timely facts. That is, even those highly motivated to advance human rights could take no action unless they could first obtain and then convey news about the plight of others beyond their own borders, either by traveling themselves to different locations or by securing news of exploitation, conquest, massacre, or other abuses in sufficient time to relieve suffering. Given the power of authoritarian rule and the lack of widespread literacy, knowledge of these abuses often could be completely suppressed. Given the limitations of technology in an age of only rudimentary transportation and communication, various parts of the world remained both geographically and intellectually isolated from each other and such information simply could not be accurately, widely, or rapidly transmitted. As one observer who lived through this period insightfully and poignantly reflected: "In the old days, news traveled slowly; one scarcely heard what was happening at the other end of the world until the following year. If blood had been spilt, the earth had time to absorb it; if tears had been shed, the sun had time to dry them."[147]

If enormous chasms thus often existed between vision and reality concerning human rights, the same cannot be said with reference to the doctrine of national sovereignty. Here theory and practice mutually reinforced each other as nation-states behaved exactly as they wished toward those under their control and human rights simply were not regarded as a matter of legitimate international concern. For several important reasons, states normally refused to become involved in disputes surrounding the treatment and well-being of people beyond their own borders. In philosophical terms, they found themselves confronting the doctrine of national sovereignty and its uncompromising claims of domestic jurisdiction. In practical terms, they found themselves largely powerless to have much of an effect on the internal affairs of others. Their own lack of resources to project their will and the complete absence of any international organization that might assist in establishing some level of minimal standards, let alone enforcement, simply reinforced this condition. Politically, they also found themselves afraid to intervene due to reciprocity, for criticism in the name of human rights within another country might well invite criticism of their own policies in return. States that made little or no effort to protect human rights of their own people at home could hardly claim justification for the protection of others abroad. These various philosophical, practical, and political factors, when combined with those many traditional ideas and practices that rejected human rights in the first place, all erected formidable obstacles in the path of anyone with visions of creating and protecting international human rights.

*   *   *

During most times and places, from the beginning of recorded history to the end of the eighteenth century, the overwhelming majority of all of those who ever lived and died found themselves confronting various forms of abuse based on gender, race, caste or class, belief, ethnicity, place of origin, or some other form of difference. They were not regarded as being fully human by those with power and privilege, and therefore never allowed to exercise whatever rights they might claim, or that others might assert on their behalf. Instead, traditional societies and imperial regimes from Asia to Africa and from Europe to South America emphasized hierarchical and patriarchal relationships, stark stratification between the strong and the weak, conformity over diversity, and obedience to existing authority rather than personal rights. The few ruled the many. Cultures reflected and reinforced patterns of dominance in many varieties of privilege and poverty, intolerance and ignorance, despotism and suppression, torture and violence, arrogance and xenophobia, persecution and segregation, and at times genocide. Human bondage and slavery were commonly accepted as the norm. Moreover, in these practices virtually all governments regarded how they treated those under their control as a matter exclusively within their own sovereign, domestic jurisdiction. Those who suffered as victims thus could not look beyond their state for any form of protection, for their fate was not regarded as a legitimate subject of any international action. This long and extraordinarily powerful legacy of reality must be understood in order to appreciate the evolution we will witness.

Yet in the midst of this hostile historical setting, and often in the face of entrenched traditional practices and fierce opposition, there were those creative and courageous enough to see visions of a different kind of world in which all people should be treated with dignity and equality. First with religious precepts, then with secular philosophical principles, and gradually with a few practical and concrete political results, there emerged visions that all men and women had responsibilities to those in need and that they possessed certain natural or inalienable rights simply as the result of being human beings. Despite all the realities and constraints aligned against them, these various visions slowly but determinedly began to grow in influence. Their strength did not derive from their ability to immediately bring about human rights for all in practice, however, but rather in keeping ideals alive for centuries during unpromising circumstances and under brutal persecution that might serve to inspire subsequent generations to develop a more sophisticated discourse about human rights and to take more determined action when possible. By the end of the eighteenth century, these visions had helped to inspire wars, revolutions, declarations, constitutions, books, hymns, the beginnings of the historically momentous transformation of individuals from subjects into citizens, and the creation of human rights NGOs, as well as personal acts of compassion. But this only set the stage for what lay just ahead, for as one observer once noted, throughout most of history liberty remains more in shadow form than in substance, "yet the shadow is itself an earnest of greater things" to come.[148]

Chapter 2
To Protect Humanity and Defend Justice

Early International Efforts

> Now there are states of affairs in which human sympathy refuses to be confined by the [old] rules, necessarily limited and conventional. . . . Let us cast aside our narrow and ill-conceived construction of the ideas of a former period . . . in order to protect humanity and defend justice.
>
> —William Gladstone of Britain

The power of visions of human rights prior to the nineteenth century could be seen largely in inspiration, in their ability to create and then nurture an ideal of compassion and respect for others simply because they were human brothers and sisters. Their capacity to influence actual behavior, however, was largely confined to specific individuals, locales, regions, or in a very small number of cases, groups within nations. Traditional practices, prejudices, vested interests, and capabilities developed over the centuries all served to obstruct human rights and to confine them to exclusive domestic jurisdiction, far removed from consideration as a legitimate issue for serious international action. The seeds of visions sown in the past, often forced to lie dormant for generations, nevertheless slowly began to germinate as appeals to the conscience on behalf of rights began to fall on more fertile soil.

There are many reasons why this change began to occur, and by identifying them we can understand any number of forces that made the evolution of international human rights possible. Some of these were physical and structural. Revolutions and foreign and civil wars, for example, overthrew many power structures and vested interests from the past and thereby began to make emerging democratization possible. Industrialization and urbanization created still further pressures for change. A technological revolution enabled railroads to cross the land, steamships to ply the seas, electronic pulses to surge through telegraph wires, printing presses to mass produce newspapers and thought-provoking novels, and something as simple as the invention of an inexpensive postal stamp all enhanced the process of actually knowing something about the lives of other people and their plight. This made it possible to more fully connect humankind with each other transnationally and thereby to develop a greater sense of empathy for victims of abuse. With these developments, awareness of the fate of those who suffered in one form or another could no longer be completely silenced, isolated, or delayed as in the past. Instead, new means emerged to spread new ideas and visions of rights.

The experience of these early efforts also began to reveal a process of crossing thresholds that would become increasingly pronounced. In the first instance, activism on behalf of human rights occurred only when people empathized enough with victims to reassess the values and practices that they had inherited, to conclude that particular actions long accepted as "normal" were wrong, and to determine that these abuses should no longer be tolerated. The next step required moving beyond outrage over an injustice to the point of taking action, or, in the words of the parable of the Good Samaritan that inspired many campaigners of the nineteenth century, to "go and do likewise." This explains why so many men and women began to assign such importance and urgency to their visions of rights that they decided actually to do something personally and collectively about it, including active participation in the first large-scale human rights movements in history. The final threshold, and one that would continue to grow in importance for international human rights, required moving beyond concern for only one's own self-centered rights and focusing attention and effort on the rights of someone else.

All these features and the aspirations for rights that they generated would serve as both a catalyst and as an outcome of intense upheaval and profound change. Those visionaries devoted to advancing human rights thus found themselves as never before encouraged to confront overwhelming odds and enabled to pursue early international action by beginning to free the enslaved, to assist the exploited, to care for the wounded, and to protect the persecuted.

To Free the Enslaved

It is hardly surprising that the first systematic efforts to realize visions of human rights should focus on the tragic fate of those condemned to slavery. Nowhere were the violations of humanity and justice—however defined—more blatant or brutal. The debasement of living human beings into property and their forceful capture, restraint with chains or neck irons, violent branding and torture, and lifelong enslavement for themselves and their descendants revealed one of the most vicious and repulsive chapters in all of history.

Up to the beginning of the nineteenth century the international slave trade flourished and the power and profits from human bondage made slavery commonly practiced, legally authorized, and taken for granted in most places of the world. To fully appreciate the magnitude of the transformation that would occur, we need to understand that at the time well over three quarters of all people alive were held in bondage of one kind or another.[1] From Asia to Africa, from India to the Caribbean, from the Ottoman Empire to South America, and from Russia and Eastern Europe to North America, the overwhelming majority of men, women, and children suffered as victims of forced labor who were bought, sold, leased, and inherited. They knew no other way of life. As such, the "peculiar institution" was not slavery—it was freedom.[2]

Common practice and a widespread acceptance of slavery, however, did not mean unanimous approval. Through time, a growing number of thoughtful people refused to be swayed by the prevailing arguments of powerful and well-financed vested interests seeking to justify the owning of slaves as part of the natural hierarchy of the universe. Instead, they began to view enslavement as completely contrary to the precepts of their religious faith and/or their political philosophy—and increasingly said so. They were prepared to make that critical mental leap of imagining a world that did not yet exist and envisioning slaves not as property, but as living and suffering human beings. Abolishing slavery, it is important to observe, was not a "Western" value. Indeed, plantation owners in the West devised and practiced one of the most brutal and barbaric forms of slavery ever known, and it was widely accepted by the majority as being completely normal. What the West did possess that those with deep religious convictions among Muslims and Buddhists who denounced the holding of humans as slaves did not, however, were the means to express opposition and influence opinion as well as the political institutions with the potential for responding to challenges to the status quo. In order to free the enslaved, abolitionists understood that they had to use these advantages to achieve two difficult objectives: first, outlawing the international slave trade to stop the flow of human cargo from abroad, and then, ending slavery at home.

The first serious efforts to render the slave trade illegal occurred in the United States and Britain. Here, declared former slave trader Thomas Branagan, all citizens had to confront the stark contrast between their stated principles and their practice of the slave trade, which made them "butchers of their brethren, destroyers of liberty and the rights of man, promoters and supporters of legal barbarity."[3] The intellectual and moral strength of this argument, along with a growing sense of guilt, a crusading zeal of evangelical Christianity, a fear of the consequences of importing more slaves, and the emergence of new economic interest groups unconnected with or even hostile to slavery, all combined to exert pressure. Importantly, the opponents of the slave trade began to realize that simply detesting abuse was not enough, and that they now needed to take the next and necessary step of action.

Toward this end, many organized themselves into early NGOs and became dedicated activists. They pledged that they would not use armed force or violence to achieve their goal, but instead rely on the peaceful means of moral persuasion. It would have been extraordinarily difficult for them not to be overwhelmed by the task at hand and by the resistance aligned against their cause. They knew that they would confront long tradition, accepted practice, entrenched political forces, and economic interests, many of which would stop at nothing to prevent any diminution of the power, influence, or profits and government revenue that came from the trade in human beings. Nevertheless, these new activists refused to be swayed, particularly those who volunteered for the Society for Effecting the Abolition of the Slave Trade. Foremost among these was Thomas Clarkson, an innovative organizer and indefatigable campaigner, a courageous individual when facing danger from those opposed to him, and a man of deep religious conviction described by the poet Samuel Taylor Coleridge as "the moral steam engine" of the crusade.[4] He was joined by William Wilberforce, who possessed something that Clarkson lacked: access to political power. As a member of Parliament he could speak out in the House of Commons, submit petitions, draft legislation, and form coalitions—and he did. Together, they and their colleagues pioneered many of the tools and techniques that human rights activists still use today to arouse and mobilize outrage against abuse. These include writing pamphlets, delivering public speeches, organizing meetings and marches, recruiting volunteers, preaching sermons, raising funds, using wall posters and lapel pins with a message, investigating and collecting information on violations of rights, launching letter-writing and media campaigns, gathering signatures on petitions, lobbying politicians, participating in economic boycotts, and initiating acts of protest. It is for this reason that the leading expert on the members of the Society for Effecting the Abolition of the Slave Trade goes so far as to describe them as "the greatest of all human rights movements."[5]

Persistent and often coordinated efforts and agitation by NGOs in both America and Britain gradually began to transform public attitudes about the slave trade in the name of "the common rights of humanity."[6] This, in turn, began to transform politics. Indeed, President Thomas Jefferson, in his 1806 message to Congress, explicitly used the language of rights when he urged lawmakers "to withdraw the citizens of the United States from all further participation in those violations of human rights which have been so long continued on the unoffending inhabitants of Africa, and which the morality, the reputation, and the best interests of our country, have long been eager to proscribe."[7] By the next year the strength of those who wanted to end their own nation's involvement in the slave trade had reached such proportions as to force votes in both Congress and Parliament. In the United States the result took the form of the 1807 Act to Prohibit the Importation of Slaves, making those who brought persons seized from Africa for slavery subject to losing their ships and cargo and facing possible fines and imprisonment. In Britain the 1807 Act for the Abolition of the Slave Trade similarly made it illegal to trade in, purchase, sell, barter, or transport human beings for the purpose of slavery.[8] It remarkably brought an end to a practice that had sustained the largest slave-trading nation in the entire world, had involved four continents, and had lasted three centuries. As such, it is easy to understand why these two acts gave hope to millions of human beings on both sides of the Atlantic.[9]

Both of these laws provided a necessary beginning to eliminating the slave trade, but neither could solve all the difficulties at once. As human rights activists of later generations would discover from their own experiences, acts in and of themselves often are not sufficient. These national laws from the United States and Britain, for example, applied only to their own areas of jurisdiction and lacked enforcement that could significantly influence the behavior of others beyond their own borders. In order to address this larger problem, therefore, those who wanted truly to end the slave trade turned their attention and energies toward international action.

Almost all of the major breakthroughs in the long struggle for international human rights, as we shall see repeatedly, emerged in the wake of upheavals, wars, and revolutions. Although visions of rights served as absolutely essential elements in these efforts, they rarely were sufficiently powerful in and of themselves to move governments into effective action. More often than not, they needed the testing of existing institutions and values by disruption or chaos, significant shifts of power, or the destruction of previous sources of resistance to create new opportunities for significant change. Those activists of the early nineteenth century had seen this with their own eyes in the cases of the American and French revolutions, the slave revolt in Haiti, the Irish rebellion, and upheavals in Latin America producing new constitutions that explicitly spoke of liberty, equality, duties, and "the rights of man."[10] But peace conferences at the end of major wars offer even more. Peacemaking provides opportunities to fulfill promises made during wartime, to be reminded of the fact of international relations that the fate of one country and its people is tied to that of others, and, finally, to address the hopes of those who have made great sacrifices of creating a more enduring peace or a world made new.[11] Those activists who worked to abolish the slave trade began to appreciate this relationship between human rights and peace conferences, and thus directed their energies on influencing the diplomats restructuring the international order after the lengthy Napoleonic wars at the Congress of Vienna in 1814–1815.

The leadership in this effort was taken by William Wilberforce and Thomas Clarkson. Wilberforce initiated correspondence with leading political and literary figures, arranged for private meetings with Tsar Alexander I of Russia, and instigated the largest petition campaign in all of British history to politically pressure Parliament to insist that the Congress of Vienna be used as the forum to abolish the slave trade. Clarkson simultaneously prepared a special abridgment of his earlier report entitled *Evidence on the Subject of the Slave Trade* that could be easily read and immediately understood. Here, and of particular importance, he also reproduced one of the most famous political images of all time: the drawing of the slave ship *Brookes* with its living and dying people stacked like cordwood and chained from head to toe in suffocating and terrifying conditions. It forced viewers to confront not sterile charts, graphs, maps, or accounting legers—but human beings. The precision and eloquent starkness of this illustration gripped not only the mind but the emotions, and revealed the power of images to evoke that essential ingredient of empathy. It allowed readers to see and feel what previously could hardly be imagined in terms of the raw fear, terror, and pain experienced by so many innocent victims. Then a particular verse from "Amazing Grace" came to their minds: "[I once] was blind, but now I see." Clarkson's materials were widely translated and a preface encouraged all leaders to seize the opportunity to finally conclude that the slave trade was no longer acceptable.[12] Lord Castlereagh, the chief British delegate, found all of this and the public pressure that it aroused to be irritating interference, complaining bitterly that it was wrong "to force it upon nations, at the expense of their honor and of the tranquility of the world."[13]

Delegates at the Congress of Vienna could not ignore this mounting pressure, however, and consequently established a special committee to deal with the international slave trade. They quickly found themselves locked into a battle between power, principle, and prejudice. Here they made and heard contesting arguments about human rights, religious imperatives, economic profits, comparative strategic advantages, the unreliability of other nations, and the continued claims of national sovereignty. These knew that they had to avoid the Scylla of achieving nothing and thereby provoking the wrath of public opinion and the Charybdis of accomplishing too much and thereby antagonizing serious vested interests. Through a complicated combination of threats and bribes ranging from money to territory, the delegates finally agreed to sign the Eight

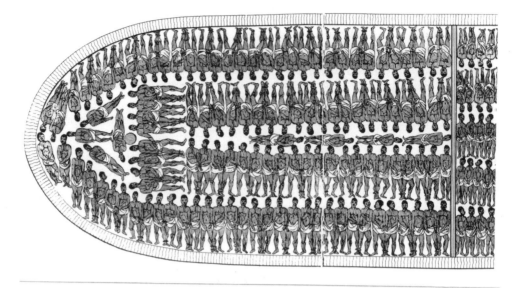

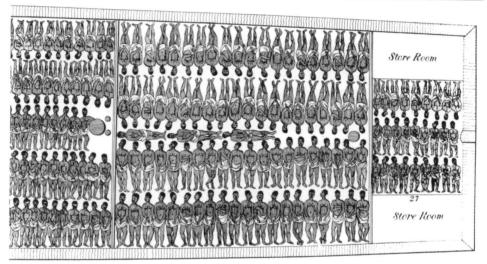

Figure 3. Human Beings as Property: The Horrors of Slavery. Thomas Clarkson, *Evidence on the Subject of the Slave Trade.*

Power Declaration acknowledging that "the public voice in all civilized countries calls aloud for its prompt suppression," proclaiming that the international slave trade was "repugnant to the principles of humanity and universal morality," and recognizing that they had a responsibility to abolish the trade as soon as practicable.[14] This language, in turn, served to stimulate another treaty provision in which Britain, Russia, Austria, Prussia, and France pledged themselves to consider further measures "for the entire and definitive abolition of a Commerce so odious and so strongly condemned by the laws of religion and nature."[15] Britain and the United States similarly declared in the

Treaty of Ghent during the same year that the traffic in slaves "is irreconcilable with the principles of humanity and justice."[16]

Many abolitionists hailed these new international declarations and pledges as tremendous accomplishments. Never before had powerful sovereign nations been willing to discuss openly such a difficult subject as trading in human cargo. Never before had they been willing to acknowledge any sense of responsibility to end the slave trade in order to protect humanity and defend justice. At the Congress of Vienna they did. Nevertheless, they also began to reveal what other international human rights efforts all would realize in turn: agreement was easier to obtain on solemn words than on the specific provisions of enforceable commitments. The final texts of 1815, for example, did not make the slave trade illegal, sanction the arrest of slavers, provide machinery for enforcement, or authorize any activity that might challenge national sovereignty.

Interestingly enough, however, even Wilberforce concluded that such declarations marked a significant beginning and that, given the long history of the slave trade and the powerful vested interests of the time, they represented all that could reasonably be expected in the world of practical politics and diplomacy. Rather than taking the line of least resistance by quitting in disgust or cynicism, he and his British colleagues in the Society for Effecting the Abolition of the Slave Trade and the Aborigines Protection Society, along with American activists in the Society for the Suppression of the Slave Trade and the Association of Friends for Promoting the Abolition of Slavery as well as French members of the Société des Amis des Noirs and the Société de la Morale Chrétienne, determined to build on the words of these first declarations and to press onward to secure the "teeth" to abolish the trade. They unceasingly wrote letters, organized meetings, sponsored lectures by fugitive slaves, conducted investigations, supported boycotts of slave-produced goods, communicated with each other through the pages of the *Christian Observer*, and, convinced of the growing power of the printed word, launched press campaigns and published and distributed thousands of copies of Clarkson's *The Cries of Africa to the Inhabitants of Europe; Or, A Survey of That Bloody Commerce Called the Slave Trade*, which they translated into French, German, Spanish, Portuguese, Dutch, and Arabic. They rejoiced when the pope finally issued instructions to all Catholics to abstain from the slave trade. They appealed to national leaders, petitioned governments, and pressured diplomats to consider such actions as making the slave trade an act of piracy, granting navies the right to search ships, and creating an international agency with a maritime force and authority to halt the slave shipments at their source. In addition, they organized the British and Foreign Anti-Slavery Society (later the Anti-Slavery International for the Protection of Human Rights and acknowledged as the longest standing human rights NGO in the world) and in 1840 sponsored their first World Anti-Slavery Conference in order to arouse and mobilize global opinion.[17] Even today this effort is described as "one of the great moral revolutions in human history."[18]

The British government proved to be the most responsive to this kind of public pressure, and thus came to be the leading crusader to abolish the international slave trade. For years it stood nearly alone among nations doing so. Inspired by moral principles, and acting contrary to its economic interests, Britain committed naval squadrons and thousands of troops, shouldered heavy financial costs, and risked seriously damaging their own empire and relations with other countries by seizing slave ships.[19] They established a special Slave Trade Department within the Foreign Office to entice, cajole, and coerce others into signing agreements to suppress slave trading. As a result of their efforts over several decades, more than fifty bilateral treaties were signed with all of the Atlantic maritime powers and countries throughout Europe, North and South America, the Middle East, and rulers in Africa and Asia to do precisely this. These proved to be of considerable importance in not only creating a maritime police force for enforcement, but especially in establishing the beginnings of international human rights law. Collectively they created an unprecedented network of antislavery courts presided over by judges from different countries who met on a continuing basis and applied emerging international law for humanitarian objectives. It is estimated that over the course of more than 600 cases they freed nearly 80,000 slaves found aboard illegal slave trading ships. As such, they were the very first international human rights courts designed to hold individuals accountable for certain abuses under the law.[20]

These international courts and their domestic equivalents made remarkable contributions in their own time and pointed the direction toward the development of international human rights law and international criminal law for the future. But they demonstrated limitations as well. They could restrain only certain activities and always had to confront problems of smuggling, maritime claims, colonial and commercial rivalries, nonparticipation, and, at a time of the growth of nationalism, the sensitivities of national sovereignty and pride.[21] Most significantly, they starkly revealed the fact that the necessary prerequisite for completely abolishing the slave trade abroad hinged on one important condition: abolishing the market that fed it by ending the practice of slavery and emancipating slaves at home.

The great abolitionist campaign insisting that slavery was no longer acceptable now began in earnest. More and more people demonstrated the capacity to change their minds and say: "this is not right." New leaders such as Thomas F. Buxton in Britain and Augustin Cochin in France, as well as new NGOs such as the Confederação Abolicionista in Brazil emerged with intensity and determination. In the United States the issue of slavery increasingly tore the nation apart. Here William Lloyd Garrison, a passionate activist who spoke out against injustice, emerged as one of the leading abolitionists. His vision was based on his religious conviction that the enslavement of another human being was a sin and his political belief that the rights enshrined in the American Declaration and Bill of Rights should be seen as natural, as equal, and as universal for everyone. As he declared in one famous—and fearless—public speech:

Fifty-three years ago, the Fourth of July was a proud day for our country. It clearly and accurately defined the rights of man; . . . it shook, as with the voice of a great earthquake, thrones which were seemingly propped up with Atlantean pillars; it gave an impulse to the heart of the world. . . . But what a pitiful detail of grievances does this document present, in comparison of the wrongs which our slaves endure! . . . Before God, I must say, that such a glaring contradiction as exists between our creed and our practice the annals of six thousand years cannot parallel. In view of it, I am ashamed of my country. I am sick of our unmeaning declamation in praise of liberty and equality; of our hypocritical cant about the unalienable rights of man.[22]

Garrison's vision and his call for action immediately provoked resistance. Opponents threatened and physically attacked him. Nevertheless, he adamantly refused to be silent and determined, in his own words, "to turn the world upside down."[23] To mobilize outrage he created the American Anti-Slavery Society and a newspaper entitled *The Liberator.* In the first issue he announced that his purpose was to advance "the great cause of human rights" and bodly declared: "I *will be* as harsh as truth, and as uncompromising as justice. On this subject, I do not wish to think, or speak, or write, with moderation. No! no!. . . . I am in earnest—I will not equivocate—I will not excuse—I will not retreat a single inch—AND *I WILL BE HEARD!*"[24]

Others joined this effort, and a movement began to grow. Abolitionists such as Theodore Weld motivated action by compiling the widely read *American Slavery as It Is: Testimony of a Thousand Witnesses* that gathered direct, personal accounts about the horrors of slavery.[25] Others wrote articles and editorials in journals entitled *The Rights of All, The Genius of Universal Emancipation,* and *Human Rights.* Some courageously campaigned to free those Africans held captive on the slave ship *Amistad* by bringing their plight to trial before the Supreme Court itself in a case that would help alter the nation's history. Still others sought to enter the political arena directly and created the Liberty Party in 1841, announcing their vision of achieving "Liberty—the liberty that is twin born with justice—the liberty that respects and protects the rights, not of the weak only, or of the strong only, but of the weak and the strong; and simply because they are human rights."[26] Former slaves Frederick Douglass and Sojourner Truth delivered hundreds of public speeches encouraging their listeners to become activists and join in the cause for the "rights of man" and "human rights."[27] Henry David Thoreau attracted others by publishing *Civil Disobedience* and declaring himself to be an abolitionist, publicly burning copies of the U.S. Constitution, and risking severe punishment for helping slaves escape through the Underground Railroad.

The abolitionist movement grew even more when in 1852 a diminutive woman named Harriet Beecher Stowe, deeply committed to her religious faith and moved by her personal encounters with fugitive slaves, published her remarkable and evocative *Uncle Tom's Cabin.* This book is described to this day as "probably the most influential novel ever published in the United States."[28] She created powerful images of slaves being ruthlessly beaten to death by heartless owners and fleeing across the ice on rivers, with babes in arms and bloodhounds baying at their heels, in order to be free. Such scenes stirred emotions and, importantly, evoked empathy. Moreover, her explicit dialogue about Christian values called readers to be faithful to their religious responsibilities. Within the first year alone, Stowe's book sold more than 300,000 copies, keeping eight rotary presses with the latest steam-driven technology operating around the clock. In Britain its circulation quickly passed the million mark, and its translation into twenty languages extended the impact by mobilizing international outrage against slavery.[29]

Such growing outrage, whether inspired by compassion and empathy, religious principle and a sense of responsibility, or political conviction about human rights, provided essential components in the process of abolishing slavery and freeing the enslaved. It began to move people from passivity into action and the movement began to grow.

But as people became activists, they increasingly realized that they confronted not only determined resistance but a serious debate about *means*. That is, they struggled among themselves over a fundamental question that still confronts all those who work on behalf of human rights: Should they use reason and moral persuasion to gradually change minds and behavior, or should they employ violence to force power and privilege from those unwilling to share them? Clarkson, Wilberforce, Garrison, Stowe, and many others, believed that they could realize their vision by the peaceful and nonviolent means found in the power of beliefs and ideas, rational discourse, procedures of liberal democracy, moderation, and moral persuasion. People, they pointed out, certainly are capable of changing. Others argued that some people may change by such means, but not all are willing or able to do so and must be forced to. They pointed out the historic strength and fierceness of resistance and the extent to which opponents of human rights had gone to crush those who opposed them. As one man asserted while threatening an activist: "We cannot afford . . . to let you and your associates succeed in your endeavor to overthrow slavery. . . . We mean, sir, to put you Abolitionists down,—by fair means if we can, by foul means if we must."[30] With this in mind, they agreed with the fiery John Brown who raided an arsenal to seize weapons for the cause, that the only language opposition clearly understands is armed force and violence. When asked his opinion about this difficult issue, Frederick Douglass thought carefully. Although not prone to violence himself, he certainly understood it and appreciated that it might sometimes be necessary. He concluded:

The whole history of the progress of human liberty shows that all concessions yet made to her august claims have been born of struggle. . . . If there is no struggle there is no progress. Those who profess to favor freedom and yet depreciate agitation are men who want crops without plowing the ground, they want rain without thunder and lightning. They want the ocean without the awful roar of its many waters. . . . Power concedes nothing without a demand. It never did and it never will.[31]

Although the debate between moral persuasion and violence raged with strong adherents on both sides, the fact remains that for better or worse slavery largely ended due to transformations brought about by tumultuous wars, revolutions, or upheavals. All of these tore down the existing structures of those who had been unwilling to share their power voluntarily. As such, they shifted power, opened up space for dialogue about human rights, and created new opportunities for change. In the Spanish colonies of Costa Rica, El Salvador, Guatemala, Honduras, and Nicaragua, slavery was abolished only after Spain and its empire fell as a result of invasion from the French army on land, attacks from the British navy at sea, armed uprisings from revolutionaries at home, and military defeats abroad during the wars for independence, some led by "The Liberator" Simón Bolívar. The British emancipated slaves in their colonies ranging from the West Indies to the southern tip of Africa and the Indian Ocean from 1833 to 1838, but only in the wake of a violent slave revolt in Jamaica and a dramatic shift of political power at home that resulted in the Great Reform Act of 1832, expanding the electorate and giving voice to anti-slavery opinion. France ended slavery in its colonial possessions only after the bloody Revolution of 1848. Civil and foreign wars surrounded the abolition of slavery in Argentina, Colombia, Equador, Peru, and Venezuela during the 1850s. In the United States, President Abraham Lincoln's Emancipation Proclamation of 1863 announced abolition as a war aim of the Union during the Civil War. This paved the way for the Thirteenth Amendment to the Constitution, which abolished slavery in 1865, but it was made possible only after military victory destroyed the power of slave-owning states and inflicted what remains to this day the most devastating conflict in the nation's history. Cuba and Brazil did not free their slaves until additional wars and struggles forced them to do so in the late 1880s.[32] The abolition of serfdom, as we shall see, followed a similar pattern. One observer saw all these events as portions of an international whole, parts of "a great fight going on the world over . . . between free institutions and caste institutions, Freedom and Democracy against institutions of privilege and class."[33]

With these upheavals, the relationship between emancipation and the fate of the slave trade became apparent for the world to see. Once nations outlawed slavery within their own domains, the slave trade had no market; and once they withdrew their active support for or passive acquiescence in the trade, this commerce in human beings could no longer survive. Those who had been so actively involved in slave trading realized that politically, diplomatically, economically, intellectually, and morally they simply could sustain it no longer. Recognition of these facts, in addition to continued pressure from anti-slavery NGOs and religious leaders such as Cardinal Lavigerie of France and his Œuvre Antiesclavagiste, finally brought these nations together to search for international solutions. By 1885 they agreed under the Berlin Act that they shared a responsibility to declare that "the trading in slaves is forbidden."[34]

More significantly, a number of states negotiated what became the 1890 General Act for the Repression of the African Slave Trade. Representatives ranging from Europe, the United States, and the Scandinavian countries to the Ottoman Empire, Persia, the Congo, and Zanzibar professed their intention "of putting an end to the crimes and devastations engendered by the traffic in African slaves, of efficiently protecting the aboriginal population of Africa, and of securing for that vast continent the benefits of peace and civilization."[35] Their convention bound them to repress the slave trade at places of origin as well as at sea and along inland caravan routes by searching slave ships, punishing offending slave captors and dealers, liberating slaves and granting them protection, and creating for the first time an enforcement mechanism known as the "slave trade bureaux," located in Zanzibar. This marked a culmination of the struggle to associate the major powers with a comprehensive legal agreement to end a practice that had existed for centuries. Despite its challenges to national sovereignty and its defects, the act revealed the capacity to change normative values by embodying the principle that an international responsibility existed to abolish the trade and enslavement of human beings. As such, it marked an important step in establishing a moral standard for behavior and legitimacy by which the powers might judge each other and the rest of the world might judge them, thereby setting a most significant precedent in the evolution of international human rights.[36]

When one looks back on the successes of these many efforts to abolish the slave trade and slavery in the face of such seemingly impossible odds, it is almost difficult to believe. In the case of the British, the anti-slavery movement that began as a mere fringe group accomplished its goals within the span of little more than a single lifetime. For others it took slightly longer, but the results were the same. "We have seen something absolutely without precedent in history," concluded the astute French observer Alexis de Tocqueville well before the process was even over. "If you pore over the histories of all peoples, I doubt that you will find anything more extraordinary."[37]

To Assist the Exploited

Visions of protecting humanity and defending justice, once awakened, have a way of inspiring others. It is precisely for this reason that freeing the enslaved inspired those wanting to assist the rights of other victims who were abused and exploited. The successes of abolishing the slave trade and breaking the chains of slavery created momentum and greatly encouraged and enabled activists to launch further movements that challenged injustices and broadened a rights agenda. Slavery became an image, a metaphor, and a lens through which to view other cases of exploitation. As such, it raised with renewed vigor that question that would continue to grow in importance: rights for whom? If the fate of slaves heretofore without any hope could be so dramatically changed, then why not the fates of countless others who also suffered? Indeed, by the early nineteenth century the overwhelming majority of the world's population still found itself exploited in one way or another and denied basic human rights because of race, gender, or class.

The powerful impact of race on human affairs, for example, continued to plague those who truly held a vision of equal rights for all, irrespective of skin color. They watched in both frustration and sorrow as the abolition of the institution of slavery often brought not an end to prejudice but rather an extension of racist ideology and exclusion in the form of racial segregation and discrimination. In one of the great paradoxes of the nineteenth century, racism actually increased as democracy expanded, demonstrating that the evolution of human rights does not always proceed in a straightforward, linear progression.[38] The loss of slave status did not always bring with it a diminution of caste status, for freedom from slavery often exacerbated existing prejudices. Emancipation in the West Indies, for instance, created a curious system of caste based on gradations of color. Freed blacks in the United States, despite new Constitutional amendments guaranteeing equal protection under the law and the Civil Rights Act of 1866, faced intense discrimination. "The Master he says we are all free," declared one former slave, "but it don't mean we is white. And it don't mean we is equal."[39] In anger many former slaves demanded: "Let's have our rights!"[40] Strenuous and often courageous attempts in the face of determined opposition were made to assist them in finding employment, creating educational opportunities, fighting the "black codes" of racial segregation, and obtaining protection from lynchings through organizations such as the National Equal Rights League. Yet, given the power of traditional vested interests and the prerogatives of sovereignty and domestic jurisdiction at the time, these efforts rarely could move beyond the narrow confines of national borders.

Some early efforts did seek to address racial matters internationally, however, and these focused on indigenous peoples. One of the most striking features of the nineteenth century, for example, was the outburst of imperialist activity by white Europeans and their cousins in North America, Australia, New Zealand, and South Africa against those whom they described as less-than-fully human "inferior races" and "lesser breeds of color."[41] With an intensity that is still astonishing to recall, these Westerners rushed into Africa, Asia, the Pacific, and North America, dispossessing, debasing, exploiting, and even exterminating the nonwhite native inhabitants. Not everyone, of course, supported these policies and instead decided to follow in the footsteps of Las Casas by declaring that it was no longer acceptable for their governments to violate the rights of millions of indigenous human beings. Rather than trying to act alone, however, they formed larger organizations to mobilize their efforts for more effective action. Some launched the great missionary movement of the nineteenth century, taking seriously the biblical injunction to "go ye into all the world."[42] Hundreds of new organizations such as the Friends Foreign Mission Association, Société des Missions Évangeliques, Berliner Missionsgesellschaft, Russian Missionary Society of the Orthodox Church, American Board of Foreign Missions, Canadian Baptist Foreign Mission Board, Evangelical Union of South America, and World Missionary Conference emerged at this time and joined their Catholic Jesuit counterparts in sending out missionaries. By foot, horseback, cart, canoe, ship, or eventually train, they made efforts to reach people from the Eskimos in Alaska to the Zulus in Africa, from the Chinese and Koreans in Asia to the Amerindians in Latin America, and from the Blackfeet in the American West to the Maori in New Zealand.[43] Others created NGOs such as the Aborigines Protection Society in Britain, the Société des Amis des Noirs in France, the Aborigines' Rights Protection Society in Africa, the Anti-Imperialist League, and the Indian Rights Association founded by Herbert Welsch, a devout Episcopalian who articulated a vision "to secure to the Indians of the United States the political and civil rights already guaranteed to them by treaty and statutes."[44]

Although the members of these organizations always risked the very real danger of being used and manipulated by national governments eager to advance their own political, economic, and strategic interests, Christian missionaries and humanitarians nevertheless made earnest efforts, often at the cost of their own lives, to assist those of other races exploited far from their own shores. They attempted to bring the needs of these peoples to international attention through publications such as the *Missionary Review of the World, Journal des Missions Évangéliques*, and *Allgemeine Missionszeitschrift*. Their efforts resulted in hospitals and schools, food and relief supplies, orphanages for children and stations for lepers, rescue homes for young girls and aged women, missions for former slaves, instruction for the blind and deaf, and the extension of legal protections for the rights of indigenous peoples through treaty law. In Britain they pressured Parliament into creating the Aborigines' Committee to consider "the native inhabitants of countries when British settlements are made, and to the neighboring tribes in order to secure to them the due observance of justice and the protection of their rights."[45] In New Zealand they established the position of Protector of Aborigines and passed the Native Rights Act of 1865 to defend the rights of the Maori. In India they inspired the Caste Disabilities Removal Act, and in Canada the 1880 passage of the comprehensive Act Respecting Indians.

In the United States, human rights activists not only helped to secure the position of the Commissioner of Indian Affairs but were quick to draw attention to two famous court decisions and one celebrated speech. The first came from the Supreme Court itself, stating explicitly, "By the protection of the law human rights are secured; withdraw that protection, and they are at the mercy of wicked rulers, or the clamor of an excited people."[46] A circuit court then went on to break new ground by ruling: "That an Indian is a 'person' within the meaning of the laws of the United States, and has, therefore, . . . the inalienable right to 'life, liberty, and the pursuit of happiness.' "[47] At the same time, Chief Joseph of the Nez Perce tribe declared in a moving speech:

Treat all men alike. Give them all the same law. Give them all an even chance to live and grow. All men were made by the same Great Spirit Chief. They all are brothers. The earth is the mother of all people, and people should have equal rights upon it.[48]

The momentum of these different national efforts began to grow. In 1885 fifteen different nations pledged in the Berlin Act to provide guarantees for the right of freedom of religion in their possessions and promised to "watch over the preservation of the native tribes and to care for the improvement of their moral and material well being."[49] The Brussels Act of 1890 reiterated this concern for "native welfare" and committed seventeen nations to "efficiently protecting the aboriginal population of Africa."[50] During the same year the black American missionary George Washington Williams published a scathing account of Belgian atrocities in the Congo, calling for international action to protect the rights of natives and, in one of the earliest uses of the expression, accused the perpetrators of "crimes against humanity."[51]

These various international activities and treaty provisions, it must be acknowledged, did not always produce the intended result for the exploited of different races. The adoption of policies and their actual fulfillment can be two very different matters. Mixed motives, changing circumstances, and unscrupulous white settlers unwilling to abide by the promises of treaty law continually revealed the familiar human rights problem of the gap between theory and practice, or between vision and reality. Through time some missionaries found themselves more interested in securing their own converts than in advancing the interests of indigenous peoples. Humanitarians came to realize that it often did not take much for ideals of "trusteeship" to degenerate into arrogant paternalism or forced assimilation into a presumed "superior" culture. Invaders alone could define the meaning of rights declared in treaties and decide whether, when, and to what extent they would be applied. Moreover, governments bent on imperial conquest learned soon enough that expressions about "advancing civilization" also could be used as an excuse for carving up of spheres of influence and seizing territory around the world. Those who genuinely devoted themselves to the early efforts on behalf of indigenous peoples thus came to realize an important lesson: namely, that words of promise in declarations or treaties provided essential beginnings, but without the political will to honor and enforce them they would remain forever insufficient to realize visions of international human rights in practice.

Other visions focused on those suffering exploitation on the basis of gender. The nineteenth century began much as did all of its predecessors, with a long and encrusted tradition of the subordination of women to men and gendered inequalities that appeared as though they would continue forever. Even in the most progressive societies of the time, females could not vote or hold elective office, speak in public, participate in political organizations, own or inherit property, manage their earnings, sue in court, enter most professions or schools, leave an abusive marriage, maintain custody of children if divorced by a husband, or have the right to personal autonomy and bodily integrity when legally regarded as their husband's personal property. To be husbandless was to be stateless. The status and treatment of females in nondemocratic countries elsewhere in the world was much, much worse. Yet, the subject of the rights of women began to emerge with particular force when the emancipation of slaves forced serious discussion about the meaning of rights for free blacks. Members of each group might be technically recognized as citizens, but were nevertheless still regarded as being less-than-fully human and therefore not deserving of the basic rights enjoyed by white males.[52] Race and gender thus became linked.

Many of those who became famous in the early campaign for women's rights in fact began their careers as activists in the abolitionist movement. Here they became acutely conscious that both race and gender were determined by genetic factors over which they had no control. They began to see the significance of the interrelationship of rights and genuine equality, and the experience of a successful challenge gave them hope. If slaves had rights, then why not women? "In striving to strike his irons off," observed Abby Kelley Foster referring to black slaves, "we found most surely, that we were manacled ourselves."[53] Here they discovered the support of at least some men such as George Thompson in Britain and William Lloyd Garrison and Frederick Douglass in the United States who, through publications like the *Liberator, The Genius of Universal Emancipation, Human Rights,* and *The Rights of All,* championed the exploited—whether they were slaves or women. Here they also gained experience, developed leadership skills, and learned practical techniques that empowered them to raise public consciousness through speeches and publicity, gather petitions, organize political protest and agitation, mobilize resources and sympathetic churches, challenge traditional boundaries of what was considered to be appropriate feminine behavior, and develop visions with the courage of their convictions. All of these became essential when they found themselves forced to confront powerful resistance and intimidation from those who pelted them with rotten eggs, hit them with rocks, and burned buildings where they tried to speak.

This could be seen in the efforts of the deeply religious and committed abolitionist Angelina Grimké, who courageously argued that the struggle was one for human rights—not man's, not woman's, but equal rights for all human beings whatever their color, sex, or station. "This is part of the great doctrine of Human Rights," she wrote, "and can no more be separated from Emancipation than the light from the heat of the sun; the rights of the slave and the woman blend like the colors of a rainbow."[54] Her influential sister, Sarah Grimké, published a manifesto in 1838 entitled *Letters on the Equality of the Sexes and the Equality of Woman,* starkly comparing the exploitation of women with that of slaves, demanding equal rights in the name of religious and moral principles, and arguing that rights must be coupled with responsibilities.[55] Elisha Hurlbut expressed the same vision in her suggestive book *Essays on Human Rights*.[56]

In this setting an event took place that would have a great impact on women's rights. It began when two American Quakers, Elizabeth Cady Stanton and Lucretia Mott, traveled to the 1840 World Anti-Slavery Conference meeting in London. Having made the arduous trip across the Atlantic to even attend, they were shocked to discover that they were not allowed to be seated. Why?—because they were women. The majority of men in control did not regard them as being fully human and capable of serving as full-fledged participants. Stanton and Mott were outraged. Here was a conference ostensibly addressing human rights and liberating victims from oppression and exploitation, but at the same time unwilling to acknowledge the rights of women. Such discrimination, they insisted, would no longer be tolerated. They thus determined to turn both their anger and their strong religious convictions into action—"to do and dare anything," as they said—by organizing the very first convention in history devoted solely to the rights of women.[57] Under their leadership, nearly three hundred delegates gathered in 1848 in the Wesleyan Chapel at Seneca Falls, New York. Here they produced the famous Declaration of Sentiments asserting: "The history of mankind is a history of repeated injuries and usurpations on the part of man toward woman, having in direct object the establishment of an absolute tyranny over her." In language modeled after the revolutionary Declaration of Independence, they claimed their rights to "which the laws of nature and nature's God entitle them," asserting:

We hold these truths to be self-evident: that all men *and women* are created equal; that they are endowed by their Creator with certain inalienable rights; that among these are life, liberty, and the pursuit of happiness; that to secure these rights governments are instituted, deriving their just powers from the consent of the governed. Whenever any form of government becomes destructive of these ends, it is the right of those who suffer from it to refuse allegiance to it. . . .
They thus called for agitation and action, demanding "the equality of human rights."[58]

This historic declaration—like all declarations of human rights—proclaimed a vision seen of what might be. It was a bold vision of equal rights for women. The signatories were under no illusion about the resistance they would face. But they were determined. "In entering upon the great work before us," they announced, "we anticipate no small amount of misconception, misrepresentation, and ridicule; but we shall use every instrumentality within our power to effect our object."[59] Such determination to see this vision of the Declaration of Sentiments realized emerged during exactly the same year as the bursting into print of a journal in Europe entitled *Voix des Femmes* (*Voice of Women*) and a newspaper called *Frauen-Zeitung* (*Women's News*), as well as the founding of a new NGO called the Society for the Emancipation of Women. These developments launched the women's rights movement.

Momentum began to build as philosophers and reformist writers contributed their voices as well. The influential proponent of liberalism John Stuart Mill, for example, argued in *On Liberty* (1859) that human rights possessed an empirical value both for the achievement of individual happiness and for the advancement of society as a whole. Drawing evidence from a vast array of historical examples ranging from

Europe to Asia, he developed a broad theory of rights based on mankind freed from unwarranted interference by others or from the arbitrary actions of governments and balanced between individual freedom and social necessity. His growing outrage over gender inequalities prompted him to collaborate with his wife, Harriet Taylor, in *The Subjection of Women* (1869), comparing women to slaves and addressing the injustices in marriage, divorce, property, and law that denied rights to women.[60] The translation of these works rapidly spread these ideas abroad, but writers from other countries also made their own contributions. The founder of the Bahá'í faith, Mírzá Husayn 'Ali, or Bahá'u'lláh, shocked many of his contemporaries in the Middle East by advocating equality between men and women based on his beliefs about the oneness of humankind and the necessity for justice. In China, Tan Sitong wrote about *ren*, or benevolence, and stressed the importance of securing gender equity. In Japan, Toshiko Kishida published her remarkable essay entitled "I Tell You, My Fellow Sisters," insisting that all people should enjoy equal human rights.[61] Rosa Guerra similarly championed equality for women throughout Latin America through her periodical *La Camelia*, asserting: "We are entering an era of liberty and there are no rights which exclude us!"[62]

These treatises, declarations, and manifestos all provided essential expressions of grievances and inspiration to those who fought for the rights of women. But in order for their visions to be realized, they required significant transformations not only in thought, but also in the political, economic, and social patterns of the past. The powerful, wrenching turmoil of the Industrial Revolution, July Revolution of 1830 in France (evocatively portrayed by Eugène Delacroix in his famous painting not of a man but of a courageous woman at the forefront of struggle entitled *Liberty Leading the People*), European revolutions of 1848, Crimean War, India Mutiny, American Civil War and abolition of slavery, insurgencies and wars throughout Latin America, Taiping Rebellion in China, demise of the Tokugawa shogunate and civil war in Japan, revolutionary Paris Commune during the Franco-Prussian War, Maori-Pakeha wars in New Zealand, and collapsing strength of the Ottoman Empire, among other upheavals, ignited just such a process and set into motion dramatic changes.[63] They disrupted, distorted, and in some cases actually destroyed traditional structures of power and thought, thereby providing new spaces for human rights discourse and new opportunities to liberate many of those exploited in one way or another due to race, gender, or class.

British women, to illustrate, seized these openings and successfully pressured Parliament to reform laws governing marriage, age of consent, and control of their property and bodies. In France females secured the right to legalized divorce. German reformers Helene Lange and Gertrud Bäumer and their Allgemeiner deutscher Frauenverein gained remarkable improvements in educational opportunities and in labor conditions for working women. Swedish crusaders obtained equal property rights in marriage, and the right for women to work without their husband's permission. In India women secured the abolition of *suti*, or the burning to death of living widows with the corpses of their dead husbands, and the Hindu Widows' Remarriage Act legalizing intercaste marriages. Chinese women began to achieve reforms allowing them to hold supervisory offices in the bureaucracy and restricting the ancient and painful practice of mutilation of their feet by footbinding. In Argentina women gained recognition of certain civil rights in a new constitution. Women gradually secured gains in the United States as well, made all the more visible by the efforts of activists who organized the American Equal Rights Association to advance their cause and launched their own newspaper entitled *The Revolution*, published with the motto "Men, their rights and nothing more; women, their rights and nothing less!"[64] They began slowly to break down the door that prevented female suffrage by obtaining the franchise in Wyoming, Colorado, Utah, and Idaho. Then, in 1893, after many years of unswerving effort by Kate Sheppard and her colleagues in the Women's Christian Temperance Union, New Zealand became the very first country in the world to make the extraordinary breakthrough of giving women the right to vote. This inspired countless other women to hope that they, too, might someday secure the same right for themselves.

Just like the other early efforts to promote and protect human rights, these activities for women's rights usually focused on conditions within particular countries. Activists understood all too well that the many domestic obstacles and resistance at home presented formidable enough challenges without having to confront the prerogatives of national sovereignty or worry about the world at large. Nevertheless, some increasingly began to believe that they did have larger responsibilities to sisters (and brothers) beyond their own borders, and ventured out to address the global issue of the exploitation of women. Using the new technological inventions of steamships and telegraphs, as well as printing presses and inexpensive postage stamps, activists such as Jenny d'Héricourt of France, Margaret Bright Lucas of Britain, Stanton and Susan B. Anthony of the United States, and Sheppard of New Zealand, among others, achieved international stature as speakers and writers of women's rights. Together they refused to let their differences divide them or to let the gains they had made in their own countries remain isolated from the rest of the world by reaching out to like-minded campaigners, sharing their visions and experiences, and creating transnational networks of advocacy. They circulated a common body of literature in translation, including Stanton's *The Woman's Bible*, d'Héricourt's *The Emancipated Woman*, written for "the equality of all before the law" by one "who believes in the unity of the human family," and Swedish author Fredrika Bremer's novel, *Hertha, or the Story of a Soul*, about a heroine who imagines women across the world from China to Europe all rising up against centuries of subordination and being told by a chorus: "Your vision will be victorious."[65]

The international dimensions of this growing movement could be seen in still further ways. Widespread attention was given to Norwegian playwright Henrik Ibsen's feminist drama *A Doll's House*, especially upon its explosive turning point when the character of Nora finally decides that she will no longer tolerate her abused life. She dramatically renounces her assigned role of unquestioned obedience to male domination, and says as she slams the door and walks out:

But our home has been nothing but a play-room. I've been your doll-wife, just as at home I was Papa's doll-child. . . . It's no good your forbidding me anything any longer. . . . I believe that before everything else I'm a human being—just as much as you are![66]

Such language was scandalous for the times and provoked enormous controversy, but it struck a powerful chord. The play was widely translated and quickly led to the formation of "Nora Societies" throughout Europe and Asia composed of women who saw in Ibsen's character a stark reflection of their own fate—and their possible future. In Egypt, jurist Qasim Amin published a book entitled *The Liberation of Women,* forcing a debate about women's rights within Islamic consciousness that continues to this day. In addition, advocates from fifty-three American organizations and from eight countries, including India, organized the first International Council of Women in 1888. Here they sought to assess progress already made in assisting females to escape their "slave status" and to lay the foundation for what they called "universal sisterhood" among those who advocated women's rights around the world.[67]

Still other visions and movements of assisting the exploited focused on divisions of class. In fact, when the nineteenth century began, most people viewed their world in terms more of classes than of nations. Abuses derived either from traditional patterns of dominance tenaciously left over from the past or new ones created by modern capitalism and the Industrial Revolution. Among the former, rigid class distinctions by feudal or semi-feudal societies positioned what were described as "perpetual serfs" at the absolute bottom of a hierarchy where for generations they faced the hardships of forced labor.[68] Masters regarded them as their permanent property to be exploited, bought and sold, exiled, or subjected to oppressive deprivations and severe punishments. As such, little appreciable distinction existed between serfdom and slavery.

As the nineteenth century progressed, however, these practices increasingly came to be questioned. Some challenged serfdom as an impediment to the development of a trained army or to a free labor force required by industrial development. Others began to see the exploitation of serfs and the ownership of one human by another as not only inhumane but morally wrong, concluding that it was "the evil of evils."[69] Novels—once again—played an important role in transforming attitudes about such practices no longer being acceptable, for as Nikolay Gogol demonstrated with *Dead Souls* and Ivan Turgenev with *Sportsman's Sketches,* they allowed readers to see something to which they heretofore had been blind by portraying serfs as actual human beings and thereby eliciting empathy for their tragic plight. For the first time many saw themselves and their own emerging social consciousness through the lens of these novels and sometimes from the mirror of insight so often gained from an international or comparative perspective. If slaves had rights, then why not serfs? As one Russian recounted in his memoirs: "One day we were sitting quietly on the terrace listening to the reading aloud of *Uncle Tom's Cabin,* a [recently translated] book which was then in fashion. My sisters could not get over the horrors of slavery and wept at the sad fate of poor Uncle Tom. 'I cannot conceive,' said one of them, 'how such atrocities can be tolerated. Slavery is horrible.' 'But,' said Bunny in her shrill little voice, 'we have slaves too.' "[70]

As in so many other cases, such a realization provided an essential element for considering and then directing change, but it ultimately took the wars, revolutions, and upheavals of the nineteenth century to break practices of the past. Liberation came to the serfs in Prussia after Napoleon's 1807 military victory over their country. Serfdom ended in the Austro-Hungarian Empire following the revolutions of 1848. The defeat of Russia in the Crimean War led Alexander II, the "Tsar-Liberator," to launch the "Great Reforms" and sign his dramatic Decree of Emancipation in 1861, freeing the serfs across the vast empire and granting them "all the rights of free cultivators." The abolition of serfdom in Russia, and then in Poland, marked a development of unprecedented scale. It liberated at least fifty million serfs. By comparison, emancipation of all the slaves in the United States just a few years later freed four million.[71] The collapse of the Tokugawa shogunate in Japan shortly thereafter led to the abolition of feudalism, a new Meiji constitution with provisions about "rights and duties," and the growth of the Jiyū minken undō, or Popular Rights Movement.[72] At exactly the same time, Iranian reformer Mirza Yusef Khan began writing about equality before the law regardless of class and Huquq-i Insani, or basic human rights.[73]

Not all class divisions during the nineteenth century, of course, centered on hereditary serfs or peasants toiling the land in agriculture. The Industrial Revolution created many beneficial developments, but also brought the emergence of an exploited working class among the urban proletariat. In factories and textile mills, millions of men, women, and children suffered in wretched squalor, thick smoke and soot, disease-infested water, overcrowded slums, misery, and oppressive working conditions. Five-year-old boys chained around the waist hauled carts of coal in mines, while girls of eight worked underground in complete darkness for twelve hours a day to open and close passage doors. Women stood on swollen feet for fifteen hours a day changing the thread on bobbins attached to power looms with no safety devices at all. Men labored under similar conditions, received pitiful payment for their efforts, remained at the mercy of those who owned the means of production, and suffered back-breaking hardships of almost unimaginable duration. Estimates place the average workweek in Europe by midcentury at an appalling eighty-four hours.[74]

The exploitation of these workers with its attendant starvation, poverty, crime, prostitution, epidemics, family dislocations, and the enormous chasm between the extreme wealth of the rich and the extreme poverty of the poor became so glaring that it simply could not be hidden. Personal observations, exposés in newspapers, reports from official commissions of inquiry, provocative portrayals of poverty in Friedrich Engels's *The Condition of the Working Class* and Caroline Norton's *A Voice from the Factories*, and the misery dramatized by such widely read and translated novelists as Honoré de Balzac and Charles Dickens all contributed to a burgeoning public consciousness about the extent of human suffering and its relationship to rights. One of Dickens's characters in *Hard Times*, for example, pleads:

Oh, my friends and fellow-countrymen, the slaves of an iron-handed and a grinding despotism!. . . . I tell you that the hour is come when we must rally round one another as One united power, and crumble into dust the oppressors that too long have battened upon the plunder of our families, upon the sweat of our brows, upon the labor of our hands, upon the strength of our sinews, upon the God-created glorious rights of Humanity.[75]

These words increasingly came alive when enhanced by images. As we saw in the cases of the slave trade and slavery, visual representations have a way of literally allowing people to see—and emotionally feel—the reality of abuses. Indeed, workers used this as a model when they carried a banner at protest rallies showing an image of a maimed factory worker with these words: "Am I Not a Man and a Brother?"[76] Stark pen-and-ink drawings of artist Gustave Doré similarly depicted sullen-eyed children, emaciated fathers holding starving children in their arms, or destitute men and women languishing along gutters. But this was only a foretaste of what would now come, for after midcentury a new invention appeared that would eventually have an enormous impact on the evolution of human rights: photography. Actual images enabled viewers to look for the first time into the faces of real victims, to see their plight, to have empathy for them as human beings and feel their pain, and to imagine themselves in the same situation. This power to elicit outrage was dramatically revealed by the widespread reaction generated by Jacob Riis's collection of photographs entitled *How the Other Half Lives*, showing the brutal reality of slums and the despair in the haunting eyes of those in destitution.

Such obvious and severe misery ignited new and profoundly serious questions about the meaning of human rights. If slaves and women had rights, then why not workers? What good were civil rights such as the freedom of speech or political rights of voting, to people who had no food, no home, no clothing, no medical care, or no prospect of an education? What were the benefits of freedom from slavery or serfdom if the alternative was "wage slavery" or destitution as "factory slaves"? Was an individual's right to private property compatible with the need to protect society's less fortunate members? Did this mean that the declarations of human rights represented no more than the abstract ideas of philosophers, parchment prose, or the hollow concepts and empty platitudes of politicians? Or, when all was said and done, did human rights really remain no more than the exclusive possession of the rich ruling class marching under the banner of untrammeled laissez-faire and the "iron law" of wages?[77] With these questions in their minds, the have-nots of the working class and their leaders increasingly began to speak out not just about "negative" or "freedom from" rights to be protected from unwarranted government interference but also about more "positive" or "freedom to" or "freedom of" rights.

Interestingly enough, Thomas Paine had raised these very issues in *Rights of Man*, advocating what has been described as "a new vision."[78] But when he proposed them at the end of the eighteenth century, few people listened. Now, with the extent of human suffering caused by the Industrial Revolution, they did. Outspoken critic William Cobbett charged during the 1830s, for example, that the poor had been cheated of their rights, and demanded before agitated crowds: "the right to have a living out of the land of our birth in exchange for our labor duly and honestly performed; the right, in case we fell into distress, to have our wants sufficiently relieved out of the produce of the land, whether that distress arose from sickness, from decrepitude, from old age, or from inability to find employment."[79] It is out of this context of class exploitation that we thus discover the significant emergence of the movement for the rights of workers and a second generation of human rights known as social and economic rights.

These problems and claims of the exploited poor once again raised the extremely serious debate among activists over how best to realize their visions of human rights. They understood that they faced fierce resistance from those who benefitted from this system of class divisions, who insisted on doing anything that they wanted with their own property even if others were harmed in the process, or who argued in the name of Social Darwinism that the poor were not fully human and needed to be weeded out because they were lazy or unfit. But to confront this opposition, should they rely on the strategy of moral persuasion and gradual reform? Or, should they employ more radical action, mobilize resistance, or even turn to violence and revolution to achieve their ends?

When faced with these choices, many advocates of economic and social rights turned to the path of moral persuasion, direct assistance, and liberal reform within civil society. Indeed, the century was marked by an unprecedented reforming impulse described as universal "service to humanity" based upon strong religious convictions.[80] The Ramakrishna Movement in India, for example, denounced the rigid caste system and spoke out on behalf of rights of the exploited poor, seeking to reduce social injustice and economic inequality on the basis of the Hindu precept of *sādhanā*, or social service.[81] Many Buddhists did the same. Activists in the West, particularly among upper- and middle-class women, found inspiration in what they called the Social Gospel, or a strong sense of Christian responsibility to assist "the least of these." They thus created a wide variety of charitable organizations and movements such as the Salvation Army, Young Men's Christian Association, Young Women's Christian Association, Women's Christian Temperance Union, and the Paulist Fathers, making extraordinary efforts to provide direct relief to the needy and to work for social reform.

As the century unfolded, additional religious voices joined in as well. For years the deep concerns of local Catholic clergy and laity about severe social problems had met only silence from a Vatican frequently identified with reaction. But in the face of overwhelming evidence of human deprivation and in light of his own personal observations of the sufferings of the exploited, Pope Leo XIII issued his remarkable and seminal 1891 encyclical *Rerum Novarum* (Of New Things), explicitly addressing what he called "the natural rights of mankind." Here he warned that "the first concern of all is to save the poor workers from the cruelty of grasping speculators, who use human beings as mere instruments for making money. It is neither justice nor humanity so to grind men down with excessive labor as to stupefy their minds and wear out their bodies." For this reason, he declared, human rights

must be religiously respected wherever they are found; and it is the duty of the public authority to prevent and punish injury, and to protect each one in the possession of his own. Still, when there is question of protecting the rights of individuals, the poor and helpless have a claim to special consideration. The richer population have many ways of protecting themselves. . . . [But] wage-earners, who are, undoubtedly, among the weak and necessitous, should be specially cared for and protected by the commonwealth.[82]

A few years later, Protestants found their consciences stirred by one of the best selling novels of the time, *In His Steps*, written by Charles Sheldon, who asked his readers to answer one simple question when confronted with destitution among the poor: "What would Jesus do?"[83]

Some held visions of economic and social rights but were motivated more by liberal political philosophy than by religious principles. One of these was John Stuart Mill. He believed strongly in private property and that people should be free from government interference. Nevertheless, he argued that the worst excesses of the Industrial Revolution needed to be tempered with some safety net, and that relief for the working poor should be regarded as "an absolute right."[84] Henry George's influential book entitled *Progress and Poverty* added yet another voice to this argument. Others such as Henri de Saint-Simon, Charles Fourier, and Robert Owen sought to bring about economic and social justice by establishing ideal or "utopian" towns and factories in which owners and workers cooperatively shared in management, benefits, and risks by peaceful means.

Others activists addressed these problems of the exploited poor and their rights by more militant action. Impatient at the slow pace of moderate reform, and angered by repressive laws forbidding unionization and what they perceived as economic theories seeking to justify exploitation under the "law" of supply and demand and laissez-faire capitalism, more radical workers channeled their discontent into labor agitation, protest, trade unionism and collective bargaining, pickets, strikes, factory sabotage, and clashes with police and troops. The Chartist Movement, for example, attracted throngs of impoverished and alienated British workers and middle-class radicals. In the face of persecution, imprisonment, and exile, they issued a "People's Charter," signed by more than three million people, denouncing rich exploiters, calling for universal suffrage and the elimination of property qualifications to vote or hold office, and demanding their rights. Some workers turned to the more radical approaches of the fiery Irish organizer Feargus O'Conner or the new theories of socialism expounded by Louis Blanc and Pierre-Joseph Proudhon from France and Ferdinand Lasalle and August Bebel from Germany challenging capitalist greed, rejecting private property, and advocating radical resistance.

Still others grew weary of words, theories, and mere protest and turned instead to revolutionary violence. The upheavals throughout Europe in 1848 fueled new demands for rights and forged a clarion call for worldwide revolution, as advocated by Karl Marx and Friedrich Engels. Their powerful and widely translated *Communist Manifesto* inspired European workers and then, during the next century, fired the imagination of Communists throughout Asia, Latin America, Africa, and Europe. Influenced by G. W. F. Hegel in his *Philosophy of Right*, they saw contradictory dialectic forces constantly competing with each other and viewed the struggle between the rich and the impoverished proletariat as class warfare that was global in scope. With their own materialist interpretation of history, they argued that liberal conceptions of the right to private property and civil and political rights, which sought to protect individual autonomy and liberty by limiting the power of the state, were hopelessly egotistical and a part of "bourgeois democracy" representing no more than a "narrow bourgeois horizon of rights" that should "be left far behind."[85] Marx and Engels proposed a more radical communitarian or communist society that focused on economic and social rights, but insisted that it could be achieved in only one way:

The Communists everywhere support every revolutionary movement against the existing social and political order. . . . They openly declare that their ends can be attained only by the forcible overthrow of all existing social conditions. Let the ruling classes tremble at a Communist revolution. The proletarians have nothing to lose but their chains. They have a world to win. WORKING MEN OF ALL COUNTRIES, UNITE![86]

In issuing this charge, Marx and Engels argued that only an international strategy would enable exploited workers to secure these rights. They thus founded in 1864 the International Working Men's Organization, or First (Communist) International, exhorting their followers to ignore their nation in an age of nationalism and instead form a "bond of brotherhood . . . between the workingmen of different countries" and "to master themselves the mysteries of international politics; . . . [and] to counteract them, if necessary, by all means in their power."[87]

These vastly different approaches to economic and social rights produced vastly different results. Violence, at least in the short term, begat violence, as evidenced by the repression against the radical Paris Commune in 1871, which claimed the lives of fifteen thousand people in a single week, or the bloody Haymarket Square riot of 1886 in Chicago. But other early efforts clearly resulted in direct and very specific measures to assist exploited workers and their families, and in the process helped to launch what has been called the "revolution in government": state-supported regulation and welfare relief designed to provide the greatest good to the greatest number.[88] Settlement houses were created to provide food to the hungry, shelter to the homeless, and, influenced in part by pamphlets like *The Rights of Infants*, maternity care for mothers and their young babies. Any number of national laws in a variety of countries prohibited the employment of children under nine years old, limited working hours for teenagers, and banned women and children from labor in underground mines. These were followed by legislative regulations designed to provide better working conditions, reduced hours in a workday, minimum wages, safety inspection measures, accident insurance, the right of labor to organize and bargain collectively, and the lowering of property qualifications for voting. Others made provision for the beginnings of child welfare, better sanitation, standards for food and drink, prison reform, and public education opportunities. Today, in most countries, these protections and services are regarded as normal functions of government and society and as a part of everyday life. At the beginning of the nineteenth century, they did not exist.

To Care for the Wounded

Ever since men began fighting each other, they left the wounded victims of armed combat scattered across countless blood-soaked battlefields, destined to be killed or captured by enemies, assisted by their comrades if possible, or simply left to fend for themselves as best they could. The vanquished remained at the mercy of the victor— and mercy was rare. Although as early as the fourth century B.C. the Chinese military theorist Sun Tzu wrote in *The Art of War* about the obligation to care for prisoners and the wounded, nations remained unable or unwilling to restrict their behavior in war by establishing any mutually acceptable rules. Those unfortunate soldiers wounded in battle had no international society, no organization, no law to which they could turn for any protection or care. They hence remained largely forgotten and without rights, condemned to suffer and very likely die.

A number of developments during the nineteenth century began to seriously challenge and transform these traditional practices. One of these was the number of early successes from the visions and movements in other areas of human rights that we have explored, for they provided hope that still other advances could be made. At the same time, the size of armed forces and numbers of men in uniform expanded as nations increasingly drew upon drafted conscripts. Technology produced by the Industrial Revolution played a particularly significant role, for it began the mechanization of warfare. Railroads made it possible to transport large numbers of troops from one location to another and have them arrive ready to fight. Steamships made it possible to do the same with sailors at sea. Artillery made it possible to rain death from considerable distances. Rifles firing expanding bullets (as compared to muskets firing solid metal balls) made it possible to greatly increase accuracy and the volume of fire, with devastating results for the victims. The lethality of these weapons made it possible to kill more people than ever before in history. Moreover, the advent of photographs showing piles of bodies strewn across battlefield, severed limbs, and mutilated bodies did much to influence public opinion about the actual conditions (as compared to artistic paintings attempting to convey excitement and glory) of war. Many observers concluded that the result was no longer war—but carnage.

It is in this setting that the fate and the rights of the wounded came to be of such great concern. As such, it would serve as yet another example that it often takes the worst, in the form of brutality or atrocities, to bring about change in the evolution of human rights. This could be seen in the empathy, compassion, sense of responsibility, and pioneering efforts of three courageous and extraordinary women. Grand Duchess Elena Pavlovna of Russia organized a group of nurses known as the Sisters of Mercy during the Crimean War, earning the gratitude of thousands of soldiers and the public. Clara Barton provided similar service in the American Civil War and became widely known as "the Angel of the Battlefield."[89] The one who made the greatest impact was the dedicated and strong-willed British nurse Florence Nightingale. A granddaughter of a Member of Parliament who had championed the rights of factory workers, defended Jews and Dissenters, and supported abolitionists, she believed that she had been called into Christian service. Over the objections of her parents (who considering nursing as "beneath" her "station" and as shamefully exposing her to the naked bodies of men), she traveled to the Crimea to aid British soldiers. Here she witnessed thousands of victims tormented by painful battle wounds, dysentery, cholera, and starvation in conditions of chaos and indescribable filth. Nightingale's experience changed her life and eventually that of a nation insofar as it cared for the wounded. She worked day and night giving care, wrote to Queen Victoria and leading politicians, and campaigned in the press to bring the rights of these victims before a broad public and into the homes of readers for attention. Her remarkable successes in these efforts, visual images of her holding a candle or lantern as she cared for her patients, and the many reports from returning soldiers who believed that they owed their lives to her, made Nightingale one of the most important and influential women of her time. Indeed, she came to be described as a visionary "whose heroic efforts on behalf of suffering humanity will be recognized and admired by all ages as long as the world shall last."[90]

One of those directly inspired by her efforts was J. Henry Dunant, a deeply compassionate man of strong religious conviction who had helped to establish the Young

Men's Christian Union in Geneva. While traveling in 1859, he found himself in a town in northern Italy and quickly concluded that he was in the wrong place at the wrong time. Here he unexpectedly encountered the horror of the monumental Battle of Solferino, fought between the combined forces of the Italians and French against the Austrians. Three hundred thousand troops ferociously battled along a ten-mile front for fifteen hours in suffocating heat. But there was more, for they fought with the weapons produced by the Industrial Revolution. When the fighting finally stopped, Dunant witnessed the catastrophe of thousands of wounded soldiers mixed with the dead, sprawled across the destroyed landscape, and suffering in total exhaustion and excruciating pain with almost no hope of medical assistance. The horror of this forced him to confront a revealing and brutal fact: armies of the time had four veterinarians for every thousand horses but less than one physician for the same number of men.

The care of these wounded soldiers attracted Dunant's attention more than anything else. He became haunted by their horrible fate and decided to speak out in 1862 by writing an intensely moving memoir entitled *A Memory of Solferino*. There are times when a single book can alter the course of history by changing minds. This was one of those. Here Dunant recounted his empathy, his shock, and his outrage at what he saw, writing not to glorify war but rather to describe its butchery. His first-hand descriptions speak for themselves:

One poor wounded man has his jaw carried away; another his head shattered; a third, who could have been saved, has his chest beaten in. Oaths and shrieks of rage, groans of anguish and despair. . . . Brains spurt under the wheels, limbs are broken and torn. . . . [Men are] left behind, lying helpless on the naked ground in their own blood! . . . Heart-rending voices kept calling for help. Who could ever describe the agonies of that fearful night!"[91]

Dunant went on to describe the hideous wounds, painful sufferings, amputations conducted without anesthesia, infections, nauseating sounds and smells, vermin-covered bodies, and limbs rotting with gangrene. The numbers of wounded completely overwhelmed all efforts made by a pitifully small group who attempted to care for them. In this heroic endeavor, Dunant found himself struck with the fact that suffering made no distinction between the wounded of the victors and those of the vanquished. "Men of all nations lay *side by side* on the flagstone floors of the churches of Castiglione—Frenchmen and Arabs, Germans and Slavs," he observed, providing graphic evidence of the Italian phrase *Tutti fratelli*, "All are brothers," and that "Our Lord Jesus Christ made no such distinctions between men in doing well."[92]

This personal experience moved Dunant to see a vision. It was a vision of a world that ought to be: a world acknowledging that soldiers did not completely surrender their basic human rights simply because their countries forced them to put on military uniforms. Toward this end, he made a proposal in the single most important passage in his book by asking whether it would it not be desirable "to formulate some international principle, sanctioned by a Convention inviolate in character, which, once agreed on and ratified, might constitute the basis for societies for relief of the wounded?"[93] He envisioned creating an international body of trained and dedicated providers with affiliates in all countries to care for the rights of the wounded as fully human beings without any distinction as to nationality, class, race, or other form of difference.

Dunant's vision became an instant topic of the day, aroused public opinion, and launched one of the important movements in the history of human rights. His book was read, reviewed, quoted, published in second and third editions, passed from hand to hand, and translated into several languages. It made the fate of the wounded in war a tangible—and unacceptable—reality to those who read it, and attracted the attention of literary, political, and financial figures who offered to provide support. His own hopeful optimism, persuasiveness, simple dignity and genuineness, energy, and sense of duty to Christian service and the message of the Good Samaritan attracted others to this movement of creating a permanent system for international humanitarian assistance. An organizing committee, not without a little audacity, then decided to invite governments to send representatives "to transpose Monsieur Dunant's ideas from the realm of theory to that of practice."[94] The resulting Geneva International Conference met in 1863 and attracted delegates from fourteen different nations and four philanthropic societies. Although none of these participants possessed any authority to bind their countries to an agreement, they agreed to establish auxiliary medical societies in their own countries to assist in carrying this vision forward. They chose as their emblem the Swiss flag in reverse, placing a red cross on a white background, and created a new humanitarian organization. They called it the International Committee of the Red Cross. During a Nobel Peace Prize ceremony it eventually would be described as "one of the great miracles in human history."[95]

The members of this committee strongly believed that human rights were natural, equal, and universal, and thus should apply to *all* soldiers. But at the same time they understood that their vision could never be fully realized without the political support of governments and their respective armies interested in protecting their national sovereignty by resisting any legally binding treaties. Nevertheless, Dunant and the other members of the committee refused to be deterred. They worked tirelessly to persuade government leaders of the necessity to take action. Success came when they convinced representatives of sixteen nations to attend an international conference in 1864 and negotiate the path-breaking Geneva Convention for the Amelioration of the Condition of the Wounded. This was the first multilateral treaty in history establishing the rights of soldiers in times of war. It required all signatories to respect the immunity of Red Cross personnel from attack or captivity in order that they might provide equal medical care to combatants regardless of nationality when unable to fight because of sickness or wounds and thereby conduct their work around the world in the name of common humanity.[96]

This Geneva, or Red Cross, Convention ignited a human rights movement. Immediately on ratification of the treaty, national Red Cross societies began to multiply, preparing for the time when their services would be desperately needed. This came soon enough. Indeed, even before the details had been fully prepared, the Red Cross emblem appeared for the first time on the battlefield during the 1864 Prussian-Danish War. Trained personnel, stocks of dressing material, surgical instruments, and horse-drawn ambulances quickly found themselves being mobilized to care for the wounded of the Austro-Prussian War of 1866 and the Franco-Prussian War of 1870–1871. In fact, their work so impressed eyewitness Clara Barton that she returned home to establish the American Association of the Red Cross. The demands of the Russo-Turkish War of 1877–1878 encouraged the creation of the Red Crescent Society.[97] Not long thereafter the Nippon Sekijuji Sha, or Japanese Red Cross Society, was formed. Subsequent adherents to the convention soon included Siam, China, most of the Latin American countries, and the United States. Whenever a new war or armed conflict broke out, Red Cross units were there: the Serbo-Bulgarian War of 1885, Sino-Japanese War of 1894–1895, and Spanish-American War of 1898. In each case, these early efforts sought to protect the wounded and establish the principle of universality for the rights of all soldiers, "recognizing man as man, without any distinction whatever."[98]

These evolving norms inspired additional international legal protections. During the 1899 Hague Peace Conference, for example, delegates ranging from Europe to Latin America and from Asia to the United States who could agree on practically nothing else, publicly committed themselves to "the laws of humanity and the requirements of the public conscience" and adopted a Convention Respecting the Laws and Customs of War on Land.[99] The text spoke explicitly of "rights"—the right of the wounded to receive medical treatment, the right of prisoners of war to be given food and clothing and protection under the law, the right of individuals to be considered inviolable if they carried a white flag and sought to communicate their intention to surrender, and the right of civilians to be protected in times of war. The treaty also established provisions recognizing the right of relief societies like the Red Cross to visit camps and provide medical care, inform home countries of individuals' whereabouts and physical condition, arrange correspondence with families, and facilitate the repatriation of the most seriously wounded. At the same time, representatives signed the Convention for the Adaptation to Maritime Warfare of Principles of the Geneva Convention, guaranteeing the neutrality of hospital ships and their staffs and extending protection to individuals wounded at sea.[100]

These legal conventions were necessarily gradual and tentative. Given the context and the tension between broad international humanitarianism and parochial national interests, they could hardly be expected to be otherwise. All nations continued to insist that there would be no compromise with their own interpretations of national sovereignty and that they were free to either ratify or to reject the treaties as they wished. They seemed to be motivated more by elemental self-interest and brutal calculations of utility rather than larger principles of humanity, and thus refused to include specific enforcement provisions within the texts. Particularly troublesome to the International Committee of the Red Cross was the tendency of governments to distort and subvert the vision of universal care for all wounded by intoxicating their respective national Red Cross societies with the heady brew of nationalism and xenophobia that sought to provide exclusive attention only for their own nationals.[101] Moreover, and ironically, these conventions also demonstrated that it was war rather than peace—the care of soldiers rather than civilians—that stimulated such international efforts for human rights.[102]

Despite these difficulties, the fact remains that all of these developments marked changes in normative values and the beginning of what is known as international humanitarian law, or Red Cross law, in armed conflict.[103] In contrast with earlier "laws of war" that focused on the use of *objects* such as weapons or ships, this new form of law focused on *people*. As such, it marked dramatic advances for visions of human rights. These early efforts began by acknowledging the "dictates of the public conscience" and articulating the principles of the "laws of humanity." For the first time, they created positive law in treaties establishing certain rights for the protection of victims of war: the rights of combatants wounded in battle and then the rights of those captured as prisoners of war. Through time, as we shall see, they expanded the scope of rights still further by including civilians, refugees, displaced persons, others victimized by human or natural disasters, and prohibitions against torture, mutilation, pillage, attack on undefended dwellings, and destruction of places of worship. Together, they all helped to lay the critical foundation of humanitarian law recognizing that individuals possessed certain basic human rights, even in times of war, and that their protection required international action.[104]

To Protect the Persecuted

Most of these efforts to advance some dimension of international human rights during the nineteenth century required the voluntary cooperation and compliance of sovereign nation-states. That is, attempts to free the enslaved, to assist the exploited, and to care for the wounded in the world could not succeed unless the governments agreed to cooperate. Given the political realities of the time, the definitions of internal affairs, and the principles of the doctrine of sovereignty, independent nations had to be willing on their own accord to sign and abide by the terms of international treaties or to allow international relief organizations into their countries in order for human rights to be promoted and protected. Otherwise, nothing would change. One important exception to this took the form of humanitarian intervention.

A number of the early founders of international law had addressed the complicated question of whether any nation or group of nations should ever actively intervene in the internal affairs of others when the mistreatment of victims became so brutal that it exceeded the limits of acceptable behavior. Writing in the sixteenth century, Alberico Gentiti maintained that resort to arms could be justified when defending the "common law of humanity," for "in the violation of that law we are all injured, and individuals in turn can find their personal rights violated."[105] Hugo Grotius went on to argue that the use of armed force could be justified if defending subjects "from injuries by their ruler" or from a tyrant's "atrocities towards his subjects, which no just man can approve."[106] Emerich de Vattel similarly wrote in the eighteenth century that "any foreign power may rightfully give assistance to an oppressed people who asked for its aid."[107] Through time, they and others who stressed that rights were universal contributed to the theory that if any state persecuted its own people to such an extent that it generated international outrage, then intervention by others to protect those rights could be considered legitimate.

This idea of humanitarian intervention, of course, immediately clashed with other theories of international relations, especially those of sovereignty and its uncompromising corollaries of domestic jurisdiction and nonintervention. It went far beyond merely protecting alien nationals,[108] and proposed to deal directly with the protection of the citizens or subjects of other countries. Humanitarian intervention also confronted both practical and political realities of power. Any nation considering launching an unwelcomed and uninvited intervention into another understood perfectly well that it possessed limitations on its ability to actually project sufficient power abroad to coerce behavior. In addition, intervening in another state in the name of human rights might well invite criticism of abuses at home and dangerously risk prompting others to reciprocate with their own interventions in return. Nevertheless, by the nineteenth century, a growing concern about severe abuses, enhanced by the technological means to gather and transmit information, increasingly encouraged governments to reevaluate at least some of their traditional reluctance to consider domestic abuse as a matter of legitimate international concern and to envision a new level of direct action on behalf of the persecuted.

Not surprisingly, the fate of minorities persecuted for their religious convictions or ethnic affiliations would most likely draw the interest of members of the same group elsewhere. They would be the ones most interested in protecting the right of religious freedom by humanitarian intervention if their coreligionists were threatened with persecution. In the past, these concerns received only slight international attention from states unwilling to challenge any prerogatives of national sovereignty.[109] This began to change at the Congress of Vienna, when diplomats explicitly recognized the beginnings of an international right of religious freedom and acknowledged that intolerance might jeopardize other aspects of international peace and security. Here they pledged themselves to maintain "religious equality" and "assure equal protection and favor to every sect" in Belgium, and to guarantee "without any distinction of Religion . . . the same political and civil rights which are enjoyed by [other] inhabitants" in Switzerland.[110] At the same time, they agreed to "an amelioration in the civil state of those who profess the Jewish religion in Germany," paying "particular attention to the measures by which the enjoyment of civil rights shall be secured and guaranteed to them."[111] The fact that these provisions occurred as integral parts of multilateral, negotiated treaties provided an important early step in establishing the principle and practice of international guarantees to protect such rights.

This issue rose with particular force in the nineteenth century over the fate of Christians living in the Ottoman Empire. Given the volatility and diversity ranging from Algeria across North Africa through the Middle East and to Asia Minor and the Balkans, the Ottomans could maintain internal peace only by recognizing the interests of the *millets*, or religious communities, of Greek Orthodox and Armenian Christians, Muslims, and Jews. Yet, even under this system, the *dhimmis*, or non-Muslim subjects, suffered various forms of discrimination.[112] Among these victims, however, only the Christians had powerful friends concerned and informed about their fate and able to project power beyond their own borders.[113] The Great Powers of Europe alone possessed the capabilities of exerting influence, if they so chose, by employing a variety of means ranging from diplomatic pressure to humanitarian intervention.

Europeans who already had taken measures to ensure greater religious toleration with the Catholic Emancipation Acts of 1829 and 1832 and the Religious Disabilities Act of 1846 in Britain, and the relaxation of many legal restrictions against Jews in several other countries, increasingly turned their attention abroad. This could be seen with expressions of concern and formal protests about the treatment of Christian subjects within the Ottoman Empire. Many Ottomans responded with resentment, claiming blatant interference into their internal affairs. Interestingly enough, some reform-minded government officials actually welcomed this international pressure and used it as a means of bringing about change. The result was the *Hatti-i Sherif* promulgated by Sultan Abdulmejid in 1839. This famous decree, read for the first time before an assemblage of foreign diplomats, guaranteed certain legal, social, and political rights to "all our subjects, of whatever religion or sect they may be; they shall enjoy them without exception."[114] Further pressure forced Sultan Abdul-Aziz to sign the 1856 Treaty of Paris accepting an international obligation to honor "the welfare of his subjects . . . without distinction of religion or race" and "his generous intentions towards the Christian population of his Empire."[115]

When diplomatic protests proved to be insufficient to protect the persecuted, European states were prepared to use direct military intervention. After several years of watching extensive human suffering and the slaughter of many Greek Orthodox Christians at the hands of the sultan's forces, to illustrate, Britain, France, and Russia resolved in 1827 to ignore the claim by the Ottomans that the conflict was an "internal affair" and sent naval vessels and troops to Greece. Their motives, they announced in a most unusual formal agreement, could be found in their desire of finally "putting a stop to the effusion of blood" and "re-establishing peace . . . by means of an arrangement called for, no less by sentiments of humanity, than by interests for the tranquility of Europe."[116] By the subsequent London Protocol of 1830, they affirmed the rights of Christians in the Ottoman Empire and the rights of Muslims in Greece. Further efforts occurred in the wake of persecution and murder of perhaps as many as eleven thousand Christian Maronites by Muslim Druze from Syria during 1860, which evoked what was described as "universal reprobation."[117] Indeed, observed one diplomat, these "calamities" caused such a "profound emotion" of outrage that governments found themselves forced to confront the question of whether or not they had certain international responsibilities to protect the persecuted.[118] Austria, France, Britain, Prussia, and Russia, with the agreement of the Ottoman Turks themselves, consequently authorized a collective military force of six thousand men to intervene and protect the persecuted. These six powers also created a ground-breaking international commission to investigate the causes and the extent of the abuses, to assist the victims and punish the guilty, to draft a new constitution guaranteeing religious freedom, and to prevent persecutions in the future.[119] Said the British secretary of state for external affairs: "It is to be hoped that the measures now taken may vindicate the rights of humanity."[120]

This was just the beginning, however. Years of notorious misrule and unrelenting persecution of Christians in Bosnia, Herzegovina, and Bulgaria finally exploded in revolts in the 1870s. When the Ottoman Empire sent in troops to crush the rebellion, their attacks against non-Muslims provoked international horror and outrage.

Eyewitnesses told of unrestrained killing, looting, raping, burning, pillaging, and torture. The massacre of no fewer than twelve thousand Christians during a single month
prompted observers to describe it "as the most heinous crime that had stained the
history of the present century."[121] Newspaper accounts and drawings of Turkish troops
burning homes and slaughtering innocent women and children provided words and
visual images that aroused widespread empathy and provoked public outrage.[122] William Gladstone, the future British prime minister, published a book entitled *The Bulgarian Horrors* that sold forty thousand copies in just three days describing "the horror
and infamy" of victims "murdered, or worse than murdered, by thousands." He spoke
of "rights and duties," telling his readers that this kind of persecution was no longer
acceptable and urging them to consider their larger responsibility to "protect humanity and defend justice." "For the purposes of humanity alone," Gladstone concluded,
the fleet should be sent "in concert with the other Powers, for the defense of innocent
lives."[123] Such action, he believed would convey one simple message: "You shall *not* do
it again!"[124]

This determination by the Great Powers to take action to protect the persecuted
played a major role when negotiating the path-breaking 1878 Treaty of Berlin at the
end of the war between Russia and the Ottoman Turks. It imposed upon the Ottoman
Empire and the new states of Bulgaria, Serbia, Montenegro, and Romania important
provisions on civil and political rights, including religious freedom and the protection

Figure 4. Images of Persecution. *Illustrated London Times*, 1876.

of Christians and Jews. Interestingly enough, the treaty also recognized "the rights and interests" of ethnic minorities, such as the Armenians.[125] The same powers then went on to sign the International Convention of Constantinople, guaranteeing the right of Muslims to freely practice their religion with complete equality in territories given to Greece.[126] Such provisions designed to protect human rights within particular countries by international treaties marked striking early departures from traditional practices.

Their efforts did not stop here. Within just two years, the signatory powers of the Treaty of Berlin issued a highly publicized collective note to Sultan Abdul Hamid, strongly criticizing his persecution of Armenians. He resented such interference and threats of further intervention from what he described as "over-zealous people" and argued that his government was being unfairly singled out for criticism of practices "which naturally occur in every country in the world."[127] He nevertheless could not ignore this international pressure, and began to make changes. Other nations renewed their protests during 1895 and 1896 when further massacres occurred not only in distant rural areas but within full view of the diplomatic community in Istanbul itself. Britain, France, and Russia publicly demanded a commission of inquiry and an immediate halt to all such bloodshed and violations of human rights.

Persecution of minorities within the Ottoman Empire provided a highly visible focal point for international attention, condemnation, and action, in much the same way that the atrocities of the Third Reich in Germany, apartheid in South Africa, and "ethnic cleansing" in Yugoslavia would do in the next century. But similar violations of human rights in other countries also prompted widespread outrage and criticism. Considerable pressure was placed on the government of tsarist Russia for its brutal suppression of Poles and on the Hungarians over their persecution of religious and ethnic minorities (including Roma) through a policy of forced assimilation known as "Magyarization." The Evangelical Alliance, composed of churches from throughout Europe and the United States, focused attention to new variants of "Russification" that deliberately persecuted non-Orthodox believers. Jewish groups also urged governments to take action that might protect their coreligionists from discrimination, expulsion, persecution, and murder in anti-Semitic pogroms, particularly in Romania and Russia. When the United States formally protested on one of these occasions, it announced that it could not remain silent in the face of this abuse of rights and the "claims of our common humanity."[128]

Along with the hope held out to victims, these early experiences with humanitarian intervention at the same time revealed troubling difficulties and serious dangers. Saving lives could cost lives. Intervention in the name of "humanity" could be legitimate and beneficial, but it also could provide a convenient pretext for coercion or a guise for masking more suspicious motives of self-interest and aggrandizement. Similarly, nations taking action against others were likely to be guilty of abuses of their own, thus opening themselves up for accusations of hypocrisy and having arbitrary standards that applied to some but not to all. The Great Powers who demonstrated such eagerness to protect the rights of the persecuted in the Ottoman Empire, to illustrate, also happened to be the same ones known to persecute indigenous peoples whom they regarded as less-than-fully human within their own overseas empires. In addition, whereas carefully negotiated and solemn treaty provisions concerning human rights indicated a strength of desire, the lack of enforcement by means of permanent institutions or mechanisms whereby victims could initiate complaints revealed a lack of will. "Whether use will be made of this . . . opportunity which has been thus obtained . . . by the interposition of the Powers of Europe," conceded one diplomat, "or whether it is to be thrown away, will depend [ultimately] upon the sincerity with which the Turkish statesmen now address themselves to the duties of good government and the task of reform."[129] Finally, and not surprisingly, those who engaged in this activity had reason to worry about what they described as "the inconveniences and dangers which an intervention of this kind might produce."[130] One of these was precedent, for it could well be turned against those who used it, thereby threatening their own independence, domestic jurisdiction, territorial integrity, and national sovereignty. In addition, humanitarian intervention, however worthy, always carried the danger that it could provoke even worse reactions against the very people it desired to protect.

Even though such problems clearly existed, these early efforts contributed heavily to the growing theory and practice of protecting the rights of the persecuted. They helped develop the emerging legal principle that certain fundamental *lois de l'humanité* (laws of humanity) must be honored, and that there were certain limits to the impunity states could enjoy under international law when it came to how they treated their own nationals. Legal scholars described these in terms of natural law and human rights, arguing that it was no longer acceptable for other states to be passive in the face of such serious violations. Pressure and force, they insisted, should be used by nations acting collectively to protect the rights of victims in another state unable to defend themselves from their own government if the abuses became so egregious as to exceed the limits of reason and justice and "to shock the conscience of mankind." In addition, and very importantly, the whole issue began to suggest the possibility that the violation of human rights in one country might well endanger the peace and security of other countries.[131]

*   *   *

Those visionaries and activists of the nineteenth century who worked so hard to claim, to articulate, to extend, and to protect human rights experienced both the pain and frustration of problems as well as the elation of successes. From the very beginning they had to confront the harsh reality and strength of countervailing old sources of resistance arising from entrenched traditions, racism, male domination, vested interests, class discrimination, and national sovereignty. Added to these were opposing forces that became more pronounced during their own day, including imperial conquest and doctrines of manifest destiny, unrestricted laissez-faire, "scientific" explanations for sexism and racism, anti-Semitism, and extreme nationalism that strongly opposed any internationalist visions whatsoever. They had to face the cruel paradox that attention to human rights tended to become most intense when abuses were the most obvious and egregious: in slavery, in exploitation, in war, and in persecution. Like all pioneers, they had to proceed without any clear guidelines and in the face of great uncertainty where progress was rarely linear but always incremental and often erratic and unpredictable. They also had to encounter the existence of serious differences between themselves and to realize that they came from highly diverse religious, philosophical, and political points of departure. Those who believed that human rights fundamentally came from God or from natural law, to illustrate, increasingly found themselves challenged by those who argued that the source of rights could be found instead in liberalism, rationalism, utilitarianism, secularism, materialism, or humanism. They similarly engaged in severe arguments about whether to choose the means of moral persuasion and gradual reform or the path of revolution and violence.

At the same time, they had to face the fact that there were different visions, and that rights did not always form a single and consistent package in practice. Those who claimed that human rights were always natural, equal, and universal, and thus belonged to all people without distinction and as interconnected and indivisible parts of a seamless web, for example, often found themselves confronted by those who instead insisted that some people were not fully human and thus did not deserve the same rights. Support for the rights of slaves and serfs, to illustrate, did not necessarily guarantee an extension of concern for the rights of women, the rights of racial or ethnic minorities, the rights of the working poor, the rights of indigenous peoples, or the rights of strangers persecuted in other lands.

In the face of these obvious limitations and inconsistencies and often severe challenges, the early efforts on behalf of international human rights made remarkable achievements. Never before had so many people been able to use the forces of the time and to cross the thresholds of determining that certain behavior was wrong and no longer acceptable, that outrage needed to be followed by action, and that the rights of others beyond themselves needed to be protected. Never before had they been so willing to examine such dark places and practices in the world and to confront abuses long taken for granted. Never before had they been so willing to work together in great movements to take action in the name of human rights. Whether in broad-based or in single-issue campaigns, they began to experiment, develop networks, open space to explore expanded definitions of human rights, build a larger sense of responsibility toward humanity as a whole, establish political precedents, challenge traditional boundaries of domestic jurisdiction and national sovereignty, and create practical mechanisms for enforcement. In this regard, and particularly important for the evolution of international human rights, these experiences marked a new willingness of government representatives to go beyond the traditional provisions in treaties limited to territories, borders, and states and their leaders to now include among their responsibilities people, populations, and victims of abuse.

At the beginning of the nineteenth century, slavery was common and the slave trade flourished, often with government sanction and support. Hereditary systems of inequality and traditional exploitation due to race, gender, or class continued unabated. The wounded in war were left to suffer and die where they fell on battlefields. Moreover, states could engage in persecution against their religious or ethnic minorities with impunity and without the slightest fear of criticism from abroad. When the century ended, most of the living victims of slavery, the slave trade, and serfdom were emancipated and those who suffered from exploitation, warfare, and persecution possessed a prospect of being helped in some, perhaps even significant, ways from others beyond their own immediate borders. These successes, made in the face of seemingly overwhelming obstacles, demonstrated that normative values could be changed and that certain goals might not be just desirable—but actually *possible*. As such, they laid a foundation, established a direction, and created hope for those who would carry further visions of human rights forward into the new century.

Chapter 3
Entering the Twentieth Century

Visions, War, Revolutions, and Peacemaking

> We must do away with boundaries of nations and unify the world, do away with boundaries of class and make all people equal, do away with boundaries of race and render all races the same, do away with boundaries of sex and protect individual independence, . . . [and] do away with boundaries of suffering to reach universal harmony.
>
> —Kang Youwei of China

The experience of entering a new century invariably provides rather special opportunities to reflect on the process and meaning of historical continuity and change. In this regard, those with visions of human rights at the beginning of the twentieth century—one that eventually would be called the "People's Century"[1]—had reasons for both worry and hope. They knew that the old forces of resistance, prejudices, vested interests, and national sovereignty with domestic jurisdiction would not simply disappear. At the same time the successes gained during the previous century gave them a newfound confidence, and they hoped that the momentum could be not only sustained but even accelerated. What they did not and could not know, of course, was that within just a few years World War I would explode around them. This would cause unprecedented suffering and death, serious violations of rights, revolutions, and the destruction of empires. It also would create new states from the ashes of old monarchies, shift the world balance of power, loosen the bonds of imperialism, bring about a peace conference, create a new global organization, and help to advance the evolution of international human rights.

Modernization, Internationalization, and Visions of Rights

The new century unleashed bursting discovery, change, development, creativity, energy, and visions to the world. "Thought had more than once been upset, but never caught and whirled about in the vortex of infinite forces," wrote intellectual Henry Adams. His essay "A Law of Acceleration" vibrated with expressions of energy and motion: "dynamic theory," "unlimited power," "new forces," and, more important, "the inadequacy of old implements of thought."[2] Visitors at the 1900 International Exposition rushed to see the technological inventions transforming the nineteenth "Century of Steam" to the new "Century of Electricity" before their very eyes. In theoretical physics the quantum theory of energy and Albert Einstein's dissertation on relativity opened heretofore unimagined perspectives on mass, time, and space. In philosophy William James's *Pragmatism* and Henri Bergson's *L'Évolution créatrice* provided dramatic shifts toward the practical needs of people. In music Claude Debussy and Arnold Schoenberg inspired composers who called themselves "modernists." In art a style emerged known as *art nouveau*. In design the pioneering work of Frank Lloyd Wright and Walter Gropius emphasized function over ornamentation. All this encouraged new thoughts about historical transformation and the possibilities of change. The process came to be widely known as "modernization." Its advocates could be heard from Europe to the Americas, from Brazil to China, from Japan to Iran, and from Russia to Egypt, urging that traditional restraints be abandoned and that "modern" ideas and practices be embraced.

Popular imagination was captivated by applied science and technology in the form of railroads capable of transporting people and goods across continents, steam ships able to travel across oceans without regard to wind, the "magic" of telegraph to connect the world, and the amazing invention of airplanes to actually fly. These all appeared to nullify many previous ideas about distance, time, geographical barriers, and national boundaries. As such, they began to "shrink" the globe, and people and places once seemingly far removed suddenly became much closer than ever before. Technological developments made it possible to think differently about a mental construct of "the world" as a whole and to consider the possibilities of more expansive interactions with others far beyond their own locale or country. It is for this reason that observers increasingly spoke of "world politics," "global affairs," and "internationalization."[3]

The results could be seen in many ways. Within just a few years, maps in the *Annuaire diplomatique* that placed all of Asia on a single page, showing Japan with only five cities, were transformed into mores sophisticated representations of China, Japan, and Korea virtually covered with place-names, cities, and towns. Similar maps appeared of the United States, Latin America, Africa, and the islands of the Pacific.[4] None of the countries nor their cities were new, of course, but in the past they had simply been ignored. It became increasingly evident that this would no longer be possible. At the same time, global perspectives suggested global solutions to common problems. This explains the remarkable emergence of interest in coordinated action across borders over a wide variety of issues including telegraph and wireless communication, rail transportation, postal services, shipping regulations, navigational charts and signals, law enforcement, scientific discovery, business transactions, trade unionization, suppression of opium, and sporting events, among many other matters requiring some form of international cooperation. It is exactly during these years that one sees the inaugural publication of the *American Journal of International Law* and the creation of bodies such as the International Association of Chambers of Commerce, the International Institute of Agriculture, and the World Missionary Conference. Indeed, the formation of the Union of International Associations itself provided a visible capstone of this activity as it began to coordinate the scheduling of the programs and conferences of these many organizations, as well as publishing its own journal appropriately named *La Vie Internationale*. As one observer noted, the impact of science and technology, the "logic of history," and "world-wide repercussions" of events all produced a new environment in which "the affairs of the world now interest all the world."[5]

These two forces of modernization and internationalization played vital roles in shaping visions of international human rights. They made it easier to see local abuses as part of larger patterns, to view events in distant places as being interrelated to each other, and to develop networks of like-minded individuals across borders who shared similar experiences of discrimination, injustice, or oppression.[6] When the NGO of the Ligue des Droits de l'Homme, which had been formed in response to the notorious anti-Semitic Dreyfus affair, issued its first publication in 1901, it thus announced its vision of liberty, equality, fraternity, and justice applying not just to those in France—but "to all humanity."[7] Activists in the Ligue published studies and exposés, pressured governments, and organized conferences on religious and ethnic persecution, the rights of indigenous peoples, victims of brutal regimes, class inequalities, and the oppressed. Their attention went wherever abuses occurred, whether in France, Algeria, China, the Ottoman Empire, Ivory Coast, Senegal, the Balkans, Indochina, Madagascar, or the Congo, pledging their constant support for the rights "of all human beings, without exception."[8]

Other visionaries engaged in similar discourse in different parts of the globe at exactly the same time. In Iran Talibov-i Tabrizi wrote his *Izāhāt dar Khusus-i Azādi* (Explanations Concerning Freedom), discussing the relationship between the rights of individuals vis-à-vis the state, the teachings of Islam, and the comparative practices of other countries.[9] In North America the Lake Mohonk Conference of Friends of the Indian expanded its concern about rights to the international level and in 1904 added a new expression to its official name: "and Other Dependent Peoples."[10] Chinese intellectuals wrote passionately about human rights, or *renquan*, leading one authority to conclude, "Early twentieth-century China was imbued with an enthusiasm for human rights, ranging from a concern with the nature of the family and its components of individual persons, and the status of women in society, to the balancing of the rights of individuals with the community as a whole."[11] Chinese philosopher and exponent of modern Confucianism Kang Youwei began publishing his path-breaking *Datong shu* (Book of Great Harmony) promoting individual liberty, freedom, equality, and the natural rights of all humanity. He argued that the achievement of these universal rights and the alleviation of suffering required eliminating the barriers of gender and liberating women, abolishing all divisions based on race and class, and erasing national boundaries so as to view the world and its people as a single entity.[12]

Visions of international human rights also received attention from some governments under pressure to use the power of states for progressive reform to assist and protect the exploited, the wounded, and the persecuted.[13] This explains the founding of the International Association for the Protection of Labor, with the International Labor Office as its executive organ. Under this auspices, governments successfully negotiated and opened for signature two innovative conventions in 1906: the International

Convention Respecting the Prohibition of Night Work for Women in Industrial Employment and the International Convention Respecting the Prohibition of the Use of . . . Phosphorus in the Manufacture of Matches. Both focused on economic and social rights and created obligations under international law on governments vis-à-vis each other concerning the treatment of their own citizens. The same year witnessed the new and expanded Red Cross Convention for the Amelioration of the Condition of the Wounded and Sick. In 1907 delegates to the second Hague Peace Conference extended this coverage of humanitarian law by securing the signatures of forty-four nations from Asia to the United States and from Latin America to Europe on the Convention Respecting the Laws and Customs of War on Land and the Convention for the Adaption to Maritime Warfare of the Principles of the Geneva Convention. The International Office of Public Health also was created to advocate a global right to health and to provide protection from the threat of diseases such as cholera with the potential for causing worldwide epidemics.[14]

These years marked an increase as well in interest in international humanitarian intervention to protect the rights of the persecuted. In several cases of egregious abuses sufficient to attract outside attention and provoke outrage, nations refused to remain silent in the face of persecution, and thereby further challenged the doctrines of national sovereignty and domestic jurisdiction. Austria, France, Britain, and the United States, for example, complained to the Romanian and Russian governments over the discrimination and persecution of their Jewish populations. Protests were made in 1906 against the sultan of Morocco and his use of torture against political opponents, demanding that he "observe henceforth the laws of humanity."[15] Formal complaints were issued to Peru on behalf of the rights of aborigines who had been subject to cruel and inhumane treatment, as well as to Belgium protesting abuse against native peoples in the Congo. Renewed atrocities against Christians in the Ottoman Empire prompted more than words, and several nations joined to actually force reforms for protecting rights.[16] In addition, a new outbreak of persecutions against Armenians by the Turks prompted a strong American protest accompanied by a presidential message about "the interest of humanity at large" and the "fundamental rights" of all people, with the following fascinating observation:

Ordinarily it is very much wiser and more useful for us to concern ourselves with striving for our own moral and material betterment here at home than to concern ourselves with trying to better the condition of things in other nations. We have plenty of sins of our own to war against. . . . Nevertheless there are occasional crimes committed on so vast a scale and of such peculiar horror as to make us doubt whether it is not our manifest duty to endeavor at least to show our disapproval of the deed and our sympathy with those who have suffered by it. The cases must be extreme in which such a course is justifiable. There must be no effort made to remove the mote from our brother's eye if we refuse to remove the beam from our own. But in extreme cases action may be justifiable and proper.[17]

Such thoughts and endeavors concerning international obligations to protect human rights across borders attempted to address a number of serious problems, but certainly not all. To those who still suffered in one form or another, and to those excluded from the coverage of treaties or the attention of humanitarian interventions, these efforts were seen as steps in the proper direction but as insufficient. Governments, declared the critics, still continued to exclude those victimized due to their race, gender, or class. To change this situation, activists determined to expand the boundaries of existing visions and to increase their efforts even further.

Racial discrimination, not surprisingly, drew the immediate attention of those concerned about human rights. In fact, after the turn of the century, long-standing prejudice actually escalated with talk about "superior whites," "the rising tide of color," "lesser breeds," "inferior blacks," "savage reds," "ignorant browns," the "yellow peril," "racial destiny," "racial purity," and possible "race wars."[18] Consequently, during the first Pan-African Congress meeting in 1900, the talented black intellectual and activist W. E. B. Du Bois (who had written his doctoral dissertation on the abolition of the slave trade) rose to give a speech. Here he made his much-celebrated statement repeated countless times around the world: "The problem of the twentieth century is the problem of the color line—the relation of the darker to the lighter races of men in Asia and Africa, in America and the islands of the sea."[19] Dissatisfied with the accommodationist approach of Booker T. Washington for securing rights, he helped organize the Niagara Movement for more aggressive action. This led to the formation of the National Association for the Advancement of Colored People (NAACP), designed to overturn the color bar of discrimination, to stop the horrifying practice of lynching, and to obtain all manner of equal rights as guaranteed by the Constitution. "We will not be satisfied," thundered Du Bois,

to take one jot or tittle less than our full manhood rights. We claim for ourselves every single right that belongs to a freeborn American, political, civil, and social; and until we get these rights we will never cease to protest and assail the ears of America. . . . It is a fight for ideals, lest this, our common fatherland, false to its founding, become in truth the land of the thief and the home of the slave—a byword and a hissing among the nations for its sounding pretensions and pitiful accomplishment.[20]

Many miles away, but at the same time, Mohandas Gandhi began his public protest against racial discrimination toward Indian immigrants in South Africa, attracting international attention by non-violently resisting the 1907 Asiatic Registration Act and by articulating his vision of justice and the value of every human being that eventually would lead him to be described as the man who "made humility and truth more powerful than empires."[21] This helped to reveal the global scope of racial prejudice and resulted in the first meeting of the Universal Races Congress in 1911 committed to securing basic human rights for all regardless of the color of their skin.

Race also pervaded imperialism with its language of "the white man's burden" and the necessity to conquer "backward colored races." For this reason a number of activists who struggled to advance international human rights focused on ending Western imperial conquest and promoting the rights of indigenous peoples. Many participated in NGOs such as the Anti-Imperialist League. Others wrote vehement attacks against colonial exploitation, including two powerful books that appeared in 1902. One of these was J. A. Hobson's pioneering *Imperialism* which condemned wealthy men and financial monopolies, politicians who served as their willing accomplices, national and racial chauvinists, and all others who turned their backs on religious and humanitarian principles and instead benefitted from "the perils, pains, and slaughter of fellowmen."[22] The other was Joseph Conrad's literary masterpiece *Heart of Darkness*, a novel painfully exploring racism, graphically portraying the brutal realities of imperial conquest, and emotionally evoking empathy for its suffering victims by seeing them as human beings. In one remarkably revealing passage one of his characters observes:

We are accustomed to look upon the shackled form of a conquered monster, but there—there you could look [and see that] . . . the men were—No, they were not inhuman. Well, you know, that was the worst of it—this suspicion of their not being inhuman. It would come slowly to one. They howled, and leaped, and spun, and made horrid faces; but what thrilled you was just the thought of their humanity—*like yours*.[23]

Perhaps nowhere was the determination to defend the rights of those exploited by imperialism revealed with such passion as the case of E. D. Morel. A quiet and unassuming clerk in a shipping company just doing his job, he hardly seemed a likely candidate to become one of the most influential human rights visionaries of his time. Nevertheless, as he did the accounting, he became aware that the amounts on the ledgers did not match those reported by King Leopold and the Belgian government. As he investigated further, he discovered that ships arriving from the Congo were filled with valuable ivory and rubber; yet when they left to return, they did not carry goods for repayment but soldiers and firearms. It dawned on Morel that there was no trade going on at all, and that he was suddenly staring into the face of the only possible explanation: slavery. When confronted with such a fateful realization, he was morally outraged. This was made even worse when company and government agents tried to bribe and then coerce him. Morel refused to be silent. At great personal risk and financial hardship, he quit his job and set about what he described as his "determination to do my best to expose and destroy what I then knew to be a legalized infamy . . . accompanied by unimaginable barbarities and responsible for a vast destruction of human life."[24]

At that moment Morel devoted himself to the protection of human rights. He formed the Congo Reform Association as an NGO in 1904 and began writing books, dozens of pamphlets, and hundreds of articles and letters to editors. He developed techniques later used by Amnesty International and others, of giving as widespread publicity to abuses, but with meticulous and verifiable accuracy. He also discovered the power of photographs—images of piles of bodies, heads mounted on fenceposts, and mutilated children sitting next to their severed feet and hands—that no amount of official propaganda could possibly refute.[25] Taken with an early model Kodak camera by missionary Alice Harris, they gave a broad public a visual encounter with atrocities in distant lands for the first time in history. They evoked empathy, stirred the conscience, and provoked outrage sufficient to move others into determining that such brutality was no longer acceptable, that they would take some kind of action, and that they would act on behalf of others far beyond themselves whom they did not even know. Indeed, these photographs and facts, as well as Morel's own personal courage, integrity, and crusading passion, inspired nearly three hundred gatherings a year in Britain, some of which attracted almost five thousand participants, and more than two hundred meetings across the United States. Thousands signed petitions designed to exert relentless pressure to change course in Africa and to protect the rights of its inhabitants. "Almost never," according to the leading authority on Morel, "has one man, possessed of no wealth, title, or official post, caused so much trouble for the governments of several major countries."[26]

Many victims of imperialism also began to rise up themselves, demanding their independence and attacking those who would deny them their rights. The Ashantis launched an uprising against the British in the Gold Coast (now Ghana), Hottentots and Hereros rose up against the Germans in South-West Africa (now Namibia), Congolese and Indochinese rebelled against the French, Ethiopians and Somalis initiated attacks against the Italians, Filipinos fought against the Americans, and members of the Boxer Rebellion in China violently struck against Westerners. Japan's stunning defeat of Russia in their 1904–1905 war provided a particularly dramatic psychological turning point, for as described by one contemporary, it represented "the most important historical event which has happened, or is likely to happen, in our lifetime: the victory of a non-white people over a white people."[27] The charismatic French socialist leader Jean Jaurès took all of these developments as signs of what was to come and declared: "There are all these people of all races who have seemed inert . . . and sunk deep in an eternal sleep, who are now awakening, demanding their rights, and flexing their muscles."[28]

Advocates for the rights of women also contributed their voices and efforts with renewed vigor during this period, confirming Lady Frances Balfour's opinion of "new winds blowing hard through society."[29] They looked to the general emancipation of women by seeking equality in marriage, access to education, the opportunity to own property, improvement of working conditions in sweatshops, and birth control, often under the slogan of "Let us be our sisters' keepers."[30] Many efforts in the West focused on gaining the right to vote, not just as an end in itself but as a means of securing access to the political process and thus to a broad range of other rights. Australian women obtained this goal in 1902, as did those in Finland in 1906 and Norway in 1913. But that was all. In fact, prior to World War I, these countries joined New Zealand as the only ones in the entire world where women possessed the right to vote. Under the influence of the Progressive movement and the efforts of the National Woman's Party, the franchise had been extended to females in eleven of the western United States by 1914, but it did not apply to the nation as a whole. When other so-called democratic governments refused to enact similar legislation, many suffragettes lost patience with the promises of moderation and gradual reform and turned to more aggressive tactics, bold activism, and even violence. In Britain Emmeline Pankhurst and her daughters (often described as "unladylike") formed the Women's Social and Political Union with the motto "Deeds, Not Words!" and began a campaign of militancy by organizing protest parades, disrupting meetings, smashing windows, chaining themselves to the gates of Parliament, setting fires, and holding hunger strikes that led to more than one thousand arrests and highly publicized force-feedings by the police.[31] Others believed that the best way to secure their rights could be found in mobilizing not just nationally but globally and, with the help of tireless crusaders like Susan B. Anthony and Carrie Chapman Catt, created the International Woman Suffrage Alliance with affiliates in many nations.[32]

For women who lived in countries without parliamentary forms of government, of course, the right to vote represented a vision far removed from any immediate prospect of reality. They worked instead to liberate themselves during these years from centuries of gender oppression. For them, the issue of women's rights was linked with the larger movements of modernization and political change and often with struggles of self-determination against Western imperialism. The revolutionary feminist Qiu Jin organized the first women's association in China, spoke out against abuses within the traditional patriarchal system, and launched the journal *Zhongguo Nübao* (Chinese Women) to advocate "equal rights for women," openly declaring: "We want our emancipation! Men and women are born equal, why should we let men hold sway?"[33] She

Figure 5. A Woman's Struggle for Equal Rights: Emmeline Pankhurst Under Arrest. Culver Pictures.

and many others rejoiced over the success of the antifootbinding campaign, which within a single generation officially banned a brutal, culturally embedded practice of symbolic and physical control over women that had lasted almost a thousand years.[34] In Japan, Hideko Fukuda began publishing her *Sekai Fujin* (Women of the World), reporting on the activities of the recently created Society for the Reinstatement of Women's Rights and suffragist movements overseas; Raicho Hiratsuka organized a group called Seitosha (Bluestockings) to promote equality for women; and revolutionary Suga Kanno shouted: "Rise up, women! Wake up!"[35] Concepción Felix formed the Asociación Feminista Filipino in the Philippines and its publication of *Filipinas*, devoted entirely to "the rights of women."[36] In Turkey, Ahmet Agaoglu forcefully argued that women's rights were completely in accordance with the tenets of Islam cleansed of its misinterpretations, while Nuriye Ulviye Mevlan organized the Ottoman Association for the Defense of Women's Rights. Similar efforts appeared in Ceylon, Egypt, India, Indonesia, Iran, Korea, and Vietnam.[37]

Still others formed new NGOs to address the rights of those women and girls treated like property and forced into "involuntary sexual slavery" and the white slave trade. They worked at closing down bordellos and combating what they regarded as the injustice of state-supported prostitution that placed restrictions on women but not on their male customers. These reformers assisted in hiring social workers to meet incoming ships and offer assistance to females traveling under suspicious circumstances. They also successfully pressured thirteen governments to negotiate and ratify two pathbreaking international agreements that actually created agencies to monitor and prosecute those who traded in women and girls across national borders.[38]

Champions of economic and social justice deeply concerned about the fate of workers and the poor victimized by class discrimination also intensified their efforts during these years. They strongly resisted any notion that rights somehow belonged only to people of wealth or property. Many worked as reformers within their existing systems to extend the franchise, elect representatives sympathetic to economic and social rights, provide social security benefits, and organize labor unions. In Britain they supported the Fabian Society, formed the new Labour Party, and secured the National Insurance Act of 1911 protecting workers against the worst ravages of accident, sickness, and unemployment. By 1912 German reformers made the Social Democratic Party the largest parliamentary group in the Reichstag. Belgian activists obtained old-age pensions, compensation for accidents, and improvements in housing and public services. Their counterparts in Sweden acquired universal men's suffrage for elections to the lower house and a reduction of the property qualification for election to the upper house. Members of the Ramakrishna Movement in India worked to provide humanitarian service and to reduce social and economic inequalities. Progressives within the United States, many of whom were either outraged by the troubling photographs of Lewis Hine revealing exhausted children exploited in factories and mines or inspired by *Christianity and the Social Order* written in 1912 by Walter Rauschenbush, a young minister from Hell's Kitchen in New York City, aroused the public's conscience sufficient to create a whole new array of legislation pertaining to food, housing, education, children, public health, labor conditions, and electoral reform. Not content with these national gains, many reformers developed transnational networks, working closely with the International Association for the Protection of Labor and creating new NGOs and organizations such as the International Ladies' Garment Workers' Union.

Not all of those dedicated to advancing the rights of the economically or socially exploited were persuaded by these efforts or by their reformist sponsors who sat cheek by jowl with the upper classes in parliaments. They found extensions of voting, social legislation, and trade union activity to be helpful, but fundamentally inadequate. For them, visions of true emancipation for workers and a full realization of their rights could be accomplished not in the moderation of voting or collecting insurance funds, but only through the "direct action" of militant strikes, sabotage, and industrial combat that would one day paralyze capitalism and ignite revolution. They were the ones who formed the more radical Confédération Générale du Travail in France, followed the Marxist Karl Kautsky in Germany, and created the Industrial Workers of the World in the United States. A number of radical socialists felt so disaffected by the reformist trend of the Second International that they turned to the more extremist positions of exiled Russian revolutionary V. I. Lenin, whose 1902 pamphlet *What Is To Be Done?* castigated the reformers who would "bourgeoisify" the class struggle and called for revolution as a means of securing the rights of the oppressed and exploited of the world.

Revolutionary upheaval, however ideologically inspired, significantly marked these years of anticipation and ferment in the evolution of human rights. The explosion of the 1905 Russian Revolution began this process when a protest march erupted after troops opened fire on hundreds of people. The bloodshed immediately led to general strikes, peasant revolts, and military mutinies, forcing a reluctant tsar to grant a legislative assembly, a constitution limiting autocratic power, decrees abolishing restrictions on the personal liberties of peasants, and protections for the rights of freedom of the press, of speech, and of assembly. The Young Turk Revolt followed in 1908, compelling the despotic sultan Abdul Hamid to grant elections for a parliament, constitutional changes promising to modernize Turkey into a more liberal state, and the extension of certain political rights. The Mexican Revolution followed in 1910, setting off a series of uprisings, the emergence of Emiliano Zapata and his landless followers demanding their rights, several years of civil war, and what would become the first major social revolution of the twentieth century. All of these upheavals, in turn, helped to inspire others. This certainly proved to be the case in China, where leaders such as Sun Yat-sen and others associated with the Revolutionary Alliance launched the 1911 Chinese Revolution, bringing an end more than two millennia of imperial history. They deposed the last emperor of the Qing dynasty, created a new republic, established a constitution, committed themselves to moving toward greater political and social equality, and announced that they henceforth would promote "the equalization of human rights."[39]

War, Revolutions, and Rights

This ferment of change exploded with the outbreak of World War I in 1914. Years of building modern armaments, forming rigid alliance systems, designing war plans, and engaging in imperial rivalries all created conditions that turned a few shots from a political assassination in Sarajevo into a conflagration of global proportions. The results took the form not only of a "total" war of states and peoples but of revolutions, complete with unanticipated consequences that both grossly violated human rights and greatly enhanced human rights.

The slaughter of human life unleashed from 1914 to 1918 was unprecedented in history. Machine-gun fire, artillery capable of hitting targets several miles away, poison gas, land mines, torpedoes, submarines and battleships, aircraft, and armored tanks all produced by science and industry in the service of war unleashed staggering death. An average of 5,500 casualties per day occurred for more than four years, often leaving little meaningful difference between the "victor" and the "vanquished." In the end, the military dead alone included two million Germans, almost as many Russians, a million and a half French, more than a million Austrians, about the same number of English, half a million Italians and nearly as many Turks, and more than one hundred thousand Americans. At least thirty million others remained wounded, maimed, disfigured, or incapacitated for the rest of their lives.[40]

The revolutionary magnitude of this kind of bloodshed and carnage forced people as never before to envision the value of rights and humanitarian law during times of war. Indeed, the International Committee of the Red Cross accurately predicted at the outbreak of hostilities: "From now on, the Red Cross movement will have to commit itself to a degree of activity unprecedented in its intensity."[41] Its members came to devote their lives to others in operating the agency, amassing an index file containing seven million cards, sending nearly two million parcels, assisting in the repatriation of captured medical personnel and the severely wounded, condemning the use of chemical warfare and deliberate attacks on hospital ships, and constantly reminding all belligerents of their obligations under the Geneva Convention concerning rights. In addition, they created the International Prisoner of War Agency to care for those whose fate had yet to be regulated by the convention, to collect and forward correspondence and gifts at the rate of nearly thirty thousand per day, and to serve as intermediaries for the exchange of information between prisoners and their anxious families. Membership in national Red Cross societies increased dramatically and new linkages were forged among them that demonstrated once again the practical importance of international cooperation beyond national borders.[42]

Not only the numbers but the composition of the armed forces during World War I greatly escalated demands for human rights. The consumption of young men at such a devastating rate over such a long period forced belligerent governments to conscript ever-larger quantities of soldiers and sailors from minority races and working or peasant classes to fill the ranks. It thus is not surprising that while risking their very lives in warfare these drafted young men would begin to ask not whether— but rather *when*—the rights enjoyed by some of their countrymen would be extended to them. Labor unions, for example, increasingly began to insist on greater social and economic rights in return for military service by their members. In France, no other segment of society was so hard hit by mobilization as the peasantry, who, contemporaries noted, "went into the war docile and resigned, [and] came out resentful and ready to complain."[43] The multiethnic empires of Russia and Austria-Hungary similarly experienced vociferous protests for rights among their minorities when called upon to fight.

Such demands became even more pronounced when the United States entered the war with black troops, which eventually constituted nearly one-third of the entire armed forces. In some cases draft boards actually exempted single white men but conscripted black fathers. Many of those who served believed that President Woodrow Wilson's promise of a "war to make the world safe for democracy" would bring the rights of citizenship to them. Even Du Bois accepted this vision, and in a famous essay encouraged his readers to "close ranks shoulder to shoulder with our white citizens and the allied nations that are fighting for democracy" in order to achieve their rights.[44] If this hope were not enough to stimulate such thinking, then enemy propaganda provided a constant reminder of the failure of America to fulfill its promise of equality. "Do you enjoy the same rights as the white people in America, the land of Freedom and Democracy," asked a German leaflet scattered over segregated black troops, "or are you rather not treated over there as second-class citizens? . . . Is lynching and the most horrible crimes connected therewith a lawful proceeding in a democratic country?"[45] All of this fostered a growing consciousness of racial inequality—and a resolve to do something about it. Kelly Miller provided ample expression of just such determination when he wrote of the intense emotions of these black soldiers in *An Appeal to Conscience: America's Code of Caste a Disgrace to Democracy*. He followed with an even stronger treatise, tellingly entitled *The World War for Human Rights*.[46]

The internationalization of human rights was also powerfully affected by the origin and racial composition of still others who fought in the war. Although it clearly began in Europe, the armed struggle rapidly enveloped people from the overseas colonies of the British, Germans, French, Belgians, and Portuguese. Australian and New Zealand forces attacked German possessions in the Pacific, as did the Japanese in Kiaochow and the Shantung Peninsula in China. British troops fought throughout the Middle East, and its sailors in the Atlantic and Indian Oceans. Not content with taking the war to Africa and Asia, Europeans took Africans and Asians to the war. Desperate for manpower, they determined that they could use their imperial subjects as soldiers in Europe. It is estimated that nearly two and a half million colonials fought for Britain, and thousands more served as noncombatants. They came from India, British East and West Africa, Egypt, the West Indies, South Africa, Mauritius, and Fiji. France pressed into service hundreds of thousands from Algeria, Morocco, Senegal, and Dahomey in Africa and still others from French Indochina, while the Russians drafted Muslims from Central Asia. It did not take much imagination for these troops to realize immediately that they all were regarded as fully human when it came time to fight and die—but not for immigration, voting, equal protection under the law, or other forms of basic human rights.

This extensive participation of nonwhites and non-Westerners in combat proved to be of revolutionary importance in the development of African and Asian nationalism, demands for self-determination, and visions of human rights. It helped to destroy the myth of "superior" and "invincible" whites, accelerated discourse about rights, and greatly politicized many of the combatants by heightening their collective sense of confidence and entitlement. Soldiers from diverse parts of the world established contacts for the first time with like-minded individuals also drawn unwillingly into the war, who began to expand their horizons and consider what this war might mean for their rights. In fact, several of those who would become major leaders in the decolonization movement, including Ho Chi Minh, Zhou Enlai, and Lamine Senghor, first became politically active at this time. In 1916 the Congress Party began to demand home rule for India in exchange for wartime sacrifice, and during the 1917 and 1918 Imperial War Conferences the Indian delegates explicitly demanded human rights and racial equality within the Dominions. Mohamed Duse, the editor of the first Afro-Asian journal, *African Times and Orient Review*, strongly encouraged his readers to see the relationship between war and human rights:

We are forced to observe that the once despised black man is coming to the front in the battle for freedom, and the freedom which he helps to win for the white man must also be meted out to him when the day of reckoning arrives. . . . In helping the British Empire and the French Republic in the hour of need you are helping yourselves to a freedom which cannot be denied to you and to a glory which shall be engraved upon the brazen tablets of fame which the rains of the ages shall not wash away."[47]

Among the many revolutionary features that so differentiated World War I from previous armed conflicts was the obliteration of the traditional distinction between combatants and civilians. This struggle introduced modern "total" war to the twentieth century, and the detachment that the average person enjoyed in most earlier wars now proved to be virtually impossible. Civilians discovered their lives and their rights subjected to ever-increasing levels of political centralization, economic regimentation, and control over their freedom of action, employment, diet, and even what they could say or think. Moreover, people of Belgium, northeast France, and Poland who saw their countries overrun, their homes commandeered, their farms and factories destroyed, and their families and friends held hostage by occupying forces, knew the war as intimately as the troops.[48] But they were by no means alone. It is estimated that in Russia, Serbia, and Bulgaria the civilian loss of life actually exceeded that of the military.[49] Added to these staggering deaths were the countless numbers of refugees forced to flee from their homelands, literally crying and begging for some form of help.

Such unanticipated and incalculable human suffering by so many men, women, and children completely overwhelmed the capacity of all existing private and religiously oriented relief organizations. The International Committee of the Red Cross had been organized to protect wounded combatants, not civilians, and therefore possessed no authorization or mechanism to meet this challenge. Try as they might, no organization could possibly deal with the sheer number of the homeless, sick, starving, and destitute that increased with each day. In addition, with armed combat, naval blockades, and danger in taking action across borders, no government was prepared to assume responsibility for the fate of these victims on its own.

Rather than falling victim to either apathy or despair over this catastrophe, some dedicated humanitarians who believed that these victimized civilians possessed the right to life, food, and care stepped into this breach. Under the direction of American businessman Herbert Hoover of Quaker background, they created the innovative

Commission for Relief in Belgium to address what was described as "a perfectly gigantic struggle."[50] It coordinated the work of thousands of separate volunteer committees in raising more than $1 billion, cajoling governments, collecting supplies, transferring necessities through war zones, and distributing more than five million tons of food to those in desperate need. Nearly four million signatures appeared on letters and scrolls sent directly to Hoover, as well as expressions of appreciation embroidered on old flour sacks from overwhelmingly grateful recipients.[51] In the end, the experience not only saved the lives of several million people, but contributed to the development of a mechanism and administration of international humanitarian relief and to a sense of responsibility to the human rights of those who suffer, irrespective of national borders.

Innocent civilians suffered in other ways during the war as well, for armed conflict often provided either an excuse for violence or a mask to conceal brutality against presumed enemies of the state. Ethnic and religious minorities caught between the Austro-Hungarian and Ottoman Empires in the Balkans, for example, experienced great persecution. The most egregious case occurred when the Turkish government conducted genocide against Armenian Christians on the excuse that they were aiding the Russian enemy. It began early in 1915 when Armenian leaders in Istanbul were executed and those serving in the Ottoman armies were taken out in entire groups and killed by firing squads. Armenian civilians then were rounded up, forced out of their ancestral homes, marched across deserts and mountains, and deliberately exposed to starvation and disease until they died. Many eyewitnesses recorded this calamity, sometimes with words and sometimes with photographs, including one diplomat who painfully wrote:

The passing . . . of Armenian exiles beneath the windows and before the door of the consulate; their prayers for help, when neither I nor any other could do anything to answer them; the city in a state of siege, guarded at every point by 15,000 troops in complete war equipment, by thousands of police agents [and] by bands of volunteers . . . ; the lamentations, the tears, the abandonments, the imprecations, the many suicides, the instantaneous deaths from sheer terror, the sudden unhinging of men's reason, the conflagrations, the shooting of victims in the city, the ruthless searches . . . ; the hundreds of corpses found every day along the exile road . . . ; the children torn away from their families . . . these are my last ineffaceable memories . . . memories which still . . . torment my soul.[52]

Others described the butchery as "slaughter," "race murder," "extermination," and "nothing less than the annihilation of a whole people."[53] Indeed, recent and reliable estimates place the number of Armenians killed as at least one million.[54] Genocide on such a massive and shocking scale could not possibly escape wider international attention. Protests of outrage came from around the world, insisting that it was no longer acceptable for governments to conduct such abuses while hiding behind claims of national sovereignty and demanding that the Turks be held accountable for what they now described as "crimes against humanity."[55]

It is particularly significant that this expression of the rights of "humanity" as a whole appeared. The revolutionary scale of carnage in combat, abuse of prisoners of war, sinkings of passenger ships, Zeppelin bombings of cities, deportations of more than sixty thousand Belgian civilians for forced labor in Germany, and Armenian genocide all broke the established bounds of what was called "civilized behavior" and the evolving body of "laws of humanity." Moreover, and very importantly, there began to be a growing awareness that just as *victims* are not abstract entities, but real and specific individual people, so too the *perpetrators* of abuses are not abstract entities of the state, but real and specific leaders. Consequently, during World War I both public opinion and government authorities began to take serious interest in determining which individuals might be guilty for causing such slaughter and suffering, in bringing them to trial, and in punishing them if necessary. The world, one visionary concluded,

must combine to find some sanction for the principles of international law; must make it clear that civilization does not ultimately rest upon Might but upon Right . . . . In particular the dignity and authority of international law must be asserted by the setting up of a judicial tribunal to deal with the men responsible.[56]

While some visions of human rights thus came to the fore during World War I as a result of persecution, others arose due to liberation. That is, by stretching existing institutions and practices often to revolutionary breaking points, wartime demands also released certain groups and individuals from traditional restraints. Among the most significant of these were women. The introduction of the "home front" in this war to match the efforts on the battlefront resulted from the realization that modern, protracted, total war simply could not be waged without using all available resources. As young men were sent off to combat, nations realized that they somehow had to replace their labor in factories, on farms, and in public service. Women consequently discovered dramatic transformations that changed definitions of "manpower" and opened up positions heretofore closed to them. At first with a trickle, and then with a flood, females found themselves actually being recruited to work in businesses, to turn out shells in munitions industries, to provide medical care, to buck rivets in shipyards, to drive trolleys and ambulances, and to deliver the mail. Some of those attached to the innovative British Women's Army Auxiliary Corps, served as secretaries, recruiters, nurses, mechanics, and physicians, at times with such distinction that they received military decorations. Together, these experiences opened up opportunities for liberation, silenced a number of critics with gender prejudices, and exposed past discrimination against women through what one historian has called "the great searchlight of war,"[57] all the while creating new levels of self-confidence that encouraged women to demand their rights.

Many of these demands during the war focused on the right to vote. The granting of suffrage to women in Denmark and Iceland during 1915 greatly stimulated others. The following year, Jeannette Rankin from the state of Montana became the first woman ever elected to the U.S. Congress. But continued frustration and anger over the lack of a national franchise led Alice Paul and others to engage in civil disobedience and form the more militant National Women's Party with its rallying cry: "HOW LONG MUST WOMEN WAIT FOR LIBERTY?"[58] Russia extended voting rights to women in 1917. At the same time, Sarojini Naidu actively campaigned for women's franchise in India. Pressure mounted in Britain and the Dominions from organizations such as the Dominions' Women's Suffrage Union and United Suffragists asking whether the assumption of the duties of men in war would result in the assumption of their rights as well, demanding: "Votes for heroines as well as heroes."[59] Even in Parliament, one male member observed, "Women of every station . . . have proved themselves able to undertake work that before the war was regarded as solely the province of men. Where is the man now who would deny to women the civil rights which she has earned by her hard work?"[60] By the war's end, females thus successfully secured at least partial voting rights in Britain and Ireland through the Qualification of Women Act of 1918. This considerable activity surrounding the war helped to inspire others to consider the rights of women in different settings, including the Turkish sociologist Ziya Gokalp who expressed in poetry:

All must be equal, marriage, divorce, wealth.
No nation can ever bloom if its daughters
Are not given the weight they deserve.
We have fought for and won all our other rights.
Only the family is still in its dark age.
Why do we still turn our backs on women?
Tell me, have they not a part in our struggles?[61]

World War I also accelerated the evolution of human rights by denying them. Men and women alike discovered that with the emergence of the "home front," governments increasingly gathered power to themselves and sought to silence criticisms. In the name of protecting national security and maintaining the fighting spirit, authorities subjected their people to extraordinary levels of control. This occurred both in countries with monarchies that imposed military dictatorships as well as in the democracies. The Defense of the Realm Act in Britain authorized the government to do nearly anything it pleased against citizens suspected of sins against the war effort. The act made it legal for houses to be searched without a warrant, for persons to be held liable for possessing literature considered subversive by overzealous magistrates or to be deported and interned without trial, for public meetings to be prohibited without the right of appeal, and for newspapers to be vigorously censored. The French government exerted enormous pressure against the Ligue des Droits de l'Homme to stop its protests about violations of rights during a time of wartime control, court martial, censorship, and conscription. In the United States, the 1917 Espionage Act and the notorious 1918 Sedition Act sought to enforce patriotic unity by crushing any criticism deemed to be "un-American" by effectively suspending provisions in the Bill of Rights, as predicted by dissenting members of Congress, particularly among pacifists, wartime critics, and left-wing workers. These laws imposed severe penalties of fines and prison terms for any person who would "willfully utter, print, write, or publish any disloyal, profane, scurrilous, or abusive language" about the American form of government, the Constitution, or the flag; or would in any way "incite, provoke, or encourage resistance" to the government; or "advocate . . . anything necessary or essential to the prosecution of the war."[62] Such laws made intolerance official policy and launched a wartime orgy of hysteria, witch-hunting, persecution, and mob violence that violated the rights of anyone suspected of being unpatriotic. Self-appointed vigilante groups attacked individuals on busy city streets and on isolated farms, while agents of the Department of Justice and army troops advanced on radicals in mining or lumber camps. Well over one thousand citizens were imprisoned, including the Socialist Party's presidential candidate Eugene V. Debs, for merely being accused of disloyalty. Some were even murdered, like Joe Hill of the Industrial Workers of the World. In this setting of wartime violations of rights, it is thus not surprising that membership would increase dramatically in NGOs such as the Ligue des Droits de l'Homme, or the newly created predecessor to the American Civil Liberties Union, the National Civil Liberties Bureau.[63]

Some of these governmental efforts to maintain fighting resolve by exerting ever greater control through the denial of human rights failed, and failed completely. In fact, as death, destruction, starvation, and other hardships of the prolonged conflict continued, cracks in the "home front" became chasms that resulted in revolution itself. This began in 1916 when a group of Irish nationalists launched the Easter Rebellion to wrest independence from Britain. Riots and strikes broke out in Germany, Russia, Austria, and Italy, often pitting civilians against one another, divided along class lines. Throughout the empires of Central and Eastern Europe ethnic minorities and nationalist groups including Czechs, Poles, Croatians, Slovenes, and Serbs increasingly resisted centralized authority, insisting on their right to self-determination. In addition, mutinies began to occur in the armies, as soldiers refused to follow the orders of their officers. By early 1917 one observer warned ominously: "We are living on a volcano."[64]

The eruption exploded in Russia. Long frustrated by the autocratic government of Nicholas II, the shortage of food, the lack of rights, and the absence of peace, people took to the streets in March 1917. Workers, women, peasants, soldiers, and moderate and radical politicians alike protested and rioted. This resulted in the abdication of the tsar and the emergence of elected soviets, or councils, and a provisional authority promising a constitution guaranteeing civil and political rights. In the hopes of destabilizing Russia even farther, the German High Command transported Lenin, the exiled leader of the Russian Bolsheviks, back to his homeland in order to spark a revolution. He did not disappoint them. Lenin called for Russia to withdraw from the war, for the soviets to take power on behalf of the workers and peasants, and for all private land to be nationalized. He and his followers then launched the Bolshevik Revolution, seizing control by force, and urging Communists everywhere to use the chaos of the war as a springboard to rise up against their oppressors, to assert their rights, and to overthrow the capitalistic order around the world.

Such massive disruption resulting from the combination of both war and now revolution immediately produced renewed and serious discussions about war aims and human rights. Why was the war still being fought after all, and what could people expect in victory or in defeat? Would their many sacrifices and sufferings in wartime provide an extension of their rights as promised, or would they be ignored once the emergency passed? Would anyone make a stand on principle and address any visions of human rights? The Ligue des Droits de l'Homme in France, the Women's Social and Political Union and United Suffragists in Britain and the Dominions, the All-Russian Jewish Conference, the National Association for the Advancement of Colored People and the National Civil Liberties Bureau in the United States, the Society for the Advancement of Women in the Philippines, the Patriotic Women's League in Korea, the Indies Social Democratic Party in Indonesia, and the Congress Party in India, among many others, all added their voices, as did writers such as Du Bois in the pages of *Crisis* and Duse in *African Times and Orient Review*. As early as 1915 a number of British citizens created an NGO with the declared aim "to preserve Human Rights for generations to come."[65] In an important and widely discussed speech, Japanese premier Shigenobu Okuma declared that for peace and for "the harmonization of different civilizations of the east and the west," practices of "inferiority must end," announcing that his country was determined to champion the basic right of racial equality.[66] In 1917 the Mexican government announced a new constitution with radical provisions for economic and social rights that were the first of their kind, not only in Latin America but in the world.[67] At the same time, Chilean jurist and diplomat Alejandro Alvarez drafted a document entitled "International Rights of the Individual" arguing for the need to establish international human rights for all and asserting that individuals possess rights based not on their citizenship in a given state but on their membership in the human family.[68]

Statements about the meaning of rights in this world of war and revolutions also emerged from the political leaders of those two countries destined to greatly shape future global affairs: the United States and Russia. President Woodrow Wilson gave great encouragement to those with visions of rights by announcing with stirring eloquence that his country was fighting this war "to make the world safe for democracy" and to create a "new diplomacy" and that it "puts human rights above all other rights."[69] Toward this end, he promised in his Fourteen Points to support individual liberty and freedom and the equality of rights across national borders. Lenin also spoke of rights, but with extremely significant differences. Instead of civil and political rights, he focused on economic and social rights. Instead of evolutionary democracy, he fiercely declared that they could be obtained only through revolutionary Communism. Despite these sharply differing approaches, however, both Wilson and Lenin envisioned what would eventually be called a third generation of rights: "collective" or "group" rights. These initially focused on the right of a people to determine their own form of government. "Self-determination is not a mere phrase," asserted Wilson. "It is an imperative principle of action, which statesmen will henceforth ignore at their peril."[70] Lenin had made the argument even earlier in *Imperialism, the Highest Stage of Capitalism* and *The Right of Nations to Self-Determination*, insisting that this right was inextricably connected with the class struggle and that it should apply universally to all, from Europe to "the Orient, Asia, Africa, [and] the colonies."[71] Such a position would go on to greatly influence decolonization and national liberation movements, but at the moment there was still a war to fight and a revolution to conduct. Here Lenin gave a certain credibility to his words when he seized power by issuing the Declaration of the Rights of the Peoples of Russia abolishing all privileges and disabilities based on nationality or religion and granting the right of self-determination.

All these visions, words, and policies involving human rights became even more pronounced during the final and chaotic stages of war and revolutions in 1918 and

1919. The All-Russian Congress of Soviets, for example, adopted what it called the Declaration of Rights of the Toiling and Exploited Peoples, boldly pledging "to suppress all exploitation of man by man, to abolish forever the division of society into classes, ruthlessly to suppress all exploitation, and to bring about the socialist organization of society in all countries."[72] In Germany, soldiers fled from the front, sailors mutinied onboard ship, and workers demonstrated in the streets launching the German Revolution, deposing kaiser Wilhelm II from the throne, and beginning a halting experiment with rights in a democracy. When the Austro-Hungarian Empire collapsed in defeat and revolution, its ruler abdicated, new leaders declared a republic, and throngs of nationalists declared their independence in the name of the right of self-determination. Revolutionaries proclaimed republics in Bavaria and Hungary. Uprisings occurred in colonial empires scattered from Asia to Africa. In each and every one of these events, discussions and claims of human rights proceeded with unparalleled intensity and vigor. Given the circumstances of the time, however, the actual realization of any of these visions would be determined initially not so much by the people in the streets or behind the barricades but rather by those who would assemble to negotiate an international peace settlement.

Peacemaking and Human Rights

The great and the small, the famous and the unrecognized who gathered at the Paris Peace Conference beginning in January 1919 were, for a brief moment in time, the arbiters of the world. Their decisions influenced countless numbers of people scattered throughout the far reaches of the globe. Here the silent influences of the more than ten million dead joined with the tumultuous demands of the living. Here nations, empires, races, men and women, political parties, pressure groups, NGOs, and the representatives of indigenous peoples met to vie with each other over both power and principles. Du Bois noted with excitement: "THIRTY-TWO NATIONS, PEOPLES, AND RACES. . . . Not simply England, Italy, and the Great Powers are there, but all the little nations. . . . Not only groups, but races have come—Jews, Indians, Arabs, and All-Asia."[73] Another observed: "Chinamen, Japanese, Koreans, Hindus, Kirghizes, Lesghiens, Circassians, Mingrelians, Buryats, Malays, and Negroes and Negroids from Africa and America were among the tribes and tongues forgathered in Paris to watch the rebuilding of the political world system and to see where they 'came in.' "[74] Although some of the more callous among them believed that they were only cleaning up the folly of a world gone mad and needed to grab whatever they could, others saw themselves as making the world anew by advancing human rights. "We were journeying to Paris," wrote one diplomat, "not merely to liquidate the war, but to found a new order. . . . We were preparing not Peace only, but Eternal Peace."[75]

Peacemaking at the end of wars and human rights are closely interconnected. There are several reasons for this. One of these is the existence of *disruption and destruction*. Since wars disrupt and destroy, they tear down power structures and previous sources of resistance to change. World War I destroyed millions of lives, four empires, centuries-old monarchies, and the traditional balance of power controlled by Europe.

It also significantly challenged the psychological myths that countries could remain completely isolated from each other, that discrimination against women could be maintained, and that one race was superior to another (for in combat, everyone died the same). Here destruction brought liberation and opened international discourse to voices with new visions of human rights heretofore excluded. Second, one of the characteristics of modern war is that in an effort to mobilize their full resources, governments make *promises*. During the course of World War I promises were made to create a "new diplomacy" of justice, to make the world "safe for democracy," and to extend rights to those who had suffered and sacrificed for the war effort. This explains why millions of women, racial and ethnic minorities, workers, and those subjected to imperial conquest now demanded that the promises so solemnly made—be kept. Third, modern wars and peacemaking, by their very nature, reveal an intimate *international interconnectedness*. World War I, after all, had demonstrated the global dimensions of shared life and death and that the fate of one country and its people and their rights are tied to those of others. Similarly, the peacemaking at Paris could not possibly escape decisions and responsibilities that extended far beyond national borders. Finally, at the end of wars, peacemakers quite naturally desire to do what they can to avoid another war by creating a settlement reflecting *normative values designed to enhance peace*. They want the sacrifices made in war to be worth something. In the wake of World War I, some leaders vowed that this could be accomplished only by taking power and territory away from their former adversaries and exploiting their victory. Others, however, began to envision peace in a much broader perspective and to argue that peace needed to be seen as more closely connected with security, justice, and respect for human rights.

The tensions between these positions could be seen immediately at the Paris Peace Conference over the issue of the collective right to choose one's own form of government. In fact, U.S. Secretary of State Robert Lansing described it as "simply loaded with dynamite."[76] Not only had so much been promised during the war about self-determination, especially by Wilson and Lenin, but groups of Poles, Czechs, Serbs, Armenians, Jews, Arabs, Indians, Senegalese, and Vietnamese, among many others, descended on Paris to exert pressure for these promises to be kept.[77] Nothing at an international conference, even in the best of times, produces greater anguish or emotion than taking power, people, and territory from one country and giving them to another. In this case, war and revolutions had destroyed the German, Austro-Hungarian, Russian, and Ottoman empires, and many claimants now clamored for the vast spoils that now seemed to be at their disposal.

Negotiations over this right of self-determination proceeded along tortuous routes at Paris due to the volatile mixture of issues and forces pulling in different directions.[78] Like so many other cases in the evolution of international human rights, those making decisions here both carried and confronted a variety of mixed motives. In addition to the desire to keep promises and to satisfy the legitimate claims from nationalist groups were the more calculating and brutal motivations of Realpolitik. Carving up old empires into new states could honor the principle of the right of self-determination and, at exactly the same time, exact revenge upon defeated enemies for losses sustained in the war and create allies who owed their very existence to these victorious peacemakers. Moreover, if such changes took place in Central and Eastern Europe, they also could erect a *cordon sanitaire*, or "sanitary barrier," to quarantine what some in the West perceived as the infectious disease of Communism emerging from Lenin's Russia.

Arriving at a just settlement in the midst of these mixed motives, complicated issues, and competing claims not only between nations but between individual and group rights in the wake of war and revolutions would have profoundly challenged the most brilliant, well-meaning, and experienced diplomats. At Paris the tasks overwhelmed the participants. The peacemakers came to understand that one of the tragic ironies of history is that it is so often easier to destroy than to build, and that peace is much more complicated than war. They might be able to reach agreement on abstract principles, but actually applying them in practice was another matter. In the end, this caused serious problems and inconsistencies. Nevertheless, the resulting peace treaties dramatically liquidated multinational empires, redrew borders, and extended independence to the Finns, Estonians, Latvians, Lithuanians, Poles, Czechs and Slovaks, Hungarians, and Albanians. Then, in an arrangement fraught with potential danger, leaders at Paris combined the Serbs, Slovenians, Bosnians, Croatians, Herzegovinians, and Montenegrins into what they called Yugoslavia. Never before had so many nation-states been created at one time in the name of the right of self-determination.

But the right of self-determination for some can raise grave dangers for the rights of others. What if collective rights threaten individual rights? What if the dominant majority of a country decide to persecute or discriminate against a minority? The persecution of religious or ethnic minorities, as we have seen, emerged well before the war, but concern had greatly intensified by the recent genocide against the Armenians, wartime atrocities, and postwar violence against Jews. It became even more acute when the very act of redrawing national borders in territories with complicated intermixtures of populations could not help but create sizeable numbers of ethnic, religious, and linguistic minorities within the new states. The peacemakers worried—as well they should—that in the name of national unity, individual and group rights among these minorities could easily be victimized with lethal consequences. If this occurred, serious threats could arise for both domestic and international stability. "Nothing," acknowledged Wilson, "is more likely to disturb the peace of the world than the treatment which might in certain circumstances be meted out to minorities."[79] The realization thus slowly began to emerge (although it would take another world war for it to be appreciated more fully) that violations of human rights at home ran perilous risks of jeopardizing peace and security abroad. This could be seen in the number and scope of proposals submitted to the Paris Peace Conference by official representatives, NGOs, and private citizens alike on behalf of the rights of minorities. "All citizens without distinction as to race, nationality, or religion," one insisted, "shall enjoy equal civil, religious, political, and national rights."[80] The critical factor, of course, was not their assertion of rights but rather their call for responsibilities. For this reason, all these proposals strongly urged members of the international community to cross that important intellectual and political threshold imposed by strict definitions of national sovereignty and now establish a larger sense of responsibility to protect the rights of minorities beyond their own borders.

After lengthy and difficult negotiations, the peacemakers determined to create an international legal foundation for such protection through a series of highly innovative agreements known as the Minorities Treaties. This protective regime began with five treaties requiring Poland, Czechoslovakia, Yugoslavia, Romania, and Greece, as beneficiaries of the peace settlement, to assume obligations to respect the rights of all their citizens. Other treaties imposed similar responsibilities on four of the vanquished states from the war, including Austria, Bulgaria, Hungary, and Turkey. These treaty provisions, along with others that would follow, required the signatories "to assure full and complete protection of life and liberty . . . without distinction of birth, nationality, language, race, or religion." They guaranteed the rights of all minorities, including Jews and Muslims, to equal protection under the law, to use their own language and customs, and to practice freedom of worship. Of particular importance, these treaties explicitly recognized that such protection "*constitute obligations of international concern* and shall be placed under the guarantee of the League of Nations."[81]

Those who gathered at the peace conference also devoted significant time discussing the human right to life. The memory of those millions recently killed and the never-ceasing reminders of those refugees and other victims of war and revolution thrust this issue to the fore. Especially after the successful efforts of the Commission for Relief in Belgium, it appeared unconscionable for the world now simply to turn its back on these men, women, and children suffering and dying on an unprecedented human scale. In addition, some political leaders feared that continued death and starvation would only breed turmoil and chaos. "It is impossible to discuss the peace of the world," warned Herbert Hoover in discussing the fate of an estimated 125,000,000 people, "until adequate measures have been taken to alleviate the fear of hunger."[82] These arguments led the peacemakers to create the Supreme Council of Supply and Relief to distribute tons of food, clothing, and other supplies to those in need.[83] The U.S. Congress subsequently passed the 1919 Relief Bill, establishing the American Relief Administration and authorizing $100 million on behalf of those who suffered. Such new international endeavors, declared those who envisioned and then created them, resulted from a "high sense of human duty and sympathy" and for the "humanitarian purpose of saving lives."[84]

Economic and social rights received significant attention during the Paris Peace Conference in other ways. Workers had sacrificed much during World War I and, in order to recruit soldiers, strengthen war production, and maintain unity on the "home front," governments had made many promises for the extension of these kinds of rights once hostilities ceased. Between 1914 and 1919 all of the major British, French, Belgian, and American trade unions, among others, had announced detailed plans to improve the condition of workers and allow them to share in the benefits of democracy for which the war was presumably being waged. No fewer than twelve international conferences had been convened by trade unions, socialist organizations, and other reformist groups to explore ways of advancing social welfare, establishing conventions governing working conditions, including representatives of labor in the peace negotiations, and, interestingly enough, creating a basic "charter" of fundamental rights.[85] The fires of revolution in Russia and Germany at precisely this time added yet another dimension to the discussion, causing a number of the leaders to fear what might happen if class unrest spread into their own countries. As delegates from the American Federation of Labor told Wilson in no uncertain terms, "*something must be done*" to secure workers' rights in the peace treaties and "*organized labor must have this recognition*" or serious consequences would follow.[86]

Once again, a variety of pressures impinged on the peacemakers, and in response to mixed motives they created a Commission on International Labor Legislation to give them advice. Comprised of representatives from different countries, it met on thirty-five separate occasions, in its own words, to address "the sentiments of justice and humanity."[87] The delegates listened to a variety of appeals ranging from moderate to radical workers' organizations, the International Women's Council, and the Conference of Allied Women Suffragists. Despite the many differences expressed, however, they all agreed on two fundamental propositions: that peace and economic and social justice were indissolubly linked, and that these could be achieved only through international action. The commission thus boldly produced a highly unusual draft convention for the establishment of a permanent organization for international labor legislation. Its purpose would be to promote "lasting peace through social justice" by improving the conditions of working men—and women. Its members still would be nation-states but they would be uniquely represented by a tripartite delegation composed of representatives of government, management, and labor sitting side by side and enjoying equal status. They also created a statement known as the Labor Charter, declaring that workers "should not be regarded merely as a commodity or article of commerce" but as human beings entitled to "a reasonable standard of life." It called for the adoption of an eight-hour workday, abolition of child labor, inspection of factories, the right of association for the employed as well as for employers, and the right of women to receive equal pay for equal work. Such proposals were regarded as truly radical measures. Thus it came as a surprise to many when the negotiators at Paris not only actually adopted the recommendations but made them integral parts of the peace treaties themselves.[88] This established for the first time a permanent body called the International Labor Organization (ILO) devoted to economic and social rights well beyond national borders.

The peacemakers also wrestled with the difficult question of whether national leaders could be held personally responsible for criminal offenses against the laws and customs of war. After weeks of contentious debate, the special Commission on the Responsibilities of the Authors of the War and Enforcement of Penalties, composed of fifteen distinguished international lawyers, issued their final report holding out a vision and forcefully declaring:

there is no reason why rank, however exalted, should in any circumstances protect the holder of it from responsibility when that responsibility has been established before a properly constituted tribunal. This extends even to heads of states. . . . If the immunity of a sovereign is claimed . . . it would involve laying down the principle that the greatest outrages against the laws and customs of war and the laws of humanity, if proved against him, could in no circumstances be punished. Such a conclusion would shock the conscience of civilized mankind.[89]

Their recommendation to create an international criminal tribunal, however, proved to be too radical for some. The United States, in particular, firmly resisted. Lansing argued that such a proposal was "unknown in the practice of nations," stating that the views of his country differed "so fundamentally and so radically" from those of the majority that he issued a formal dissent.[90] "The essence of sovereignty," he famously asserted, "is the absence of responsibility."[91] In the end, the peace treaties contained path-breaking provisions for establishing an international criminal tribunal holding individuals leaders accountable for their actions. Nevertheless, given this level of resistance, they would never be seriously implemented. Powerful states were not yet prepared to run the risks of jeopardizing their own national sovereignty.[92]

There is no question that the peacemaking process up to this point produced any number of remarkable treaty provisions on human rights. Many, many people, with justifiable reason, eagerly anticipated an enormous extension of their rights. But not all. Others who also had sacrificed during the war examined the terms and wondered just where their rights "came in." Why, they asked poignantly, did the protection of rights for minorities not extend to minority races and indigenous peoples in Asia, Africa, the Middle East, Latin America, the United States and Canada, or the Pacific? Where were the tons of food and relief supplies for the refugees and needy outside Europe? Why was there so little mention in the treaties about the rights of women? What were the advantages of international labor legislation to pre-industrial societies of peasants barely surviving on the land? And, especially, where was the solemn principle of the right to self-determination when it involved the colonial possessions of the victors?

These were precisely the kinds of questions that individuals and NGOs insisted on raising at the international level. Du Bois, for example, deliberately organized the Pan-African Congress to meet in Paris at exactly the same time as the peace conference, to demand adherence to human rights, and to bring "all pressure possible on the delegates at the Peace Table in the interest of the colored peoples of the United States and the world."[93] Jane Addams, Jeannette Rankin, and Gertrude Baer wanted to link visions of women's rights more closely with visions of peace, and thus held a simultaneous conference of their own. Men, they declared, "are seldom representative of modern social thought and the least responsive to changing ideas" who must be told of "the importance of certain interests which have hitherto been inarticulate in international affairs."[94] To accomplish this task, they formed the Women's International League for Peace and Freedom and vowed to exert unrelenting pressure on governments. Still others critics decided to hold their tongues for just a little longer, waiting to see whether their visions of rights might be realized by the negotiations involving the much-anticipated Covenant of the League of Nations.

The Covenant: Rights Proclaimed and Rights Rejected

Great hope and drama surrounded the creation of the League of Nations. For generations, there had been dreams of some kind of international organization that might be able to bring security, peace, justice, and human rights to the world. The trauma of recent war and revolutions focused attention on this idea even further, particularly when advocated by Woodrow Wilson. He had promised that he would devote himself to ushering in a "new diplomacy" and creating "a general association of nations" for just such a purpose.[95] This vision inspired millions of people who greeted Wilson when he arrived in Europe, hung his portrait in their homes, held parades in his honor, and hailed him as "the spokesman for world humanity."[96]

Wilson's insistence on creating this new organization and his position as chair of the Commission on the League of Nations made discussions on this subject a vital part of the entire peacemaking process. In fact, the delegates determined to make its governing Covenant an integral legal component of the peace treaties themselves. There was great hope that the League, with its Secretariat composed of civil servants whose loyalties would be placed beyond their own nation-states, and its sister bodies such as the International Court of Justice, would protect human rights through collective action. It is for this reason that the negotiators in Paris assigned the League responsibilities for guaranteeing the borders drawn in the name of the right of self-determination, enforcing the provisions of the minority treaties, assisting in the distribution of relief supplies, and providing financial support for the International Labor Organization, among other significant new departures.

Peacemakers also crafted other provisions within the Covenant related to evolving visions of international human rights. All members of the League of Nations, for example, pledged "to secure and maintain fair and humane conditions of labor for men, women, and children, both in their own countries and in all countries." They promised to enforce agreements relating to the traffic in women and children, trade in opium and other drugs, and the right of freedom in communication and transit, as well as to promote the right to health. They committed themselves to expanding humanitarian law and encouraging national Red Cross societies in their efforts for "the mitigation of suffering throughout the world." Finally, and in fascinating language that was to raise more questions than it answered, they pledged "to secure just treatment of the native inhabitants of territories under their control."[97]

Careful observers of these developments wondered just how far the delegates would go. Here the fundamental question emerged over and over again: rights for whom? If the Covenant was truly designed to govern the new international organization responsible for security, peace, justice, and human rights for the great and the small alike, then why did it favor the interests of the victors? If human rights were truly natural, equal, and universal, should not the rights of everyone be included? Should there not be more provisions, for example, dealing with the rights of women or with the right of religious believers to worship as they chose? One draft proposal, to illustrate, suggested that the League of Nations recognize "religious persecution and intolerance as fertile sources of war" and therefore agree "that they will make no law prohibiting or interfering with the free exercise of religion, and that they will in no way discriminate, either in law or in fact, against those who practice any particular creed, religion, or belief."[98] But in the end, this nondiscrimination proposal failed, primarily because of the great fear that it might create a dangerous precedent for opening an even more controversial issue of international human rights: racial equality.[99]

Perhaps no single issue at the Paris Peace Conference attracted more genuinely global attention than race. For the millions of people still exploited by colonialism, excluded by immigration restrictions, persecuted by prejudice, and victimized by segregation and the long-term effects of slavery, racial discrimination was of fundamental importance.[100] Indeed, this is exactly why Du Bois described it as "*the* problem of the twentieth century."[101] Even less passionate observers identified racial inequality as "the burning question" "filled with explosives."[102] To explicitly address this issue, the representatives of NGOs such as the NAACP, National Equal Rights League, Universal Negro Improvement Association, and International League of Darker Peoples made their way to Paris (often having to evade government efforts to keep them away).[103] But at a time when human rights NGOs still remained small and could be easily excluded, all they could do was to speak from the outside and hope someone would listen to them. They needed an advocate on the inside of the conference itself, some official government delegation not be afraid of challenging white supremacy by championing racial equality. They found such a voice in Japan.

Victims of all previous generations seeking to combat discrimination on the basis of race at the international level always could be excluded from diplomatic negotiations because they possessed little power or influence. Suddenly, in 1919, this was no longer the case. Among the victors of World War I was Japan, the first nonwhite country ever to participate in such a momentous gathering—and one determined to speak out as a victim of racial prejudice itself. "As to the terms of peace, Japan should insist on the equal international treatment of all races," wrote the Tokyo newspaper *Asahi*. "No other question is so inseparably and materially interwoven with the permanency of the world's peace as that of unfair and unjust treatment of a large majority of the world's population." "If the discrimination wall is to remain standing," it concluded, "then President Wilson will have spoken of peace, justice, and humanity in vain, and he would have proved after all only a hypocrite."[104]

Although acknowledging that "the question of race prejudice is a very delicate and complicated matter involving the play of keep human passions," the Japanese delegation of Kimmochi Saiongi and Nobuaki Makino considered that the process of peacemaking presented the best opportunity to raise this issue of human rights and believed that "what was deemed impossible before is about to be accomplished."[105] They therefore sought to include a single clause in the Covenant of the League of Nations establishing not an immediate realization, but rather an international recognition, of the principle of the right to racial equality.

Their efforts met with instant and intransigent opposition from prejudiced whites. Wilson, who long had supported immigration exclusion against the "Yellow Peril" abroad and racial segregation within the United States, thwarted their efforts at several turns.[106] The British foreign secretary exclaimed that he simply did not believe that all men were created equal and most certainly "not that a man in Central Africa was created equal to a European."[107] The abrasive Australian prime minister, representing a country that persecuted Aborigines, had campaigned on the platform: "Our chief plank is, of course, White Australia. There's no compromise about *that*." He insisted that he "would not deviate an inch" from this position, and declared that if the Covenant contained any provision on racial equality his government would refuse to join the League itself.[108] New Zealand's prime minister voiced the same attitude, supported by newspapers such as the *Otago Witness* printing the opinion that "though the American Declaration of Independence begins by asserting all men are born equal in the sight of God, it makes no mention of niggers and Japanese."[109]

Such stark statements immediately prompted angry reactions, especially among those who had been hailed as "close allies" during the recent war. Thirty-seven Japanese NGOs mobilized a mass meeting in Tokyo and organized the new Association for the Equality of Races, declaring that any perpetuation of racial discrimination would not only strike against the great principles of liberty and equality but would endanger all future international relations. "As long as this remains unchanged," they asserted, "all peace conferences, leagues, and agreements will be as a house built on the sand, and no true peace can be hoped for."[110] The Chinese delegate, Wellington Koo, proclaimed that the people of China were "profoundly interested" in this fundamental question of human rights and "in full sympathy" with the movement to secure racial equality.[111] Similar expressions came from throughout colonial possessions in Asia, Africa, and Latin America who listened in outrage as they heard delegates refer to them as less-than-fully human "primitive" and "racially inferior" peoples, "savage tribes," and too "backward" for self-government. Within the United States, the National Association for the Advancement of Colored People publicly and pointedly asked Wilson, with reference to his famous statement about saving the world: "Mr. President, why not make America safe for democracy?"[112]

Global attention thus focused on the meetings of the Commission on the League of Nations designed to resolve this highly symbolic and critical issue of international human rights. Wilson desperately had hoped to avoid voting at all, even if the Japanese were willing to water down their original proposal. His own prejudices were well known, and he believed that the U.S. Senate would never ratify a treaty if it contained any article about racial equality. But the Japanese and their supporters insisted that the larger principle was too important, and forced Wilson to call for a vote. The count revealed eleven of seventeen in favor of a provision in the Covenant on racial equality—a clear majority. Confronted with this result, Wilson, as the chair, suddenly declared that the proposal had failed. It could not be adopted, he announced, because it had been unable to secure unanimous approval. The legal expert quickly announced to the stunned participants, now in an uproar, that there was no such thing as a unanimity "rule" and that a majority had just voted in support of the principle of racial equality. Wilson was forced to admit this fact, but said that in this particular case there simply were "too serious objections on the part of some of us" to have it inserted into the Covenant.[113] He therefore refused to accept any challenges and adamantly declared the debate to be over.

This unilateral and shocking decision on such an emotionally charged subject by such a presumed champion of human rights created storms of international reaction and protest. Newspaper headlines blared: "PEACE DELEGATES BEAT JAPAN'S PROPOSAL FOR RACIAL EQUALITY."[114] Du Bois watched in astonishment—and then burned with anger. He accused Wilson of blatantly betraying the very principles for which the war had been fought and completely turning his back on promises made to black soldiers. In seething outrage he shouted:

We stand again to look America squarely in the face and call a spade a spade. We *return*. We *return from fighting*. We *return fighting*. Make way for Democracy! We saved it in France, and by the Great Jehovah, we will save it in the U.S.A. or know the reason why![115]

Race riots broke out in a number of cities throughout the United States, including the nation's own capital, Washington, D.C., and according to no less than the leading historian of race relations in America, "ushered in the greatest period of interracial strife the nation had ever witnessed."[116] Other critics elsewhere lashed out at what the *Asahi* and the *Nichinichi* in Japan called "the paralyzed conscience" and hypocrisy of the "so-called civilized world" of the Anglo-Saxons, and decided to create their own League of the Abolition of Race Discrimination.[117] "The root of [the problem] lies in the perverted feeling of racial superiority entertained by the whites," reflected an Asisan diplomat. "If things are allowed to proceed in the present way, there is every likelihood that the peace of the world will be endangered. It, therefore, behooves all well-wishers of mankind to exert their utmost to remove their gross injustice immediately."[118]

Once this decision about racial equality was made, it sealed the fate of millions of nonwhites who mistakenly thought that if the right of self-determination could be authorized for those in Europe, then surely it would be granted for those who suffered even worse from oppression and exploitation in the colonies. They too had sacrificed in the war and been promised by Wilson himself that "a free, open-minded, and absolutely impartial adjustment of all colonial claims" would take place in which "the interests of the populations concerned must have equal weight" with those of the imperial powers.[119] These hopes were now crushed. When Wellington Koo asked the Western powers to end their special privileges in China, he was told that it "was out of the question."[120] To the great anger of the Arab world (and in a decision that would have enormous consequences), the British and the French partitioned Palestine and took control of Lebanon, Syria, Transjordan, Iraq, and the Persian Gulf territories. They then seized former German possessions in Tanganyika (now Tanzania), the Cameroons, and Togo. Not to be outdone, the Belgians extended their control into Ruanda-Urundi (now Rwanda and Burundi), the Italians seized a sphere of influence in western Turkey, and the South Africans took South-West Africa (now Namibia). The Japanese extended their influence on the Shantung peninsula, in Manchuria, and over Pacific islands north of the equator formerly occupied by Germany. Australia and New Zealand grabbed what they could in the South Pacific, and the United States held on to the Philippines.

Lest all this taking and trading appeared too crass, the powers often called their new acquisitions "mandates" rather than possessions, promising to care for "the well-being and development" of the inhabitants, but declaring that they would govern until such time as these "backward" peoples were "able to stand on their own feet in the strenuous conditions of the modern world."[121] Confided one diplomat in a moment of rare candor at Paris: "However fervid might be our indignation regarding Italian claims to Dalmatia and the Dodecanese, it could be cooled by reference, not to Cyprus only, but to Ireland, Egypt, and India. We had accepted a system for others which, when it came to practice, we should refuse to apply to ourselves."[122] In this regard, the settlement seemed to make the world safe not for democracy but for empire.

When the details of the peace treaties and Covenant of the League of Nations became known, widespread demonstrations broke out throughout the world among those who saw their wartime service dishonored and promises unfulfilled. Oppressed peoples perceived nothing but manifest racial prejudice and new schemes for continued control, describing the mandate system as "the crudity of conquest draped in the veil of morality," and no more than "fig leaves" designed to conceal the nakedness of imperialism.[123] The Destour Party formed immediately in Tunisia to struggle for independence from France. Riots broke out in Egypt and Palestine against the British, and demonstrations erupted in Korea against the Japanese for their own blatant hypocrisy concerning equal rights and imperial conquests. Ho Chi Minh realized that these decisions at Paris confirmed a "bright shining lie": that the right of self-determination did not apply to everyone—only whites and "not to the brown and the yellow peoples of Asia or to the blacks of Africa."[124] In India, where more than one million troops and noncombatants had served in the war, protests for freedom sparked the massacre at Amritsar when British troops opened fire and killed four hundred unarmed civilians. Within three weeks, mass riots erupted in China as well, beginning first with students in Tiananmen Square and then spreading throughout the country, igniting what came to be the May Fourth Movement. Among the most significant demands of the protestors, in the words of one of the movement's intellectual founders, Chen Duxiu, were two: "equality and human rights."[125]

*   *   *

When the peace conference finally ended in June 1919 and the delegates returned home, observers came to understand that the evolution of international human rights rarely proceeds in a direct or linear path uncomplicated by mixed motives or unintended consequences. Those who had championed rights found cause for both deep disappointment and genuine celebration. The many expectations, often encouraged by political leaders themselves, that somehow all the sacrifices made in wartime would be rewarded and thereby suddenly transform rights around the globe did not materialize. Moreover, those who believed that the perceived righteousness of their cause would somehow be sufficient to bring about their dreams came to realize the enormous power of vested interests, resistance, revenge, greed, prejudice, and national sovereignty. According to the terms of the peace treaties and the Covenant, the standards and obligations to protect human rights did not fall on all equally, the benefits did not extend universally to everyone, the enforcement provisions remained uncertain, and the locus of authority largely continued to reside in sovereign nation-states who could choose to join the new League of Nations—or not. On the other hand, these same legal instruments, despite their messy inconsistencies, also marked several striking achievements. Never before in history had a peace conference produced so many treaties or programs with so many provisions reflecting normative values about the right of self-determination, the right of minorities to be protected, the right to receive humanitarian relief, and economic and social rights, or produced an international organization with responsibilities for protecting these rights. Never before had the global community made such a direct connection between security, peace, justice, and human rights, or, in the case of the Minorities Treaties, to challenge traditional claims of national sovereignty and domestic jurisdiction. For the beneficiaries, these results held out extraordinary promises. For those still excluded and denied these rights, they provoked a even stronger determination to continue struggling until they realized their visions as well.

Chapter 4
Opportunities and Challenges

Visions and Rights Between the Wars

> Considering that at the present moment these rights might be so formulated as to ensure that every inhabitant of a State should have the right to the full and entire protection of his life and liberty, and that all the citizens of a State should be equal before the law and should enjoy the same civil and political rights, without distinction of race, language, or religion; Expresses the hope that a world convention may be drawn up under the auspices of the League of Nations, ensuring the protection and respect of such rights.
>
> —Delegation to the League of Nations from Haiti

Those who survived a world war, revolutions, and a peace conference reached different conclusions. The all-too-recent experiences of death, devastation, monumental human suffering, and sense of betrayal certainly provided unmistakable warnings about what the future might hold. If the forces of extreme nationalism, state power over citizens, prejudice, and modern technology in the service of war or persecution were unleashed again, then the prospects for security, peace, justice, and human rights appeared bleak indeed. "I see how peoples are set against one another, and in silence, unknowingly, foolishly, obediently, innocently slay one another," says a young solider in Erich Maria Remarque's *All Quiet on the Western Front*. "I see that the keenest brains in the world invent weapons and words to make it yet more refined and enduring. And all men of my age . . . throughout the whole world, see these things."[1] But others considered these same experiences as a prod for humanity to redeem itself and as a chance for hope. They revealed instead the capacity to see visions in desperate times, to create treaties to protect people, and even to establish an international organization to guide the world into a better future. These sharply contrasting opinions came to influence the course of events between the wars as they revealed both great opportunities and serious challenges in the evolution of international human rights.

A Flourishing of Visions

One of the most striking features of this period was a dramatic flourishing in the number and scope of open and frank discussions about human rights around the globe. As such, it seemed to provide further evidence of the paradox that advances in human rights often follow in the wake of trauma and tragedy. Visions of international human rights, of course, have always required the capacity to consider responsibilities extending beyond national borders and to visualize the world as a whole. In this regard, the global dimensions of World War I and the experiences of its participants who had traveled far from their own shores to fight in it made an indelible impression that lasted long after the fighting ceased. Advances in communication and transportation technology also contributed to this perspective by inexorably bringing people and places, heretofore far removed from each other, much closer together. The flow of goods, services, and capital from one continent to another did the same. Moreover, the creation of the League of Nations with responsibilities for the world enhanced this view even further, prompting expressions about the "international idea," a "new world order," and "internationalism."[2] As one commentator noted, all this "implies a new international attitude: the attitude of sacrifice as the earnest of its reality, the attitude of universalism as the pledge of its continuity."[3]

For many thoughtful women and men, an essential element of this enhanced international perspective centered on human rights. They envisioned the rights of one person as being directly related to the rights of others, irrespective of place, and truly universal in scope. They sought to expand the scope of two particular dimensions: *what* should be included in human rights and *who* should be included in human rights. Rather than being deterred by the actions (or inactions) of their own governments, for example, they created new NGOs such as the Women's International League for Peace and Freedom with headquarters in Geneva and sections ranging from Mexico to New Zealand, from Japan to Peru, and from Sweden to the United States. Its members worked to promote a wide range of human rights, in the words of Jane Addams, "to inaugurate a new type of international life in the world" and advance "the hopes of mankind." "They all alike had come to realize," she noted with great insight, "that every crusade, every beginning of social change, must start from small numbers of people convinced of the righteousness of a cause."[4]

Such convictions certainly motivated those who focused on women's rights. In 1919 and 1920 females secured the right to vote in Germany, Austria, the Netherlands, Luxembourg, Czechoslovakia, Poland, and Canada. The passage of the Nineteenth Amendment to the Constitution in 1920 finally enfranchised twenty-six million women of voting age in the United States. This stimulated the introduction of the Equal Rights Amendment stating that "Equality of rights under the law shall not be denied or abridged by the United States or any State on account of sex."[5] These accomplishments inspired Ichikawa Fusae to organize the Fusen Kakutoku Domei (Women's Suffrage League) in Japan. Other women's movements emerged in Turkey, Iran, India, Ceylon, Indonesia, the Philippines, China, Korea, and Vietnam. Women in Muslim countries found further encouragement when Kemal Atatürk asserted:

Let us be frank: society is made of women as well as men. If one grants all the rights to progress to the one and no rights at all to the other, what happens? Is it possible that one half of the population is in chains for the other half to reach the skies? Progress is possible only through common effort.[6]

New organizations such as the Women's International League for Peace and Freedom, the International Council of Women, and the International Alliance of Women all emphasized the necessity for gender equality around the world, witnessing the successful extension of the right to vote in some form for women in Burma, Ecuador, Greece, Hungary, Mexico, Mongolia, and Sweden.[7] The first campaigns against female genital mutilation (FGM) began in Africa.[8] At the 1923 Conference of the American Republics in Chile, delegates agreed to study how women could achieve full civil and political rights, and at their next conference in Cuba they established the Inter-American Commission of Women for just this purpose.[9] These were also the years when Margaret Sanger of the United States, Ellen Key of Sweden, and Ishimoto Shizue of Japan launched their campaign for reproductive rights, often in the face of great opposition, by providing information about birth control to mass audiences for the first time in history and asserting rights for women wherever they might be.[10]

At exactly the same time, an English primary school teacher named Eglantyne Jebb focused her vision of rights upon children. She was horrified and outraged at how much young boys and girls suffered during war, revolutions, famine, and disease. She saw that children were the most invisible, least powerful, and most vulnerable of all victims. As a consequence of this, and her own deeply held religious convictions, she realized that they were completely dependent upon others with a sense of responsibility to speak for them when they were voiceless and to defend them when they were defenseless. Jebb determined that past practice was no longer acceptable and refused to be passive. With a selfless passion so strong that she was described as "humanity's conscience" and "the White Flame," she created the Save the Children Fund, launching a movement that continues today.[11] Although accused of "anti-patriotic activities" for assisting children beyond her own national borders, and even arrested for distributing leaflets with photographs showing starving "enemy" infants of the Germans or Bolsheviks, she devoted the her life to the universal principle that all children regardless of nationality, race, or faith were entitled to certain basic rights. "The only international language," she said, "is a child's cry."[12]

Other visionaries devoted themselves to advancing international human rights as a whole. The prestigious Institut de Droit International began as early as 1921 to consider creating a worldwide declaration of rights. Under the leadership of the courageous Victor Basch, the French Ligue pour la Défense des Droits de l'Homme contacted former German enemies to seek reconciliation. Among those was Carl von Ossietsky, chair of the recently formed Deutsche Liga für Menschenrechte, who would later be killed by the Nazis. They brought other NGOs and leaders into contact, including Miguel de Unamuno, who founded the Spanish rights organization; Italian human rights leader Giacomo Mateotti, who would be assassinated for resisting the Fascists; and a representative from China. Together they established the Fédération Internationale des Droits de l'Homme (FIDH) in 1922 to develop a central bureau of information and assistance, promote and defend human rights (including those of indigenous peoples under colonial domination), and bring pressure on the League of Nations. Its members also actively began to advocate the idea of an international declaration of human rights for all people.[13]

Activists who viewed themselves as parts of this larger and dynamic movement emerged in a myriad of diverse places. Chinese campaigners contributed to progressive journals such as *New China, New Youth, New Dawn,* and *Human Rights (Renquan)* and joined the new liberal and democratically oriented NGO known as the China League for Civil Rights founded by Cai Yuanpei and Lu Xun. Those impatient with gradual reform turned to the revolutionary Chinese Communist Party and its leader Mao Zedong, who predicted that "several hundred million peasants will rise like a mighty storm, like a hurricane, a force so swift and violent that no power, however great, will be able to hold it back. . . . They will sweep all the imperialists, warlords, corrupt officials, local tyrants, and evil gentry into their graves."[14] The dramatic 1925 Japanese electoral law instituted universal adult male suffrage, thereby increasing the electorate from three million to more than twelve million with a single stroke and initiated intensive discussion about the nature and extent of rights.[15] At the same time, pioneering jurist Alejandro Alvarez from Chile worked on behalf of international human rights through his extensive publications and active participation in the League of Nations, Institut de Droit International, American Institute of International Law, and Carnegie Endowment for International Peace.

Elsewhere in the world this movement for rights became part and parcel of efforts to gain the right of self-determination from colonial rule. Gandhi increased his civil disobedience against the British in India, developing his belief in the redemptive power of love to convert even brutal opponents by its *satyagraha,* or "soul force," and declaring that he would use passive resistance as a means "of securing rights."[16] In Indonesia, Sukarno (who would become the first president of his country) led various groups in the struggle to secure independence from the Dutch. In Vietnam, Ho Chi Minh (who would become the leader of his nation) and the Communist Party mobilized revolutionaries and others who worked for the rights of peasants, workers, and women, along with those seeking freedom from the French. Leaders of the Soviet Union similarly saw vast opportunities in such potent combinations of the discontent and exploited, and through the Third (Communist) International, or Comintern, encouraged those trying to unite revolution with national liberation. Young activists in Accra created the National Congress of British West Africa, while those in the French colonies formed NGOs to promote visions of independence. This vibrant period also marked the beginning of the political education of a number of those who would eventually lead their countries into independence throughout Africa, including Nnamdi Azikiwe in Nigeria, Kwame Nkrumah in the Gold Coast (now Ghana), Jomo Kenyatta in Kenya, Kenneth Kaunda in Zambia, and Habib Bourguiba, who made a connection between self-determination and other human rights by declaring: "The Tunisia we mean to liberate will not be a Tunisia for Muslim, for Jew, or for Christian. It will be a Tunisia for all, without distinction of religion or race, who wish to have it as their country and to live in it under the protection of just laws."[17]

These assertions of the right to independence often often coupled with demands to be free from racial discrimination. No issue raised more complications, for race was not only closely tied to class but all too intimately related to imperial domination and exploitation in the colonies and policies of immigration exclusion. It is thus not surprising that discourse of human rights between the wars would entail visions of racial equality. In fact, new NGOs were created for just this purpose. Activists formed the League for the Abolition of Race Discrimination in Japan and the Pan-Asian Society in China to address the rights of "1,000 million souls of Asia" who suffered "from the oppression of the white races of Europe and America."[18] Several Pan-Asian conferences insisted on racial equality and demanded that those basic human rights discussed in the West be extended elsewhere. In 1925 representatives from Japan, China, India, the Philippines, East Indies, the Malay states, Egypt, and Turkey created what they called the "Colored International" to support "the abolition of racial discrimination in the immigration policies of certain white nations, and to combat the assumption of . . . superiority by the white races."[19] In India, Gandhi and B. R. Ambedkar courageously launched campaigns against the entrenched caste system and its discrimination against "untouchables."[20] At the same time, the Institute of Pacific Relations was formed to address regional problems, especially those of race. Walter Nash of the New Zealand delegation (who would become an outspoken advocate for rights in the International Labor Organization and the formative years of the United Nations), returned from the 1927 meeting so convinced that he took a highly unpopular stand by urging his country to "look behind the mask of race and color and nation" and extend equal rights to all.[21]

Demands for racial equality came from other sources as well. Those who created the Ligue Universelle pour la Défense de la Race Noire dedicated themselves to protect the rights of those victimized because of the color of their skin wherever they might be. Jean Price-Mars and Aimé Césaire of Haiti and Léopold Senghor of Senegal adopted the same cause under the banner of what they called "Négritude," developing journals such as *L'Étudiant Noir* and *La Revue du Monde Noir* to give expression to their visions. Du Bois and others instituted the Pan-African Association and issued their "Declaration to the World" demanding "the absolute equality of races"—"in Asia, in Africa, America, and the isles of the sea."[22] More radical elements followed Marcus Garvey, who founded the Universal Negro Improvement Association for public agitation. His International Conventions of the Negro Peoples of the World attracted delegates from around the globe, and his newspaper *The Negro World* appeared in English, French, and Spanish and was distributed over several continents until banned by many colonial governments. "Up, you mighty Race!" Garvey exhorted. "Now we have started to speak and I am only the forerunner of an awakened Africa that shall never go back to sleep."[23]

Visionaries of international human rights also emerged in many other places and with other organizations. In fact, a remarkable array of individuals with considerable experience became publicists and activists.[24] These included Alejandro Alvarez, the outspoken advocate of international law to protect individual rights; André Mandelstam, who had served as a diplomat and legal expert in the Russian Ministry of Foreign Affairs; Antoine Frangulis the jurist and diplomat, who had represented Greece at the

League of Nations; Eduard Beneš, the Czech leader who would become president of his country; and Colonel Edward House, diplomatic advisor to Woodrow Wilson in the United States. Along with others, they created the Académie Diplomatique Internationale (ADI) in 1926 and almost immediately set up a commission to explore the international protection of human rights. Its members concluded that the obligations delineated in the Minorities Treaties should serve as a model for others, and thus recommended that *all* inhabitants (not just those belonging to a minority) of *all* states should have the right to receive full and complete protection of life and liberty, equality before the law, and the enjoyment of civil and political rights without distinction as to race, language, or religion. The academy accepted this recommendation in 1928 and called for an international convention that would ensure the protection of these basic human rights.[25]

Simultaneous with these efforts, the Institut de Droit International invested significant time and energy in envisioning the role that human rights should play in the world. Mandelstam, who served as the rapporteur of its Commission for the International Protection of the Rights of Man and Citizen and of Minorities, took the initiative for this effort. With determination he campaigned for extensive measures and argued for a three-step strategy: a declaration, a convention, and then sanctions to ensure the observance of norms. After lively discussion over the course of nearly eight years, and consistent with its position that international law encompassed more than just the relationships between states, its members adopted in 1929 what they called the Declaration of the International Rights of Man. They asserted that "the juridical conscience of the civilized world demands the recognition for the individual of rights preserved from all infringement on the part of the state," and declared: "it is essential to extend international recognition of the rights of man to the entire world." Specific articles called for protecting the rights to life, liberty, and property "without distinction of nationality, sex, race, language, or religion." By taking this public stand, the Institute saw itself as speaking out on behalf of humanity as a whole, challenging the claims of national sovereignty, and thereby marking a significant point of departure for a new era of international human rights.[26]

This Declaration of the International Rights of Man inspired and emboldened other individuals to speak out as well, especially those who themselves had suffered at the hands of governments or been forced into exile. These included Russian Boris Mirkine-Guetzévitch, a former professor of international law and a victim of the Bolsheviks, and Antoine Frangulis, who had been forced to flee from the Greek military dictatorship, both of whom thrust themselves into highly public debates about human rights and national sovereignty. In particular, Mandelstam, an exile and a minority, with his intense and scholarly eyes focused through wire-rimmed glasses, wrote, taught, and worked unceasingly. His articles in leading legal journals, his 1931 book *Les Droits internationaux de l'homme*, and his university courses offered to eager students all gave expression to his visions.[27] Moreover, he constantly encouraged NGOs such as the Institut de Droit International, Académie Diplomatique Internationale, Fédération International des Droits de l'Homme, and International Institute of Public Law to become more active in protecting basic human rights.[28]

Other visions came not from reflections in academies or law offices, but from the brutal hardships caused by the Great Depression. As misery and suffering spread first across the industrialized West and then to seemingly far-removed locations, so too did calls for economic and social rights. Moderates and reformers looked to religious or charitable groups, NGOs, states, or the League of Nations to secure rights to food, housing, jobs, and medical care. Some turned to labor and socialist political parties or the International Labor Organization and International Federation of Trade Unions. Still others moved to more militant action by launching strikes or to the extremes of the Third (Communist) International, believing that these rights could be secured only through means of violence and revolution.

All these developments contributed tributaries into a ever-growing river of intense interest in human rights and encouraged activists and NGOs to push even farther. Members of the International Union of Associations for the League of Nations, for example, mobilized citizen groups to exert pressure to create a general convention for international human rights. They declared that the principle of legal equality between people as well as states required a global acceptance of responsibility for protecting rights, including the use of humanitarian intervention if necessary.[29] Its members included Mandelstam, Jacques Dumas of France, and Henri Rolin of Belgium (who later as a delegate to the 1945 San Francisco Conference insisted that the United Nations Charter begin with the words, "We the peoples," and eventually became the president of the European Court of Human Rights). Similarly, the Fédération Internationale des Droits de l'Homme with the support of its affiliates around the world endorsed the Institut de Droit International's Declaration of the International Rights of Man.[30] This, in turn, inspired the Ligue pour la Défense des Droits de l'Homme and its members (including René Cassin who later would help draft the 1948 Universal Declaration of Human Rights) to produce its own Complement to the Declaration of the Rights of Man and of the Citizen, proclaiming, "The international protection of human rights must be universally organized and guaranteed in such a manner that no state can deny the exercise of these rights to any human being living on its territory."[31]

In addition, and precisely at this same time, a dedicated group of international lawyers and scholars drafted statutes, wrote books and articles, and spoke out about yet another vision: the protection of human rights through the creation of an international criminal court with jurisdiction over "offenses committed contrary to the laws of humanity."[32] They worked with the Inter-Parliamentary Union and International Law Association, and then founded their own Association Internationale de Droit Pénale to advance the idea of an international tribunal to confront what they described as "the ingrained habit of centuries"[33]—namely, the culture of impunity for those political leaders who seriously abused human rights.

Almost all of these visions came from individuals acting on their own or as members of NGOs. But on a few occasions governments made contributions as well. During a series of Inter-American Conferences, for example, some from Latin America sought to articulate definitions of individual rights beyond nation-states and to explore ways in which those rights might be protected regionally and internationally. They created the Inter-American Commission on Women focusing on gender discrimination and began to address the rights of indigenous peoples, workers, and immigrants. Representatives adopted the Lima Declaration in Favor of Women's Rights and then a more broadly based statement entitled "Defense of Human Rights."[34] In these efforts, they and others increasingly found themselves turning to the opportunities provided by the new League of Nations.

Opportunities for New Departures

Much of this flourishing of visions can be attributed to the emergence of the League of Nations, described as "the great innovation of the peace."[35] Created in the wake of devastating war and revolutions, it generated extraordinary expectations among millions of people around the world. It held out the hope of a fresh beginning, a chance to correct existing flaws on an international scale, and the prospect of advancing security, peace, justice, and human rights. When delegates first assembled at Geneva in 1920, they excitedly spoke of the event as being of "unprecedented greatness," presenting a "unique opportunity," one that "will have a permanent influence on the evolution of the nations," and planting "the divine seed of future harvests, the witness of the world to be."[36] "Let us dedicate ourselves to humanity," declared one representative. "Working together, let us seek to prepare and step by step to achieve the reign, so long awaited, of international morality and human rights."[37]

In attempting to realize these visions, the League immediately discovered a remarkable array of opportunities for new departures. Specific provisions within the Covenant and the peace settlements assigned a wide variety of highly unusual responsibilities in several different areas of human rights. The League was expected to guarantee the provisions of a whole series of new Minorities Treaties regarding nondiscrimination and equal protection in civil and political rights. It was charged with protecting the right of self-determination and political independence of all its members and for fulfilling its "sacred trust of civilization" to administer a new mandate system of territories who wanted to become independent. It was required under the Covenant to create a Permanent Court of International Justice, to promote cooperation among Red Cross societies, and to secure "fair and humane" working conditions, obtain "just treatment" for native inhabitants under their control, check international traffic in women and children and dangerous drugs, and protect freedom of communication and transit.[38] What all of this would mean in actual practice, of course, was completely unknown as the League set about in the absence of experience and with few road maps to begin its work, turning ambiguous language over delicate political issues into purposeful action, and exploring both the possibilities and the limits of politics and diplomacy that lay ahead.

Among the first efforts were those involved in creating, and then activating, the International Labor Organization. Designed to promote the rights of workers in the name "of justice and humanity" and supported by funds from the League of Nations, this body set out with energy and determination. Under the direction of Albert Thomas, the dynamic French Socialist,[39] it set out with an ambitious program of establishing an International Labor Office, investigating working conditions, publishing the

International Labour Review, considering complaints, organizing international conferences, coordinating contact between national labor unions, promoting economic and social justice, drafting treaties, and creating a Committee of Experts on the Application of Conventions to serve as the prototype of a treaty-monitoring body. By 1933, it had prepared and submitted to governments an extraordinary forty separate international conventions. These addressed a wide array of issues, including limits on the hours of work, maternity leave, unemployment, conditions of labor at night for women and children, equality of treatment in workers' compensation, compulsory labor, insurance, medical examinations, and the right of association. Such agreements had never been achieved before on an international scale. It appeared entirely appropriate therefore for them to be described as an integral part of "the great evolutionary movement" of human rights.[40]

Other opportunities for new departures arose as a result of the legal protections of the Minorities Treaties. When first signed, these applied only to Czechoslovakia, Greece, Poland, Romania, and Yugoslavia, and to the vanquished from the war of Austria, Bulgaria, Hungary, and Turkey, establishing that such protections "*constitute obligations of international concern* and shall be placed under the guarantee of the League of Nations."[41] These provisions marked a beginning, but pressure for further extensions arose immediately. Countries subjected to the treaties, not surprisingly, complained that they were being unfairly singled out and held to standards not applied to all. At the same time, others began to have a growing sense of responsibility that the rights of minorities should be recognized as a universal human right and therefore protected much more broadly.[42] Toward this end, they made admission into the League for certain states actually contingent on protecting minority rights. Finland, Albania, Lithuania, Latvia, Estonia, and Iraq all faced this requirement before they could become members. The League also actively encouraged states to sign bilateral agreements protecting minority rights between them, as in the case of the 1922 German-Polish Convention on Upper Silesia, which, as we shall see, would assume tremendous importance. Then, in a famous resolution, the Assembly expressed its hope

that the States which are not bound by any legal obligations to the League with respect to Minorities will nevertheless observe in the treatment of their own racial, religious, or linguistic minorities at least as high a standard of justice and toleration as is required by any of the Treaties.[43]

As a result of these many efforts, including the creation of special mechanisms and procedures, minority groups now possessed some means whereby they could bring complaints against states that violated their rights before the international community. Indeed, hundreds of petitions were submitted on behalf of protecting minorities.[44] If the secretary-general considered that a charge possessed merit, he could recommend that a Minorities Committee investigate and try to reach a settlement. If this failed, the complaint could be sent to the Council as a whole or to the Permanent Court of International Justice. This is precisely what occurred with the *Minority Schools in Albania* case, in which the court insisted that equality must be maintained in fact as well as in law.[45] The German-Polish Convention on Upper Silesia, to use another important example, not only guaranteed equal protection for the rights of minorities but also set up a Minorities Office and established two other bodies, each with an independent president appointed by the League Council. One of these was the Mixed Commission which focused on conciliation. It handled more than two thousand cases during the fifteen years of its existence. The other was the Arbitral Tribunal, a judicial body with competence to hear claims by individuals and render judgments binding on the courts and administrative authorities of the two countries. Serious differences were submitted to the Permanent Court of International Justice, as occurred with the 1928 *Rights of Minorities in Upper Silesia* case when the court ruled that any racial, linguistic, or religious criterion for school admission was a violation of equal protection and thus completely unacceptable.[46]

In addition to these activities, the Council, the Assembly, and the numerous committees of the League regularly devoted considerable time debating the issue of minorities. Over and over again delegates confronted an increasingly familiar tension: their interest in maintaining national sovereignty and domestic jurisdiction on the one hand, and their growing sense of responsibility for protecting minority rights on the other. As one official described it, "No debate in Committee is more animated or is followed with closer interest than the yearly discussion on Minority questions."[47] These intense discussions, when combined with the new treaty obligations, rulings, opinions, resolutions, and mechanisms, all marked new departures on behalf of international human rights. Indeed, it is estimated that as early as 1924 fifty different minorities with a total of thirty million people had come under the League's protection.[48]

Members of the League of Nations also turned their attention to protecting the rights of indigenous peoples in Africa, the Near East, and the Pacific brought under the new mandates system, trying to determine the meaning of such vague expressions in the Covenant as "the well-being and development" of these people and the "sacred trust of civilization." To begin this task, they created the Mandates Commission and decided to make it composed strictly of experts nominated by the Council rather than representatives of governments, along with an independent assessor from the International Labor Office, to signal that it was no longer acceptable to allow imperial powers to have complete free rein as in the past. Wellington Koo of China was named as its first chair. It held two long sessions every year, collecting materials, receiving petitions, examining reports, calling often-reluctant and resistant governors and other high officials before it, promoting humanitarian assistance, issuing reprimands against those who violated the letter of the law or the spirit of responsibility, and giving wide publicity to abuses through its published annual reports. As early as 1922, for example, South Africa found itself publicly criticized for abusing the rights of native tribes in South-West Africa. The Mandates Commission worked to secure the right of self-determination for Iraq, Syria, Lebanon, and Transjordan. In these efforts, the commission and the Assembly worked to place colonial administrators under continuous watch and open criticism, in the words of Lord Balfour, "to make it quite impossible that any transaction of general interest should take place except in the full glare of the noonday sun of public opinion."[49] In this way the majority of the League began distancing themselves from the old practice of direct, no-questions-asked, colonial annexation and abuse of native peoples, working instead to develop international norms establishing forcible conquest as no longer acceptable and a greater sense of responsibility for the rights of indigenous peoples.[50]

This growing concern for human rights focused attention on the matter of slavery as well. The Covenant specifically required nations with mandates to prohibit any remnants of the slave trade in territories under their control. To meet this responsibility, members of the League created a whole series of mandate treaties for the British, French, and Belgian in the Cameroons, Togoland, and East Africa, each of which contained explicit provisions dealing with slave trading, slaves, and forced labor. Similar terms appeared in those treaties creating the British, Australian, New Zealand, and Japanese mandates in the Pacific.[51] The League then established a Temporary Slavery Commission consisting of eight experts, instructing them to institute all necessary inquiries and make proposals for eradicating the last vestiges of slavery and the slave trade wherever they still existed. Their discovery of royal slaves, domestic servitude, and compulsory labor in Ethiopia, the Belgian Congo (now the Democratic Republic of the Congo), India, Sierra Leone, Rio de Oro, Borneo (now parts of Indonesia, Malaysia, and Brunei), New Guinea, Burma, Afghanistan, and the Hedjaz (now part of Saudi Arabia) convinced the commission that further action was necessary.[52] They thus created the comprehensive and far-reaching 1926 International Convention on the Abolition of Slavery and the Slave Trade with the formal obligation to progressively bring about "the complete abolition of slavery in all its forms."[53] The purpose, noted one observer, was to establish the international norm that personal freedom "is the rightful possession of every human being."[54]

Some of the most dramatic new departures by the League addressed the rights of women and children. The Covenant spoke of both only in the context of working conditions and illicit traffic, but this provided an opening that was quickly seized. NGOs such as the Women's International League for Peace and Freedom, Association Féminine Internationale, Union Internationale des Ligues Féminines Catholiques, and International Alliance of Women played extremely important roles in giving support for extending the franchise and in keeping the issue of equal rights constantly before the League, as they said, on behalf "of the whole world."[55] They took enormous pride in watching women's rights advance during the 1930s in Brazil, Ceylon, Chile, Cuba, India, Nicaragua, Peru, the Philippines, Romania, South Africa, Siam (now Thailand), Turkey, and Uruguay.[56] They also were pleased that the League made participation on the Council, Assembly, commissions, and secretariat open to females as well as males and began to address prostitution, consent in marriage, the exploitation of women, and the welfare of families. The League went on to successfully produce the International Convention for the Suppression of the Traffic in Women and Children in 1921 and the International Convention for the Suppression of the Traffic in Women of Full Age in 1933.[57] The delegations of Argentina, Bolivia, Cuba, Dominican Republic, Haiti, Honduras, Mexico, Panama, Peru, and Uruguay then all urged the League to extensively study the legal status and rights of women wherever they might be, Africa, the Americas, Asia, Europe, and the Pacific.[58]

Those attentive to women's rights often found themselves concerned about the rights of children as well, and many spoke of a relationship between being a woman and being a nurturing mother. As we have seen, one of the constant questions in human rights always has been: rights for whom? Up to this point in history, children had rarely even been considered in discussions about rights. But now, the pioneering work of Eglantyne Jebb and new NGOs such as Save the Children Fund, Jewish Association for the Protection of Girls and Women, Union Internationale de Secours aux Enfants, and Association Catholique Internationale des Œuvres des Protections de la Jeune Fille, pressure mounted on behalf of those least able to defend or care for themselves.[59] The League responded by creating the Advisory Committee for Child Welfare to address life and health in early infancy and childhood, while the International Council of Women asked the world to envision of the "inalienable rights" of every child.[60]

This vision of the natural, equal, and universal rights of all children led the League of Nations to create the very first declaration ever adopted by an international organization of sovereign nation-states on an issue of human rights: the 1924 Geneva Declaration of the Rights of the Child. Here, in language drafted by Jebb, the rights of children were coupled with the responsibilities of governments to the most vulnerable members of society, recognizing

that mankind owes to the Child the best that it has to give, declare and accept it as their duty [to act] beyond and above all considerations of race, nationality, or creed. . . . The child that is hungry must be fed; the child that is sick must be nursed; the child that is backward must be helped; the delinquent child must be reclaimed; and the orphan and the waif must be sheltered and succored.[61]

For the delegate from Japan, this declaration, along with other actions by the League, accurately reflected the universal concern for the rights of children across all other barriers and demonstrated how "so many nations in the different continents—nations of most varied customs, traditions, systems of morality, and civilizations—have joined forces, with that sense of responsibility of the human conscience which is the spiritual treasure of all mankind."[62]

Delegates used similar expressions as they began to address what they described as the right of all people to a minimum level of health. As difficult as it was to believe, recent explosions of influenza, typhus, cholera, and typhoid had been so severe that they actually claimed more lives than those killed during all of World War I. In order to care for the sick and to prevent such loss of life in the future, they created the innovative Health Organization of the League of Nations. Composed of skilled medical personnel from Europe, the Americas, and Asia, this body drew on leading scientific institutes and individual experts who often gave freely of their knowledge and time. It became one of the League's most successful operations and one whose output of work far exceeded its financial resources. Indeed, it was the Health Organization that often made the League a reality in distant places where it otherwise would have remained no more than an abstraction. With energy and zeal, it launched an international campaign against epidemics and leprosy, organized conferences on world health, sent missions to the Middle East and Asia, prepared studies of tropical diseases in Africa, drafted conventions for sanitation control, and established standards for vaccines. In light of new discoveries with vitamins and minerals, it also initiated pioneering studies on nutrition.

These startling reports publicized the fact that even in the richest countries, large numbers suffered from serious undernourishment, and that millions of people around the world were denied, through poverty or ignorance or government policy, their right to obtain the food necessary for basic life and health.[63] All of these efforts helped to establish the foundation of the World Health Organization of today. The League also created the Advisory Committee on Traffic in Opium and Other Dangerous Drugs to conduct investigations, criticize governments who colluded with traffickers, and draft the International Opium Convention of 1925 and the Convention for Limiting the Manufacture and Regulating the Distribution of Narcotic Drugs of 1931 for the first time giving an international body legal authority to regulate the importation of drugs.[64]

Members of the League of Nations also viewed issues of the right to life and health as applying not only to civilian populations but to military combatants. It is for this reason, and in the name of human rights, they worked to extend the coverage of humanitarian law. More specifically, they sought to establish that no one would ever become a victim of new and horrifying chemical and biological weapons. The League therefore created the famous Geneva Protocol of 1925 prohibiting the use in war of asphyxiating, poisonous, or other gases and of bacteriological agents. Although criticized at the time for being overly idealistic, it established a successful regime and led, in turn, to the 1929 Geneva Convention Relative to the Treatment of Prisoners of War, stipulating the obligations of states to guarantee that the captured and wounded "shall at all times be humanely treated and protected" with the right to receive medical attention and food and the right to be free from torture.[65]

The League launched even more new departures in human rights by assisting refugees. World War I had produced a flood of human victims, but the revolutions, civil wars, military coups, and other upheavals that followed unleashed even more. From Russia alone, at least two million men, women, and children were forced to flee from the new Bolshevik regime, warfare, and famine. War and violence in Turkey then drove more than one million Turks, Greeks, Armenians, and Assyrians out across borders. Wherever these refugees appeared, their desperate needs completely overwhelmed the capacities of national governments and all other private relief organizations. As one eyewitness painfully reported:

we found ourselves confronted with 140,000 Russians who had arrived . . . on some 75 ships in a starving condition. It was a sight I shall never forget. . . . Then some 75,000 Turkish refugees arrived. Hearing of the misery amongst them I went to visit some of the camps myself. A more pitiable sight I never saw. We then tried to help these unfortunate people. . . . Our task seemed hopeless. The calls for charity could not continue. The Americans were feeding some 17,500 Russians a day. The British Relief were feeding some 10,000 Russians and 10,000 Turks a day. The future became black indeed. Funds were exhausted. . . . The situation became very serious. . . . There appeared to be no machinery capable of dealing with this avalanche. . . . The death rate was appalling, reaching some 1,500 a week.[66]

Political philosopher Hannah Arendt described their fate in these words: "Once they had left their homeland they remained homeless, once they had left their state they became stateless, once they had been deprived of their human rights they were rightless."[67]

In the face of such tragic human suffering and lack of sufficient relief from any other source, appeals poured into the League to take action. But nothing in the Covenant obligated the organization to accept such magnitude of responsibilities. Nevertheless, after considerable debate, the majority became convinced that they simply could not turn their backs on these most unfortunate victims crying out for assistance. They concluded that refugees had "become a question of international importance," and thus decided to create the Refugee Organization.[68]

This body set out to meet these desperate needs. Its overworked and underfunded staff received much energy from its first commissioner, the dynamic Fridtjof Nansen of Norway. He turned those special qualities of courage, resoluteness, and inventiveness that had made him such a famous Arctic explorer facing the elements of nature now to the elements of people. He refused to be deterred by the odds or swayed from his vision of protecting the rights of refugees. Since they possessed no clear guidelines for this new departure, Nansen and his staff constantly experimented and did what they could, often taking great risks in their faith that somehow funds would come in. He constantly received personal appeals like the one pleading: "Those of us . . . who see this suffering and injustice at first hand, feel it keenly and the shame it casts on a so-called civilized age, beg you most earnestly to use your influence to end this impossible situation, something which no one else seems to have the power to do."[69] Time and time again, he responded by saying, "It must be possible to find some definite solution of the problem. . . . Whatever happens, we cannot allow this people to starve, that is obvious."[70] The Refugee Organization worked with the International Labor Organization and hundreds of dedicated volunteers from relief societies to send money, distribute food and clothes, provide medical attention, secure housing, seek employment, prepare legal documents, assist in evacuations, search for parents and children, and intervene with governments for the repatriation of individual refugees. Their activities extended from Asia to the Middle East and from Europe to Latin America. In addition, they invented something called the "Nansen Passport," a certificate that enabled stranded refugees stuck at border crossings to find an escape to freedom. The successes of these efforts established the foundation for what is now the United Nations High Commissioner for Refugees. In addition, they earned Nansen a Nobel Peace Prize and led others to describe him as a "creative genius" and a "saint" who "deserves the gratitude of all mankind" for saving "from misery and often from death hundreds of thousands of human beings."[71]

Other developments emerged as well. These included creating the International Relief Union, assisting victims of disasters through the International Committee of the Red Cross and the recently formed International Federation of Red Cross and Red Crescent Societies, marking the beginning of international refugee law with the Convention Relating to the International Status of Refugees, and founding the International Penal and Penitentiary Commission to work for the rights of prisoners.[72] In addition, the League wrestled with an always-difficult philosophical and political issue: the relationship between individual rights and responsibilities. As it poignantly noted,

While the Assembly recognizes the primary right of the Minorities to be protected by the League from oppression, it also emphasizes the duty incumbent upon persons belonging to racial, religious, or linguistic minorities to cooperate as loyal fellow-citizens with the nations to which they now belong.[73]

All of these many and varied activities marked significant new departures. The League launched out, seized unique opportunities, and increasingly brought together what had been a number of single-issue struggles into broader visions of interdependent and indivisible human rights. Its efforts on behalf of the rights of workers, the rights of ethnic and religious minorities, the rights of indigenous peoples in mandates, the rights of those still enslaved, the rights of women and children, the rights of all to a minimal standard of health, the rights of combatants, and the rights of refugees, among others, benefitted thousands upon thousands of people.

Persistent Problems and Challenges

Not all people embraced this "spirit of Geneva" and its visions of international human rights, however. In fact, many individuals and nations actively opposed any efforts to pursue this historical evolution. Instead, they squirmed, temporized, condemned the League of Nations as either no more than unrealistic sentiment or a dangerous threat, and firmly resisted any changes that might destroy their privileges. The persistence of vested interests, fear of the unknown, selfishness, skepticism, greed, prejudice, money and power, and the claims of national sovereignty all presented enormous challenges to those who worked on behalf of human rights.

In order to appreciate both the successes and the failures of the League, it is essential to understand that the organization, as a product of politics and diplomacy, reflected many uneasy compromises from the beginning. It resulted from the Versailles Treaty, tied to the end of a specific war, and authored by victors. Significant differences thus existed between the universalists who wanted all to participate and the exclusionists who wanted to restrict membership according to who won and who lost in World War I. The Minorities Treaties marked the differences between the idealists who wanted to promote a principle and the politicians desiring leverage over the vanquished and the weak. The composition and scope of its Mandates Commission represented the conflicts between the interests of the imperial powers who wanted to retain their colonial possessions and those who envisioning the right of self-determination. Moreover, constant struggles existed (as they would later under the United Nations) between those who desired to give the League expansive authority to extend human rights around the world and, on the other hand, those who felt no responsibility toward others whatsoever and who refused to move beyond the prerogatives of the sovereign nation-state.

Further problems existed from the outset. Despite Wilson's support for the organization, the United States not only refused to join the League at all, but during the early years, did much to deliberately obstruct its activities and diminish its effectiveness. Germany and the Soviet Union were initially denied membership. Britain and France held fundamental differences about what the organization should be allowed to do. Since it was composed of nation-states claiming sovereignty, the League never possessed any more authority or means than its members were willing to give it. The Council, composed primarily of the Great Powers, held considerable power over the larger and more representative Assembly, but in both cases no action could be taken without unanimity among all its members. The Covenant made provision for important exemptions by stating that certain subjects remained "solely within the domestic jurisdiction" of member states.[74] There were times when it was made clear that some agreements were not binding, but instead operated at the "discretion" of governments and served "as a recommendation only."[75] Such factors hardly boded well for the protection of human rights.

Beyond these immediate limitations of the League of Nations itself, however, were challenges of some old, larger, and perhaps more serious problems of history and global politics. This is precisely what Secretary of State Lansing meant when he described the lack of "altruistic cooperation" in the world and the "national selfishness and the mutual suspicions which control international relations."[76] These proved to be formidable obstacles, and came to confront every single one of the efforts made by the League. In so doing, they revealed the nature, strength, and persistence of the problems that would continue to reappear and, as we shall see, later plague the United Nations in its own struggles to advance international human rights.

The very creation of the League and its internationalist approach, for example, directly threatened the sovereignty of nation-states and their prerogatives as the major actors in international affairs. If an organization, however structurally flawed or compromised, could claim to speak on behalf of the people of the world as a whole, then the exclusive privileges held by nations thereby would be placed in jeopardy. What if the League somehow found a way to restrict the power of a state to unilaterally advance its own national interests or control its own people? What would happen if it suddenly decided to take action on behalf of the rights of racial or religious minorities, indigenous peoples, women, children, workers, refugees, immigrants, or anyone else heretofore regarded as subjects of domestic jurisdiction? When faced with such questions, some began to dig in their heels and resist. As one official complained:

I would say that it is much to be hoped that attempts . . . to regulate matters which are national in character, will be brought to an end, and that the League will in future more and more concern itself only with those tasks provided for in the Covenant.[77]

Others, like Australian Prime Minister Hughes, were even more direct, observing that matters "solely within the domestic jurisdiction of a nation" could not be "the proper subjects for inquiry" by the League. "We must choose," he declared, "between doing our way . . . [or] having the matter taken out of our hands."[78] Americans simply refused to be a part of the enterprise altogether. Raising all kinds of fears, Senator James Reed of Missouri posed a problem in language that speaks for itself: "Think of submitting questions involving the very life of the United States to a tribunal on which a nigger from Liberia, a nigger from Honduras, a nigger from India . . . each have votes equal to that of the great United States."[79] His colleague Henry Cabot Lodge, who led the fight for isolationism, declared bluntly, "We do not want a narrow alley of escape from jurisdiction of the League. We want to prevent any jurisdiction whatever."[80]

Resistance occurred in other ways as well. Despite the creation of the International Labor Organization and the series of treaties to protect the rights of workers, for example, governments presented one challenge after another. Albert Thomas, his staff, and their supporters were constantly accused of wasteful administration, of utilizing international labor legislation to interfere into the domestic affairs, of spreading class warfare propaganda, and of pushing beyond the organization's original intent or authority. One proposal elicited this response:

I say . . . this conference has no more jurisdiction over the question of the distribution of raw materials . . . than it has over the question of discovering a way of navigating from the earth to the moon. It might just as well be clearly understood that the nations . . . will deal with them as they believe fair and in the national interest . . . and they will not accept international regulations with reference to the control of their private property.[81]

Bitter complaints arose when the ILO granted small states the same vote as large states. Many business interests strongly resisted the imposition of the eight-hour day, changes in working conditions, international investigations or interference into their activities, or any other "dangerous innovations," and frequently placed considerable pressure on their governments to not ratify treaties for the rights of workers. More rabid critics engaged in what labor leaders described as reactionary "sinister attacks," publicly denouncing those involved with the International Labor Organization as being full of Communist revolutionaries, bent on destroying free enterprise, capitalism, national sovereignty, and the nation-state itself.[82]

Extremely serious problems also confronted those administering the Minorities Treaties—something described as "a hard and thankless task."[83] The politically explosive controversies surrounding the role of the League in enforcing these rights of racial, religious, and linguistic minorities were enormous. Those countries subjected to the provisions vehemently resisted providing protection, subverting enforcement when they could and complaining that they were being unfairly held to standards not applied to others. Indeed, by refusing to establish the universality of minority rights, the victors undermined the moral as well as the political basis for the international protection system.[84] As India reminded everyone, "there are minority questions outside Europe," pointing to those suffering discrimination in South Africa, and arguing for the need to believe "in one truth and one justice, universal for all men."[85] The Chinese delegate similarly insisted that this issue "raised not only the question of nationalities but that of races, and consequently directly concerned China."[86]

Several governments therefore proposed a resolution in 1925 to create a general convention obligating all members of the League to guarantee the rights of minorities. It met with immediate rejection. Two other attempts, one in 1930 and another in 1932, resulted in the same fate. Each time the powerful argued that the rights of minorities raised "very delicate matters" and "touched sensitive spots in many countries," declaring that they had no intention of surrendering control over their own citizens or subjects to an international organization. One government official, for example, tellingly revealed that, "even at the risk of a little local suffering," efforts to help protect minority rights should be avoided, for "as long as these people imagine that their grievances can be aired before the League of Nations they will refuse to settle down."[87] In addition, although the Minorities Committees agreed to receive petitions, the League's influential members insisted that such communications be regarded as simply informational reports rather than legal appeals, and that delegations of minority populations never be allowed to appear before the Council where only the accused governments could be represented and where they could prevent any punishments against themselves. To make matters even worse, it was always possible for states to make bilateral agreements on their own and actually force the hand of the League, as did the Greeks and the Turks with a convention in Lausanne that brutally expelled large numbers of minority populations between them.[88]

One of the reasons why some states so firmly resisted any international attention to minority protection, as the Chinese among other non-Europeans quickly pointed out, was the persistent problem of race. Many nations, especially those of white settlement, possessed significant racial minorities (or even majorities) descended from indigenous peoples, slaves, or, more recently, immigrants. Most of these people suffered as victims of prejudice, experiencing severe racial discrimination through variations of segregation or apartheid, denial of civil and political rights, unequal protection under the law, and exclusion. Those very states who had prevented a racial equality clause in the Covenant of the League at the Paris Peace Conference did not change their minds or their hearts. In fact, they actually intensified their policies and their abrasive public statements about "race wars," "racial alliances," "racial purity," and the "Yellow Peril," insisting that all such matters remained exclusively within their domestic jurisdiction.[89] "The 'racial equality' question in its present state," stated one confidential and blunt memorandum from the British Foreign Office,

primarily concerns the following countries: Japan, China, British India, United States of America (especially California and the Pacific States), Canada, Australia, New Zealand, South Africa. The first three countries demand the right of free immigration and freedom from discrimination disabilities for their nationals in the territories of the last five countries. The question can be regarded from an economic or from a political point of view, but in its essence it is a racial one. . . . The white and the colored races cannot and will not amalgamate. One or the other must be the ruling caste.

The report concluded that the international racial issue would remain "highly combustible," presenting a problem for which there was "no solution" and "no cure."[90]

Attitudes such as these more than manifested themselves when groups suffering from racial discrimination approached the League of Nations for assistance. If they came from countries under the Minorities Treaties, they likely would be allowed to at least submit a petition. If they came from any other nation, however, and operated under the mistaken assumption that the provisions about nondiscrimination in these treaties somehow would apply to them as well, they faced rejection. When the National Colored World Democracy Congress asked the League to support the principle of racial equality and "the ultimate ascendancy of the Right over Might," their request was denied.[91] When Du Bois and the Pan-African congresses called on the League to "turn its attention to the great racial problem," to "promote Peace and Justice," and to "take a firm stand on the absolute equality of races," it refused to budge.[92] The same refusal confronted Marcus Garvey and his Universal Negro Improvement Association claiming members in Africa, the West Indies, South and Central America, North America, Europe, and Asia when they approached the League stating: "Your Petitioners desire to impress upon you the fact that the four hundred million Negroes of the world are no longer disposed to hold themselves as serfs, peons, and slaves, but that it is their intention to look forward to the higher benefits of human liberty, human rights, and true democracy."[93] More petitions poured in from South Africa, Australia, New Zealand, India, France, Cuba, Canada, and the United States, among other countries. Regardless of whether they were typed and eloquent in their use of language, or arrived handwritten on notepaper with misspellings and improper grammar, they all demanded the same thing: racial equality.

These many petitions and pleas placed the League of Nations in a most difficult position and exposed a serious dilemma. As internal staff noted, "They have a real case which we cannot totally ignore and should not greatly encourage." If the League tried to respond positively to the petitioners, it would exceed the authority given to it by its members, threaten vested interests, and alienate powerful states. To address letters from the United States drawing attention to the horrifying practice of lynching, for example, warned one official confidentially, "might antagonize many of our friends in America, who might think that the League was meddling in the Negro question in the States, where this question is a very burning one."[94] Yet, if it did not respond, the League would violate its own stated principles of higher purpose and the expectations of millions of people around the world, thereby subjecting itself to charges of double standards and hypocrisy.

When faced with this dilemma, the majority of members refused to let the League provide any assistance. Consequently, when Du Bois, Garvey, the Maori leader from New Zealand T. W. Ratana, or others traveled to Geneva to personally deliver their pleas, they were told over and over again that "the rules of procedure" did not allow for consideration of their requests and that "it is not possible for the Secretariat to take up this question."[95] When Deskaheh, a leader of the Six Nations Iroquois Confederacy, tried to present a petition that he called *The Redman's Appeal for Justice*, he received a sympathetic hearing from Persia, Ireland, Estonia, and Panama, but anger from Canada, which described it as "absurd," and from Britain, which blocked any formal consideration by warning that it constituted "impertinent interference in internal affairs."[96] In fact, the flood of petitions about racial discrimination proved so embarrassing that a majority in League found it necessary in 1928 to reaffirm national sovereignty and domestic jurisdiction by declaring their determination "to insure that states with a minority within their borders should be protected from the danger of interference by other powers in their internal affairs."[97]

Similarly, despite the often heroic efforts of the Mandates Commission, the imperial powers continually resisted any international attempts to interfere in their control over indigenous peoples. Some of them spoke openly in the Assembly itself of those under their jurisdiction with black, yellow, brown, or red skin color as the less-than-fully human "savage races," "uncivilized races," and "savage hordes"—rather than as people.[98] One delegate even included in the official records a suggestion made to impose a system of segregation in the mandates and "to prevent equality between white and black, to uphold the status of the white men."[99] Others described the commission as "an unfriendly intruder" and "an unwelcomed critic," arguing that the League could only advise on the mandates but most certainly not exercise control.[100] Some simply could not restrain their hostility toward those who struggled for independence from empire or sought the League's assistance in gaining the right of self-determination. Winston Churchill in Britain vehemently reacted to what he described as "the nauseating and humiliating spectacle of this one-time Inner Temple lawyer, now seditious fakir, striking half-naked up the steps of the Viceroy's palace, there to negotiate and parley on equal terms with the representative of the King-Emperor," declaring that "Gandhism and all it stands for must ultimately be . . . finally crushed."[101] With attitudes like these, decolonization would have to wait until yet another world war shattered the strength of imperial powers beyond recognition or repair. But until this occurred, the majority of the League's membership would stay in the hands of white Europeans.

Resistance to human rights occurred in other ways as well. When negotiating the International Convention on the Abolition of Slavery and the Slave Trade, to illustrate, several states worked to restrict enforcement and challenged the very competence of the League to even address this matter. "In all questions of this nature," declared the Belgian government with many skeletons in its own closet, "the League of Nations and its organizations cannot engage in any investigation except through the intermediary of the States directly concerned."[102] When dealing with women's rights or the Geneva Declaration of the Rights of the Child, some delegates expressed dismay over the interest in women in the first place, protested that children either had no rights at all (or that if they did they had no place in the deliberations of an international organization), or that all matters of family relationships should remain exclusively within the domestic jurisdiction of nation-states. Even in seemingly neutral matters of the right of health, opposition occurred. India, the Dutch East Indies, the Malay states, and other British, French, and Portuguese possessions that drew revenue from the opium trade all resisted strict international controls, and countries with powerful pharmaceutical industries such as Switzerland opposed limitations on narcotic drug manufactures. The Refugee Organization generated opposition from those who argued that they should not be asked to contribute funds or assistance to "foreigners" when their "own people" were starving and out of work. Human rights activists in NGOs such as the Fédération International des Droits de l'Homme and the Women's International League for Peace and Freedom constantly found themselves unwanted and criticized by governments who resented their "interference" and "pushful energy."[103]

Opposition also arose when it appeared that progress was about to be made. When the League sponsored a conference on the progressive development of international law, for example, a Jewish lawyer from Poland by the name of Raphael Lemkin (who would eventually coin the word "genocide") proposed a treaty making the destruction of national, religious, or ethnic groups a crime. States adamantly refused to accept his proposal.[104] Similarly, as a result of the shocking assassinations of the king of Yugoslavia and the foreign minister of France, delegates at the League reached a ground-breaking decision in 1937. They agreed to draft a treaty for the prevention and punishment of terrorism, including an enforcement provision known as the Convention for the Creation of an International Criminal Court to try offenses.[105] Nevertheless, government leaders regarded this as too threatening to the prevailing culture of impunity and their claims of national sovereignty. In the end, not one ratified the convention.

Such persistent and determined resistance by so many governments insisting on their own sovereignty, in addition to the structural limitations of the League of Nations itself, made the struggle for human rights exactly that—a struggle. The many committees, commissions, affiliated bodies, NGOs, declarations, and treaties launching new departures all sought to bring visions of human rights into reality. But in the near absence of enforcement capabilities, these efforts fundamentally depended on moral suasion and voluntary cooperation. At times these worked. On other occasions, as one report noted in frustration, "these were often not enough."[106]

The Gathering Storm

The frustrations caused by these problems and challenges soon began to be replaced by fears, for even more severe and foreboding storm clouds gathered ominously on the horizon. With the emergence of Benito Mussolini and the Fascist Party in Italy, the dictatorship of Joseph Stalin in the Soviet Union, the rise of militarism in Japan, and Adolf Hitler and Nazism in Germany, those who held visions of international human rights had reasons for profound concern. None of these regimes believed in internationalism, "universal laws of humanity," the "conscience of mankind," the League of Nations, gender equity, or racial equality. None cared about protecting the rights of individuals. Instead, they all sought to overthrow the international order by glorifying the nation-state and its sovereignty, increasing power over people, securing discipline through submission and blind obedience, gaining territory by conquest, and literally destroying those at home or abroad who stood in their way.

Mussolini lashed out at any foreign criticism of his actions as unwarranted interference. When the League condemned Japanese aggression against Manchuria in 1931, Japan simply walked out and severed all connections with the organization and its values. Even before coming to power, Hitler had used his autobiographical *Mein Kampf* (My Struggle) to promote the German nation and its superior "master race," denounce Communists and liberals, curse Jews, and describe the League of Nations as a worthless body of idealists with "pious hopes" foolishly chasing after a "phantom." Visions of international human rights, individual worth, compassion for others, care for the persecuted or exploited, responsibilities beyond borders toward victims of abuse, and racial or gender equality, he asserted, were "drivel" invented by cowards, weaklings, religious fanatics, bleeding hearts, and fools—"for Nature does not know them." Armed struggle alone is the father of all things, wrote Hitler, declaring: "When the nations on this planet fight for existence . . . then all considerations of humanitarianism . . . crumble into nothingness."[107]

It did not take long for such attitudes to dramatically impact policy. Indeed, immediately on assuming power in January 1933, Hitler set about to put these ideas into practice and build the edifice of the Third Reich. A series of acts and ordinances enabled him to rule by decree and thereby make himself a dictator. He abolished civil and political rights, unleashed the police and his own storm troopers to sow fear and terrorize opponents, arrested alleged enemies of the state at will, and made anti-Semitism official state policy. Jews were removed from the civil service, the professions, businesses, and education. The regime declared that all these actions fell within the prerogatives of national sovereignty and, thus, that it could do exactly as it wished.

To the German government's shock, however, this position was suddenly challenged by a single man who decided to transform this domestic matter into an international issue by taking his case directly to the League of Nations. His name was Franz Bernheim, a thirty-two-year-old German national of Jewish descent who declared that he had been unfairly and illegally discharged from his job in Upper Silesia solely as a result of Hitler's decrees. This action, he claimed, represented a serious violation of his rights and of the specific minority clauses of the German-Polish Convention guaranteeing equal protection of the law without discrimination as to race, language, or religion. Bernheim also argued that the convention assigned the League authority to pronounce judgments on either individual or collective petitions addressed to it by members of a minority. Consequently, he submitted a petition requesting the Council to declare these Nazi measures against Jews to be null and void for Upper Silesia, and then to issue instructions that the victims be "reinstated in their rights."[108]

This sudden, direct, and highly public petition from "an unknown Jew" threw down the gauntlet—both to Hitler and to the League.[109] Some viewed it as remarkably courageous. Others saw it as dangerously foolhardy and likely to cost Bernheim his life. It directly challenged Hitler, and thus the German delegate in Geneva was instructed in no uncertain terms: "Debate on the Jewish question in the League Council is absolutely undesirable, and is to be avoided at all costs."[110] But it also challenged the credibility of the League of Nations itself. If it did nothing, then no international treaty dealing with human rights was safe and the League's reputation would be in shambles; but if it did something, and actually enforced the treaty, then national sovereignty would be diminished and this would set a precedent that might affect other member states. Here was a dramatic contest before the eyes of the world between international human rights on the one hand and the claims of national sovereignty on the other.

The League thus found itself forced to address one of the most fundamental of all issues of international human rights: how can states, even when acting collectively, respond to abuses in other countries? As such, predicted one correspondent, it "may turn out to be the most important matter to come before the seventy-second session of the Council of the League of Nations."[111] Unprecedented time consequently was devoted to what the representative of Mexico described as "the great difficulties" raised by this case.[112] Here their debate ranged from very specific questions over whether Bernheim had legal standing and could submit a petition in the first place, to much larger issues such as whether the League possessed the competence or the "moral right" to deal with this matter, the difficulty posed by protecting minorities in some countries gutmachung geleistet werde.

VI./　　　Der unterzeichnete Franz Bernheim bittet
ferner, das Generalsekretariat des Völkerbundes,
dieser Petition <u>Dringlichkeit</u> zuzuerkennen.

　　　Er begründet diese Bitte damit, dass, wie die
oben zitierten Gesetze und Verordnungen beweisen,
die Durchführung des Grundsatzes der Ungleichheit
gegenüber den Reichsangehörigen nichtarischer,
also jüdischer Abstammung, systematisch auf allen
Gebieten des privaten und öffentlichen Lebens fort-
gesetzt und durchgeführt werden, dass bereits eine
Unzahl von jüdischen Existenzen vernichtet wurde,
und dass bei fortgesetzter Anwendung dieser heute
im Deutschen Reiche geltenden Tendenzen in kür-
zester Zeit sämtliche Juden in ihrer Existenz dau-
ernden Schaden gelitten haben werden, sodass irgend-
eine Wiedereinsetzung und Wiedergutmachung dann
unmöglich sein wird, und viele Tausende und Zehn-
tausende in ihrer Existenz vollkommen zugrunde ge-
richtet sein werden.

8 Beilagen
Prag, am 12. Mai 1933

Franz Bernheim

Osvědčuji !

Figure 6. A Single Individual Appeals to the International Community: The Bernheim Petition.
Archives de la Société des Nations.

but not all, the relationships between international and municipal law, the conflicting claims of international organizations and national sovereignty, and the likely reaction of world public opinion if the League obfuscated or refused to take any meaningful action. After careful consultation with the Committee of Jurists, the Council decided that the discrimination as charged was a breach of treaty obligations and that Bernheim should receive compensation. It also and importantly ruled that the interests of a minority *could* be represented by one individual, and that an offense against an individual was ipso facto against the entire minority to which he or she belonged.[113] This decision opened the floodgates for even more serious and intense debate.

When the Assembly of the League took up this matter during its sessions of September and October 1933, the lines were more sharply drawn. By this time the delegates had become much more aware not just of Bernheim but of the much larger problem of persecution throughout Nazi Germany; and some, especially those from Denmark, Sweden, and Norway, were fully determined to bring this matter to international attention. If they did not evince sufficient concern about the fate of these victims, or privately admitted that they were "very much averse from raising this question at Geneva in any form,"[114] then individual citizens and NGOs such as the Federation of League of Nations Unions or the World Jewish Congress applied pressure to take action.[115] Reports revealed increased physical violence and coercion, serious deprivations of rights, and growing numbers of refugees tragically forced to flee their country. The sudden and sensational personal appearance of Joseph Goebbels, the Nazi propaganda minister who often served as Hitler's mouthpiece, in Geneva itself raised the stakes even higher. What price were the members of the League prepared to pay for the principle of meeting their international responsibilities to protect the human rights of minorities? The German government argued that this was "a purely internal affair," insisting that the "Jewish problem" fell exclusively within its domestic jurisdiction and thus remained completely outside the authority of the League.[116]

This kind of argument and these developments profoundly troubled those concerned about international human rights, and did so for good reason. They watched in alarm and outrage as the League found itself confronted with the Bernheim petition, the seeming inability to protect minorities, and reports of brutal abuses by totalitarian regimes. Unwilling to simply sit by and watch this gathering storm rise and their visions collapse in the process, they determined to speak out. One of these was Haiti's representative Antoine Frangulis, who would soon be described as "the delegate of the rights of man."[117] He insisted that human rights were natural, equal, and universal; but despaired over the fact that recent experience revealed these rights "so ardently desired for the nations has not yet been given any real international guarantee in the domestic sphere of the different countries."[118] Frangulis believed that the place to begin was in the recognition that

there is not only one category of citizens of a State, described as a minority, which deserves attention, but . . . all the citizens of which human communities are made up are entitled to the same freedom and the same protection, [and] the League of Nations must consider the problem as a whole from the aspect of the rights of man—that is to say, of the rights which men possess as such, whether they belong to a minority or a majority—and it must seek the solutions which are necessary.

He therefore proposed that the League draft a comprehensive, universal "world convention" for the protection of human rights everywhere.[119] Other delegates offered support as well.

But once again, these proposed plans on behalf of human rights confronted their old adversaries of vested interests, prejudice, and national sovereignty. Despite whatever diplomatic niceties governments might say in public sessions, or denunciations that they might level against Nazi behavior against Jews, once these proposals were sent into committee behind closed doors, opposition reared its head. The majority of members might profess loyalty to the principle of minority protection, but they had no interest at all in any general convention with enforcement mechanisms that might be used against them. They began by trying to discredit the human rights activists in NGOs as "people of no great importance."[120] More seriously, they feared that if they extended protection to minorities not yet covered by the treaties, the obligations incurred might risk outside intervention into their own domestic affairs, force them to eliminate immigration restrictions, and encourage racial minorities or separatists within their own countries or indigenous peoples within their colonies to be more assertive in demanding rights.[121] As one British official said, he "did not wish to be quoted," but declared that "the acceptance of such a proposal by His Majesty's Government would be entirely impossible in view of our colonial empire."[122] He and other opponents knew that the League itself possessed no power other than that given to it by member states—and they were willing to give very little. In the end, the Assembly could muster enough votes only to reaffirm "the hope" that all nations would treat minorities with justice. Proposals for more universal protection for human rights, thus, in the words of one delegate, "fell to the ground."[123]

To make matters even worse, Hitler then abruptly announced that Germany would completely withdraw from membership in the League of Nations and would treat its minorities exactly as it wished. This immediately cast long shadows elsewhere, for it encouraged Poland, Hungary, and Romania to declare that now they no longer needed to honor their commitments to protect the rights of their own minorities either. The storm clouds grew all the more ominous.

But this represented only part of the picture, for unparalleled assaults on human rights occurred on several fronts. In the Soviet Union, Stalin ruthlessly imposed his dictatorship. He forced the disposition and deportment of millions of peasants and "class enemies" into government-controlled collective farms against their will. Resistance led to execution or death by starvation. The complete disregard for human life is revealed by the fact that the state published statistics on the number of deaths of livestock—but not people. Writer Boris Pasternak describes the sheer magnitude of this assault as so horrendous as to "not fit within the bounds of consciousness."[124] Stalin further initiated what is still known as the "Great Terror," sending his secret police out as agents to persecute, to purge, to exile into prison camps in the Siberian Gulag, and to kill through mass extrajudicial executions those who opposed him. The precise numbers will never be known, but estimates of human lives lost under Stalin's regime run into the millions.[125]

After suppressing human rights throughout Italy, Mussolini in 1935 launched a war against Ethiopia, itself a member of the League of Nations, deliberately bombing hospitals marked with the Red Cross insignia, shamelessly using outlawed mustard gas, and attacking defenseless women and children, all while describing black Ethiopians as less-than-fully human. He then issued his infamous Manifesto of Fascist Racism, openly declaring: "It is time that the Italians proclaimed themselves frankly racist."[126] In 1936 General Francisco Franco initiated a civil war in Spain that would destroy liberty in that country and bring the international conflict between democracy and dictatorship to new intensity. At the same time, and in complete violation of the rule of law and obligations of the Versailles Treaty, Hitler announced rearmament for the German army, the creation of an air force, and the occupation of the demilitarized Rhineland.

While these events stunned Europe and Africa, Japan's lust for conquest led to terrible assaults on human rights in Asia. Its deliberate 1937 bombardment against innocent civilians in Shanghai was soon followed by its brutal "Rape of Nanking." Here, the word "rape" is not used figuratively—but literally. The reason for this is that it accurately describes the horrific atrocities perpetrated against ten of thousands of victims at the hands of Japanese soldiers, repulsively captured on photographs. As Iris Chang, who has studied this case carefully, writes:

> it is shocking to contemplate that the deaths at Nanking far exceeded the deaths from the American raids on Tokyo . . . and even the combined death toll of the two atomic blasts at Hiroshima and Nagasaki. . . . The rape of Nanking should be remembered not only for the number of people slaughtered but for the cruel manner in which many met their deaths. Chinese men were used for bayonet practice and decapitation contests. An estimated 20,000–80,000 Chinese women were raped. Many soldiers went beyond rape. . . . So sickening was the spectacle that even the Nazis in the city were horrified, one proclaiming the massacre to be the work of "bestial machinery."[127]

To make the situation even worse, further human suffering occurred simultaneously with the ravages of the Great Depression. Serious unemployment, poverty, starvation, homelessness, and economic and social collapse all severely stressed democratic institutions and international efforts by the League. Many governments began to question why they should expend money and effort on foreigners beyond their borders when they could not even feed or house or employ their own nationals suffering at home. For this reason, they voted to close to the critical Refugee Organization and refused to contribute any further funds, leaving helpless victims in a state of desperation.

Those with visions of international human rights watched these developments with horror. Much of the world and many of their accomplishments seemed to be falling apart before their eyes as dictatorships displaced democracies, depression crushed prosperity, hatred overrode compassion, violence (especially armed force against innocents) overpowered reason, and isolationism and extreme nationalism overwhelmed international cooperation. The majority of members of the League of Nations would not bring themselves to grant sufficient authority to the organization to keep its commitments or fulfill its responsibilities, to have international law cover the relation of the citizen to the state as well as the relations between states, to impose sanctions, or to take meaningful collective action. Instead, they sought refuge in narrow definitions of interests and security, reduced support for projects that might cause political problems, and worried that if they interfered with the sovereignty of other states they would become victims themselves. "The trouble with the League," observed one human rights advocate from Brazil in frustration, "is not the *League*, it is the *Nations*."[128] When the League's High Commissioner for Refugees realized that national governments were only ignoring his reports about horrendous abuses and his observations about the connection between human rights at home and international peace and security abroad, he announced that he could no longer remain silent and publicly resigned in the name of "common humanity."[129] "We had hoped," sighed an exhausted Nansen, "for a disarmament of souls: but the spirit of hostility and national hatred is growing worse than ever. . . . Everything that happens seems to hasten the catastrophe. We have decided for a policy of words."[130] At this stage, members of the League expressed only "concern," "noted" aggression, and "deplored" violations of human rights.

This lesson was not lost on the dictators and those bent on aggression. Seeing no visible international restraints to keep them in check either at home or abroad, they believed that they could proceed as they wished without fear of serious consequences. Hitler, in particular, directed the mechanisms of the state to escalate the process of "Aryanization" to secure "racial purity." The venomous publication *Neues Volk* poured out articles praising Mussolini's racist policies in Ethiopia, America's segregation and lynching as well as the "efficiency" of earlier genocide against Native Americans, British and French conquest of indigenous colored peoples, exclusion of Asians through immigration restrictions, and intense hatred against Jews.[131] State-sponsored anti-Semitism ignited the ferocity and brutality of Kristallnacht (Night of Broken Glass) in November 1938 when Nazis and their supporters launched an orgy of violence—not in dark corners but rampaging through the streets in full public view. Arrests, beatings, the burning and dynamiting of synagogues, and looting and destruction of Jewish businesses received official endorsement. As an ominous sign of even more tragic events to come, several thousand Jews were shipped off to concentration camps bearing names that would soon bring terror when spoken: Dachau, Sachsenhausen, and Buchenwald. That same year, Hitler seized Austria and, with the open assistance of those who appeased him, dismembered Czechoslovakia. In March 1939 he marched into Prague. All this simply whetted his appetite for more. He consequently instructed his generals to prepare for the coming war in words that speak for themselves:

I have put my death-head formations in place with the command relentlessly and without compassion to send into death many women and children of Polish origin and language. Only thus can we gain the living space that we need. Who after all is today speaking about the destruction of the Armenians?

"Close your hearts to pity," he ordered, and "act brutally." [132]

*   *   *

Given these incredibly hostile times, severe limitations, and the active resistance of so many governments between the wars, the surprise should not be that in the end the

League of Nations collapsed (for so did the whole international system)—but that it accomplished anything at all. That the League did so is remarkable testimony to those men and women with visions who, despite the limited means at their disposal, seized the opportunities, confronted the problems and challenges, and labored so hard to make the enterprise work. Especially in the technical and specialized fields, the achievements of the International Labor Organization, the Minorities Committees and supervision of the Minorities Treaties, the judgments of the Permanent Court of International Justice, the determined and courageous investigations of the Mandates Commission, the work of the Slavery Commission and its International Convention on the Abolition of Slavery and the Slave Trade, the active promotion of the rights of women and the Geneva Declaration of the Rights of the Child, the hands-on care and extensive studies of the Health Organization, the Geneva Protocol and Conventions on humanitarian law in times of war, and the tenacious assistance the Refugee Organization provided to many thousands of suffering human beings all bear witness to remarkable efforts in the face of extraordinary difficulties. Never before in history had members of the global community ventured so far into what had long been held to be matters exclusively within the domestic jurisdiction of states or attempted so much in the name of international human rights. These efforts would provide invaluable practical experiences, establish several institutional foundations that last to this day, and eventually inspire those who followed with the United Nations holding visions of their own. Before any of this could happen, however, the world would experience still further—and staggering—horrors of war and genocide.

Chapter 5
A "People's War"

The Crusade of World War II

> This is in very truth a people's war. It is a war which cannot be won until the fundamental rights of the peoples of the earth are secured. In no other manner can a true peace be achieved. . . . We must pursue this with courage and with vision.
>
> —Sumner Welles of the United States

The trauma of World War II shook the world to its very foundations. Never before in human history had any armed conflict resulted in so many deaths, such massive devastation, or so much global upheaval. For six brutal years, this total war extended to most parts of the world, consumed the financial and material resources developed over generations, ignited what many called an international "race war," fanned hatreds that produced horrifying genocide, mobilized science and the mysteries of the atom into instruments of mass destruction, and exposed entire populations of men, women, and children to horrifying death. Very important, more civilians lost their lives than did combatants. For this reason, participants often described this war as a "people's war"[1] that consumed not only those in uniform but everyone caught in its inferno.

It is difficult to imagine that a war of this magnitude, lasting for so long, spreading across the globe, and causing the deaths of perhaps sixty million human beings could ever possibly create, at the same time, new and unanticipated opportunities for the advancement of international human rights. But it did. World War II was a test not only of weapons and warriors, but of values and ideas. Its horrors exposed, as nothing else had ever been able to do, the ultimate consequences of allowing nations to hide behind the shield of national sovereignty. It forced people as never before to examine themselves, their past, and their values in a mirror, and to begin the process of redefining the meaning of "security," "peace," "justice," and "human rights." It also provided confirmation of the adage that "war is the great equalizer," for by requiring the total mobilization of all resources, the war brought about the emergence—and sometimes even the liberation—of many victims heretofore subjected to race, gender, or class discrimination as well as smaller nations and colonial populations. They had been excluded in the past, but now were enabled to be heard. Moreover, by becoming a "people's war," this struggle compelled governments to enunciate the principles and aims for which they were fighting and to bring them into the mainstream of political discussion. This elaborate process, with its many interconnecting variables forged in the intense crucible of war, became a crusade that set into motion what would become a veritable revolution in international human rights.

War, Genocide, and Self-Reflections

When World War II began in 1939, only the most idealistic few could possibly hold out any hope for the future of human rights. The aggressors operated nearly at will. Mechanized forces of the Third Reich crushed Poland with a *Blitzkrieg* lasting only a few weeks. They quickly conquered Denmark, Norway, the Netherlands, Belgium, and Luxembourg, and then marched under the Arc de Triomphe in Paris itself as France capitulated. Seemingly invincible, Hitler launched the Battle of Britain and ordered the deliberate use of aerial bombardment to pound civilian populations into submission. German forces then moved to assist Mussolini's troops in the territorial conquest of Yugoslavia, Greece, Crete, and North Africa. In June 1941 Hitler invaded Russia, declaring that this would be no ordinary military conflict but a war of extermination requiring unmerciful, unrelenting ruthlessness. Toward this end, he gave orders to the *Einsatzgruppen*, or mobile killing squads, for "special tasks": round up innocent civilians in occupied territories, march them naked toward open ditches (such as those in the ravine outside Kiev known as Babi Yar), and then kill them by the hundreds of thousands. International jurists estimated that perhaps two million defenseless human beings in Russia alone were murdered in this way, describing it as "a crime of such unprecedented brutality and such inconceivable savagery that the mind rebels against its own thought image and the imagination staggers in the contemplation of a human degradation beyond the power of language to adequately portray."[2]

Not content with this kind of murder, the Nazis determined to pursue their obsession of "cleansing" presumed "inferiors" from the face of the earth in an "ideological and biological" struggle of race undeterred by any legal or moral limitations. Hitler appointed Heinrich Himmler as the Reichsführer SS and gave him the power to engage in whatever "special treatment" might be necessary. This took the form of segregation, expropriation, internment, forced labor, deportation, and murder of all Jews, "degenerate-looking Orientals," "the Asian-Mongol virus" of Slavs, and others deemed to be racial *Untermenschen*, subhumans.[3] When it appeared that the mass shootings and mobile asphyxiation vans would not be sufficient for the task, camps began to be constructed at places such as Auschwitz, Chelmno, Belzec, Sobibor, Majdanek, and Treblinka for one terrifying purpose: massive and systematic extermination.

The military triumphs of the Germans in Europe and North Africa whetted the appetites of Japanese expansionists. The fall of the Netherlands and France, and the absorption of Britain in her own survival, meant that these countries could not possibly defend their Asian and Pacific colonial possessions that now appeared ripe for the taking. Thus undeterred, Japanese troops invaded Indochina and Thailand, again attacking innocent civilians. At this stage the only power standing in the way of further conquest in the Philippines, Burma, Singapore, the Malayan Peninsula, and Indonesia was a very uncertain United States.

The United States, of course, had not played a significant role in international affairs since the Paris Peace Conference twenty years earlier. It had refused to join the League of Nations at all, obstructed a number of international human rights efforts, and pursued a policy of isolationism. The military successes of the aggressors, however, shattered the illusion that it could remain aloof from global affairs. This forced President Franklin Roosevelt to begin serious self-reflection and to formulate a response. To do this, he sent Under Secretary of State Sumner Welles on a critical fact-finding mission. Welles, who soon would work hard to promote human rights during the war, reported back that he saw only increasing drift and an absence of security. "What is imperatively required," he pointedly told Roosevelt, "is statesmanship of the highest character, marked by vision, courage, and daring."[4]

The president responded to this challenge in a message to Congress and the nation by speaking forcefully not just about the interests of the United States, but about the world at large. Here he discussed the relationship between domestic liberties and international security, peace, and justice. He proclaimed that he sought to secure "four essential human freedoms": freedom of speech and expression, freedom of worship, freedom from want, and freedom from fear—"everywhere in the world." "Freedom," he declared, "means the supremacy of human rights everywhere. Our support goes to those who struggle to gain those rights or keep them." This, he concluded, "is no vision of a distant millennium. It is a definite basis for a kind of world attainable in our own time and generation."[5]

To move in this direction, Roosevelt became increasingly aware of the fact that, although his country was technically still a nonbelligerent, he needed to formulate with Prime Minister Winston Churchill a joint strategy and to respond to growing pressure from within their respective countries to declare a common purpose.[6] They agreed to meet secretly in August 1941 "somewhere in the Atlantic."[7] Roosevelt and Churchill, traveling along with their staffs (including Sumner Welles), rendezvoused off the Newfoundland coast under heavy naval protection.[8] They had corresponded with each other at length and admired each other from afar, but now met each other for the first time and joined together for a Sunday morning religious service on the quarterdeck, with several hundred sailors and marines standing under the imposing barrels of fourteen-inch guns singing "Onward, Christian Soldiers" and "O God, Our Help in Ages Past." As Churchill later described the event with obvious emotion, "Every word seemed to stir the heart. It was a great hour to live. [Yet] nearly half those who sang were soon to die."[9]

Together they discussed the details of the United States serving as "the arsenal of democracy," of lend-lease assistance to Britain and Russia, and of strategies to combat the aggressors in Europe, North Africa, and Asia. They also issued an eight-point declaration of less than 400 words known as the Atlantic Charter, the most famous result of their meeting. It had been initially suggested by Roosevelt and a draft on stationery from 10 Downing Street had been written by a somewhat reluctant Churchill. Here they held out an expansive vision of "their hopes for a better future": freedom of trade

Figure 7. The Crusade Begins: Roosevelt, Churchill, and the Atlantic Charter. Franklin D. Roosevelt Library.

and of the seas, "the right of all peoples to choose the form of government under which they will live," the right to have "improved labor standards, economic advancement, and social security" in all nations, the right of "all" to "live out their lives in freedom from want and fear," and "a wider and permanent system of general security" for the world.[10] By having the leaders of two such powerful nations publicly speak out on behalf of individual rights rather than only the traditional interests and prerogatives of nation-states, and by emphasizing that these rights applied within as well as across national borders, in the recent words of one authority, the Atlantic Charter "was positively revolutionary."[11]

Both Roosevelt and Churchill sought to use the Atlantic Charter to delineate a sharp contrast between themselves and their adversaries and to provide principles around which their people could rally for a crusade. Both knew from their own experiences in leading their nations through difficult times about the power of visions and words, and thus sought to bring them to bear. The Voice of America quickly seized the Charter as a banner to rally forces around the globe, and Welles described it as "the agreement that was to bind together the United Nations."[12] It immediately received the enthusiastic endorsement of the first meeting of the Inter-Allied Council and of more than thirty countries meeting at an International Labor Organization conference. It also greatly impressed two New Zealand leaders with strong religious and labor backgrounds who soon would make very significant contributions to international human rights far out of proportion to the size of their country. One of these, Peter Fraser, who had been imprisoned for opposing conscription during World War I, but now as prime minister participated in the War Cabinet discussions in London, viewed it as a most welcomed contribution to international human rights. His close colleague and deputy Walter Nash described it as "a modern charter of human liberties" and without hesitation predicted that it constituted nothing short of "a declaration more potent for good than any other in the records of human history."[13] In addition, its universal principles greatly impressed a young black lawyer in South Africa named Nelson Mandela, who writes in his autobiography:

The Atlantic Charter of 1941 . . . reaffirmed faith in the dignity of each human being and propagated a host of democratic principles. Some in the West saw the Charter as empty promises, but not those of us in Africa. Inspired by the Atlantic Charter and the fight of the Allies against tyranny and oppression, the ANC [African National Congress] created its own Charter, called African Claims, which called for full citizenship for all Africans, the right to buy land, and the repeal of all discriminatory legislation. We hoped that the government and ordinary South Africans would see that the principles they were fighting for in Europe were the same ones we were advocating at home.[14]

Not all reactions to the Atlantic Charter were so enthusiastic. The Germans, Italians, and Japanese, as might be expected, considered it as nothing more than a wartime "maneuver" or "propaganda bluff" that lacked substance and smacked of hypocrisy.[15] Others expressed deeper concerns and asked tough questions. How, asked isolationists and those belonging to organizations such as the America First Committee, could the president commit to such a declaration without drawing their country down a slippery slope toward international entanglements and closer to war? How, asked those with vested interests, could pledges for liberalized trading practices be given without jeopardizing protective tariffs, or for improved labor standards and social security without spreading dangerous socialism? What, asked those skeptical of words, was the value of declarations without legally binding commitments? Would these principles, asked others, apply to the domestic laws of racial segregation or immigration restrictions based on race in the United States, Canada, Australia, New Zealand, or South Africa? Or, would the pronouncements about universalism and the right of self-determination actually apply to the indigenous people in the colonial possessions of Britain, France, the Netherlands, Portugal, Spain, and the United States extending over the four hemispheres of the globe?

These difficult questions about what the visions would mean in practice immediately assumed greater significance when the Japanese attacked Pearl Harbor on 7 December 1941. The torpedoes launched from planes sunk not only U.S. battleships but, ultimately more momentous, the strength of American isolationism. In a stunned and angry response, Congress dramatically reversed its policies, declaring war against Japan, and then against Germany and Italy. Thus, within only a few days the United States found itself wrenched completely away from its policies of the recent past and engaged in a global war. But for the moment, the military advantage remained with the Japanese. Their invasion of the Philippines led to staggering brutality against captured survivors, including the Bataan Death March in which thousands died of beatings, starvation, and exposure. Other conquests followed in Singapore, Burma, Sumatra, Java, Borneo, New Guinea, Wake, and Guam, and the Japanese seemed poised to invade India, Australia, New Zealand, or Alaska if they chose. For those facing this aggression and for those possessing any visions of human rights at all, the future appeared bleak indeed.

In order to hold out hope, however, and to mobilize all the resources necessary to mount a people's war against the Axis powers, twenty-six different nations agreed to sign the Declaration of the United Nations on 1 January 1942. Here, the United States, Soviet Union, Britain, and China joined with Canada, Haiti, Cuba, India, New Zealand, and South Africa, among others, in making a highly public pledge. They promised to devote their full resources to World War II, to refrain from signing any separate agreement with their enemies, and to adhere to the principles of the Atlantic Charter. By the end, a total of forty-six nations signed this declaration, adding their names and their reputations to engage in the "common struggle against savage and brutal forces seeking to subjugate the world." They announced their commitment to secure "decent life, liberty, independence, and religious freedom" for the world. In addition, and in a particularly important breakthrough, they solemnly pledged "*to preserve human rights and justice in their own lands as well as in other lands.*"[16] Roosevelt assered that this was nothing short of a global struggle against "tyranny and cruelty and serfdom" in which there could be no compromise "between good and evil" and where "only total victory" could bring about the realization of human rights.[17] Within just a few weeks, the Ministers of Foreign Affairs of the American Republics reaffirmed these principles.[18] Many of those who now entered the war strongly believed in the objectives of this crusade, and when the war finally ended after staggering losses and sacrifices they fully intended to insist that their governments honor their promises.

In the evolution of international human rights, World War II thus provided the opportunity and the motivation not only to enunciate basic principles but to make certain public pledges as well. But it did far more than this. The experience of war and genocide also greatly heightened awareness of human rights by the sheer magnitude and brutality of their violation. Indeed, this is what demonstrated as never before in history the extreme consequences of the doctrine of national sovereignty and ideologies of superiority. This, in turn, forced the belligerents to look in a mirror and see their own reflections. Here they saw that there were not only *differences* between the Grand Alliance and the Axis Powers—but *similarities* as well.

No case so dramatized the horrors of pain and suffering inflicted on other human beings as deliberate state policy more than the Third Reich. Hitler began his persecutions in Germany immediately on seizing power and escalated his program of securing "racial purity" by means of mass murder once his armies invaded other countries. In January 1942 (the very month of the Declaration of the United Nations), Nazi officials at the Wannsee Conference determined to step up their systematic genocidal extermination. They even provided a name for their program: the "Final Solution of the Jewish Question." Within several weeks, the first group of Slovakian Jews arrived at Auschwitz, followed by others from the ghetto of Lublin sent to Belzec. Although even the propaganda minister Joseph Goebbels described the program as "barbaric,"[19] it gathered frightful momentum. The Nazis—along with their many non-German, anti-Semitic collaborators—rounded up those whom they regarded as less-than-fully human in France, Belgium, the Netherlands, Luxembourg, and Norway. They abducted others from Austria, Italy, Poland, Russia, Latvia, Estonia, Lithuania, Czechoslovakia, Hungary, Romania, Bulgaria, and Greece. These helpless victims were crammed into suffocating cattle cars and then sent on their way to the specially prepared camps that awaited them.

Once they arrived, these terrified men, women, and children ripped apart from their families, homes, and countries, met a fate described by eyewitnesses as follows:

The first train arrived . . . 45 freight cars with 6,700 people, of whom 1,450 were already dead on arrival. . . . A large loudspeaker blares instructions: undress completely, take off artificial limbs, glasses, etc. Hand in all valuables. . . . Women and girls to the barber, who cuts off their hair in two or three strokes and stuffs it into potato sacks.

Then the line starts moving. . . . At the corner a strapping SS-man announces in a pastoral voice: Nothing will happen to you! Just breathe deeply inside the chambers, that stretches the lungs; this inhalation is necessary against the illnesses and epidemics. . . . For a few of these unfortunates a small glimmer of hope which suffices to have them take the few steps

Figure 8. Toward the "Final Solution." International Military Tribunal.

to the chambers without resistance—the majority knows what is ahead, the stench tells their fate. . . .

The wooden doors are opened. . . . Inside the chambers, the dead are closely pressed together, like pillars of stone. . . . They still hold hands, so they have to be torn apart to get the chambers ready for the next occupants.[20]

It is estimated that as many as eleven million human beings were killed, including six million Jews and a nearly equal number of others ranging from children to the aged, homosexuals, Slavic slave laborers, prisoners of war, Communists, members of the German resistance, handicapped, Roma, and Jehovah's Witnesses.[21] Such a policy and such staggering numbers seem so grotesque, so perverse, so inhuman, and so self-defeating that they defy credulity. But tragically, the horrors of this Holocaust and its assault on humanity were all too real.

The language of superiority, exclusivity, and racial hatreds, however, was most certainly not confined during World War II to the German Nazis. In their attacks against other peoples in Asia and the Pacific, for example, Japanese practices and pronouncements also defied human rights. Like their counterparts in the West, and despite their earlier efforts at the Paris Peace Conference in the name of equality, the leaders of Japan declared their own superiority as *shido minzoku*, or the leading race. At home, they spoke of "racial purity" and "racial destiny," as well as engaging in a "race war" to secure land for the superior "Yamato race." This prejudice and intolerance extended to non-Japanese Asians subjected to conquest as well as to Caucasians characterized as subhuman "devils," bestial "monsters," and "savages."[22] These attitudes, in the judgments of most Asian historians, produced horrendous brutality and human rights abuses by Japanese troops against captured soldiers and civilians alike in the form of forced labor, experiments with germ warfare, sex slave "comfort women" and rape, mutilations, and murder.[23]

Leaders and ideologues in Japan also deliberately manipulated the highly emotional issue of race to mobilize support in Asia against what they called the "White Peril." They spoke not of common humanity or universal principles, but instead portrayed the war as a battle of the East versus the West and as a "holy war" to "liberate East Asia from white invasion and oppression."[24] As such, they claimed that their conquests should not be viewed as victories against their neighboring brothers and sisters, but rather as humiliations against the Americans, British, French, and Dutch. To those who had long suffered from racial discrimination, exploitation, imperialism, and immigration restrictions, these claims often struck a responsive chord. Indeed, for some they provided a sense of racial solidarity, pride in ties of blood and color, and a chance to inflict a "great disgrace on the white race" that outweighed the fact that the Japanese discriminated against them and that old conquerors simply were being replaced by new ones.[25] "Although my reason utterly rebelled against it," admitted one Asian, "my sympathies instinctively ranged themselves with the Japanese in their fight against the Anglo-Saxons."[26]

The Western allies also contributed heavily to this international racial hatred. Once the war began in all its global dimensions, their actions—and inactions—often spoke far louder than their many words about human rights. Despite their vigorous condemnations of the Third Reich's policy of genocide, for example, none of the Allies would take measures to provide relief to Jews trapped in Hitler's inferno. They rejected efforts to revise immigration restrictions, to grant asylum to those who might escape, to consider rescue attempts, or to provide emergency aid. In one early case that attracted considerable attention, nearly one thousand Jewish refugees onboard ship were forced out of port by immigration officials first in Cuba, then the United States, who refused to let them enter, prompting the *New York Times* to editorialize that such behavior "cries to high heaven of man's inhumanity to man."[27] The heroic actions of Swedish diplomat Raul Wallenberg, who saved the lives of tens of thousands Jews in Hungary by issuing special travel permits, were not matched by others. Protestant churches, except for those in Scandinavia, remained noticeably silent in the face of the Holocaust, and Pope Pius XII steadfastly refused to issue any public protest against the Nazi atrocities, let alone take any action. Stalin himself was a virulent anti-Semite, and many high-ranking British and American officials harbored poorly concealed abhorrence toward Jewish refugees, describing them as "these useless people" and as part of the "racial problem."[28] Moreover, when the battles of the Pacific began, governments and the popular press in the West quickly created an image of the Japanese as a "racial menace" of scheming, "murderous little ape men" or "vermin," as "yellow bastards," and as savage, slant-eyed "subhumans."[29] The Hearst newspaper chain appallingly declared: "The war in the Pacific is . . . the War of Oriental Races against Occidental Races for the Domination of the World."[30]

Lest these expressions be somehow dismissed as simply wartime rhetoric against opponents, it is important to recognize that similar attitudes by the West were revealed with reference to nonwhite allied partners and friends as well. Despite the publicly praised status of China and India as members of the Grand Alliance, for example, the United States, Canada, Australia, New Zealand, and South Africa all blocked immigration by their nationals during most of the war because of the color of their skin. "Why be apologetic about Anglo-Saxon superiority [to other races]?" said a brazen Churchill, "We are superior."[31] When he was asked whether the right of self-determination proclaimed in the Atlantic Charter would apply to colonial peoples sacrificing on behalf of the war effort, he declared: "We mean to hold our own. I have not become the King's First Minister to preside over the liquidation of the British Empire."[32] When passing through Allied Africa, U.S. military commanders continued to refer to people there as "fuzzy wuzzies" and "niggers."[33] Moreover, when Ruth Benedict published her famous wartime pamphlet *The Races of Mankind* warning about the dangers of international racism, especially as practiced by whites, it was banned by the U.S. Army and denounced in Congress.

Tragically enough, this revelation of such racial prejudices by so many in the West toward enemies and allies alike even applied to some of their own citizens and soldiers. Throughout the Western hemisphere, for example, men, women, and even children of Japanese descent were viewed as potential enemies solely because of their race. In Mexico and Peru, immigrants from Japan were rounded up and confined in special camps. In Canada, more than twenty thousand were evicted from their homes and interned. In the United States, the situation was even worse when in February 1942

Roosevelt signed Executive Order 9066 authorizing the exclusion, removal, and then detention of U.S. citizens of Japanese origin. With no legal charges being made, more than one hundred thousand Japanese-Americans accused of belonging to "an enemy race" found themselves forced out of their jobs and homes, then herded into "relocation centers," or what government documents described as "concentration camps" surrounded by barbed wire and armed guards.[34] Even those in combat against the Axis in the name of freedom faced discrimination. Colored colonial troops certainly did not receive equal treatment during war. Blacks providing military service for the United States quickly realized that their country wanted them as soldiers, but not as complete citizens or human beings deserving full equality, as evidenced by segregated units, the banning of "subversive" black newspapers from military bases, surveillance, and even discriminatory medical treatment. As Representative John Rankin of Mississippi explained, any mixing of plasma in field hospitals would "mongrelize America" and he would never allow anyone to "pump Negro or Japanese blood into the veins of our wounded white boys."[35] Similar experiences confronted blacks in South Africa when commanded by white Afrikaners committed to a separation of the races through apartheid.

The claim by the Allies that they were engaged in a universal crusade for human rights, while at the same time flagrantly violating some of those very rights both at home and abroad, rang hollow, revealing a glaring chasm between words and deeds. Indeed, the distance was so great that it became impossible to dismiss or ignore. The Axis certainly did their best to draw widespread attention to this hypocrisy.[36] More important, attention focused on this problem because of its painful truthfulness. Virtually all citizens and those within their vast colonial empires in this "total" war faced restrictions on their freedom and liberties. Women confronted gender barriers, and even those working in defense industries did not receive equal pay for equal work. Differences of religion, nationality, and ethnicity persisted. Class distinctions continued, for the poor were more likely to be drafted into military service than the rich. And, of course, nothing could hide the highly visible discrimination based on racial prejudice. When people asked how these attitudes and practices compared with those of their opponents, they not only posed troubling questions but held up a mirror to their leaders—and to themselves. For precisely this reason, the war was a battleground for ideas and values as well as for warriors and weapons. The editors of the *Negro Quarterly* understood this very well and were attuned to the powerful deceptions of political rhetoric in time of war, observing:

This war has brought about the greatest upset of human values and assumptions the world has ever known. The plans of Roosevelt and Churchill are mocked by a vision of the world they flirt with but fear to embrace. Liberal Democracy plays Hamlet, while the "great sickness" spreads from within, allowing Fascism at the very moment it begins to lose battles, to win its greatest victories. For the Four Freedoms is a vision that must be embraced wholly or else it changes its shape to confound us.[37]

When these criticisms came from such a widespread base, Allied governments found themselves forced—as never before in the mainstream of public discussion—to confront the similarities as well as the differences with their adversaries and thereby to acknowledge their hypocrisy. In Britain, the Foreign Office had to admit that very legitimate grounds existed for complaint about violations of human rights.[38] The secretary of state for the colonies even went so far as to declare: "If we are fighting for liberty, we cannot set the bounds to the advance of other races. . . . We must avoid any reproach that, when we blame Hitler for his poisonous doctrine of the Herrenvolk, we had a similar doctrine lurking in our own hearts."[39] Australia and New Zealand leaders were similarly forced to ask: "Are we afraid to do justice?"[40] In South Africa, General Jan Smuts reluctantly admitted: "I have heard natives saying, 'Why fight against Japan? We are oppressed by the whites and we shall not fare worse under the Japanese.' "[41] Others were compelled to acknowledge publicly the role that human rights abuses played in perpetuating empire and international racial tensions.[42]

The forced self-reflection from this wartime mirror became virtually impossible to avoid, especially in the United States which saw itself as leading the crusade itself. Vice President Henry Wallace admitted openly that the country could not honestly campaign for human rights around the world and at the same time deny the right to vote for millions of black Americans. "The nation," warned Eleanor Roosevelt, "cannot expect colored people to feel that the United States is worth defending if the Negro continues to be treated as he is now."[43] How, asked Gunnar Myrdal again and again as he prepared his monumental wartime study entitled *An American Dilemma: The Negro Problem and Modern Democracy*, could the country oppose the racial policies of the Nazis and Fascists with such vehemence abroad, yet support them so vociferously at home?[44] This penetrating and unrelenting question forced many to the conclusion that they had reached a critical turning point. "Today it is becoming increasingly apparent to thoughtful Americans that we cannot fight the forces and ideas of imperialism abroad and maintain a form of imperialism at home," acknowledged titular head of the Republican party Wendell Willkie. "The war," he conceded in a remarkably revealing message,

had done this to our thinking. . . . So we are finding under the pressures of this conflict that long-standing barriers and prejudices are breaking down. The defense of democracy against the forces that threaten it from without has made some of its failures to function at home glaringly apparent. Our very proclamations of what we are fighting for have rendered our own inequities self-evident. When we talk of freedom and opportunity for all nations the mocking paradoxes in our own society become so clear they can no longer be ignored.[45]

Because these striking contrasts could not be ignored, individuals, NGOs, and sometimes even governments themselves fighting in this crusade of a "people's war" turned to the task of developing visions and drafting proposals on the subject of international human rights.

Crusaders, Visions, and Proposals

The first elaborations of visions for human rights during World War II, not surprisingly, came from individual crusaders rather than governments. Building on the inspiration and efforts of the League of Nations, they saw the war as a struggle against totalitarian regimes characterized by their complete disregard for human life and liberty through aggression abroad and dictatorship at home. The prominent British utopian writer (and, hence, no stranger to imagining visions of worlds that might be) H. G. Wells, for example, immediately launched a public human rights campaign. At the age of seventy-three he began by writing a letter to the *Times* declaring:

> At various crises in the history of our communities, beginning with the Magna Carta, and going through various Bills of Rights, Declarations of the Rights of Man and so forth, it has been our custom to produce a specific declaration of the broad principles on which our public and social life is based. . . . The present time seems particularly suitable for such a restatement of the spirit in which we face life in general and the present combat in particular.[46]

To do this, Wells drafted a "Declaration of Rights." He then formed a committee of well-known citizens to help attract notice and secured the willingness of the *Daily Herald* to publish a series of articles under the title of "The Rights of Man."[47] He delivered public lectures, wrote numerous articles, worked to gain the support of NGOs, and in 1940 published his significant *The Rights of Man, or What Are We Fighting For?* It has been described as "one of the twentieth century's most influential books."[48] Here he called on people to spread the idea of human rights around the world, and with the intensity of a crusader declared emphatically: "There is no time to waste. Do not wait for 'leaders.' Act yourself."[49]

Wells sought to make his vision international in scope. He made sure that *The Rights of Man* received widespread distribution throughout forty-eight countries and that his declaration appeared in many translations ranging from all of the European languages to Chinese, Japanese, Arabic, Urdu, Hindi, Bengali, Gujerati, Hausa, Swahili, Yoruba, Zulu, and Esperanto. His ideas of human rights received considerable attention from the press, especially when they were attacked by Mussolini's *Popolo d'Italia* and on Goebbels's propaganda radio. Not content with this coverage, Wells spoke or corresponded with many leaders, including Franklin and Eleanor Roosevelt, Dorothy Thomson (America's best-known female journalist of the time), Jan Masaryk and Eduard Beneš of Czechoslovakia, Chaim Weizmann of the Jewish Agency, Jan Smuts of South Africa (who eventually would draft the preamble of the United Nations Charter), Gandhi and Jawaharlal Nehru of India, and several philosophers in China. He also conducted a highly publicized lecture tour throughout the United States. In this process, Wells learned much about the relationship between rights and duties and about the importance of incorporating different philosophical traditions into any broad vision of international human rights for the world.

Other individuals and NGOs contributed to these visions as well. The American League of Nations Association created a special Commission to Study the Organization of Peace. Under the leadership of James T. Shotwell, the eminent historian at the Carnegie Endowment for International Peace who had served on the U.S. delegation at the Paris Peace Conference, this group devoted considerable energy in publishing studies and arousing public support for international human rights. Activists in London similarly organized themselves as the Atlantic Charter Society to bring its principles of rights into practice. The journalist Clarence Streit published *Union Now: A Proposal*, urging all democratic nations to unite on behalf of what he called "the rights of man."[50] In 1940 the Movement for Federal Union published a pamphlet entitled *How Shall We Win?* proposing an international charter of freedoms for all peoples. The Catholic Association for International Peace advocated that "the rights of man and of peoples must be defined and recognized, and an institutional way established to ensure human rights" while at the same time promoting the creation of an international bill of rights.[51]

Private citizens established the International League for the Rights of Man (subsequently the International League for Human Rights) as did legal expert Quincy Wright and others who founded the World Citizens Association and produced a report entitled *The World's Destiny* calling for recognition of the "new rights of man."[52] The British Labour Party went on record as supporting a statement of "The Rights of Man," and J. L. Brierly of Oxford University proposed "an international bill of rights" for all people.[53] Lecturing in exile, Beneš addressed the same theme and declared: "After the present war a charter of Human Rights throughout the whole world should be constitutionally established and put into practice."[54] A widely circulated statement by the National Conference of Christians and Jews concerning "inalienable rights" in early 1942 and the publication of a book by Jacques Maritain entitled *Les Droits de l'Homme et la Loi Naturelle* stimulated still further discussion.[55] These many men and women who created visions and proposals on behalf of human rights became even more convinced of their crusading mission when Roosevelt commemorated the first anniversary of the Atlantic Charter by declaring that all the continents of the earth have united to form

a great union of humanity, dedicated to the realization . . . of purposes and principles set forth in the Atlantic Charter. . . . Their faith in life, liberty, independence and religious freedom, and in the preservation of human rights and justice in their own lands as well as in other lands, has been given form and substance and power through a great gathering of peoples now known as the United Nations. . . . When victory comes, we shall stand shoulder to shoulder in seeking to nourish the great ideals for which we fight. . . . We reaffirm our principles.[56]

Such broad declarations of principle and proposals for bills or charters of guarantees marked steps in a general direction. They did not always possess precision in terminology, sophistication in concept, consistency, or agreement on ends and means. What they did was to contribute to a process of developing language and meaning that provided essential elements for the larger evolution of international human rights. Nevertheless, for some activists they were still too abstract and did not offer sufficient specificity. They believed it was necessary to take the generalities of these visions and focus them on very concrete problems. Toward this end, they consciously drew on the theme of a "people's war" and directed their energies to the specific needs and rights of peoples around the world.

Enormous attention, for example, focused on the fate of those millions of indigenous peoples still suffering as conquered subjects under colonial empires. The promise of the right of self-determination stirred their hopes: Du Bois and George Padmore of the Pan-African movement, Nkrumah of Ghana, Azikiew of Nigeria, and

Amy Jacques Garvey who wrote for the *Negro World* and the *African* were all greatly encouraged in their visions of freedom in Africa, as were NGOs such as the Universal African National Movement and Council on African Affairs. Harold Moody and his League of Colored Peoples proposed a "Charter for Colored Peoples" claiming their right to self-determination.[57] At the same time, military victories by Japan against the Americans, British, French, and Dutch stripped away the facade of presumed Western superiority in Asia, providing inspiration for independence heretofore considered virtually impossible. For the first time, colonial peoples saw the prospect of a different future. Everything, recalled Sutan Sjahrir of Indonesia in *Out of Exile*, "was shaken loose from its moorings. . . . All layers of society came to see the past in another light. If these [Japanese] barbarians had been able to replace the old colonial authority, why had that authority been necessary at all? Why, instead, hadn't they handled the affairs of government themselves? . . . [Now] national self-consciousness . . . developed a new and powerful drive beyond anything known before."[58]

For their part, the Japanese encouraged these visions by cultivating nationalist leaders like Subhas Chandra Bose of India, Ba Maw of Burma, José Laurel of the Philippines, and Sukarno of Indonesia. Pearl S. Buck, the widely read author and interpreter of Asian affairs to the West, watched all these developments carefully and warned: "The deep patience of colored peoples is at an end. Everywhere among them there is the same resolve for freedom and equality that white Americans and British have, but it is a grimmer resolve, for it includes the determination to be rid of white rule and exploitation and white race prejudice, and nothing will weaken this will."[59]

Raising the issue of race abroad, of course, elevated it at home. Aborigines in Australia, Indians and Inuits in Canada, blacks in South Africa, and Maori in New Zealand, among many others, wanted to know how the proclaimed principles of human rights would apply to them.[60] In this light, the Institute of Pacific Relations called on the Allies to establish "conditions of racial, political, and economic justice and welfare" for all.[61] The issue arose with enormous force in the United States where equal rights had been contested ever since the nation's founding and now escalated with the active participation of several million blacks in the armed forces and defense industries. During 1942 the Congress of Racial Equality launched its first political action campaigns. At the same time, the National Association for the Advancement of Colored People launched what they called the "Double V Campaign": victory over fascism and imperialism abroad and victory over racism at home. Race riots and galling segregation, even within the armed forces and on military bases, made the disparity between visions and actual practice all the more stark. "Just carve on my tombstone," declared one draftee with pointed anger, "Here lies a black man, killed fighting a yellow man, for the protection of the white man."[62] These sentiments were given widespread attention, and thus helped to generate a growing number of specific proposals, including those for the right to vote without poll taxes, equal protection through a federal anti-lynching law and Justice Department intervention in cases of civil rights violations, the elimination of Jim Crow segregation, an end to colonial possessions, and desegregation of the armed forces.[63] The activities of the Indian Rights Association and the formation of the more militant National Congress of American Indians on behalf of both individual and indigenous "tribal rights" added still further momentum to this movement.[64]

Other proposals focused specifically on the rights of women. Not only did females suffer whenever civilian populations were attacked in this total war, but they contributed heavily to volunteer activities, the work force, and actual military service and armed resistance against occupation forces. In these circumstances, it is not surprising that there would be demands for equal rights. The Mongolian People's Republic, Dominican Republic, and French Provisional Government in Algiers all extended the right to vote for women, and these examples served to inspire others.[65] Struggles of war also stimulated visions of liberating women in China, as reflected by the well-known writer Ding Ling in her influential essay "Thoughts on 8 March [International Women's Day]" and a proposal for "raising women's political, economic, and cultural position in society on the basis of the fundamental principle of equality between the sexes."[66] In the United States, the government and media suddenly changed their traditional criticisms of females who worked outside the home, and instead embarked on a campaign to encourage them to enter the work force in the name of patriotic duty. Over six million women subsequently took jobs in the workforce where they watched their efforts praised with popular images of "Rosie the Riveter" and their economic independence and self-confidence grow as never before. Indeed, the Women's Bureau declared this to be "one of the most fundamental social and economic changes" in the nation's history, and indicated that women had every intention of insisting on the full extension of their rights when the war finally ended.[67]

Women also played a particularly significant role during the war as advocates for the rights of children. As in virtually all other cases in the evolution of international human rights, a consciousness of victimization provided the essential impetus. It became increasingly clear that innocent children were starkly incapable of defending themselves against the ravages of war and horrors of genocide. Their tragic plight could hardly be ignored by Allies crusading in the name of the value of human life and rights. At first, efforts such as those of the National War Orphans Shelter Association in China sought to provide immediate assistance of food, clothing, and refuge for girls and boys deprived of their parents and without any other form of protection. NGOs in the West devoted to the welfare of children, including many based on religious belief, took similar action in the face of such obvious need. As the war progressed and as the number of infant and young victims mounted, other efforts began to focus on establishing increased international recognition of rights for children. The Inter-Allied Conference of Educational Experts, the Pan American Child Congress, and the U.S. Children's Bureau, for example, all proposed some form of a "Children's Charter" addressing the rights of the child.[68]

Still other proposals for human rights emphasized class and caste. Since this "people's war" and its crusade required sacrifices from all citizens, they came to expect that their efforts would be rewarded and their rights recognized. In fact, to secure wartime support, Allied governments made precisely these promises to their people. Workers and those impoverished in the United States with vivid memories of the recent Depression certainly saw Roosevelt's pledge about freedom from want, especially in the context of his New Deal social legislation, in just such a light and welcomed his call for a new "Economic Bill of Rights" that would complement the Constitution's traditional Bill of Rights.[69] Some looked at this as a more expansive "New Deal for the world."[70] People in Australia and New Zealand heard their leaders speak again and again about how the war, although a calamity, was being fought on "a moral issue" to extend justice and the rights "of all mankind" to economic and social justice as "the rightful heritage of all human beings."[71] The formation of the Mahila Atmaraksha Samiti in India at the same time held out a vision of eliminating the great disparities between castes.[72] One of the most influential of all such wartime proposals was the 1942 Beveridge Report in Britain. "Now, when the war is abolishing landmarks of every kind," it declared, "is the opportunity for using experience in a clear field. A revolutionary moment in the world's history is a time for revolutions, not for patching."[73] It argued that economic and social security should be the reward for service and sacrifice, and therefore proposed the right of all citizens to have a decent level of subsistence through family allowances, disability benefits, national health insurance, old-age pensions, and a minimum income. This report came to serve as the conceptual foundation of the modern welfare state and its authors found themselves being praised for their "pioneering vision."[74]

These proposals about rights to minimum levels of protection and to freedom from fear and want assumed particular poignancy when it came to masses victimized by wartime destruction, disruption, and dislocation, made all the more extensive and spread across continents by the weapons of modern science. Graphic accounts and photographs of displaced, huddled human beings in pain from starvation, exposure, destitution, and illness from around the world moved humanitarian activists to consider their responsibilities and render assistance. Private groups, religious charities, and the Red Cross rushed to provide critical relief, and did so until they simply were overwhelmed. In an attempt to address this undeniable emergency, forty-four nations agreed to create the United Nations Relief and Rehabilitation Administration (UNRRA), described as "the first and in some ways the most fruitful of broadly based international organizations" to emerge from the war.[75] By contributing their collective resources they sought to provide humanitarian aid in ways that none of them could possibly accomplish on their own. Its members and workers dispensed tons of food, built hundreds of hospitals, prevented epidemics of diphtheria and cholera, and cared for an estimated one million displaced persons. Moreover, they pledged that they would never use relief as a political weapon and never make distinctions because of race, gender, creed, class, or belief. This principle of nondiscrimination when combined with the necessities to sustain life, they declared, constituted basic rights that belonged to all humankind.[76]

As all these incalculable needs and human vulnerabilities became increasingly apparent during the course of the war, and as the crusading dimensions of this global conflict grew in intensity, individuals and NGOs devoted even more effort to promoting visions of international human rights. The Commission to Study the Organization of Peace, composed of scholars and foreign policy experts, released a report entitled "Human Rights and the World Order," insisting on the necessity of protecting rights across national borders.[77] The International Bill of Rights Committee of the Twentieth Century Association published *The International Bill of Rights and Permanent Peace*

Concordance, and representatives from forty-seven colleges and universities throughout the United States submitted a proposal for an international bill of rights.[78] Hersch Lauterpacht, perhaps the most famous expert on international law of the time, began his advocacy of human rights with a public lecture at Cambridge University and then published his proposals in An International Bill of the Rights of Man.[79] At the same time in Latin America Ricardo Alfaro worked with other lawyers in the Inter-American Bar Association to articulate a vision of international human rights as a part of the postwar world order.

One of the most important wartime efforts to develop a vision of international human rights came from the American Law Institute. Under the guidance of its director William Draper Lewis, an advisory committee began work in 1942 on an extensive effort known as the International Bill of Rights Project. Although most of the participants were from the United States, representatives from Europe, Canada, Latin America, and China also contributed. They took on the ambitious task of trying to identify those rights that might be considered universal in nature and that might provide a blueprint for an international bill of rights. After considerable labor, and vigorous political and philosophical arguments, in 1944 they released their *Statement of Essential Human Rights.* This advisory report (which would serve as one of the principal sources in drafting the Universal Declaration of Human Rights) articulated a vision of individual rights including not only civil and political rights but also social and economic rights. It also made explicit the duty of states to protect these rights. At the same time, it called on peoples and leaders to recognize that "at this crucial moment in human history . . . new concepts [of human rights] affecting the future development of man and society are being crystallized."[80]

Greatly encouraged by these many proposals, the International Labor Organization sought to add its voice to this groundswell of support for human rights. Under the leadership of Walter Nash, its members from forty-one countries enthusiastically endorsed what they called The Declaration of Philadelphia. Here, they spoke with a sense of great urgency and need to see themselves as "the conscience of mankind" and to create "a people's peace." They reaffirmed the universal applicability of the principles of the Atlantic Charter, reiterating that all have the right to pursue their material well-being and spiritual development in conditions of freedom and dignity, economic and social security, and equal opportunity. Nash spoke of "a vision of a different post-war world unfolding truly amazing possibilities of a better life for all of us." Toward this end, he movingly declared that "there are no superior people" and that "there can be no justification for discrimination." "Men and women of all races, of all creeds, of all nationalities, and of all classes," he insisted, henceforth must be treated equally. The experience of the war, Nash concluded, revealed that there cannot be genuine security, peace, or justice without a genuine recognition of human rights.[81]

All of these proclaimed visions constituted what René Brunet, a former delegate to the League of Nations, described as a "vast movement of public opinion" that "grew incessantly in force and in scope as the war rolled on." Through "hundreds of political, scholarly, and religious organizations," he noted, the crusaders fervently believed in their mission and sought to build momentum and bring as much influence to bear on governments as they could. Through their many publications, manifestos, and appeals for action, Brunet concluded, they created visions and proposals that "have spread and impressed the idea that the protection of human rights should be part of the war aims of the Allied Powers, and that the future peace would not be complete if it would not consecrate the principle of international protection of human rights in all States and if it would not guarantee this protection in an effective manner."[82]

It was precisely this effectiveness, of course, that constituted the critical problem. How to actually guarantee and enforce protection for human rights plagued every one of the visions emerging from World War II, as acknowledged by the influential Commission to Study the Organization of Peace in its path-breaking 1944 report *International Safeguard of Human Rights*. Hard-hitting and highly critical of both the horrifying abuses of rights by the Axis as well as the double standards practiced by the Allies, it argued that the world stood on the verge of a new era. It emphasized that change could begin only if people and governments first acknowledged the intimate connection between human rights and world peace, then took deliberate international action to implement and safeguard those rights. Toward this end, the commission proposed to convene a United Nations Conference on Human Rights without delay, establish a permanent Commission on Human Rights to develop standards and methods of protection, recognize the right of victims to petition this body, and develop effective means of enforcement. It fully recognized that such tasks would not be easy, for traditions inhibit innovation, prejudices run deep, fear of the unknown is strong, and diplomatic agreement is hard to achieve. But among all of the obstacles, the report singled out one for special attention: "the bogey of national sovereignty." This is what allowed states to claim a special privilege of domestic jurisdiction and to hide within a culture of impunity that regarded any criticism about abuses of rights as unjustifiable interference into their own internal affairs. In the past, observed the report, the guarantee of human rights remained the separate, exclusive, and independent responsibility of each nation. Individual victims thus had to rely on their own governments—the most likely sources of abuse in the first place—for protection and could not look beyond its borders for help. The commission vowed that in the name of international human rights, after the experience of war and genocide, this simply would no longer be tolerated. They thus declared with as much intensity as they could possibly command:

We are determined that hereafter no nation may be insulated and wholly a law unto itself in the treatment of its people.[83]

The acceptance or rejection of this vision would be determined not so much by those many individuals or NGOs who proposed it, however, but by the very claimants of national sovereignty, namely the governments of nation-states themselves.

Human Rights Versus National Sovereignty in Postwar Planning

The many visions of international human rights generated during World War II presented Allied governments with an unanticipated and serious dilemma. On the one hand, all the discussions about rights provided enormous advantages. They helped to make a dramatic and positive distinction between themselves and their wartime adversaries as well as to provide principles capable of inspiring their people to make sacrifices on behalf of a universal crusade. Yet, at the same time, such discussions also presented difficult problems. They created a troublesome mirror that reflected their own abuses of rights, raised dangerous expectations that might not be met, and potentially threatened their own power and claims of national sovereignty. It did not take long for governments, particularly as they began to plan for the postwar world, to be confronted by this contest between international human rights and national sovereignty, and to recognize the profound difficulty of trying to have it both ways.

There were times during the war when some Allied governments actually appeared enthusiastic in leading the crusade for rights. The visionary language of the Atlantic Charter and then the forceful Declaration of the United Nations marked dramatic advances in the evolution of international human rights. Innumerable public addresses by Winston Churchill and his Secretary of State for Foreign Affairs Anthony Eden in Britain, Charles de Gaulle and René Cassin of the Free French National Committee, Prime Minister William Mackenzie King of Canada, Madame Chiang and Minister of Foreign Affairs T. V. Soong of China, Prime Minister Robert Menzies and his Minister for External Affairs Herbert Evatt of Australia, Peter Fraser and Walter Nash of New Zealand, Jan Smuts of South Africa, President Manuel Camacho of Mexico, and especially Franklin and Eleanor Roosevelt, Sumner Welles, and Secretary of State Cordell Hull in the United States, among many others, all spoke about principles of human rights in official and highly visible ways.[84] At times the Allies even dropped copies of H. G. Wells's *The Rights of Man* behind enemy lines.[85] Additional encouragement came from Latin American governments when their Inter-American Juridical Committee issued its Recommendation on Postwar Problems stating the need to change traditional interpretations of national sovereignty by taking into account moral law and social justice within a larger international community.[86] More evidence appeared when several Allied governments signed the 1942 United Nations Declaration on Jewish Massacres, publicly condemning Hitler's violation of "the most elementary human rights" and solemnly promising to punish those responsible for atrocities.[87] Their pledges to establish a new United Nations organization, to support the UNRRA in alleviating human suffering, and to create an international criminal tribunal gave even further credence to their pronouncements about international human rights.[88]

Other statements and actions, however, revealed a very different direction. When pressed, most of those leaders who spoke so eloquently about rights quickly noted that statements in the Atlantic Charter and Declaration of the United Nations represented only goals rather than legal agreements that might jeopardize national interests or national sovereignty. It is in this context that Churchill made his statement about not allowing the principle about the right of self-determination to precipitate the liquidation of the British Empire, describing the Atlantic Charter as "no more than a simple, rough and ready, war-time statement of a goal" toward which the supporting governments meant "to make their way" instead of a firm commitment.[89] When H. G. Wells lectured abroad to promote a vision of international human rights, officials in the Foreign Office contemptuously referred to him as "a somewhat senile, half-extinct prophet . . . much better kept at home."[90] Governments reacted with similar hostility when in an essay on rights entitled "Your Sovereignty—or Your Nation's?" Clarence Streit challenged them by reminding all of those fighting this "people's war" that states were made for the benefit of people rather than the reverse.[91] Moreover, and as we have seen, the Allied governments refused to take any serious action that might threaten their colonial empires or protect indigenous peoples, assist Jews caught in Hitler's Holocaust, modify their immigration restrictions, release those interned solely because of their race, or change their domestic policies of segregation. It must be acknowledged that in doing so these government officials understood perfectly well that they did not act in political isolation but enjoyed the support of large numbers of their own citizens who clearly did not want other countries telling them what they could or could not do and wanted no part of this particular crusade. As one study attempting to promote human rights sadly noted: "There are many voters to whom national sovereignty is a very dear thing. They will surrender it [if at all] . . . only after long argument, and even then with reluctance."[92]

This tension between those who advocated human rights and those unwilling to surrender national sovereignty revealed itself in any number of ways, not the least of which could be found in postwar planning. Most of the Allied governments created special, official, interdepartmental committees to analyze the profoundly changing nature of relations among states and the forces at work within and between them, anticipate future peace and security, and prepare for the vast and complicated problems that eventually would confront them and the world on the conclusion of the war. The most elaborate of these occurred in the United States when Roosevelt authorized the creation of the Advisory Committee on Postwar Foreign Policy. Its membership came from the Department of State, Congress, the White House, the War and Navy Departments, the Joint Chiefs of Staff, and, as if to confirm the theme of a "people's war," several individuals serving in their personal capacities. These included Hamilton Fish Armstrong, editor of *Foreign Affairs*; Anne O'Hare McCormick, foreign affairs analyst of the *New York Times*; Norman Davis of the American Red Cross and Council on Foreign Relations; James Shotwell from the Commission to Study the Organization of Peace; and representatives of the American Federation of Labor, among others. The most important part of this committee was the Subcommittee on Political Problems chaired by Sumner Welles.[93]

Welles brought a wealth of experience and valuable assets with him to postwar planning. He had traveled widely, served in diplomatic posts and on special assignments from Asia to Latin America and Europe, held the position of Under Secretary of State, and enjoyed a long personal friendship with Roosevelt. He had played important roles in the historic negotiations of the Atlantic Charter, the Declaration of the United Nations, the endorsement of the Atlantic Charter by the Ministers of Foreign Affairs of the American Republics, and, as Hull suffered from increasing illness, he effectively became the secretary of state. In addition, Welles fervently believed in international human rights. Both in private conversations and in highly publicized speeches, he spoke frequently and intensely about a vision of humanity, the needs of those who suffered, equality, responsibilities beyond national borders, the importance of ending colonial empires and supporting indigenous peoples, the rule of law, and the necessity of using this "people's war" to advance the inherent rights of every human being, "guaranteed to the world as a whole—in all oceans and in all continents."[94] Under his direction, therefore, it is hardly surprising that the Subcommittee on Political Problems would turn its attention to the relationship between security, peace, justice, and human rights.

Consequently, the first drafting group for postwar planning received the charge of considering the possibility of an international bill of human rights. Known as the Special Subcommittee on Legal Problems,[95] it became perhaps the very first governmental group of a nation-state ever to address this subject in such detail. It met at least once a week for months in confidential deliberations. Indeed, most of its documents were marked "Secret. Not to be removed from the State Department building." Encouraged by Welles, the members assumed that the international recognition and, within each state the guarantee, of basic human rights would be conducive to peace and security. They therefore formulated a set of rights that they thought would be universally respected, even if not formally subscribed to by all states, in a forceful statement of principles. In doing so—and appreciating the value of understanding the experiences of history—they consulted texts of the English Bill of Rights, U.S. Bill of Rights, French Declaration of the Rights of Man and Citizen, Declaration of the International Rights of Man adopted by the Institut de Droit International, proposals of the Fédération Internationale des Droits de l'Homme, and suggestions from the American Institute of International Law and the Commission to Study the Organization of Peace, among others. Based on both the letter and the spirit of these documents and proposals, along with their own visions, members of this group produced drafts that included both traditional civil and political rights as well as social and economic rights that were becoming increasingly important to people engaged in the war. At the end, they recommended that an international bill of rights conclude with these words:

These human rights shall be guaranteed by and constitute a part of the supreme law of each state and shall be observed and enforced by its administrative and judicial authorities, without discrimination on the basis of nationality, language, race, political opinion, or religious belief, any law or constitutional provision to the contrary notwithstanding.[96]

The critical difficulty with this draft, of course, came from the language "shall be observed and enforced . . . any law or constitutional provision to the contrary notwithstanding." "It becomes immediately apparent," observed legal advisor Durward Sandifer, that "the principal problem is that of implementing the guarantees contained in any bill of rights."[97] Words and phrases were one thing, he pointed out to the other members of the subcommittee not eager to hear him, but implementation and enforcement were something quite different. International guarantees of human rights, by their very nature, would impinge on the claimed prerogatives of national sovereignty and domestic jurisdiction. Confronted with this conflict, Sandifer advised against any proposal that might involve international sanctions and cited the earlier opinion of André Mandelstam in *Les Droits Internationaux de l'Homme* who, even as a strong advocate of human rights, also reluctantly acknowledged the power of national sovereignty when he wrote:

The signature, by all states, of a general convention of the rights of man would be at present unattainable, if such a convention should include any sanctions. . . . In fact, it would be falling victim to strange illusions to imagine that at the present time, when the Powers have not yet reached an understanding on the subject of the establishment of collective sanctions against the state which breaks its solemn obligations to maintain the *external peace*, that the same Powers would consent to the institution of a juridical system permitting the international community to render judgements followed by sanctions in the demand of *internal peace*.[98]

Sandifer thus recommended that a bill be promulgated—but without any provisions for enforcement. "This would represent the simplest and least complicated method of putting an international bill of rights into effect," he wrote in a document classified as secret. "It is a device used many times in the past. States agree on the adoption of new rules of law or a formulation of existing rules and proclaim them to the world in a formal international agreement. Reliance is placed primarily upon the good faith of the contracting parties. . . . Such a procedure has the advantage of provoking the minimum of opposition, which is important in a step as radical in character as giving universal legal recognition to individual human rights."[99]

Other planners confronted exactly the same problem. Members of the Territorial Subcommittee, for example, knew that complicated questions would soon arise over border readjustments, the desire of victors to hold strategic possessions, and the promised right of self-determination to indigenous peoples in mandated areas or colonial empires. They also knew that most of those imperial powers were the very military allies still necessary for defeating common enemies and not at all interested in surrendering their possessions or their prerogatives of national sovereignty. Similarly, when the members of the Special Subcommittee on International Organization began their planning under the chairmanship of Welles, they believed strongly in making human rights an integral part of the postwar world and regarding the individual as well as the nation-state as both the object and subject of the international organization that would follow. To do this, however, they realized that they simply could not avoid what they unequivocally called "the underlying question": "*How* do we limit sovereignty?"[100]

Every single one of the postwar planners found it extremely difficult to find satisfactory answers to this question. They spent months carefully drafting a proposed charter for a postwar international organization, for example, including specific provisions on human rights. These included the enumeration of civil and political rights regarding freedom of conscience, speech, press, petition, association, and assembly, and safeguards of persons accused of a crime. The draft also provided for economic and social rights, including the right to participate in public education, property rights, and the right to minimum standards of well-being. One of the most important articles addressed the right of equal protection and nondiscrimination on the basis of race, nationality, language, political opinion, or religious belief. Such a provision, members of the committee believed, was "fundamental because without it no person's rights are assured and those of all may be undermined."[101] Yet, when one internal evaluator provided an assessment, she soberly noted that this provision suffered from several problems. One of these was the absence of any mention of discrimination on the basis of gender, "because agreement on this point could not yet be attained." She also feared that such language would never be allowed to "interfere with the laws of some of our states for the segregation of the races." For these reasons, among others, the draft revealed what she called "the most notable omission": namely, "the absence of guarantees or measures of enforcement." Any provisions regarding the enforceable protection of human rights, she predicted, would raise "constitutional or political difficulties in various states," be "politically unacceptable," interfere with domestic jurisdiction and national sovereignty, and thus would be completely "out of the question at the present time."[102]

Avoiding challenges to national sovereignty by means of international human rights certainly resonated with the cautious and sometimes cynical Secretary of State Cordell Hull. He and his supporters continually praised their own "realism" when addressing power politics while portraying Welles as no more than a Don Quixote tilting at windmills, criticizing him for his unrealistic visions spawned by "idealism" and "crusading liberalism."[103] Neither Hull nor Welles could hide their considerable differences of personality or policy, and their smoldering conflicts that sometimes flared out in the open provided a vivid reminder of the fact that governments and their officials rarely speak with the same voice. This became particularly evident over the issue of human rights. Although they both could deliver magnificent public speeches about the importance of rights, Hull did so to mobilize wartime support rather than out of genuine conviction. He used the authority of his office to reiterate that no nation should interfere in the domestic affairs of another, that the colonial powers should not be forced to dismantle their empires too precipitously, that the proposed United Nations organization should not have too much power, and that the doctrine of national sovereignty should not be sacrificed on any altar of human rights. When presiding over one of the postwar planning meetings, for instance, he specifically attacked the proposed international bill of human rights and reminded all of those present (including most pointedly Welles) that no self-respecting nation would ever allow other countries to determine its relations with its own people, accept a concept of rights that applied vertically from the world down to the local level, permit enforcement to be imposed by outsiders, or surrender its basic sovereignty. "Any proposal requiring a derogation of national sovereignty," he announced firmly, would "meet the opposition" of the United States.[104]

Opposition from the Great Powers

The wrenching struggle of World War II forced most nations into a dramatic realization that they must find solutions on an international scale. Even the strongest among them came to understand that traditional national borders, geographical barriers, and reliance on their own resources alone simply could no longer protect them. "We have learned," observed Franklin Roosevelt, "that we cannot live alone . . . ; that our own well-being is dependent on the well-being of other nations far away."[105] Without the combined might of all the members of the Grand Alliance, they each would fall victim to aggression. Without the collective efforts of the United Nations Relief and Rehabilitation Administration, they each would be completely unable to provide humanitarian aid to helpless victims. And without such newly created multilateral institutions as the World Bank and the International Monetary Fund, they each would be at the mercy of global market forces over which they individually could have no control. The impact of this absolute necessity for cooperation assumed even greater urgency when Allied successes in the Pacific, Soviet advances westward, and the Anglo-American D-Day invasion of Normandy in 1944 brought the war closer to the point where the final battles would be fought to decision. Now the coalition partners found themselves forced to give even more serious and urgent attention to the postwar world that their victory would bring. It is for this reason that the Great Powers among the Allies decided that it was imperative for them to meet and draft a charter for a new international organization that would become known as the United Nations.

Representatives of the United States, Britain, the Soviet Union, and China thus met from August to October 1944 at Dumbarton Oaks on the secluded outskirts of Washington, D.C. Prophetically, an inscription on the mansion wall read: *Quod severis metes* ("You shall reap what you sow.")[106] Here they sought to negotiate the design of an organization that would replace the League of Nations. They held their conversations in phases—and in secret.[107] Among themselves they reached agreement over Roosevelt's concept of the "Four Policemen," or the idea that those nations with the most preponderant strength would act as guardians over all the rest. As described by Hull, the "major responsibility" for maintaining peace and security after the war "must inevitably" be borne by these powers, and no possibility existed for a successful international organization unless these four supported it.[108] Their preliminary charter of the United Nations therefore provided for a powerful Security Council, that they, as the Great Powers, would dominate. They designed a considerably weaker General Assembly composed of representatives of all nations, an Economic and Social Council, and an International Court of Justice. Moreover, they also completely agreed that in this new organization the principle of national sovereignty would be firmly respected.[109]

Irrespective of the significant differences between them on other matters, the Great Powers also agreed to oppose any meaningful provisions on international human rights. Despite all the solemn declarations, moving speeches, crusading rhetoric during the "people's war," and even Roosevelt's own reported opinion that some provision about human rights was "extremely vital,"[110] the movers and shakers at Dumbarton Oaks resisted anything in the charter that might give the United Nations authority to actually enforce rights. The only exception to this (and particularly ironic given the claims of subsequent regimes about the "imposition" of rights by the West on the rest of the world) was China. The Chinese announced in advance that they would be willing "to cede as much of its sovereign power as may be required" in order to help the organization accomplish its tasks for the world.[111] In addition, and fully aware of the ignoble fate of the Japanese proposal for racial equality at the earlier Paris Peace Conference, they declared their firm determination to again raise the issue of race and human rights. "I am particularly grateful to you," wrote Chiang Kai-shek to Roosevelt, "for the insistence on the necessity of China's being represented. . . . Without the participation of Asiatic peoples, the conference will have no meaning for half of humanity."[112] The Chinese then officially proposed that the new organization "shall be universal in character," support social justice and the right of self-determination, and uphold "the principle of equality of all states and all races."[113] Wellington Koo, head of the delegation, proudly described the contributions of Confucius, Mo Tze, and Sun Yat-sen to human rights, explaining that "the thought of universal brotherhood has been deeply rooted in the minds of the Chinese for more than two thousand years."[114] His colleague H. H. Kung further declared in a speech given considerable publicity that China wanted "to strive toward the realization of a world commonwealth, in which all nations, great and small, will live in peace and equality, and all peoples are protected in their inalienable rights."[115]

China's proposal drew fire at once from the other Great Powers who shared a deep concern over "the equality of race question" specifically and the larger issue of human rights in general. The United States delegation no longer included Sumner Welles at the helm of postwar planning, for he had been forced to resign. Instead, they now received instructions from Hull and his new, handpicked Under Secretary of State Edward Stettinius directing them to reject previous State Department postwar planning proposals with strong provisions of human rights and any starkly explicit article about equality.[116] The Soviets opposed the Chinese proposal immediately. Sir Alexander Cadogan representing Britain worried about its dangerous implications. In order to get around the impasse, he suggested a solution that separated words from deeds:

Recognition of the principle commits us to nothing more than we have always stood for. . . . These are, of course, . . . matters of domestic jurisdiction and would be covered if a satisfactory solution of this question is reached. We may be sure that if it were thought that such questions were involved by the recognition of the principle, the United States Delegation would oppose it.[117]

This was a safe bet. The United States considered the possibility of authorizing the United Nations to conduct studies and make recommendations concerning human rights, but certainly not to take action or have any power of enforcement.[118] Stettinius was willing to support a general statement of principle about rights, but not one that would threaten national sovereignty or speak explicitly about racial equality. If the United Nations formally recognized the principle of equality, it could seriously challenge America's domestic jurisdiction on such matters as segregation and immigration based on race. The Senate, House of Representatives, and Republican presidential candidate Thomas Dewey and his foreign affairs advisor John Foster Dulles all conveyed warnings about granting too much "coercive power" to the United Nations. They and many other elected officials knew that super-patriotism always lay just below the surface for many voters who could be counted on to oppose any "foreigners" telling them what they could or could not do. In addition, military victories began to change the attitude of the Joint Chiefs of Staff regarding the right of self-determination, and they thus increasingly resisted suggestions about surrendering Pacific islands of strategic importance captured from the Japanese. All of these factors represented what Welles described as "the powerful influences" opposed to granting too much authority to the United Nations.[119] The United States consequently tried to have it both ways by proposing a statement reading: "The International Organization should refrain from intervention in the internal affairs of any state, it being the responsibility of each state to see that conditions prevailing within its jurisdiction do not endanger international peace and security and, to this end, to respect the human rights and fundamental freedoms of all its people and to govern in accordance with the principles of humanity and justice."[120]

The British and the Soviets would not even support this statement that took away with one hand what it gave with the other. They feared that any language about human rights and fundamental freedoms in the section on general principles for the United Nations would open a Pandora's box, releasing dangerous forces that would seriously threaten their sovereignty and power. The British representatives worried that it would greatly endanger their vast empire, would lead to the creation of "an international detective service" to monitor compliance with rights protection, "would be asking for trouble," and would create "a degree of interference with municipal law that no State, and certainly no Great Power, is likely to tolerate."[121] Soviet officials also understood perfectly well that Stalin's dictatorial regime of forced collectivization, ruthless purges, state terrorism, and the Gulag could never possibly survive any serious human rights scrutiny. In addition, despite innumerable wartime pledges, Stalin had no intention of honoring the rights of Poles or Germans that he captured or the self-determination of peoples in territories that he was about to annex with the might of the Red Army. Andrei Gromyko, the dour Soviet representative, bluntly declared that any reference to individual rights and basic freedoms "is not germane to the main tasks of an international security organization."[122]

By the time the Chinese began their direct participation in the second phase of the Dumbarton Oaks negotiations, therefore, the United States, Britain, and the Soviet Union already had agreed to bury any mention of human rights deep within the text and confine it to an innocuous phrase about social and economic cooperation alone.[123] They also agreed to completely eliminate any mention of racial equality as proposed by China. In anger and frustration, Koo bitterly complained that "nothing was said about justice" or "humanity at large," and then explained the necessity of combining both pragmatism and principle:

The new organization aims at the maintenance of peace and security throughout the world. . . . For the successful attainment of this object, the faith, understanding, and cooperation of all peoples will be needed. As a means of promoting this . . . it will be highly desirable to consecrate the principle of equality of races as of states in the fundamental instrument of the new institution. Reference to this principle . . . in the preamble of the new charter will not only give moral satisfaction to the greater part of humanity, but will also go far to pave the way for the realization of the ideal of universal brotherhood inseparable from the ideal of permanent world peace.[124]

The other Great Powers opposed this position, telling Koo in no uncertain terms that they simply would not approve it. This presented a serious dilemma for the Chinese. If they accepted the draft text, they risked losing the principles at stake. If they pushed the issues of race or of colonies too strongly, however, they risked attracting criticism of their own regime of Chiang Kai-shek and alienating the very allies on whom they depended. The cost was especially high when considering the United States, who served as China's vital benefactor of military and financial assistance in wartime and sponsor of diplomatic status in postwar planning. Churchill, for example, had opposed even inviting the Chinese to attend the Dumbarton Oaks negotiations, dismissing them as not being a world power at all but only a "faggot vote on the side of the United States."[125] In the end, the Chinese decided that they could not be allowed to jeopardize their immediate strategic and political needs by offending the other Great Powers, particularly since they knew they already had been outvoted. They did not remain silent, however. Although he avoided the sensitive word, *race*, Koo spoke directly about all of the sacrifices that people had made during the war, the great body of public opinion around the world, and the need to adopt basic principles of justice and humanity for international conduct—matters to which China "attached a great deal of importance." "It would be highly desirable to do everything possible," he observerd, "to remove any suspicion on the part of the peace-loving peoples of the world that this new organization . . . might eventually degenerate into an organization of power politics" by providing a "moral tone" and respecting human rights.[126]

For the moment, these words of the Chinese largely fell on deaf ears at Dumbarton Oaks. The draft charter that emerged from the Great Powers emphasized Realpolitik and revealed their intention of creating something that they could control. As described by one leading authority, "the Big Three saw the defense of their own security, the protection of their own interests, and the enjoyment of the fruits of their victory in the world war as more important than the creation of an international organization to maintain world peace."[127] They planned to dominate the powerful Security Council with their permanent membership and vetoes capable of thwarting any action against themselves or their interests. They also designed a much weaker General Assembly in which all states would sit, but one that largely would confine itself to discussion rather than action. In the confidential words of Roosevelt (as thus not designed for public consumption), this assembly "should meet about once a year" and enable "all the small nations . . . to blow off steam at it."[128] In addition, they wanted to ensure that an emphasis would be placed on the rights of states rather than individuals; that no reference would be made about race, about gender, about religion, or about indigenous peoples in colonial possessions at all; and that no mention would be made about basic human rights either in the principles of the organization as a whole or in the functions of the Security Council and General Assembly. Instead, they permitted the only reference to human rights and fundamental freedoms to appear within the confines of general economic and social cooperation. When one member of the Chinese delegation dared to ask for an explanation of what the Great Powers meant by this single mention, Hull's associate Leo Pasvolsky of the Department of State replied that the details would be left to the organization itself. After making appropriate studies, he observed, it might propose international agreements with regard to the observance of human rights, but that any such accords would become effective only when accepted by the respective sovereign states. "This," he bluntly concluded, "would not be likely to happen for some time."[129]

*   *   *

Most of the representatives of the Great Powers who drafted a charter for the United Nations at Dumbarton Oaks thus seemed to have little understanding of, or appreciation for, the power of visions of human rights generated during World War II. As a result of unintended consequences, they came to realize much sooner than they ever anticipated, however, that crusades of rights and freedoms once unleashed are not easily reined in or halted. Expectations had been raised, promises made, and proposals of visions seen during this "people's war"—and these were not about to be denied. Countless men and women, including those who suffered from discrimination on the basis of race, gender, or class, as well as those from smaller nations and indigenous peoples in colonies, had come to hear the crusading message of human rights over and over again during the course of war. Although the language and terminology of "human rights" was still evolving and not yet well-defined as it is today, the concept had captured enormous attention and led people to believe that they had been fighting for a purpose and that their many sacrifices would be rewarded. Advocates for human rights thus reacted with immediate shock, resentment, and then outrage when they read the proposals emanating from the Great Powers containing all the old provisos about national sovereignty but almost nothing about rights. Welles, perhaps with a broader perspective gained from considerable experience, responded by suggesting to them that not everyone had yet been heard on this subject. There would not be any "signing on the dotted line," he said, "by nations that have not yet been given a chance to take part in conferences and who may not be willing to accept the general lines in the proposals of Dumbarton Oaks."[130] This is exactly what happened, for those who had been excluded up to this point now fully determined that they would not remain passive in the face of Great Power opposition or silent on the subject of human rights as the time approached for a more broadly based international conference designed to create a "people's peace."

Chapter 6
A "People's Peace"

Peace and a Charter with Human Rights

As we have had a people's war, so shall we now have a people's peace.
—Walter Nash of New Zealand

After enduring so much suffering, surviving so much devastation, and hearing so many promises from their leaders about human rights for such a sustained and intense period of the most calamitous war in history, it is hardly surprising that many of those who sacrificed so much during World War II would make demands upon the peace that would follow. Indeed, although the expression, "human rights," had been explicitly used ever since the eighteenth century, as we have seen, it was the experience of this war and this genocide that propelled it into widespread popular use. Millions of people had fought in a crusade for a purpose, and with their adversaries on the verge of collapse and the end in sight, they were not about to let pledges be broken or their visions of what might be created now be denied. The diplomacy at Dumbarton Oaks and the strategic positioning of armed forces around the globe revealed that the Great Powers already were seeking to mold the postwar world in particular ways that had little to do with the wartime promises of peace and justice for all people. In fact, their actions gave every appearance of having everything to do with geopolitics and almost nothing to do with normative values about peacemaking and human rights. Consequently, an unprecedented number of voices arose to protest what they regarded as a betrayal and to reassert their own proposals and visions. To do this, they sought to reshape the discourse about the United Nations Charter by insisting that sacrifices made in the "people's war" now be rewarded with a "people's peace" that advanced human rights.

Insisting on a Peace with Rights

The expectations for the Dumbarton Oaks negotiations had been exceedingly high. After all, victory seemed assured and the Great Powers already had pledged before their own people and the world to honor the principles of human rights. The very fact that the meetings were held in the United States, the "arsenal of democracy" and the home of Franklin Roosevelt who had done so much to bring visions of human rights to popular attention during the war, provided additional hope. Public statements by the participants themselves about creating a new international organization to establish peace and justice generated even further enthusiasm. "We meet at a time when the war is moving toward an overwhelming triumph for the forces of freedom," declared Cordell Hull. "It is our task here to help lay the foundations upon which, after victory, peace, freedom, and a growing prosperity can be built. . . . This war moves us to search for an enduring peace—a peace founded upon justice and fair dealing for individuals and for nations."[1]

Perhaps the very height of these expectations made the fall so precipitous when they failed to materialize. Instead of the promises made during the war and suggested anew by the grandiose speeches of Hull and others, the Dumbarton Oaks proposals revealed something quite different. Once these plans became known, especially among human rights activists, they opened up a vociferous public debate and launched a storm of protest. In the minds of those who advocated a new kind of peace with human rights, the meetings were an affront that exposed the same old crass, national self-interests of the Great Powers. The prominence of the Security Council, the diminution of the General Assembly, the emphasis on states rather than individuals, the absence of any provision at all about colonial empires, and the single mention of human rights buried in the text and confined to social and economic cooperation provoked shock, resentment, and outrage. As one diplomat described it, the proposals were "very little more than an undertaking by the . . . Great Powers to meet from time to time . . . and to decide what they thought might best be done, and in taking this course they expected the assistance and collaboration of the smaller powers." If the United Nations were to be founded on these bases, he warned, it would be the very "negation in the international field of those principles of democracy for which this war is being fought."[2]

Many state members of the alliance, NGOs, and private citizens thus felt an enormous sense of betrayal at the hands of the Great Powers. For this reason, they reacted with language that spoke of pledges dishonored. When Peter Fraser addressed the Canadian House of Parliament, for example, he referred to the catastrophes, cynicism, and despair that resulted when governments ignored promises made during World War I and warned that it must never happen again. Principles of rights, he declared, "are not platitudes" and they "must be honored, because thousands have died for them." He reminded his listeners that millions of people had sacrificed on land and sea, in the air, in workshops, on farms, in mines, and in factories because they believed in what their leaders told them. If these promises now turned into lies and visions of rights transformed into dust, he said with passion, "we shall be undoing in peace what has been won on the battlefield."[3] It was the possibility of just such an "undoing" that seriously worried so many others, particularly among colonial peoples and minority groups, who vehemently complained that the Dumbarton Oaks proposals flagrantly violated both the letter and the spirit of the promises made about human rights for the peace that would follow victory.

New Zealand proved to be one of the most vigorous and vocal opponents. Exercising an influence far out of proportion to the size or strength of their country, staunch advocates for human rights like Fraser and Nash reacted with immediate indignation. They had believed in the crusade for rights from the very beginning and used their considerable energy and passion to fight for them wherever they went. They envisioned an international organization that could keep the peace by treating nations equally, practicing collective security against aggression, and developing a system of trusteeship for colonial possessions that advanced "the well-being and development of native peoples" and self-determination. They also strongly believed in advancing economic and social justice and promoting the "moral principles" of human rights on a global level, thereby creating a "people's peace" for the world.[4] Mincing few words, Carl Berendsen, New Zealand's ambassador to the United States, expressed his criticisms directly:

Too much emphasis on Great Powers and not much real machinery for joint action. . . . Too much vagueness. No guarantees, no pledges, no undertaking except in general terms. . . . With the emphasis on the Great Powers no adequate opportunity for small countries like New Zealand to exercise influence or express views. . . . Too much emphasis on Council, too little on Assembly. . . . No adequate machinery for securing peaceful change and economic justice—only words.

Consequently, he tersely concluded: "It aims too low."[5]

Other allies also voiced objections to what they regarded as the elitism and heavy-handedness of the Dumbarton Oaks proposals. They complained that the plans of the Great Powers simply smacked of Realpolitik and imperialism from the past, reeked of arrogance and the presumption of permanent predominance, and completely ignored promises made. India protested that absolutely nothing appeared regarding the right of self-determination or racial equality. Australia, Canada, and South Africa wanted to know why, despite all their contributions to the war, they had been excluded and why their views had been so completely dismissed. In an attempt to influence future discussions, representatives from Australia and New Zealand met in November 1944 to formulate a joint position to press for a greater role for the small powers and the General Assembly, the creation of an international trusteeship system on behalf of indigenous peoples under colonial empires, and explicit provisions relating to human rights. "The Charter of the Organization," they collectively declared, "should make clear to the peoples of the world the principles on which the action of the Organization is to be based," and draw on "the essential principles" regarding rights delineated during the war.[6] Now the shoe was on the other foot, and the British did not like it at all. "In our view," they announced in a sharply worded comment, "in a matter of this kind all members of the British Commonwealth ought to take every care to coordinate as far as possible their respective views before entering public declarations of policy. We can only express our regret that this public announcement has been made on behalf of the Australian and New Zealand governments without prior consultation with, or warning to us."[7] The responses from both Australia and New Zealand to this protest from London, in the words of even the polite official history, "were, to say the least, unrepentant."[8]

Countries in Latin America complained loudly as well. A long history of outside exploitation, colonialism, and intervention already had made them sensitive to abuse at the hands of the Great Powers. Moreover, they felt particularly betrayed by the United States, which had not invited them to Dumbarton Oaks despite promises that as allies in the Western Hemisphere they would be fully consulted on any plans on a postwar organization. Thus, when the proposals were released, it did not take much to provoke their reaction. Brazil, Guatemala, Panama, and Uruguay all expressed their support for a new international organization, but only one that stood for genuine equality, liberty and justice, and respect for the dignity of each human person.[9] Mexico insisted on including statements of principle about the rights and duties of nations and individuals, citing the influence of the visions seen by the French Declaration of the Rights of Man and the Citizen, the writings of André Mandelstam and Alejandro Alvarez, the efforts of the League of Nations, the promises made during World War II, and the American Law Institute's *Statement of Essential Human Rights* and the Commission to Study the Organization of the Peace's *International Safeguard of Human Rights*.[10] Venezuela complained that the Dumbarton Oaks proposals created a "fundamental defect," and called for provisions on the disposition of colonies and protection of their inhabitants and "the great and humanitarian principles" of human rights.[11] These criticisms became so vociferous, in fact, that the governments throughout Latin America decided to call an extraordinary meeting to create a united front and exert as much pressure as possible.

For this reason, the representatives of twenty nations assembled at Chapultepec Castle in Mexico City in February 1945 for the Inter-American Conference on Problems of War and Peace, determined to make a difference. Here, they examined the Dumbarton Oaks proposals, in the words of one observer, "paragraph by paragraph."[12] Although the United States sent a large delegation, this hardly deterred the other nineteen from expressing their criticisms about Great Powers dominance, the relationship between regional arrangements and the larger international organization, economic and social problems, and human rights.[13] The delegates submitted more than one hundred and fifty draft resolutions, and used the occasion to express their visions that were followed closely by the world press and by China.[14] Sometimes forgetting their own less than exemplary records, they contended that if the wartime crusade was in the name of democratic principles, then surely the new international organization should be based on democracy. Bolivia argued for the need to define rights and responsibilities. Venezuela championed a global system of law, justice, and equity that supported human rights. Licenciado Alfonso García Robles of the Mexican Ministry for Foreign Affairs vigorously advanced a program for the Protección de los Derechos Internacionales del Hombre, or Protection of the International Rights of Man. He acknowledged the visions of human rights seen by H. G. Wells, the Institut de Droit International, and the American Law Institute who had gone before, and insisted that now that the time had come to make them a reality.[15] One of the female members of the Mexican delegation, along with Minerva Bernardino of the Dominican Republic who served as president of the Inter-American Commission of Women, spoke strongly on behalf of women's rights. Cuba submitted two elaborate proposals, a Draft Declaration

Figure 9. Speaking Out for a "People's Peace" with Human Rights: The Latin Americans at the Chapultepec Conference. Organization of American States.

of the International Duties and Rights of the Individual and a Draft Declaration of the Duties and Rights of Nations, that spoke of the "conscience of the civilized world" and addressed a wide array of civil, political, economic, and social rights. "It is important," concluded the Cuban vision, "to extend to the whole world the international recognition of these rights of man."[16]

In the end, all delegates agreed to a set of resolutions and the text of the Final Act of the conference. These ranged from continued military cooperation and the punishment of war crimes to the incorporation of international law into municipal legislation and proposals for a new international organization that emphasized human rights. Taking a deliberate jab at the Great Powers, they reminded everyone that "the Republics here represented . . . did not take part in the Dumbarton Oaks Conversations." They agreed that the proposal could serve as a basis for discussion, but declared that it "must reflect the ideas and hopes of all peace-loving nations participating in its creation."[17] Toward this end, the delegates subscribed to the promises made during the war, the rights of women and children, the right of freedom of access to information, economic and social rights, and a resolution recommending "every effort to prevent racial or religious discrimination." They also endorsed a list of fundamental principles including the sovereign equality of all states, international law as a standard of conduct, repudiation of territorial conquest, support for the principles of democracy, justice, and "the rights of man." Instead of stopping there, however, they went on to strongly declare their support for "a system of international protection of these rights" and called on the Inter-American Juridical Committee to advance their draft Declaration of the International Rights and Duties of Man.[18]

The Latin American countries hailed this declaration as a significant contribution toward the vision that human rights possess a universal moral validity across all national boundaries. Indeed, some of the attendees at Chapultepec even spoke of the "spiritual experience" and "zeal and devotion" of their gathering. They expressed the hope that it would help in the creation of a "people's peace" that addressed the rights of "the common man" and all the "peons, coolies, and other social outcasts throughout the world" and thereby advance the process of transforming the individual from being merely the object of international pity to the actual subject of international law.[19] The Great Powers reacted differently. Stalin's Soviet Union, for example, already guilty of killing millions of its own people and currently occupying Eastern Europe, certainly had no intention of endorsing principles of democracy or any broad application of civil and political rights at all. The British noted disparagingly that, "although considered of great importance by the Mexican Delegation, it is not clear what practical application it will have."[20] Edward Stettinius, now as U.S. secretary of state, hailed the declared "principles of humanity" with a flourish before the press, but in private the delegation discounted the declaration as no more than a means of embarrassing the United States or dismissed it as a mere sop designed to satisfy Mexican prestige.[21] Moreover, the Department of State chose not to publish the declaration at a time or in a place along with other resolutions and results of the conference as a whole.[22] Serious questions thus persisted about the true intentions of the Great Powers with reference to the role human rights should play in the new international organization and in the peace.

Governments were not the only ones asking these questions. Many NGOs and private citizens joined in as well. The invitation to representatives from various citizen groups normally excluded from diplomatic affairs to observe the Chapultepec Conference, for example, certainly facilitated this process. Within the United States, some of the most serious questioning actually occurred as an unintended consequence. Roosevelt, Stettinius, and their advisors remained acutely aware of Woodrow Wilson's failure to secure American participation in the League of Nations at the end of World War I, and desperately sought to avoid any repetition with the new United Nations. The Department of State consequently launched a vigorous program marking a significant departure in its relations with the public. Its Office of Public Affairs sent people out across the country to deliver addresses, hold seminars, and lead discussions in a campaign to build popular support for the Dumbarton Oaks proposals. In slightly more than a month, more than one hundred separate sessions were sponsored in a number of widely scattered cities. Officials met with business and labor leaders, education and women's associations, farm groups, service clubs, churches, and specialists in international relations. Audiences listened—but they also asked pointed questions. Officials received an unexpected earful as the public wanted to know how the secretary of state himself could use the expression, "a people's peace," and yet at the same time be so blind as to exclude international human rights.[23]

In these public discussions, NGOs such as the American Bar Association, American Federation of Labor, American Law Institute, Congress of Industrial Organizations, Brookings Institution, Farm Bureau Federation, NAACP, and Carnegie Endowment for International Peace, among many others, all voiced their concerns about human rights. Members of the newly formed Americans United for World Organization widely distributed the American Law Institute's *Statement of Essential Human Rights*.[24] The influential Commission to Study the Organization of Peace used these occasions to advance the visions recently presented in their *International Safeguard of Human Rights.* Pulling no punches, they forcefully argued for the necessity of moving beyond the Dumbarton Oaks proposals. They specifically and prophetically called for more provisions about human rights in the Charter, the convocation of a United Nations Conference on Human Rights, the promulgation of an international bill of rights, the creation of a permanent Commission on Human Rights to develop standards and methods of protection, and the promotion of effective means of enforcement.[25] At the same time, the Federal Council of Churches, American Jewish Congress, and Synagogue Council of America all endorsed the establishment of a specialized agency under the proposed Economic and Social Council with specific responsibility for human rights and the creation of an international bill of rights.[26]

Religious values also played a powerful role in the response of the Commission on a Just and Durable Peace set up by the Federal Council of Churches. Representing forty-five denominations, this NGO issued a report entitled *Christian Standards and Current International Developments* analyzing the "omissions and shortcomings" of the Great Powers' proposals and suggesting ways "to bring the Dumbarton Oaks plan into closer harmony with Christian ideals." It endorsed those "purposes of justice and human welfare which are set forth in the Atlantic Charter and which reflect the aspirations of peoples everywhere," the development of the rule of law, the limitation of armaments, and the protection of the weak from the strong. In addition, it advocated the creation of a special Commission on Human Rights that would protect, among other rights, those of religious and intellectual freedom and "equal and unsegregated opportunity for all races." Moreover, it directly called on all colonial powers to renounce their empires and proclaimed their support for the right of self-determination and freedom for indigenous peoples by declaring: "We cannot in good conscience, be a party to the dismantling of Japanese colonial possessions without at the same time insisting that the imperialism of the white man shall be brought to the speediest possible end. We cannot have a sound or stable community so long as there is enforced submission of one people to the will of another in Korea, in India, in the Congo, in Puerto Rico or anywhere else."[27]

Individuals joined in this rising chorus of criticism as well. Through letters to editors, speeches, press conferences, sermons, and other forms of protest, they complained about the meager results and their resentment over Great Power diplomacy. Congresswoman Clare Boothe Luce, for example, criticized the absence of any female delegates from the United States, Britain, the Soviet Union, or China during the negotiations.[28] Others focused on race, noting: "In the preliminary peace talks at Dumbarton Oaks only one colored group participated, the Chinese, and [thus] the equality and basic problems of Negroes and colonial colored people were not on the agenda."[29] Professor Rayford Logan of Howard University openly complained that the proposals completely ignored the rights of colonial peoples.[30] Du Bois weighed in as well, castigating the Great Powers for rigging control over the new organization and for neglecting human rights. In his famous essay "Human Rights for All Minorities," he pointedly noted that the world's minorities "*together form a majority*," and specified what was at stake. Turning the wartime promise of universalism back on itself, he argued that universal principles required universal application. Unless the problems of colonial empires and racial discrimination were addressed, he argued, the United Nations would never be able to create or maintain a lasting peace.[31]

These many criticisms of the Dumbarton Oaks proposals, whether originating with governments, NGOs, or private individuals, profoundly contributed to the evolution of international human rights in two significant ways. The first of these was to elevate human rights to new heights on the global agenda as the war neared its end. They did this by recalling the promises made during the "people's war" and by serving notice that these could not—and would not—be dismissed in the creation of the United Nations. Second, they placed visions of human rights directly at the center of concepts of peace. For them, peace defined exclusively and narrowly in terms of Great Power interests in a geopolitical balance of power would no longer suffice. Instead, they proposed an infinitely broader "people's peace" that included collective security, justice, and the international protection of certain basic human rights.

This vision of a peace with rights owed a great deal to the recent and profound traumas of the Depression, Hitler and the Third Reich, and World War II. Many of the survivors believed that they could learn lessons from history, and thus sought to create a peace that would avoid perceived mistakes of the past. They came to regard the painful hardships suffered during the course of the Depression, for example, as contributing heavily to the rise of fascist regimes, deadly competition, and ultimately to the outbreak of war itself. For this reason, those concerned about the long-standing and pernicious divisions of class or caste—such as Fraser, Nash, Du Bois, the American

Federation of Labor, and various socialist and communist parties—despite their many differences, all insisted that the maintenance of a genuine "people's peace" required a guarantee to protect certain economic and social rights. They believed that poverty, unemployment, and misery anywhere bred instability elsewhere and thereby threatened peace. This is why Roosevelt's language about freedom from want resonated so strongly with them and why the ILO Declaration of Philadelphia could state with conviction that "experience has fully demonstrated the truth . . . that lasting peace can be established only if it is based upon social justice." Peace, in their mind, required that "all human beings, irrespective of race, creed, or sex, have the right to pursue both their material well-being and their spiritual development in conditions of freedom and dignity, of economic security, and equal opportunity."[32]

Many also began to define peace as more clearly entailing the protection of civil and political rights for all people. They now were no longer willing to meekly accept the old proposition that how a government treated its own people remained an exclusive matter of "domestic jurisdiction." The crushing of opposition, the denial of freedom of speech and assembly, the elimination of due process, and the expansion of the power of the state by Hitler, Mussolini, and the militarists in Japan—all behind the protective shield of national sovereignty—convinced them that the abuse of rights at home could all too quickly spill over borders. In their support for human rights, the Commission to Study the Organization of Peace argued that

it has become clear that a regime of violence and oppression within any nation of the civilized world is a matter of concern for all the rest. . . . [T]he government that rests upon violence will, by its very nature, be even more ready to do violence to foreigners than to its own fellow citizens, especially if it can thus escape the consequences of its acts at home. The foreign policy of despots is inherently one which carries with it a constant risk to the peace and security of others. In short, if aggression is the key-note of domestic policy, it will also be the clue to foreign relations.[33]

The ordeal of this particular war similarly contributed to the belief that any lasting peace would require respecting the right of self-determination. Part of this, of course, resulted from the many wartime promises made by the Allies to contrast themselves from their adversaries and to solicit support for the larger crusade. The Atlantic Charter, the Declaration of the United Nations, countless speeches, and the Declaration on Liberated Europe emerging as late as February 1945 from the Yalta Conference between the United States, Britain, and the Soviet Union all fostered this belief.[34] But there was something more. The war produced millions of new European victims of Axis aggression. As a result of their own first-hand experiences, they became much more sympathetic to the sufferings of others forced to live under conquest and subjugation, including indigenous peoples within their own colonial empires. Thus, many in the West began to support Gandhi of India, Ho Chi Minh of Indochina, Nkrumah and Kenyatta of Africa, Romulo of the Philippines, and Fonoti of Western Samoa, among others, who vowed that there could never be international peace as long as they were denied their freedom.[35]

New visions of peace also entailed the right to equal treatment and protection under the law without discrimination. Press coverage and attention by the League of Nations and many NGOs over Hitler's abuses had raised international awareness of this problem even before the war began. Yet, as the stench of the Holocaust began to seep from under the earth of unmarked mass graves, it became nearly impossible to ignore the connection between persecution and genocidal war. This appeared all the more evident when their own actions and statements during the war forced the Allies to look into a mirror and see their own reflections of blatant and often violent prejudice.[36] Opinion thus increasingly concluded that the persecution of any individual or group anywhere potentially threatened the peace everywhere. It is for this reason that nearly all serious proposals for peace emerging from governments, NGOs, and individuals alike—with the notable exception of the Dumbarton Oaks proposals from the Great Powers—contained explicit provisions for the fundamental right of all people to nondiscrimination.[37] The proposal from the American Jewish Committee, for example, used precisely this language in its *World Charter for Human Rights*.[38] As those assembled for the Inter-American Conference on Problems of War and Peace formally declared: "World peace cannot be consolidated until men are able to exercise their basic rights without distinction as to race or religion."[39]

Finally, and not surprising given the crusading nature of the war, new proposals from activists continually argued that peace could be neither created nor sustained unless it contained elements of "justice." Definitions of international justice appeared in many different forms. For some, it meant freedom from aggression and that small states would be treated if not equally, then certainly fairly, by the Great Powers in the postwar world. For others, it entailed the rule of law, principles of democracy, an international court of justice, free trade, or the reduction of armaments. Yet, for most, a "people's peace" required the protection of some form of human rights, however defined. "The relation between human rights and a just peace," proclaimed the Commission to Study the Organization of Peace, "is close and interlocking."[40] The Commission on a Just and Durable Peace argued exactly the same point. Here, economic and social rights, civil and political rights, the right of self-determination, and the right to nondiscrimination all played prominent roles. But other dimensions appeared as well. These included visions for gender equity, the rights of children, the right to be protected in times of war, the right of refugees and displaced persons to have access to relief, and the rights of indigenous peoples and ethnic minorities, among others. Those who asserted such rights, either singularly or together, invariably did so in the name of the relationship between peace and justice.[41]

These various visions of peace with rights could never be realized, of course, unless and until the peoples and the governments of the world agreed to implement them. Although World War II contributed as never before to the concept of duties far beyond one's own national borders, any discussion about how these might be applied in peace remained speculation until the fighting actually ceased. But by spring 1945 this seemed to be a distinct possibility, and it became vital for nations to gather and negotiate a plan for an international organization. "This time we shall not make the mistake of waiting . . . to set up the machinery of peace," said Roosevelt in drawing a lesson from recent history. "This time, as we fight together to get the war over quickly, we work together to keep it from happening again. . . . We shall have to take the responsibility for world collaboration, or we shall have to bear the responsibility for another world conflict."[42]

This plan suddenly was placed in doubt when Roosevelt died only thirteen days before the conference was scheduled to meet. Many feared that a new president with almost no experience in foreign affairs would have any interest in or appreciation for such an enterprise. They need not have worried. Little did they know that ever since he was a young man Harry Truman had kept a poem by Alfred Tennyson in his wallet reading:

For I dipt into the future, far as human eye could see,
Saw the Vision of the world, and all the wonders that would be. . . .
Till the war-drum throbb'd no longer, and the battle-flags were furl'd,
In the Parliament of man, the Federation of the world.[43]

As the first decision of his presidency, Truman announced that the conference would proceed. Fifty nations thus sent their representatives—and their plans for peace—to San Francisco.

Politics and Diplomacy at the San Francisco Conference

The opening speeches of the United Nations Conference on International Organization delivered in the elegant San Francisco Opera House during April 1945 conveyed both a spirit of extraordinary euphoria and a sense of serious responsibility. Flushed with military victories against their adversaries and excited about what they knew would be one of the century's most historic events, representatives and their staffs could hardly contain their enthusiasm. Never before in history had so many nations of such various sizes been so widely represented at such an international conference. Never before had Asia and the Pacific Rim been given so much recognition. At the same time, they understood that the occasion also came with heavy responsibilities. They perceived that they had been given a second chance after the failure of the Paris Peace Conference at the end of World War I, and knew that war-weary people expected them this time to create a viable international organization to keep the peace. "For there can be no doubt anymore," said the seasoned Prime Minister Jan Smuts of South Africa, "that for us, for the human race, the hour has struck. Mankind has arrived at the crisis of its fate, the fate of its future as a civilized world."[44] "If we should pay mere lip service to the inspiring ideals and then later do violence to simple justice," declared President Harry Truman in exactly the same tone, "we would draw down upon us the bitter wrath of generations and yet unborn. . . . We must build a new world—a far better world—one in which the eternal dignity of man is respected."[45]

Other delegates also spoke about both the opportunities and the responsibilities for now creating a "people's peace." They urged each other to put past practices behind them, to rise above parochial national self-interests, to honor the pledges made during the war, and to create an organization founded not on power politics but on principle. Participants were encouraged to be guided by "the vision of the ideal" and commit themselves "to vindicate the fundamental rights of man, and on that basis to found a better, freer world for the future."[46] Interestingly enough, some delegates also warned about the dangers in settings such as this of excessive oratorical flourishes that might create a false sense of euphoria, conceal serious problems, or ignore the reality of global politics and diplomacy. Ramaswami Mudaliar of India responded by arguing that, given the promises made and the pressures unleashed during the war, those who would define "reality" solely in geopolitical terms would be making an error of equal seriousness. "We are all asked to be realists," he said; but noted, "There is only one great reality":

one fundamental factor, one eternal verity which all religions teach, which must be remembered by all of us, the dignity of the common man, the fundamental human rights of all beings. . . . Those rights are incapable of segregation or of isolation. There is neither border nor breed nor color nor creed on which those rights can be separated as between beings and beings. And, speaking as an Asiatic, may I say that this is an aspect of the question which can never be forgotten, and if we are laying the foundations for peace we can only lay them truly and justly. . . . Those fundamental human rights of all beings all over the world should be recognized and men and women treated as equals in every sphere.[47]

Following all the opening ceremony and initial speeches, the participants set about to address the many and challenging tasks at hand. Nearly three hundred official delegates labored with the help of twenty-five hundred advisors, while over two thousand journalists and radio announcers reported the deliberations to the world. The organization of work into several commissions and committees created a unique and democratic process that provided many more opportunities for vigorous debate and discussion than any other diplomatic conference ever held before. In this setting, the different agendas of the participants thus became quickly apparent. The Great Powers insisted on adhering as closely as possible to their original Dumbarton Oaks proposals that would enable them to permanently dominate the Security Council, possess the power to veto any action that might be taken against them, create a weak General Assembly, emphasize the rights of states rather than individuals, and exclude any reference to colonial possessions at all. In addition, their plan would allow only one reference to human rights, and that would be confined to economic and social cooperation alone. In fact, a lengthy, elaborate, and carefully indexed briefing book prepared for the U.S. delegation on all conceivable subjects did not contain a single agenda item for human rights.[48] The earlier meeting at Yalta confirmed that the United States, Britain, and the Soviet Union intended to stick with the Dumbarton Oaks proposals.[49] Indeed, when the United States merely suggested that they perhaps reconsider their collective position on colonial territories, Churchill exploded, declaring that he would never "consent under any circumstances to the United Nations thrusting interfering fingers into the very life of the British Empire."[50] Seeking to avoid any further surprises and maintain as much solidarity as possible, the Great Powers agreed to have constant communication with each other and to hold private evening consultations in Secretary of State Stettinius's penthouse apartment. They also cooperated closely within committees, as revealed somewhat perversely by Sir Alexander Cadogan of the British delegation, who privately described the process in these words: "I generally sit next to the American . . . and we conspire together to try to whack obstructionists on the head. . . . I tell him he's our heavy artillery and I am the sniper. It works quite well and we wiped the floor with a Mexican last night: I think we must have shut him up for a week or so."[51]

Despite such callous bombast, however, these delegates of the Great Powers knew perfectly well that they had serious differences between themselves and understood that if push came to shove they might not always be able to speak with the same voice. The Americans, Chinese, and Soviets might find common ground in their opposition to the British Empire, for example, but discover many other areas of disagreement such as regional defense, the nature of democratic regimes, or the meaning of human rights. Particularly troublesome was the growing level of tension between the United States and the Soviet Union. On the very first day of the San Francisco Conference, their troops met each other at the Elbe River in Europe and enjoyed a brief moment of celebration that symbolized their cooperation as allies in a successful coalition. Once Nazi Germany surrendered, however, the one element of a common enemy that had brought them together fell apart and both nations began to perceive that they no longer needed each other. This change appeared in Molotov's opening speech which accused some of those very nations listening to him of having turned the League of Nations "into a tool of various reactionary forces and privileged powers" and warned about the "many irreconcilable enemies in the camp of the most aggressive imperialists."[52] Truman reciprocated this hostility and told his advisors in his own blunt way that "if the Russians did not wish to join us they could go to hell."[53]

Disagreements also existed even within the delegations of the Great Powers. In order to avoid the bitter partisanship suffered by Wilson at the end of previous war, for example, the U.S. delegation consisted of rival Democrats and Republicans, including individuals as different as former isolationist Senator Arthur Vandenberg, Senator Tom Connally who had thwarted anti-lynching and fair employment bills, and John Foster Dulles. Virginia Gildersleeve of Barnard College served as the only female on an otherwise all-white, male delegation and saw herself as representing the interests of women and the public at large. In fact, she was lobbied to help secure rights for "the world's most long-suffering minority—women."[54] To make matters even more complicated, they were very much aware of many criticisms already leveled at their Dumbarton Oaks proposals and of the amendments officially submitted by others insisting on changes. Alice McDiarmid of the Department of State already had prepared a secret memorandum noting the widespread complaints from "various governments and private organizations" for a greater stress on standards of justice and rights. "Religious groups have been particularly emphatic in demanding that the Charter be strengthened in the field of human rights," she wrote, "newsmen have demonstrated keen interest in freedom of information; and groups of lawyers and others interested in international relations have put forward proposals for an international bill of rights."[55] Her colleague Leo Pasvolsky similarly informed the delegation that the absence of references to human rights "had caused a great deal of difficulty" and would continue to do so.[56] The British delegation also knew the criticisms they faced. In some respects, wrote one Foreign Office advisor, the Dumbarton Oaks proposals "either represent a retrogression as compared with the Covenant [of the League of Nations] or fail to deal with practical problems having a legal aspect which proved during the interwar period to be of substantial importance." "We cannot afford to forget," he suggested, "that the tentative proposals can be made a reality only by the release of moral and political forces." He therefore offered the not particularly welcomed advice to dedicate the international organization to a "high purpose" beyond power politics that "will ring through ages to come as a challenge . . . to establish right and justice as the basis of the world community."[57]

The medium and small nations of the world also sent representatives to San Francisco with their own national and/or personal agendas. Australia and New Zealand were not at all timid in announcing their objectives in advance. News releases from India and the Philippines revealed their intentions. The very large Latin American contingent had widely circulated their recommendations from the Chapultepec Conference. Despite their many differences of geography, politics, culture, language, race, religion, and ethnicity, all of these countries shared a desire to shape the new United Nations into an organization that reflected both their particular interests and their visions of peace. Thus, in sharp contrast with the Great Powers, they sought to reduce the influence of the proposed Security Council, increase the authority of the more widely representative General Assembly, provide more explicit statements about purposes and principles, and make sure that the organization committed itself in a variety of different ways to support international human rights. They wanted definite changes—and said so.

Delegates from these countries therefore submitted amendments regarding human rights provisions in the UN Charter, starting with the very first chapter. Such formal proposals from governments could not be easily ignored or quickly dismissed. Although there was no necessary consensus in form or content, they all expressed great dissatisfaction with the vague statements, stark omissions, and tight parameters of the Dumbarton Oaks plan. The declared purposes of the new organization, they argued, should go beyond old concepts of peace and security defined only in narrow geopolitical terms, and include those principles of justice and rights promised during the war. Consequently, the governments of Egypt, Mexico, France, Guatemala, Paraguay, and South Africa all submitted amendments proposing that human rights be established as one of the essential purposes of the United Nations.[58] Next came proposals from India, New Zealand, Norway, Lebanon, and Cuba, all seeking to insert explicit provisions supporting international human rights.[59] As the Egyptians argued, "the principles of the Atlantic Charter have fostered so much hope throughout the world that they ought to be put forward as the aims of the new World Organization."[60]

In this effort to include human rights in the Charter, these medium and small powers received enormous support from many NGOs. Indeed, one of the major characteristics of the San Francisco Conference and its efforts to create a "people's peace" was the unprecedented influence of groups and individuals not a part of any government who came to advance the interests of people rather than those of states. Some of these operated from a considerable distance, such as the World Trade Union Congress, Provisional World Council of Dominated Nations, West Indies National Council,

Sino-Korean People's League, and Council of Christians and Jews headquartered in London. The last (composed, in the words of one Foreign Office official, of "some heavy backers" such as the archbishop of Canterbury, the archbishop of Westminster, the Chief Rabbi, and the moderator of the Church of Scotland) issued a petition urging that human rights be given prominence by the British delegation.[61] The Non-European United Committee from South Africa printed "A Declaration to the Nations of the World" on behalf of several million black Africans, Indians, and those of mixed color, proclaiming that unless the United Nations addressed racial equality, all individuals other than whites in South Africa would "live and suffer under a tyranny very little different from Nazism."[62] The Six Nations Iroquois Confederacy similarly pressed the Canadian government to support the rights of indigenous peoples and racial justice in the Charter.

No nation experienced more pressure from activist NGOs than the United States. Freedom of speech and assembly, an open and active press, and geographical proximity all contributed to this development. Moreover, the Department of State wanted to use NGOs to generate public support, and therefore took the unusual move of trying what was called "an experiment in democracy in action on the diplomatic level" by actually inviting forty-two NGOs to send representatives serving as "consultants."[63] These included Clark Eichelberger of the American Association for the United Nations, Helen Reid of the American Association of University Women, David Simmons of the American Bar Association, Robert Watt of the American Federation of Labor, Joseph Proskauer of the American Jewish Committee, James Shotwell of the Carnegie Endowment for International Peace and the Commission to Study the Organization of Peace, Walter Van Kirk and Lutheran pastor Frederick Nolde of the Federal Council of Churches, Richard Pattee of the National Catholic Welfare Conference, and Jane Evans of the National Peace Conference. The NAACP sent Walter White, W. E. B. Du Bois, and Mary McLeod Bethune who supported an international bill of human rights, the dismantling of colonial empires, a racial equality clause similar to that proposed by the Chinese, and, in the case of Bethune, the rights of women.[64] Many other NGOs not invited to enjoy formal consultant status such as the Fraternal Council of Negro Churches, Council on African Affairs, and the Universal Negro Improvement Association, simply sent members to San Francisco on their own in order to make their influence felt and to prevent only white, middle- and upper-class males from dominating the discussions.[65]

Much to its surprise—and sometimes to both its pleasure and its unanticipated annoyance—the Department of State came to realize that when people are given the opportunity to express their opinions, they just might do so. These consultants came from different backgrounds and did not always speak with the same voice, but they believed passionately in their various visions and most had spent years of their lives as political, social, and religious activists. They most certainly were not the type to meekly sit by, be mere spectators, take an oath of silence, or be content, in the words of one of them, to serve as "window dressing" for the benefit of their government's public image.[66] They energetically held news conferences, issued press releases, spoke in local churches, sought allies, lobbied foreign delegations, and applied pressure as aggressively as they could. On one particularly dramatic occasion, they insisted on meeting as a group with secretary of state himself. His own assistant recorded the event as follows:

Mr. Stettinius was in the chair. Human rights was the topic of discussion. I see it all as if it had happened yesterday. I can see Judge Proskauer rise to his feet and address an impassioned plea. . . . "It isn't enough," he said, "for the charter to speak of universal respect for and observance of human rights. If there is to be freedom in this world, and peace, human rights must be safeguarded and there must be machinery within the United Nations to promote such freedom, to make fundamental human rights a reality. It is for you, Mr. Secretary," he continued—he pointed at him—"it is for the American delegation to take the lead in this matter, to live up to what is best in our traditions, to write into the charter a provision which would give meaning to the articles which pledge the nations of the world to promote human rights and fundamental freedoms." [His] appeal was taken by other people at the meeting—people representing different races, creeds, and political opinions. I accompanied Mr. Stettinius at the end of that meeting to a meeting of the American delegation. We went straight there. And all the way up in the elevator, then way down the long corridor . . . , down the corner room, where the American delegation was meeting, he didn't say a word. He was obviously moved.[67]

It is impossible, of course, to know the precise impact of this single meeting or whether Stettinius manipulated the consultants for this own purposes or ever admitted that "he had no idea of the intensity of the feeling on this subject,"[68] but other governments did not patiently wait to find out. Instead, they applied pressure to include explicit provisions in the Charter concerning equal protection and nondiscrimination. The new organization, in the words of the amendment submitted by India—and advanced with vigor by the dynamic female excluded from the official delegation, Vijaya Lakshmi Pandit—should promote "fundamental human rights for all men and women, irrespective of race, color, or creed, in all nations and in international relations and associations of nations one with another."[69] The Philippines proposed that the United Nations follow the principles of the Atlantic Charter and commit itself to develop "the spirit of brotherhood and racial equality among nations," while Iraq argued that racial discrimination constituted a "Nazi philosophy" that had to be "discarded forever."[70] Brazil, the Dominican Republic, and Mexico also submitted an amendment calling for human rights without any discrimination against race, sex, condition, or creed.[71] The American and Chinese women delegates felt very strongly about the right of equal treatment and stressed that "women should be regarded as human beings."[72] Uruguay proposed endorsing "the essential rights of mankind, internationally established and guaranteed," while Panama suggested inserting a "Declaration of Essential Human Rights" and a clause guaranteeing equal protection against discrimination because of race, religion, sex, "or any other reason."[73] And, unique among the Europeans at this stage, France advanced a similar amendment.[74] In every one of these proposals, nondiscrimination was seen as absolutely essential to any provision about international human rights. Then, in a move that surprised many, the Soviet Union announced that it would support a clause in the Charter prohibiting discrimination. U.S. representatives interpreted this as being motivated purely by politics, dismissing Soviet behavior as no more than "playing up to the small nations."[75]

Yet it was precisely these "small nations," most of whom were nonwhite, that had suffered so much in the past from discrimination, exploitation, and exclusion from international deliberations. Their people, who consistently found their rights abused or denied, long had been the victims, the subjects, and the pawns in the great chess game of diplomacy. Now at the San Francisco Conference, and after all the promises of the crusading war, they and their supporters demanded change. They did so with particular vehemence over the issues of the right to self-determination and the welfare of indigenous peoples in colonial empires, insisting that these principles must be applied universally and not just confined to territories formerly belonging to wartime adversaries. "Otherwise," noted the representative of Australia pointedly, "native peoples would be in a better position merely because they had once been under enemy sovereignty."[76] China now reentered the public debate on this issue that it alone had raised before at Dumbarton Oaks, insisting again for the equality of all races and their right to self-determination.[77] This time the Chinese found themselves surrounded by many supporters. General Carlos Romulo of the Philippines, for example, reminded all delegates that many different races and peoples had fought in World War II together. "This is a victory for the whole world," he stated, "not for one race, one nation, or one leader, but for all men. . . . I toured the Asiatic territories and I learned from the leaders and from the people of the flame of hope that swept the Far East when the Atlantic Charter was made known to the world. Everywhere these people asked the questions: Is the Atlantic Charter for the Pacific? Is it for one side of the world, and not for the other? For one race and not for them too?"[78]

So strong was the pressure on this point deliberately excluded by the Big Three at Dumbarton Oaks that the majority of other delegates formed an entirely new committee to address the human rights of people in colonies and dependent territories.[79] They created the Trusteeship Committee and elected Peter Fraser as its chair. He threw himself into this assignment with conviction and a deep sense of responsibility, using it to advance what he called the vision of "the fundamental rights of men and women" around the world.[80] Even before the conference began, he and Herbert Evatt of Australia had announced their support for an international system of trusteeship that would support the welfare and the economic, social, and political development of indigenous peoples. Now other delegations endorsed having a strong Trusteeship Council within the United Nations that would have the authority to compel the colonial powers to begin the process of decolonization and eventually dismantle their empires. Others opposed this plan as being too slow and too patronizing, demanding instead immediate self-determination for all peoples under imperial domination. Those holding colonies, of course, resisted and argued that the organization must never be allowed to engage in the "theft" of their possessions. Harold Stassen of the U.S. delegation, warned that independence was "a dangerous word."[81] Such sharply conflicting positions revealed an intensity of politics and diplomacy rarely matched elsewhere at the conference, resulting in contentious debate, vicious maneuvering, and what Fraser himself described as "protracted negotiations" so difficult that they often had to take place in private "outside the Committee."[82]

Simultaneous with these efforts, many delegates also worked to increase both the number and the scope of human rights provisions in other sections of the United Nations Charter. They lobbied hard to increase the influence of the General Assembly where all nations would have an equal vote, by giving it the authority to consider any international issue, including the explicit power to initiate studies and make specific recommendations concerning human rights.[83] In addition, those who believed strongly in a connection between peace and justice sought to make the proposed Economic and Social Council a "principal organ" of the United Nations itself and possessing clear responsibilities in the area of international human rights. These included such matters as economic and social justice, cultural affairs, the right of self-determination, and nondiscrimination, as well as humanitarian relief activities. But here a great controversy arose between those who represented labor governments such as Australia and New Zealand wanting to include statements about the right to "full employment," and those such as the United States who regarded such provisions as "too socialistic."[84]

Such extraordinary pressures to place provisions on international human rights squarely within the UN Charter were not only exerted over a period of months but, in the words of one State Department official, created a "stampede."[85] When confronted with the barrage of public statements, private conversations, official speeches, NGO activities, formal proposals, and the actual votes of other governments from around the world concerning human rights—and the intensity with which they were presented—the Great Powers realized that they had no choice but to go into further deliberations. Spurred on by its own consultants who argued that human rights represented "a matter of tremendous importance" requiring "much greater emphasis" in the Charter, and by members of its own delegation like Virginia Gildersleeve, the United States suggested to the other authors of the Dumbarton Oaks proposals that certain changes had to be made.[86] As a result of intense discussions among themselves, and for a variety of mixed motives, they agreed to submit a new package of amendments. It incorporated many suggestions advanced up to this point, including specific provisions on human rights and nondiscrimination as they related to the purposes of the organization, the terms of reference for the General Assembly, arrangements for international economic and social cooperation, and the functions and powers of the Economic and Social Council. They still refused, however, even to mention the fate of colonies or to include any enforcement provisions concerning human rights. In fact, they insisted on inserting an explicit provision reaffirming national sovereignty and domestic jurisdiction to prevent outside interference from the United Nations itself.[87]

In the midst of this debate, a powerful and emotional element suddenly appeared. It was captured with particular poignancy in a single issue of *Life* magazine. The issue began, as it always did, with letters to the editors, ads, and stories of the previous week's events. Readers correctly anticipated full coverage of the start of the San Francisco Conference. Then, without any warning, they turned a page and saw something that they had never seen before in their lives. One word led the title: "Atrocities." The language still speaks for itself:

Last week the jubilance of impending victory was sobered by the grim facts of the atrocities which the Allied troops were uncovering all over Germany. For 12 years since the Nazis seized power, Americans have heard charges of Germany brutality. Made skeptical by World War I "atrocity propaganda," many people refused to put much faith in stories about the inhuman Nazi treatment of prisoners.

Last week Americans could *no longer doubt* stories of Nazi cruelty. *For the first time there was irrefutable evidence. . . .*

Eyewitnesses commented: "The memory of what we saw and heard will haunt us," the truth is so horrific "you couldn't print it," and "the lowest point in human degradation to which humanity has yet descended." The editors then introduced what was to follow with these words:

With the armies in Germany were four *Life* photographers whose pictures are printed on these pages. The things they show are horrible. They are printed for the reason [that] . . . "Dead men will have indeed died in vain if live men refuse to look at them."[88]

The photographs enabled readers to see what they could never have imagined on their own—and they were absolutely shocked at what they saw. Graphic images showed broken prisoners deformed by malnutrition, charred remains, several thousand emaciated corpses laid out in long rows on the grounds of extermination camps, guards knee-deep in decaying human flesh and bones, and a young boy walking along a dirt road virtually numb to all the dead bodies with bulging lifeless eyes piled along the side. If one ever needed evidence of the power of photographs to evoke empathy, to arouse the conscience, to provoke outrage, to move people into determining that certain behavior is completely unacceptable, and thereby to serve as a catalyst for action, this was surely it.

The first widespread knowledge of the Holocaust and its message that some people and nations—if left completely unchecked—could inflict unimaginable atrocities against other human beings thus entered public consciousness at precisely the same time as the opportunity to create a new international organization designed to create and maintain peace and security. This particular combination inextricably tied visions of human rights with visions of peace, security, and justice. When added to the changes to the Dumbarton Oaks proposals already made under pressure, the amendments from governments, and proposals from NGOs along with the personalities and the nations who presented them, it greatly intensified the volatile mixture of politics and diplomacy in the weeks that followed at the San Francisco Conference. Indeed, it presented one of those several forces, in the words of one delegate, "which none of the statesmen present could ignore, since in the long run, power is a moral as well as a physical entity."[89]

But other important and strategic factors also weighed heavily. Neither vigor of protest nor urgency of argument could alter the fact of Great Power dominance. The delegates understood perfectly well that, for better or worse, the United Nations could never be created or sustained unless the most powerful nations agreed to give their support, and that this would come only at a cost of certain conditions.[90] Similarly, they realized that no organization seeking to claim universal principles would ever emerge unless endorsed by the medium and small powers who had their own agendas and could claim to speak for the overwhelming majority of people in the world. The Latin Americans alone held twenty out of fifty votes at the conference.[91] In addition, all delegations knew all too well of the many domestic critics and pressures that would scrutinize their decisions once they left the exciting mood of an international meeting and the quaint Victorian homes and cable cars of San Francisco. This was particularly true of the United States, where the delegation was constantly reminded that Senate approval would be necessary for ratification of any treaty and where opposition party members declared again and again that national sovereignty and domestic jurisdiction must never be compromised.[92] Moreover, and of particular importance to human rights, since governments are usually the most egregious violators of such rights, their representatives came to realize that they were being asked to consider provisions that might actually restrict the ability of their own governments to treat their own people as they wished. Whatever arguments they made at the conference might well come back to haunt them. The complicated interplay of these many forces, factors, and motives finally came to seen in the text of the United Nations Charter itself.

The Charter of the United Nations

Exactly two months after opening the San Francisco Conference, the delegates reached an agreement. On 26 June 1945, they all assembled before a throng of excited correspondents and photographers. Under an imposing backdrop of their many national flags, the heads of each delegation gathered behind a massive desk placed on a bright blue circular carpet. When the hands of the clock stood together at noon, Wellington Koo stepped forward to represent the country that had suffered the longest as a victim of the war. With a traditional Chinese ink brush in his hand, he inscribed the characters of his name on the leather-bound copy of the text.[93] The rest followed in turn. At the end, they presented a blueprint for the most ambitious experiment in international organization ever attempted in history: the Charter of the United Nations.

In many ways the Charter resembled the Dumbarton Oaks proposals. It established a powerful Security Council with primary responsibility for the maintenance of peace and security, dominated by the Great Powers through their permanent membership and veto. It created a General Assembly where all nations possessed equal votes in matters of common concern, an Economic and Social Council, and an International Court of Justice as the judicial organ to deal with state-to-state disputes. It also established a Secretariat administered by a secretary-general and a staff. In other ways, the Charter marked a notable departure from the Dumbarton Oaks proposals submitted by the Great Powers. This was particularly evident and most dramatic in the area of international human rights.

The very first sentence of the Charter announced the departure. Rather than traditional language about the plenipotentiaries of nation-states, yet entirely consistent with visions of a "people's peace," the Preamble declared:

WE THE PEOPLES OF THE UNITED NATIONS
DETERMINED
to save succeeding generations from the scourge of war, which twice in our lifetime has brought untold sorrow to mankind, and

to reaffirm faith in fundamental human rights, in the dignity and worth of the human person, in the equal rights of men and women of nations large and small, and

to establish conditions under which justice and respect for the obligations arising from treaties and other sources of international law can be maintained, and

to promote social progress and better standards of life in larger freedom . . .

HAVE RESOLVED TO COMBINE OUR EFFORTS
TO ACCOMPLISH THESE AIMS.

This resolve was immediately carried into Article 1 where the signatories boldly pledged themselves and their organization to new responsibilities:

To develop friendly relations among nations based on respect for the principle of equal rights and self-determination of peoples, and to take other appropriate measures for international peace;

To achieve international cooperation in solving international problems of an economic, social, cultural, or humanitarian character, and in promoting and encouraging respect for human rights and fundamental freedoms for all without distinction as to race, sex, language, or religion. . . . [94]

Such explicit provisions regarding human rights—especially with the language "for all"— provided a dramatic beginning. But the Charter went on to say much more. It gave the General Assembly considerably more authority than originally proposed by the Great Powers to discuss virtually any matter, including that of human rights, and to initiate studies and make recommendations for assisting in the realization of these rights without racial, sexual, linguistic, or religious discrimination. This meant that although a recommendation from the Assembly would not possess the binding force of law, any resolution dealing with human rights most certainly had the potential of significantly impacting the United Nations as a whole. Very importantly, the Charter linked security, peace, justice, and human rights. It instructed the Security Council to act in accordance with the larger purposes and principles of the organization and to determine whether serious human rights violations constituted a "threat to the peace." They thus were authorized to decide what action might be required, including the possibility of humanitarian intervention.[95]

The majority of delegates also made certain that the Charter addressed a broad spectrum of economic and social rights. Indeed, in the words of Peter Fraser, "No section of the Dumbarton Oaks proposals underwent more extensive changes for the better than that which dealt with international cooperation in economic and social matters."[96] The text explicitly drew a connection between human well-being and international peace, reiterated support for the principle of equal rights and self-determination, and committed the organization to promote universal respect for, and observance of, human rights and fundamental freedoms without discrimination—"for all." To achieve this, it elevated the Economic and Social Council to be one of the principal organs of the United Nations and authorized it to initiate studies, make recommendations, prepare draft conventions, organize conferences, and consult with human rights NGOs. In addition, and in the only such provision in the entire Charter, this body was mandated to create a Commission on Human Rights.[97]

Then, in a radical departure from the original proposals from the Great Powers, the Charter explicitly addressed one of the most contentious issues of the entire conference: the rights of indigenous peoples. The text began with a broad-based provision entitled the Declaration Regarding Non-Self-Governing Territories recognizing the principle "that the interests of the inhabitants of these territories are paramount" and accepting "as a sacred trust" the obligation to promote their well-being "to the utmost." Toward this end, the signatories pledged themselves to ensure just treatment and protection against abuses, to assist in developing self-government, to take due account of their aspirations, and to help in the progressive development of their free political institutions.[98] At the same time, the Charter also provided for the creation of an International Trusteeship System assisted by a Trusteeship Council with the authority to consider reports, accept petitions, and provide for periodic visits for observations. It was charged with securing peace, security, "equal treatment," the "administration of justice," and

the political, economic, social, and educational advancement of the inhabitants of the trust territories, and their progressive development towards self-government or independence as may be appropriate to the particular circumstances of each territory and its peoples and the freely expressed wishes of the peoples concerned

and

respect for human rights and for fundamental freedoms for all without distinction as to race, sex, language, or religion, and . . . recognition of the interdependence of the peoples of the world.[99]

Never before in history had any treaty ever given human rights such a prominent place as did the Charter of the United Nations. Those government delegates and their allies among NGOs, individuals, and colonial peoples who had worked so hard to insert these provisions thus had many reasons for a sense of remarkable accomplishment. They had done their best to keep the promises made during the war. They had not been deterred by Great Power pressure or by criticisms that their visions were only idealistic, naive dreams in a world dominated by power politics. And they had successfully resisted the attempts to eliminate what their opponents called the "controversial" and "offensive" articles about human rights.[100] But it was not over. In order to secure these provisions, they had to concede others. Thus, a more detailed reading of *all* the provisions in the Charter revealed that the politics and diplomacy of the San Francisco Conference also produced important qualifications, omissions, and other problems that would confront the evolution of international human rights for many years to come.

The much-heralded International Trusteeship System with its goal of extending the rights of indigenous peoples, for example, did not apply to all colonies. Indeed, those states possessing empires insisted that it apply only to former League mandates, territories detached from enemy states, and those areas voluntarily placed under the system with conditions to be determined by nations responsible for their administration. Such a qualification, of course, allowed Britain, France, Portugal, Spain, the Netherlands, Belgium, and the United States to retain and exploit whatever colonial possessions they wished. In addition, the Charter allowed certain territories under trust to be designated "strategic areas" and placed under the auspices of the Security Council, where the Great Powers could maintain exclusive control (a method quickly employed by the United States with the Caroline, Mariana, and Marshall islands in the Pacific). Moreover, they sought to restrict the powers of the Trusteeship Council and keep it from pushing colonial powers further than they wanted to go.[101]

The Charter also spoke in new and eloquent ways about responsibilities of the United Nations in the area of international human rights. It provided unparalleled specificity for a treaty of this wide-ranging nature in language against discrimination on the basis of race, gender, language, and religion—"for all." But it did not define precisely what was meant by the broad and general expression, "human rights." Due to politics and diplomacy, not the least of which involved the growing tension between the democratic and capitalist states against those who advocated Communism, the Charter did not discuss any details or conditions of civil and political rights or economic and social rights. Similarly, it did not explain what was actually meant by "fundamental freedoms," "just treatment," "political, economic, social, and educational advancement," "independence as may be appropriate," or "humanitarian character." The language of the Charter remained very generous but also very vague on each of these points.

A much greater problem emerged over enforcement. Several representatives, especially those of the Great Powers, indicated a willingness to include lofty words about rights, but not provisions for practical or effective means of enforcing them. Any proposals that the United Nations be required to actively "safeguard," "protect," "preserve," "guarantee," "implement," "assure," or "enforce" human rights died an unceremonious death in committee.[102] Instead, the only verbs that could gain acceptance were "should facilitate," "may discuss," "initiate studies," "make recommendations," "consider," "reaffirm," "assist," "encourage," and "promote."[103] Even then, delegates carefully explained that they did not want these words to assume any greater meaning or authority than they already possessed. As the Costa Rican representative bluntly announced during deliberations: "The propagation of ideas and principles . . . is of immense value to mankind; but surely if the word 'promote' is understood as implying the ability to coerce states . . . not one of the states concerned will recognize this principle."[104]

International human rights, once again, thus confronted the formidable rock of national sovereignty. This came as no surprise. In fact, many observers had accurately predicted in advance that this problem, which had plagued so many efforts on behalf of human rights in the past, would resurface with a vengeance once negotiations began for the United Nations. "We have taught the layman to worship the arch-fiction of the sovereign state," forewarned legal scholar Philip C. Jessup, "and thereby have built a Maginot line against the invasion of new ideas in the international world, and behind that rampart the demagogue and the reactionary are enthroned."[105] James Shotwell similarly cautioned in the *International Safeguard of Human Rights* that "each state, jealous of its sovereignty, had regarded any expression of foreign interest in the welfare of its citizens at home, as an interference in its own affairs," and would continue to do so unless stopped. The recent experience of the war, he argued, demonstrated once and for all the disaster of this approach, and thus urged all delegates to now overcome their traditional defense of national sovereignty for the sake of international peace and human rights.[106] This would not be easy, for as Arthur Vandenberg of the U.S. delegation candidly announced in the beginning, national sovereignty and the prevention of outside interference into domestic affairs were matters "dear to our hearts."[107]

The fundamental difficulty and ultimate paradox, of course, stemmed from the fact that those very governments most guilty of violating the human rights of their own people were being asked to provide protection against themselves. For this reason, the majority of states remained unwilling to sacrifice elements of their sovereignty for the sake of human rights by authorizing the international community to intervene in their internal affairs. The United States could speak eloquently about civil rights around the world, for example, but not if they exacerbated what Dulles called "the Negro problem in the South."[108] The British had no trouble supporting the principle of extending political rights, but not if it applied to their empire. The Soviets could champion economic and social rights, but not if they imposed any restrictions on Stalin's dictatorship. The Chinese could strongly advocate the rights of self-determination and racial equality, but not if they entailed drastic reforms at home. But this could not simply be laid at the doorstep of the Great Powers alone. The Australians and New Zealanders could endorse a broad extension of human rights for the globe, but not if this jeopardized control over their immigration policies against Asians or their respective populations of Aborigines or Maori. Jan Smuts of South Africa could enthusiastically draft language about rights for the Charter's preamble, but not if it committed his country to giving equal treatment for blacks. The Indians could argue passionately for the rights of all people, but not if required them to eliminate their caste system. The Iranians could declare their agreement with principles of equality and justice, but not if it forced them to modify their policies toward women. The Cubans had no trouble supporting a declaration of rights and duties, but not if it threatened the strong-armed rule of Fulgencio Batista.[109] As Herbert Evatt remarked during an extremely candid moment, "Every country represented in this conference has its own internal problems, its own vital spheres of domestic policy in which it cannot, without forfeiting its very existence as a state, permit external intervention."[110] The international protection of human rights seemed perfectly acceptable if extended over the domestic jurisdiction of other nations—but not of their own.

For precisely these reasons, and despite all the other features of the Charter as described, some government representatives insisted on a feature that would protect the interests and prerogatives of their states. Although the language of the preamble spoke of "We the Peoples," the fact was that governments and not peoples conducted the negotiations. This explains why, in the end, they made certain to insert in the chapter on fundamental principles one of the most critical and sweeping of all provisions in the entire text, Article 2 (7) reading:

Nothing contained in the present Charter shall authorize the United Nations to intervene in matters which are essentially within the domestic jurisdiction of any state or shall require Members to submit such matters to settlement.[111]

With such language, they hoped that they could defend the national sovereignty of their own nations and prevent the new organization from interfering with their own particular domestic affairs. In the words of one delegate from the United States, this provision "was sufficient to overpower all other considerations."[112]

When one reads this article on domestic jurisdiction it is easy to conclude that the delegates who drafted and signed the Charter engaged in nothing less than deliberate duplicity. That is, they cynically and capriciously took away with one hand what they had given with the other. They could claim that they had supported human rights, while at the same time knowing full well that the organization now could not interfere with the way that they treated their own people. There is some truth to this argument. But it is insufficient as a full explanation and does not do justice to the complexities of the issues or the range of motivations among the participants, many of whom believed that without Article 2 (7) the Charter would have never been approved, and thus the United Nations never created in the first place. The evidence suggests that many delegates, trying to be conscientious in representing competing interests—and thus balance pressures on them—either did not completely understand the full implications of their decisions or somewhat naively believed that they just might be able to have their cake and eat it too. They wanted to ensure that individuals would be protected from severe violations of their rights at the hands of governments, while wanting to make sure that the new international organization did not have the authority to intervene in their own domestic affairs.[113] Some fell victim to their own wishful thinking and convinced themselves that all of the provisions and principles in the Charter were internally consistent. Still others believed that, if nations cooperated with each other in good faith, the problems created by the necessity of compromise somehow would work themselves out through time. Nevertheless, most did not appreciate the fact that they had created a profound inherent contradiction. If the *international* human rights provisions "for all" regardless of their nationality enshrined in Article 1 were completely protected, then the claims of state sovereignty would be undermined. If, on the other hand, *national* sovereignty as enshrined in Article 2 was completely protected, then international efforts to assist victims of human rights abuse in any given state would be undermined. The subsequent evolution of international human rights has been a struggle between these two diametrically opposed principles ever since.

Differing Reactions and Assessments

The final provisions of the Charter of the United Nations, including those specifically dealing with human rights, as might be expected, produced a wide variety of differing reactions and assessments. For many, they marked unprecedented achievement. Never before in history or in the annals of diplomacy had issues of international human rights been so openly discussed, strongly advocated, or made such an integral part of a negotiated agreement with formal obligations and enlarged responsibilities. Never before had so many countries, cultures, and races participated in such momentous negotiations. Never before had women played such an active role in the deliberations. Never before had human rights NGOs been so visible or vigorous. Those with visions of rights had refused to be intimidated by pressure, to be dismissed by the skeptics as mere idealists, or to be silenced for the sake of expediency. They had done their best to keep promises by creating a "people's peace" in which the rights of individuals would be respected. The actual inclusion of explicit provisions in the Charter for human rights and fundamental freedoms, equality and nondiscrimination, justice, economic and social advancement, humanitarian assistance, self-determination and independence, the welfare of indigenous peoples, and a Commission on Human Rights seemed simply unbelievable.

For these reasons, the concluding speeches of many delegates and the private assessments that followed spoke profusely of "one of the great moments in history," an "epoch-making document," and a "milestone in the evolution of human freedom." They discussed the historic role of their conference and the unprecedented contributions of human rights NGOs. They praised the Charter as one of the most important agreements ever negotiated in the entire history of the world and hailed it as representing the embodiment of highest aspirations of men and women everywhere. They enthusiastically embraced its wider definitions of global peace and security that included justice, the welfare of "untold millions" of people, and human rights. "The words upon its parchment," declared one participant, "chart the course by which a world in agony can be restored and peace maintained and human rights and freedoms can be advanced."[114]

Others reacted much differently and accused the delegates of not doing enough and producing a Charter of little or no value. *Time* magazine compared the idealistic promises made during the war with the end result and concluded that the final agreement represented no more than "a charter for a world of power."[115] Seasoned activist Rayford Logan characterized it as a "tragic joke."[116] He noted that the organization just created lacked the power to implement or enforce the human rights provisions, allowing even the signatories themselves to continue violating the full rights of their own citizens and subjects. The domestic jurisdiction clause, of course, drew immediate criticism for appearing to slash with a single stroke the very life out of all the articles dealing with human rights. As E. B. White of the *New Yorker* wrote in despair, the fundamental problem could be identified in the "steady throbbing" of one theme: "sovereignty, sovereignty, sovereignty."[117] In addition, indigenous peoples who believed that they had been promised the right of self-determination were furious to learn that the colonial powers could still retain their empires. Du Bois, who had just published *Color and Democracy*, declared before the Senate Foreign Relations Committee that the Charter reflected nothing more than "the national interests, the economic rivalries, and the selfish demands" of governments represented at San Francisco. The new United Nations, he argued, should be created to serve "not only white peoples" but "the yellow, brown, and black peoples of America, Asia, and Africa." Toward this end, he concluded, it should make a "clear and unequivocal" stand "for race equality, and the universal application of the democratic way of life, not simply as philosophy and justice, but to save human civilization from suicide. What was true of the United States in the past is true of world civilization today—we cannot exist half slave and half free."[118]

Instead of complaining that the Charter accomplished too little, some critics took just the opposite position, angrily charging that it did far too much. They feared that the delegates had created some kind of world government or super-state that would jeopardize the prerogatives of their own nation. Particularly when reading the explicit provisions about human rights, they worried that even the domestic jurisdiction clause would not be "water tight" and might not be able to sufficiently protect complete national sovereignty from interference. Given the increasingly close relationship between foreign and domestic affairs, they wondered, who would actually determine the precise definitions of "intervene" or "domestic jurisdiction"? Or, even more difficult, who would decide the meaning of "essentially" within the domestic jurisdiction of member states? Would this decision rest with each government, the Security Council, a majority of the General Assembly, the Commission on Human Rights, or the International Court of Justice? Would it be made on the basis of established law or by the politics of the moment? Thus, depending on their particular interests and problems, national governments worried aloud how the Charter would affect their treatment of indigenous peoples in colonial areas, of those seeking immigration, or of those discriminated against due to their race, gender, language, or religious beliefs.[119]

Still other participants and observers viewed the Charter and its human rights provisions as neither a simply magnificent achievement that suddenly would create heaven on earth nor a horrendous tragedy that would destroy the cherished nation-state. Instead, they saw it in the context of the time and considered it to be a remarkable accomplishment in the evolution of international human rights. They regarded politics and diplomacy as the art of the possible, balanced somewhere between the cynics and the perfectionists, and knew that no nation or group could obtain everything they wanted during a mere two months of negotiation. They believed that those who assembled at San Francisco had accomplished about as much as—if not more than—could realistically be expected given the heavy legacies of the past, the circumstances of the war, the magnitude of the tasks, the sharp divergence between the Great Powers and others, the differences between states and NGOs, the prejudices of the time, and the often exaggerated hopes for the future. No one, they concluded, reasonably could expect the delegates, even if they had nothing else to do, to agree on a precise definition or enumeration of human rights—let alone draft an actual bill or charter of rights as proposed by some—in such a politically complex and philosophically diverse world within just a few weeks. "We cannot indeed claim that our work is perfect or that we have created an unbreakable guarantee of peace," said Lord Halifax. "For ours is no enchanted palace to 'spring into sight at once' by magic touch or hidden power."[120] He observed that the newly forged organization would enhance peace and security only if nations were ready to make sacrifices for the common good, and that only time would tell whether their efforts rested on shifting sand or solid rock. Jan Smuts and Peter Fraser reached the same conclusion, describing the Charter as an imperfect document, full of compromises over difficult and tangled problems, but nevertheless a substantial advance over any previous plan ever created and the best possible hope of realizing a vision of peace with human rights around the world.[121]

In his concluding speech at the final session of the San Francisco Conference, President Truman offered a similar assessment. He explained that in his judgment the Charter represented somewhat of a wonder to have been even negotiated at all. Many pressures had been exerted on the participants to keep them from making concessions or reaching compromises. The result was not perfect, he acknowledged, but it most certainly marked an essential first step in moving toward the future. "This Charter, like our Constitution," he said, "will be expanded and improved as time goes on. No one claims that it is now a final or a perfect instrument. It has not been poured into a fixed mold. Changing world conditions will require readjustments—but they will be readjustments of peace and not of war." Then, significantly, Truman publicly declared what many others believed they had learned from experience: namely, that security, peace, justice, and human rights were inseparably connected. "The Charter is dedicated to the achievement and observance of human rights and fundamental freedoms," he concluded. "Unless we can attain those objectives for all men and women everywhere—without regard to race, language, or religion—we cannot have permanent peace and security in the world.[122]

*   *   *

There are times in history when powerful forces converge at precisely the same moment. The end of World War II marked one of those times. Visions of creating a "people's peace" that contained provisions for human rights would not be denied. Too many people had endured too much suffering, made too many sacrifices, heard too many promises, and witnessed too much of the staggering capacity of modern states to oppress, torture, and kill millions of their own fellow human beings around the world ever to return to an unchanged past. The United Nations Charter thus sought to address their concerns, and, by providing explicit provisions focused on human rights in a formal treaty as never before, dramatically challenged and changed some of the most essential parameters of international discourse and behavior. Those who negotiated the Charter, however, discovered themselves caught in the vortex of a dramatic and powerful struggle between a long tradition of national sovereignty and a dynamic new movement demanding international human rights. They were unable and unwilling either to completely abandon a conservative past or to wholeheartedly embrace a potentially radical future. For this reason, they simultaneously wrote provisions into the Charter containing language about both domestic jurisdiction and human rights,

Figure 10. Creating a "People's Peace" and the United Nations Charter: The San Francisco Conference. United Nations Photo.

about both governments and individuals. Assuming responsibilities to respect "the principle of equal rights and self-determination" and to promote "universal respect for, and observance of, human rights and fundamental freedoms for all without distinction as to race, sex, language, or religion," while at the same time avoiding any provisions for practical enforcement and prohibiting intervention "in matters which are essentially within the domestic jurisdiction of any state," appeared confusing at best and completely contradictory at worst. The existence of these unresolved difficulties set into motion an intense global debate about the philosophical and political meanings of these expressions and the precise nature of duties beyond national borders that continues to this day. This process began to transform the evolution of international human rights into a revolution.

Chapter 7
Proclaiming a Vision

The Universal Declaration of Human Rights

> Are human rights essentially within the domestic jurisdiction of the State? My answer is no, and a hundred times no. I submit that by the San Francisco Charter human rights have been taken out of the province of domestic jurisdiction and have been placed within the realm of international law.
> —Ricardo Alfaro of Panama

Those who negotiated and signed the United Nations Charter opened a veritable floodgate to new possibilities of expanding international human rights as never before in history. Explicit provisions suddenly placed the organization and its members on public record and in international law as supporting universal respect for and observance of human rights—"for all." They formally pledged themselves to promote these rights without any distinction as to race, sex, language, or religion. Just how these objectives would be met in practice, of course, remained to be seen. There were those with expansive hopes that human rights now would be actively advanced beyond all previous experience. Yet there also were others committed to vested interests and national sovereignty who, armed with the domestic jurisdiction clause, vowed to resist change, at least insofar as it involved their own country. Both sides believed that any resolution of their sharply conflicting positions would take time and would depend on changing historical circumstances, but few anticipated just how soon the contest would be joined. It began immediately, for those who demanded change refused to wait and sought to proclaim a vision of international human rights to the world.

The Revolution Begins

The activists saw in the language of the Charter and the momentum that created it unprecedented opportunities to advance international human rights and threw themselves into action. They were absolutely determined not to accept the proposition that the domestic jurisdiction clause precluded any challenges to national sovereignty. Instead, they insisted that the Charter imposed both legal and moral obligations on all member states to transform individuals from mere objects of international pity into actual subjects of international law.[1] Thus, even before the United Nations formally met for the first time, they launched a variety of new efforts. These produced fear among those governments and individuals who opposed them, but brought hope to those who shared their visions.

Within only days of the signing of the Charter, for example, the Pan-African Federation, the Federation of Indian Associations in Britain, the West African Students' Union, the Ceylon Students' Association, and the Burma Association organized the All-Colonial Peoples' Conference to demand their rights of self-determination and racial equality. The Fifth Pan-African Congress met shortly thereafter, attracting representatives from Antigua, Barbados, Bermuda, British Guiana (now Guyana), Gambia, the Gold Coast (now Ghana), Jamaica, Kenya, Liberia, Nigeria, Nyasaland (now Malawi), St. Kitts, St. Lucia, Sierra Leone, South Africa, Tanganyika, Tobago, Trinidad, and Uganda, among others, including Du Bois from the United States. Reflecting both the radicalizing effect of World War II and the expectations raised by the Charter, they too announced that they were no longer willing to ask modestly for some slight favor from on high, but now to demand independence, an end to racial discrimination and exploitation, and respect for human rights. From their ranks emerged leaders such as Nkrumah and Kenyatta. In a resolution entitled "The Declaration to the Colonial Peoples of the World," they asserted their determination to seize their freedom by force if necessary and issued a call echoing the *Communist Manifesto*: "Colonial and Subject Peoples of the World—Unite!"[2]

This, of course, marked only the beginning. Not all peoples possessed the patience to wait for the results of declarations from NGOs or resolutions from the as yet untested United Nations. Instead, they sought to take matters into their own hands, utilizing the unique conditions and destroyed power structures that existed in the aftermath of war. They launched armed campaigns against the British in Burma, Egypt, India, Iraq, Malaya, and Palestine; the French in Algeria, Indochina, Lebanon, and Syria; and the Dutch in Indonesia. Violent race riots erupted within the United States when black ex-service men and women returned in no mood to live again in a Jim Crow society with segregation, the Ku Klux Klan, and lynching. As Walter White saw it, all these struggles against exploitation, imperialism, and racism were global in nature and closely interrelated, whether they occurred in Asia, Africa, the Middle East, the Pacific, North or South America. "A wind *is* rising," he wrote, "—a wind of determination by the have-nots of the world to share the benefits of freedom and prosperity which the haves of the earth have tried to keep exclusively for themselves. That wind blows all over the world. Whether that wind develops into a hurricane is a decision which we must make now."[3]

Others also suddenly became much more active in criticizing the abuses of human rights at home and abroad. The African National Congress publicly condemned the practice of apartheid in South Africa. The World Jewish Congress and the Conseil Représentatif des Juifs de France exerted pressure for peace treaties with former adversaries to provide equal protection. A Texas radio station broadcast programs about unequal treatment of Hispanics, claiming that such discrimination clearly violated the new Charter of the United Nations. India joined with the NAACP and the Indian

Rights Association in castigating racial segregation in the United States with newspaper headlines such as "A Shameful Act" and "Treatment of Negroes a Blot on U.S." Czechoslovakia criticized the Soviet Union for suppressing rights in Eastern Europe. China drew attention to the immigration policies of Australia, Canada, and New Zealand. The Soviets condemned the West for violating the economic and social rights of the poor. Iraq, Egypt, and most of the Latin American countries, among many others, condemned the British, French, and Dutch for trying to perpetuate their colonial empires and deny human rights to indigenous peoples.[4] At the same time Uruguay protested the abuse of civil and political rights of the people of Argentina by their own government, declaring that national sovereignty and its traditional culture of impunity could no longer "shield without limitation the notorious and repeated violation by any republic of the elementary rights of man and of the citizen, nor the nonfulfillment of obligations freely contracted by a state with respect to its external and internal duties and which entitle it to be an active member of the international community."[5]

Those states subject to such criticism, of course, reacted swiftly and vehemently. They claimed that how they treated their own people was strictly their own business, regardless of whatever new pledges had been made. The long-standing doctrine of national sovereignty and the Charter's own Article 2 (7) about domestic jurisdiction, they insisted, precluded any outside interference whatsoever into their internal affairs. The government of Argentina, to use just one example, declared that any accusation against its human rights record was as "unexpected as it is dangerous," "extraordinary," threatened traditional practices, and raised the specter that members of the international community could intervene in the domestic affairs of any state whenever they wished. It thus adamantly announced that it would never accept the proposition that its own policies at home might somehow be "subject to the will or the judgement of foreign powers."[6] Such expressions of resistance threw fuel on the fire of the escalating global debate and mobilized those with visions of international human rights to vow that they would challenge the traditional claims of national sovereignty even further and in any forum possible.

A variety of international meetings therefore provided perfect opportunities to raise these issues. When a conference met in the autumn of 1945 to create a new constitution for the International Labor Organization, the delegates determined to go "beyond the nation-state" and address the rights of all people, especially economic and social rights. They focused on labor inspection, freedom of association, equal remuneration for men and women, freedom from forced labor, nondiscrimination, minimum standards of living, and the need for colonial powers to implement rights for those under their control.[7] Similarly, when diplomats established the United Nations Educational, Scientific, and Cultural Organization (UNESCO), they felt compelled to comment on the causes of the catastrophe they all had just experienced. They easily could have blamed territorial ambition, economic greed, the accumulation of armaments, the absence of collective security, or the lack of prudent statecraft, but did not. Instead, they focused on only one factor, and poignantly concluded in a most remarkable statement: "The great and terrible war which has now ended was a war made possible by the denial of democratic principles of the dignity, equality, and mutual respect for men, and by the propagation in their place, through ignorance and prejudice, of the doctrine of the inequality of men and races."[8] To counteract these practices, they committed themselves to devoting their educational, scientific, and cultural resources toward the promotion of international human rights.

No assemblage in the autumn of 1945 attracted more attention that the opening of the International Military Tribunal at Nuremberg. Never before in history had a legal proceeding attempted to make government leaders internationally responsible for crimes covering so much time, so many nations, or so many people. The prosecutors knew all too well that they possessed far more than sufficient evidence to charge the remaining Nazi leaders with crimes against the peace, war crimes, and, in addition, an important category of abuses: extermination, enslavement, and other inhuman acts so heinous that they constituted "crimes against humanity."[9] "The wrongs which we seek to condemn and punish," declared Justice Robert Jackson in his opening statement, "have been so calculated, so malignant, and so devastating, that civilization cannot tolerate their being ignored, because it cannot survive their being repeated." He spoke about the extraordinary violations against the "inalienable rights" of members of the human family and predicted without exaggeration: "Our proof will be disgusting."[10]

It was. Meticulous records revealed the names and the numbers of those helpless human victims exterminated like insects. Shocking testimony described the massive deportations, forced labor, torture, death camps, and unspeakable medical experiments that made even the strong avert their eyes and turn away. Grotesque photographs of the "Final Solution" displayed mounds of human bones, piles of eyeglasses and gold teeth fillings, and grooves in solid concrete made by the clawing fingers of those about to be gassed to death. Gruesome newsreels showed bulldozers unceremoniously shoving heaps of naked and limp bodies of men, women, and children into mass graves. To make it worse, the defendants claimed that they could not be held responsible, and Hitler's deputy Hermann Goering declared: "But that was our right! We were a sovereign State and that was strictly our business."[11]

The lurid evidence and personal testimony presented at Nuremberg forced the world to stare down into the abyss of overwhelming horror that claimed the lives of millions of human beings. For most, it produced unprecedented revulsion and outrage. For some, it also produced profound sense of guilt. After considerable soul-searching, for example, German pastor Martin Niemöller would express his own shame in these words:

First they came for the Communists, but I was not a Communist so I did not speak out. Then they came for the Socialists and the Trade Unionists, but I was neither, so I did not speak out. Then they came for the Jews, but I was not a Jew so I did not speak out. And when they came for me, there was no one left to speak out for me.[12]

Whether motivated by empathy for the victims, outrage, or guilt, many came to realize what could happen if people remained silent in the face of abuses or allowed leaders to remain immune under claims of national sovereignty. For them, the horrors revealed at Nuremberg provided a defining and irrevocable turning point where they concluded that such abuses must *never* be allowed to occur again.

Figure 11. "We Were a Sovereign State and that was Strictly Our Business": The Holocaust. U.S. Holocaust Memorial Museum.

Activists vowed that they would turn their emotional reaction into action on behalf of others. Many of these worked at the national level, successfully producing important and often dramatic changes within their own states. In Canada the High Court of Ontario in the *Re Drummond Wren* case dismissed racially restrictive real estate covenants. In New Zealand activists' efforts led to the Maori Social and Economic Advancement Act and, in the United States, to what would become the Indian Claims Commission to consider redress for Native Americans.[13] New constitutional provisions on rights appeared in Albania, Brazil, Ceylon, China, Ecuador, France, Japan, Panama, and Yugoslavia, immediately affecting the rights of millions of people, particularly women. Bolivia, Guatemala, Hungary, Italy, Liberia, and Portugal all granted women the right to vote.[14] The new Japanese constitution turned its back on centuries of tradition by prohibiting discrimination because of race, creed, social status, family origin, or sex, prescribing "the equal rights of husband and wife."[15] The British elected a Labour government promising to reduce class divisions at home and to consider the rights of indigenous peoples abroad by implementing "a revolution in Imperial attitude."[16] Moreover, the Council of Foreign Ministers deliberately used the language of the United Nations Charter to include guarantees for human rights within the peace treaties with Bulgaria, Hungary, Italy, and Romania, arguing that how nations treat their own people now must be seen as an international responsibility.[17]

Many of those with visions of international human rights focused their hopes and energies on the new United Nations itself. Here they launched full-scale debate within the General Assembly on several highly explosive and controversial issues. During the very first session in 1946, delegates charged that states were abusing individuals in Bulgaria, Greece, Hungary, Spain, and the Soviet Union. Egypt introduced a resolution condemning racial and religious persecution and calling on all governments to take prompt and energetic action to end discrimination. Others quickly rose to lend their support, describing this matter as a "burning question," a "vital" issue of "immense importance," and as "one of the most important questions which the conscience of this august Assembly must face." Emilio Saint-Lot of Haiti passionately spoke of the need to proclaim the value and the dignity of each individual, while the delegate from India argued that global peace and security must be based "on freedom for all people, on the recognition of human dignity, on the fact that the human soul has the same value whether it is encased in a white, brown, or black body."[18] The force of this principle in light of the provisions in the Charter could hardly be denied, and the Assembly unanimously passed the resolution of principle condemning persecution and discrimination.

Enormously encouraged by this strong international support for racial equality, India determined to raise the stakes. It decided to single out a specific country for condemnation and a call for action. To launch the campaign, it sent the intense and articulate Vijaya Lakshmi Pandit, the first woman leader of any delegation to the General Assembly, to the first session. Standing erect at the podium, she threw down the gauntlet by accusing the white minority South African government of abusing the basic human rights by its policies of gross racial discrimination, in contradiction of the Charter. She declared that this was not simply a matter between two countries, but one with consequences for the entire globe and for the integrity of the United Nations itself, calling on her fellow delegates to listen to their conscience and to rise to their new international responsibilities. Her speech produced an immediate reaction from Jan Smuts of South Africa, who had clashed with Gandhi over this issue before and was furious over having his reputation and that of his country now put on trial for all the world to see. He shouted that his country was protected by Article 2 (7) of the Charter. The treatment of Indians, coloreds, and mixed races, he said, was a matter of "domestic jurisdiction." Smuts warned ominously that if the United Nations intervened, an extremely dangerous precedent would be set for doing the same in any other state, thus destroying national sovereignty. Pandit arose again and dismissed this argument about domestic jurisdiction as "late in the day and far-fetched" and as making a mockery of the principles enunciated in the Charter:

Millions of voiceless people, who because of their creed or color, have been relegated to positions of inferiority, are looking to us for justice, and it is only on the foundation of justice that we can create a new world order. . . . We must remember that, in the present case, the minds of millions of people in India and in other parts of Asia and Africa have been moved to intense indignation at all forms of racial discrimination which stand focused upon the problem of South Africa. This is a test case.[19]

All sides agreed that it was indeed a test case. It pitted Article 1's international human rights against Article 2's national sovereignty, and the outcome would establish a critical precedent. Several other states rallied behind India's position. Wellington Koo of China argued that all Asians took a great interest because they wanted to see racial discrimination eliminated from the face of the earth. The Mexican delegate rose in strong support and described the issue as "one of the most important questions of our time," and Carlos Romulo of the Philippines called it "a moral question of the first magnitude" that could be ignored only at great risk. Ricardo Alfaro of Panama argued passionately that he would never consider human rights as the exclusive prerogative of states hiding behind the cloak of domestic jurisdiction, insisting that the Charter gave birth to the new principle that individuals as well as states now were subjects of international law. In sharp contrast, South Africa angrily lashed out against those who dared to interfere in its internal affairs, and in heated debate described the General Assembly as a "mere political forum" of activist troublemakers. Australia, Britain, Canada, and the United States, among others, fearful that their own discrimination might attract international attention, supported the South African position, arguing that the United Nations possessed no jurisdiction in these matters. In the end, the resolution passed with the necessary two-thirds majority.[20] As such, it marked a revolutionary departure and signaled to the world that the members of the United Nations would no longer be silent on this issue or be swayed by the old argument that how a nation treats its own people is somehow its own business.

Within only days of passing this resolution, for example, the General Assembly turned its attention to the issue of genocide. Once again, the initiative came not from white nations or the Great Powers but from those who had been victimized. Cuba, India, and Panama led the charge, but were quickly joined by others. They observed that extermination had existed for centuries, including the tragic cases of the Hereros in Africa, Aborigines in Australia and Tasmania, Armenians in Turkey, and native Indian tribes in North and South America. But they argued that the extreme nature of genocide during the "Final Solution" demonstrated an enormous danger that simply could no longer be tolerated. They took considerable interest in the words at Nuremberg from Justice Jackson who surprisingly (given the fact that his country had dropped atomic bombs on Hiroshima and Nagasaki only three months earlier) raised the prospect of a larger legal precedent when he declared: "The idea that a state, any more than a corporation, commits crimes, is a fiction. Crimes always are committed only by persons." "We must never forget," he continued, "that the record on which we judge these defendants today is the record on which history will judge us tomorrow. To pass these defendants a poisoned chalice is to put it to our own lips as well. . . . We are able to do away with domestic tyranny and violence and aggression by those in power . . . only when we make all men answerable to the law."[21]

They consequently determined to place genocide squarely on the international agenda by speaking out, reaffirming the right of all to a human existence, and advancing international law. They seized upon the final judgment of the Nuremberg Tribunal as well as the ongoing deliberations of the Tokyo War Crimes Trials, declaring in significant language that genocide "is a crime under international law which the civilized world condemns, and for the commission of which principals and accomplices—whether private individuals, public officials, or statesmen, and whether the crime is committed on religious, racial, political, or any other grounds—are punishable."[22] They also recognized that if these war crimes trials were to be more than mere vengeance or "victors' justice," they must lead toward a broader system of jurisdiction dealing with offenses whenever they might occur, and therefore created a special Committee on the Progressive Development of International Law. Its purpose was to help change the traditional culture of impunity by codifying the principle that individuals—and not just nations—would be held responsible and that rights would be protected.[23] For this reason, Nuremberg, despite its many flaws, provided an essential element of a "juridical revolution" of human rights and thus has been described as "a colossus in the development of international human rights law."[24]

But there was more here than the technicalities of law. The horrifying evidence revealed at Nuremberg forced many to examine their larger moral values and sense of responsibility. This was encouraged even further when the final judgment concluded that "just following orders" was no longer acceptable as a defense for the reason that "individuals have international duties which transcend the national obligations of obedience imposed by the individual state."[25] Such a position was particularly poignant when considering "crimes against humanity." As one authority writes, "these were crimes that the world could not suffer to take place anywhere, at any time, because they shamed everyone. They were not, for that crucial reason, crimes against Germans . . . ; they were crimes against humanity, because the very fact that a fellow human being could conceive and commit them diminishes every member of the human race."[26] One thoughtful contemporary wrote of what he regarded as the real meaning of Nuremberg:

an immense revolutionary effort to give utterance to a collective human conscience, to bring into being a collective standard by which gross violations of that conscience can be punished. . . . Some may gibe that I am speaking of a "human conscience" and a "moral sense" that are vague and formless, things on which no body of law can be built. I submit that they are the only things that a body of law ever rests on. The surest basis of a future world society lies in the sense of our common plight. When a Negro is lynched, all of us are strung upon that rope. When the Jews were burned in the Nazi furnaces, all of us were burned.[27]

Simultaneous with these developments on the new human rights agenda were others of great drama focused on the right of self-determination. World War II had released powerful psychological and political forces in Africa, Asia, the Caribbean, Middle East, and the Pacific demanding an end to colonial empires and respect for the rights for indigenous peoples. The Charter reflected these pressures by providing the Declaration Regarding Non-Self-Governing Territories, the principle that the interests of the inhabitants of these lands were paramount, the pledge to work toward self-government, and the creation of an International Trusteeship System. But the majority within the General Assembly were not satisfied and decided to push further. They elected such well-known opponents of colonialism as China, Iraq, Mexico, and the Soviet Union to serve on the Trusteeship Council. They battled over the text of every trusteeship agreement, strongly criticizing most proposals from the colonial powers, but praising the commitment from New Zealand to give Western Samoa "a self-contained Bill of Rights for the inhabitants."[28] They adamantly rejected the plan by South Africa to annex South-West Africa and passed two important resolutions. One of these sought to take reports about the conditions within the trust territories and place them in the hands of the General Assembly as a whole where they could be discussed by determined and vocal advocates of decolonization. A second resolution called on those who administered trust territories to convene special conferences of representatives of the peoples living in these lands in order that they might articulate their wishes and aspirations for self-government.[29]

Not content with all these efforts, delegates to this very first session of the United Nations also turned attention to the issue of gender. Inspired by the Charter's language prohibiting discrimination on the basis of sex that stood in such marked contrast with centuries of historical practice, a number of members sought to push the world even further toward genuine equality. They began by creating a permanent Commission on the Status of Women, declaring:

The position which women hold today has not been won without hard and often bitter struggle and a great deal of work is still required. But today for the first time in history the women of the world have in the Commission an international body solely devoted to achieving complete equality for them.[30]

Well-known activists such as Bodil Begtrup of Denmark, Minerva Bernardino of the Dominican Republic, Fryderyka Kalinowska of Poland, W. S. New of China, and Agnes McIntosh of New Zealand stressed that unless the United Nations took a stand on gender equity, women in country after country would be forced to fight long and bitter battles by themselves to secure equal rights and that international human rights would never be advanced. After months of work, these women and their male supporters gathered enough votes to secure a General Assembly resolution recommending that all states fulfill the purposes of the Charter by granting political rights to women.[31] As Secretary-General Trygve Lie said during the debates: "We will not rest until women everywhere enjoy equal rights and equal opportunities with men."[32]

The General Assembly threw itself into debating the relationship between human rights and freedom of information as well. According to Carlos Romulo, the rights of citizens were most likely to be respected in countries with an unfettered press. He knew that abusers always had thrived when they could control or limit knowledge of their actions. Recent experience with totalitarian governments demonstrated all too well the dangers of propaganda and censorship that destroyed rights and, as described by Aase Lionaes of Norway, "poisoned the minds of millions."[33] Delegates thus referred to their "moral obligation" to address this issue by calling for an international conference on the press and the new technological inventions of radio and film. They declared their conviction that "freedom of information is a fundamental human right and is the touchstone of all the freedoms to which the United Nations is consecrated."[34]

In addition to political and civil rights, delegates spent enormous time discussing their collective responsibility to address basic social and economic rights. Under the leadership of Peter Fraser, the Third Committee (Social, Humanitarian, and Cultural Affairs) considered human rights in two ways: as *ends* in themselves as well as *means* toward larger security, peace, and justice. Their recommendations led the General Assembly to create a whole series of mechanisms to help those who suffered. To assist the hundreds of thousands of refugees and displaced persons of the time, they responded to what was described as "the first opportunity and the duty to demonstrate in a practical way the true significance of the Rights of Man, so often extolled during the years of war, and also often referred to after victory," by establishing the International Refugee Organization (IRO).[35] To help children, they created the United Nations International Children's Emergency Fund (UNICEF). To secure fair and humane conditions of labor, they brought the International Labor Organization (ILO) into a relationship with the United Nations as a specialized agency. To raise levels of nutrition and standards of living, they did the same with the new Food and Agricultural Organization (FAO). To raise knowledge, they repeated the process with the United Nations Educational, Scientific, and Cultural Organization. To collect and distribute relief, they gave assignments to the office of the secretary-general, the Economic and Social Council, and the specialized agencies, while encouraging close cooperation with the Red Cross and Red Crescent societies in rendering humanitarian assistance. And, to provide essential medical care, they urged member governments to accept the constitution of the World Health Organization (WHO) reading: "The enjoyment of the highest attainable standard of health is one of the fundamental rights of every human being without distinction as to race, religion, political belief, economic or social condition."[36]

Finally, and in the middle of this already extraordinary first session, delegates significantly raised the issue of an international bill of human rights. Visions of such a bill, as we have seen, had emerged at the time of the League of Nations, throughout the crusade of World War II, and certainly during preparations for a "people's peace."

Even President Truman had urged that it be created and become "as much a part of international life as our own Bill of Rights is a part of our Constitution."[37] But up to this point there had never been enough time to draft such a document or enough political will to secure acceptance. The many decisions made by the United Nations during this first year, however, revealed that the mood had changed dramatically and that the time was now ripe to make more determined efforts. Consequently, Cuba and Panama seized the initiative by submitting statements on the rights and duties of states and draft declarations on human rights. Strong endorsement came from Chile, Ecuador, Egypt, France, and Liberia, among others. The General Assembly thus decided to support the idea, but given the complex nature of such an international bill of rights, instructed the Economic and Social Council to forward it for study and action to the new Commission on Human Rights.[38]

Members of the United Nations invested considerable time and care in creating this Commission on Human Rights as mandated by the Charter. They knew that many people throughout the world with visions of human rights would be watching them carefully and that expectations ran high. The U.S. Secretary of State even predicted that the creation of the commission "may well prove one of the most important and significant achievements of the San Francisco Conference. . . . It is a promise from this generation to generations yet unborn that this war, fought in the cause of freedom, will not have been fought in vain."[39] One official in the British Foreign Office anticipated that "the work of this commission may be of considerable importance, and that many subjects of particular concern to this country, in particular subjects such as the rights of colonial peoples, may be raised."[40] Consequently, governments approached their task of establishing this body very seriously.[41] To provide professional staff support, the secretary-general created the Human Rights Division. His assistant Henri Laugier, who once served as president of the Fédération Internationale des Droits de l'Homme, named Canadian professor of international law John Humphrey as the division's first director with the promise that the assignment would prove to be "a great adventure."[42] The Economic and Social Council then named nine individuals to a special "nuclear," or preparatory, commission. This group immediately elected as its chair none other than Eleanor Roosevelt, the remarkable former First Lady of the United States already well known for her activism and often courageous positions on human rights for women, the poor, and racial minorities.

With intelligence, compassion, graciousness, commitment, and determination, Eleanor Roosevelt set about to guide this commission. Her enormous popularity and prestige attracted attention, but it was her refreshing idealism, lack of cynicism, and contagious enthusiasm for the goodness in people and for a world that might be that generated inspiration and offered hope. Indeed, according to her son, even in her most private moments her nightly prayer always concluded with these words: "make us sure of the good we cannot see and of the hidden good in the world. . . . Save us from ourselves and show us a vision of a world made new."[43] She possessed that rare combination of a deep appreciation of pragmatic politics with an even deeper understanding of the power of visions of human rights. She believed in an international community that respected the value and variety of all human life where no nation or individual person—including those who she described as the "everyday people" in local communities and villages—could be truly free as long as others were not. People sensed her profound sincerity and compassion, and thus wrote to tell her that they shared her hope in the United Nations and its potential.[44] She thus quickly became aware of the fact that "this Commission means a great deal to a great many people" who yearned for a new set of international norms, telling her colleagues that "they look upon us, regardless of the governments that we spring from, as *their* representatives, the representatives of people of the world." But she knew that neither she nor the commission could please everyone and that not everyone would like the results. "Sometimes issues arise," she said, "where one has to advocate something that may be difficult for one's own government to carry through, and yet, if one believes it is right, I think one should advocate it, hoping that if it would be good for the world, it would, therefore, in the end, be good for one's own government and one's own people too."[45]

With precisely this in mind, Roosevelt and her committee made several recommendations. They suggested creating three subcommissions: one for Freedom of Information and of the Press, one for Protection of Minorities, and another for Prevention of Discrimination. In addition, and most daring, they recommended that the Commission on Human Rights itself be composed of individual experts rather than representatives of governments in order that it might acquire greater independence and integrity, and that it be empowered to assist the Security Council by pointing out cases where violations of human rights constituted threats to peace.[46] Some of these recommendations received ready acceptance, but as Roosevelt had predicted, others produced immediate hostility among those who regarded them as far too ambitious and too threatening to their own national sovereignty. The delegate from Britain, for example, received ciphered instructions to be very careful about this "extremely delicate" subject while at the same time being warned "not to give the impression that we are being obstructive. We suggest our right course is to play for time, leaving it as far as possible to other delegations to bring out the difficulties."[47] They need not have worried, for others quickly jumped into the fray, including the Soviets, who adamantly stated that they would never accept individual experts acting in their own capacity instead of state-appointed representatives. With this kind of pressure, it was decided to establish the commission as a permanent body, composed of eighteen members representing their respective governments. They would be responsible for submitting proposals, recommendations, and reports regarding international declarations or conventions on civil liberties, the status of women, freedom of information, and similar matters; the protection of minorities; and the prevention of discrimination on grounds of race, sex, language, or religion. But before any of this could take place, the commission was instructed to give the highest priority to one particular task: drafting an international bill of human rights.[48] This, in turn, immediately raised extremely daunting issues of both philosophy and politics, thereby confirming the judgment of one veteran observer that "no part of the Economic and Social Council contains more explosive material than the Commission on Human Rights."[49]

Challenging Questions of Philosophy

It is likely that no issues of public policy in the world raise more difficult philosophical questions than those of human rights. Nevertheless, up to this stage in the evolution of international human rights, diplomats had only been on the margins of serious philosophical discourse. In their more private moments they may have pondered philosophy and ethics, but as representatives of nation-states they rarely ventured beyond immediate political interests. They never before had been required to provide any precise definition or articulation of the meaning of "human rights" or "fundamental freedoms," to wrestle with moral diversity on a global scale, nor to thoughtfully consider what the extension of rights might mean for the world as a whole. Instead, visions of rights largely had come from religious visionaries, philosophers, or men and women with a sense of responsibility toward victims of abuse and determined to act on principles very different from that of national sovereignty. This changed dramatically once the United Nations decided that its Commission on Human Rights, composed of government representatives, should draft an international bill of rights capable of securing universal acceptance. Such a formidable task suddenly presented a whole array of inescapable and challenging questions of philosophy.

Those who understood something about the nature of international human rights clearly anticipated that these philosophical issues would arise with force and with drama. Thus, when the commission first met in January 1947, observers packed the visitors' seats to capacity in order to witness what they knew would be a fascinating discussion. Even more telling, governments appointed not political flunkies but a remarkable collection of individuals of unusual quality and stature who they believed would be thoughtful, articulate, and intellectually capable of understanding the complicated questions that would confront them. Several held Ph.D. degrees. China named Dr. Peng-chun Chang (Zhang Pengjun), a career diplomat and former professor with a powerful intellect, highly knowledgeable about the West, Islam, and Arabic culture, yet deeply committed to Confucianism and the values inherent in Asian culture and philosophy. Lebanon appointed Dr. Charles Habib Malik, a former professor of philosophy and a brilliant scholar, born into a family of Greek Orthodox Arabs, raised at a crossroads of many cultures, and personally and professionally shaped by both Christianity and Islam. France designated Dr. René Cassin, a widely published professor of international law and skilled legislative draftsman who had been raised by a devout Orthodox Jewish mother and an intensely antireligious father, represented his country at the League of Nations, served as a long-standing member of the Ligue Française des Droits de l'Homme, lost many of his own relatives to the Holocaust, and would later become president of the European Court of Human Rights. The Philippines selected the dynamic Carlos Romulo, an experienced public official, a devoted Catholic, a brigadier general, and recipient of a Pulitzer Prize for journalism. Charles Dukes, a trade unionist and former Member of Parliament with extensive service, represented Britain. Hansa Mehta, a Hindu and determined advocate for human rights, especially those of women, who had been arrested for civil disobedience, came from India. Chile appointed Don Felix Nieto del Rio, a career diplomat, former editor of

El Mercurio, and acknowledged as his country's most knowledgeable writer on foreign affairs. Panama named Dr. Ricardo Alfaro, its own foreign minister, former professor of history and law, and judge on the Permanent Court of Arbitration at The Hague. Iran appointed Dr. Ghasseme Ghani, a distinguished author, member of parliament, former minister of culture, and fluent in Persian, Arabic, and French. Dr. Don José A. Mora represented Uruguay. The Soviet Union eventually appointed Alexander Bogomolov, a former professor, experienced diplomat, and the recipient of the Order of Lenin. Vladislav Ribnikar, a son of the owners of the newspaper *Politica* who had joined the partisans during the war and became a Communist, represented Yugoslavia. The United States named Eleanor Roosevelt, and her prestige was such that even this distinguished group unanimously elected her to lead them.[50]

This group quickly came to realize that philosophy—like politics—does not speak with one voice. Indeed, profound philosophical differences about the individual, the state, and ethical values surfaced immediately. In opening the first session, for example, Laugier announced that with the General Assembly's recent vote on India's complaint about discrimination in South Africa, the international community had determined that principles of human rights for each person would now take precedence over the principle of national sovereignty and that individual victims could seek protection from their own governments. Ribnikar challenged this position, arguing as an orthodox Marxist that abuses stemmed from the errors of bourgeois, individualistic philosophy generated during the eighteenth and nineteenth centuries rather than some eternal verity. In the modern world, he insisted, the rights of the state superseded the so-called rights of the individual. Malik responded that it had been precisely the states of totalitarians that had so egregiously destroyed human rights, and that their excesses now needed to be curbed by affirming that the individual human person was infinitely more valuable than any group or state to which he or she belonged. Dukes retorted that unrestricted individual liberty was virtually impossible in any organized society, and stressed the value of trade unions that could play a critical role in moderating between the state and each person.

Further debates raged over whether human rights derived from God, from natural law, or from the authority of the state. Some insisted that an emphasis should be placed on political rights such as voting and civil rights such as freedom of religion and the right to own property, while those of a Communist or Latin American socialist persuasion heatedly countered that nothing compared to the basic economic and social rights of employment, shelter, social security, and health. Others passionately argued whether rights were natural, universal, and equal or completely context-dependent on particular times, places, and circumstances.[51] All this presented, in the words of one observer, "an astonishing spectacle." "Here was a body preoccupied mainly with ideas, trying to deepen moral concepts, philosophical doctrines, and legal and sociological theses in a common effort to build a new soul for the international body."[52]

Thus, from the very first meeting of its first session, the Commission on Human Rights confronted fundamental and not easily answered philosophical questions that had been asked for centuries and that continue today. What exactly are "human rights" and what is their source? Do they come from God, or Nature, or something else? And what exactly is meant by "God," "Nature" and "by nature," "inalienable," "inherent," "reason," "conscience," "morality," or "general welfare" when viewed through the lenses of various philosophical, religious (and nonreligious), and ideological perspectives? To whom should these rights apply? Could they be universally claimed by all people as a metaphysical inherence without distinctions as members of the larger human family? Or in a world with different forms of government and value systems, are they restricted to membership within a given state, culture, or stage of development? Do rights apply only to individual people, or can states claim them? What is the relationship, if any, between human rights for individuals and "security," "peace," and "justice" for the world? Should states largely stay out of the lives of people and give them as much freedom as possible, or should they intervene and take active steps to guarantee rights? Do the rights of individuals possess greater value than the rights of collective groups, or are they truly indivisible and interdependent? Are some human rights more "fundamental," antecedent, and necessary to other rights, or must they all be respected in equal measure? If all human rights have the same value and are ultimately indivisible, then what happens if the claims of one vision of human rights conflict with those of another vision?

These questions only began the discussion, for they raised countless others. How does one justify human rights? Does the simple assertion of a right make it so, or must it be tested against some established norm? Are human rights absolute, or must they be modified by particular circumstances? What if the right of free speech is used to inflame racial hatred, goad class antagonisms, arouse religious intolerance, or incite war? What is the precise relationship between individual rights and collective responsibilities for the rights of others? Is it possible to establish international normative standards of behavior while at the same time respecting different philosophical and cultural values? And, is there any value in proclaiming a vision of international human rights if means are not simultaneously provided for their implementation?

Any answers to these vexing questions, as accurately described by those who wrestled with them, "were far from clear," particularly since they consciously sought to discover universal principles by creating a discourse "wherein no regional philosophy or [single] way of life was permitted to prevail."[53] Indeed, their extraordinary and pioneering efforts not only to consider— but actually solicit—a wide range of opinions and values belies later charges that they somehow conspired to "circumvent fundamental differences" or engaged in "moral chauvinism" and "cultural imperialism."[54] Far from feeling a sense of "Western triumphalism," their all-too-recent experience with the horrors of war and genocide made them approach their task with an unusual soberness and humility. For this reason, the drafters determined to broaden their perspectives by deliberately drawing on different sources far beyond whatever instructions they received from their governments. Some of them—Cassin, Malik, and Chang— already possessed highly respected credentials to guide discussions, to command respect when they spoke, and to understand the pluralistic philosophical and cultural traditions of Europe, Latin America, the Middle East, and Asia. Laugier and Humphrey from the Secretariat provided a wide range of information on the laws and customs of many different states. Experts from the International Labor Organization, UNESCO,

World Health Organization, and the preparatory International Refugee Organization gave valuable insights.[55] Lawyers from the Nuremberg and Tokyo war crimes trials offered assistance as to how emerging definitions of crimes against humanity might contribute to the evolving meaning of human rights.[56] Governments, NGOs, and private individuals such as legal expert Hersch Lauterpacht contributed ideas, provided formulations of theory, sent copies of the writings of Alejandro Alvarez and H. G. Wells, made suggestions, and even offered detailed proposals for an international bill of rights.[57]

Then, and in one of the most unusual developments in the entire history of diplomacy, UNESCO called upon a group of experts to provide advice on this critical matter of international policy. They considered convening a lengthy "Conference of Philosophers," but the immediacy of drafting a bill pushed them toward soliciting opinions directly. They knew that they could not rely simply on Western philosophy but needed to obtain wide-ranging perspectives from around the world. They thus invited one hundred and fifty very different leading intellectuals to send their thoughts on the specific philosophical questions raised by international human rights. Their invitation began with a dramatic challenge that revealed the complexities at hand:

The world of man is at a critical stage in its political, social, and economic evolution. If it is to proceed further on the path towards unity, it must develop a common set of ideas and principles. One of those is a common formulation of the rights of man. This common formulation must by some means reconcile the various divergent or opposing formulations now in existence. It must further be sufficiently definite to have real significance both as an inspiration and as a guide to practice, but also sufficiently general and feasible to apply to all men, and to be capable of modification to suit peoples at different stages of social and political development while yet retaining significance for them and their aspirations.[58]

The responses poured in. Although deep philosophical differences often existed between them, each respondent attempted to address the nature of humankind, the purpose of governments, the efficacy of natural law, the relationship between the individual and the larger society and world in which they live, the necessity to curb abuses, the importance of shaping policy according to moral values, and whether it was even possible to create an international bill of human rights in the first place. Some, like the Italian philosopher and historian Benedetto Croce, doubted the entire enterprise; while the author of *Values for Survival*, Lewis Mumford of the United States, strongly urged creating a truly universal vision of rights. F. S. C. Northrop, a professor of philosophy at Yale University who had written *The Meeting of East and West*, provided similar endorsement; but warned that ethnocentrism must be avoided by incorporating the ideologies and values of many different cultures and schools of thought into any final document. Jacques Maritain, a former philosophy professor from France influenced by the writings of Thomas Aquinas and author of *Les Droits de l'homme et la Loi naturelle*, cautioned that no bill of rights could ever be exhaustive or final, and by necessity must always be a function of the state of moral conscience at any given time in history. Anthropologist A. P. Elkin of Australia, author of *Wanted: A Charter for the Native Peoples*, stressed the importance of the rights of indigenous peoples. Physical and biological scientists such as J. M. Burgers of the Netherlands argued for the necessity of freedom of expression.

Others from non-Western perspectives made suggestions based upon their own religious and cultural traditions. These included Bengali Muslim poet and philosopher Humayun Kabir, who wrote on "Human Rights: The Islamic Tradition and the Problems of the World Today," and political scientist S. V. Puntambekar of India, who authored "The Hindu Concept of Human Rights." Le Zhongshu from Nanjing University in China penned "Human Rights in the Chinese Tradition" and sent a personal letter to U.S. Secretary of State George Marshall declaring: "I believe that the Declaration of the Rights of Man for the entire world is required."[59] Many of these respondents also stressed the need of recognizing the relationship between rights and responsibilities.[60] Among these, Gandhi wrote most pointedly: "I learned from my illiterate but wise mother that all rights to be deserved and preserved came from duty well done. Thus the very right to live accrues to us only when we do the duty of citizenship of the world. From this one fundamental statement, perhaps it is easy enough to define the duties of Man and Woman and correlate every right to some corresponding duty to be first performed."[61]

Once these opinions and commentaries were received, UNESCO convened the special Committee on the Philosophic Principles of the Rights of Man during the summer of 1947. Their purpose was not to achieve doctrinal consensus but rather to see whether a formulation of basic rights might be found sufficient to draft an international bill. They gathered as much information as they could about the differing religious, philosophical, political, and cultural values spread across the vastness of the globe and analyzed several centuries of the historical evolution of concepts of rights in different times and places. Their survey persuaded them that, despite many differences, a core of "common convictions" did exist and that the United Nations had a solemn obligation "to declare, not only to all governments, but also to their peoples, the rights which have now become the vital ends of human effort everywhere." Among these they included certain basic political, civil, economic, and social rights, the right to life, and the right to rebel against oppressive regimes. These rights, they argued, "must no longer be confined to the few," but now must be extended to everyone. "All the rights which we have come slowly and laboriously to recognize," they concluded, "belong to all men everywhere without discrimination of race, sex, language, or religion. They are universal." As the committee recognized at the end of the report, however, it would be extremely difficult to take these abstract principles of philosophy and actually apply them in a world of politics.[62]

Difficult Problems of Politics

Those men and women who served on the Commission on Human Rights, of course, hardly needed to be reminded of politics. Despite all the discourse of philosophy and expressions of goodwill, they operated within the intensely political environment of an organization comprising nations with highly divergent systems of government. This forced them to confront politics at every turn. Each and every one of the rights identified by the Committee on the Philosophic Principles of the Rights of Man raised a political problem of some kind. If the United Nations attempted to implement any of these rights it would provoke states to insist on their domestic jurisdiction under Article 2 (7) of the Charter, and thereby exacerbate the already existing contradiction with Article 1. In addition, the members of the commission came to realize all too well that they served not as individuals free to make their own decisions but rather as official representatives of their governments who provided them with "position papers" and "letters of instruction" to support highly politicized agendas.[63] Their meetings consequently became the focus of what the participants themselves called not only "fireworks"—but major "battles."[64]

Problems of politics surfaced immediately. Indeed, even before it formally began its meetings, the Commission on Human Rights found itself the unexpected recipient of a veritable flood of petitions. Literally thousands of people from all across the globe sent appeals begging for help against the abuses of their governments and pleading that the principles of the Charter be applied to them.[65] Because of her stature and integrity, her emerging reputation as the "First Lady of the World," the vision she represented, and the hope she inspired, many of these petitions were addressed personally to Eleanor Roosevelt.[66] It is difficult to read these without feeling the pain, sensing both desperation and hope, and being reminded of the human face of human rights among those writing to her. They pleaded with her to help those who suffered from racial prejudice or religious persecution, women who confronted discrimination, survivors of concentration camps, conscientious objectors, and children lacking food, shelter, or medical care. A telegram sent in the name of five thousand displaced Ukrainians, for example, spoke about the need for justice, and while struggling with grammar but not with conviction, expressed their belief "that you venerable lady and the committee you preside over will protect us from any acts of ill treatment and violation of the rights of man just now a time of hard trial arrived and your assistance most necessary."[67]

Under these circumstances, virtually all governments quickly realized that none of them could remain immune from criticism. If petitions could be received and considered by the United Nations, they calculated, it would only fuel dissent at home or in the colonies, embarrass them in front of the entire world, and increase the risk of outside interference into their internal affairs. Thus, over the objections of Romulo, Mehta, Cassin, and Roosevelt who responded with sympathy toward these urgent and often desperate appeals, governments explicitly instructed their representatives to declare that the commission had "no power" to take any action in regard to individual complaints alleging violations of human rights.[68] This precluded the possibility of reprisals against the authors of such petitions, but it also prevented the commission from making serious charges public. Politics from the very beginning, therefore, forced the commission, in the words of one authority, to make "a critical declaration of impotence" with reference to petitions.[69]

Nevertheless, even these pronouncements about the lack of jurisdiction and efforts to stop petitions could not halt the flood of appeals. In fact, they seemed to make some challenges all the more necessary. One of the most striking of these occurred when the indefatigable and nearly eighty-year-old Du Bois determined to submit a carefully crafted complaint on behalf of the National Association for the Advancement of Colored People describing the long history of racial discrimination and the solemn obligations regarding human rights incumbent under the new Charter. Walter White privately warned Eleanor Roosevelt that the press "from all over the world" wanted advance copies of this explosive document, observing that "the matter cannot be kept secret, so great is the interest."[70] Du Bois, of course, did not want secrecy or quiet diplomacy, and presented the petition in October 1947 with full publicity. He gave it a provocative title: "An Appeal to the World: A Statement on the Denial of Human Rights to Minorities in the Case of Citizens of Negro Descent in the United States of America and An Appeal to the United Nations for Redress."[71] With fire in his voice, Du Bois shouted that justice could no longer be denied and appealed to the representatives to stand by their promises on human rights.[72] In taking this action, the NAACP clearly appreciated that the original cause of the petition represented "primarily an internal and national question," but argued with considerable insight that it "becomes inevitably an international question, and will in the future become more and more international." "The eyes and ears of the chancelleries of the world," they predicted,

will be focused and attuned to this petition. For depending upon what stand the United Nations takes in this appeal will determine in part, the policy to be followed and the measures to be adopted by the colonial powers in their future relations with their wards, and the procedures to be put into practice by countries who practice some form of discrimination. While on the part of submerged and underprivileged groups, it is likely to inspire and stimulate them to carry their cases directly to the world body in the hope of redress.[73]

This is exactly what governments feared, and they understood the possible consequences immediately. The petition confirmed what would become some of the most difficult and sensitive political problems in the world. If the United Nations became a gigantic "complaint bureau" for human rights, then there would be no end of challenges to national sovereignty. With or without justification, individuals or groups could go over the heads of their own governments and seek help from the international community, thereby seriously challenging the traditional meaning of domestic jurisdiction and greatly increasing the power and authority of the United Nations. The global publicity given to Du Bois's petition by journalists demonstrated just how embarrassing such issues might be for other governments as well. The intensity with which delegates from Asia and Africa viewed it as their own in the name of the right to racial equality and to self-determination revealed that the existence of all colonial empires could be in serious jeopardy. Moreover, the eagerness with which the Soviet Union drew attention to this petition as a means of exploiting flaws of the United States offered dramatic proof that human rights also could be used as political ammunition in the struggle rapidly becoming known as the Cold War.[74]

Those who founded the United Nations knew perfectly well that the organization could succeed only if the Great Powers collaborated in peace as they had during the war.[75] Yet even before the ink was dry on the Charter, the pledges of cooperation began to give way to suspicion and hostility. Disputes about the suppression of freedom and imposition of an Iron Curtain in Eastern Europe by the Soviet Union, exclusive possession of the atomic bomb and occupation of Japan by the United States, and crises in Greece and Turkey all propelled the wartime allies into implacable enemies. When the United States enunciated the Truman Doctrine in March 1947 declaring that the world now faced a choice between freedom or Communist totalitarianism, the Soviets responded by describing it as "hostile and bellicose" and designed "to interfere in the affairs of other countries on the side of reaction and counter-revolution."[76] This venomous animosity quickly carried over into the United Nations and affected virtually all discussions about human rights. The United States accused the Soviets of punishing dissidents without trial, persecuting religion, imposing censorship, forcing refugees to return against their will, and suppressing citizen committees designed to monitor human rights violations, among many other abuses. The Soviets responded by charging the United States with making "false and slanderous allegations," supporting imperialism, and crushing basic economic and social rights by means of "a clique of magnates" from "capitalist monopolies," and resorted to personal attacks against Eleanor Roosevelt by accusing her of being a "meddling old woman" and "hypocritical servant of capitalism."[77] Then, in what proved to be its most powerful and effective argument, they accused the United States of being a hypocrite of the worst sort by talking boldly about human rights while at the same time violating the fundamental rights of its Native American and black citizens guaranteed by its own constitution, a result of the festering sore of racial discrimination.

Suddenly, the United States found an issue heretofore regarded as exclusively a domestic matter not only exposed—but deliberately exploited—as its vulnerable Achilles' heel for all the world to see.[78] Under the scrutiny of this new international attention—made all the more acute by its own desire to be seen as the leader of the "free world" in the Cold War—it could no longer hide from its failure to extend voting rights to blacks, prohibit blatant segregation, or prevent the insidious practice of lynching. Indeed, even President Truman's own Committee on Civil Rights, in their report *To Secure These Rights*, described by one authority as "one of the most outspoken and impressive documents of all time bearing upon human rights,"[79] reached the same conclusion. "Throughout the Pacific, Latin America, Africa, the Near, Middle, and Far East," they warned, "the treatment which our Negroes receive is taken as a reflection of our attitude toward all darked-skinned peoples" and "plays into the hands of Communist propagandists. The United States is not so strong, the final triumph of the democratic ideal is not so inevitable that we can ignore what the world thinks of our record."[80]

Political problems were hardly confined to the Cold War, however. In fact, virtually every one of the activities of the United Nations in the area of human rights—by their very nature—threatened existing policies and practices, and thus suddenly confronted governments with a whole range of new and unexpected difficulties with severe political implications. When the General Assembly debated South Africa's policies of apartheid and the Sixth Committee (Legal Affairs), the Ad Hoc Committee on Genocide, and the Committee on the Codification of International Law started to draft a convention on genocide, for example, every government with minority populations within its borders or under its control began to realize that it, too, would be subject to greater international scrutiny than ever before. When the Secretariat appointed the black American and determined advocate of human rights, Ralph Bunche, as the first director of the Trusteeship Division, it served notice that colonial empires with their racial discrimination and exploitation would be challenged. When the Commission on the Status of Women initiated its survey, all governments began to understand that their policies toward gender would receive unprecedented global attention. When the Sub-Commission on Prevention of Discrimination and Protection of Minorities began asking questions about the status of Aborigines in Australia, Maori in New Zealand, Inuits and Metis in Canada, and Amerindian tribes in Latin America, every country with populations of indigenous peoples realized that sooner or later they would come under examination. Even something as "simple" as preparing the seemingly innocuous *Yearbook on Human Rights* produced difficulties. Never before in history had governments been asked to provide information about rights in their countries for all the world to see and examine. This request suddenly forced them all to agonize over how much they would reveal and how much they would conceal about abuses. They therefore began to realize that an aggressive pursuit of international human rights would likely attract global attention to their own problems and seriously jeopardize their own national sovereignty.

In the wake of these developments, government officials began to speak of the use of human rights violations as "weapons," to condemn "irresponsible if not actually hostile groups" who wanted to embarrass them, and to criticize the "careless idealism of certain members" of the Commission on Human Rights "willing to agree to anything, possible or impossible, in order to advance the cause of human rights."[81] Some accused the United Nations of being in a disastrous "violent hurry" in the pursuit of rights.[82] Smuts of South Africa complained that much of this was the result of becoming dominated by the "colored peoples" of the world.[83] Officials in the Department of State accused commission members such as Cassin as "manifesting fellow-traveler tendencies" and being "crypto-Communist."[84] Soon-to-be U.S. Secretary of State Dean Acheson distrusted the internationalists, criticized the Charter as "impracticable," regarded the United Nations Secretariat as no more than "a crowded center of conflicting races and nationalities," and revealed his prejudice toward gender roles by asking Vijaya Pandit, who became the first female president of the General Assembly, "Why do pretty women want to be like men?"[85] The fears of these critics were only exacerbated when John Humphrey, the Director of the Division of Human Rights, declared in a moment of unusual candor:

Human rights are largely a matter of relationships between the state and individuals, and therefore a matter which has been traditionally regarded as being within the domestic jurisdiction of states. What is now being proposed is, in effect, the creation of some kind of supranational supervision of the relationship between the state and its citizens. . . . What the United Nations is trying to do is revolutionary in character.[86]

Still other political problems arose as a result of NGOs who had been emboldened by their influence during the San Francisco Conference. They often could mobilize considerable domestic pressure at home and, as the United Nations emerged as a forum for international discourse, could generate significant embarrassment abroad. Most wanted to push governments much, much farther than they wanted to go. The International League for the Rights of Man, Fédération Internationale des Droits de l'Homme, Committee on Human Rights of the Commission to Study the Organization of Peace, Joint Committee of American Agencies on Human Rights, Inter-American Bar Association, and Women's International League for Peace and Freedom were particularly outspoken in their criticisms. The International Committee of the Red Cross, International Missionary Council, and many religious groups, drew attention to failures in providing humanitarian protection and relief. The International African Institute, Centre Against Imperialism, and Pan-African Congress mounted pressure for the right of self-determination. The International Alliance for Women for Equal Rights and Equal Responsibilities, Pan-American Women's Association, and World Woman's Party for Equal Rights focused on gender discrimination. The World Jewish Congress and World Council of Churches mobilized pressure for religious freedom, while the International Union for Child Welfare and Save the Children unrelentingly criticized violations of the rights of children. The Worker's Defense League, World Federation of Trade Unions, and International Federation of Christian Trade Unions all launched campaigns to expose abuses of economic and social rights.[87]

At the same time, other NGOs, described by one experienced official as the "enemies . . . of the United Nations human rights program," applied political pressure in exactly the opposite direction.[88] Within the United States, for example, the Republican Party and Southern Democrats waged fierce campaigns of resistance. The American Bar Association launched a particularly aggressive effort to oppose an international bill of human rights, claiming that it was part of a scheme to destroy national sovereignty, domestic jurisdiction, "the free enterprise system," "the laws of our country," and "the American way of life."[89]

All these pressures came to bear on the Commission on Human Rights at every step of the way as it attempted to meet its charge of producing an international bill of human rights.[90] Even procedural issues generated controversy. After considerable debate over Australian Colonel W. R. Hodgson's opinion that "no concrete results could be achieved by a drafting committee composed of government representatives expressing different points of view,"[91] it was decided to have Roosevelt, Chang, and Malik work on an initial draft. Protests emerged immediately from those determined not to be excluded.[92] This resulted in the addition of representatives from Australia, Chile, France, Britain, and the Soviet Union—an arrangement described as "strictly political";[93] but one that nevertheless brought together West and East, Communist and non-Communist, industrialized and developing countries. They exhaustively pored over a four-hundred-page compilation of all the rights identified in various proposals or in existing national laws along with a draft text initially prepared by John Humphrey.[94] They frequently met all night long, arguing over both philosophy and politics, and trying to decide exactly what might be meant by an "international bill of rights." Should such a bill be in the form of a treaty, which on ratification would be binding and become an integral part of the basic law of nations? Or, should it be a declaration of principles, enumerating and explaining the still-undefined meaning of "human rights," that would take the form of a recommendation? This was no simple dilemma, and feelings ran strong in the committee. The Soviet representative warned sternly of the danger of "embarking on a voyage which would lead it in a direction where it might cross the border which divides international from internal law—the border which divides the inter-relationships of governments from the field where the sovereign rights of nations must prevail."[95] In sharp contrast, with passion that far exceeded any authorization from her government, Hansa Mehta decried any timidity regarding enforcement, and let the committee know in no uncertain terms that, "Unless it is binding on the states Members of the United Nations it will have no meaning."[96] Observed one official watching all this very closely:

The setting up of international machinery to protect individual human rights would be one of the greatest international achievements in history. It would assert that just as the real purpose of a State's government is to ensure the welfare of the individual human being, so the real concern of international law is with the welfare of individuals. It would at the same time be a more drastic limitation of sovereignty than any State has yet been prepared to accept.[97]

Others reached exactly the same conclusion—and it terrified them. Thus, in the midst of these deliberations, Eleanor Roosevelt received most unwelcome instructions. She was told to focus only on a non-binding declaration of principles of human rights, where the United States felt "on safer ground." Anything involving legal obligations and enforcement, she was instructed, "should be kept on a tentative level and should not involve any commitments by this Government."[98] This kind of pressure explains why it was determined at the second session of the Commission on Human Rights in late 1947 that the international bill of rights would be composed of three sequential parts: a declaration, a binding convention, and, finally, specific measures for implementation. Its members thus spent arduous months of work producing a Draft International Declaration on Human Rights, a Draft International Covenant on Human Rights, and suggestions on ways in which these might be implemented.[99] They hoped that the result might become "the basis of one of the most significant documents in history: a charter of the fundamental rights and freedoms of men and women the world over."[100]

Before any parts of this vision could be realized in practice, of course, these drafts needed to be circulated to all nations in order to give them opportunities to shape the language and the content through suggestion or amendment and to secure their approval. This inclusive process both revealed and escalated the difficult problems of politics even further, for the drafts had captured the headlines of the world, created high public expectations, and necessitated responses that could not be hidden. Governments thus were forced into a true test of conviction about what they would—or would not— be willing and able to do on behalf of international human rights. This required that they devote considerable time and energy to studying the language of the drafts, considering the philosophical premises on which they were based, and analyzing what they described as "practical politics" at home and "the international political situation" abroad should the texts be adopted.[101] Toward this end, governments often exchanged views with each other, asked for advice, received unsolicited

opinions from individuals and NGOs, and at times even created elaborate committees
to help them work through the challenges. The British instituted a special Working
Party on Human Rights, the United States established an Interdepartmental Committee on International Social Policy (ISP) with a Subcommittee on Human Rights, and
New Zealand formed its own Human Rights Committee.[102] Some sought to work collectively in order to formulate common or regional responses, as did the Latin Americans who adopted what would become the highly influential "American Declaration
of the Rights and Duties of Man" during their Ninth International Conference of
American States meeting in Bogota.[103] Throughout this entire process, governments
found themselves constantly pressured by the public for some measure of achievement, by activists who wanted to energize a revolutionary program for the international protection of human rights, and by those who resisted any restrictions on their
national sovereignty or invested interests.

These arguments continued within the United Nations as representatives lobbied
for their positions and as they found themselves caught—once again—between wanting to achieve something on behalf of human rights while at the same time protecting what one diplomat described as "their own sacred cows."[104] Many governments
expressed their opinions directly to the secretary-general.[105] South Africa wrote that
the proposed draft "trespasses upon matters which should be left where they belong,
in the domestic sphere of the member states," declaring it to be "completely unacceptable."[106] Others approached the staff of the Division of Human Rights or the members
of the Sub-Commission on Prevention of Discrimination and Protection of Minorities,
the Sub-Commission on Freedom of Information and the Press, the Commission on
the Status of Women, and especially the Commission on Human Rights,[107] where it was
reported that governments sometimes presented "violent objection" and "determined
opposition" to certain proposals as well as strong support of others.[108]

These many problems easily could have overwhelmed members of the commission
at any time. Nevertheless, despite the seemingly overwhelming odds against them, they
persevered. Eleanor Roosevelt's attitude toward visions seen set the tone:

We make our own history. It is more intelligent to hope than not to hope, to try rather than not
try. Nothing is achieved by the person who says it can't be done.[109]

The Commission on Human Rights seriously considered all of the reactions, comments, and suggestions during its third session in May-June 1948, including China's
proposal for provisions on the right of equality without discrimination, freedom of
conscience, and freedom of speech and expression.[110] After intensive work, it finally
agreed on a draft declaration consisting of a preamble and twenty-eight articles. These
they submitted to their much larger parent body, the Economic and Social Council,
for further deliberation during July and August. Here, long and contentious meetings
revealed sharp and continuing differences. Some wanted to weaken the text, which
they feared would challenge their sovereignty by legitimating outside interference into
their internal affairs. Others sought to defer the declaration until agreement had been
reached on a covenant and system of implementation as well. Still others argued that
any attempt to reach consensus on such a complicated package involving enforcement

of the constantly evolving totality of human rights would only lead to a loss of momentum and a long delay in the proclamation of the declaration, and perhaps even a watering down of its contents. They believed that if they insisted on getting both a declaration and a covenant at the same time, and tried to enforce undefined norms against unwilling states, they would obtain nothing at all. In the end, ECOSOC, then under the presidency of Malik, decided to transmit the draft declaration as it stood to the General Assembly for consideration and decision.[111]

The Universal Declaration of Human Rights

When the General Assembly met in Paris from September to December 1948, it did so in a mood that juxtaposed the extremes of both fear and hope. On the one hand, the ominous fall of Czechoslovakia to a Communist coup, an escalating strategic arms race with weapons of mass destruction, and the frightful risk of war resulting from the Soviet blockade of Berlin created a plummeting and terrifying frigidness in the Cold War. Exploding anticolonial uprisings, tense division on the Korean peninsula, advances by Mao Zedong's forces in China, violence between India and Pakistan, and armed conflict in Palestine between the new state of Israel and its Arab neighbors made the situation even worse. On the other hand, two years of extraordinary effort and extensive preparation involving countless individuals, many NGOs, the Secretariat staff, and all governments members of the United Nations had produced a draft declaration on human rights for all people in the world. The majority thus decided that, despite all the other difficulties and problems that pressed so heavily upon them, too much had been invested and too much was at stake to allow this unique opportunity to pass. With an overwhelming sense that time was running out and that the future hung by a thread, they determined to address what was described as the "great debate" on the "miracle" of the Universal Declaration of Human Rights.[112]

Most of this serious and impassioned debate occurred within the General Assembly's Third Committee responsible for social, humanitarian, and cultural affairs, described as "perhaps the most turbulent body in the United Nations."[113] Here, representatives of over fifty nations, including some of the same individuals who served on the Commission on Human Rights,[114] participated in nearly ninety meetings that considered one hundred and sixty-eight different resolutions containing amendments and took nearly 1,400 separate votes. Here, too, non-Western and smaller nations presented powerful voices. Knowing of their significant impact on including human rights provisions in the Charter, they were determined to be active participants and ardent advocates for their own views once again. They came from Asia, the Pacific, the Middle East, Africa, Europe, and Latin America, representing an incredibly wide range of religious, philosophical, political, and cultural opinion. Some were democratic, many were not. Islamic culture was represented by Afghanistan, Egypt, Iran, Iraq, Pakistan, Saudi Arabia, Syria, Turkey, and Yemen, and to some extent by India and Lebanon. Buddhist influences came from Burma, China, and Siam. The most ardent champions of economic and social rights were the Communists and Latin Americans. The Soviets stressed nondiscrimination. Egypt was responsible for the strong statement about universality. Denmark, the Dominican Republic, and India fought to have rights expressed in gender-neutral language, and the delegate from Pakistan (who herself had been the victim of discrimination) spoke out strongly for women's rights and against child marriage. Poland called attention to human trafficking and all forms of slavery, while the representative of the Philippines argued for a strong prohibition against torture.[115]

Even normally bland official accounts described the setting of these debates as one in which delegates "thrashed out" their differences and pored over the draft text— "line by line" and "word by word."[116] They spent six days on the first article alone. Due to the philosophical issues raised by human rights, the participants engaged in vigorous and fascinating debates most unusual for diplomacy about spiritual values and religious belief, whether there should be any reference to the divine origin of human beings, the relationship between an individual and larger society, conscience, the connection between rights and responsibilities, universalism and cultural relativism, natural law, human nature, the purpose of the state, when life begins and whether children have rights, justice and morality, definitions of "freedom" and "democracy," and the meaning of "the public good" and "the dignity and the worth of the human person." And, owing to the highly political nature of human rights, they exchanged accusations over whether human rights were abused more in colonial empires or behind the Iron Curtain or in the segregated United States, argued about national sovereignty and whether abuses could be "essentially within the domestic jurisdiction of any state," and discussed what one Soviet delegate described as "the destruction of governments" should the United Nations push too far.[117]

Most of these arguments had been heard before, but time and previous debate in no way diminished the intensity or passion of those who believed in the necessity of proclaiming a vision or visions of international human rights. They refused to be dissuaded by whatever philosophical questions still remained, by old and new political problems, or by not obtaining everything that they wanted. Despite the fact that they came from different backgrounds and had conflicts between them, the overwhelming majority of delegates were determined to do what had never been done before: create a declaration of universally accepted norms of human rights, developed after serious consideration of the philosophies, cultures, and political systems of the world, and to establish what Eleanor Roosevelt described as a common standard valid "for all peoples and all nations."[118] To do this, they often labored well after midnight in order to secure agreement. Less than one week before the closing date of the session, the Third Committee finally reached consensus that the text should be submitted to the plenary as a whole.[119]

The proposed declaration was introduced to the entire General Assembly by Malik of Lebanon. The crowd of delegates, reporters, and onlookers fell silent as he approached the podium and began to speak. Drawing on his skills as a diplomat, a professor, and a philosopher, he began to explain the vision before them. Its origins could be found in the values and the rights traditions contributed from around the globe, he explained, but unlike previous declarations that had sprung from particular cultures, this was something new:

Thousands of minds and hands have helped in its formation. Every member of the United Nations has solemnly pledged itself to achieve respect for and observance of human rights. But, precisely what these rights are we were never told before, either in the Charter or in any other national instrument. This is the first time the principles of human rights and fundamental freedoms are spelled out authoritatively and in precise detail. I now know what my government pledged itself to promote, achieve and observe. . . . I can agitate against my government, and if she does not fulfil her pledge, I shall have and feel the moral support of the entire world.[120]

The language was designed not to meekly suggest—but to boldly proclaim—a vision. The drafters did not intend for it to become a narrow "document for lawyers," but rather a declaration of principles that could be readily understood by ordinary people in all walks of life and in any city or village of the world and inspire them for action.[121] Toward this end, and to stress its morally binding nature on all peoples as well as all nations, the text deliberately used the more expansive word "universal" in its title rather than "international." It began with philosophy, setting the tone of the entire document by proclaiming that rights were natural, equal, and universal. It spoke of the "inherent dignity" of each person and the "inalienable rights of all members of the human family" as the foundation of freedom, justice, and peace in the world. By declaring that rights came as a moral birthright of being human, it rejected the view that rights were man-made or can only be conferred by governments.[122] It then addressed lessons of recent history, observing that "disregard and contempt for human rights have resulted in barbarous acts which have outraged the conscience of mankind," that the United Nations has affirmed "equal rights for men and women," and that all member governments have pledged themselves to promote universal respect for and observance of human rights and fundamental freedoms. After looking back, it then looked forward, asserting that a "common understanding of these rights and freedoms is of the greatest importance for the full realization of this pledge."[123]

To articulate this understanding and to create "a common standard," the document presented thirty articles for consideration. Of particular importance, and in language that merits considerable attention and reflection, it insisted that "*all* human beings are born free and equal in dignity and rights." To emphasize the point, most articles began with exactly the same simple—but extremely powerful—word: "*Everyone.*" In addition, the text significantly expanded the principle of nondiscrimination established in the Charter by declaring that all the rights set forth be applied to everyone "without distinction of any kind, such as race, color, sex, language, religion, political or other opinion, national or social origin, property, birth, or other status." Lest any question still remain about the universal intent or the particularities of East or West, South or North, and to give expression to the rights of those not yet represented in the United Nations under colonial rule, the language further proclaimed that no distinction could be based on the political, jurisdictional, or international status of any country or any territory to which a person belongs.[124]

The vision then enumerated different kinds of human rights. Many of the articles addressed civil rights. These included the right to life, liberty, and the security of each person; the right to be free from slavery or servitude; and the right to be free from torture and cruel or inhumane punishment. They encompassed the right to equality and equal protection as a person under the law, the right to a fair trial, the right to be free from arbitrary arrest or exile, and the right to be presumed innocent until proven guilty. Everyone, it proclaimed, possessed the right to freedom of movement, opinion, expression, conscience, and religion, as well as the right to peaceful assembly and association. Other provisions entailed the right to marry and form a family, equal rights in marriage for men and women, and the right to own property and to be free from any arbitrary deprivation of that property.[125]

Political rights also were prominently featured. In what has been described as "a revolution within a revolution," one of the most critical articles declared the right of all people to take part in the government of one's own country, either directly or through freely chosen representatives.[126] Moreover, in language that would cause considerable difficulty for many regimes, the text explicitly stated that the "will of the people shall be the basis of the authority of government" and that everyone had the right to vote in periodic and genuine elections with universal and equal suffrage.[127] These articles thus referred to what must not be done *to* people.

Significantly, a number of articles addressed economic, social, and cultural rights, thereby placing them on the same level as civil and political rights. These articulated what ought to be done *for* people. They included the right to an adequate standard of living, including food, clothing, housing, medical care, necessary social services, the right to assistance for motherhood and childhood, and the right to security in the event of unemployment, sickness, disability, widowhood, old age, or other lack of livelihood as a result of circumstances beyond one's control. Additional articles spoke to the right to work and the free choice of employment, the right to just conditions of work, the right to equal pay for equal work, and the right to education, including at least free elementary education, and equal access for all, on the basis of merit, to higher education, and the right of each person to participate freely in the cultural life of his or her community. Another provision proclaimed the right of everyone "to a social and international order in which the rights set forth in this declaration can be fully realized."[128]

The declaration then directly addressed the issue of the relationship between individual rights and collective responsibilities, or what has been called "the other side of the coin."[129] The many authors who contributed to the final text wanted to acknowledge that "everyone" was not an autonomous, solitary bearer or claimant of rights but a person in broader community, and thus that the enjoyment of rights entails responsibilities to others. For some, the motivation for including such a provision derived from their religious sense of duty to those in need beyond themselves. For others, it came from a belief that the needs of society at large were more important than those of the individual. Thus, despite different points of departure, the text declared: "Everyone has duties to the community." It asserted that in the exercise of their own rights, each individual has the responsibility to respect the same rights of others and to meet the just requirements of morality, public order, and the general welfare.[130]

Great care, countless meetings, extensive discussions, compromises accommodating differing ideologies from around the world and diverging viewpoints in the Cold War, and incalculable effort all had been given to bring this vision of international human rights to this point. Some delegates still argued that the text contained too many rights, while others claimed that it embraced too few. They argued about its likely benefits and possible curses. The Soviets proposed to delay consideration and introduced a number of desperate amendments, but could gain only the support of their Communist allies in doing so.[131] But finally, at four minutes before midnight on 10 December 1948—the date now celebrated as Human Rights Day—Herbert Evatt of Australia, serving as president of the General Assembly, announced that the time had come for the entire membership to cast their votes. Acutely sensing that they were about to make history, conveyed by excited murmurings throughout the normally solemn chamber of the Palais Chaillot, each delegation watched for the votes of others with anticipation and prepared to cast their own. In the end, the final vote was announced: forty-eight in favor with eight abstentions. Not one country opposed.[132] In the midst of spontaneous rejoicing, the delegates arose and gave Eleanor Roosevelt a standing ovation. Then they and members of the news media left the large assembly hall to announce that the United Nations had just proclaimed a vision on behalf of all peoples to be known as the Universal Declaration of Human Rights.[133]

This proclamation unleashed an enormous sense of achievement and a flood of praise. To Cassin who had worked on the drafting from the very beginning, the Universal Declaration represented "a milestone in the long struggle for human rights," "the first international document of ethical value," and a "beacon of hope for humanity."[134] Hernan Santa Cruz of Chile hailed it as being of "exceptional importance," and Malik praised it as "destined to mark an important stage in the history of mankind."[135] Chang declared that China greatly welcomed the declaration as establishing normative standards that were truly universal and applied to all countries and all cultures. Evatt lauded it for marking the first time in the entire course of history that the community of nations had ever made a declaration of universal human rights on behalf of millions of people in every corner of the globe who could now turn to it for help, guidance, and inspiration.[136] Other delegates added to this chorus of acclaim, such as Belarmino de Athayde of Brazil who described it as a "remarkable achievement" possessing "great moral authority," and Mohammed Khan of Pakistan who hailed it as "an epoch-making event."[137] The representative of Norway praised it as finally putting to rest the claim that human rights somehow fell within the exclusive jurisdiction of states.[138] Eleanor Roosevelt acknowledged that it was not perfect, but one that "may well become the international Magna Carta of all men everywhere." She spoke of "the moment of achievement" and concluded: "We stand here today at the threshold of a great event both in the life of the United Nations and in the life of mankind. . . . At a time when there are so many issues on which we find it difficult to reach a common basis of agreement, it is a significant fact that . . . [so many] states have found such a large measure of agreement in the complex field of human rights."[139] Many NGOs and individuals also rejoiced at the approval of the Universal Declaration, describing it as an unprecedented accomplishment in the evolution of international human rights and praising it for achieving "the very near impossible."[140]

Nevertheless, not all reactions were so positive. Indeed, the critics who represented those forces of vested interests and tradition, the power of states over the lives of

Figure 12. The "Magna Carta of Mankind": Eleanor Roosevelt and the Universal Declaration of Human Rights. United Nations Photo.

individual people, or domestic jurisdiction and national sovereignty all reacted sharply to this revolutionary proclamation. Communist governments, for example, consistently complained that it tried to challenge their authority and restrict their power. They criticized the Universal Declaration for being too "vague" and ambiguous on certain points, too specific on others, and possessing "many gaps," internal tensions, and "deficiencies" such as failing to provide means for practical implementation.[141] The representative of Poland went so far as to accuse it of being "a step backward" in the movement for genuine human rights.[142] Andrei Vyshinsky of the Soviet Union, who often clashed publicly with Eleanor Roosevelt, reluctantly admitted that it would probably assist the lives of "little people," but soundly condemned it for having "serious defects" and for not addressing "the sovereign right of States."[143] South Africa, on its way to becoming a global pariah, vehemently complained that the Universal Declaration went "far beyond" the rights contemplated by the UN Charter and thereby seriously interfered with the domestic jurisdiction of member states. Its delegate feared—correctly, as it turned out— that this proclamation would be interpreted as an authoritative definition of fundamental rights and that, if this happened, those states who voted for the Universal Declaration would feel bound in the same manner as if they had signed a convention embodying those principles.[144] The president of the American Bar Association similarly declared that it represented a revolutionary concept in the field of law and government that would drastically threaten the U.S. constitutional system of federal-state relations and the principle of national sovereignty.[145]

Exactly as its advocates hoped, and as its critics feared, the Universal Declaration enormously accelerated the evolution of international human rights. Despite many efforts to portray it as a "mere" statement of principle with no legally binding authority at all,[146] the vision proclaimed struck a chord and rapidly began to take on a life of its own. It quickly came to assume, as we shall see, growing moral, political, and even legal force through customary law. This, in turn, inspired a veritable revolution in international, regional, and national actions on behalf of human rights. In fact, it is precisely for this reason that the vision of the Universal Declaration of Human Rights is still described as "the greatest achievement of the United Nations" and as "one of the greatest steps forward in the process of global civilization."[147]

*   *   *

In creating the Universal Declaration of Human Rights, an international body representing the community of nations for the first time in all of history agreed on a comprehensive vision of human rights for all men, women, and children everywhere in the world. Remarkably, the participants joined together both to reflect and to transcend their many different political and economic systems, social and judicial structures, religious and cultural backgrounds, philosophical and ideological beliefs, stages of development, and histories of exclusive national sovereignty in such a way as to speak of the "human family" as a whole and to establish a set of normative standards for "all peoples and all nations." The fact that there was no single author, but rather hundreds—or, arguably, even thousands—who contributed to drafting the text, gave the vision even greater authority and prestige. Indeed, according to Abdul Rahman Kayala, a Sunni Muslim from Syria, "It was not the work of a few representatives . . . it was the achievement of generations of human beings who had worked toward that end."[148] In this sense it represented a culmination of thinking about human rights as it had evolved over the long history of the preceding centuries. At the same time, it was directed toward the future. This vision proclaimed that "everyone" possessed certain basic and identifiable rights, that universal standards existed for people everywhere, and that human rights were matters of legitimate international concern and no longer within the exclusive domestic jurisdiction of states as in the past. Yet, as those familiar with the long struggle for human rights knew from experience, tremendous distances often exist between abstract theory and rhetoric and actual practice. In fact, it is essential to understand and appreciate that at the time of the adoption of the Universal Declaration of Human Rights no place on earth accepted the proclaimed package of rights unanimously and no state—*not one*—regardless of location, system of government, level of development, laws or cultures, could meet its standards of achievement.[149] Champions and opponents of human rights alike thus wondered what would happen and what it all would mean. The answer, of course, would depend on whether, when, and how the world decided to transform this bold vision into reality.

Chapter 8
Transforming Visions into Reality

The First Fifty Years of the Universal Declaration

> The Universal Declaration of Human Rights [has] . . . inspired, guided, and directed national and international energies toward the achievement of a worldwide awareness of the human person . . . as well as standards and machinery to protect human rights; and these have far outstripped the vision of many at the time of the proclamation. The universality and continuing relevance of the Universal Declaration of Human Rights in a vastly changed world is not due to its legal style or precision, nor to the expertise of its authors [but] . . . because it reflects profound truths about human nature and the requirements of human dignity.
>
> —Jan Mårtenson of Sweden

The many women and men who worked so hard to draft and then secure international approval for the Universal Declaration of Human Rights wanted to make certain that the proclaimed vision would be transformed into reality. They knew that without action the text would remain only wishful thinking or abstract verbiage. In fact, their concerns only intensified when critics and detractors immediately attacked their achievement as "mere" words, "only a declaration," "solely a statement of ideals" devoid of any force, and "just dreams."[1] But time and experience would reveal that the Universal Declaration made two extremely significant contributions. The first is that it articulated and affirmed a vision that ought be for those willing to act to secure rights for themselves and for others. The second is that since official government representatives from around the world had publicly pledged themselves and the United Nations to the universal and effective observance of human rights by progressive national and international measures, it established legitimacy. Exactly as one official predicted, once member states adopted the Universal Declaration, "it will always be open to argument how far 'Human Rights' can be regarded as protected by Article 2 (7)."[2] These factors combined to change assessments of possibilities and thereby amplify that essential element that would profoundly influence the subsequent evolution of international human rights: *hope*. Indeed, the Universal Declaration quickly assumed ever-greater and critical importance by serving as a powerful and authoritative source of inspiration and direction, establishing normative standards by which to judge behavior and the human condition, building institutions, acquiring significant moral and political force, influencing legal instruments and measures of implementation, and becoming the very foundation of contemporary international human rights law. Copies were sold out as soon as they became available, and the Universal Declaration became the most translated single document in history.[3] The world began to respond to both the promise and the challenge of the Universal Declaration by seeking to transform its vision into reality not in one but many different ways by extending, protecting, promoting, and enhancing international human rights.

Extending Rights and Setting Standards

Champions of the Universal Declaration possessed few illusions about the tasks before them. As one insightfully observed: "What we are called upon to do is to change attitudes and re-orient . . . values in nearly all parts of the world."[4] But how should this be done? In order to appreciate the magnitude of their accomplishments, it must be recognized that they had no consensus on priorities, no agreement on means or methods, and no central plan for action. Moreover, their major organization for affecting change, the United Nations, possessed only whatever power its sovereign state members were willing to give it. Although inspired by a vision, they thus were forced at every turn to experiment in the face of the unknown, to adjust to change and opportunities, to confront their own differences, and to discover what they could—and could not—do in the face of constant restraints and determined forces of resistance.[5]

Despite these challenges, the Universal Declaration began to have an immediate impact. New laws and constitutions, including those of Costa Rica, El Salvador, Haiti, Indonesia, Jordan, Libya, Puerto Rico, and Syria, incorporated its specific language or principles into their texts. Judicial opinions from national courts as well as from the International Court of Justice referred to its vision. Indigenous peoples in colonial possessions seized on its proclaimed rights. Japan committed itself "to realize the objectives of the Universal Declaration of Human Rights."[6] Bilateral treaties and complaints by one government to another about abuses explicitly mentioned the Universal Declaration. Inspired by its vision, some countries, such as Canada, created a Special Senate Committee on Human Rights and Fundamental Freedoms to draft its own national bill of rights. Schools and universities provided special instruction on the proclaimed rights, and public events sought to attract even greater publicity. Newspaper articles, radio broadcasts, posters, photographs, and the new technological medium of television did the same. Over and over again the General Assembly, ECOSOC, Commission on Human Rights, Division of Human Rights, UNESCO, and other specialized agencies found their work driven by references to its vision. Indeed, one surprised observer concluded that "there is an impressive amount of evidence to show just how much influence this Declaration has exerted throughout the world . . . since it was adopted and proclaimed."[7]

But this was only the beginning. The Universal Declaration and its explicit language about the rule of law struck a powerful chord, and the resonance greatly assisted in the important process of formally setting standards, or establishing norms, for other declarations and legally binding conventions covering abuses against some of the world's most highly vulnerable victims who were unable to protect themselves. Its vision of human life, for example, encouraged states to begin ratifying the Convention on the Prevention and Punishment of the Crime of Genocide, which established genocide as a crime under international law and held those who committed or incited extermination responsible for their actions.[8] Such ratification, as the treaty's chief author and advocate, Raphael Lemkin, described it, was "a matter of conscience" and a test of "moral responsibility."[9] The Universal Declaration then helped to shape the four momentous 1949 Geneva Conventions and their principles of *jus in bello*, or justice in war, that now serve as the modern basis of humanitarian law protecting sick and wounded combatants, prisoners of war from "grave breaches" such as torture, and civilian populations in time of armed conflict.[10]

These were quickly followed by two treaties long-sought by advocates for women's rights: the International Labor Organization's 1951 Convention Concerning Equal Remuneration for Men and Women Workers and the 1952 Convention on the Political Rights of Women. Further negotiations led to the 1954 Convention Relating to the Status of Stateless Persons. The 1956 Supplementary Convention on the Abolition of Slavery, the Slave Trade, and Practices Similar to Slavery then sought to augment and intensify previous agreements by going beyond concepts of "classical" slavery and giving greater status to other forms of servitude such as debt-bondage, serfdom, servile marriage, and the transfer of children for the purpose of exploitation. The texts of each of these specifically cited the vision of the Universal Declaration by name.[11]

It is within this context of particularly innovative standard-setting that two additional and extremely important treaties also were created. The first of these began when the Consultative Assembly of the newly established Council of Europe recommended that a convention "be drawn up as soon as possible, providing a collective guarantee, and designed to ensure the effective enjoyment of all persons residing within their territories of the rights and fundamental freedoms referred to in the Universal Declaration of Human Rights."[12] This resulted in the landmark 1950 European Convention for the Protection of Human Rights and Fundamental Freedoms focusing on civil and political rights,[13] described by its leading scholar as "without doubt, the most notable achievement of the Council of Europe."[14]

The other was the 1951 Convention Relating to the Status of Refugees, frequently described as "The Magna Carta for Refugees." It fell under the supervision of the United Nations High Commissioner for Refugees which the previous year began operations to protect the rights of those victims uniquely positioned at the intersection of international and domestic politics and caught between states. It referred explicitly to the Universal Declaration as the basis of its efforts and defined a refugee as anyone outside his or her country of normal residence as a result of a well-founded fear of persecution because of race, religion, nationality, social group, or political opinion. This was followed by the 1967 Protocol acknowledging that the plight of refugees could not confined to Europe, as originally conceived, but posed human rights issues that were truly global in scope and "without any geographic limitation."[15] Together, this convention and its protocol provide the cornerstones of modern international refugee protection today, for they impose obligations on states to move beyond empathy and take action.[16] It is this acknowledgment that inspires the poster pointedly reading:

You are not to blame if a man becomes a refugee.
You are, if he continues to be one.[17]

All these innovative treaties broke significant new ground, providing extremely important contributions and precedents for much of what would still come. But many of the champions of rights desired more and wanted a broader-based covenant directly tied to the wide-ranging provisions of the Universal Declaration. They understood the necessity of putting words into action and knew that the original plan had called for an international bill of rights with three parts: a declaration, a covenant to set more precise standards, and, finally, measures of implementation. They therefore urged the United Nations to proceed immediately toward the next stage and adopt the draft "International Covenant on Human Rights." Even intimate insiders believed that such a treaty lay just around the corner.[18] They were wrong.

The adoption of the Universal Declaration and the early groundbreaking treaties created a wave of euphoria among rights advocates that temporarily masked several underlying problems and countervailing forces of resistance. States willing to adopt declarations of principle, for example, did not always share a similar enthusiasm for accepting binding obligations that might challenge their vested interests or threaten their national sovereignty. They intensely argued over the highly controversial and emotionally charged question of whether the proclaimed vision of the Universal Declaration imposed legal commitments or not.[19] Politics within the United Nations itself created particularly complicated problems. The United States and its allies in the Cold War increasingly feared that the organization was falling under the influence of Communists. At exactly the same time, the Soviet Union and its allies came to believe that the United Nations was bowing to anti-Communist, imperialistic, and capitalist forces, especially when if refused to seat the representative of the People's Republic of China after the 1949 revolution. This East-West confrontation soon affected nearly everything that the United Nations attempted, including what has been called "The Deep Freeze" for international human rights.[20]

Of particular importance, and despite their extremely serious differences, however, the two superpowers of the Cold War ironically shared one critical characteristic in common: both greatly feared efforts by the United Nations on behalf of human rights that might threaten their national sovereignty. The Soviets vehemently opposed any international scrutiny of their one-party state, secret police, suppression of freedom of speech, persecution of religion, forced labor, or political prisoners confined to the Gulag's brutal prisons, arguing that such action would be contrary to Article 2 (7) of the Charter protecting domestic jurisdiction. They adamantly refused to respond to the thousands of letters received by the Commission on Human Rights from women regarding their sons and husbands still imprisoned against their will and against the principles of the Universal Declaration.[21] The Soviets repeatedly argued that civil and

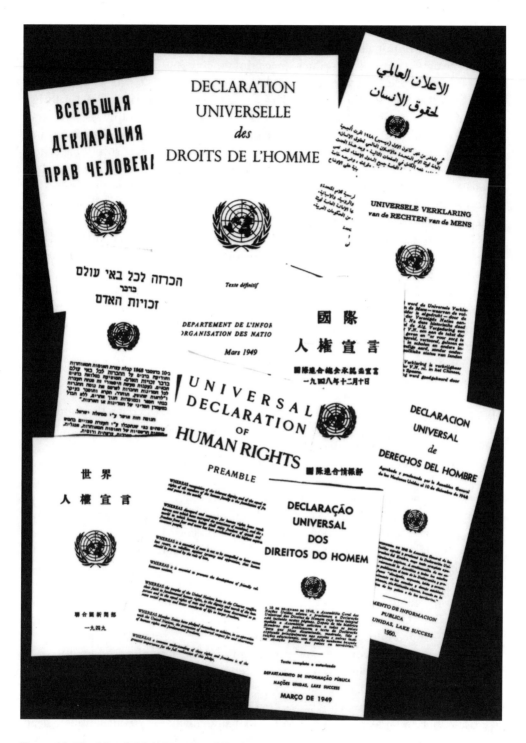

Figure 13. The Most Widely Translated Single Document in History.

political rights represented nothing more than meaningless "bourgeois" values. They and their allies continually resisted anything that might establish a system of "international pressure" that could introduce "spies" into their country or become "an instrument of interference" into their internal affairs.[22]

Similar arguments emerged in the United States. Here, the rise of McCarthyism with its rabid nationalism, xenophobia, and anti-Communism portrayed the specter of a United Nations infested with foreign enemies. The American Bar Association issued ominous warnings about international agreements usurping the constitutional system of federal and state law and openly opposed the Genocide Convention and the draft covenant on human rights. The Daughters of the American Revolution did the same, while issuing personal attacks against Eleanor Roosevelt. Many business and political leaders insisted that economic and social rights represented an insidious "scarlet hue" designed to destroy free enterprise. In addition, segregationists continued to oppose any efforts of the United Nations and its colored "alien elements" to bring about changes in Jim Crow or racial immigration laws.[23] Republican Senator John Bricker thus introduced legislation demanding that the United States withdraw from all treaties having anything to do with human rights. "My purpose," he declared, "is to bury the so-called covenant on human rights so deep that no one holding office will ever dare to attempt its resurrection."[24] He described international human rights as subversive, dangerous, "completely foreign to American law and tradition," and as nothing less than a "U.N. Blueprint for Tyranny."[25] Bricker stridently announced: "I do not want any of the international groups, and especially the group headed by Mrs. Eleanor Roosevelt, which has drafted the covenant of Human Rights, to betray the fundamental, inalienable, and God-given rights of American citizens enjoyed under the Constitution. That is really what I am driving at."[26]

Powerful political forces of resistance such as these joined with others to confront the Commission on Human Rights every step of the way. For precisely this reason, it took years to reach any agreement on setting standards for a covenant. But then, as one participant noted, this attempt to create global protection of human rights "represents a radical departure from traditional thinking and practice." "We are in effect asking States to submit to international supervision their relationship with their own citizens, something which has been traditionally regarded as an absolute prerogative of national sovereignty."[27] Representatives disagreed on almost everything and argued strenuously about the meaning, relationship, applicability, enforceability, and priority of rights. Britain and the United States, for example, argued that only civil and political rights should be included in a legally binding treaty. The Soviets protested, insisting that any covenant contain only economic and social rights. These disputes raged on and on as the antagonists pursued their own agendas, accusing the other of human rights abuses while ignoring their own failures and picking through the Universal Declaration's thirty carefully integrated articles, choosing which rights they liked and which ones they disliked, and thereby breaking a single vision into many. Finally, to prevent complete deadlock, an uneasy compromise was arranged whereby not one, but two, separate treaties would be created: the International Covenant on Civil and Political Rights and the International Covenant on Economic, Social, and Cultural Rights.

But once again, differences, pressures, and resistance emerged immediately, turning the Commission on Human Rights into what has been described as "a forum of political conflict."[28] Representatives argued over whether governments themselves should be considered as oppressors or protectors, whether special escape clauses should be included for "emergencies," and whether international enforcement machinery was even necessary in the first place. The Soviet Union, for example, insisted that national institutions alone should enforce any provisions, warning that anything else would impinge on domestic jurisdiction. Australia, on the other extreme, advocated an International Court of Human Rights with authority to protect individuals from their own governments. Colonial powers heatedly debated with those committed to decolonization about the right of self-determination, while Britain decided on a strategy "to prolong the international discussions, to raise legal and practical difficulties, and to delay the conclusion of the Covenant as long as possible."[29] With reference to the right of freedom of speech, the United States with support from the American Civil Liberties Union argued that no limits should exist on expression, whereas delegates from the nonwhite world and Europeans victimized by Hitler's propaganda strongly believed that the covenant should prohibit any advocacy of racism or war. Some lobbied for provisions guaranteeing equal protection against discrimination, but others with serious racial problems, such as the United States and South Africa, opposed any possibility of interference into their internal affairs. Indeed, it was precisely this concern that prompted President Dwight Eisenhower and his Secretary of State John Foster Dulles in 1953 to refuse to reappoint Eleanor Roosevelt to the Commission on Human Rights (even though she still had two years left in her term) and to shockingly announce that the United States would not become a party to *any* human rights treaty approved by the United Nations.[30] With this, the issue was no longer one of personal hurt, but of policy. She thus publicly and bluntly declared: "We have sold out to the Brickers and McCarthys. It is a sorry day for the honor and good faith of the present Administration in relation to our interest in the human rights and freedoms of people throughout the world."[31]

To those who sought to transform the vision of the Universal Declaration into reality, these developments produced disappointment, frustration, and anger. In their minds, valuable time had been squandered. It seemed to them that nations appeared more interested in protecting their own national sovereignty and in fighting the Cold War rather than in advancing human rights. They would have felt even worse if they had known that the decision by Eisenhower and Dulles to sack Eleanor Roosevelt and to turn her country's back on the entire enterprise of covenants would set a tone and direction that would be followed by Republican and Democratic successors alike, thereby largely removing the United States from a constructive role in the evolution of international human rights that it could have played for the next two decades. The Soviets seized on this as an incredible gift for their propaganda, now arguing that since the United States would not become a party to the covenants, it had no right to lecture others on the subject of human rights. "The hopes," wrote one disheartened observer, "have been so far sadly frustrated" and concluded that this deadlock would likely continue for many years to come.[32]

What he and many others could not fully anticipate was the impact on the evolution of international human rights of one of the most powerful developments ever seen: the emergence of newly independent nations and peoples in the wake of collapsed colonial empires. In this regard, the vision proclaimed in the Universal Declaration would be both profound and revolutionary as it began to extend to literally millions of men, women, and children around the world. It could hardly be otherwise if one honored the words of "the equal and inalienable rights of all members of the human family" that applied to "everyone." Inserted as a result of pressure from Asian, African, and Latin American countries who themselves had suffered as victims, one particularly important article proclaimed that "no distinction shall be made on the basis of the political, jurisdictional or international status of the country or territory to which a person belongs, whether it be independent, trust, non-self-governing territory or under any other limitation of sovereignty."[33] Given this unequivocal language, many governments, activist members of the Trusteeship Council, colonial peoples, and NGOs such as the International Committee of the Congress of Peoples Against Imperialism concluded that subjugation was no longer acceptable and began to plan how to bring about the collapse of all colonial empires.[34]

Indigenous peoples who sought independence and their supporters elsewhere did not require the Universal Declaration to launch decolonization. The desire for freedom, especially among those under foreign domination, is a powerful force at any time. But, as we have seen, promises of self-determination had been made during World War II. In addition, the war seriously weakened two important elements critical to the maintenance of empire. One of these was the political, economic, and military strength of Western powers that enabled them to hold on to their imperial possessions. The other was the myth of white invincibility. These factors greatly increased the self-confidence of indigenous peoples. Moreover, the United Nations Charter itself had included the Declaration Regarding Non-Self-Governing Territories. Yet it was the Universal Declaration that gave them hope by affirming their vision for freedom and—since the colonial powers themselves had voted for it—by providing a new and widely acknowledged legitimacy to their efforts. Those with imperial possessions understood the implications perfectly well, and thus deliberately attempted to delay any publicity about, or application of, the Universal Declaration overseas. The British Colonial Office, to illustrate, sent a secret dispatch to governors in the colonies telling them that it was "a source of great embarrassment" that would produce only "difficulties" and "undesirable implications."[35] Others warned that it would be "seized on by agitators to further their own ends and to cause unrest" and of the "danger that politically inclined school teachers would . . . use the Declaration to confuse pupil's minds."[36] This explains why many in the West complained about the "widespread anti-colonial bias in the United Nations."[37]

In this setting, there is no question that the human rights efforts of the United Nations played a critical role. The Trusteeship Division under Ralph Bunche could not have been more committed to decolonization. The same could be said about many of those serving on the Trusteeship Council who significantly adopted procedures for periodic visits, special missions, and petitions drawing attention to violations of human rights. With the support of the Fourth Committee (Trusteeship Affairs) and especially the Third Committee, where the issue of the right of self-determination was raised most directly, they also created the Special Committee on Information from Non-Self-Governing Territories.[38] Then, under a joint initiative taken by Afghanistan, Burma, Egypt, India, Indonesia, Iran, Iraq, Lebanon, Pakistan, the Philippines, Saudi Arabia, and Syria, and with constant reference to the Universal Declaration, the General Assembly voted to include articles on self-determination in the two emerging human rights covenants. They also specifically asked the Commission on Human Rights to make recommendations on the right self-determination for all peoples.[39] In addition, the General Assembly increasingly became willing to apply political and diplomatic pressure, engage in economic boycotts, and provide various forms of assistance to those struggling for independence. Fierce debates raged between the colonial powers and most others, and between the United States and the Soviet Union who competed for the affections of emerging nations. The whole subject, in the words of one staff member, was full of "political complexities."[40] Those who watched all these powerful forces at work concluded that sooner or later "something is going to happen."[41]

It did. The process that began in the aftermath of the war when the United States granted independence to the Philippines, when the French pulled their troops out of Lebanon and Syria, and when the British relinquished their control over Jordan and Palestine and then over India, Pakistan, Burma, and Ceylon (now Sri Lanka) grew into a tidal wave. Millions determined that subjugation under colonial rule was no longer acceptable—and determined to secure their freedom as well. At this juncture intense arguments raged over that difficult question of means that we have already explored: are human rights best advanced by moral persuasion and reform or by violence? Gandhi stressed the former, emphasizing the practical and the spiritual benefits of nonviolence. But others, such as Ho Chi Minh, took the opposite position, insisting that if they did not receive their freedom as a gift from their colonial masters, then they would take it—by armed force if necessary. This explains the eruption of insurgent guerrilla movements and wars of national liberation. As a result, the Dutch were forced to surrender a colonial possession they had held for three and a half centuries by granting independence to Indonesia in 1949, why the French suffered the same fate with Laos in 1953 and with Cambodia and South Vietnam shortly thereafter, and why the British left Malaya in 1957. In the midst of these struggles, a meeting was convened at Bandung for what host Indonesian President Sukarno described as a "new departure" and "the first international conference of colored peoples in the history of mankind."[42] Such notables as Romulo of the Philippines, Nehru of India, and Zhou Enlai of China, despite their highly divergent ideological differences on other matters, discussed human rights at length and referred specifically to the vision of the Universal Declaration. They announced their determination to act as agents of history by advancing self-determination and racial equality, and to make sure that those rights obtained in Asia would be extended in Africa as well.[43]

In order to appreciate the magnitude of this transformation, it is important to recognize that at the time of the creation of the United Nations only one country—only one—in all of Asia was free from foreign control, and that was China. Similarly, as late as 1955, only five countries in the entire African continent could claim to be independent: Egypt, Ethiopia, Liberia, Libya, and South Africa. All other peoples remained under colonial rule. But they saw powerful forces for change sweeping the world, ranging from the vision of the Universal Declaration to diplomatic pressure from the United Nations and the use of armed force. All this led them to a clear conclusion: the colonial powers would not be able to "cling on to their imperial ermine" forever and that "time had run out."[44] Some Europeans, reminded of their own words about human rights and frightened by forces they could no longer control, came to the same realization. Thus, in a dramatic shift of policy, France reluctantly relinquished control in Tunisia and Morocco and Britain conceded independence to Sudan. In 1957 Kwame Nkrumah announced with tears in his eyes that the colony once exploited for its gold and black slaves would gain self-determination under the name of Ghana. Vowing that he would work to extend this right to others, he organized the All-African Peoples' Conference the next year, inviting representatives from anglophone West and East Africa, francophone black Africa, the Belgian Congo, and Arab lands to the north. Not about to miss an historic opportunity like this, ninety-year-old Du Bois demonstrated that age in no way had diminished his passion for rights as he exhorted: "You have nothing to lose but your chains! You have a continent to regain! You have freedom and human dignity to attain!"[45]

A veritable revolution resulted, for within just a few short years cracks in the edifice of empire became chasms. Guinea gained independence in 1958. But the dam burst in 1960, frequently described as "The Year of Africa."[46] Suddenly, the people of seventeen separate states gained the right of self-determination. These included Cameroon, Central African Republic, Chad, Congo-Brazzaville (now Republic of the Congo), Congo-Kinshasa (then Zaire, now Democratic Republic of the Congo), Dahomey (now Benin), Gabon, Ivory Coast, Madagascar, Mauritania, Mali, Niger, Nigeria, Senegal, Somalia, Togo, and Upper Volta (now Burkina Faso). Sierra Leone and Tanganyika secured their freedom the next year, while Frantz Fanon published his powerful and angry book entitled *The Wretched of the Earth* supporting revolutionary violence if necessary to secure self-determination.[47] Algeria (after a particularly gruesome war marked by the use of torture by French forces, portrayed so graphically in the film *The Battle of Algiers*),[48] Burundi, Kenya, Malawi, Rwanda, Uganda, Zambia, and Zanzibar (which united with Tanganyika to form Tanzania) soon followed. Elsewhere, Cyprus, Jamaica, Kuwait, Malaysia, Mongolia, Tobago, and Trinidad also obtained their independence. Bahrain, Qatar, United Arab Emirates, and Yemen would be added shortly thereafter. Never before had so many people gained emancipation in such an incredibly short period of time. In just a few years, decolonization destroyed empires often built up over centuries, liberated vast territories from colonial rule, transferred power from whites to nonwhites, and secured the right of self-determination for more than one billion people. Indeed, one participant describes it as nothing short of "the greatest extension and achievement of human rights in the history of the world."[49]

This revolutionary destruction of colonial empires and emergence of many independent nations and peoples resulted in revolutionary changes. Careful observers noted that when these new countries participated and voted in the United Nations "for the first time," there would be "new tendencies and new relations" that "may provoke reactions which we cannot yet estimate."[50] This was an understatement, for their influence—described as an "irrepressible force"[51]—dramatically transformed the composition, character, tone, language, and much of the agenda of the United Nations itself. In sheer numbers alone, they now captured the majority and hence voting strength within the organization. They thus elected U Thant from Burma as the first non-Western, nonwhite, and Buddhist secretary-general. But more importantly, they brought a new and shared determination to extend certain aspects of international human rights. In order to appreciate this factor, it is essential to understand that this Afro-Asian group represented the most heterogeneous bloc within the United Nations. Geographically, its members ranged from Japan on the Pacific to Morocco on the Atlantic and from Tunisia on the Mediterranean to Madagascar on the Indian Ocean. Religiously, they varied from Hinduism to Islam and from Christianity to Buddhism. Politically, they spanned the distance from pro-West Thailand and Lebanon, to vociferously nonaligned Egypt and Indonesia, to pro-Communist Mongolia, and many found themselves sharply divided in the Sino-Soviet split. Some had gained their independence through peaceful means, and others by violence. Some believed in democracy, some did not. In other words, they held often sharply divergent visions of rights. But what they did share was that at the time of independence they all praised the Universal Declaration by name or incorporated some of its provisions into their new constitutions[52] and they all held a particular passion for two intimately intertwined issues: the right of self-determination for those people not yet free from colonial domination and the right to equality for those still suffering from racial discrimination. To address these problems directly, they set out to finally break the deadlock that had immobilized the entire process of standard setting for international human rights.

With the knowledge that they controlled a majority within the United Nations, and with the conviction that they had a responsibility to do whatever they could to facilitate the historical process of emancipation, eighty-nine states from Africa, Asia, Latin America, the Middle East, and all the Communist countries along with others in Europe joined together in 1960 to adopt a resolution entitled the Declaration on the Granting of Independence to Colonial Countries and Peoples.[53] Its vision boldly proclaimed that the subjugation of peoples to domination, discrimination, and exploitation constituted a flagrant violation of the Universal Declaration and an impediment to world peace. Supporters then established a new and special committee to explore ways in which this declaration might be implemented and set about their task with vigor and determination. Over the objections of Australia, Britain, and the U.S., but with the full support of Secretary-General U Thant who criticized any policy of "the ruler and the ruled, the master race and the subhuman" as completely unacceptable,[54] the committee took the dramatic decision to invite petitioners from colonial territories to come and bear witness about the violations of their human rights before representatives of the United Nations. They organized meetings in places such as Addis Ababa, Dar-el-Salaam, Lusaka, and Tangier, and made explicit recommendations on how to transform the vision of the Universal Declaration into reality.[55]

Throughout all of these efforts, the new delegates never lost sight of the related issue

certain to unite them: the right to racial equality. The long and heavy legacy of subjugation, exploitation, enslavement, segregation, and exclusion made them extremely sensitive to human rights violations based on racism. They consistently cited the Universal
Declaration's vision when they met at the Asian-African Conference in Bandung, the
All-African Peoples' Conference in Accra, the Summit Conference of Independent African States creating the Organization of African Unity in Addis Ababa, the Afro-Asian
Peoples' Solidarity Organization in Cairo, and United Nations meetings in New York
and Geneva. As Carlo Romulo declared with emotion:

We of Asia and Africa are emerging into this world as new nation-states . . . [and] besides the issues of colonialism and political freedom, all of us there are concerned with the matter of racial
equality. . . . In the United Nations [we] have again and again forced this on the unwilling attention of the other members. There we could see palpably the extent to which Western men have
become defensive about the past racist attitudes. . . . They have yet to learn, it seems, how deeply
this issue cuts and how profoundly it unites non-Western people who may disagree on all sorts
of questions. [We need to provide] a sober yet jolting reminder to them that the day of Western
racism is passing along with the day of Western power over non-Western people.[56]

The intensity of their feeling grew even more as they witnessed the determined refusal of whites to give up power in territories controlled by Portugal, Southern Rhodesia, and South Africa; the persistent marginalization of indigenous peoples; and the
immigration policies of "White Australia," "White New Zealand," and "White Canada."
There was a very personal dimension to this as well, for when these non-white delegates
came to the United States to represent their countries at the United Nations, they
suddenly confronted the fact that, regardless of their own distinguished accomplishments at home, they often were refused service and subjected to discrimination simply
because of the color of their skin. This made them conclude that what they had heard
about racism in America was not just Soviet propaganda—but reality.

In addition, there was the unrelenting racial segregation, exploitation, and persecution known as apartheid against an overwhelming majority of blacks, Asians, and
those of mixed race by a small, white minority regime in South Africa who regarded
them as being less-than-fully human. When police attacked unarmed black civilians
at Sharpeville in 1960, it proved to be more than the Asian and African countries
would tolerate. They were outraged and called for a special emergency session of the
Security Council to address the dangers that apartheid presented for security, peace,
and justice. This prompted the white South African prime minister to lash out at what
he called the "international forces" interfering within his country's domestic jurisdiction.[57] In sharp contrast, the charismatic black leader Nelson Mandela embraced this
external pressure, proclaiming simply but powerfully before being sentenced to life
imprisonment: "The Universal Declaration of Human Rights provides that all men are
equal before the law."[58]

With all these violations of racial equality, the new majority determined that it was
time for them to do whatever they possibly could to help transform this vision into
reality. They began by creating the Special Committee on the Policies of Apartheid
and called on all nations to pressure South Africa by severing diplomatic relations,

boycotting its products, embargoing goods (including weapons), and prohibiting its ships or aircraft from using port facilities.[59] They then adopted the important Declaration on the Elimination of All Forms of Racial Discrimination, condemning any ideology or policy that resulted in racial segregation or apartheid and calling for concrete action against them. "We are not forgetting for a single instant," said one delegate, "that even the best resolutions are of value only in so far as they are effectively applied. . . . The hour for decisive action has struck. Let us not allow it to pass by."[60] Toward this end, and again citing the Universal Declaration, they created the ground-breaking International Convention on the Elimination of All Forms of Racial Discrimination in 1965. For the first time in history, states negotiated a standard-setting treaty that defined racial discrimination, pledged themselves to adopt all necessary measures to prevent and eradicate it, and agreed to hold themselves subject to criticism from other states party to the convention and to individual petitioners.[61]

These actions finally broke the stalemate that had prevented completion of the covenants. They proved that if the political will existed among the majority, the United Nations could move forward in extending rights and setting standards. As the Colombian delegate observed,

the change is not purely numerical. . . . There has been a change of ideas, modes of expression, attitudes, objectives, and even ideals. There has been an awakening of the world conscience to a duty that cannot be denied, an awakening of peoples to a clear right—that of strengthening the foundations of justice, society based on equality, the obligations of States to promote conditions that will permit every person the full enjoyment of his rights.[62]

Consequently, and with the full and active support of an ever-growing number of NGOs, work now started in earnest to complete the international bill of human rights that would make respect for the proclaimed rights a legal responsibility of states. An indication of this new determination can be seen in the fact that it took only the single, pivotal year of 1966 for both the historic International Covenant on Civil and Political Rights and the International Covenant on Economic, Social, and Cultural Rights to be adopted by the General Assembly and opened for signature.[63] Both treaties begin by referring to the Universal Declaration. They unequivocally state that human rights are essential matters of international concern, hence no longer reside within the exclusive confines of the domestic jurisdiction of parties to the covenants. They also prohibit discrimination based on race, color, gender, language, religion, political or other opinion, national or social origin, property, birth, or other status. In addition, both covenants provide not just for the human rights of individuals but for what increasingly came to be known as a third generation of rights: "group" or "collective" rights relating to the right of self-determination, a healthy environment, subsistence and development, and the right to control their natural resources. Moreover, each establishes a distinct and compulsory international enforcement system designed to ensure that the parties comply with their obligations. Participants thus described them as marking a "historic event," "a major advance," and "a new era, a new epoch in the development of positive international concern for human rights."[64]

The International Covenant on Civil and Political Rights, originally supported by

Western governments but opposed by Communists, builds on the vision of the Universal Declaration but provides much greater juridical specificity and expands on the number of rights enumerated. A total of fifty-three articles address the right to life, liberty and security; a fair trial; privacy; freedom of thought and religion; freedom of conscience and expression, assembly, association, movement, voting and political participation; equal protection; and the right of all to be regarded as a person before the law, among others. Obligations are established for states to provide for the right of detained persons to be treated with humanity and not to deny ethnic, religious, or linguistic minorities the right to their own culture, to profess and practice their own religion, or to use their own language. Provisions are made for rights of children to have a name, acquire a nationality, and be protected against discrimination on the basis of race or gender. The General Assembly also created a separate treaty known as the Optional Protocol, making provision for individuals claiming to be victims to file complaints against states parties to its terms. Later they opened a Second Optional Protocol establishing commitments to abolish the death penalty.[65]

The International Covenant on Economic, Social, and Cultural Rights also significantly broke new ground in standard setting. Its articles, originally pushed by the Soviet Union and its allies and states sympathetic to social welfare, gradually gained the support of others. The International Labor Organization, for example, stressed provisions for the right to work, UNESCO for the right to education and participation in cultural life, WHO for the right of all people to health, and the Food and Agricultural Organization for the right to be free from hunger. The political factor that tipped the scales for final adoption by the General Assembly, however, and that confirmed the connection between the extension of rights and the setting of standards, was once again the emergence of those new countries just released from the bonds of colonialism and vitally interested in securing progressive development. The thirty-one articles of the covenant define these rights in considerable detail, including the right to work, the right to equal pay for equal work, the right to join trade unions, the right to social security, the right to protection of the family with special assistance to mothers and children, the right to an adequate standard of living and food, the right to the highest attainable standard of physical and mental health, the right to education, and the right to take part in cultural life.

The new majority, along with their supportive colleagues in other delegations, took much justifiable pride in adopting these two standard-setting covenants. They knew that their collective effort had been responsible for finally breaking the long and debilitating political deadlock. This success encouraged them to embark on even more activity, including changing the composition of the Commission on Human Rights itself. In 1967 they were able to enlarge the membership to thirty-two, and thereby secure influence in determining priorities. Perhaps more important in terms of emphasizing the universal nature of the enterprise, a new formula allocated seats in accordance with a regional distribution, with Africa securing eight, Asia six, Eastern Europe four, Latin America six, and Western Europe and all others eight.[66] At the same time they found themselves agreeing with Seán MacBride of the International Commission of Jurists that the vision of the Universal Declaration needed to be made "the Charter of liberty of the oppressed and the downtrodden" wherever they were in the world.[67]

This momentum and the commitment to internationalize human rights by an expanding number of states could be seen almost immediately. As early as 1968 the General Assembly adopted and opened for signature the Convention on the Non-Applicability of Statutory Limitations to War Crimes and Crimes Against Humanity.[68] By 1973 its members agreed on the International Convention on the Suppression and the Punishment of the Crime of Apartheid dealing with the highly emotional issue of race, declaring that apartheid "is a crime against humanity" and establishing particular measures to implement its provisions and punish those judged guilty.[69] They then created the landmark 1979 Convention on the Elimination of All Forms of Discrimination Against Women, defining gender discrimination as "any distinction, exclusion, or restriction made on the basis of sex" that impairs the enjoyment by women of their human rights "in the political, economic, social, cultural, civil, or any other field." The text requires that states party to this treaty "modify the social and cultural patterns of conduct of men and women, with a view to achieving the elimination of prejudices and customary and all other practices which are based on the idea of the inferiority or the superiority of either of the sexes or on stereotyped roles for men and women." Significantly, by holding them responsible for discrimination by "any person, organization, or enterprise," it moves states beyond the public into heretofore private spheres of economic, social, and family life.[70]

Other important standard-setting treaties followed in rapid succession. With the unceasing prodding and assistance from a number of NGOs, the overwhelming majority of delegates to the United Nations wanted to turn their outrage into action by clearly establishing that the egregious violations of basic human rights caused when governments employ torture against their opponents simply was no longer acceptable. For this reason, they adopted the 1984 International Convention Against Torture and Other Cruel, Inhuman, or Degrading Treatment or Punishment, making the language as clear and unequivocal as it could possibly be with an absolute prohibition:

No exceptional circumstances whatsoever, whether a state of war or a threat of war, internal political instability or any other public emergency, may be invoked as a justification for torture.[71]

They went on to adopt the International Convention on the Protection of the Rights of All Migrant Workers and the groundbreaking 1989 Convention on the Rights of the Child, which today holds the distinction of being the most widely ratified treaty in history.[72]

Never before in history had so many standard-setting treaties been created so quickly on behalf of international human rights. Moreover, every single one specifically cited the vision of the Universal Declaration by name. Of particular importance is the fact that all of them resulted from the approval of representatives from one hundred to more than one hundred and fifty states (as compared to the fifty-one that had created the United Nations), and thus became all the more remarkable for reflecting the normative values not of a particular group or narrow region of states but of the broader international community and its collective sense of responsibility toward those who suffered abuse. Once they achieved this, the next task—and the ultimate test in the face of continued abuses—became one of avoiding mere lip service by actually protecting these enumerated rights through implementation.

Protecting Rights Through Implementation

Those familiar with the struggle for international human rights knew from long experience of the constant problem posed by the distance between theory and practice. For this reason, they took great pride in actually being able to extend rights and to establish new standards following the proclamation of the Universal Declaration. But they also knew that serious difficulties still lay ahead. What would be the practical effect of all these efforts on the lives of individual people if states simply refused to ratify these treaties, thereby preventing them from ever entering into force and establishing the rule of law? As one delegate noted, the challenge would be to acknowledge the achievements while at the same time avoiding "pompous statements" and "tempting promises" by seeing to it "that these new covenants are strictly observed everywhere."[73]

International human rights covenants and conventions depend upon governments to put domestic laws and legislation into place that provide protection against abuses. They become binding, contractual treaties with the authority of law only when the necessary and predetermined number of states agree to accept the obligations contained therein. This usually begins with the signature by state representatives in a public ceremony and then with subsequent ratification or accession in accordance with the law of each country, with some involving the approval of only a small number of leaders and others, like the United States, requiring a two-thirds majority of the Senate. It is this second phase that generally presents the most difficult problems, for here the influences of domestic politics, personalities, and vested interests play powerful roles. In addition, some states will not ratify treaties unless or until their own national laws are in conformity with the international agreements. This explains why there often is such a lag between standard setting and actual treaty implementation in the form of compliance and enforcement. Fundamentally, the determining factor in whether treaties are ratified rapidly, after a long delay, or not at all—and whether these commitments are then honored—is political will.

The European Convention for the Protection of Human Rights, for example, demonstrated extraordinary will among its liberal and conservative parties alike not only to work with a Committee of Experts on Human Rights to set standards, but to implement the treaty through ratification that placed limits on their sovereignty.[74] They recognized the value of institution building and established the unusually successful European Commission on Human Rights and European Court of Human Rights for judicial enforcement, marking the first time in history that states were willing to give an external tribunal the power to require changes in their domestic legislation and where petitions against contracting states for alleged violations of their rights could be presented and where decisions would be binding.

Similarly, the International Convention on the Elimination of All Forms of Racial Discrimination gained such strong support from Asian, African, Arab, and Latin

American countries that it entered into force only four years after adoption. Significantly, its monitoring body known as the Committee on the Elimination of Racial Discrimination (CERD) created the first international mechanism for monitoring implementation of a UN-sponsored treaty in the field of human rights. Its members are elected by the states parties to the convention but, importantly, serve in their individual capacities rather than as government representatives in assessing the periodic reports legally required of all parties and in making recommendations. Specific provisions also give them the authority to receive interstate complaints and provide an optional protocol for individual petitions. The members of CERD quickly conveyed their view that racial discrimination was not a monopoly of whites against blacks and refused to accept inadequate reports from governments trying to hide from their obligations.[75]

Such political will is not always easy to find. The important Covenant on Civil and Political Rights, by contrast, took a full decade to enter into force in 1976, for many of those states who signed the text in public resisted assuming binding obligations. This included a number of the originally enthusiastic new leaders of Asia and Africa who, once they began to exercise power themselves, demonstrated a troublesome unwillingness to accord these rights to their own citizens, often trying to invoke self-determination or Third World nationalism as an excuse for immunity from international scrutiny.[76] Some of the national liberators became rights violators. Nevertheless, a sufficient number of states did ratify its terms, making them subject to the jurisdiction of the mechanism of the Human Rights Committee (HRC) composed of independent experts. This they did with vigor, as revealed by their thorough examination of protection measures, use of information provided by human rights NGOs, administration of an interstate complaint mechanism, receipt of individual petitions as provided under the Optional Protocol, adoption of advisory opinions, and development of a valuable body of case law. Indeed, one evaluator concluded: "Even the most skeptical observers have been impressed by the apparent seriousness that many states from different parts of the world, with diverse political systems, have taken toward their reporting obligations, as reflected by the quality of the reports and the calibre of the representatives, as well as their willingness to answer the Committee's questions."[77]

Once the International Covenant on Economic, Social and Cultural Rights entered into force, states party to this treaty also committed themselves to submitting obligatory reports on the measures taken to protect these rights. At first the Economic and Social Council provided the monitoring mechanism, but its sheer size and the fact that its members were representatives of governments subjected to constant political pressures inhibited its ability to perform the required tasks objectively. Consequently, and with remarkable political courage, it was decided in 1985 to create the Committee on Economic, Social, and Cultural Rights (CESCR), composed of eighteen individuals acting in their own personal capacities. Members of this committee have devised an elaborate and obligatory reporting system to determine whether states are honoring their commitments and annually submit recommendations to ECOSOC for consideration and action.

The successes of these monitoring mechanisms of experts established a pattern followed by other international conventions. When the Convention on the Elimination of

All Forms of Discrimination Against Women entered into force in 1981, its parties created the Committee on the Elimination of Discrimination Against Women (CEDAW). When the International Convention Against Torture became law in 1987, they created the Committee Against Torture (CAT) to administer a required reporting system as well as an optional interstate and individual complaint mechanism. Of particular importance, and a potential source of considerable enforcement power, it possesses the authority in certain cases to undertake actual investigations of suspected abuses. In addition, when the Convention on the Rights of the Child entered into force in 1990, the Committee on the Rights of the Child (CRC) was instituted to monitor compliance, particularly against abuses of sexual and economic exploitation, use as child soldiers in armed conflict, abandonment, and ill-treatment. Together, these various treaty bodies have created a comprehensive legal framework in which states are obligated to engage in often rigorous international scrutiny of human rights implementation within their own countries.[78]

As impressive as these legal instruments and treaty bodies might be, however, they most certainly could not solve all problems of implementation. Governments could refuse to ratify the new agreements or protocols and thus remain outside the established commitments. Or they could become parties to the treaties, but only with attached conditions or reservations. Or, when pressures became too great, they could try to claim special privileges, refuse to acknowledge the competence of monitoring bodies, or take refuge under a "derogation clause" exempting them from obligations in times of emergencies. For all these reasons, the advocates of international human rights, whether serving as state officials, members of NGOs, or individuals understood that they could not rely exclusively on their achievements in creating these various legal instruments or rest on their accomplishments in creating convention-based mechanisms. The realization of the vision of the Universal Declaration required more. Toward this end they set about to establish a number of extremely significant non-treaty procedures and mechanisms as well.

One of the most critical features in the evolution of international human rights has always been whether individuals are able to bring complaints about violations to the attention of others for possible action and protection. Throughout most of history, people wanting to draw attention to abuses had no organization to which they could turn, found themselves denied recognition or standing and thus excluded and ignored, or were silenced by their own governments hiding behind claims of national sovereignty. Only in very unusual circumstances, as we saw with the Bernheim petition to the League of Nations, did this ever change. In fact, for many years the United Nations itself followed the well-established pattern. When confronted with a flood of petitions conveying abuses, governments fearful of political consequences instructed their representatives to insist that the Commission on Human Rights possessed "no power to take any action in regard to any complaints concerning human rights."[79]

Remarkably, despite this widely publicized policy and its appearance of complete futility for seeking remedy, individuals and NGOs acting on their behalf nevertheless wrote constantly to the Commission on Human Rights. They bitterly cried out that this system was designed to protect governments rather than people and was "most unfair,"[80] but continued to write because they had no place else to turn and because they hoped that the United Nations might eventually be able to transform visions of rights into reality. Some pleaded on behalf of particular individuals (both those known only to their families and immediate neighbors as well as those globally recognized such as Nelson Mandela or Martin Luther King, Jr) or groups.[81] Still others petitioned for broader subjects such as the protection of minorities, the right of people to self-determination, freedom of religion, the right of asylum, freedom from forced labor, prevention of discrimination, conscientious objection, or protection of civilians during war. Letters poured in every day of every year from virtually every country in the world. Indeed, during one year alone, the commission received more than twenty-five thousand communications alleging violations of human rights.[82]

Members of the Economic and Social Council thus faced a serious dilemma. For political reasons, they could not take action on these petitions; but, by the same token, they could not completely ignore them. After all, many of the communications contained references to the Universal Declaration by name, the principles of which their own governments had endorsed. One insightful observer put his finger precisely on the problem by writing that this issue of petitions raised "the whole question of state sovereignty" and provided

a constant invitation to the United Nations to intervene in what may properly be regarded as the internal affairs of a sovereign state. Nevertheless, it is this very encroachment of the international community into the affairs of states which lies at the root of all progress in the field of human rights.[83]

To begin working their way through this delicate dilemma, they created a system whereby the staff of the Human Rights Division would compile a confidential list of the communications and then convey them to the Commission on Human Rights or the Commission on the Status of Women. Member states not represented on these bodies would be informed of the substance that directly concerned them, but the identity of the authors would be kept secret unless they chose to reveal themselves. Yet access to this list was severely restricted, information could never be used to initiate remedy in specific cases, and the entire process provoked resentment. The possibility of petitioning against alleged violations of human rights thus remained deadlocked for years under the early "no power" decision with only the slightest of modifications.[84] Like so many other efforts in the long evolution of international human rights, action could proceed only when a problem of such magnitude arose that it simply could no longer be ignored. This occurred—once again—over an extremely emotional subject: racial discrimination.

When confronted not only with the continued injustice of apartheid but also the refusal of some white governments to change their policies of colonialism or discrimination despite all the resolutions, declarations, and embargos to the contrary, the new and determined majority within the United Nations decided to take further action. First they created a Working Group of Experts to investigate the treatment of prisoners in South Africa, Namibia, Southern Rhodesia, and Portuguese territories in Africa, as well as to invite victims to bear witness to abuses. Then, in order to focus global

Figure 14. A Voice Finally Gained: Bearing Witness to Abuses Before the World. United Nations Photo.

attention on racism and to go far beyond the diplomatic parlance of substituting general criticisms of "certain countries" for references to specific violators, states from Africa and Asia, with the strong support from Latin America and Arab countries, passed a most significant resolution. They authorized the Commission on Human Rights "to examine information relevant to gross violations of human rights and fundamental freedoms, as exemplified by the policy of apartheid as practiced in the Republic of South Africa" and to make recommendations.[85]

This action opened a critical door that had been slammed shut from the beginning, and thereby made possible many other efforts that went far beyond apartheid. Broader discussions followed quickly about racial discrimination, segregation, the vestiges of colonialism, abuses of a military junta in Greece, brutality of the Duvalier regime in Haiti, and, in a problem that increasingly would attract attention: Israeli policies in occupied Palestinian territories after the 1967 war. Several Western members of ECO-SOC then mobilized sufficient political will to encourage the passage in 1970 of the landmark Resolution 1503. Over the strong objections of some states who argued that it would threaten national sovereignty, they created a procedure for receiving petitions and determining whether they "appear to reveal a consistent pattern of gross and reliably attested violations of human rights requiring consideration."[86] Then, in an extremely important decision, and referring specifically to the Universal Declaration, it was decided to open the door still wider by establishing that these communications would be admissible if

there are reasonable grounds to believe that they reveal a consistent pattern of gross and reliably attested violations of human rights and fundamental freedoms, *including* policies of racial discrimination and segregation and of apartheid *in any country, including* colonial and other dependent countries and peoples.[87]

The widespread possibilities—and challenges—of giving voices to victims created by this new 1503 procedure were seen immediately. When the chief of the Communications Unit of the International Instruments and Procedures in the Human Rights Division brought the first collection before the commission in 1974, he carted more than two thousand pages into the room. Members who hitherto had been involved in the somewhat more abstract issues of standard setting rather than practical implementation were stunned. The shocking and politically sensitive content of this material struck like a bombshell, and they quickly realized why they had been instructed to close this kind of meeting to the public.[88]

With this auspicious beginning, the Commission on Human Rights started to work its way through a process of receiving, considering, and acting on what is described as "thousands, thousands, and thousands" of communications.[89] Some governments, such as those of the Shah of Iran, Fidel Castro of Cuba, and Ferdinand Marcos of the Philippines, launched a counter-offensive to divert the commission from focusing on specific cases by swamping it with more general issues, claiming that only collective abuses such as colonialism should be considered. But the number of complaints increased dramatically, for added to the petitions from individuals were those generated by massive letter-writing campaigns and extensive information provided by human rights NGOs. Although the procedure was designed to address large-scale and systemic violations rather than single individual abuses, the files and archival records demonstrate once again the fact that victims are always individual human beings.[90] In addition, and despite the requirement for confidentially, any number of highly visible and politically charged "situations" attracted considerable international attention that generated demands for action. These included apartheid by the white minority regime of South Africa, the Israeli treatment of Palestinians, the torture of opponents by dictator Augusto Pinochet of Chile, and the launching of the "dirty war" by a military junta in Argentina. The creation of new procedures and mechanisms for implementation, and their modifications through time, enabled the Commission on Human Rights to address many complaints wherever they occurred, ranging alphabetically from Afghanistan, Argentina, Armenia, and Azerbaijan to Uganda, the United States, Vietnam, and Zaire.[91]

Those who have participated in this evolution bear testimony to the striking impact of the 1503 procedure. Prior to this mechanism, states generally responded to complaints charging them with human rights violations with a single sentence tersely reading: "The Government of _____, views such charges as slanderous propaganda, libelous allegations, a threat to our national sovereignty, and unwarranted interference into our internal affairs as protected by Article 2 (7) of the Charter."[92] Such replies are no longer acceptable. Today, governments know that they cannot get away with claiming that they are immune from scrutiny under established standards. None are anxious to go through an elaborate and highly embarrassing process that names and shames them before other representatives capable of launching formal investigations against them. For this reason, they often send their ministers of foreign affairs or justice, prime ministers, or even presidents to respond to charges. On some occasions, they have even forgone their prerogatives of confidentiality and voluntarily opened their files in order to clear their name.[93]

Not content with even these remarkable developments, the majority of the Commission on Human Rights decided to create still other non-treaty procedures and machinery to implement the vision of the Universal Declaration. With the encouragement from activist Theo van Boven who became Director of the Division of Human Rights in 1977, they determined not to let abusers hide simply because they might not be a party to a particular treaty. To do this, they successfully established new means collectively described as "special procedures" designed to examine and bring to public attention particularly egregious cases of abuse. These included working groups dealing with such thematic topics as enforced or involuntary disappearances, arbitrary detention, structural adjustment programs for economic, social, and cultural rights, and the right to development. Special rapporteurs were appointed to report on such wide-ranging issues as summary or arbitrary executions, torture, religious intolerance, the use of mercenaries, child prostitution and pornography, constraints on freedom of opinion and expression, violence against women, racism and xenophobia, internally displaced persons, independence of the judiciary, the illicit movement and dumping of toxic and dangerous products, threats to the cultural property of indigenous peoples, discrimination against people with HIV or AIDS, and forbidding conscientious objection.

In creating these procedures, the majority on the commission refused to back away from some of the most sensitive abuses within specific countries and found sufficient political will to establish special rapporteurs for Afghanistan, Burma (Myanmar), Cambodia, Cuba, Haiti, Iran, Iraq, Palestine, Rwanda, Somalia, Sudan, and the former Yugoslavia, among others.[94]

These many efforts of protecting rights through implementation, and those that would soon follow with the creation of international criminal tribunals, marked a tremendous change on the road of transforming visions into reality. For centuries, traditional international law had enshrined a horizontal system between states in which only they possessed legal standing. Individuals remained completely excluded. But these new legal instruments of binding conventions with their treaty bodies and mechanisms increasingly created a more vertical arrangement of great significance to human rights: the transformation of individual victims from objects of international pity into subjects of international law. Indeed, while looking back on these advances, one experienced lawyer concluded, "A hundred years from now, jurists may well be saying that the most important, most radical indeed, development in international law in the [last half of the] twentieth century was the growth of an international law of human rights."[95]

Promoting Rights

Advocates of human rights firmly believed that the vision of the Universal Declaration could never be realized in practice without widespread support based upon information. As one observer noted: "It must be pointed out . . . that in the course of our history . . . attempts at reform and modernization have been frustrated by stubborn resistance on the part of certain persons or groups of persons who wished to keep the population in ignorance for their own ends."[96] Knowledge is power, and this explains why publicity and promotion are so important. "Governments move slowly, except under the pressure of opinion or events," noted a member of the UN Secretariat, concluding that without a public informed of abuses, efforts on behalf of human rights would lose "the most important factor." "This latent potential demand must be organized, if we are to succeed."[97] With precisely this in mind, member governments and officials of the United Nations, NGOs, and individual activists launched serious efforts to make the promotion of human rights around the world "top priority."[98]

Toward this end, they sought to carry the vision into lives of men, women, and children in nearly every part of the globe by translating the Universal Declaration into as many different languages as possible and printing millions of copies for distribution. UNESCO produced study guides, films, posters, radio and television programs, exhibits, and books such as *Human Rights: Comments and Interpretations*. Others used the universal language of music by holding special concerts to honor human rights. The United Nations designated 10 December of each year as "Human Rights Day" to commemorate the anniversary of the Universal Declaration and rededicate the collective commitment to its vision through public observance. Many other efforts followed in rapid succession. In fact, when political obstacles prohibited other efforts, promotional activities became the primary focus of the Commission on Human Rights itself.[99]

Publications became one of the most effective means of promotion. The Secretariat placed a high priority on producing the annual *Yearbook on Human Rights* in which each country's record was given wide publicity. Articles about human rights appeared regularly in the *United Nations Chronicle, Refugees* from the United Nations High Commissioner for Refugees, *Human Rights Newsletter* produced by the Center for Human Rights, the ILO*International Labour Review,* and UNESCO *Courier* and *Chronicle.* The Sub-Commission on Prevention of Discrimination and Protection of Minorities sponsored a series of special publications including the *Study on Racial Discrimination, The Realization of Economic, Social, and Cultural Rights,* and the comprehensive *United Nations Action in the Field of Human Rights,* making them widely available to libraries. On major anniversaries of the Universal Declaration, the Secretariat published *Human Rights: A Compilation of International Instruments,* containing all conventions, declarations, and recommendations adopted by the United Nations and its specialized agencies. Annual publications of *Human Rights: Status of International Instruments* describing the signatures, ratifications, and accessions to human rights treaties followed.[100] In addition, books, reports, and documentation published by regional, intergovernmental organizations such as the European Commission on Human Rights, Inter-American Commission on Human Rights, and African Commission on Human and Peoples' Rights contributed still further to this expanding body of information. In fact, as one librarian wrote, the sheer amount of material about human rights exhibited "a state of explosion, not just explosive growth, but explosion."[101]

The power of publicity came to be seen by others as well. One of these was Peter Benenson, a man with years of activist experience and strong religious convictions who worked as a lawyer in London. One day as he turned the pages of his daily newspaper, reading stories of local and international affairs, his eyes focused on an article about two students who just had been sentenced to seven years' imprisonment by the dictatorial Salazar regime in Portugal for treason. Their crime? They went to a bar, had a beer, and simply raised their glasses in a toast "to freedom!" They had not gone on strike, rioted in the streets, or attacked anyone. Benenson knew perfectly well that the Portuguese government had voted for the Universal Declaration, including its provision about freedom of expression. He could have followed the well-trod path of shrugging his shoulders in disgust and turning to the next page, shaking his head in cynicism, or saying that these unfortunate students were in another country and thus not his responsibility. Instead, he concluded that this violation of rights was no longer acceptable, that his outrage must be turned into action, and that these victims needed help. But what could he do? As improbable as it seemed, he thought that a publicity campaign that would name and shame governments might halt their abuses. He described his vision in these words:

Open your newspaper any day of the week and you will find a report from somewhere in the world of someone being imprisoned, tortured, or executed because his opinions or religion are unacceptable to his government. . . . The newspaper reader feels a sickening sense of impotence.

Yet if these feelings of disgust all over the world could be united into common action, something effective could be done. . . . Experience shows that in matters such as these governments are prepared to follow only where public opinion leads. Pressure of opinion a hundred years ago brought about the emancipation of the slaves. It is now for man to insist upon the same freedom for his mind as he has won for his body.[102]

Despite much ridicule that simply writing letters could never possibly have any impact, Benenson worked with friends to launch a one-year campaign entitled an "Appeal for Amnesty, 1961," urging people to write on behalf of "forgotten prisoners of conscience" calling for their release. The surprising success and grassroots support for this publicity led to the creation of Amnesty International. It adopted as its logo a symbol designed to convey the value of promotion: a candle burning inside a string of barbed wire to give visual expression to a Chinese saying: "It is better to light a single candle than to curse the darkness."[103]

One candle grew to inspire many, for multiple efforts tended to reinforce each other as they developed new strategies and engaged new constituencies. Amnesty International eventually grew into one of the most well-known human rights NGOs in the world. Its *Report* was soon joined by *The Review* of the International Commission of Jurists, publications from the Asian Forum for Human Rights and Development, *Human Rights Africa Bulletin, Human Rights Watch World Report, Human Rights Bulletin* of the International League for Human Rights, and *Human Rights Monitor* of the Human Rights Service, among many others, in drawing attention to abuses. One of the most important features of these reports, especially when combined with new journals of independent scholarly research such as *Human Rights Quarterly* and *Human Rights Law Journal*, was that since they did not represent governmental positions, they could be hard-hitting in their criticisms. As one activist expressed it: "Surely the United Nations is not merely a body for the mutual preservation of the vested interests of the Member States; it has to become a body representing humanity as a whole if the Universal Declaration is to be translated into reality."[104] In this regard, NGOs with transnational networks often revealed themselves to be particularly effective in gathering information, conducting research, and promoting rights by speaking truth to power without the restraints of "quiet diplomacy." This, of course, provoked harsh reactions from governments. The Soviet delegate, for example, accused the International League for the Rights of Man of being "one of the most odious organizations" for waging "a systematic campaign of slander and subversion" and protecting "plotters, kidnappers, criminals, murderers, detainees, fugitives, and refugees." "It throws mud," he complained, "at member states."[105]

Despite pressure to silence the critics, however, this momentum for promotion continued to accelerate, and those who championed visions of human rights became enormously heartened by the convergence of several different developments. Some occurred when Australia, Canada, and New Zealand began to enact new immigration laws and policies toward indigenous peoples, publicly acknowledging "that the winds of change are blowing" and declaring their desire to conform more closely with the vision of the Universal Declaration.[106] At the same time, Pope John XXIII issued his powerful encyclical *Pacem in Terris*, praising the Universal Declaration as "an act of the highest importance" and asserting that for peace and justice the global community must have "as its special aim the recognition, respect, safeguarding, and promotion of the rights of the human person." He described these rights as "universal, inviolable, and inalienable."[107]

Nearly simultaneous with this pronouncement, over two hundred thousand people gathered to protest in Washington, D.C. before a memorial dedicated to Abraham Lincoln who had issued the Emancipation Proclamation. When the eloquent black preacher Martin Luther King, Jr. approached the podium, the huge crowd grew silent in anticipation of what he might say. With determination and passion in his voice, he drew pointed attention to the abject failure of the United States to keep its promises to protect the inalienable rights of all Americans, especially its citizens of color. But then, instead of leaving his listeners in anger and despair, King held out a hope for a future far better than the past by declaring that he had a vision. He called it a dream. Drawing upon religion, philosophy, politics, and history, he said that it was a dream deeply rooted in the American dream that all are created equal. "I have a dream," he exclaimed: a dream that "the sons of former slaves and the sons of former slave owners will be able to sit down together," a dream that injustice and oppression will be transformed into justice and freedom, and a dream that his own children will be judged by the "content of their character" rather than the "color of their skin." Rising to a crescendo, he shouted: "Let freedom ring!"

When we allow freedom to ring, when we let it ring from every village and hamlet, from every state and city, we will be able to speed up that day when all of God's children—black men and white men, Jews and Gentiles, Catholics and Protestants—will be able to join hands and to sing in the words of the old Negro spiritual, "Free at last, free at last, thank God Almighty, we are free at last."[108]

This vision and the civil rights movement that it inspired stirred the conscience of the nation. Despite resistance, sometimes presented by police with clubs, tear gas, water cannon, and dogs, King and his many black and white colleagues and supporters, insisted on using moral persuasion rather than violence to achieve their goals. Just as the hymn, "Amazing Grace," had expressed an imperishable hope to those who campaigned to end the slave trade in a previous century, these activists turned to music as they sang: "Oh, deep in my heart, I do believe, *we shall overcome someday*."[109] As a result of their efforts, millions were able to watch in astonishment when the landmark 1964 Civil Rights Act and the 1965 Voting Rights Act entered into law in the United States while President Lyndon Johnson declared: "There is no issue of states' rights or national rights. There is only the struggle for human rights."[110]

These extraordinary changes, at precisely the time that the entire process of decolonization and the extension of the right of self-determination reached the force of a tidal wave, occurred so rapidly that serious assessment was frequently difficult. The achievements were not always fully appreciated or understood—nor were the problems. Among the latter, for example, the signing of international human rights treaties did not necessarily ensure ratification, and implementation mechanisms often required adjustments. In addition, many new Asian, African, and Arab nations came to realize, sometimes with considerable difficulty, that independence did not automatically produce civil or political rights or provide economic or social justice. In order to address these issues, the General Assembly declared 1968 as the International Year for Human Rights. Determined to make this effort "truly universal," they created a committee of representatives from different geographical regions, ideological orientations, religious faiths, cultures, and stages of development and charged them with organizing a major gathering to assess human rights.[111]

The resulting International Conference on Human Rights was held in Teheran in 1968. Participants included delegations from eighty-four nations, staff from the United Nations and its specialized agencies, officials from regional bodies such as the League of Arab States and the Organization of African Unity, and activists from NGOs ranging from the Society for Human Rights in Iraq and the Sudan National Committee on Human Rights to the All India Women's Conference and the Korean League for the Rights of Man, and from the International Alliance of Women and the League of Red Cross Societies to the World Council of Churches, World Jewish Congress, and the World Muslim Congress. With worldwide media attention, they evaluated the effects of the Universal Declaration, called upon all states to ratify the existing treaties, and devoted considerable effort to the issues of racial and religious discrimination, apartheid, self-determination, humanitarian law in armed conflicts, discrimination against women, and protection for families and children. Some also raised the problem of double standards, as indicated by the request that the participants consider "rendering justice not only to the Jewish victims of the Nazis but also to the [Palestinian] victims of the Jews as well as other governments who are guilty of such crimes."[112] Significantly, the delegates went on to declare that "since human rights and fundamental freedoms are indivisible, the full realization of civil and political rights without the enjoyment of economic, social, and cultural rights is impossible." They urged "all peoples and governments to dedicate themselves" to the Universal Declaration and to "redouble their efforts" to transform its vision into reality. Moreover, and of particular interest given later attempts by certain governments to characterize international human rights as a "Western invention," all of the majority of non-Western, non-white, and non-affluent states solemnly proclaimed:

The Universal Declaration of Human Rights states a common understanding of the peoples of the world concerning the inalienable and inviolable rights of all members of the human family and constitutes an obligation for the members of the international community.[113]

To promote these rights further, the members of the General Assembly decided to focus widespread attention on particular problems for an entire decade. They thus designated 1973 as the beginning of the Decade to Combat Racism and Racial Discrimination "to promote human rights and fundamental freedom for all, without distinction of any kind on grounds of race, color, descent, or national or ethnic origin," and with the aim of eliminating the persistence of racist beliefs and policies wherever they might exist.[114] They agreed on a specific and ambitious Plan of Action that included such concrete measures as providing assistance to victims, denying political and diplomatic support to governments guilty of racial discrimination, seeking ratification and implementation of relevant standard-setting instruments, and sponsoring the World Conference to Combat Racism and Racial Discrimination.[115]

These efforts opened up new spaces for discourse and action and encouraged others. The Decade for Women was launched in 1976 following the World Conference of the International Women's Year held in Mexico City. Working closely with the Commission on the Status of Women and many NGOs, the participants focused on problems that had confronted women's rights for centuries, including education, employment, health, family planning, and domestic violence. Their studies revealed that "while women represent 50 percent of the world's population, they perform nearly two-thirds of all working hours, receive only one-tenth of the world income, and own less than 1 percent of world property."[116] In addition, they successfully worked on behalf of the Convention on the Elimination of All Forms of Discrimination Against Women with its treaty-monitoring body of CEDAW. The World Conference to Review and Appraise the Achievements of the UN Decade for Women held later in Nairobi attracted close to fourteen thousand participants to a NGO forum and more than fifteen hundred official representatives from one hundred fifty-nine nations. Here they adopted a program of action entitled Forward-Looking Strategies for the Advancement of Women that in the words of the secretary-general "constitute the principal instrument of overall policy of the United Nations in the promotion of the rights of women."[117]

Sometimes the promotion of human rights comes from completely unexpected sources. Space technology during these years, for example, provided people the opportunity for the first time in history to view photographs of their own planet.[118] Model globes and theoretical projections were one thing, but actual images something else. From the unique perspective afforded by thousands of miles of distance, viewers could marvel in wonder at this orb in the heavens with its magnificent oceans, icecaps, mountains, deserts, islands, and continents. But one particularly striking feature also stood out above all others: no bold lines of political borders separated its inhabitants from one another. Discovery in space thus allowed a different kind of discovery of Earth. It made it easier to imagine what human beings shared in common and therefore for the vision of the Universal Declaration of Human Rights to be seen with new eyes.

The same period also witnessed an extremely significant development that came to be known as the Helsinki Human Rights Movement. Following several years of intense consultations, thirty-three European nations as well as Canada and the United States agreed to participate in the Conference on Security and Cooperation in Europe (CSCE).[119] Despite strong resistance from the Soviet Union, which described the subject as "interference in internal affairs" and an "unjustified waste of time,"[120] the majority insisted on making human rights an integral part of any negotiations. Some delegates called this issue "the centerpiece," and even insisted that the entire enterprise be described as "the Helsinki Human Rights Conference."[121] Time and time again they referred to the vision of the Universal Declaration and argued that a link existed between security, peace, justice, and human rights. In this regard, they spoke of the "indivisibility of security": that security of the individual person, security of the nation, and security of the international system are all inextricably interconnected. Indeed, this was the part that has been described as "the most spectacular innovation of the Helsinki process" and one "nothing short of revolutionary."[122] When the Helsinki Final Act was thus signed in 1975, it contained explicit language recognizing "the universal significance" of human rights and pledging the participating states to promote and encourage the effective exercise of civil, political, economic, social, and cultural rights. Of what came to be of particular importance, the signatories promised to "confirm the right of the individual to *know* and *act* upon his rights and duties in this field."[123]

Armed with this highly publicized agreement, activists began to organize NGOs they called Helsinki Committees to promote human rights and monitor compliance with these promises. The Helsinki Final Act gave them a vehicle of legitimacy and hope, and victims trapped under oppressive Communist regimes seized upon it. Yuri Orlov, for example, formed the Moscow Helsinki Group where he and other noted dissidents such as Andrei Sakharov and Yelena Bonner spoke out at great personal risk—but with the knowledge that others could help. "We do not have the means by which to reach our [own] government. My appeal to Brezhnev probably got as far as the regional KGB office," Orlov explained. "The crucial question," however, was now the Soviets could be reached "through the governments of other countries."[124] This critical feature of the value of international human rights norms for national human rights problems was realized by others as well. It inspired dissident (and future president) Václav Havel to create Charter 77 in Czechoslovakia, Polish activists to establish Helsinki Watch, and others to form Human Rights Watch and the International Helsinki Federation for Human Rights to draw attention to violations of rights. Although persecuted, arrested, battered at labor camps and psychiatric hospitals, and exiled by their own governments, they courageously persisted and watched with anticipation as the seeds sown at Helsinki began to dramatically change the life they had known behind the Iron Curtain.[125]

Momentum for promotion continued to increase in the United States as well. It started in Congress. Outraged over the support given by President Richard Nixon and his Secretary of State Henry Kissinger for the coup against a democratically elected government in Chile and the war in Vietnam, Congressman Donald Fraser began holding hearings about violations of internationally established standards and published a report entitled *Human Rights in the World Community: A Call for U.S. Leadership*. He and many of his colleagues contended that a vital connection existed between security, peace, justice, and human rights, and thus that America's own national interests necessitated a disassociation from dictators and repressive regimes. For this reason, Congress passed important legislation tying military and economic aid to rights performance and requiring the Department of State to produce annual "Country Reports" on the status of rights in each nation. This immediately challenged the prevailing Cold War paradigm, for it drew attention not only to abuses conducted by Communist foes but to those of anti-Communist allies, including American-supported death squads of military dictatorships in Latin America, Augusto Pinochet in Chile, the Shah of Iran's secret police, apartheid in South Africa, and Israeli occupation policies. Human rights activists played an important role in this process not only by providing information but in forming new NGOs to address issues of feminism, homosexuality, torture, and the environment. The Ford Foundation began funding human rights programs.[126]

The election of Jimmy Carter then brought attention to human rights that the nation had not seen since the days of Eleanor Roosevelt. "As President," Carter later wrote, "I hoped and believed that the expansion of human rights might be the wave of the future throughout the world, and I wanted the United States to be on the crest of this movement."[127] He announced that human rights would serve as the core and "soul" of his foreign policy. To do this, he appointed determined activist Patricia Derian to head the newly created the Bureau of Human Rights and Humanitarian Affairs within the Department of State, black civil rights leader Andrew Young as ambassador to the United Nations, and Jerome Shestack of the International League for Human Rights as representative on the Commission on Human Rights. Carter then pressed both adversaries as well as authoritarian allies alike to improve their human rights practices. He drew attention to the Universal Declaration to reiterate that no nation—including his own—could hide any longer behind the excuse of national sovereignty in the treatment of its citizens.[128]

At the same time, Archbishop Oscar Romero delivered public sermons in Latin America about respecting rights, and the American Convention on Human Rights entered into force with the establishment of the Inter-American Court of Human Rights. The World Council of Churches appointed a Human Rights Advisory Group and began a major program of publicity. Amnesty International's receipt of the Nobel Peace Prize gave marked visibility to human rights NGOs. This was enhanced with the widespread attention given to developments in Argentina. One was the publication of Jacobo Timerman's book *Prisoner Without a Name, Cell Without a Number* describing horrifying torture at the hands of the military junta. The other was those women from quite ordinary backgrounds but possessed of extraordinary courage who formed the Mothers of the Plaza de Mayo, confronting possible death by defiantly carrying banners and poster-sized photographs of their "disappeared" children.[129] Shortly thereafter, human rights activists in China risked imprisonment by creating the "Democracy Wall" of protest in Beijing. Then, encouraged by the collapse of the last remnants of the Portuguese empire and the emergence of a black majority government in Zimbabwe, the Organization of African Unity (now the African Union) made specific reference to the Universal Declaration and adopted the "Banjul Charter," or the African Charter on Human and Peoples' Rights.[130]

Promotion occurred in other areas as well, each time expanding the agenda and casting a wider net around those to be included in human rights. The United Nations increasingly worked with the World Health Organization, for example, to draw attention to the rights of those with physical, intellectual or sensory impairment, medical conditions, or mental illness. Toward this end, they produced the 1975 Declaration on the Rights of Disabled Persons and established the Decade of Disabled Persons from 1983–1992 with its program of action that led to the Standard Rules on the Equalization of Opportunities for Persons with Disabilities.[131]

All of these developments inspired others and greatly strengthened the belief that promotion was essential to the progressive evolution of international human rights. Indeed, when he became Under Secretary-General of Human Rights, Jan Mårtenson described promotion as one of the three "pillars" of the United Nations human rights

Figure 15. The Courage to Speak Out: Mothers of the Plaza de Mayo. Enrique Shore-Woodfin Camp, and Associates.

program, the other two being standard setting and implementation. "A key element in the realization of human rights," he declared, "is the knowledge by each person of his or her inalienable rights and the means that exist to protect them."[132] With the launching of the UN World Public Information Campaign for Human Rights in 1988, the release of Amnesty International's *Global Report on Human Rights* charging that gross violations had increased in proportion to the amount of government lip service, and the creation of new NGOs such as Americas Watch, Asia Watch, Africa Watch, and Middle East Watch, these activities grew even more. The new and expanded Center for Human Rights (replacing the former Division of Human Rights) began publishing the *Human Rights Newsletter*, cosponsored a large NGO World Congress on Human Rights in New Delhi, and worked with the Commission on Human Rights and a special preparatory committee to plan for a major conference designed to assess the entire status of international human rights.

Not all governments welcomed this plan. In fact, some worked to thwart the efforts of Ibrahima Fall of Senegal and scores of others organizing the event and to prevent it from taking place at all. They believed that this kind of promotion would result in embarrassing criticism of their own abuses before the eyes of the world. Even documents usually noted for using polite diplomatic language described the confrontations between the supporters and the opponents of the conference as "difficult," "divisive," and "intense."[133] The Chinese government, for example, still furious at the criticism of their 1989 Tiananmen Square massacre, occupation policies in Tibet, imprisonment of human rights activist Wei Jingsheng, and other abuses of civil and political rights, staked out a hard-line position to stop the entire process. It worked with similar-minded governments to create a "gag rule" forbidding any finger-pointing at specific violations by individual member states, sought to exclude human rights NGOs, and fought to keep the Dalai Lama from addressing the conference at all.[134] In addition, China led a movement that followed a 1990 attempt known as the "Cairo Declaration of Human Rights in Islam" to support what they called the "Bangkok Declaration" which challenged the very basis of the Universal Declaration by asserting the relativity of norms derived from the "particularities" or differences of nation, region, history, culture, and religion.[135]

These maneuvers provoked strong reactions among human rights advocates within other governments and most certainly among NGOs. Among the latter, those in Asia were particularly incensed. They accused the ruling elite of these countries of being interested in nothing more than creating a shield under the expressions of "Asian values" or "cultural relativism" to protect themselves against accountability and to use the specter of "foreign" values to divert attention away from domestic abuses. Said one spokesman, they came up with this argument because they "have something to hide on the protection of human rights in their own countries."[136] They noted that no region in the world has ever had a monolithic set of values and, for this reason, fundamental debates and contests about human rights have taken place as much *within* cultures as *between* them. More than one hundred Asian-Pacific NGOs, in fact, went so far as to publicly issue their own parallel declaration, strongly supporting the vision of the Universal Declaration. They warned others to be aware of the legitimate claims of differences and cultural pluralism, but not to be seduced into thinking that these somehow allowed repressive regimes to set their own norms as it suited them and to absolve themselves from internationally established standards.[137] The Burmese activist, Buddhist, and pacifist Aung San Suu Kyi subsequently declared that claims of "cultural relativism" by her government and others were only cynical manipulations "intended to justify the policies and actions of those in power." "If ideas and beliefs are to be denied validity outside the geographical and cultural bounds of their origin," she insightfully observed, "Buddhism would be confined to north India, Christianity to a narrow tract in the Middle East, and Islam to Arabia."[138] The serious differences, she said bluntly, were not between cultures but rather between universal norms of human rights and the unrestricted exercise of power.

Despite all the obstacles and arguments designed to kill the entire enterprise, the will of the majority of the United Nations prevailed to the point that they could hold the World Conference on Human Rights in Vienna in 1993. Acutely aware of its highly visible, promotional mission, Secretary-General Boutros Boutros-Ghali of Egypt announced that the event "marks one of those rare, defining moments when the entire community of States finds itself under the gaze of the world. It is the gaze of the billions of men and women who yearn to recognize themselves in the discussions that we shall be conducting and the decisions that we shall be taking in their name." He challenged all participants to rise above their differences, avoid "verbal battles" and "sterile polemics," and recommit themselves to the worth of each and every human being.[139] But with the presence of over two thousand delegates from one hundred seventy-one nations, heads of state and other government officials, representatives from specialized agencies and intergovernmental bodies, and nearly four thousand activists from over eight hundred NGOs, as well as all those who demonstrated in the streets outside the conference, it is not surprising that many serious and contentious problems arose. Nevertheless, the delegates finally agreed on the Vienna Declaration and Program of Action in whcih they invoked what they described as "the spirit of our age and the realities of our time" supporting international human rights. They openly recognized that they all came from different cultures and backgrounds, but turned their backs on the argument of relativism by reaffirming the Universal Declaration as a common standard of achievement "for all peoples and all nations" and by unequivocally and authoritatively declaring: "The universal nature of these rights and freedoms is beyond question." Moreover, they boldly rejected the old claims of domestic jurisdiction by asserting that *all* human rights represented a legitimate international concern. In addition, they acknowledged the indivisible and interrelated nature of human rights and stressed the necessity of taking specific action to protect victims. Finally, they urged support for democracy and development, encouraged NGOs to become even more active, and recommended that more resources be devoted to the Center for Human Rights and that the process of institution building be enhanced by creating a new position of High Commissioner for Human Rights to provide strategic direction and coordination for as many new expanding activities as possible.[140]

Expanding Activities and Enhancing Rights

Standard setting, implementation of treaties, and promotion all played vital roles in helping to transform the vision of the Universal Declaration into reality. But those committed to international human rights were not content with these developments, and thus set out to develop a wide array of other activities to enhance rights even further. Many of these centered within the United Nations where the Division of Human Rights, then the Center for Human Rights, along with the specialized agencies, created what they called Advisory Services in the Field of Human Rights to offer practical assistance. They provided expert advice on how to administer fair elections and how to prepare women for participation in political affairs. They offered fellowships, seminars, and training programs to those politicians, civil servants, and educators involved with social welfare and development, health, the administration of justice, drafting national legislation, protecting minorities and aboriginal populations, helping to secure equal pay for women workers, assisting refugees, and providing relief to victims of disaster. Of particular importance, United Nations personnel took these programs wherever they received an invitation, from Japan, India, Mongolia, the Philippines, and Thailand in Asia to Cameroon, Ethiopia, Ghana, and Zambia in Africa, and from Argentina, Chile, Colombia, and Mexico in Latin America to Austria, Britain, Italy, and Poland in Europe.[141]

It is impossible to know the precise impact of these many activities, of course, but there is no question that they had a cumulative effect and, when combined with events of consequence, helped to sow seeds that would bear fruit. One of the most notable of these was the monumental upheaval of the "Velvet Revolution" of 1989 that brought about the fall of the Iron Curtain, the collapse of Communist regimes in Eastern Europe and of the Soviet Union and its empire, and the end of the Cold War itself—events all strongly inspired by visions of human rights. Indeed, this is precisely why people were willing to gather in public squares, stand on the Berlin Wall, and link hands in a human chain of an estimated two million men, women, and children that stretched all the way from Tallin in Estonia to Vilnius in Lithuania in defiance of oppression.

Harkening back to both the Universal Declaration and the Helsinki Final Act and the Helsinki Human Rights Movement that it encouraged, and building upon the momentum of a decade of follow-up meetings to monitor compliance, NGOs and the member states of CSCE sought to take full advantage of this unparalleled window of opportunity. Indeed, some of these states themselves were now represented by human rights activists who formerly had been persecuted. They immediately organized three Conferences on the Human Dimension. One of these produced the 1990 Charter of Paris, remarkably declaring "democracy as the only system of government of our nations," thereby recognizing the legitimacy of the constitutional order *within* states as a matter of agreement *among* states.[142] Participants in the 1991 conference held in Moscow and hosted by Mikhail Gorbachev referred to human rights as being "in the soul of man," spoke about the power of visions to change the world, and affirmed that they "categorically and irrevocably" declare human rights as "matters of direct and legitimate concern to all . . . and *do not belong exclusively to the internal affairs of the State concerned.*"[143] Such direct statements marked yet further erosions of the claims of domestic jurisdiction under Article 2 (7) of the UN Charter.

In order to help manage the dramatic and historic changes taking place around them, the participants of CSCE then determined to set a new course by establishing the Organization for Security and Cooperation in Europe (OSCE). Today it includes fifty-six states from Europe, Central Asia, and North America; stretches from Vancouver to Vladivostok; and is the largest regional security organization in the world. Of particular importance, the members committed themselves to a broad concept of security beyond politico-military elements by explicitly acknowledging that security, peace, justice, and human rights are inextricably intertwined.[144] At exactly the same time, former states of the Soviet bloc and former regions of the Soviet Union itself were allowed to become full-fledged members of the Council of Europe—but only under the critical condition that they also become parties to the European Convention on Human Rights and subject themselves to the jurisdiction of the European Court of Human Rights. Throughout this dynamic process many of the participants knew from their own experience the enormous practical value of advisory services and technical assistance, and thus created the Office for Democratic Institutions and Human Rights to assist in holding free elections, establishing the rule of law, developing local democracy, and protecting freedom of religion and expression.[145]

Extraordinary changes were taking place in South Africa at the same time, for here what had once appeared to be inconceivable became a reality. Years of apartheid had caused so much oppression and so much hatred that people spoke openly about the "inevitability" of a "bloodbath" of violence, "brutal" conflict, and a "race war" in which "millions will die."[146] But shifting geopolitics, economic hardship resulting from sanctions, and the cumulative effects of countless international efforts now began to force the minority regime into making unprecedented reassessments of their alternatives and attitudes. As white President F. W. De Klerk would describe it, the time had come to acknowledge in one's conscience that apartheid was "morally unjustified."[147] In a particularly dramatic move, he announced in 1990 that he would release Nelson Mandela from prison—alive. With this, the same international community that had used whatever tools it could devise in the anti-apartheid struggle in the past now offered political and diplomatic support, financial investment, and assistance for South Africa's first ever nonracial democratic election in 1994. This enabled twenty-eight million previously disenfranchised blacks to vote for the very first time in their lives. Mandela emerged as their new president, the result of a peaceful election rather than a war. His victory signaled not only the end of apartheid but also of more than three centuries of white domination. With joyous elation, an emotional Mandela finally could proclaim to South Africa and to the world: "Free at last!"[148]

All of these developments encouraged the international community to strengthen its efforts in expanding activities and enhancing rights in other areas as well. Among these, the creation of the UN High Commissioner for Human Rights proved to be one of the most significant. In 1993 the General Assembly established this position long sought by many human rights NGOs and activists. They assigned it the "principle responsibility" for providing strategic direction and coordination to the evolving and ever-growing number and scope of United Nations human rights efforts, playing an active role in preventing abuses, strengthening international human rights and mainstreaming them into the United Nations system, and promoting and protecting human rights—"for all." Moreover, they insisted that the person holding this post possess expertise in human rights and "knowledge and understanding of diverse cultures" and be "of high stranding and personal integrity."[149]

The impact of this new position could be seen immediately and in very practical ways. As soon as they named José Ayala Lasso from Ecuador as its first UN High Commissioner for Human Rights in 1994, he and his staff made sure that the Program for Action emerging from the World Conference on Human Rights specifically highlighted the value of advisory services and technical assistance.[150] For this reason, and with the new UN Fund for Technical Cooperation in the Field of Human Rights, Lasso and his staff launched a series of activities to build national and regional human rights infrastructures, strengthen democratic institutions, draft new constitutions, explain treaty obligations, reform penal institutions, train officials and security forces, conduct seminars for judges and lawyers, develop educational strategies and materials, and assist the media in covering human rights. They also provided direct assistance to the African Commission on Human and Peoples' Rights, the African Center for Democracy and Human Rights Studies, and the Arab Institute for Human Rights, as well as creating field offices in Georgia, Burundi, Cambodia, Colombia, Gaza (at the request of the Palestinian Authority), Malawi, Mongolia, and elsewhere.[151]

Special field operations were also instituted to address particularly gross violations of human rights. In response to the Haitian crisis of military dictatorship, for example, the General Assembly authorized the United Nations to participate with the Organization of American States in the International Civilian Mission to Haiti. They then created the United Nations Mission for the Verification of Human Rights in Guatemala. Responding to the shocking brutality and "ethnic cleansing" in Bosnia and Herzegovina, they instituted the Human Rights Field Operation in the Former Yugoslavia. In response to the slaughter inflicted by Hutus against Tutsis, the Commission on Human Rights and the High Commissioner for Human Rights established the Human Rights Field Operation in Rwanda. Each was staffed with specialists mandated to investigate breaches of international human rights and humanitarian law, assist refugees and internally displaced persons, help NGOs, offer expertise on reforming law enforcement, and provide public information and education on behalf of democratization initiatives and human rights.[152] Indeed, the extraordinary range, geographical scope, and complexity of these many activities became so extensive that great effort needed to be made to coordinate them all.

Much of this activity could be traced directly to the increasingly energetic efforts of those who served on the Commission on Human Rights itself. The original eighteen members grew to fifty-three and its agenda grew as never before. With the assistance of the High Commissioner for Human Rights, it drafted new standard-setting instruments and declarations, sought further ratifications of existing treaties, dealt with complaints about abuses, developed extra-conventional mechanisms or special procedures, dispatched fact-finding missions, supported advisory services and technical assistance, worked with NGOs and regional intergovernmental bodies, made recommendations for further action, and assisted in such promotional activities as the 1995 World Conference on Women held in Beijing, the Third Decade to Combat Racism and Racial Discrimination (1993–2002), the UN Decade for Human Rights Education (1995–2004), and the International Decade of the World's Indigenous People (1995–2004). The commission's work also attracted growing numbers to the Palais des Nations at Geneva, including delegations from member states, representatives from most other countries in the world (often including high-ranking government officials), staff from the newly created Office of the High Commissioner for Human Rights and specialized agencies of the United Nations, the secretary-general himself, and activists from many NGOs trying to find a place just to stand in the packed room.

Such an assemblage at the open meetings of the Commission on Human Rights, sometimes numbering over eight hundred, began to provide its own kind of enhancement of human rights. That is, it created an influential deterrent value, for few nations relished the prospect of standing before this huge and potentially hostile audience and being called on to defend their record on human rights in light of internationally established norms before the eyes of the world. In fact, and despite the commission's own political problems, it normally proved sufficient to compel most governments to expend considerable energy trying to comply with at least some of the standards in advance. If this failed, they then found themselves having to work very hard to keep the commission from taking action against them. In a particularly heated debate during the 1997 session, to illustrate, China lobbied intensely for a motion of "no action" to prevent any investigation of violations of the rights of assembly and expression, of fair trials, and of the religious and cultural rights of Tibetans. The Chinese ambassador found himself nearly smothered by news media and placed in the unenviable position of accusing most human rights advocates of "outrageous distortion" and "sanctimonious posturing," arguing that national sovereignty was more important than universal standards, and ominously threatening economic retaliation against those who might vote against his country.[153] Most states made considerable effort to avoid being placed in this kind of situation in the first place.

Other international bodies, the specialized agencies, and the United Nations Office for the Coordination of Humanitarian Affairs also enhanced human rights with their many expanded activities. UNESCO focused on the right to an education, cultural rights, and human rights education. The Food and Agricultural Organization stressed the right to sustain life by providing food. UNICEF concentrated on the rights of the child and helped the General Assembly organize the World Summit for Children. The UN High Commissioner for Refugees expanded its operations on behalf of the rights of refugees and displaced persons, providing assistance during the 1990s to a staggering twenty-seven million victims a year.[154] The World Health Organization centered its activities on the right to health and the United Nations Development Program on human rights and human development. The ILO focused on the rights of labor and the rights of children against exploitation. The International Committee for the Red Cross and the International Federation of the Red Cross and Red Crescent Societies continued their often courageous efforts to protect the rights of both civilians and combatants through humanitarian law and humanitarian relief, as well as working for the abolition of land mines. Moreover, the World Bank and the International Monetary Fund began conducting human rights impact assessments prior to making investments and loans.

Among the more unexpected of these many new and expanding activities were those initiated by members of the Security Council. When the United Nations was first created, many believed that issues of human rights would remain narrowly defined and confined to the Economic and Social Council. Only when confronted with such egregious violations as the oppression against blacks by the white minority regime in Rhodesia in 1966 and 1968, and apartheid in South Africa with the Soweto massacre in 1976 and the murder of black activist Steven Biko the following year that attracted the attention of the world, would the Security Council ever act in this area and in ways that increasingly reshaped traditional concepts of national sovereignty. Through time, however, and now freed from stalemates of the Cold War, members increasingly became convinced that gross violations of human rights *within* states ultimately and seriously threatened *international* security and peace. For this reason, according to close observers, the council began to exhibit what was described as "a dramatic new vision of human rights" that included a willingness to launch several innovative initiatives at both the operational and jurisdictional levels.[155] Its mandates establishing and deploying United Nations peace-keeping forces, for example, steadily incorporated important human rights components as a part of their mission, including those sent to Namibia, El Salvador, Cambodia, Mozambique, Bosnia, Herzegovina, and Croatia. Moreover, it explicitly identified violations of human rights as the reason for authorizing humanitarian intervention in Somalia and imposing sanctions against Saddam Hussein in Iraq and the Taliban in Afghanistan.

The Security Council then took extremely significant action in creating the path-breaking International Criminal Tribunal for the Former Yugoslavia in 1993 and the International Criminal Tribunal for Rwanda in 1994 to prosecute violations of the laws or customs of war, genocide, and crimes against humanity, including—for the first time—sexual violence and rape against women. Tellingly, the resolutions establishing both tribunals declared that the members were *"determined to put an end to such crimes and to take effective measures to bring to justice the persons who are responsible for them."*[156] The trials produced several precedent-setting decisions, not the least of which was the conviction of Rwanda's former prime minister Jean Kambanda, marking the first time in history that any head of government had ever been convicted and punished by an international criminal court for genocide and crimes against humanity.[157]

With these successes in mind, members of the global community, legal experts on the International Law Commission, and human rights activists in NGOs increasingly began to believe that the world simply could not continue indefinitely going from one human rights crisis to another, creating ad hoc criminal tribunals for each specific case only if and when unique political forces allowed it. They knew that the International Court of Justice had been designed to focus on state-to-state disputes, not the protection of individual victims of rights abuses. They also knew perfectly well that tyrants like Pol Pot of Cambodia (who executed a fifth of his own people), Idi Amin of Uganda, and Augusto Pinochet of Chile, among others, never faced trial for heinous human rights abuses. As British Foreign Secretary Robin Cook observed, the ultimate paradox was that those who murdered one person are "more likely to be brought to justice than those who plot genocide against millions."[158] To address this serious problem, government representatives met in Rome in 1998. They agreed that the culture of impunity with its unqualified claims of national sovereignty to shield leaders from responsibility was no longer acceptable. Instead, they concluded that an independent, permanent international criminal court was necessary to protect human rights, to deter future atrocities, and to facilitate the rule of law for peace and justice. Kofi Annan observed:

In the prospect of an international criminal court lies the promise of universal justice. That is the simple and soaring hope of this vision.[159]

The final vote revealed the support of one hundred and twenty nations, the abstention of twenty-one, and the opposition of seven. Thus, the delegates adopted the landmark Rome Statute of the International Criminal Court (ICC) declaring their intention to try *individuals*—not states—for war crimes, genocide, and crimes against humanity, including newly codified sexual and gender crimes. They invited all nations to ratify the treaty and thereby bring the vision of the Universal Declaration one step closer to reality.[160]

This extraordinary momentum continued to grow. Governments created special offices within their foreign ministries to deal specifically with human rights issues, and some created truth and reconciliation commissions to confront abuses.[161] When the Center for Human Rights produced their first CD-ROM under the title *Human Rights: Bibliographical Data and International Instruments*, it contained seventeen thousand references to United Nations documents and publications.[162] New human rights NGOs emerged around the world, including Africa, Asia, Latin America, and the Middle East.

A most remarkable event then occurred. In 1998 the House of Lords ruled against Augusto Pinochet. While on a personal visit to Britain, he was arrested and held under custody in response to a warrant from a determined Spanish judge for offenses committed while he brutally governed Chile. Pinochet, in the words of one observer, "was, so he thought, clad in the impregnable armor of state sovereignty, which had for centuries shielded every tyrant against legal attack," and therefore demanded to be released.[163] The judges, however, ruled that under evolving international law, he no longer could claim immunity from prosecution for torture and crimes against humanity. United Nations High Commissioner Mary Robinson from Ireland immediately hailed their momentous decision as one that "will hearten human rights defenders around the world," acknowledging that it "would have been unthinkable not so long ago."[164] *Le Monde* perceptively concluded in words that need to be carefully read:

Whatever ultimately becomes of it, this decision of the 25th of November 1998 will always mark an important date in history. For one simple reason: *fear began to change sides.* Fear, the means by which all dictatorships govern, the ultimate weapon of all forms of state terrorism, is now no longer reserved for the victims. . . . For dictators this marks the transition from the age of impunity to the age of illegality.[165]

Amnesty International also praised the ruling, declaring that it "signals the birth of a new era for human rights" and observing: "On the eve of the 50th anniversary of the Universal Declaration of Human Rights, victims of human rights violations and human rights defenders the world over could not have wished for a better reaffirmation of the principles contained in the Declaration."[166]

*   *   *

In a period of fifty years the world witnessed a veritable revolution in transforming visions of international human rights into reality. Never before in history had there been so many achievements in extending rights, setting standards and establishing customary law, protecting rights through binding treaties and special procedures, promoting rights through education and naming and shaming abusers, enhancing rights through advisory services for those who suffered, and expanding activities to break the former culture of impunity. Never before had there been such an intrusion into what historically had always been regarded as purely domestic affairs. Together these new actions and policies helped millions of people gain their independence and assisted unknown numbers of others by preventing abuses, securing freedom from torture or prison, acquiring access to monitoring bodies and humanitarian aid, and obtaining national and international legal protections for their rights. In addition, they inspired national constitutions and domestic laws, regional intergovernmental organizations, and states to use the observance or violation of human rights by others as a criterion for their policies. In almost every one of these endeavors, reference was made to the Universal Declaration and the power of its vision to change the world.[167] Indeed, it opened a whole new era of international history and its impact led the British Broadcasting Corporation news to describe the Universal Declaration as nothing short of "our century's greatest achievement."[168] It is likely that Eleanor Roosevelt, René Cassin, Charles Malik, and Peng-chun Chang, among the many others who worked on the draft of the declaration during the most precarious of times, could have never imagined this level of achievement in their wildest dreams.

Nevertheless, these many remarkable successes, however impressive, certainly did not complete the struggle for human rights. They did not abolish all abuses, eradicate all resistance, protect all victims, or solve all problems. In fact, in some places gaping chasms grew between rhetoric and reality. For this reason, when ten million signatures were submitted to Secretary-General Kofi Annan from Ghana on the occasion of the fiftieth anniversary of the Universal Declaration of Human Rights, they not only praised the achievements but insisted that the evolution must continue.

Chapter 9
The Continuing Evolution

I have walked that long road to freedom. But I have discovered that after climbing a great hill, one only finds that there are many more hills to climb. I have taken a moment here to rest, to steal a view of the glorious vista that surrounds me, to look back at the distance I have come. But I can only rest for a moment, for with freedom comes responsibilities, and I dare not linger, for my long walk is not yet ended.
—Nelson Mandela of South Africa

A unique and compellingly symbolic event occurred in 2000 when nearly all the leaders of the world met in New York City for what they called the Millennium Summit. Their purpose was to articulate and affirm their visions at the dawn of the twenty-first century before them. Based upon the lessons they had learned from the past, they quickly acknowledged the existence of a close and integral relationship between security, peace, justice, and human rights. Using the image created by Nelson Mandela, they looked back at the remarkable distance they had come in the light of centuries of historical experience—but then looked forward to recognize that the journey was not yet over. To confront the abuses that still exist, they agreed that they all had a "shared responsibility" to fully uphold the Universal Declaration of Human Rights, the rule of law, and "the full protection and promotion in all our countries of civil, political, economic, social, and cultural rights for all."[1] What made this task even more daunting was the fact that in addition to old problems of resistance they faced a new barrage from skeptics who pronounced "the end of human rights," declaring that the evolution was over and would never continue.[2] They were wrong.

International Law, the Responsibility to Protect, and Challenges to Sovereignty

Human rights campaigners long have understood that societies need not only principles but laws. Whether national law at the domestic level or international law at the regional or global level, they have been acutely aware how critical it is to create safeguards with legally binding standards enforced through sanctions or punishment. By providing restraints upon government leaders and others who might otherwise arbitrarily and abusively use their power, they seek to address the premise that those least favored in life should be most favored in law. When states agree to become parties to a treaty, they willingly bind themselves to its terms and thereby agree to restrict a certain measure of their sovereignty, or their freedom to treat people exactly as they wish. As this has increased dramatically in recent years, it has accelerated that evolutionary process of changing traditional international law that benefited only *states* into new forms of law that benefit *individuals*, thereby transforming victims of human rights abuse from mere objects of international pity into actual subjects of international law.

This certainly can be seen with the continuing evolution of international human rights law. In order to offer legal protection to those unable to protect themselves, more and more states are agreeing to additional conventions or to protocols that expand existing treaties, invariably referring to the vision of the Universal Declaration. They thus adopted the Optional Protocol to the Convention on the Elimination of Discrimination Against Women establishing a mechanism to consider complaints by independent experts serving on CEDAW. This was followed by two protocols to the Convention on the Rights of the Child, the first prohibiting the use of child soldiers in armed conflict and the second making the sale of children, child prostitution, and child pornography illegal. They supported the Optional Protocol to the International Convention Against Torture creating a special system of international and national bodies to inspect the treatment of those held in detention or imprisonment. Then the International Convention on the Protection of the Rights of All Migrant Workers and Members of Their Families entered into force with the treaty-monitoring body of the Committee on Migrant Workers (CMW). In 2006 they opened two new treaties for signature: the International Convention for the Protection of All Persons from Enforced Disappearance and the International Convention on the Rights of Persons with Disabilities, along with an optional protocol permitting the treaty-monitoring body of the Committee for the Rights of Persons with Disabilities (CRPD) to receive and consider complaints. In 2008 they adopted the Optional Protocol of the International Covenant on Economic, Social, and Cultural Rights providing similar mechanisms for those claiming to be victims of abuse under the terms of the treaty.[3]

These developments are being accompanied by others at the regional level. The most notable of these is the new and expanded structure of the European Court of Human Rights with full-time judges meeting in Strasbourg, France, monitoring compliance with the European Convention on Human Rights. Since all forty-seven members of the Council of Europe are required to be parties to the convention, this opens up the judicial protection of rights to over eight hundred million people. States, NGOs, and—uniquely—individuals can bring charges before the court against contracting parties for violations of human rights. Thousands of cases have been tried, with some rulings seriously challenging powerful states and traditional claims of national sovereignty, including judgments against Britain for its unlawful treatment of persons alleged to have ties to terrorism and against Russia for the disappearances, torture, and extrajudicial executions of victims in Chechnya.[4] The court is today widely acknowledged as "the pre-eminent system of international human rights protection which exists anywhere in the world."[5]

The Inter-American Court of Human Rights is serving as the judicial system of the Organization of American States for interpreting and enforcing the American Convention on Human Rights and other related treaties. Cases against states are brought to court in San José, Costa Rica, either by the Inter-American Commission on Human Rights or by a state party.[6] One of its decisions encouraged the Argentine Supreme Court in 2005 to annul earlier amnesty laws and thereby prosecute military and government leaders responsible for thousands of "disappearances" and other egregious abuses. The year 2006 marked the first meeting of the African Court of Human and Peoples' Rights created by the African Union. Although still at a rudimentary stage, this court based in Arusha, Tanzania, is designed to provide legal protections for the African Charter on Human and Peoples' Rights and other human rights conventions.[7]

New advances also are being made in international humanitarian law[8] and international refugee law. Beginning with the Guiding Principles on Internal Displacement and the Global Consultations process of the UN High Commissioner for Refugees and its Agenda for Protection, to illustrate, many nations, intergovernmental organizations, NGOs, and independent experts are working to increase legal safeguards to cover not only refugees *outside* their home country but also internally displaced persons (IDPs) fleeing *inside* their own countries. Although these uprooted civilian victims (80 percent of whom are women, children, and the elderly) are theoretically under the "protection" of their own government, it is often that very government that has been the cause of their flight in the first place or has shown itself unable or unwilling to save them from violence or marauding rebel groups. The examples of Colombia, the Democratic Republic of the Congo, Iraq, and Sudan come immediately to mind. Any international actions to protect the human rights of these vulnerable groups, of course, cannot help but challenge the national sovereignty of the states in question. In addition, the UNHCR increasingly is being called upon to go beyond its original mandate by assisting victims of natural disasters, as evidenced by its extensive efforts after the 2004 Indian Ocean tsunami, the 2005 Pakistan earthquake, the 2008 Burmese cyclone and Chinese earthquake, and the devastating 2010 earthquake in Haiti.[9]

Among all of these developments in the continuing evolution of the rule of law, perhaps none is so dramatic as those in international criminal law. It is here that one finds a growing determination to insist that *no one*—rulers and the ruled alike—is above the law and thereby hold some of the worst abusers of human rights responsible for their crimes. Recently created international criminal law, jurisdiction, and procedures increasingly have served notice that the world is no longer willing to let dictators hide behind the claims of sovereignty or within the traditional culture of impunity. The arrest of Augusto Pinochet marked a critical threshold in this change. Although released from Britain due to his deteriorating medical condition, once he returned to Chile in 2000 he was stripped of his immunity from prosecution, placed under house arrest, and formally charged in his homeland for kidnaping, torture, and murder committed by his "Caravan of Death."[10] This prompted President Abdoulaye Wade of Senegal to announce that he would turn over former Chadian leader Hissène Habré, known as "Africa's Pinochet," for trial to answer criminal charges for some forty thousand executions and the torture of perhaps two hundred thousand victims during his eight-year rule.[11] These actions encouraged others. In 2002 Sierra Leone requested United Nations help in instituting a further new departure in international jurisprudence by creating a special court with both national and international judges to prosecute those who inflicted serious abuses on civilians and conscripted child soldiers during that country's brutal civil war, including Charles Taylor the former president of neighboring Liberia accused of using "blood diamonds" to fuel and fund that conflict. The same year a rights tribunal in Indonesia sentenced Lt. Col. Soejarwo to imprisonment for atrocities committed in East Timor. Additional criminal tribunals have been established in Cambodia and Kosovo. In each of these cases, history—as memory and as a source of evidence—continues to play a vital role.

At the same time, the two tribunals established by the Security Council attract considerable attention. The International Criminal Tribunal for Rwanda, after its path-breaking conviction of former Prime Minister Jean Kambanda for the crime of genocide, continues to tackle additional cases involving senior military commanders, government officials, prominent business executives, journalists, and other influential leaders. In the process, it has created a unique and sophisticated witness protection program for Africa and is forging a substantial body of case law.[12]

A continent away, the International Criminal Tribunal for the Former Yugoslavia continues to judge and to punish those found guilty of crimes, including mass rape and systematic sexual violence, thus enabling women victims to finally testify publicly about their chambers of horrors. In a dramatic development, Serbia extradited its former head of state and commander-in-chief Slobodan Milosevic to the tribunal under charges of grave breaches of the Geneva Conventions, violations of the laws and customs of war, and, most seriously, genocide and crimes against humanity. Shocking documentation and painful eyewitness accounts presented evidence of horrific abuses of expulsions, forced labor, mutilations, rape, torture, and executions in the name of "ethnic cleansing" in Bosnia, Croatia, and Kosovo, including the massacre of an estimated eight thousand Muslim men and boys at the Bosnian town of Srebrenica.[13] For this reason, the chief prosecutor referred to the "savagery," "calculated cruelty," and "unspeakable suffering" inflicted by Milosevic, observing that his policies were "not local affairs" but ones that affected the world:

These crimes touch every one of us, wherever we live, because they offend against our deepest principle of human rights and human dignity. The law is not a mere theory or an abstract concept. It is a living instrument that must protect our values and regulate civilized society and for that we must be able to enforce the law when it is broken. This tribunal, and this trial in particular, gives the most powerful demonstration that no one is above the law or beyond the reach of international justice.[14]

Such reach applied to others as well. In 2003 Biljana Plavsic, Bosnia's former "Iron Lady" president, was sentenced to imprisonment for her crimes against humanity. In 2008 Radovan Karadžic, the former Bosnian Serb leader described by the Public Broadcasting Service as "the most wanted man in the world," was arrested and sent to trial before the court for ordering rape, torture, and massacres against Muslims, Croats, and other non-Serbs throughout Bosnia.[15]

The continued growth and intensity of this vision of the rule of law to deter future perpetrators can be seen in the number of ratifications of the Rome Statute of the

International Criminal Court. Given the often tortuous history of ratifications, even some of the most optimistic supporters believed it would take decades for a sufficient number of states to ratify the treaty. Remarkably, it took less than four years. The treaty entered into force in 2002, marking, in the words of one authority, "a breathtaking international innovation."[16] The court appointed its first chief prosecutor (Luis Moreno-Ocampo, who had successfully prosecuted human rights violations by senior military commanders in Argentina), began its first investigations in 2004, issued its first arrest warrants in 2005, and then initiated its first trial (against Thomas Lubanga Dyilo of the Democratic Republic of the Congo). It now exists as an independent, permanent, treaty-based mechanism to try individuals responsible for those abuses taken most seriously by the international community—war crimes, genocide, and crimes against humanity—if and when national authorities cannot or will not prosecute. Human Rights Watch describes this achievement as "a major historical development" marking "the most important human rights institution that has been created in fifty years."[17]

An overwhelming majority of nations now participate in the International Criminal Court. Others are likely to join as well. But in sharp contrast to this widespread support, some countries continue to oppose the entire effort. These include China, Iran, Israel, Pakistan, and Russia. The United States, which worked so actively to establish the tribunals for Yugoslavia and Rwanda, also remains in opposition of having these standards applied to itself for fear of diminishing its sovereignty and the possibility of having its own leaders or military personnel held accountable to international jurisdiction. President Bill Clinton signed the Rome Statute but refused to forward it to the Senate for ratification where one senator described the ICC as a "monster that we need to slay."[18] More vociferously, President George W. Bush took the unprecedented and deliberately provocative step of "un-signing" the treaty in 2002, announcing bluntly: "We do not intend to ratify it and therefore we are no longer bound in any way to its purpose and objective."[19] This was followed by an aggressive campaign to pressure others into rejecting the court by withholding military and financial assistance to those who joined, to seek special immunity for U.S. service members abroad, and to secure legislation authorizing the president to "use all means necessary" to physically free any American that might ever be held in custody by the ICC.[20] Even though in 2009 Secretary of State Hillary Clinton under a new Barack Obama administration expressed "deep regret" about this hostile policy, the United States today remains one of the very few democratic governments in the world that refuses to participate in the International Criminal Court.[21]

That claims of national sovereignty should be used to resist the continuing evolution of international human rights, of course, is hardly new. Indeed, as we have seen, they have been used time and time again to oppose any international norms that would place limits on the behavior of national leaders. Yet, as we also have seen, challenges to both the arguments and the practices of sovereignty have been mounted over the course of generations. What has become increasingly different from the past, however, is the growing scope, speed, and intensity of such challenges. Some of these are conceptual in nature. "State sovereignty, in it most basic sense, is being redefined," observed former Secretary-General Kofi Annan:

States are now widely understood to be instruments at the service of their people, and not vice versa. At the same time individual sovereignty—by which I mean the fundamental freedom of each individual, enshrined in the Charter of the UN and subsequent international treaties—has been enhanced by a renewed and spreading consciousness of individual rights. When we read the Charter today, we are more than ever conscious that its aim is to protect individual human beings, not to protect those who abuse them.[22]

Still other challenges to national sovereignty come from the forces of technological and economic globalization that often completely bypass traditional national borders, from non-state actors playing major roles in world affairs beyond nations, and from humanitarian intervention.

With the ever-growing value placed on human rights in international politics and in international law, for example, many government leaders have become less and less willing to allow themselves to remain impotent bystanders, turning their backs on victims who suffer, and letting gross and systematic violations of human rights continue unchecked. They have assumed a growing sense of responsibility after their earlier failures to intervene in Rwanda while eight hundred thousand people died in genocide or in Srebrenica with the massacre of thousands as painful historical lessons of the disastrous mistakes of inaction. Consequently, they increasingly have taken direct action designed to alleviate or prevent abuses. Some have passed domestic legislation and adjusted their courts in the name of "universal jurisdiction" in order to prosecute accused violators of human rights outside of their own borders on behalf of common humanity. Others have worked more closely with international bodies to accomplish the same goal.

This explains the Security Council's new activism in linking particularly egregious cases of human rights violations with threats to international peace and security and engaging in enforcement action. The result can be seen in its willingness to do more than sending humanitarian relief to victims. Instead, it has taken action to stop violence and prevent further abuses themselves, as seen by sending the case of genocide in Darfur to the International Criminal Court, using economic and military sanctions against the dictatorship in Burma and the Taliban in Afghanistan, dispatching peace-keeping forces with human rights missions in Sierra Leone and the Democratic Republic of the Congo, and deploying the armed International Force for East Timor in the name of humanitarian intervention. NATO employed the same principle in using military force against the regime of Milosevic when Serbian forces displaced, raped, and killed thousands in Kosovo. This action, as expressed by Václav Havel, was taken "out of respect for a law that ranks higher than the law that protects the sovereignty of states" and one that "places human rights above the rights of the State."[23] Said one Muslim victim in grateful response, "Intervention was the only hope for us."[24]

But such actions designed to enhance international human rights by challenging national sovereignty also can cause new problems that jeopardize those rights themselves. For better or worse, national governments remain the major source of rights protection, and collapsed or failed states in anarchy or incapable of governing simply cannot and do not protect human rights. It thus may be necessary to learn how to help build the capacity of nations to become strong enough to protect the rights of their own citizens. In addition, military interventions and even the recently conceived "smart sanctions" against specific targets, are blunt instruments not easily controlled that can result in unintended consequences, mask other agendas of powerful states against the weak, and harm the very people they are designed to help. They also raise anew that inherent contradiction within the UN Charter between the revolutionary affirmation of international human rights of the Preamble and Article 1 and the traditional reaffirmation of non-interference into the domestic affairs of member states of Article 2. As former British Prime Minister Tony Blair observed:

The most pressing foreign policy problem we face is to identify the circumstances in which we should get actively involved in other people's conflicts. Non-interference has long been considered an important principle of international order. . . . But the principle of non-interference must be qualified in important respects. Acts of genocide can never be a purely internal affair.[25]

Considerable attention and controversy thus surround problems of when, how, and under whose authority humanitarian intervention should take place. Here, some of the first efforts to establish policy began not with the West or the North, but rather when members of the African Union who had so vehemently defended national sovereignty in the days of decolonization shifted in 2000 to the point of declaring "the right of the Union to intervene in a member State pursuant to a decision of the Assembly in respect of grave circumstances" that egregiously abuse human rights.[26] The next year, the International Commission on Intervention and State Sovereignty issued a path-breaking report with three words in its title that now are part of the lexicon of international human rights: *Responsibility to Protect*. It called on the community of nations to rise to the occasion when it becomes necessary to provide practical protection for ordinary people whose lives are at risk because their states are unwilling or unable to protect them.[27]

Of particular interest, when the largest gathering of national leaders ever assembled in history met at the 2005 World Summit, they spoke explicitly about this issue. Despite their differences of political structure, stages of development, and cultural settings, they dramatically and unanimously agreed on the "values and principles" of human rights, reaffirmed "the universality, indivisibility, interdependence, and interrelatedness of all human rights," and acknowledged their responsibility to enforce international law and provide protection. "We are prepared," they announced, "to take collective action, in a timely and decisive manner through the Security Council . . . and in cooperation with regional organizations as appropriate, should peaceful means be inadequate and national authorities manifestly failing to protect their populations from genocide, war crimes, ethnic cleansing, and crimes against humanity."[28] The Security Council unanimously reaffirmed precisely this position in a landmark decision on protecting civilians in armed conflict.[29] Since then, the concept of Responsibility to Protect—increasingly known as "R2P"—has continued to evolve by providing assistance and capacity-building abilities to others, as evident by the increasing use of something that would have been completely unacceptable just a few years ago: the international monitoring of domestic elections. Further efforts occurred in 2009 with the creation of a new NGO called the International Coalition for the Responsibility to

Protect.[30] For all of these reasons, and despite many practical and political problems, Secretary General Ban Ki-moon observes: "the Responsibility to Protect—and now to deliver—is an idea whose time has come."[31]

Globalization, Development, Terrorism—and Torture

Among other characteristics of our time that have an impact on human rights is that of globalization. This expression is used to describe a world increasingly interconnected by shared challenges, norms, laws, institutions, technology, and practices. Its economic dimensions, for example, are characterized by the surging international network of trade, exchange of services, and finance. Successful returns on investment, access to capital and technology, lower consumer prices, a growing market economy, employment, improved economic and social standards, and increased productivity and prosperity are enjoyed by many. But its benefits are not shared equally, and its costs are unevenly distributed. Countless others—sometimes described as "the disposable people" of a "new slavery"—experience abuses not so much from the *state* as from the *market* in the form of displacement, loss of bargaining leverage, poverty, crushing debt, exploitation, marginalization, loss of land, alienation, disruption of family and community life, diminished health, and environmental degradation.[32] Economic globalization sometimes encourages the evolution of democratic institutions and civil society that respect rights and challenge traditional claims of national sovereignty by rendering nation-states less important. At other times it exacerbates the gap between rich and poor and bolsters authoritarian regimes that offer promises of stability and low labor costs favored by external investors.[33]

It is in this competitive global setting that sustainable economic and social development becomes such a serious challenge. Nevertheless, the leaders who met both at the Millennium Summit and the World Summit committed themselves to achieve what they called the Millennium Development Goals by reducing the poverty of those millions of people whose income is less than a dollar a day and who suffer from want, hunger, disease, and lack of education. They have substantially increased their financial contributions to the United Nations Development Program and the United Nations Assistance Framework in order to mobilize financial and human resources for development, encourage trade and investment, reduce debt, improve health and education, and restructure and strengthen the commodity sectors in developing countries. The International Monetary Fund, World Bank, and Asian Development Bank also have increasingly tied funding for development projects to human rights practices. But the distance between the rich winners and the poor losers in the globalized economy is formidable and the tasks are extremely complicated. They become even more difficult at a time of global recession and when the efforts for rapid development conflict with protecting the environment from the consumption of natural resources, pollution, and climate change. For all of these reasons, a *Human Development Report* concludes that, in the continuing struggle, "bold new approaches are needed to achieve universal realization of human rights in the 21st century—adapted to the opportunities and realities of the era of globalization, to its new global actors, and to its new global rules."[34]

One striking indication of such new actors and new rules can be seen today with the growth of transnational corporations (TNCs) from the private sector. These non-state, for-profit actors challenge the national sovereignty of states and operate with enormous power and influence. Indeed, some possess revenue that far exceeds the national economies of most nations, and their leaders have a much greater impact on individuals and global events than many heads of governments. If they possess a sense of social responsibility, they can use their power to enhance human rights by attaching conditions to investment, instituting standards and codes of business practices, and allowing monitors to view their operations in developing countries. If, on the other hand, they are interested solely in profit or market considerations without any regard for human rights, they can seriously harm children and women in forced labor, the health of those affected by sweatshop conditions and environmental destruction, the rights of indigenous peoples when their resources are extracted by outsiders, or the political and civil rights of those abused by brutal but economically cooperative regimes. This explains why discourse about international human rights has expanded once again to now involve TNCs. In recent years the votes of concerned stockholders, widespread negative publicity about "unethical behavior," and the economic consequences of consumer boycotts have helped to change corporate policies, as evident in the cases of Royal Dutch Shell, Nike, Reebok, and Starbucks. Private citizens and NGOs also continue to push businesses into using their economic power to pressure abusive governments, such as the military dictatorship in Burma over its treatment of human rights activist Aung San Suu Kyi.[35] At the same time, the international community has launched a series of large scale initiatives. These include the Secretary General's Global Compact, the International Labor Organization's Social Dimension of Globalization, and especially the draft UN Norms on the Responsibilities of Transnational Corporations and Other Business Enterprises with Regard to Human Rights declaring:

Within their respective spheres of activity and influence, transnational corporations and other business enterprises have the obligation to promote, secure the fulfillment of, respect, ensure respect of and protect human rights recognized in international as well as national law, including the rights and interests of indigenous peoples and other vulnerable groups.[36]

If any illusions about the capacity of non-state actors to impact contemporary global affairs and to challenge national sovereignty still remained after all these developments, they should have been irrevocably shattered by the terrorist attacks of 11 September 2001. Within less than two hours, three thousand people were killed in New York City, Washington, D.C., and rural Pennsylvania, revealing the power of terrorist organizations to destroy human lives and wreak havoc. Terrorism had been a security problem for years, but never before had a single episode captured so much attention or made the world so aware of its collective vulnerability. Although the main target was the United States, eighty different countries lost citizens in the attack on the World Trade Center, and the international community reacted with outrage. "All of us," said Kofi Annan, "feel deep shock and revulsion at the cold-blooded viciousness of this attack. . . . A terrorist attack on one country is an attack on humanity as a whole. All nations of the world must work together to identify the perpetrators and bring them to justice."[37]

This terrorist attack and its aftermath—like other assaults and suicide bombings before and since—dramatically revealed the fragility of human rights in times of crisis and continued to raise extremely troubling questions. In the first instance, it simply strains the mind and the soul to imagine how any person or group could deliberately extinguish the most basic of all human rights, namely the right to life, especially among unsuspecting and vulnerable civilians, and then seek to somehow justify it. For this reason and its violation of the Universal Declaration of Human Rights provision that "everyone has the right to life, liberty, and security," and for the complete rejection of the rule of law by terrorists, both the General Assembly and the Security Council condemned the attack in the strongest possible terms. They reaffirmed that terrorism presented one of the most dangerous threats to human rights in the world and set about to develop immediate and far-reaching measures to combat international terrorist acts.[38]

They understood that terrorism threatened them all, and thus that the question was not *whether* but rather *how* to combat it. Worthy ends do not justify unworthy means. If an anti-terrorist campaign is based on a genuine attempt to combine the demands of security with the demands of human rights and is waged on the basis of accepted norms and legal restraints designed to prevent the uninhibited use of government power, it is widely acknowledged to be legitimate. "We must," observed German Chancellor Angela Merkel, "find answers to how we can combat terrorists effectively without calling our own fundamental principles and beliefs into question."[39] For this reason, the General Assembly built upon the Security Council's Counter-Terrorism Executive Directorate and the Secretariat's Counter-Terrorism Implementation Task Force and adopted the historic United Nations Global Counter-Terrorism Strategy. It marks the first time that member states have ever agreed to a comprehensive, global, strategic framework and plan of action against terrorism, while at the same time upholding human rights norms and the rule of law. The Inter-American Commission on Human Rights followed in the same path when it advised the Organization of American States: "The very object and purpose of anti-terrorist activities in democratic society is to protect democratic institutions, human rights, and the rule of law—not to undermine them."[40]

Not everyone accepted this approach, however. In the heated passion for revenge and the "war on terrorism" directed at Osama bin Laden, the al-Qaida network, the Taliban in Afghanistan, Iraq, and anyone else accused of offering support to terrorists, it quickly became apparent that some states and their leaders would ignore the law. Russia, China, Uzbekistan, and other repressive regimes, for example, discovered that it provided a convenient pretext to claim their political opponents were not just adversaries but "terrorists," and that this excused them from complying with human rights norms. Abuses occurred within the United States with intensified intolerance, the demonization of certain religious groups, warrantless surveillance, and other violations of civil rights and long-standing legal protections and abroad with the harm inflicted upon civilians in wars against Afghanistan and Iraq.[41]

Among the many abuses of human rights in the name of anti-terrorism, perhaps nothing captured the attention of the world more forcefully than the American use of torture. Recently released documents reveal decisions from the George W. Bush administration declaring that although the United States was a party to the unequivocal Geneva Conventions and the International Convention Against Torture (defined by the text as "any act by which severe pain or suffering, whether physical or mental, is intentionally inflicted on a person for such purposes as obtaining from him or a third person information or a confession"),[42] these treaties, military and civilian law, the protections of any court of the United States, any court of any foreign nation, any international tribunal, and international humanitarian law were "quaint" and did not apply in the "war on terrorism."[43] In a practice known as "extraordinary rendition," suspects were apprehended and sent off to clandestine "black sites" in defiance of the law where they were not only denied due process and habeas corpus, but tortured. Detention centers of Abu Ghraib in Iraq, Bagram Prison in Afghanistan, and Guantanamo Bay in Cuba, according to documented reports and depositions from victims as well as interrogators, employed what was euphemistically described as "enhanced interrogation techniques" designed to gain information by inflicting unbearable, excruciating mental and physical trauma.

The shocking extent of such violations of human rights norms and breaches of legal obligations and the rule of law by the United States resulted in widespread condemnation from close allies, other governments, the International Committee of the Red Cross, the Committee Against Torture, members of both political parties in the U.S. Congress, a bipartisan Senate Armed Services Committee report, officials within the Department of State and Department of Justice, human rights NGOs, civilian attorneys, official investigators, international and regional organizations, and, particularly striking, a number of retired generals, admirals, military lawyers, and intelligence officers.[44] Indeed, as revealed by Central Intelligence Agency's own Inspector General, some of the interrogators themselves seriously worried about "the possibility of recrimination or legal action," that "a human rights group might pursue them," and they "might end up on some 'wanted list' to appear before the World Court for war crimes."[45]

Yet, the impact of whatever was said with words to describe these abuses pales next to the outrage produced by photographs that one might expect from dictatorships not democracies. One shows a prisoner standing alone barefooted on a box, his head covered with a hood, and his outstretched arms attached to wires in such a way that electrical shocks could be sent pulsating into his body. Others graphically bear witness to men bloodied and broken, tied in stress positions or spent from simulated drowning by "waterboarding." Still others exhibit chained prisoners attacked by dogs or piles of men in enforced nakedness and submission stacked on a concrete floor as their interrogators pose behind their helpless victims with cigarettes in their mouths or green latex gloves on their hands, flaunting their acts even further by actually smiling at the camera and gloating over something they wanted to have recorded.[46] Even though President Obama announced in 2009 that the United States would no longer engage in secret detentions and torture, the impact of these damning photographs and the policies that they reflect will not quickly go away, but will be felt for many years to come, both at home and abroad.

Terrorism and anti-terrorism also will continue to present enormous challenges to those who think seriously about human rights and think seriously about security. Here there will be a fierce debate. Some will insist that the "idealism" of rights and the "realism" of security are complete opposites. They will argue that even in the best of times individual rights and national security coexist in uneasy tension; but when there is a life-and-death struggle, military necessity under a war paradigm prevails, no rules or laws apply, and one must choose one or the other. Thus, if rights need to be sacrificed for security, then the price simply must be paid. This was the choice that he made, said former Vice President Richard Cheney, and the choice that he would make again "without hesitation."[47]

At the same time, there will be others who insist that this "choice" between human rights or security is a false choice. They are likely to quote Benjamin Franklin's statement that "They who can give up essential liberty to obtain a little temporary safety, deserve neither liberty or safety."[48] Indeed, their argument will be that these elements are actually dependent upon each other: that security cannot be achieved without peace, that peace cannot be achieved without justice, and that justice cannot be achieved without respect for human rights. They will maintain, in other words, that there is not an antithetical *contest* but rather a necessary *relationship* between international security, national security, and individual security. As such, torture will be seen not as advancing an anti-terrorism campaign, but actually undermining it by ignoring the rule of law, by serving as a recruitment tool for more terrorists, by placing service men and women in greater jeopardy, by alienating others who could help, and by diminishing the nation's own honor and values. Similarly, their argument will again raise the difficult question of whether terrorist attacks could be avoided if long-standing violations of human rights did not exist in the first place. Political exclusion, repression, poverty, inequality, violence, and foreign occupation of their own or neighboring countries breed, feed, and shape terrorism itself.[49] As such, serious human rights abuses will continue to be danger signals, warning of future conflict just over the horizon.

New Human Rights Institutions and Organizations

Some of these challenges in the continuing evolution of international human rights are being addressed by new human rights institutions and organizations. Among these is the United Nations Human Rights Council, created in 2006. Despite its many and often extraordinary accomplishments, as discussed in previous chapters, the Commission on Human Rights over the years had developed several serious problems. Some of these were practical in nature. They resulted from the fact that the expansive growth of activities and initiatives in promotion, standard setting, implementation through treaty-based mechanisms, and special non-treaty procedures, as well as the expanding membership of the Commission, simply overwhelmed the small and seriously underfunded staff assigned to them. To make matters worse, the Commission was only authorized to meet once a year for a frenzied period of six weeks. This not only was insufficient time to address all of the violations of rights at hand, but allowed abusing governments to stall and delay any action against them. Other problems were created by politics, as evident by its close association with the 2001 World Conference

Against Racism held in Durban, South Africa, and its intense clashes over the legacy of slavery, the Israeli treatment of Palestinians, and the meaning of anti-Semitism and Zionism. Further problems resulted from a voting procedure that set a low threshold for membership and allowed regional blocs in backroom deals to forward candidates to the Economic and Social Council for approval without any debate about their commitment to human rights. During 2001, for example, Sudan, Sierra Leone, Uganda, and Togo were all elected as members despite their well-known abuses. In 2003 the Zimbabwe of widely condemned dictator Robert Mugabe secured a seat and the representative of Col. Muammar Gaddafi's Libya known to support terrorists was elected chair of the Commission. At the same time, the United States in the midst of its invasion of Iraq and "war on terrorism" shielded its allies of Israel, Pakistan, Saudi Arabia, Turkey, and Uzbekistan from action by the Commission; invoked claims of national sovereignty and special American "exceptionalism" against international scrutiny; and (despite overwhelming evidence to the contrary) consistently denied torturing prisoners or in any other way violating the rule of law.[50]

It is thus hardly surprising that when serious discussion took place from 2004 to 2006 about the necessity of wide-ranging reforms at the United Nations, enormous attention would focus on this problem. Indeed, in the debates about security, peace, justice, and human rights that transpired, the Commission on Human Rights was described as the "litmus test," "the centerpiece," and "the linchpin."[51] For this reason, when Secretary General Annan released his highly publicized report announcing his vision of replacing the old Commission on Human Rights with a new Human Rights Council, Human Rights Watch responded by declaring that he had done "the unthinkable" and called his proposal "courageous."[52] Other human rights advocates and NGOs described his recommendation as "bold," a "bombshell," and precisely the remedy that could have "a transformative impact on human rights worldwide."[53]

After months of labor, assessment, consultations, negotiations, and intense politics and diplomacy among leaders at the World Summit and then representatives at the United Nations as a whole, the General Assembly made its decision in March 2006.[54] 170 nations resolved (over the objections of Israel and the United States which voted no, and Iran and Venezuela which abstained) to create a new Human Rights Council, vowing to make it more universal, more transparent, and more effective than its predecessor. As a result, its status was elevated and its work mainstreamed into the organization as a whole. In order to provide more sustained and serious attention to human rights problems, to act preventively, and to respond more quickly to new crises, it is based in Geneva, mandated to meet no fewer than three times a year, and enabled to hold special sessions for urgent situations. Its number is limited to forty-seven members, the first time that a UN body has ever been reduced in size to achieve greater effectiveness. Membership is open to all states, but they must be competitively and genuinely elected by individual and direct votes and must gain ninety-seven votes from the entire General Assembly rather than the mere twenty-eight in the Economic and Social Council as in the past. In order to provide some measure of protection against coercion, this voting is now by secret ballot. Similarly, term limits now prevent any state from holding a permanent seat. A new geographical distribution of members now reflects the population realities of evolving international life in the twenty-first century, especially in Asia and Africa. In addition, those engaged in this process of institution building who created the new Human Rights Council took a most unusual step by actually mandating a broad-based review in 2000 of its mechanisms and work in order to provide an opportunity for assessment and further improvement.

Of particular importance is the fact that the actual behavior of governments now serves as the criteria for membership. The founding resolution declared the principle—seemingly intuitive, but never before officially pronounced—that members must uphold standards of human rights themselves and must "fully cooperate" with the Council and its norms, mechanisms, and procedures or face possible expulsion. They thus are required to subject themselves to be first in line for scrutiny under an entirely new and Universal Periodic Review "based on objective and reliable information" of their own human rights record during their term on the Council. This provision provides, for the first time, the opportunity to examine the human rights record of even the most powerful countries (including permanent members of the Security Council) and thereby provide a mechanism for addressing the double standards that the former Commission often was accused of using. Louise Arbour, High Commissioner for Human Rights at the time, noted this critical difference immediately and announced: "No country will be beyond scrutiny, and no longer will countries be able to use membership on the premier UN human rights body to shield themselves or allies from criticism or censure for rights breaches."[55]

The energetic sessions of the Human Rights Council are held in a vast, circular room at the Palais des Nations in Geneva especially constructed for them. They attract hundreds of active participants and observers. These include member states, observing governments, staff of the Office of the High Commissioner of Human Rights, representatives of specialized UN agencies, experts on the new Human Rights Council Advisory Committee serving in their personal capacities, security personnel, and various non-state actors vitally concerned about international human rights. Considerable attention is devoted to the unique Universal Periodic Review (UPR) process.[56] Under this mechanism first launched in 2008, the human rights records of every single one of the 192 members of the United Nations must be reviewed every four years, and every member of the Council must be reviewed during their period of membership. These assessments are carried out by a Working Group composed of all forty-seven members of the Council, and each is facilitated by a group of three states drawn by lot. Each review, despite a number of shortcomings, provides for interactive dialogue and incorporates not only information from the governments under examination, but also credible and reliable reports provided by other governments, independent human rights experts, special procedures, human rights treaty bodies, various United Nations entities, NGOs, and other interested stakeholders. For this reason, they range in discussing positive achievements and best practices, constraints, challenges, and serious failures in living up to human rights obligations. The Council as a whole then evaluates the review and decides on the outcome, including a follow-up review to assess the actual implementation of recommendations. There has never been anything like this before in history.

In addition to the review process, sessions also devote considerable time to what is

Figure 16. The Universal Periodic Review: No Country Beyond Scrutiny. Arkibong Bayan.

described as "human rights situations that require the attention of the Council."[57] Although politics is never absent from the process, members address systematic human rights violations in specific countries such as China, Colombia, Iran, Israeli-occupied Palestinian territories, Russia, Sudan, Uganda, or Zimbabwe. Sometimes they focus on abuses against specific individuals. At other times their attention is directed at such specific thematic issues as religious intolerance, terrorism, racism, freedom of speech and assembly, the rule of law and civil society, torture and arbitrary arrest, the death penalty, indigenous peoples, contemporary forms of slavery, sexual orientation, migrant workers and refugees, development, rights of the disabled, and the environment and climate change, among many others. Moreover, there are occasions when the Council, with assistance from the new Petitions Team of the Office of the High Commissioner for Human Rights, holds closed sessions to consider individual communications or petitions filed under a more streamlined victims-oriented complaint procedure.

Members of the Council have opportunities in all of these activities to work closely with many other actors that exist to promote human rights. Some of these are national human rights institutions (NHRIs) in the form of agencies, commissions, or ombudsmen established by constitutional or legislative authority designed to provide a link between internationally established norms and apply them in practical and concrete ways within their own domestic settings. They often play critical roles in protecting human rights by monitoring implementation at the national and local levels where people live their lives. They exist in all regions of the globe, from the Canadian Human Rights Commission, National Commission for Human Rights of Rwanda, and National Human Rights Commission of the Republic of Korea to the Ombudsman of Ecuador and the Human Rights Defender of Armenia.[58]

Other institutions include the international treaty-monitoring bodies, the African Center for Democracy and Human Rights Studies, Arab Institute for Human Rights, the Council of Europe's active and outspoken Commissioner for Human Rights, the European Union's European Instrument for Democracy and Human Rights (EIDHR), the Inter-American Commission on Human Rights, and OSCE's Office for Democratic Institutions and Human Rights, among many others, who engage in promotion, reporting, providing advice and technical assistance, election monitoring, and capacity building. Grateful Ukrainian judges and attorneys noted recently, "If it were not for the important lobbying role of our international partners . . . Ukraine would not have been able to establish its system of administrative justice" to protect rights— "an outcome that would have been unthinkable a few years ago."[59]

Among the most important non-state actors with whom the Council can collaborate are human rights NGOs. Never before in history have their numbers and the intensity of their involvement been so great. Indeed, they have created what has been described as an "advocacy revolution."[60] Their growth has been explosive, especially in developing countries. One estimate places the figure as high as twenty-six thousand human rights NGOs.[61] Some of these have a global reach, including Amnesty International, Human Rights Watch, Fédération Internationale des Droits de l'Homme, and International Commission of Jurists. Some focus on regional issues, such as the Afro-Asian Peoples' Solidarity Organization, Asian Coalition of Human Rights Organizations, Arab Organization for Human Rights, Inter-African Network for Human Rights, and Association Africaine de Défense des Droits de l'Homme. Still others address national or local grassroots problems, such as the Democracy Network of Iran, Coordinadora Nacional de Derechos Humanos in Peru, Civil Liberties Organization of Nigeria, Moroccan Organization for Human Rights, International Campaign for Tibet, Independent Human Rights Organization of Uzbekistan, and Zimbabwe Lawyers for Human Rights. Some are secular in orientation, such as WOMANKIND Worldwide and Médecins sans Frontières (the largest medical relief effort in the world today), while others are based upon religious belief, such as the Baha'i International Community, Commission of the Churches on International Affairs of the World Council of Churches, Friends (Quakers) World Committee for Consultation, International World Conference on Religion and Peace, Rabbis for Human Rights, World Fellowship of Buddhists, World Jewish Congress, and Muslim Women Lawyers for Human Rights. Some devote themselves to broad issues such as racial discrimination, development, indigenous peoples, environmental protection, refugees, and migrant workers, while others focus upon specific problems such as child soldiers, child labor, the sexual exploitation of children, violence against women by rape or female genital mutilation, torture, prisoners of conscience, the International Criminal Court, forced labor, HIV/AIDS, sexual orientation, disabilities, and the death penalty, among many, many others.

The dedicated and persistent women and men in these thousands of human rights NGOs work to expose abuses, monitor compliance with international norms and seek to hold government leaders accountable to their promises, serve as visionaries and "moral spurs," mobilize public opinion, offer humanitarian relief and legal assistance to victims and their families, and apply pressure for further action agendas. They gather information through independent investigations, sponsor training and educational programs, file human rights complaints, and provide treaty bodies with documentation and evaluation of whether national laws and practices meet existing obligations, often submitting hard-hitting material normally not included in official state reports. In addition, these activists offer support and praise to those governments and transnational corporations who contribute to the evolution of international human rights, as well as sharp and highly public condemnation of those who do not, in what is sometimes called "the mobilization of shame" before the eyes of the world.[62] The trend toward this wide range of activities, the determination with which they are pursued, and the capacity to network with others across borders is unmistakable and highly likely to continue.[63]

These various institutions and organizations, whether comprising government representatives or NGO activists, will continue to be called upon to confront blatant abuse and easily identified resistance. But even more will be required, for some issues of human rights are not so direct or simple. Instead, they are multi-layered, laden with contradictions, morally ambiguous, philosophically complex, and fraught with risk to other values. As human rights increasingly have become a fundamental and integral dimension of contemporary international politics and globalization, they have created new practical and political complexities, more subtle and nuanced dilemmas, and difficult questions for principle and policy.

What exactly does it mean, for example, to have a responsibility to protect against egregious human rights violations? Under whose authority should action be taken? If time, energy, and resources are limited, which cases of abuse should take precedence over others and what are the reasonable prospects for success? What happens when there are conflicts or collisions between human rights norms? What if the vigorous pursuit of immediate criminal justice and punishment undermines the long-term objective of reconciliation and stability in, say, Cambodia, Chile, or Uganda? What if support for the right of self-determination for, say, the Kurds or the Chechens, comes at the price of considerable loss of human life? Are sanctions the best way to address human rights abuses in China, or will engagement through liberalized trade provide better opportunities for reform? How can states seriously claim to combat terrorism without at the same time addressing those human rights violations that may have spawned violence in the first place? Should respect for human rights be considered as a part of what it means to be a legitimate government, and thus a core component of modern state sovereignty itself? What should be done if the most powerful states refuse to honor their obligations to protect human rights? If consistency in human rights protection is not always possible, is more damage done to claims of universal norms by selectively taking some action as compared to doing nothing at all? Those who work on behalf of international human rights will have to seriously wrestle with such questions as international human rights continue to evolve.

Technology and Political Will

Perhaps nothing is so visibly dramatic in this evolution as that of modern technology. Technological means, to be sure, have created dangerous weapons of mass destruction and the capacity for unprecedented surveillance and invasions of privacy. But they also have broken the historical cast in which the egregious violators of human rights thrived on darkness, on distance, on ignorance and superstition, on silence, and on their capacity to hide or deny abuses. Today's hand-held computers or smartphones, intelligence-gathering satellites, laptop computers, fax machines and scanners, video and digital cameras, along with many other mobile and wireless devices, all possess the capabilities to record and transmit words, sounds, or images to expose human rights abuses throughout the world. They can override government control, transcend national borders and geographic and cultural barriers, break down ignorance and disbelief, turn silence into debate, plead for protection, and give victims a voice. The capabilities of this technological globalization enable news from the most remote locations and circumstances to be uploaded, transmitted, and then downloaded from cyberspace to the Internet within seconds and then to international organizations, governments, broadcasting networks, NGOs, Web sites and their links, social networking sites such as Facebook and Twitter, file exchange and video sharing sites such as YouTube, or personal e-mail accounts and blogs. This enables extraordinary monitoring, collection, and dissemination of vast amounts of information about flagrant abuses as well as the promotion of human rights as never before. Indeed, here the contrast with the past and the present could not be more striking.

Sophisticated satellites equipped with multi- and hyper-spectral sensors and synthetic aperture radar, for example, are able to reveal when military forces attack civilians. This was demonstrated recently when high-definition composite images provided to the UN Operational Satellite Applications Program by DigitalGlobe marked the precise positioning of artillery shelling in Sri Lanka, proving that the government was lying.[64] Similar geospatial technology currently is being used by Google Earth to map the movement of refugees and the Science and Human Rights Program of the American Association for the Advancement of Science to discover the location of abuses in Burma, Darfur, Lebanon, South Ossetia, and Zimbabwe.[65] Digital photographs, video feeds, and photostreams from unmanned reconnaissance drones or by people on the ground with smartphones or cameras increasingly provide information, images, and sounds about abuses to human rights treaty-monitoring bodies and human rights activists. Technological capabilities thus make it possible for the world to catch abusers in the act: to know almost immediately when an eighteen-year-old young woman in Pakistan is gang raped, when a woman in Nigeria is stoned to death, when an innocent Israeli boy on his way to school is killed on a bus by a terrorist bomber, when an innocent Palestinian girl in a playground in Gaza is killed by military air attacks, when a father is abduced at the hands of Colombian security forces, when an indigenous tribe is forced off its land, when a university student is imprisoned in China for speaking out on behalf of human rights, or when in 2009 a young woman named Neda bleeds to death on a street in Tehran after being shot while protesting rigged elections in Iran.

These images and vast information all become readily available to those involved with the evolution of international human rights and in the development of a global citizenry and civil society. During the debates of the Human Rights Council, for instance, members, observer governments, national human rights institutions, NGOs, and others constantly consult extensive databases and Web sites available at their fingertips from hotspots in a Wi-Fi environment or when tethering their laptop computers to

Figure 17. Images Giving Victims a Voice: Protesting in Iran. AP/Wide World Photos.

their smartphones. The Office of the High Commissioner for Human Rights maintains the Human Rights Council Extranet using Internet protocols and network connectivity to provide Electronic Data Interchange (EDI), technical support for interactive conferences, a powerful public Web site, electronic means for submitting complaints and petitions, and a 24–hour "Human Rights Hot Line" at an e-mail address for victims needing to establish urgent, potentially life-saving contact with the Special Procedures Branch.[66] The International Criminal Court uses up-links that enable victims in remote towns in the Congo to watch live Webcasts of the Lubanga trial taking place in The Hague.

Technology also provides tools to greatly assist human rights activists in establishing horizontal links to like-minded people around the world and critical vertical links between victims at the local grassroots level to national, regional, and international bodies.[67] They are now able to create global networks or coalitions relatively inexpensively by using Internet connectivity to pool their resources, exchange and disseminate information, develop strategies for coordinated campaigns, mobilize pressure against abusers, and share their visions across national and cultural frontiers, thereby drawing ever-wider audiences into discourse about international human rights.[68] Similarly, the Web sites of such NGOs as Amnesty International, Human Rights Watch, Human Rights Internet, and Derechos Human Rights, among many others, are able to contain extensive information and analyses on international treaties and tribunals, specific reports on every country and government, testimony and reports from human rights defenders, and breaking news from around the globe.[69] Other sites are devoted to carefully monitoring the activities of the Human Rights Council and how states are responding to the new Universal Period Review.[70] But there is more than the words of information. Digital photography can use the evocative power of visual images in new ways to rally outrage, as demonstrated when Amnesty International USA created a "virtual tour" of a prisoner's cell at Guantanamo Bay.[71] This continuing technological revolution has been described with one word: "Unstoppable."[72]

What is done with all this information and these images once obtained through modern technology, of course, is a matter of political will. "The problem is not lack of early warning," observes Pierre Sané of Senegal, "but lack of early action."[73] The same can be said of the opportunities provided by international law, the principle of Responsibility to Protect, human rights institutions, and human rights organizations. It is infinitely easier to invoke human rights than to implement them. When confronted with tragic violations of human rights, are people actually willing to do what they say they will do?

At times it is evident that such will is seriously lacking or absent altogether. The price of realizing visions may appear too high and too threatening to special privileges, vested interests, the exercise of power, profits, or national sovereignty. When Human Rights in China applied for consultative status as an NGO at the United Nations, the Chinese delegation blocked its way, describing the organization as a "hostile force," a threat composed of "criminals," and "splittists" "aiming at overthrowing the Chinese government."[74] When the United States found its treaty obligations never to engage in torture inconvenient in its "war on terrorism," it declared that they were "quaint," "obsolete," and thus did not apply.[75] When former UN High Commissioner for Human Rights Mary Robinson courageously spoke out by "standing up to the bullies," those sensitive to criticism exerted pressure on her to resign, as they have on her successors.[76] When the International Criminal Court issued an arrest warrant in 2009 for President Omar Hassan al-Bashir of Sudan on the charge of crimes in Darfur, members of the African Union refused to cooperate. When a number of journalists in Russia have publically criticized their government for human rights abuses, they have been killed. When the recent Goldstone Report accused both Israel and Hamas fighters of war crimes, Israeli leaders lashed out by denouncing it as gross interference with their national sovereignty and "filled with lies."[77]

There are other times, however, when people do reveal a strong and determined will to act. These are the ones on the front lines willing to dodge bullets, speak out against brutality and tyranny, search for the "disappeared," write letters on behalf of the imprisoned and tortured, defend the exploited and repressed, seek to stop carnage and genocide, offer eyewitness accounts at criminal trials, protect the weak or impoverished, and work in common ways to bring human rights to life. They are the ones willing to participate in a vast new field of action in which ordinary but dedicated people—either as individuals or as members of NGOs—are constructing human rights projects, organizing practical training sessions in local communities, and sharing their knowledge with others through education.[78] They are the CEOs and boards of transnational corporations willing to create codes of human rights conduct for their globalized operations or to withdraw business from countries that systematically abuse their people. They also are courageous individuals such as Sergio Vieira de Mello, sometimes described as "the conscience of the world," who, as UN Special Representative to Iraq, was willing to risk his life on behalf of human rights before he was killed by a suicide bomber.[79]

In addition, they are the leaders of those governments with sufficient political will to ratify human rights treaties, bind themselves to obligations, submit to international scrutiny, apprehend war criminals, work with NHRIs and NGOs, support regional efforts such as the Inter-American Court of Human Rights or the Charter of Fundamental Rights of the European Union, and in many other ways try to make human rights a vital component of their collective policies and programs. Without political will, the rule of law, the principle of Responsibility to Protect, institution building, and the practice of international election monitoring never would have developed. Without political will, it never would have been determined that impunity for perpetrators of the most serious crimes was no longer acceptable and the International Criminal Court never would have become a reality. Without political will, those states in Europe with significant Roma minorities never would have joined together to create the Decade of Roma Inclusion from 2005–2005. Without political will, the leaders meeting at the World Summit never would have agreed to double the budget of the Office of the High Commissioner for Human Rights and the General Assembly never would have determined to adopt the Declaration on the Rights of Indigenous Peoples in 2007 or to mainstream human rights into all aspects of the work of the United Nations.[80] Without political will, the Security Council would never have engaged in increased activism on behalf of human rights, would never have consulted with hard-hitting special procedures rapporteurs, and would never have declared in its historic resolution of 2008 that rape and sexual violence in armed conflict against women are no longer acceptable and now can constitute war crimes and crimes against humanity.[81] Without political will, Navi Pillay (a prominent judge of international criminal tribunals who began her work defending the opponents of apartheid in South Africa) would never have been appointed UN High Commissioner for Human Rights, and well-known attorney Hina Jilani (imprisoned and threatened with death for her advocacy of the rights of women in Pakistan) would never have been named as Special Representative for Human Rights Defenders. Without political will, especially when secured at exactly the time of the "war on terrorism" and intense religious and regional antagonisms, the Human Rights Council would never have been created and would never have established the new Universal Periodic Review to examine the human rights record of every nation in the world.

*   *   *

That so much global attention now should be given to the political will necessary to advance human rights is itself a testimony to the profound and hard-won evolution that has and continues to occur. In fact, even the normally callous *Economist* devoted an issue to the intensified interest in international human rights and the widespread consciousness about the inherent dignity of each person, under the suggestive title, "The World Is Watching." It is. "Victims are no longer seen as someone else's business," reported the journal, concluding that such a development "marked a genuine turning point in world affairs."[82] As a result of the powerful forces and individuals that we have explored in each chapter of this book, the world no longer turns its collective face away from seeing human rights abuses as it did throughout most of history. But the evolution most certainly is not over. As Mandela observed, many hills remain to be climbed and challenges lie ahead. When faced with this fact, one report concluded:

The world community needs to return to the audacious vision of those who dreamed of the Rights of Man and of the Citizen and drafted the Universal Declaration of Human Rights. A new millennium is just the occasion to reaffirm such a vision—and to renew the practical commitments to make it happen.[83]

Successes in this endeavor may well depend on how well we understand what conclusions can be reached about the past and what lessons can be learned for the future about the evolution of international human rights and visions seen.

Chapter 10
Toward the Future

It is not enough merely to call for freedom, democracy, and human rights. There has to be a determination to persevere in the struggle, to make sacrifices in the name of enduring truths, to resist the corrupting influences of desire, ill will, ignorance, and fear. Saints, it has been said, are the sinners who go on trying. . . . It is his capacity for self-improvement and self-redemption which most distinguishes man from the mere brute. At the root of human responsibility is the concept of perfection, the urge to achieve it, the intelligence to find a path towards it, and the will to follow that path. . . . It is man's vision of a world fit for rational, civilized humanity which leads him to dare and to suffer to build societies free from want and fear.
—Aung San Suu Kyi of Burma

The evolution of international human rights, as we have seen throughout this book, is a history of the long and persistent struggle for freedom and dignity. It is one inspired by visions of what it means to be truly human and have a sense of responsibility to others. It is a history brought about by visionaries and by those determined men and women willing to make sacrifices and sometimes take considerable risks in confronting vested interests, privilege, prejudice, and the claims of national sovereignty. Moreover, it is one in which revolutions, wars, upheavals, and even atrocities have played often critical roles in accelerating the process, accentuating the influence of politics, and helping visions become reality. Such a history not only is valuable in its own right but capable of providing insights and perspectives about what can be anticipated and evaluated as international human rights evolve toward the future.

The Nature and Power of Visions

Visions, by their very nature, defy and offer alternatives to the existing order. They challenge our imaginations, cause us to reexamine our assumptions, and often raise profound and disturbing questions about our own values and our behavior. They address some of the most complex issues of life and pose difficult questions that do not always lend themselves to simple solutions or conclusive answers. At precisely the time that they seek to address the best in people, for example, they generally are forced to confront the worst. Paradoxically, visions of human rights have always gained the greatest support during times of the greatest human abuses, including slavery, torture, segregation and apartheid, war, conquest, or genocide. In these most trying of circumstances, how is one to determine the genuine nature of human beings and what is possible? Do we possess certain basic rights simply because we are all human? If so, what exactly are these rights and do they have universal applicability? Are some rights more important than others, or are they really indivisible and interdependent? And, what is the relationship between the individual and the larger community in which we live, and does the enjoyment of rights entail corresponding responsibilities?

Visions also challenge us by presenting hypothetical possibilities of what might be rather than of what is or has been. This is why they and those who see them are so often and accurately described as "ahead of their time." They require both a willingness and an ability to go beyond existing experience by a leap of human imagination. But capacities and means to do this vary greatly, and what might be seen by one visionary in his or her own mind or conscience may not be at all clear to others or may be subject to different interpretations. Some, for example, are not at all receptive or able to imagine in the first place. They consider or feel their own pain, but not that of others. They know their own personal experience, but cannot see beyond it. Others can go far beyond themselves, seeing visions in their minds through sophisticated philosophical theories, through a carefully crafted "paradigm of rights," through intellectually articulated doctrines, or through the compelling language of declarations of human rights. They find words sufficient for the strong to imagine what it is like to be weak or for those who have no pain to imagine the suffering of those who are tortured

Others see visions of rights best in their hearts due to a sense of compassion or, as Mencius believed, a basic, human emotional empathy with suffering. The philosopher Diderot and the former slave Equaiano identified it in the same way: an "interior feeling" of intuitions and emotions.[1] This is exactly what Harriet Beecher Stowe sought to arouse when writing about slavery in *Uncle Tom's Cabin* by asking:

If it were *your* Harry, mother, or your Willie, that were going to be torn from you by a brutal trader, tomorrow morning,—if you had seen the man, and heard that the papers were signed and delivered, and you had only from twelve o'clock till morning to make good your escape,—how fast could *you* walk?[2]

Still others need more than words. They must literally see something with their own eyes in order to imagine new possibilities. This explains why photographs and other visual images have played such a powerful role in the evolution of international human rights. They attract riveting attention by capturing a precise event and laying bare something that up to that moment seemed too horrible to be true. They have the power to put the "human" in human rights by giving the abstract concept of violence a tangible and very intimate face, by removing claims of deniability and exposing abuse, by revealing the agony of an actual person with a name and a family, and by enabling the viewer to look another in the eye and have an emotional encounter and sense of participation with the victim. This is what gives them the power to evoke empathy and provoke outrage. Thomas Clarkson discovered this with his pen and ink drawing of helpless victims crammed into a slave ship, as did E. D. Morel with his early photographs looking directly into the terrified eyes of a slave trapped under a net or a Congolese girl with her severed hand lying on the ground before her. These came to be followed by the images of a young boy holding up his hands pleading for mercy from conquering soldiers, a man about to be tortured with a hot branding iron, a Kurdish grandmother holding her grandchild burned by Iraqi chemical weapons, and a woman watching her husband and son being marched into the woods for "ethnic cleansing." But it is not just these victims in pain that make viewers want to shield the eyes of their children, for some images show the perpetrators as well: the political leader issuing the order to kill opponents, the soldier waiting his turn to rape, the extermination camp warden in a proper vest standing in a yard amidst piles of corpses, the prison guard crouched over bloodied and broken bodies victimized by torture, or the crowd standing at the base of a tree from which the limp body of a lynched black man hangs as they perversely smile at the camera.[3]

It is exactly these difficult, emotional, thought- and conscience-provoking dimensions that endow visions of human rights with a power that encourages, enables, or actually forces us to challenge our existing values, reexamine our assumptions, and sometimes change our minds and our actions. This has been called "moral prestige" or "moral capital."[4] It is a resource that, if deemed by others to be worthy of esteem because of the normative value that it places on human life, can be mobilized for influence and service. This is precisely why those witnesses of the evolution of international human rights have commented over and over again on the remarkable power of visions to transform society by "stirring the conscience of humanity" and "changing patterns of thought," even those entrenched with centuries of encumbered tradition behind them.[5] They have the capacity to cause people to consider that the existing state of things might not necessarily be inevitable and that an alternative reality is possible. They pointedly raise the possibility that kings and emperors might not be "divine," that certain races or classes might not be inherently "superior," or that slavery might not be part of the "natural order" of things. They offer the prospect that women deserve the same rights as men, that indigenous peoples are fully human beings, or that torture and genocide are ethically reprehensible and must not be tolerated. Similarly, they ask people to imagine that government leaders need not be allowed to claim that the way they wish to treat others is strictly their own business and that international norms and concepts of legitimacy can be transformed.

In addition, these visions possess a remarkable power to inspire, for they serve as carriers of hope for the future. They all present an alternative to the status quo and say simply: we can do better than this. It is not at all difficult to understand how dreams of a world community with security, peace, and justice as a result of respect for basic rights can generate inspiration. They see the best in us rather than the worst, even at the most horrific of times when human rights are known more for their deprivation than their expression or realization. They look toward the possibilities of what might be rather than what is or what has been in an imperfect world, and call us to rise above the limitations and experiences of the past. These visions consider what we share as members of the same human family and what brings us together rather than what drives us apart. They see a world of common humanity without borders where the worth and dignity of each man, woman, and child is honored. They imagine the elimination of suffering based on distinctions of gender, race, caste or class, belief, ethnicity, or nationality. Moreover, they point the way toward behavior based on ethical norms and values rather than the exercise of raw power and brutal force. All this helps to explain why visions provide such enduring inspiration to those seeking human rights.

Indeed, these are the reasons why certain visions have touched people in powerful ways at their core, uplifted the human spirit, and enabled us to dream of what might be, even at times of great peril. They inspired countless numbers to follow those religious leaders who preached the brotherhood and sisterhood of all human beings. They encouraged others to embrace the visions of philosophers who spoke of ethical values and justice that respected the dignity of each person everywhere. These visions gave hope to those who dreamed of freeing the enslaved, assisting the exploited, caring for the wounded, and protecting the persecuted, wherever they might be. They provided strength to millions seeking a time when women would enjoy the same rights as men, when racial discrimination and apartheid would end, and when colonial empires would crumble. In addition, these visions inspired those who hoped that the international community would someday be able to create an organization that placed a value on people rather than just states and that could develop normative standards of human rights that would be universally accepted and applied around the world.

These same visions that inspire some, however, also enrage, produce fear, and provoke resistance in others. To imagine a world in which each and every individual is treated with respect and dignity, receives equal protection, enjoys freedom, and is accorded social justice is to threaten virtually any tradition or practice based on privilege and hierarchy, birth or wealth, exclusivity or prejudice. The reason is not difficult to explain, for as one experienced observer notes succinctly: "The struggle for human rights has always been and always will be a struggle against authority."[6] Visions of human rights, by their nature, defy the legitimacy and threaten the existence of all forms of political, economic, social, or cultural despotism, tyranny, dictatorship, oligarchy, or authoritarian control. They are capable of presenting a potent focal point and a resounding rallying cry for those who want change. This is why these visions have been described by those who resist them as "upsetting public order," "endangering national unity," "threatening the natural order," "inciting discontent," "challenging tradition," and, in the case of women's rights, as "disturbing stability" in the social fabric or "spreading immorality." Moreover, if they seek to apply principles to the world as a whole, they challenge the jealously guarded claims of national sovereignty, "cultural relativism," and "national exceptionalism," and are accused of "moral imperialism" and "interfering into internal affairs." Visions of human rights have always presented profound threats to special privilege. They still do.

Given these factors, the power of visions should never be underestimated. History certainly demonstrates that ideas know no boundaries and have the capacity to change the world. Men and women who draw inspiration from visions of human rights understand this—as do those who fear them. In fact, it is for precisely this reason that visionaries and those who follow them so frequently face enormous pressure to keep their visions to themselves and to remain silent. At times they may be ridiculed as naive idealists or criticized as impractical dreamers, as discovered by the Buddhist *bodhisattvas,* Mo Tze when he wrote about moral philosophy, Al-Farabi when he described his vision of virtue from the perspective of Islam, Thomas Clarkson when he imagined ending the slave trade, Alejandro Alvarez and André Mandelstam when they dreamed of formulating international standards of rights, and Peter Benenson when he considered forming Amnesty International. Sometimes they may be reviled and coerced, as experienced by Jean-Jacques Rousseau when forced into exile, Thomas Paine when burned in effigy, Emmeline Pankhurst when imprisoned and force-fed in jail, or Nelson Mandela when sent into confinement for twenty-seven years. On other occasions, they may be viewed as dangerous heretics or revolutionaries with death the price to be paid for their visions, as experienced by Jan Hus when burned at the stake, Olympe de Gouges when guillotined, Mohandas Gandhi and Martin Luther King, Jr. when assassinated, or Steven Biko when killed in a South African jail. The same fear of the power of visions of human rights exists today, as evidenced by all those victims censored, punished for their beliefs, arbitrarily arrested, imprisoned without trial, tortured, starved, killed, or otherwise coerced into being silent about human rights.

Despite all the historical evidence of the capacity of visions of human rights to inspire, create normative authority, transform attitudes and behavior, and provoke resistance, and despite the fact that this is readily recognized by both dedicated proponents and determined adversaries, it is still surprising how few understand or appreciate the potency of this power. This often appears to be particularly striking among those observers and practitioners of international relations who describe themselves as "realists." They quite appropriately appreciate the influence of politics, yet nevertheless and contemptuously dismiss visions of human rights as "just dreams," "only words," "merely statements," "quixotic notions," "ephemeral ideas," "sentimental fiction," or the "impractical speculations" of "utopian fanatics" unlikely to create anything more than a ripple on the course of human events. Those who measure power in military or economic terms alone fail to see this other critical dimension, often at great cost to themselves and their countries.

There were those, for example, who confidently believed that their empires could never be seriously threatened by the ideas in a Declaration on the Granting of Independence to Colonial Countries and Peoples or a Declaration of the Asian-African Conference, that their monarchies and aristocracies could never be dangerously contested by the concepts in some Declaration of the Rights of Man and Citizen, or that their gender discrimination could never be significantly changed by statements in a Declaration of Sentiments or a Declaration of Mexico on the Equality of Women. There were those who simply could not imagine that racism might be profoundly challenged by the words in a speech entitled "I Have a Dream" and a Declaration on the Elimination of All Forms of Racial Discrimination, or that national sovereignty and domestic jurisdiction might be critically jeopardized by the text of some Atlantic Charter, or that the Soviet Union would help sow the seeds of its own destruction with the principles enunciated in the Helsinki Final Act, or that laws might actually be created on the basis of ideas expressed in international declarations. Upon the adoption of the Universal Declaration of Human Rights, for example, any number of commentators sought to denigrate the achievement. They described the text as "a mere declaration" and "a statement of principles devoid of any obligatory character."[7] John Foster Dulles noted contemptuously that the Universal Declaration "merely sets up a standard."[8] Others of the same mind dismissed it as "innocuous," "ineffectual," "purely declaratory," "of no more value than a recommendation," "a mere statement of political and moral principle," and "a grandiloquent incantation" destined only for "futility."[9] In the light of the subsequent impact of the vision of the Universal Declaration of Human Rights, it is unlikely that they would hold these opinions today. Through time, some things that were entrenched came to be seen as no longer acceptable, and what was considered utopian became practical.[10]

People of Vision and Action

Although visions possess an extraordinary degree of transformative power and influence, they do not have the capacity to spring to life on their own or bring themselves to fruition. For this task they need people, or what Nelson Mandela calls the heroes and heroines. Such people may be quiet religious leaders teaching through prophecy or parables, they may be contemplative philosophers or poets inspiring through the written word, they may be eager activists engaging in civil disobedience, they may be unlikely citizens reluctantly propelled by dramatic forces or events to become involved, or they may be government leaders setting and implementing policy.

Without these people there would be no such thing as the evolution of international human rights. It has required thoughtful men and women serving as visionaries—not only capable of imagining possibilities beyond existing experience themselves, but of then persuading others to share their visions for change. They may achieve this through their teachings, as in the messages of the prophets Isaiah and Muhammad, the parables of Jesus, the instructions of Kong Qiu, or the lessons of Siddhartha Gautama. They may use the speeches of Cicero or Franklin Roosevelt, the poetry of Sultan Farrukh Hablul Matin or Ziya Gokalp, the letters of Abigail Adams or Eglantyne Jebb, the manifestos of Karl Marx, the journals of Hideko Fukuda, the photographs of Louis Hine, the pamphlets of Thomas Paine and H. G. Wells, the decisions of the judges presiding over the International Military Tribunal at Nuremberg, the encyclicals of Pope John XXIII, or the music and the lyrics of "Amazing Grace" and "We Shall Overcome." These visionaries may transmit their ideas to others by means of books such as those of Bartholomé de Las Casas, John Locke, Mary Wollstonecraft, or Kang Youwei. Or they may convey visions through resolutions such as the Universal Declaration of Human Rights.

For many, however, actions speak louder than words. It is clear from the experiences of history that one of the most effective ways of conveying visions of human rights to others has been by means of personal example. The actual behavior of dedicated and courageous women and men believing in the face of fear and doubt that they might make a difference and therefore willing to make great sacrifices—sometimes including their lives—on behalf of human rights provides credibility and inspiration that cannot be matched in any other way. Such people include a Francisco de Vitoria willing to risk imprisonment by criticizing his government's extermination of indigenous peoples. They include a Julia Ward Howe who wrote in "The Battle Hymn of the Republic" that "As He died to make men holy, let us die to make men free," and a Angelina Grimké willing to suffer in order to free slaves, believing that

If persecution is the means which God has ordained for this great end, EMANCIPATION, then . . . I feel as if I could say, LET IT COME; for it is my deep, solemn, deliberate conviction that *this is a cause worth dying for.*[11]

They include a Florence Nightingale willing to risk her own health by tending to the needs of wounded soldiers, a Qiu Jin willing to risk torture by organizing the first woman's movement in China, and a Fridtjof Nansen willing to put himself in danger by helping refugees. They include a Franz Bernheim willing to risk persecution by drawing international attention to the plight of Jews under the Nazi regime, a W. E. B. Du Bois willing to risk lynching by criticizing racism in the United States before the world, a Kwame Nkrumah willing to risk his life by standing up to the mighty British Empire, an Andrei Sakharov and Yelena Bonner willing to risk severe punishment by speaking out on the abuses of rights by the Soviet Union, and a Wei Jingsheng willing to risk imprisonment by drawing international attention to the violations of human rights by their governments. They include an Aung San Suu Kyi willing to suffer under a military dictatorship on behalf of democracy and a Shirin Ebadi willing to risk her life in order to advance the rights of women in Iran and throughout the Islamic world. They also include International Red Cross workers willing to risk their own lives by investigating a prison where torture occurs and a staff member of the High Commissioner for Refugees willing to risk possible death in order to protect mothers and their children fleeing from a civil war. As Václav Havel observed after long and painful experience: "There are certain causes worth suffering for."[12]

Indeed, this characteristic of personal commitment, strength of spirit, courage, and sacrifice in action has been one of the most distinguishing features of the most noted visionaries. They believed that lives could be saved by action—or lost by the failure to act. They believed that minds and behavior, and thus the future, could be changed. "The future," Gandhi told his followers, "depends on what we do in the present."[13] Although scorned, reviled, jailed, exiled, persecuted, or tortured by contemporaries, they nevertheless persisted against all odds. As Eglantyne Jebb exhorted those who worked with her on behalf of the rights of children: "Let us clearly understand that this is *not impossible.*"[14] It is for this reason that their visions and actions have been inspiring to the point of recognition and admiration. It is interesting to note, for example, how many individuals discussed in these pages eventually were honored for their work on behalf of human rights with the Nobel Peace Prize. These include Henry Dunant of Switzerland, Fridtjof Nansen of Norway, Carl von Ossietsky of Germany, Ralph Bunche and Martin Luther King, Jr., of the United States, Andrei Sakharov of the Soviet Union, Adolfo Pérez Esquivel of Argentina, Desmond Tutu and Nelson Mandela of South Africa, the Dalai Lama of Tibet, José Ramos-Horta and Carlos Filipe Ximenes Belo of East Timor, Rigoberta Menchú Tum of Guatemala, Aung San Suu Kyi of Burma, Kim Dae Jung of South Korea, Shirin Ebadi of Iran, and Liu Xiaobo of China.

There is a reason, of course, why these particular individuals attract our attention. But it is perhaps even more important to recognize that most people do not become famous or have any desire to do so. Time and time again in the long struggle for human rights almost all have been relatively unknown and ordinary people with the normal uncertainties, imperfections, hesitations, constraints, frailties, and fears that one might expect. But in their own way they saw something wrong, listened to the voice of their conscience, and were willing to turn their outrage into action by confronting abuse on the ground where they lived and worked. These are the ones who engaged in small, daily, and often common acts on behalf of human dignity without much thought about becoming well known. As one man modestly described his own efforts that came to draw widespread attention: "The role that I had played in this affair seemed very minor to me. All I had done is what any decent person would do."[15] They are the ones described by Eleanor Roosevelt as "everyday people" who take human rights seriously, work for, and sometimes sacrifice and suffer for visions in which they truly believe. As she observed,

Where, after all, do universal human rights begin? In small places, close to home—so close and so small that they cannot be seen on any maps of the world. Yet they ARE the world of the individual person; the neighborhood . . . , the school or college . . . , the factory, farm, or office. . . . Such are the places where every man, woman, and child seeks equal justice, equal opportunity, equal dignity without discrimination. Unless these rights have meaning there, they have little meaning anywhere. Without concerned citizen action to uphold them close to home, we shall look in vain for progress in the larger world.[16]

These are not the trained specialists, international lawyers, or "the experts" on human rights, but people of determination and courage who labor without fanfare at the local grassroots level to bring human rights to life from remote villages to urban slums, who believe that individual acts, however small, in the end matter. They are the ones who voluntarily provide care for those in need, speak out in public squares, sign petitions, teach others, participate in letter-writing campaigns, engage in boycotts, passively resist, refuse to sit at the back of racially segregated buses, or march in protest to draw attention to abuses. They also are the individuals sometimes suddenly confronted with the unexpected, like the unknown man willing to risk death in the name of human rights by standing completely alone, planting his feet squarely in the path of a moving column of armored tanks in Beijing.

Most of the time, however, individual people do not need to stand entirely by themselves. Instead, they can stand out without standing alone. They can do this by drawing strength and support from other visionaries and activists in larger groups, networks, communities, NGOs, or even mass movements created and held together by shared visions. Within these they can combine their energies and resources, name and shame rights violators, give voice to the voiceless, create pressure to challenge abuses and bring about change. As Brazilian Archbishop Dom Hélder Camara observed after a lifetime of grassroots human rights struggles in the face of nearly overwhelming resistance:

When you dream alone, it is only a dream.
But when you dream together, it is the beginning of reality.[17]

Figure 18. Actions Speaking Louder Than Words: Confronting Authority in Beijing, 1989. AP/ Wide World Photos.

As we have seen, the contributions made by people working together through NGOs often have overcome seemingly impossible odds and thereby played absolutely critical roles in the evolution of international human rights. The Society for Effecting the Abolition of the Slave Trade and the Société Française pour l'Abolition de l'Esclavage, for example, proved to be invaluable in overturning centuries of practice by bringing an end to the shipment and sale of human beings as cargo and property. The International Woman Suffrage Alliance and the Fusen Kakutoku Domei made overwhelming contributions in raising awareness about equal rights for women and in securing agreements on suppressing the traffic in women and children. The Commission to Study the Organization of Peace and the Institut de Droit International provided significant assistance and mobilized powerful pressure to create human rights provisions within the United Nations Charter. The Fédération International des Droits de l'Homme and the International League for the Rights of Man, among many others, all helped enormously to shape and secure the Universal Declaration of Human Rights. The Pan-Asian Society and the Pan-African Congress contributed heavily to discussions and then actions concerning the right of self-determination and the rights of indigenous peoples. The National Association for the Advancement of Colored People and the League for the Abolition of Race Discrimination did the same for the eventual International Convention on the Elimination of All Forms of Racial Discrimination. Nothing did more than the Mothers of the Plaza del Mayo, who courageously gathered in vigils with photographs of their "disappeared" children, to expose the abuses of Argentina's military dictatorship to the world. The International Commission of Jurists provided similarly powerful contributions to the International Convention Against Torture, as did Human Rights Watch and its predecessor Helsinki Watch Committee in drawing the attention of the world to human rights violations within the Soviet empire, and the Vietnam Veterans of America Foundation and Physicians for Human Rights in successfully pressing for the Landmine Convention. It is important to recognize that not one of these NGOs began with any significant money, power, size, or influence. Instead, what they had were people of vision and action.

This can be seen even further by the remarkable the case of Amnesty International. It started with only a very small number of people, a single newspaper article, and the rather improbable idea that writing letters to ruthlessly oppressive governments might possibly help free political prisoners. Indeed, observers almost immediately described it as "one of the larger lunacies of our time."[18] But it attracted supporters, and they began to write letters and draw attention to human rights abuses. Governments in turn began to complain about interference into their own affairs, and Amnesty International found itself being accused as "traitorous," an agent of "anti-Communist subversion," and a "lackey of satanic powers."[19] Detractors quickly came to include Iran's Ayatollah Khomeini, Uganda's Idi Amin, Iraq's Saddam Hussein, Chile's Augusto Pinochet, Britain's Margaret Thatcher, China's Jiang Zemin, and NATO commanders, among many others. Nevertheless, its members refused to be intimidated and instead worked hard to document and publicize human rights abuses such as unfair trials, executions, disappearances, and torture around the world, as well as help free thousands of prisoners of conscience. Some of these freed prisoners, most notably Olusegun Obasanjo of Nigeria, Kim Dae Jung of South Korea, and Václav Havel of the Czech Republic, eventually became democratically elected presidents of their countries. These efforts and achievements inspired many others. Today Amnesty International comprises over two million members and supporters in one hundred fifty countries who collectively exert enormous influence on behalf of human rights and are often described as the "conscience of the world."[20]

One of the great advantages of individuals working together in such NGOs, of course, is the fact that they do not represent the interests or official positions of governments. They are less encumbered by the responsibilities of governing and balancing other policy considerations or by diplomatic protocol. They therefore possess the freedom to focus directly on human rights issues for their own sake and to be much more vocal, outspoken, and fiercely critical of abuses. They are free to work with governments and to work against them. As Edith Ballantyne of the Women's International League for Peace and Freedom said when informed that NGOs might not be invited to high-level meetings of government representatives who feared their influence: "If we are not invited, then too bad. We will simply attend anyway."[21] This kind of independence and the successes that it brings have been invaluable in the evolution of international human rights. Indeed, as one United Nations official observes, "Without the people of the NGOs, our program for human rights would be a mere shadow of itself."[22] They are credited with creating what has been called an "advocacy revolution" and with breaking the monopoly of nation-states to conduct international affairs as they wish.[23]

All these men and women acting either by themselves or in cooperation with others, despite the many differences and various points of departure between them, share a number of characteristics in common. Over a considerable period of time, they have been inspired by some vision of human rights emerging from religious belief, philosophical or political conviction, or their own personal experiences. They are the ones who refused to accept the prevailing behavior of their time, who envisioned a world in which people enjoyed basic human rights, who believed that they had a responsibility to do something to protect those unable to defend themselves, and who refused to be silent or passive in the face of abuse. They have known that just because their leaders spoke about "peace," "justice," and "human rights" did not mean that their policies actually advanced these objectives. They have resisted falling prey to intimidation, to ignorance or fatigue, to failures and repeated frustrations, to skepticism or cynicism generated by the imperfections in humankind and society, to the dangerous argument that patriotism requires silence or a blind eye to violations of rights, or to the seductive idea that their religious beliefs and their nation's self interests were somehow synonymous. Moreover, they all have concluded that they need not resign themselves to meekly accepting the existing state of things, thinking that nothing will work or that nothing is worth fighting for. Instead, they believed that they should speak out and that their efforts could make a difference. They were willing to confront powerful vested interests and fierce opposition, to make sacrifices, and sometimes to suffer greatly on behalf of visions of human rights in which they truly believed.

Some people of vision and action, it is important to observe, also are government officials. This may appear strange, since leaders of governments historically have been the worst violators of human rights, and none could survive a test of either consistency or untarnished achievement. As John Humphrey concluded after many years of working in this area, "in matters relating to human rights, individuals and governments are usually on opposite sides of the ring. In such matters, governments usually move when and only when they are forced to do so."[24] They are the ones, as we have seen, who traditionally have used the enormous power of the state at their disposal to retain privilege, to keep international norms and institutions weak, to hide behind the claims of national sovereignty, and to abuse rights. For this reason, they so often draw such wrath from human rights activists who describe them as "the enemy"[25] or who carry banners declaring: "Betrayed by Governments."[26] But it is also true that in the world of politics governments are the major source of rights protection. Here the most significant actors are governmental leaders, some of whom have taken actions that in their own way, whether intended or not, contributed significantly to the evolution of international human rights.

One thinks, for example, of the actions of people such as Abraham Lincoln emancipating slaves in the United States, Alexander II liberating at least fifty million serfs in Russia, and William Gladstone using pressure to protect those persecuted for their religious beliefs overseas. Others include Nobuaki Makino representing Japan and Wellington Koo representing China to make efforts to obtain a clause on racial equality in the Covenant of the League of Nations, Peter Fraser representing New Zealand and official delegates from the Latin American countries to secure human rights provisions in the Charter of the United Nations, and the many representatives including Eleanor Roosevelt, Charles Malik, and René Cassin who negotiated and then adopted on behalf of their governments the Universal Declaration of Human Rights. Further examples can be found among those leaders willing to create regional bodies on behalf of human rights and all those from Asia and Africa, along with their supporters in the West, who worked so hard to move the United Nations out of a long and debilitating deadlock into binding conventions on international human rights and the creation of the new Human Rights Council with its Universal Periodic Review.

It is important to remember that in this regard none of the many activities taken by the United Nations in the field of human rights can be done without the approval and political will of the leaders and representatives of governments. As Kofi Annan acknowledged, "The ultimate success of that effort remains, of course, in the hands of Member States."[27] One of the great paradoxes of the evolution of international human rights lies in the fact that states have been both the most significant abusers and the most significant protectors of rights—both the cause and the cure. Thus, all the standards that are set, the treaties that are drafted, the implementation mechanisms that are created, the decisions made by the Human Rights Council, the special rapporteurs that are sent to investigate abuses, the technical assistance and advisory services that are provided, and the tribunals that are created to prosecute those who commit genocide, occur because governments determine that they will. At the same time, national leaders decide whether their countries will honor their commitments in treaties, whether they will subject their own actions to the scrutiny of others, whether they will bear the costs of imposing sanctions on other governments for violations of human rights, whether they will arrest and try war criminals, and, like Jimmy Carter as president of the United States, Nelson Mandela as president of South Africa, or Mary Robinson as president of Ireland, whether they will speak out and act on behalf of rights in the world—or not.

With such a wide variety of people ranging from enraged dissidents to government leaders involved in one way or another with international human rights, it is hardly surprising that there would be vastly different visions, personalities, motives, and methods. Indeed, the champions of human rights have been no more monolithic or homogeneous in their efforts than those who resisted them. Some, for example, are motivated by religious values and sense of moral responsibility, while others are not and take action due to secular philosophical positions, various forms of political theory, or formal legal precepts. Some activists believe that all rights are completely inseparable and indivisible in inclusive and comprehensive ways, while others do not and focus exclusively on single-issue rights that are one-dimensional and self-serving. Some advocates move with humble quietness outside public attention, while others are vain, openly seek publicity, and proceed with vocal stridency and arrogant self-righteousness. Some proceed with confidence, while others are uncertain or fearful. Some champions seek targeted improvement within a system by using moral persuasion and reform, while others employ a clenched in-your-face fist determined to overthrow a system by violence and revolution. Some focus on building mass and grassroots movements, while others direct their efforts at influencing elites. Some are reflective and act on the basis of carefully considered and reasoned positions, while others are impulsive and act on the basis of emotion. Some are engaged because of hope in the best in people, while others are motivated by fear of the worst. Some proponents genuinely value the intrinsic worth of human rights for their own sake, while others give their support only if it serves an expedient purpose such as responding to unwelcomed pressure, seeking international loans or assistance, or embarrassing an adversary. In addition, historical experience reveals that people can be inconsistent, outrage can be selective, and that human beings can possess an enormous capacity to see the speck in the eyes of others while ignoring the mote in their own.

These features about people help to explain why human rights efforts sometimes appear so erratic, selective, inconsistent, myopic, confusing, self-serving, morally am-biguous, and fraught with double standards. Human rights can mean different things to different people. For this reason, there has never been one single vision—but many, and sometimes they have even contested each other. During the eighteenth century, for example, many of those who spoke so eloquently on behalf of the inalienable and natural rights had no intention at all of including women, black slaves, indigenous peoples, or the unpropertied among those who should receive protection. Not all of those who campaigned in the nineteenth century for the abolition of the slave trade or for the protection of the persecuted supported rights for exploited workers or for those subjected to colonial domination. Woodrow Wilson could advocate the right of self-determination and the right to enjoy religious freedom but simultaneously reject the principle of racial equality. During the height of the Cold War, it was not at all difficult to find politicians in the United States eager to publicly criticize the Soviet Union and its clients in Eastern Europe in the name of human rights while at the same time determinedly supporting authoritarian, anti-Communist regimes abroad and op-posing the civil rights movement in their own home states. It was not uncommon to hear Communist governments strongly supporting the right of self-determination for peoples in Western colonial empires, but fiercely resisting the extension of that same right for those under their control. Similarly, it is not unusual to hear some countries today speak loudly on behalf of economic and social rights and the right to develop-ment while at the same time restricting civil and political rights and failing to accord equal rights to women; or to support international human rights efforts against their foes but not against their political allies; or to claim to defend human rights while seri-ously abusing them in the name of fighting terrorism. But despite these serious prob-lems, inconsistencies, and differences, each in their own way, by design or by accident, has opened up new spaces for discourse, created new possibilities, and thereby made some contribution to the evolution of human rights.

Forces and Events of Consequence

None of these many individual men and women, however, existed with their visions in a vacuum. They all lived in specific historical contexts, times, places, cultures, and stages of development. During certain periods and in particular areas, change proceeded slowly and traditional patterns of behavior remained much as they had been for centuries. In these circumstances, contributions on behalf of human rights were largely confined to the realm of theory rather than practice. On other occasions, historical forces and events of wars, revolutions, upheavals, atrocities, and technological advance created the conditions for change. They drastically transformed existing structures, vested interests, habits of thought, and societal values that allowed, encouraged, or actually compelled changes enhancing international human rights.

One of the most interesting—and perhaps tragically ironic—features of this entire evolution is the fact that so often the major efforts to advance human rights have been coupled with enormous human traumas and catastrophes. In so many ways the history of human rights is a history of human wrongs written in blood. The early bills and declarations of civil and political rights, to illustrate, emerged only with the upheavals of the English Revolution, the American Revolution, and the French Revolution. The end of the slave trade came only when the horrendous brutality of the Middle Passage and the treatment of several million human beings as mere property became so gruesome that it could no longer be ignored. The abolition of slavery and serfdom resulted only after traumatic civil and foreign wars. The advancement of economic and social rights first resulted from the monumental sufferings of men, women, and children exploited by the Industrial Revolution. The creation of the Red Cross and humanitarian law came in the wake of the agony of wounded soldiers in war.

This pattern proceeded with even greater force in the twentieth century. The innovative Minorities Treaties, extension of humanitarian law, the League of Nations, refugee assistance, and efforts to promote the right to health all came in the wake of suffering from World War I, the Bolshevik Revolution, and massive epidemics. Serious discussions about international standards of human rights resulted from the extraordinary atrocities perpetrated under totalitarian regimes, especially those of Stalin and Hitler. The experience of World War II and the unimagined destruction of human life in the Holocaust's "Final Solution" that exceeded all previously known bounds and finally tipped the scales. After this, individuals, NGOs, and the governments refused to remain silent in the face of large-scale violations of human rights by creating the United Nations and adopting the Universal Declaration of Human Rights. With the subsequent destruction of colonial empires in Asia and Africa, the determination to secure international human rights grew even stronger, resulting in a multiplicity of efforts to set standards, establish binding covenants and conventions, create implementation mechanisms, and promote and enhance human rights around the world. More recently, it was when "ethnic cleansing" in the former Yugoslavia and genocide in Rwanda became so brutal as to provoke global outrage that the International Criminal Court and the principle of the Responsibility to Protect emerged. In so many ways, then, human rights emerge in the wake of human wrongs.

One of the reasons these cause-and-effect relationships occur is that events such as revolutions and wars destroy existing structures of authority, privilege, and vested interests, thus making change possible. Violence and upheaval—whether they occur in Europe, North America, Latin America, Asia, Africa, the Middle East, or islands of the Pacific—tear away power from those unwilling to share it voluntarily. The consequence is a transformation of established institutions of control, whether they are political, military, diplomatic, economic, social, or cultural in nature. Upheaval, of course, always contains the potential danger of leading to merely reshaped forms of abuse. But it also can open up new possibilities to make changes only previously imagined in dreams. Due to their duration and extent, the two world wars of the twentieth century created revolutions in their own right, destroying monarchies, authoritarian and totalitarian regimes, social hierarchies, and empires, ultimately emancipating millions of men, women, and children around the world and launching a revolutionary movement on behalf of international human rights.

But events of consequence do much more than this, for they can change habits of thought and normative values as well. They force people, as we have seen constantly throughout this book, to ask how such developments, with all their tragedies and abuses, could have happened in the first place. This reevaluation can take them out of their previously accepted ways of thinking and into considering new possibilities of how things might actually be reconstructed in accordance with convictions about how the world ought to be. Sometimes these events provide dramatic reminders that cultural values in any society can themselves be the result of the particular interests of those with power seeking to benefit from the way that culture is defined, and therefore are not immutable. They also can break down barriers between the personal and the political and between the domestic and the international.[28] In this process, the visions themselves can be transformed. "It is always when the world is undergoing a metamorphosis, when certainties are collapsing, when the lines are becoming blurred," noted one practitioner with a wealth of experience, "that there is greatest recourse to fundamental reference points, that the quest for ethics becomes more urgent, that the will to achieve self-understanding becomes imperative."[29]

Upheavals compel those who survive them to test their assumptions and habits of thought, to acknowledge the limitations of the past, to seriously assess the legitimacy of existing authority and the purposes of government, and to consider the meaning of human rights. The revolutions of the seventeenth and eighteenth centuries, for example, raised questions about a first generation of human rights focused on civil and political rights. The socialist and Marxist revolutions of the nineteenth and first half of the twentieth centuries provoked discussions about a second generation of economic and social rights. World War II did much to radically transform the thinking of many women, racial minorities, and indigenous peoples from colonial empires who up to this point had been taught to think that they were somehow inferior and less-than-fully human. As Reverend Ndabaningi Sithole writes of the experience from Africa:

During the war the African came in contact with practically all the peoples of the earth. He met them on a life-and-death basis. He saw the so-called civilized and peaceful and orderly white people mercilessly butchering one another just as his so-called savage ancestors had done in tribal wars. He saw no difference between the primitive and the civilized man. In short, he saw through the European pretensions that only Africans were savages. This had a revolutionary psychological impact upon the African.[30]

The subsequent anticolonialist revolutions continued this evolving process by drawing attention to yet a third generation of human rights, concentrating on such collective rights as those of self-determination, economic and social development, and environmental health.[31]

Traumas and catastrophes, especially those caused by atrocities, also affect patterns of thought in still another, perhaps more powerful, way. That is, they often shockingly and painfully reveal just how cruel some people can be to other humans, and thereby change perceptions of human rights. Shackled men and women packed like cordwood on board slave ships, soldiers and civilians writhing in pain, floods of helpless refugees fleeing for their lives from persecution, bodies and minds mutilated by torture, unearthed graves of victims of summary executions, and mounds of corpses piled high as a result of genocide seize attention. Whether witnessed personally with horrifying directness or viewed through pen-and-ink drawings, photographs, the printed word, or digitalized images and sounds now sent instantaneously around the world by modern technology, these staggering scenes elicit empathy and make others realize that this could happen to them. They demonstrate perhaps as nothing else can the consequences of apathy, of ignoring abuses, or of allowing leaders to hide behind a shield of national sovereignty and behave completely as they wish. As such, they have the capacity to produce outrage and to force people to confront their thinking and their values.

For those sensitive to the dignity and worth of each life, the horror and pain of these disasters often brings them to transformative thresholds that take them from passivity to participation. They find their individual and collective conscience stirred at these points of unimagined cruelty to reconsider the meaning of justice, of freedom, of responsibility to others, and of being truly human. It is here that the "only" words and "mere" declarations of principle in visions of human rights find their greatest strength in drawing upon, articulating, and projecting moral force in the face of contrary traditions, prevailing assumptions, pressures from vested interests, and resistance aligned against them. Time and time again, those either eagerly or reluctantly involved with the evolution of international human rights have spoken about this feature of forces and events of consequence and their power to move what they have called "global moral opinion," stir "the conscience of mankind," and create "a revolution in the public mind" by eliciting empathy and then provoking outrage at the pain inflicted upon another human being—whether close to home or at another end of the earth.[32] As one activist describes that precise point of decision in his own experience:

My motivation fundamentally emerges from a religious perspective. Having been given life, I believe we are called to do things that edify life. . . . Human rights entered my vocabulary on 11 September 1973 when it was suddenly denied [by the dictatorship of Pinochet] to one-third of the Chilean population. That was a watershed. That defining moment has sustained my vision of what abuses of human rights are about. It has driven me.[33]

For those more interested in the exercise of political, military, or economic power than moral force, these catastrophes, interestingly enough, create a similar threshold of decision. Horrific and brutal events of consequence bring people to points of hard-headed calculations about the ultimate price to be paid for turning a blind eye to abuse in ways that routine circumstances simply do not. If states support human rights because of calculations that it is in their national interests to do so, not because of moral or legal arguments,[34] these are precisely the events that cause them to do so. Barbarous acts of genocide and the discovery of mass graves in another country, for example, force them to seriously calculate whether the danger might spread and place their own tenuous security at risk. Violent terrorist actions or military attacks against innocent civilians in other cities or villages make them consider whether their own peace is threatened. Floods of desperate refugees fleeing widespread persecution or torture across borders compel them to assess whether their own stability and economic prosperity are in jeopardy. In such critical cases as these, decision makers in otherwise diverse cultural traditions, forms of government, and levels of development may well reach the conclusion that they might or might not share a set of aspirations but certainly share a capacity to be harmed at the hands of those who grossly abuse others.[35] Crises, in other words, force them to consider that support of international human rights might well be in their own best interest.

Process, Politics, and Perspective

For these visions, people, forces, and events to combine in ways that advance human rights a process must occur. If we look carefully, it appears from historical evidence that when steps are deliberate, there must be movement across at least three critical, transformational thresholds. The first of these is crossing *from indifference or toleration to non-acceptance.* Sometimes like erosion over a long period, and other times like an earthquake at a precise instant, people exhibit empathy with victims and determine that certain behavior formerly regarded as normal is wrong and will no longer be accepted.[36] It is at these times of momentous shifts that they refer to "an aroused conscience," moral codes, normative values, "the conscience of mankind," and "the conscience of humanity." We have seen this with virtually every challenge to a long-standing abuse, from hereditary systems of inequality to absolute monarchies, from slavery to violence against women, from discrimination based on race to that of class, from the exploitation of workers or children to the conquest of indigenous peoples, from genocide to torture, and from the claims of national sovereignty to the culture of impunity. None of these problems just "faded away." Instead, they came to be widely seen as wrong, illegitimate, and, thus, no longer acceptable.

The second threshold is behavioral and entails crossing *from outrage to action.* Anger over an injustice, while a necessary beginning, is in and of itself not sufficient to advance human rights. The essential next step requires moving from passivity to participation and actually doing something to stop abuse.[37] We have seen this with virtually every effort to find remedy and protect victims, from speaking out and naming and shaming abusers, from articulating declarations of rights to creating laws to guarantee them, from negotiating conventions to establishing treaty-monitoring bodies and tribunals, and from providing humanitarian assistance to protecting refugees.

The third threshold is one of scope and involves crossing *from concern about one's own rights to the rights of someone else.* It is easy to understand why people would work for their own rights. To go beyond self-centeredness and interest requires, however, an infinitely broader stretch and sense of responsibility to protect others, including those beyond one's own borders. Activists who campaigned to abolish the slave trade, for example, focused on the rights of strangers not only of a different class and a different race but of a distant continent and ocean away.[38] Many other campaigners followed in their footsteps as they attempted to see visions of common humanity and integrate norms into a broader international society. Indeed, without this dimension, there would be no such thing as the evolution of international human rights.

But history and life do not always unfold in ways that are so deliberate. The dynamic evolution of international human rights has been—and continues to be—one of considerable complexity, involving interaction among visions, people, forces, and events in ever-changing and often unanticipated ways. Visions possess considerable power, but they differ widely, and are constantly subject to modification, and what is seen clearly by some may remain completely invisible to others. Those women and men and involved with human rights play absolutely critical roles, but they vary greatly in their personalities, motives, and methods ranging from moral persuasion to armed force. Although revolutions, wars, and upheavals provide often necessary conditions for change, they remain highly volatile and unpredictable. At the same time, paradoxes, ambiguities, and contradictions abound in that people and the very forces and events that advance human rights can seriously violate them as well.[39] Just as it is people who lie at the center of human rights visions and actions, for example, it is people who lie at the center of resistance to those rights and people who abuse.

For all these reasons, the evolutionary process most certainly has never been orderly, predictable, linear, self-evident, consistent, or teleologically pre-determined. There is no such thing as an "unbroken chain," a seamless web, or a direct, straight line of triumphal progress. Instead, there have been twists and turns, fits and starts, false starts, advances and setbacks, progressive movement and detours, changing arenas, ambiguities, intended and unintended consequences, agreements and controversies, contradictory patterns, complexities, and paradoxes, all enabled and constrained by local, national, regional, and international politics.

Political factors, as we have explored from the very beginning, play critical roles in the process of how human rights norms are established, whether they are translated and given publicity and thereby placed on a public agenda, how they are interpreted, how they are implemented, and whether or not they are taken seriously. Politics, for example, can explain much about the determined and long-standing opposition to human rights. Most of those with vested interests, power, and special privilege at stake fiercely resist sharing what they have with others and reject acknowledging that all people possess certain basic rights simply by being human. At the global level, this tendency also applies to those states adamantly unwilling to surrender the claims of national sovereignty or cultural uniqueness and refuse to allow the international community to pass judgment on their behavior or how they treat people under their control. This can be seen not only in the past but also in the abuses and double standards that persist today against exploited women and children, racial or religious minorities, the dispossessed and unpropertied, certain ethnic groups, and political prisoners, among others. Some governments use human rights as a flag of convenience to mask other agendas. Some confine themselves to symbolic gestures and lip service, refusing to ratify, and thus be bound by, the international treaty commitments. Others ratify treaties but in practice do not comply with their obligations or do so only selectively, claiming that special circumstances make them exempt from established norms. This has affected efforts in the past and will continue to do so, including whether the new Human Rights Council and its Universal Period Review process are taken seriously or not.

Given these features, it certainly is not surprising to hear many advocates of human rights despair over the heavy influence of politics. They accuse governments of being interested only in crass "political motivations" that use or abuse rights for self-serving advantages. They express their "disappointment and consternation" over the tendency of members of the United Nations to resort to weakened compromises of political expediency rather than determined stands of principle and to selectively apply standards by criticizing comparatively small countries while allowing the big and powerful to escape serious scrutiny. They condemn official representatives on international bodies as being no more than duplicitous "striped-pants dignitaries rather than people of substance," and criticize them for playing "a ping-pong game of diplomacy between nation-states" and creating no more than a "circus of hypocrisy and rhetoric." If only it were not for "politics," they argue, international human rights would be further advanced.[40]

These arguments are understandable, for political forces have often greatly hindered and seriously obstructed the evolution of international human rights. But to argue that politics is the very antithesis of human rights is to create a false duality, for it is also the case that the advances made in this evolution are the result of politics. Regardless of the motives—both the noble and the base—none of the many achievements discussed in this book would have taken place without the political forces, political discourse, and political will necessary to make them happen. The human rights provisions in the United Nations Charter, for example, would not be there if it had not been for the political influence wielded by the small- to medium-sized states and the NGOs, and the people they represented, gathered together at the San Francisco Conference. The Universal Declaration of Human Rights and the Helsinki Final Act never would have been negotiated and adopted without political determination. It took the political will of a new majority of states from Asia and Africa emerging from the decolonization revolution to finally break a protracted deadlock and create an array of international human rights covenants and conventions. Similarly, all the treaty mechanisms, special procedures, and tribunals, as well as the several regional human rights bodies and the International Criminal Court in existence today designed to enforce human rights norms, are the result of specific and serious political decisions.

But not all developments in this evolution of international human rights have been so deliberate or the result of willed achievement. Indeed, sometimes politics play strange tricks on the unsuspecting and produce unanticipated—and unwelcome—consequences. Those slave owners who signed the American Declaration of Independence with its language about "all men are created equal" and "endowed . . . with certain unalienable rights," for example, did so to be free from the British but had no intention of losing the source of their wealth or touching off a revolution of thinking about human bondage in the "land of liberty." Those who advocated human rights in the Atlantic Charter and then the Declaration of the United Nations during the course of World War II did so to encourage a military crusade against their enemies. It most certainly was not their intention to sow the seeds of the destruction of their own empires. But this was the result and it eventually and dramatically transformed the status of colonial possessions throughout the world. As one African nationalist writes,

During the war the Allied Powers taught the subject peoples (and millions of them!) that it was not right for Germany to dominate other nations. They taught the subjugated peoples to fight and die for freedom rather than live and be subjugated by Hitler. Here then is the paradox of history, that the Allied Powers . . . set in motion those powerful forces which are now liquidating, with equal effectiveness, European domination in Africa.[41]

At the same time, in drawing attention to the attitudes of racial superiority in Nazi Germany during the war, they did not intend to have their own words used against them to overthrow their domestic policies of segregation or discrimination in postwar peace. But this was the result. Sometimes moral purposes are advanced by amoral agendas. As one observer noted with reference to the landmark Nuremberg trial, it was "an angel born in a brothel."[42]

Similarly, at the time of the adoption of the Universal Declaration of Human Rights, many governments did everything they possibly could to make sure that it was not construed to mean any more than they originally intended. They made speeches in the General Assembly, held news conferences, and issued press releases to inform all who would listen that the proclaimed vision represented "only a declaration" and a "mere recommendation." They insisted that it was "simply" a general statement of principle and contained no legal obligations or binding commitments.[43] It thus came as a great surprise—and sometimes profound shock—to them when the Universal Declaration immediately began to take on an authority and normative character of its own, serving as a model for national constitutions, influencing court decisions, assuming the status of customary international law, inspiring new international legal instruments, and arousing critics at home and abroad to challenge their claims of national sovereignty and their own records on human rights. As the British Colonial Office noted bitterly: "The F.O [Foreign Office] in the early stages were so anxious to dish the Russians that they did not think ahead to all the implications for ourselves, especially in relation to the Colonies."[44]

This same pattern continued during the Cold War when the Soviet Union enthusiastically welcomed the surprise announcement that the United States would never sign any of the United Nations-sponsored treaties on human rights. Such a decision allowed the Soviets suddenly to present themselves as the only superpower who defended the exploited and championed human rights. In their enthusiasm, they energetically supported the right of self-determination for colonial peoples, gave enormous publicity to their support for the opponents of apartheid, and then agreed to sign human rights provisions of the Helsinki Final Act. They had no intention whatsoever of jeopardizing their own repressive government or iron-fisted control over their Eastern European satellites, but thought that they could keep these visions under control. But by giving such prominence to human rights for other purposes, Soviet authorities were oblivious to the fact they were giving legitimacy to dissidents who (together with other activists from abroad) could mobilize "watch groups" against them and creating a powerful force that helped to pull down not only their empire but their entire regime. As one official later conceded, such a result from the human rights provisions was "totally beyond the imagination of the Soviet leadership."[45]

Other governments also have found themselves surprised by politics and the consequences of their own rhetoric. By framing self-determination as a human right in the anti-colonial struggle, to illustrate, leaders of Asia, Africa, and the Middle East opened themselves up to criticism about violations of other dimensions of the Universal Declaration of Human Rights. In the same way, China eagerly threw itself into the struggle for the right to racial equality, the right to development, and rights for women and children. In the name of human rights it actively supported strong punitive measures against the "pariah regimes" of the white minority in South Africa for apartheid and of Israel for its suppression of the rights of the Palestinians in occupied territories. Yet, in doing so, the Chinese leaders unintentionally gave legitimacy to their own human rights activists such as Fang Lizhi and to international critics regarding the suppression of political expression at Tiananmen Square, the repression of the rights of Tibetans and Uighurs, and other abuses.[46] They thereby came to realize that when dealing with human rights, rhetoric can take on serious substance and "words can hurt you."[47]

By the same token, human rights activists also have had to learn that some of their well-intentioned efforts can produce unintended consequences as well. There are times when attempts to defend victims have made their situation even worse, at least in the short term. Support for the right of self-determination from colonial empires, for example, sometimes brought brutal autocrats into power in Africa and Asia. International pressure upon South Africa to end apartheid at first created not compliance but more determined resistance from the white minority regime. Efforts to remove the despotic Shah of Iran and his hated SAVAC secret police paved the way for the extremism of Ayatollah Khomeini. United Nations humanitarian intervention in Somalia and its disastrous results contributed significantly to the subsequent reluctance to intervene in Rwanda when genocide was rampant. NATO's action against Milosevic to defend Kosovars against "ethnic cleansing" initially increased Serbian atrocities rather than deterred them. Promotion of the rights of ethnic minorities sometimes created secessionist movements not at all adverse to using rebel armies or terrorism and abusing the rights of others. Similarly, sanctions against the regime of Saddam Hussein in the name of protecting human rights unintentionally harmed thousands of Iraqi women and children denied food and medical supplies.

The influences of politics on the evolution of international human rights and on its unintended consequences should come as no surprise at this stage. As we have seen, they always are present, influencing the creation and implementation of all human norms, institutions, organizations, and laws. These then generate their own political pressures in turn. The reason for this is that human rights relate to human beings not as they live their lives alone—but as they live their lives together with others. Indeed, it is precisely this existence of others in community that explains why rights and duties are not separate, but intimately and necessarily interrelated.

Human rights are embedded in some of the most profound of all political issues in the world. They challenge the authority of the state over its own people, attempt to impose defined limitations upon the arbitrary exercise of power, endeavor to eliminate special privileges, and seek to hold governments accountable to certain norms of behavior. Political forces play a significant role in creating the very context and space in which the terms and the scope of human rights can be discussed, defined, and applied. Most particularly, by means of debating competing claims and interests, determining relative priorities and making choices, creating and enforcing law, and allocating resources, politics largely determine how human rights will be implemented—not in some mythical or theoretical state of nature but in the practical and daily lives of people in society.[48] Thus, human rights can never "trump, or 'bypass," or "go beyond" politics due to the fact that they are so integrally intertwined and lie at the very heart of political communities. As one observer with a lifetime of experience in this field writes, "In a sense, nothing could be more political; and it would have been quite unreal had the great international debate on human rights not reflected the deep differences which divide nations and groups."[49]

All those who sought to advance the cause of human rights had to confront this fact of politics and then decide how to deal with the challenge of trying to reconcile moral ends with concrete circumstances and the strong possibility of having to make painful choices. Some saw the magnitude of the obstacles and in fear, frustration, disappointment, or exhaustion largely gave up, declaring the task to be "impractical," "naive," or "impossible," and withdrawing themselves into the margins of verbal complaint about the imperfections of the world. Others decided to confront abuses head-on in a frontal assault with action, regardless of the consequences, and refused to ever compromise or to be intimidated or seduced by what they regarded as the "impurity," "wickedness," and "evil" of politics. Still others determined to proceed as they could by taking progressive steps, recognizing limited means and accepting politics as the art of the possible, making accommodation with the constraints of the time and place when necessary, and approaching the ideal described by poet William Butler Yeats of holding "reality and justice in a single vision."[50] As such, they acknowledged that half a loaf might be considerably better than no bread at all. They believed that desirable measures should not be postponed or rejected simply because someday there might be agreement on a perfect and complete solution, but instead should be persistently taken one step at a time beginning with successes "in *some* matters, to *some* extent, for *some* people, against *some* organ of the State."[51]

This was precisely the position taken by members of the Society for Effecting the Abolition of the Slave Trade at the end of the eighteenth century. They determined that they should not let the pursuit of the excellent (the eradication of slavery) diminish the chances of achieving the good (the end of the African slave trade) by alienating those who might be willing to take one or more steps in the right direction.[52] In the same way, the National Society for Women's Suffrage in the nineteenth century insisted that "like stroke on stroke which eventually overthrows the largest forest tree, so these strokes, dealt week by week, year by year, will eventually overthrow all opposition to the accomplishment of the just object we have in view."[53]

Similarly, when Olusegun Obasanjo reflected upon the process that personally transformed him from a political prisoner to the president of Nigeria: "It's like constant drips of water on a stone. It seems to make little difference, but over time it does."[54] Another former prisoner of conscience, Julio de Peña Valdez of the Dominican Republic, testifies to the same phenomenon when describing the seemingly improbable impact of an Amnesty International letter-writing campaign on his behalf:

When the 200 letters came, the guards gave me back my clothes. Then the next 200 letters came and the prison director came to see me. When the next pile of letters arrived, the director got in touch with his superior. The letters kept coming and coming: 3,000 of them. The president was informed. The letters still kept arriving and the president called the prison and told them to let me go.[55]

Not all efforts produce such successes; but some do, and this process of gradual, incremental steps explains much about the entire evolution of international human rights itself.

Each of the many advances occurred only as the range of choice and complex circumstances of time and place permitted. Complexities and irregularities in the process, not surprisingly, led to complexities and irregularities in the results. Consequently, no step was complete or perfect, not even the great milestones of human rights successes. But each nevertheless marked a willingness to determine that certain ideas and behavior long taken for granted were no longer acceptable, to confront prejudice and abuse, to challenge power and authority, and to take action by raising the bar of normative standards and protecting victims, thereby demonstrating that change could, in fact, occur. To fully appreciate this evolution, it is necessary to bring a sense of historical perspective to bear and to measure human rights not against a perfectionist abstraction or simply the last few years but rather against the human condition over the last five centuries or more.

There is no lack of those who draw our attention to what *has not* been achieved. They focus on the shortcomings, the inconsistencies, the failures, and the imperfections of human rights. Their observations and arguments deserve thoughtful and careful consideration, especially when they remind us of the dangers of the gaps between norms and practice and of what still needs to be done. But by themselves they are insufficient and misleading, for they provide no balance and miss the critical perspective of what *has* been achieved.

For nearly the entirety of human history, almost all of those who lived and died never knew the meaning nor the enjoyment of human rights. During most times and in most places of the world, they found themselves facing one kind of abuse or another. They confronted various forms of discrimination and patterns of dominance based on gender, race, class or caste, religion, ethnicity, or some other form of difference that divided people from one another. They encountered traditional societies, cultures, and authoritarian or despotic regimes that emphasized hierarchical relationships, sharp divisions between the few rulers and the many ruled, stratification between the powerful and the weak, and the performance of obedience rather than the exercise of rights. Misogyny, racial prejudice, intolerance, segregation, torture, conquest, and human bondage in serfdom or slavery were accepted as the norm rather than the exception. Moreover, victims of these practices suffered under governments who confidently knew that how they treated those under their control would be regarded as *internal* matters exclusively within their own domestic jurisdiction and not at all subject to criticism from distant states. Over the course of centuries, the practices, institutions, and laws of international affairs thus created a culture of immunity, remained essentially silent on the subject of rights, and precluded victims from ever having recourse to any assistance beyond their own borders. For all practical purposes and throughout most of history, international human rights did not even exist.

Today, as a result of the extraordinary evolution discussed in this book, we live in a drastically different setting. Universal normative standards have been set with the active and essential participation of people from around the world representing different cultures, systems of government, and levels of development and power. Once-fundamental and nearly sacrosanct ideas and widely accepted practices have been significantly reconfigured and transformed. Nation-states no longer are the only actors or sources of power and influence in international relations. Claims of exclusive "national sovereignty" and what was firmly regarded as "essentially within the domestic jurisdiction of any state" insofar as abuses were concerned no longer carry the conviction, weight, or legitimacy that they did for centuries, for human rights now are regarded as vital to *external* affairs and subject to international scrutiny. In fact, during a recent conference of government representatives meeting on the subject of war crimes, one spokesman declared: "There is no longer any such thing as 'domestic affairs' when it comes to human rights."[56]

The extent of other concepts has not been eroded at all but greatly expanded and enhanced. One of these is the meaning of "security." For centuries this was interpreted narrowly and exclusively in terms of the territorial integrity of states. It no longer is. As a result of the history that we have explored, there is today a growing recognition of the multi-dimensional nature of security with intimately intertwined elements in what is described as "human security" and the "indivisibility of security."[57] That is, that *international* security, *national* security, and *individual* security are not mutually exclusive, but mutually reinforcing and actually dependent upon each other. Security increasingly is seen as directly linked to human rights in this way: one cannot have security without peace, one cannot have peace without justice, and one cannot have justice without respect for human rights.[58]

Dramatic expansion also has occurred with the meaning of "responsibility." In the past, responsibility for the well-being of others focused on the behavior of individuals. Through time, this expanded to include groups of various kinds, NGOs, and even for-profit transnational corporations. Today, it also encompasses the responsibility of nation-states themselves. National sovereignty, for example, increasingly is seen as conditional, or measured by how states meet their obligations to act in accordance with human rights norms accepted by the international community. This explains why the expression, "sovereignty as responsibility," is used to convey the principle that governments have an obligation to fulfill the rights of their people; and, if they fail to do so, they forfeit their sovereignty.[59] The human tragedies caused by such failures, in turn, explain the emergence of the whole concept of Responsibility to Protect, that collective sense of being responsible for protecting victims beyond one's own borders who are unable to protect themselves from repeated, systematic, and egregious human rights abuses.

Similar transformations have occurred with the language, definitions, and meanings of "human rights" themselves. They began in rudimentary ways with habits of the heart, simple beliefs, and without precise expression or articulation. Then, as we have seen, they have been named and framed in different ways, debated, contested, refracted through many lenses, addressed through competing approaches and schools of thought, and changed to accommodate a variety of aspirations or visions among people of different locations, political regimes, traditions, and cultures as circumstances permitted within particular historical contexts. They never have been "plain" human rights, static and "settled" once and for all, or an isolated and immutable block of theories, for changing developments always have created new possibilities for new kinds and levels of rights. This explains their remarkable expansion from the local level, where they began, to their present day range and global scope. It also accounts for how today's comprehensive and widely accepted concept of universal and indivisible human rights was built upon the evolution of sequential "generations" of rights emerging out of different settings: political and civil rights, economic and social rights, and communal or group rights, or the movement to address not just politically motivated abuses but those resulting from gender violence, social control, and economic exploitation. Moreover, as the question was asked through time about rights for whom, the circle of inclusion has been ever growing: from slaves to women, from workers to wounded soldiers, from the persecuted to the discriminated, from minorities to children, from the tortured to indigenous peoples, from the imprisoned to the silenced, from the trafficked to the poor in developing countries, from refugees to the "disappeared," from the exiled and deported to the internally displaced, from migrant workers to the disabled, and from child soldiers to victims of homophobia, among many others. As such, the very idea of human rights has been an integral part of the whole dynamic process of historical change in bringing the *is* closer to the *ought*. Eleanor Roosevelt described it as nothing short of "the measure of mankind's evolving ethical sense."[60]

This dynamic and dramatic evolution has included other seismic shifts as well. As a result of modern technological developments in an age of globalization, gross violations of rights thousands of miles away can no longer remain hidden for long and can be graphically revealed in facts, in images, and at speeds unparalleled in history. At the same time, a vast array of organizations, declarations, resolutions, judicial rulings, legally binding covenants and conventions, treaty-monitoring bodies, special procedures, technical assistance, hundreds of thousands of volunteer members of NGOs, and staffs of professional experts and civil servants are now devoted to promoting and protecting international human rights. The availability of these collective norms and continuous means provide states, groups, and individuals innumerable opportunities to issue complaints and file petitions, express aspirations, and seek practical protection for their rights or those of others. In the past, victims of human rights abuses had nowhere to run and nowhere to hide. Today, and especially as a result of the evolution of international criminal law, it is increasingly the abusers who discover that it is *they* who have nowhere to run and nowhere to hide.

Never before in history has there been what is now widely described as a "universal culture of human rights" in which the rights of so many men, women, and children are given so much attention in so many diverse places under the watchful eyes of the world and in which human rights is described as "the *lingua franca* of modern political discourse" and "the common language of humanity."[61] Never before have so many victims had so many opportunities to be empowered, to make their cases known to the world, or to seek and secure protection. Never before have there been so many democratic governments, or what is called the globalization of democracy, resulting from the *quintupling* in the number of democracies during the last half century.[62] Never before has the percentage of women able to vote, hold public office, be educated, or participate in civil society and the public sphere been higher Never before have states found their human rights records so subject to scrutiny or so often used as critical criteria for establishing legitimacy, for imposing sanctions, for initiating humanitarian intervention, or for securing military assistance, economic aid, or membership in regional or international bodies of great importance to them. Never before have human rights been such a part of the political, legal, and moral landscape, or played such an important role in world affairs as they do today. Indeed, Nelson Mandela—himself transformed from prisoner to president, hence dramatically able to see visions turn into reality—declared that "human rights have become the focal point of international relations."[63]

When one considers all the differences in the world and the formidable opposition faced all along the way, the magnitude of these remarkable achievements and the prominent role now played by human rights becomes all the more impressive. Phenomenal accomplishments have been realized and many visions have become reality. Indeed, many practices and protections of today would have seemed simply unbelievable to those campaigners of previous generations. While recognizing how far the world has come, of course, it essential to acknowledge how far it still has to go. Horrifying abuses occur, ranging from those at the local level known only to the victims who suffer to those that draw widespread international attention.[64] As such, there remains what has been called "the unfinished ethical agenda of our time" and "the unfinished revolution—the revolution of placing the human person squarely at the center of national and international values."[65]

Those who engage in this unfinished revolution ahead will undoubtedly find what those who have preceded them have always found: resistance, conflict, uncertainty, cynicism, and frustration caused by gaps between normative aspirations and behavioral reality. But if Aung San Suu Kyi who herself has suffered so much is correct, it is in our very nature as human beings to try to work through these problems by persisting in our search for improvement and redemption by seeing visions of societies free from want and fear.[66] After a lifetime of working to improve the human rights of others, and after many personal experiences with failures as well as with successes, Jane Addams reached exactly the same conclusion:

What after all has maintained the human race on this old globe despite all the calamities of nature and all the tragic failings of mankind, if not faith in new possibilities and courage to advocate them.[67]

In this endeavor and in the constant vigilance and courage that always will be required to protect the rights of all men, women, and children wherever they might be, the perspective of history may offer considerable hope not only for the future but also for the power of visions seen.

The Universal Declaration of Human Rights

PREAMBLE

Whereas recognition of the inherent dignity and of the equal and inalienable rights of all members of the human family is the foundation of freedom, justice, and peace in the world,

Whereas disregard and contempt for human rights have resulted in barbarous acts which have outraged the conscience of mankind, and the advent of a world in which human beings shall enjoy freedom of speech and belief and freedom from fear and want has been proclaimed as the highest aspiration of the common people,

Whereas it is essential, if man is not to be compelled to have recourse, as a last resort, to rebellion against tyranny and oppression, that human rights should be protected by the rule of law,

Whereas it is essential to promote the development of friendly relations between nations,

Whereas the peoples of the United Nations have in the Charter reaffirmed their faith in fundamental human rights, in the dignity and worth of the human person and in the equal rights of men and women and have determined to promote social progress and better standards of life in larger freedom,

Whereas Member States have pledged themselves to achieve, in cooperation with the United Nations, the promotion of universal respect for and observance of human rights and fundamental freedoms,

Whereas a common understanding of these rights and freedoms is of the greatest importance for the full realization of this pledge,

Now, therefore, The General Assembly,

Proclaims this Universal Declaration of Human Rights as a common standard of achievement for all peoples and all nations, to the end that every individual and every organ of society, keeping this Declaration constantly in mind, shall strive by teaching and education to promote respect for these rights and freedoms and by progressive measures, national and international, to secure their universal and effective recognition and observance, both among the peoples of Member States themselves and among the peoples of the territories under their jurisdiction.

ARTICLE 1
All human beings are born free and equal in dignity and rights. They are endowed with reason and conscience and should act towards one another in a spirit of brotherhood.

ARTICLE 2
1. Everyone is entitled to all the rights and freedoms set forth in this Declaration, without distinction of any kind, such as race, color, sex, language, religion, political or other opinion, national or social origin, property, birth, or status.
2. Furthermore, no distinction shall be made on the basis of the political, jurisdictional, or international status of the country or territory to which a person belongs, whether it be independent, trust, non-self-governing, or under any other limitation of sovereignty.

ARTICLE 3
Everyone has the right to life, liberty, and security of person.

ARTICLE 4
No one shall be held in slavery or servitude; slavery and the slave trade shall be prohibited in all their forms.

ARTICLE 5
No one shall be subjected to torture or to cruel, inhuman, or degrading treatment or punishment.

ARTICLE 6
Everyone has the right to recognition everywhere as a person before the law.

ARTICLE 7
All are equal before the law and are entitled without any discrimination to equal protection of the law. All are entitled to equal protection against any discrimination in violation of this Declaration and against any incitement to such discrimination.

ARTICLE 8
Everyone has the right to an effective remedy by the competent national tribunals for acts violating the fundamental rights granted him by the constitution or by law.

ARTICLE 9
No one shall be subjected to arbitrary arrest, detention, or exile.

Article 10
Everyone is entitled in full equality to a fair and public hearing by an independent and impartial tribunal, in the determination of his rights and obligations and of any criminal charge against him.

ARTICLE 11
1. Everyone charged with a penal offense has the right to be presumed innocent until proven guilty according to law in a public trial at which he has had all the guarantees necessary for his defense.
2. No one shall be held guilty of any penal offense on account of any act or omission which did not constitute a penal offense, under national or international law, at the time when it was committed. Nor shall a heavier penalty be imposed than the one that was applicable at the time the penal offense was committed.

ARTICLE 12
No one shall be subjected to arbitrary interference with his privacy, family, home, or correspondence, nor to attacks upon his honor and reputation. Everyone has the right to the protection of the law against such interference or attacks.

ARTICLE 13
1. Everyone has the right to freedom of movement and residence within the borders of each state.
2. Everyone has the right to leave any country, including his own, and to return to his country.

ARTICLE 14
1. Everyone has the right to seek and to enjoy in other countries asylum from persecution.
2. This right may not be invoked in the case of prosecutions genuinely arising from non-political crimes or from acts contrary to the purposes and principles of the United Nations.

ARTICLE 15
1. Everyone has the right to a nationality.
2. No one shall be arbitrarily deprived of his nationality nor denied the right to change his nationality.

ARTICLE 16
1. Men and women of full age, without any limitation due to race, nationality, or religion, have the right to marry and to found a family. They are entitled to equal rights as to marriage, during marriage, and at its dissolution.

2. Marriage shall be entered into only with the free and full consent of the intending spouses.

3. The family is the natural and fundamental group unit of society and is entitled to protection by society and the State.

ARTICLE 17

1. Everyone has the right to own property alone as well as in association with others.
2. No one shall be arbitrarily deprived of his property.

ARTICLE 18

Everyone has the right to freedom of thought, conscience, and religion; this right includes freedom to change his religion or belief, and freedom, either alone or in community with others and in public or private, to manifest his religion or belief in teaching, practice, worship, and observance.

ARTICLE 19

Everyone has the right to freedom of opinion and expression; this right includes freedom to hold opinions without interference and to seek, receive, and impart information and ideas through any media and regardless of frontiers.

ARTICLE 20

1. Everyone has the right to freedom of peaceful assembly and association.
2. No one may be compelled to belong to an association.

ARTICLE 21

1. Everyone has the right to take part in the government of his country, directly or through freely chosen representatives.
2. Everyone has the right of equal access to public service in his country.
3. The will of the people shall be the basis of the authority of government; this will shall be expressed in periodic and genuine elections which shall be by universal and equal suffrage and shall be held by secret vote or by equivalent voting procedures.

ARTICLE 22

Everyone, as a member of society, has the right to social security and is entitled to realization, through national effort and international cooperation and in accordance with the organization and resources of each State, of the economic, social, and cultural rights indispensable for his dignity and the free development of his personality.

ARTICLE 23

1. Everyone has the right to work, to free choice of employment, to just and favorable conditions of work and to protection against unemployment.
2. Everyone, without any discrimination, has the right to equal pay for equal work.
3. Everyone who works has the right to just and favorable remuneration ensuring for

himself and his family an existence worthy of human dignity, and supplemented, if necessary, by other means of social protection.

4. Everyone has the right to form and to join trade unions for the protection of his interests.

ARTICLE 24

Everyone has the right to rest and leisure, including reasonable limitation of working hours and periodic holidays with pay.

ARTICLE 25

1. Everyone has the right to a standard of living adequate for the health and well-being of himself and of his family, including food, clothing, housing, and medical care and necessary social services, and the right to security in the event of unemployment, sickness, disability, widowhood, old age, or other lack of livelihood in circumstances beyond his control.

2. Motherhood and childhood are entitled to special care and assistance. All children, whether born in or out of wedlock, shall enjoy the same social protection.

ARTICLE 26

1. Everyone has the right to education. Education shall be free, at least in the elementary and fundamental stages. Elementary education shall be compulsory. Technical and professional education shall be made generally available and higher education shall be equally accessible to all on the basis of merit.

2. Education shall be directed to the full development of the human personality and to the strengthening of respect for human rights and fundamental freedoms. It shall promote understanding, tolerance and friendship among all nations, racial or religious groups, and shall further the activities of the United Nations for the maintenance of peace.

3. Parents have a prior right to choose the kind of education that shall be given to their children.

ARTICLE 27

1. Everyone has the right to freely participate in the cultural life of the community, to enjoy the arts, and to share in scientific advancement and its benefits.

2. Everyone has the right to protection of the moral and material interests resulting from any scientific, literary, or artistic production of which he is the author.

ARTICLE 28

Everyone is entitled to a social and international order in which the rights and freedoms set forth in this Declaration can be fully realized.

ARTICLE 29

1. Everyone has duties to the community in which alone the free and full development of his personality is possible.

2. In the exercise of his rights and freedoms, everyone shall be subject only to such limitations as are determined by law solely for the purpose of securing due recognition and respect for the rights and freedoms of others and of meeting the just requirements of morality, public order, and the general welfare in a democratic society.
3. These rights and freedoms may in no case be exercised contrary to the purposes and principles of the United Nations.

ARTICLE 30
Nothing in this Declaration may be interpreted as implying for any State, group, or person any right to engage in any activity or to perform any act aimed at the destruction of any of the rights and freedoms set forth herein.

Notes

Introduction: Visions and Visionaries

1. Universal Declaration of Human Rights, Preamble.
2. Zbigniew Brzezinski, *The Grand Failure* (New York: Collier, 1960), p. 256.
3. Jan Mårtenson, in Asbjørn Eide (ed.), *The Universal Declaration of Human Rights* (Oslo: Scandinavian University Press, 1992), p. 27. See also Jack Donnelly, "Relativity and the Universal Declaration," in U.S. Department of State, *eJournalUSA* 13 (November 2008): 33–37.
4. Michael Ignatieff, *The Warrior's Honor* (New York: Metropolitan, 1997), p. 8.
5. Johannes Morsink, *Inherent Human Rights* (Philadelphia: University of Pennsylvania Press, 2009), p. 1.

Chapter 1. Visions and the Birth of Human Rights

1. Veda, as cited in S. S. Subramuniyaswami, *Dancing with iva* (Concord, Calif.: Himalayan Academy, 1993), p. 195. Also see Arvind Sharma, *Hinduism and Human Rights* (New Delhi: Oxford University Press, 2004).
2. Genesis 4:9.
3. See Milton Konvitz, *Judaism and Human Rights* (New York: Transaction, 2001); Rabbis for Human Rights at www.rhr.israel.net.
4. Leviticus 9:13, 15, 18.
5. Isaiah 58:6–7; 42:1. See also the books of Amos and Micah.
6. Martin Buber, as cited in Norman Glazer (ed.), *The Way of Response* (New York: Schocken, 1966), p. 86.
7. Buddha, as cited in "Disappearance of Buddhism," *Observer of Business and Politics*, 8 August 1993.
8. Tenzin Gyatso, *Ocean of Wisdom* (Santa Fe, N.M.: Clear Light, 1989), p. 13. Also see L. P. N. Perera, *Buddhism and Human Rights* (Columbo: Karunaratne, 1991).
9. Confucius, as cited in H. G. Creel, *Confucius* (New York: Day, 1949), p. 150. Specialists debate whether Confucianism should be regarded as a philosophy or as a religion.
10. *The Analects*, XV, 23.
11. *Great Learning*, as cited in Huston Smith, *The Religions of Man* (New York: Harper & Row, 1958), p. 181.
12. Luke 10:29–37 (my emphasis).
13. Colossians 13:12; Galatians 3:28.
14. Smith, *The Religions of Man*, p. 249. See also Ann Elizabeth Mayer, *Islam and Human Rights* (Boulder, Colo.: Westview, 2006); Mahmood Monshipouri, "Islamic Thinking and the Internationalization of Human Rights," *Muslim World* (July–October 1994): 217–39.
15. Michael Perry, *The Idea of Human Rights* (New York: Oxford University Press, 1998), pp. 11–41.

16. Stanley Hoffmann, *Duties Beyond Borders* (Syracuse, N.Y.: Syracuse University Press, 1981).

17. Mohandas Gandhi, as cited in UNESCO, *The Birthright of Man* (Paris: UNESCO, 1969), p. 24. See also Robert Traer, *Faith in Human Rights* (Washington, D.C.: Georgetown University Press, 1991), p. 187.

18. Mo Zi, as cited in Henri Maspero, *La Chine antique* (Paris: PUF, 1927), pp. 253–54.

19. Mencius, as cited in Irene Bloom, "Fundamental Intuitions and Consensus Statements," in Wm. Theodore de Bary and Tu Weiming (eds.), *Confucianism and Human Rights* (New York: Columbia University Press, 1998), pp. 101–2.

20. Mencius, as cited in "Evolution of Human Rights," *Weekly Bulletin of the United Nations*, 12 August 1946. This was recited by Chinese students in Tiananmen Square in 1989.

21. Xun Zi (Hsün-tzu), as cited in UNESCO, *Birthright of Man*, p. 303.

22. Precepts for Merikare, third millennium B.C., as cited in ibid., p. 301.

23. Cited in P. Modinos, "La Charte de la liberté de l'Europe," *Revue des Droits de l'Homme* 8 (1975): 677.

24. Hammurabi, as cited in J. Roberts, *History of the World* (New York: Knopf, 1976), p. 48.

25. See www.farsinet.com/cyrus.

26. As cited in Christian Daubie, "Cyrus le Grand: Un précurseur dans le domain des droits de l'homme," *Revue des Droits de l'Homme* 5 (1972): 304.

27. See Sultanhussein Tabandeh, *A Muslim Commentary on the Universal Declaration of Human Rights* (London: Goulding, 1970), p. 5.

28. Āpastamba-Dharmasūtra II, 450–350 B.C., as cited in UNESCO, *Birthright of Man*, p. 94.

29. Micheline Ishay, *The History of Human Rights* (Berkeley: University of California Press, 2008), pp. 29, 36–37, 49–50.

30. Asvaghosa, as cited in UNESCO, *Birthright of Man*, p. 268.

31. Pampa, as cited in ibid., p. 508.

32. "Spirit of Sacrifice Ennobles Man," *Hindu Times*, 22 January 1977.

33. See the Iroquois Constitution at www.indigenouspeople.net; Donald Grinde, Jr., and Bruce Johnsen, *Exemplar of Liberty* (Los Angeles: American Indian Study Center, 1991).

34. See Robert Taylor (ed.), *The Idea of Freedom in Asia and Africa* (Stanford, Calif.: Stanford University Press, 2002); Abdullahi An-Na'im and Francis Deng (eds.), *Human Rights in Africa* (Washington, D.C.: Brookings Institution, 1990); Iba Der Thiam, "Human Rights in African Cultural Traditions," *Human Rights Teaching* 3 (1982): 4–10.

35. As cited in UNESCO, *Birthright of Man*, pp. 43, 269, 189.

36. A. H. Robertson and J. G. Merrills, *Human Rights in the World* (Manchester: Manchester University Press, 1992), p. 9.

37. Alan Rosenbaum (ed.), *The Philosophy of Human Rights* (Westport, Conn.: Greenwood, 1980), pp. 9–10.

38. Sophocles, *Antigone*, lines 453–57.

39. Marcus Tullius Cicero, *De Re Publica* (New York: Putnam, 1928), book 3, 22, p. 211.

40. Marcus Tullius Cicero, *De Legibus* (New York: Putnam, 1928), book 1, 43, pp. 345.

41. *Justinian's Institutes*, Peter Birks and Grant McLeod (trans.) (Ithaca, N.Y.: Cornell University Press, 1987), p. 37.

42. Magna Carta, in William Stubbs, *Select Charters* (Oxford: Clarendon Press, 1921), pp. 294ff.

43. See John Headley, *The Europeanization of the World* (Princeton, N.J.: Princeton University Press, 2007).

44. Christine de Pizan, *The Book of the City of Ladies*, Sarah Lawson (trans.) (New York: Penguin, 2003).

45. The impact of the printing press on human rights around the world is conveyed by a fascinating statue of Johannes Gutenberg in the city square of Strasbourg, France.

46. Jan Hus, 1415, as cited in H. Gordon Skilling, *Charter 77 and Human Rights in Czechoslovakia* (London: Allen & Unwin, 1981), epigraph.

47. Erasmus of Rotterdam, as cited in Mark Kishlansky et al., *Civilization in the West* (New York: HarperCollins, 1995), p. 392.

48. For a broad discussion see Richard Tuck, *Natural Rights Theories* (1979; Cambridge: Cambridge University Press, 1998); Brian Tierney, *The Idea of Natural Rights* (Atlanta: Scholars Press, 1997); Knud Haakonssen, *Natural Law and Moral Philosophy* (Cambridge: Cambridge University Press, 1996).

49. Peter Zarrow, "Citizenship and Human Rights in Early Twentieth Century Chinese Thought," in de Bary and Tu, *Confucianism and Human Rights*, pp. 209–33.

50. I am grateful to J. Herman Burgers for this citation of the 1581 Dutch Act of Abjuration.

51. G. E. Aylmer, *The Struggle for the Constitution* (London: Blandford, 1975), pp. 132–36.

52. Bill of Rights, in Walter Laqueur and Barry Rubin (eds.), *The Human Rights Reader* (New York: Meridian, 1989), pp. 104–6. See also Bernard Schwartz, *The Roots of Freedom* (New York: Hill & Wang, 1967).

53. John Locke, as cited in Richard Ashcroft, "Religion and Lockean Natural Rights," in Irene Bloom et al. (eds.), *Religious Diversity and Human Rights* (New York: Columbia University Press, 1996), p. 199.

54. John Locke, *Two Treatises of Government* (New York: Hafner Library of Classics, 1947), pp. 124, 128, 163.

55. Jean-Jacques Rousseau, *Contrat social, ou Principe du droit politique* (Paris: Garnier, 1900), p. 236.

56. Immanuel Kant, *Grundegung zur Metaphysik der Sitten* (Riga: Hartknoch, 1785).

57. Immanuel Kant, *Perpetual Peace and Other Essays*, Ted Humphrey (trans.) (Indianapolis: Hackett, 1983), p. 119.

58. Francis Hutcheson, as cited in Gary Wills, *Inventing America* (New York: Vintage, 1979), p. 216.

59. As cited in Stanley Chodorow et al., *The Mainstream of Civilization* (Fort Worth: Harcourt Brace, 1994), p. 547.

60. Denis Diderot and Jean Le Rond d'Alembert (eds.), *L'Encyclopédie*, as cited in Lynn Hunt, *The French Revolution and Human Rights* (Boston: Bedford, 1996), p. 37.

61. Cesare Beccaria, *On Crimes and Punishments*, David Young (trans.) (Indianapolis: Hackett, 1986, p. 23.

62. Maurice Cranston, as cited in Burns Weston, "Human Rights," in Richard Pierre Claude and Burns Weston, *Human Rights in the World Community*, 2nd ed. (Philadelphia: University of Pennsylvania Press, 1992), p. 16.

63. Abigail Adams to John Adams, 31 March 1776, as cited in Diane Ravitch and Abigail Thernstrom (eds.), *The Democracy Reader* (New York: HarperCollins, 1992), p. 104.

64. Thomas Jefferson, as cited in J. P. Foley (ed.), *The Jefferson Cyclopedia*, 2 vols. (New York: Russell and Russell, 1967), 2: 609.

65. "The Virginia Bill of Rights, 1776," in Benjamin Poore, *Federal and State Constitutions*, 2 vols. (New York: Franklin, 1972), 2:1908–1909.

66. Declaration of Independence, 4 July 1776, in John Garraty, *The American Nation*, 2 vols. (New York: HarperCollins, 1991), 2:A-1.

67. See James MacGregor Burns and Stewart Burns, *The Pursuit of Rights in America* (New York: Vintage, 1993), p. 41; Michael Zuckert, *The Natural Rights Republic* (South Bend, Ind.: University of Notre Dame Press, 1999).

68. Thomas Jefferson to James Madison, 20 December 1787, in P. L. Ford (ed.), *The Writings of Thomas Jefferson*, 10 vols. (New York: Putnam, 1892–1899), 4:477.

69. Duke Mathieu de Montmorency, 1 August 1789, as cited in Hunt, *The French Revolution and Human Rights*, pp. 73–74.

70. Stéphane Rials, *La Déclaration des droits de l'homme et du citoyen* (Paris: Hachette, 1989).

71. Lord Acton, as cited in Robertson and Merrills, *Human Rights in the World*, p. 4.

72. Frede Castberg, "Natural Law and Human Rights," in Asbjørn Eide and August Schou (eds.), *International Protection of Human Rights* (Stockholm: Almquist & Wiksell, 1968), p. 19. See also Stephen Marks, "From the 'Single Confused Page,'" *Human Rights Quarterly* 20 (1998): 459–514.

73. On this important point of the "demonstration effect," see Richard P. Claude, "The Classical Model of Human Rights Development," in Richard P. Claude (ed.), *Comparative Human Rights* (Baltimore: Johns Hopkins University Press, 1976), p. 23.

74. Déclaration des droits de la femme et de la citoyenne, 1791, in Olympe de Gouges (Marie Gouze), *Œuvres* (Paris: Mercure de France, 1986), pp. 99–112. See also Françoise Thébaud, "La Première féministe milite," *Historia* (January 2000): 62–65.

75. Leonard Levy, *Origins of the Bill of Rights* (New Haven, Conn.: Yale University Press, 2001).

76. "Federalist Paper No. 10," in Alexander Hamilton, James Madison, and John Jay, *The Federalist Papers* (New York: New American Library, 1961), p. 78.

77. Thomas Paine, *Rights of Man* (New York: Heritage Press, 1961), pp. 18, 39, 114.

78. See Lynn Hunt, *Inventing Human Rights* (New York: Norton, 2007), pp. 22–26.

79. This account is from Burns and Burns, *The Pursuit of Rights in America*, p. 71.

80. See John Keane, *Tom Paine, A Political Life* (Boston: Little Brown, 1995), pp. 335–36; Craig Nelson, *Thomas Paine* (New York: Viking, 2006), p. 228.

81. James Madison, as cited in Nelson, *Thomas Paine*, p. 284.

82. Edmund Burke, *Reflections on the Revolution in France* (Chicago: Regnery, 1955), pp. 64, 87, 90, 96, 201.

83. Ibid., pp. 313, 341; Edmund Burke, as cited in Weston, "Human Rights," p. 16.

84. Jeremy Bentham, "Nonsense upon Silts," in *The Collected Works of Jeremy Bentham*, Philip Schofield et al. (eds.) (Oxford: Clarendon Press, 2002), p. 330.

85. Thomas Hobbes, *Leviathan* (New York: Washington Square Press, 1964), pp. 84–85.

86. Ibid, pp. 120–28.

87. See Kenneth Lockridge, *On the Sources of Patriarchal Rage* (New York: New York University Press, 1992); Felicity Nussbaum, *The Brink of All We Hate* (Lexington: University Press of Kentucky, 1984); Carole Pateman, *The Sexual Contract* (Stanford, Calif.: Stanford University Press, 1988).

88. Confucius, as cited in Kumari Jayawardena, *Feminism and Nationalism in the Third World* (London: Zed, 1986), p. 167.

89. Jacob Sprenger, *Malleus Maleficarum*, as cited in Eva Figes, *Patriarchal Attitudes* (London: Faber & Faber, 1970), pp. 62–63.

90. Among many examples, see the *Kalevala*, Elias Lönnrot (comp. and ed.) (Oxford: Oxford University Press, 1999), p. 45.

91. For more discussion, see Paul Gordon Lauren, *Power and Prejudice* (San Francisco: Westview/HarperCollins, 1996), chapter 1.

92. See André Thevet, *Cosmographie universelle* (Paris: Huilier, 1575), p. 67.

93. Bartholomé de Las Casas, *In Defense of the Indians*, Stafford Poole (trans. and ed.) (DeKalb: Northern Illinois University Press, 1974), p. 362. See also "Las Casas protecteur des Indiens, défenseur des droits de l'homme," *Revue historique* 589 (1994): 51ff.; Paolo Carozza, "From Conquest to Constitutions: Retrieving a Latin American Tradition of the Idea of Human Rights," *Human Rights Quarterly* 25 (2003): 281–313.

94. J. H. Parry, *The Spanish Seaborne Empire* (New York: Knopf, 1966), p. 150.

95. Lauren, *Power and Prejudice*, chap.1; Winthrop Jordan, *White over Black* (Chapel Hill: University of North Carolina Press, 1968), p. 80.

96. See David Brion Davis, *Inhuman Bondage* (New York: Oxford University Press, 2006); James Watson (ed.), *Asian and African Systems of Slavery* (Berkeley: University of California Press, 1980); Orlando Patterson, *Slavery and Social Death* (Cambridge, Mass.: Harvard University Press, 1982).

97. As cited in Magnus Morner, *Race Mixture in the History of Latin America* (Boston: Little, Brown, 1967), p. 47.

98. Harley Ross Hammond, "Race, Social Mobility, and Politics in Brazil," *Race* 4 (1963): 4.

99. "The Fundamental Constitutions of 1669," in Poore, *The Federal and State Constitutions*, 2:1408.

100. Burke, *Reflections on the Revolution in France*, pp. 115, 344.

101. See Burns and Burns, *The Pursuit of Rights in America*, pp. 79–92; Thomas Horne, *Property Rights and Poverty* (Chapel Hill: University of North Carolina Press, 1990).

102. Locke, *Two Treatises of Government*, p. 184.

103. Jean-Jacques Rousseau, *A Discourse on Political Economy*, in *The Social Contract and Discourses* (New York: Dutton, 1950), p. 311.

104. See the discussion of property rights in Noel Coulson, "The State and the Individual in Islamic Law," *International and Comparative Law Quarterly* 6 (1957): 49–60.

105. Jean Bodin, *Les six livres de la République*, 6 vols. (Paris: Fayard, 1986), 1:179–228, 295–310.

106. Hobbes, *Leviathan*, pp. 120–28.

107. Hans Morgenthau, *Politics Among Nations* (New York: Knopf, 1978), p. 315. See also René Brunet, *La Garantie internationale des droits de l'homme* (Geneva: Grasset, 1947), pp. 29ff.

108. To the extent that states had any international legal obligations relating to individuals, these were only deemed to be owed to other states and arose either from agreements involving the treatment of foreign nationals or of certain religious groups.

109. Thucydides, *The Peloponnesian War* (New York: Random House, 1951), p. 331.

110. William Graham Sumner, *The Forgotten Man and Other Essays*, Albert Keller (ed.) (New Haven, Conn.: Yale University Press, 1919), p. 470.

111. Adam Smith, *Lectures on Jurisprudence*, R L. Meek et al. (eds.) (Oxford: Oxford University Press, 1978), p. 187.

112. "Board of Trade to the Governors of the English Colonies," 17 April 1708, in Elizabeth Donnan (ed.), *Documents Illustrative of the History of the Slave Trade to America*, 4 vols. (Washington, D.C.: Carnegie Institution, 1930–35), 2:45.

113. Adam Hochschild, *Bury the Chains* (Boston: Houghton Mifflin, 2005), p. 3.

114. David Brion Davis, *Slavery and Human Progress* (New York: Oxford University Press, 1984), pp. xvii, 51; James Walvin, *Black Ivory* (London: Wiley-Blackwell, 2001).

115. Jean-Jacques Rousseau, *Émile* (Paris: Garnier, 1964).

116. Baron de Montesquieu, *De l'esprit des lois*, book 12, chap. 2, in *Œuvres complètes*, 3 vols. (Paris: Hachette, 1908), 2:15.

117. Voltaire, as cited in William Cohen, *The French Encounter with Africans* (Bloomington: University of Indiana Press, 1980), pp. 88, 133, 137.

118. David Hume, "Of National Characters," in *The Philosophical Works*, 4 vols., T. Green and T. Grose (eds.) (London: Longmans, Green, 1882–1886), 3:252n.

119. Johann Friedrich Blumenbach, *On the Natural Varieties of Mankind* (1775; New York: Bergman, 1969), pp. 209, 264, 269.

120. Micheline Ishay, *The Human Rights Reader* (New York: Routledge, 2007), is particularly good at raising this question.

121. Hunt, *Inventing Human Rights*, p. 20.

122. Condorcet, "Sur l'admission des femmes au droit de cité," *Journal de la Société de 1789* V (3 July 1790): 2.

123. Thomas Paine, *The American Crisis*, in *Thomas Paine, Collected Writings* (New York: Library of American, 1995), p. 91.

124. See Jan Lewis, "'Of Every Age, Sex, and Condition': The Representation of Women in the Constitution," *Journal of the Early American Republic* 15 (Fall 1995): 368; Burns and Burns, *The Pursuit of Rights in America*, pp. 60–61.

125. Citations in Ronald Wright, *Stolen Continents* (Boston: Houghton Mifflin, 1992), pp. 116, 126, and 139; Richard Drinnon, *Facing West* (New York: Schocken, 1990), 98; David Stannard, *American Holocaust* (New York: Oxford University Press, 1992), p. 120.

126. Yves Bénot and Marcel Dorigny (eds.), *Rétablissement de l'esclavage dans les colonies françaises* (Paris: Maisonneuve et Larose, 2003).

127. Marcel Garaud, *La Révolution et l'égalité civile* (Paris: Sirey, 1953).

128. See Richard Schifter, "Human Rights Day, 1989," U.S. Department of State, *Current Policy* 1242 (1989): 2.

129. Abigail Adams to John Adams, 31 March 1776, as cited in Ravitch and Thernstrom (eds.), *The Democracy Reader*, p. 104.

130. Mary Wollstonecraft, *A Vindication of the Rights of Woman* (New York: Norton, 1988).

131. E. P. Thompson, *The Making of the English Working Class* (New York: Pantheon, 1964), p. 163.

132. See Christopher Leslie Brown, *Moral Capital* (Chapel Hill: University of North Carolina Press, 2006).

133. As cited in Claudius Fergus, "War, Revolution, and Abolitionism," in Heather Cateau and S. H. Carrington, *Capitalism and Slavery Fifty Years Later* (New York: Lang, 2000), p. 180.

134. Jeremy Bentham, "Emancipate Your Colonies!" in *The Collected Works of Jeremy Bentham*, p. 292.

135. Patrick Henry, as cited in *OAH Magazine of History* (Spring 1995): 40.

136. See Isaiah 61:1 and Luke 4:18.

137. Roger Bruns (ed.), *Am I Not a Man and a Brother* (New York: Chelsea House, 1983); Davis, *Slavery and Human Progress*, pp. 107–153, are good on this religious motivation.

138. Anthony Benezet, as cited in George Mellor, *British Imperial Trusteeship, 1783–1850* (London: Faber & Faber, 1951), p. 32.

139. London Revolution Society, 2 September 1792, as cited in ibid., p. 22.

140. James Beattie, *Elements of Moral Science*, 2 vols. (Edinburgh: Creech, 1793), 2:164.

141. See Prince Hoare, *Memoirs of Granville Sharp* (London: Colburn,1820), pp. 244 and 237n. See also the discussion in Hochschild, *Bury the Chains*, pp. 78–82.

142. Hochschild, *Bury the Chains*, p. 97.

143. Petition of New Hampshire Slaves, 12 November 1779, as cited in *OAH Magazine of History* (Spring 1995), p. 39.

144. Olaudah Equiano, *The Interesting Narrative and Other Writings*, Vincent Carretta (ed.) (New York: Penguin, 2003), p. 333 (citing a published letter of 5 February 1788), 51. See also Vincent Carretta, *Equiano, the African* (New York: Penguin, 2006).

145. Ibid., p. 101.

146. Hunt, *Inventing Human Rights*, pp. 35–69 is particularly insightful on this point.

147. Madame de Gasparin, as cited in Pierre Boissier, *From Solferino to Tsushima* (Geneva: Dunant Institute, 1985), p. 344.

148. R. H. Tawney, *The Agrarian Problem in the Sixteenth Century* (New York: Longmans Green, 1912), p. 44.

Chapter 2. Early International Efforts

1. Hochschild, *Bury the Chains*, p. 2.

2. Seymour Drescher, *Capitalism and Antislavery* (New York: Oxford University Press, 1987), p. x.

3. Thomas Branagan, as cited in Dwight Dumond, *Antislavery* (New York: Norton, 1966), p. 81.

4. Samuel Taylor Coleridge, as cited in Ellen Gibson Wilson, *Thomas Clarkson* (New York: St. Martin's, 1990), p. 1.

5. Hochschild, *Bury the Chains*, pp. 112–13.

6. Britain, Parliament, *Substance of the Debates on a Resolution for Abolishing the Slave Trade* (London: Phillips and Fardon, 1806), especially pp. 99–101, 146, 149, 168, 202–10.

7. Thomas Jefferson, 2 December 1806, in James D. Richardson (ed.), *A Compilation of the Messages and Papers of the Presidents*, 10 vols. (Washington, D.C.: Government Printing Office, 1896–1899), 1:408.

8. Act to Prohibit the Importation of Slaves, 2 March 1807, in U.S. Congress, *Annals of Congress*, 9th Congress, 2nd Session (Washington, D.C.: Gales and Seaton, 1852), pp. 1266–70; Act for the Prohibition of the Slave Trade, 25 March 1807, in Elizabeth Donnan (ed.), *Documents Illustrative of the History of the Slave Trade*, 4 vols. (Washington, D.C.: Carnegie Institution, 1930–1935), 2:659–69.

9. Hochschild, *Bury the Chains*, p. 307.

10. See Paolo Carozza, "From Conquest to Constitutions: Retrieving a Latin American Tradition of the Idea of Human Rights," *Human Rights Quarterly* 25 (May 2003): 281–313.

11. This point will be presented in more detail when discussing the Paris Peace Conference of 1919 and the San Francisco Conference of 1945.

12. See the discussion in Betty Fladeland, "Abolitionist Pressures on the Concert of Europe, 1814–1822," *Journal of Modern History* 38 (December 1966): 355–60; Drescher, *Capitalism and Anti-Slavery*, pp. 93–94.

13. Lord Castlereagh, as cited in F. J. Klingberg, *The Anti-Slavery Movement in England* (New Haven, Conn.: Yale University Press, 1926), p. 144.

14. "Déclaration des 8 cours, relative à l'abolition universelle de la traité des nègres," 8 February 1815, in Great Britain, Foreign Office, *British and Foreign State Papers, 1815–1816*, 3:971–72.

15. Great Britain, Public Record Office, Foreign Office (hereafter cited as Britain, PRO/FO) 92/30, "Traité défintif entre Grande Bretagne et la France," 20 November 1815.

16. "Treaty of Peace and Amity," 18 February 1815, in U.S. Department of State, *Treaties and Other International Agreements of the United States*, Charles Bevans (comp.), 12 vols. (Washington, D.C.: Government Printing Office, 1974), 12:47.

17. See Betty Fladeland, *Men and Brothers* (Urbana: University of Illinois Press, 1972); the various publications of the British and Foreign Anti-Slavery Society.

18. Matthew Mason, "Keeping Up Appearances," *William and Mary Quarterly* 66 (October 2009): 832.

19. See Chaim Kaufmann and Robert Pape, "Explaining Costly International Moral Action," *International Organization* 53 (Autumn 1999): 631–68.

20. See Jenny Martinez, *The Slave Trade and the Origins of International Human Rights Law* (New York: Oxford University Press, forthcoming).

21. See Suzanne Miers, *Britain and the Ending of the Slave Trade* (New York: Africana, 1975), pp. 3–166; for an economic interpretation, Eric Williams, *Capitalism and Slavery* (New York: Capricorn Books, 1966).

22. William Lloyd Garrison, 4 July 1829, as cited in William Cain (ed.), *William Lloyd Garrison and the Fight Against Slavery* (Boston: Bedford, 1995), pp. 61–65.

23. William Lloyd Garrison, in ibid., p. 38.

24. William Lloyd Garrison, in *The Liberator*, 1 January 1831.

25. Theodore Weld, *American Slavery as It Is* (New York: American Anti-Slavery Society, 1839). See also Margaret Keck and Kathryn Sikkink, *Activists Beyond Borders* (Ithaca, N.Y: Cornell University Press, 1998), pp. 45–48.

26. James G. Birney, as cited in Dumond, *Antislavery*, p. 301.

27. See Burns and Burns, *The Pursuit of Rights in America*, p. 109.

28. Winthrop Jordan et al., *The United States* (Englewood Cliffs, N.J.: Prentice-Hall, 1987), p. 327.

29. Gary Nash et al., *The American People* (New York: HarperCollins, 1990), p. 485; Fladeland, *Men and Brothers*, pp. 350–55.

30. William Lloyd Garrison, as cited in Cain, *William Lloyd Garrison*, p. 42.

31. Frederick Douglass, as cited in Philip Foner (ed.), *The Life and the Writings of Frederick Douglass*, 4 vols. (New York: International Publishers, 1950), 2:437.

32. See Aaron Fogleman, "The Transformation of the Atlantic World," *Atlantic Studies* 6 (April 2009): 5–28.

33. Wendell Phillips, as cited in J. B. Stewart, *Holy Warriors* (New York: Hill & Wang, 1976), p. 3.

34. General Act of the Conference of Berlin, 26 February 1885, in Edward Hertslet (ed.), *The Map of Africa by Treaty*, 3 vols. (London: Harrison & Sons, 1909), 2:468ff.

35. General Act of the Brussels Conference, 2 July 1890, in ibid., 2:488ff.

36. See Miers, *Britain and the Ending of the Slave Trade*, pp. 236–319; Davis, *Slavery and Human Progress* (New York: Oxford University Press, 1984), pp. 302–7; Gwyn Campbell (ed.), *Abolition and Its Aftermath in Indian Ocean Africa and Asia* (New York: Routledge, 2005); for a larger discussion of international normative values, see Ian Clark, *International Legitimacy and World Society* (Oxford: Oxford University Press, 2007), pp. 37ff.

37. Alexis de Tocqueville, "On the Emancipation of Slaves," in Seymour Drescher (ed.), *Tocqueville and Beaumont on Social Reform* (New York: Harper & Row, 1968), p. 138.

38. For more discussion, see Lauren, *Power and Prejudice*, pp. 32ff.

39. George King, as cited in Leon Litwack, *Been in the Storm So Long* (New York: Knopf, 1979), p. 224.

40. As cited in Burns and Burns, *The Pursuit of Rights in America*, p. 127.

41. Lauren, *Power and Prejudice*, pp. 41–48.

42. Mark 16:15.

43. For a fascinating survey of the thousands of missions established at this time, see Harlan Beach and Burton St. John (eds.), *World Statistics of Christian Missions* (New York: Foreign Missions Conference of North America, 1916).

44. As cited in William T. Hagen, *The Indian Rights Association* (Tucson: University of Arizona Press, 1985), p. 19.

45. As cited in Mellor, *British Imperial Trusteeship*, p. 249.

46. Decision in *Ex Parte Milligan*, 1866, in John Wallace (ed.), *Cases Argued and Adjudged in the Supreme Court of the United States* (New York: Banks, 1910), 4:119.

47. Decision in *United States ex rel. Standing Bear v. Crook*, 1879, Case No. 14,891, in U.S. Federal Circuit and District Courts, *Federal Cases: Circuit and District Courts, 1789–1880* (St. Paul, Minn.: West, 1896), 25:695–701.

48. Chief Joseph, speech of January 1879, reprinted in *North American Review* (April 1879): 412–33.

49. General Act of the Conference of Berlin, 26 February 1885, in Hertslet, *The Map of Africa by Treaty*, 2:468ff.

50. General Act of the Brussels Conference, 2 July 1890, in ibid., 2:488ff.

51. George Washington Williams, as cited in Adam Hochschild, *King Leopold's Ghost* (Boston: Houghton Mifflin, 1998), p. 112.

52. See Jan Lewis, "'Of Every Age, Sex, and Condition': The Representation of Women in the Constitution," *Journal of the Early Republic* 15 (Fall 1995): 359–87.

53. Abby Kelley Foster, as cited in Jordan et al., *The United States*, p. 267. Also see Blanche Hersh, *The Slavery of Sex* (Urbana: University of Illinois Press, 1978).

54. Angelina Grimké, as cited in Catherine Du Pre Lumpkin, *The Emancipation of Angelina Grimké* (Chapel Hill: University of North Carolina Press, 1974), p. 120.

55. Sarah Grimké, *Letters on the Equality of the Sexes and the Condition of Woman* (Boston: Knapp, 1838).

56. E. P. Hurlbut, *Essays on Human Rights* (New York: Greeley & McElrath, 1845).

57. As cited in Bonnie S. Anderson, *Joyous Greetings* (New York: Oxford University Press, 2000), p. 168.

58. "Declaration of Sentiments and Resolutions," in Elizabeth Cady Stanton et al. (eds.), *History of Woman Suffrage*, 2 vols. (New York: Mann, 1881), 1:70–71 (my emphasis).

59. Ibid., 1:73.

60. John Stuart Mill, *On Liberty* (London: Parker & Son, 1859); John Stuart Mill, *The Subjugation of Women* (London: Longmans, 1869).

61. See Bahá'u'lláh, *Gleanings from the Writings of Bahá'u'lláh*, Shoghi Effendi (trans.) (Wilmette, Ill.: Bahá'í Publishing, 1952); Ono Kazuko, *Chinese Women in a Century of Revolution, 1850–1950*, Joshua Fogel (ed.) (Stanford, Calif.: Stanford University Press, 1989), pp. 34–37; Mioko Fujieda, "Japan's First Phase of Feminism," in Kumiko Fujimura-Fanselow and Atsuko Kameda (eds.), *Japanese Women* (New York: Feminist Press, 1995), pp. 324–26.

62. Rosa Guerra, as cited in Anthony Esler, *The Western World* (Upper Saddle River, N.J.: Prentice-Hall, 1997), p. 540.

63. For the relationship between upheaval and human rights advances in China and Japan, see Stephen Angle, *Human Rights and Chinese Thought* (Cambridge: Cambridge University Press, 2002), pp. 101ff.

64. Eleanor Flexner, *Century of Struggle* (Cambridge, Mass.: Belknap Press of Harvard University Press, 1975), p. 153.

65. Jenny d'Héricourt and Fredrika Bremer, as cited in Anderson, *Joyous Greetings*, pp. 20, 184.

66. Henrik Ibsen, *A Dolls's House* (London: Penguin, 1965), pp. 226–28.

67. Elizabeth Cady Stanton, as cited in Elisabeth Griffith, *In Her Own Right* (New York: Oxford University Press, 1984), p. 193.

68. *Kalevala*, p. 383.

69. See W. E. Mosse, *Alexander II and the Modernization of Russia* (New York: Collier, 1962), p. 41; Jerome Blum, *Lord and Peasant in Russia* (New York: Atheneum, 1967), pp. 568, 616.

70. N. E. Wrangel, *From Serfdom to Bolshevism* (Philadelphia: Lippincott, 1927), p. 40.

71. Alexander II, Decree of Emancipation, 3 March 1861, as cited in Raymond Stearns (ed.), *Pageant of Europe* (New York: Harcourt, 1961), p. 664; Nicholas Riasanovsky, *A History of Russia* (New York: Oxford University Press, 1993), pp. 372–73.

72. Sheldon Garon, "Japan: State, Society, and Collective Goods Versus the Individual," in Taylor, *The Idea of Freedom in Asia and Africa*; Stephen Vlastos, "Opposition Movements in Early Meiji, 1865–1885," in Marius Jansen (ed.), *The Emergence of Meiji Japan* (Cambridge: Cambridge University Press, 1995), pp. 203–61.

73. See Mehrdad Kia, "Constitutionalism, Economic Modernization and Islam in the Writings of Mirz Yusef Khan Mostashar od-Dowle," *Middle Eastern Studies* 30 (October 1994): 751–77.

74. Stanley Chodorow et al., *The Mainstream of Civilization* (Fort Worth, Tex.: Harcourt, 1994), p. 628.

75. Charles Dickens, *Hard Times* (New York: Bantam, 1981), p. 129.

76. Hochschild, *Bury the Chains*, p. 353.

77. See the stimulating discussion in Burns and Burns, *The Pursuit of Rights*, pp. 75–76; George Rudé, *Ideology and Popular Protest* (New York: Pantheon, 1980).

78. Eric Foner, "Introduction," in Thomas Paine, *Rights of Man* (New York: Penguin, 1985), p. 17.

79. William Cobbett, as cited in Thompson, *Making of the English Working Class*, p. 761.

80. See especially Gustave Moynier and Louis Appia, *La Guerre et la charité* (Geneva: Cherbuliez, 1867), pp. vi, 370.

81. See Gwilym Beckerlegge, "Human Rights in the Ramakrishna Math and Mission: 'For Liberation and the Good of the World,'" *Religion* (April 1990): 119–37.

82. Pope Leo XIII, *Rerum Novarum* (New York: Paulist Press, 1939).

83. Charles Sheldon, *In His Steps* (New York: Hurst, 1897).

84. John Stuart Mill, *Principles of Political Economy with Some of Their Applications to Social Philosophy* (New York: Kelley, 1961), p. 366.

85. Karl Marx, as cited in Louis Henkin, *The Rights of Man Today* (Boulder, Colo.: Westview, 1978), p. 160 n. 74.

86. Karl Marx and Friedrich Engels, *Manifesto of the Communist Party* (New York: Socialist Labor Party, 1888), p. 28.

87. "Inaugural Address of the International Working Men's Association," 1864, in Saul Padover (ed.), *Karl Marx Library*, 7 vols. (New York: McGraw Hill, 1972–1977), 3:5–12.

88. Kishlansky et al., *Civilization in the West*, p. 689.

89. Ishbel Ross, *Angel of the Battlefield* (New York: Harper & Brothers, 1956).

90. International Conference of Red Cross Societies, as cited in Cecil Woodham-Smith, *Florence Nightingale, 1820–1910* (London: Constable, 1950), p. 592.

91. J. Henry Dunant, *A Memory of Solferino* (Washington, D.C.: American National Red Cross, 1939 ed.), pp. 20, 33, 35, 36, 51.

92. Ibid., pp. 47 (my emphasis), 54, 73.

93. Ibid., p. 93.

94. As cited in the Musée international de la Croix-Rouge et du Croissant-Rouge.

95. C. J. Hambro, 10 December 1963, Nobel Peace Prize Ceremony, as found in Hoover Institution Archives, Red Cross International Committee, Box 3.

96. See "Amelioration of the Condition of the Wounded on the Field of Battle (Red Cross Convention)," 22 August 1864, Treaty Series 377, in U.S. Department of State, *Treaties and Other International Agreements*, 1:7–11.

97. Société Ottomane de Secours aux Blessés et Malades Militaires, *Annuaire, 1877–1878* (Constantinople: La Turquie, 1878).

98. "100 Years of the Red Cross," *Daily Telegraph*, 29 December 1962.

99. "Convention with Respect to the Laws and Customs of War on Land," Hague II, 29 July 1899, which secured twenty-four signatures, in U.S. Department of State, *Treaties and Other International Agreements*, 1:247–62.

100. "Convention for the Adaption to Maritime Warfare of the Principles of the Geneva Convention," Hague III, 29 July 1899, in ibid., pp. 263–69.

101. On the Red Cross societies being used by states for their own aggressive nationalism and militarism, see John Hutchinson, *Champions of Charity* (Boulder, Colo.: Westview, 1996).

102. See David Forsythe, *Humanitarian Politics* (Baltimore: Johns Hopkins University Press, 1977), p. 7.

103. See David Forsythe, *The Internationalization of Human Rights* (Lexington, Mass.: Lexington Books, 1991), p. 146; H. Coursier, "L'Évolution du droit international humanitaire," *Recueil des Cours de l'Académie de Droit International* 99 (1960): 361–465.

104. On the convergence of humanitarian and human rights law, see David Weissbrodt, "The Role of International Organizations in the Implementation of Human Rights and Humanitarian Law in Situations of Armed Conflict," *Vanderbilt Journal of Transnational Law* 21 (1988): 313–65.

105. Alberico Gentili, as cited in Theodore Meron, "Common Rights of Mankind in Gentili, Grotius, and Suárez," *American Journal of International Law* 85 (1991): 114.

106. Hugo Grotius, as cited in Jean-Pierre Fonteyne, "The Customary International Law Doctrine of Humanitarian Intervention," *California Western International Law Journal* 4 (1974): 203–58.

107. Emerich de Vattel, *Le Droit des gens, ou principes de la loi naturelle* (Washington, D.C.: Carnegie, 1916), book 2, chapter 4, p. 298.

108. The protection of aliens under international law recognized that a nation could demand respect for the rights of its own nationals when living in another country.

109. The Peace of Westphalia (1648) stipulated an equality of rights for Roman Catholics and Protestants and the Treaty of Utrecht (1713) provided that French Protestants be released from imprisonment if held solely on the basis of religious belief.

110. Act of the Acceptance of Sovereignty of the Belgic Provinces, 31 May 1815, in Edward Hertslet (ed.), *Map of Europe by Treaty*, 4 vols. (London: Butterworths, 1875–1891), 1:38; The Vienna Congress Treaty, 9 June 1815, 1:255.

111. Federative Constitution of Germany, annexed to the Vienna Congress Treaty, 9 June 1815, in ibid., p. 205.

112. See A. R. Gibb and Harold Bowen, *Islamic Society and the West* (London: Oxford University Press, 1957), pp. 207ff.

113. As early as 1649, for example, Louis XIV unilaterally issued the Proclamation of French Protection of the Maronite Community in Lebanon. By the Treaty of Kutchuk-Kainardji of 1774 Russia claimed to be the protector of Christians in the Ottoman Empire.

114. *Hatti-i Sherif,* 3 November 1839, in Robert Landen, *The Emergence of the Modern Middle East* (New York: Van Nostrand Reinhold, 1970), pp. 38–42.

115. Peace of Paris, 30 March 1856, Article IX, in Hertslet, *The Map of Europe by Treaty,* 2:1255. Similar pressure occurred from 1866 to 1868 to protect Christians on Crete.

116. London Treaty Between Great Britain, France, and Russia for the Pacification of Greece, 6 July 1827, in ibid., 1:769–72.

117. Earl Cowley to Lord John Russell, 5 July 1860, in Great Britain, Parliament, House of Commons, Command Paper 2800, *Correspondence Relating to the Affairs of Syria* (London: Her Majesty's Stationery Office, 1861), p. 1.

118. M. Thouvenel to Count de Persigny, Paris, 16 July 1860, in ibid., pp. 3–6.

119. See Manoucher Ganji, *International Protection of Human Rights* (Geneva: Droz, 1962), p. 25.

120. Lord John Russell to Earl Cowley, 28 July 1860, in Great Britain, Parliament, Command Paper No. 2800, *Correspondence Relating to the Affairs of Syria,* p. 24. See also Gary Bass, *Freedom's Battle* (New York: Knopf, 2008).

121. As cited in Lord Kinross, *The Ottoman Centuries* (New York: Morrow, 1977), p. 509.

122. See "The War," in *Illustrated London News,* 19 August 1876.

123. William Ewart Gladstone, *Bulgarian Horrors and the Question of the East* (London: Murray, 1876), pp. 13, 17, 19–20, 43, 53. See also "Das Recht der Europaischen Intervention in der Turkei," *Die Gegenwart,* 9 December 1876.

124. William Ewart Gladstone, *Lessons in Massacre* (London: Murray, 1877), p. 80.

125. Treaty . . . for the Settlement of the Affairs of the East, 13 July 1878, in Hertslet, *The Map of Europe by Treaty,* 4:2759–69, 2796.

126. International Convention of Constantinople, 24 May 1881, in Great Britain, Foreign Office, *British and Foreign State Papers, 1880–1881* (London: Ridgway, 1885), 72:382–87.

127. Abdul Hamid, as cited in Kinross, *The Ottoman Centuries,* p. 555.

128. See Matthew Jacobson, *Special Sorrows* (Cambridge, Mass.: Harvard University Press, 1995); Secretary of State Frederick Frelinghuysen, 15 April 1882, as cited in Ellert C. Stowell, *Intervention in International Law* (Washington, D.C.: Byrne, 1921), p. 75.

129. Marquis of Salisbury, 13 July 1878, as cited in René Albrecht-Carrié, *The Concert of Europe, 1815–1914* (New York: Harper & Row, 1968), pp. 279–80.

130. C. Musurus to Lord John Russell (London), 30 July 1860, in Great Britain, Parliament, Command Paper No. 2800, *Correspondence Relating to the Affairs of Syria,* p. 36.

131. See M. Pillet, "Le Droit international public," *Revue Générale de Droit International Public,* 1 (1894); Antoine Rougier, "La Théorie de l'intervention d'humanité," *Revue Générale de Droit International Public* 17 (1910): 468–526.

Chapter 3. Visions, War, Revolutions, and Peacemaking

1. The expression began to be used by Henry Wallace during World War II and has continued, as seen by the PBS broadcast series under this title in 2000.

2. Henry Adams, *The Education of Henry Adams* (Boston: Houghton Mifflin, 1918), pp. 489–98. See also Paul Morand, *1900* (Paris: Éditions de France, 1931), pp. 71–130.

3. Paul Gordon Lauren, *Diplomats and Bureaucrats* (Stanford, Calif.: Hoover Institution Press,

1976), pp. 34–68; Maurice Paléologue, *Un grand tournant de la politique mondiale* (Paris: Plon, 1934).

4. France, Archives Diplomatiques du Ministère des Affaires Étrangères (hereafter cited as France, MAE), collection of *Annuaire diplomatique et consulaire*, and Comptabilité, Décrets et décisions ministérielles, Carton 50, No. 237, "Note pour le Ministre," 10 May 1906; Germany, Politisches Archiv des Auswärtiges Amt, Politisches Archiv und Historisches Referat (hereafter cited as Germany, PA/AA), budgets for 1903, 1904, 1905 "für kartographische Arbeiten."

5. Gabriel Hanotaux, "L'Europe qui naît," *Revue Hebdomadaire* 48 (30 November 1907): 561–70. See also F. S. Lyons, *Internationalism in Europe* (Leyden: Syhoff,1963).

6. See Jean Quataert, *Advocating Dignity* (Philadelphia: University of Pennsylvania Press, 2009), pp. 20–21.

7. Henri Sée, *Histoire de la Ligue des Droits de l'Homme* (Paris: Ligue des Droits de l'Homme, 1927), p. 11. The Ligue was formed in 1898 by Ludovic Trarieux.

8. Ibid., p. 81; and the various issues of *Bulletin officiel* from 1901 to 1914.

9. Mehrdad Kia, "Nationalism, Modernism, and Islam in the Writings of Talibov-i Tabrizi," *Middle Eastern Studies* 30 (April 1994): 201–23.

10. Larry Burgess, *The Lake Mohonk Conference of Friends of the Indian* (New York: Clearwater, 1975), pp. 6–8.

11. Peter Woo, "A Metaphysical Approach to Human Rights from a Chinese Point of View," in Alan S. Rosenbaum (ed.), *The Philosophy of Human Rights* (Westport. Conn.: Greenwood, 1980), pp. 117–18; Marina Svensson, *Debating Human Rights in China* (Lanham, Md.: Rowman & Littlefield , 2002).

12. See Kazuko, *Chinese Women in a Century of Revolution*, pp. 40–42, 212.

13. Peter J. Coleman, *Progressivism and the World of Reform* (Lawrence: University Press of Kansas, 1987).

14. See Great Britain, Parliament, House of Commons, Command Paper 3933, *Papers Relating to the Geneva Convention, 1906* (London: His Majesty's Stationery Office, 1908); "Convention Respecting the Laws and Customs of War on Land," Hague IV, 18 October 1907, and "Convention for the Adaption to Maritime Warfare of the Principles of the Geneva Convention," Hague X, 18 October 1907, in U.S. Department of State, *Treaties and Other International Agreements*, 1:631–53, 694–710.

15. As cited in Antoine Rougier, "La Théorie de l'intervention d'humanité," *Revue Générale de Droit International Public* 17 (1910): 477.

16. Ganji, *International Protection of Human Rights*, pp. 33–40.

17. Theodore Roosevelt, 6 December 1904, in James Richardson (ed.), *A Compilation of the Messages and Papers of the Presidents*, 20 vols. (New York: Bureau of National Literature, 1897–1916), 16:6924.

18. See Lauren, *Power and Prejudice*, pp. 50ff.

19. W. E. B. Du Bois, as cited in United Nations Centre Against Apartheid, *International Tribute to W. E. B. Du Bois* (New York: United Nations, 1982), p. 48.

20. W. E. B. Du Bois, in P. S. Foner (ed.), *W. E. B. Du Bois Speaks* (New York: Pathfinder Press, 1970), pp. 170–71.

21. Arthur Vandenberg, as cited in Louis Fischer, *Gandhi* (New York: Mentor, 1982), p. 8.

22. J. A. Hobson, as cited in L. H. Gann and Peter Duignan, *Burden of Empire* (New York: Praeger, 1967), p. 40. See also Henry Nevinson, *A Modern Slavery* (New York: Harper & Bros., 1906).

23. Joseph Conrad, *Heart of Darkness* (New York: Penguin, 1995), pp. 62–63 (my emphasis).

24. E. D. Morel, as cited in Hochschild's excellent *King Leopold's Ghost*, p. 186.

25. See Sharon Swilinski, "The Childhood of Human Rights: The Kodak and the Congo," *Journal of Visual Culture* 5 (December 2006): 333–63.

26. Hochschild, *King Leopold's Ghost*, p. 209.

27. Alfred Zimmern, *The Third British Empire* (London: Oxford University Press, 1926), p. 82. See also René Pinon, *La Lutte pour le Pacifique* (Paris: Perrin, 1906), p. 165.

28. Jean Jaurès, 28 June 1912, in France, Assemblée nationale, Chambre des Députés, *Débats parlementaires* (Paris: Imprimerie des Journaux Officiels, 1912), p. 923.

29. Frances Balfour, as cited in Barbara Tuchman, *The Proud Tower* (New York: Macmillan, 1966), p. 354.

30. Jordan et al., *The United States*, p. 563.

31. Anderson and Zinsser, *A History of Their Own*, 2:364–65.

32. See Jacqueline Van Voris, *Carrie Chapman Catt* (New York: Feminist Press, 1996).

33. Jiu Jin, as cited in Elizabeth Croll, *Feminism and Socialism in China* (New York: Schocken, 1980), pp. 68–69.

34. See Keck and Sikkink, *Activists Beyond Borders*, p. 64.

35. Suga Kanno, as cited in Sharon Sievers, *Flowers in Salt* (Stanford:, Calif.: Stanford University Press, 1983), p. 149.

36. See Tarrosa Subido, *The Feminist Movement in the Philippines, 1905–1955* (Manila: National Federation of Women's Clubs, 1955), p. 18.

37. See Kumari Jayawardena, *Feminism and Nationalism in the Third World* (London: Zed Books, 1986).

38. See Donna Guy, "'White Slavery,' Citizenship, and Nationality in Argentina," in Andrew Parker et al. (eds.), *Nationalisms and Sexualities* (New York: Routledge, 1992), pp. 206–8.

39. As cited in Kazuko, *Chinese Women in a Century of Revolution*, p. 88.

40. A. J. P. Taylor, *The History of World War I* (London: Octopus, 1974), p. 279.

41. As cited in André Durand, *From Sarajevo to Hiroshima* (Geneva: Henry Dunant Institute, 1984), p. 32.

42. Musée international de la Croix-Rouge et du Croissant-Rouge; Hutchinson, *Champions of Charity*, pp. 282–83; Forsythe, *Humanitarian Politics*, p. 20.

43. As cited in Gordon Wright, *France in Modern Times* (Chicago: Rand McNally, 1966), pp. 403–4.

44. W. E. B. Du Bois, "Close Ranks," *Crisis* 16 (July 1918): 111.

45. As cited in John Hope Franklin, *From Slavery to Freedom* (New York: Knopf, 1974), pp. 343–44.

46. Kelly Miller, *An Appeal to Conscience* (New York: Macmillan, 1918); Kelly Miller, *The World War for Human Rights* (Washington, D.C.: Jenkins, 1919).

47. Mohamed Duse, "Today: India and Africa," *African Times and Orient Review* (March 1917): 46.

48. Gordon A. Craig, *Europe Since 1815* (New York: Holt, Rinehart & Winston, 1971), p. 474.

49. Anthony Livesey, *The Historical Atlas of World War I* (New York: Holt, 1994), p. 182.

50. Hoover Institution Archives, Commission for Relief in Belgium, Box 1, cablegram from Herbert Hoover (Washington) to Cravath (London), 3 July 1918.

51. Based upon the archival evidence in Hoover Institution Archives, Commission for Relief in Belgium, Boxes 1–11.

52. As cited in Richard Hovannisian, "Etiology and Sequelae of the Armenian Genocide," in George Andreopoulos (ed.), *Genocide* (Philadelphia: University of Pennsylvania Press, 1994), p. 125.

53. See Peter Balakian, *The Burning Tigris* (New York: HarperCollins, 2003); Samantha Powers, *"A Problem from Hell"* (New York: HarperCollins, 2002), pp. 1–16.

54. Taner Akçam, *A Shameful Act* (New York: Metropolitan, 2006).

55. See Comités arméniens, *Aspirations et agissements révolutionaires des comités arméniens* (Constantinople: Comités arméniens, 1917), pp. 317–18.

56. "Germany and the Laws of War," *Edinburgh Review* 220 (October 1914): 297.

57. As cited in Arthur Marwick, *Women at War, 1914–1918* (London: Fontana, 1977), epigraph.

58. Nash et al., *The American People*, p. 772.

59. Marwick, *Women at War*, p. 152.

60. E. S. Montague, as cited in ibid., p. 156.

61. Ziya Gokalp, as cited in Jayawardena, *Feminism and Nationalism in the Third World*, p. 32.

62. Sedition Act of 1918, in United States, *Statutes at Large*, 40, pt. 1 (Washington, D.C.: Government Printing Office, 1919), pp. 553–54. See also Clem Work, *Darkest Before Dawn* (Albuquerque: University of New Mexico Press, 2005).

63. Craig, *Europe Since 1815*, pp. 474–80; Sée, *Histoire de la Ligue des Droits de l'Homme*, pp. 143–63; Burns and Burns, *The Pursuit of Rights in America*, pp. 204–13.

64. As cited in Hunt et al., *The Challenge of the West*, 2: 904.

65. As cited in A. W. Brian Simpson, *Human Rights and the End of Empire* (New York: Oxford University Press, 2001), p. 161.

66. Shigenobu Okuma, as cited in U.S. Congress, *Congressional Record, 1916*, 53, pt. 1 (Washington, D.C.: Government Printing Office, 1916), pp. 754–55.

67. Carozza, "From Conquest to Constitutions," p. 304.

68. See Albert Verdoodt, *Naissance et signification de la Déclaration universelle des droits de l'homme* (Louvain-Paris: Éditions Nauwelaerts, 1964), p. 41.

69. Woodrow Wilson, as cited in Norman Graebner, "Human Rights and Foreign Policy," in Kenneth Thompson (ed.), *The Moral Imperatives of Human Rights* (Lanham, Md.: University Press of America, 1980), p. 40.

70. Woodrow Wilson, 11 February 1918, in *The Papers of Woodrow Wilson*, Arthur Link (ed.), 69 vols. (Princeton: Princeton University Press, 1984), 46: 321. See also Erez Manela, *The Wilsonian Moment* (New York: Oxford University Press, 2009).

71. V. I. Lenin, *Collected Works* (New York: International Publishers, 1929–1945), 18:367.

72. Declaration of Rights of the Toiling and Exploited Peoples, January 1918, as cited in E. H. Carr, "The Rights of Man," *United Nations Weekly Bulletin*, 21 October 1946.

73. W. E. B. Du Bois, "Opinion," *Crisis* 18 (May 1919): 7.

74. E. J. Dillon, *The Inside Story of the Peace Conference* (New York: Harper, 1920), p. 6.

75. Harold Nicolson, *Peacemaking 1919* (New York: Grosset & Dunlop, 1965), pp. 31–32.

76. See Library of Congress, Manuscripts Division, Robert Lansing Papers, diary entries for 20 December and 30 December 1918.

77. France, MAE, Nouvelle série, Correspondance politique et commerciale, Congrès de la Paix, Carton 1001, Dossier 2, "Représentation des nationalités."

78. See Margaret Macmillan, *Paris, 1919* (New York: Random House, 2003).

79. Woodrow Wilson, as cited in League of Nations, *Protection of Linguistic, Racial, or Religious Minorities*, I.B. Minorities, 1931 I.B.1 (C.8.M.5.1931.I), p. 159.

80. Document No. 822, "Proposals for Protection of Minorities," 20 April 1919, in David Hunter Miller, *Diary*, 21 vols. (New York: privately printed, 1924) 8:422–23. See also Carole Fink, *Defending the Rights of Others* (New York: Cambridge University Press, 2004), pp. 133–264; Jacques Duparc, *La Protection des minorités de race, de langue et de religion* (Paris: Dalloz, 1922), pp. 141–71.

81. Société des Nations/League of Nations, Document C.L.110. 1927. I, Annex, *Protection of Linguistic, Racial, and Religious Minorities* (Geneva: Société des Nations, 1927).

82. Herbert Hoover, as cited in Hoover Institution Archives, Commission for Relief in Belgium, Box 11, letter from Woodrow Wilson to Secretary of War Newton Baker, 9 January 1919.

83. U.S. Department of State, *Foreign Relations of the United States* (hereafter *FRUS*): *The Paris Peace Conference, 1919*, 13 vols. (Washington, D.C.: Government Printing Office, 1942–1947), 2:627–725; 10: passim.

84. See Hoover Institution Archives, Commission for Relief in Belgium, Box 11, joint letter from Woodrow Wilson, David Lloyd George, Georges Clemenceau, and Vittoria Orlando to Fridjof Nansen, 9 April 1919; Box 12, Memorandum on the Economic Situation of Europe, from Herbert Hoover, 3 July 1919.

85. France, Archives Nationales, 94–AP, Fonds Albert Thomas, Cartons 357, 358, 406.

86. See U.S. Department of State, *FRUS: Paris Peace Conference, 1919*, 11:6, 71. Also see 1:149,

178, 409–412, 461, 539–42; Ernst Haas, *Beyond the Nation State* (Stanford, Calif.: Stanford University Press, 1964), pp. 140ff.

87. See Léon-Eli Troclet, *Législation sociale internationale,* 3 vols. (Brussels: Librairie Encyclopédique, 1952).

88. Treaty of Versailles, Articles 387–427, in U.S. Department of State, *FRUS: Paris Peace Conference, 1919,* 13:692–719; repeated in the other treaties.

89. Commission on the Responsibility . . . and on Enforcement of Penalties, "Report," 29 March 1919, reprinted in *American Journal of International Law* 14 (1920): 95–154.

90. Ibid., pp. 127–51.

91. Robert Lansing, as cited in James Willis, *Prologue to Nuremberg* (Westport, Conn.: Greenwood, 1982), p. 74.

92. See B. Ferencz, *An International Criminal Court,* 2 vols. (London: Oceana, 1980), 1:27.

93. W. E. B. Du Bois, *Crisis* 17 (January 1919): 130–31. See also Immanuel Geiss, *Panafrikanismus* (Frankfurt am Main: Europäische Verlagsanstalt, 1968), pp. 180ff.

94. Jane Addams, *Peace and Bread in Time of War* (New York: Macmillan, 1922), pp. 152–53.

95. Woodrow Wilson, 8 January 1918, in U.S. Congress, *Congressional Record, 1918,* pt. 1, p. 681.

96. As cited in Jordan et al., *The United States,* p. 586.

97. Covenant of the League of Nations, Articles 23 and 25, in U.S. Department of State, *FRUS: Paris Peace Conference, 1919,* 13:104–5.

98. Document No. 211, Draft Covenant, in Miller, *Diary,* 3:455.

99. See David Hunter Miller, *The Drafting of the Covenant,* 2 vols. (New York: Putnam, 1928), 1:191, 196, 267–69, 462; 2:273, 282, 555.

100. For a fuller account, see Lauren, *Power and Prejudice,* pp. 82–107.

101. W. E. B. Du Bois, as cited in United Nations, Centre Against Apartheid, *International Tribute,* p. 48; first stated in 1900 but repeated again in Paris during 1919.

102. Dillon, *The Inside Story,* p. 493; Stephen Bonsal, *Unfinished Business* (Garden City, N.Y.: Doubleday Doran, 1944), p. 169.

103. The Papers of the NAACP held in the Library of Congress document the organization's concerns and activities during 1919.

104. *Asahi,* as cited in "Racial Discrimination to End," *Japan Times,* 31 January 1919. For good discussion about mixed Japanese motives, see Naoko Shimazu, *Japan, Race, and Equality* (New York: Routledge, 1998).

105. Japan, Ministry of Foreign Affairs, Diplomatic Record Office (hereafter Japan, MOFA), Kokusai Renmei: Jinshu sabetsu teppai, File 2/4/2/2, Binder 1, Despatch No. 133.-2, from Matsui (Paris) to Ministry of Foreign Affairs (Tokyo), 14 February 1919, "Secret."

106. See Library of Congress, Manuscripts Division, Woodrow Wilson Papers, Breckinridge Long to Wilson, 4 March 1919, and Memorandum from the Japanese Government, 4 March 1919; Japan, Delegation to the Paris Peace Conference, Documents Distributed to the Public, located at the Hoover Institution.

107. Arthur Balfour, as cited in Miller, *Diary,* entry of 9 February 1919, 1:116.

108. As cited in L. F. Fitzhardinge, *William Morris Hughes* (Sydney: Angus & Robertson, 1964), pp. 116, 136; in "Equality of Races," *Age* (Melbourne), 21 March 1919.

109. "The Week: Racial Equality," *Otago Witness,* 23 April 1919.

110. Text in Japan, MOFA, Kokusai Renmei: Jinshu sabetsu teppai, File 2/4/2/2, Binder 1. See also Britain, PRO/FO, 371/3817, Despatch No. 55 from Conyngham Greene (Tokyo) to Lord Curzon (London), 6 February 1919; "Do to Others," *Japan Times,* 9 February 1919.

111. Conférence de la Paix, 1919–1920, *Recueil des actes de la Conférence,* "Secret," Partie 4, Commission de la Société des Nations (Paris: Imprimerie Nationale, 1922), p. 90; Wellington Koo Papers, Columbia University, Rare Book and Manuscript Library, Box 1, File 3, Memorandum of Interview with Col. House, 2 April 1919.

112. As cited in Franklin, *From Slavery to Freedom,* p. 352.

113. Document No. 773, in Miller, *Diary*, 8:279; Conférence de la Paix, 1919–1920, *Recueil des actes de la Conférence*, "Secret," Partie 4, passim. Voting in favor were Brazil, China, Czechoslovakia, France (2), Greece, Italy (2), Japan (2), and Yugoslavia.

114. *Sacramento Union*, 13 April 1919.

115. W. E. B. Du Bois, "Returning Soldiers," *Crisis* 18 (May 1919):13–14.

116. Franklin, *From Slavery to Freedom*, p. 356.

117. *Asahi*, as cited in "The League's Amended Covenant," in *Japan Times*, 18 April 1919; *Nichinichi*, as cited in "Anglo-Saxons Want to Dominate the World," *Japan Times*, 26 April 1919.

118. Shigenobu Okuma, "Illusions of the White Race," in K. K. Kawakami (ed.), *What Japan Thinks* (New York: Macmillan, 1921), p. 170. See also Japan, MOFA, Kokusai Renmei: Jinshu sabetsu teppai, File 2/4/2/2, Binders 2–3.

119. Woodrow Wilson, in U.S. Congress, *Congressional Record, 1918*, 56, pt. 1, pp. 680–81.

120. Wellington Koo Papers, Box 1, File 3, Note of 22 January 1919, Strictly Confidential.

121. As cited in Roland Oliver and Anthony Atmore, *Africa Since 1800* (Cambridge: Cambridge University Press, 1981), p. 161.

122. Nicolson, *Peacemaking 1919*, p. 193.

123. See H. A. L. Fisher, *A History of Europe*, 3 vols. (London: Eyre & Spottiswoode, 1938), 3:1174; Ronald Segal, *The Race War* (New York: Bantam, 1967), p. 58.

124. The words are those of Neil Sheehan, *A Bright Shining Lie* (New York: Random House, 1989), p. 147.

125. Chen Duxiu, as cited in Lin Yü-sheng, *The Crisis of Chinese Consciousness* (Madison: University of Wisconsin Press, 1979), p. 76.

Chapter 4. Visions and Rights Between the Wars

1. Erich Maria Remarque, *All Quiet on the Western Front* (New York: Fawcett, 1968), pp. 160–61; first published in 1928 as *Im Westen Nichts Neues*.

2. See Sean Brawley, *The White Peril* (Sydney: University of New South Wales Press, 1995), pp. 8–9.

3. A. Harrison, "A New Order?" *English Review* 28 (February 1919): 160.

4. Addams, *Peace and Bread*, pp. 196, 198, 224.

5. Equal Rights Amendment to the U.S. Constitution, 1923, as cited in Eleanor Flexner, *Century of Struggle* (Cambridge, Mass.: Belknap Press of Harvard University Press, 1975), p. 342.

6. Kemal Atatürk in 1923, as cited in Jayawardena, *Feminism and Nationalism in the Third World*, p. 36.

7. See UN Document 1949.I.15, *Political Rights of Women* (New York: United Nations, 1949).

8. See Keck and Sikkink, *Activists Beyond Borders*, pp. 66–72.

9. See UN Document 1948.I.10(1)F, "Pour les droits de la femme," p. 2.

10. Margaret Sanger, *International Aspects of Birth Control* (New York: American Birth Control League, 1925).

11. Dorothy Buxton and E. Fuller, *The White Flame* (London: Longmans, 1931), pp. 87–88.

12. Eglantyne Jebb, as cited at www.savethechildren.org.uk, accessed 4 January 2010.

13. Based on Henri Sée, *Histoire de la Ligue des Droits de l'Homme* (Paris: Ligue des Droits de l'Homme, 1927), pp. 188ff.; personal letter to author from J. Herman Burgers, 14 March 1966, recounting information from Daniel Jacoby, president of the FIDH.

14. Mao Zedong, "Report on an Investigation of the Peasant Movement in Hunan," 1927, in M. J. Coye et al., *China* (New York: Bantam, 1984), pp. 213–14.

15. Rhoades Murphey, *A History of Asia* (New York: HarperCollins, 1996), pp. 318, 341–42, 346.

16. Mohandas Gandhi, as cited in W. T. de Bary et al., *Sources of Indian Tradition* (New York: Columbia University Press, 1958), pp. 811, 818.

17. Habib Bourguiba, in Oliver and Atmore, *Africa Since 1800*, p. 177.

18. Britain, PRO/FO, 371/6684, Memorandum entitled "Racial Discrimination and Immigration," Confidential, 10 October 1921; *Ta Ya*, as cited in Britain, PRO/FO, 371/3823, Despatch No. 553 from Sir J. Jordon (Beijing) to Lord Curzon (London), 10 December 1919.

19. Cited in Britain, PRO/FO, 371/11700, Memorandum A.D. 35/24, "Secret," from J. G. Fearnley to Naval Secretary (Melbourne), 30 December 1925.

20. Eleanor Zelliot, *From Untouchable to Dalit* (New Delhi: Manohar, 1996).

21. Walter Nash, as cited in Keith Sinclair, *Walter Nash* (Auckland: Auckland University Press, 1976), p. 82.

22. As cited in W. E. B. Du Bois, *The World and Africa* (New York: International Publishers, 1965), p. 238. See also Geiss, *Panafrikanismus*, pp. 189ff.

23. Marcus Garvey, as cited in Edmund David Cronon, *Black Moses* (Madison: University of Wisconsin Press, 1969), p. 39.

24. See J. Herman Burgers, "The Road to San Francisco: The Revival of the Human Rights Idea in the Twentieth Century," *Human Rights Quarterly* 14 (November 1992): 447–77.

25. Académie Diplomatique Internationale, *Séances et Travaux* 2 (1928): 9, 20.

26. See André N. Mandelstam, "La Protection internationale des droits de l'homme," *Recueil des Cours de l'Académie de Droit International* 38 (1931): 205–6; Britain, PRO/FO, 372/2553, File T 14526/1761/377.

27. André Mandelstam, "Der internationale Schutz der Menschenrechte," *Zeitschrift für ausländisches öffentliches Recht und Völkerrecht* 2 (1931); *Les Droits internationaux de l'homme* (Paris: Éditions Internationales, 1931); among others.

28. See J. Herman Burgers, "André Mandelstam, Forgotten Pioneer of International Human Rights," in Fons Coomans et al. (eds.), *Rendering Justice to the Vulnerable* (The Hague: Kluwer, 2000), pp. 69–82; "André Mandelstam (1869–1949)," in Institut de Droit International, *Annuaire* 43 (September 1950): 482–84.

29. Burgers, "The Road to San Francisco," pp. 453–54; André Mandelstam, "Les Dernières phases du mouvement pour la protection internationale des droits de l'homme," *Revue de Droit International* 1 (1934): 62–69.

30. André Mandelstam, "La Protection internationale des droits de l'homme," *Cahiers des Droits de l'Homme* 31 (10 December 1931): 723–33.

31. Victor Basch, "Projets de complément à la déclaration des droits ou de nouvelle déclaration," *Cahiers des Droits de l'Homme* (1935): 342.

32. H. H. Bellot, "La Cour permanente international criminelle," *Revue Internationale de Droit Pénal* 3 (1926): 333–37.

33. Nicolas Politis, as cited in Willis, *Prologue to Nuremberg*, p. 168.

34. Lima Declaration in Favor of Women's Rights and Defense of Human Rights, of December 1938, in U.S. Department of State, *Report of the Delegation . . . to the Eighth International Conference of American States* (Washington, D.C.: Government Printing Office, 1941), pp. 123, 128–29. For previous efforts, see Samuel Guy Inman, *Inter-American Conferences* (Washington, D.C.: University Press of America, 1965).

35. René Albrecht-Carrié, *A Diplomatic History of Europe* (New York: Harper & Row, 1973), p. 379. See also Susan Pedersen, "Review Essay: Back to the League of Nations," *American Historical Review* 112, 4 (October 2007): 1091–1117.

36. Guiseppe Molta, in Société des Nations, *Actes de la première assemblée, séances plenières* (Geneva: Renaud, 1920), pp. 25–27.

37. Paul Hymans, in ibid., p. 31.

38. Covenant of the League of Nations, especially Articles 10, 14, 22, 23, 25, in U.S. Department of State, *FRUS: The Paris Peace Conference, 1919*, 13: 69–106.

39. See France, Archives Nationales, Fonds Albert Thomas (94 AP).

40. Paul Périgord, *The International Labor Organization* (New York: Appleton, 1926), p. 217.

41. Société des Nations/League of Nations, Document C.L.110. 1927. I, Annex, *Protection of Linguistic, Racial, and Religious Minorities* (Geneva: Société des Nations, 1927).

42. André N. Mandelstam, "La Protection des minorités," *Recueil des Cours de l'Académie de Droit International* 1 (1923): 367–519.

43. Société des Nations, *Journal Officiel*, supplément 9, *Résolutions et Vœux Adoptés par l'Assemblée* (21 September 1922): 35.

44. Archives de la Sociètè des Nations (hereafter cited as Archives de la SDN), Section des Minorités, S400–1 to S400–6, Petitions, 1922–1938; Britain, PRO/FO, 371/50843, Memorandum entitled "Minority Protection Under the League of Nations," RRI/101/ii, Restricted, 2 March 1945. See also Martin Scheuermann, *Minderheitenschutz contra Konfliktverhütung?* (Marburg, Herder, 2000).

45. Permanent Court of International Justice, Advisory Opinion of 6 April 1935, in *Publications of the Court*, Series A/B, No. 64, Series A/B (Leyden: Sijthoff, 1935).

46. Permanent Court of International Justice, Judgment No. 12, 26 April 1928, in *Publications of the Court*, Series A, No. 15 (Leyden: Sijthoff, 1928), pp. 46–47.

47. New Zealand, National Archives, External Affairs 2, File 114/3/2, pt. 5, Despatch No. 2315 from Thomas Wilford (London) to Prime Minister (Wellington), 6 November 1933 (hereafter cited as NANZ, EA).

48. Fink, *Defending the Rights of Others*, p. 279; Christoph Gütermann, *Das Minderheitenschutzverfahren des Völkerbundes* (Berlin: Duncker und Humblot, 1979).

49. Lord Balfour, as cited in Quincy Wright, "Sovereignty of the Mandates," *American Journal of International Law* 17 (1923): 692.

50. See League of Nations, Permanent Mandates Commission, *Minutes*, and the often hard-hitting *Reports*; F. P. Walters, *A History of the League of Nations*, 2 vols. (London: Oxford University Press, 1952), 1:121–22, 171–73, 211–13.

51. Texts in *American Journal of International Law* Supplement 17 (1923): 138–94.

52. Société des Nations, Document A.25.1924.VI, *La Question de l'esclavage, memorandum du sécrétaire général*, 4 August 1924 (Geneva: Société des Nations, 1924).

53. International Convention for the Abolition of Slavery and the Slave Trade, in League of Nations, *Treaty Series*, 60 (Geneva: League of Nations, 1926): 253–70.

54. "The Slave Trade Rapidly Vanishing," *Evening Post* (Wellington), 29 December 1927.

55. League of Nations, Council Document 23/5359/3554, "Resolution Officially Transmitted . . . from the International Woman Suffrage Alliance," 12 June 1920.

56. UN Document 1949.I.15, *Political Rights of Women*.

57. International Convention for the Suppression of Traffic in Women and Children, in League of Nations, *Treaty Series* 9 (1922): 415–33; International Convention for the Suppression of Traffic in Women of Full Age, in League of Nations, *Treaty Series* 150 (1933): 431–43.

58. See League of Nations, *Official Journal*, Special Supplement 169, *Records of the Eighteenth Ordinary Session of the Assembly* (1937): 136–37; "Status of Women," *Weekly Bulletin of the United Nations*, 16 September 1946; Britain, PRO/FO, 372 (Treaty Series)/2636, File T 1315/11/377, Minute of 6 February 1930.

59. Archives d'État de Genève, U.I.S.E., Tri/71–1, M1.1, "Les Orìgines de l'Union Internationale de Secours aux Enfants."

60. See League of Nations, Document C.264.M.103.1926.IV, "Child Welfare Committee"; International Council of Women, as cited in United Nations, Economic and Social Council, Document E/CN.5/44, *Report of the Social Commission, Third Session*, 19 February 1948, p. 45.

61. Archives d'État de Genève, U.I.S.E., Tri/71–1, M3, "Declaration de Genève."

62. Yotaro Sugimura, in League of Nations, *Official Journal*, Special Supplement 33, *Records of the Sixth Assembly* (1925), p. 131.

63. See issues of the *Bulletin of the Health Organization*; Paul Weindling (ed.), *International Health Organizations and Movements, 1918–1939* (Cambridge: Cambridge University Press, 1995); Walters, *A History of the League of Nations*, 1:181–83; 2:752–53.

64. International Opium Convention, League of Nations, *Treaty Series* 81 (1925): 317–58; Convention for Limiting the Manufacture and Regulating the Distribution of Narcotic Drugs, League of Nations, *Treaty Series* 139 (1931): 301–49.

65. "Protocol for the Prohibition of the Use in War of Asphyxiating, Poisonous, and Other Gases and of Bacteriological Methods of Warfare," League of Nations, *Treaty Series* 94 (1929): 65–74; Convention Relative to the Treatment of Prisoners of War, League of Nations, *Treaty Series* 118 (1931–1932): 345–97.

66. League of Nations, Document C.484.M.201.1923, Letter from Lieutenant General C. H. Harington, 14 July 1923, describing events beginning in 1920.

67. Hannah Arendt, *Origins of Totalitarianism* (New York: Harcourt, Brace, 1951), p. 266.

68. NANZ, EA 2, File 114/3/2, pt. 5, Despatch 2315 from Thomas Wilford (London) to Prime Minister (Wellington), 6 November 1933; UN Document LIB/96/6, *The League of Nations*, pp. 74–80; Claudena Skran, *Refugees in Inter-War Europe* (Oxford: Clarendon Press, 1995).

69. Hoover Institution Archives, Anna Mitchell Papers, Box 2, Letter from A. Mitchell (Constantinople) to F. Nansen (Geneva), undated.

70. Ibid., Letter from F. Nansen (Geneva) to A. Mitchell (Constantinople), 11 June 1925.

71. League of Nations, Document A.107.1923.IV, "Work of the High Commission for Refugees," 26 September 1923; Document A.114.1924.II, "Questions Concernant les Réfugiés, 25 September 1924; Michael Marrus, *The Unwanted* (Philadelphia: Temple University Press, 2000). In 1930 renamed the Nansen International Office for Refugees.

72. See League of Nations, *Official Journal* 8 (August 1927): 997–1035; League of Nations, *Treaty Series* 159 (1935–1936): 199–217.

73. Société des Nations, *Journal Officiel*, Supplément 9, *Résolutions et Vœux adoptés par l'Assemblée* (October 1922): 35.

74. Covenant of the League of Nations, Article 15 (8).

75. Convention of the International Labor Organization, Article 19.

76. Library of Congress, Manuscript Division, Robert Lansing Papers, Confidential Memoranda, Box 87, "Consideration as to a League of Nations," 27 October 1918.

77. NANZ, EA 2, File 114/3/2, pt. 5, Despatch No. 2315, from Thomas Wilford (London) to Prime Minister (Wellington), 6 November 1933.

78. William Hughes, as cited in Sean Brawley, *The White Peril*, pp. 41–42, 44.

79. James Reed, as cited in Ralph Stone, *The Irreconcilables* (Lexington: University of Kentucky Press, 1970), p. 88.

80. Henry Cabot Lodge, *The Senate and the League of Nations* (New York: Scribner's, 1925), p. 246, speech of 28 February 1919.

81. N. W. Rowell, as cited in National Industrial Conference Board, *The International Labor Organization of the League of Nations* (New York: Century, 1922), p. 145.

82. Périgord, *The International Labor Organization*, pp. 192–217; 118–59.

83. Arthur James Balfour, as cited in Fink, *Defending the Rights of Others*, p. 276.

84. See ibid., pp. 274 ff.; Christian Raitz von Frentz, *A Lesson Forgotten* (New York: Palgrave Macmillan, 2000).

85. Maharajah of Nawanagar, in Société des Nations, *Actes de la troisième assemblée, séances plénières* (1922), 1:176.

86. Tcheo-Wei, in League of Nations, *Records of the Sixth Assembly*, Special Supplement 39, *Minutes of the Sixth Committee* (1925), p. 19.

87. Alexander Cadogan, as cited in Simpson, *Human Rights and the End of Empire*, p. 126.

88. Convention Concerning the Exchange of Greek and Turkish Populations," 30 January 1923, at www.hri.org.

89. See Lauren, *Power and Prejudice*, pp. 108–18.

90. Britain, PRO/FO, 371/6684, Memorandum entitled "Racial Discrimination and Immigration," "Confidential," 10 October 1921, F 4212/223/23.

91. Archives de la SDN, General 40/151/78, "Petition for an Amendment to the League of Nations," 3 July 1919.

92. Archives de la SDN, Mandates, 1/15865/13940, letter from W. E. B. Du Bois, 15 September 1921.

93. Archives de la SDN, Mandates, 1/37672/21159, letter from Marcus Garvey, 23 May 1923.

94. Archives de la SDN, Mandates, 1/37672/21159, note by A. S., 12 August 1922; note from E. H. F. Abraham, 15 June 1922.

95. See Archives de la SDN, Mandates, 6A/7158/7158, passim.

96. As cited in Wright, *Stolen Continents*, pp. 323–24. See also Deskaheh (Levi General), *The Redman's Appeal for Justice* (Brantford, Ont.: Moore, 1924).

97. Société des Nations, *Journal Officiel* 9 (July 1928): 942.

98. J. S. Smit, in League of Nations, *Official Journal*, special supplement 64, *Records of the Assembly* (September 1928): 93.

99. Archives de la SDN, Mandates, 1/2444/2444, note by Robert Cecil of Britain.

100. Walters, *A History of the League of Nations*, 1:173, 211; Lord Balfour, as cited in Wright, "Sovereignty of the Mandates," p. 697.

101. Winston Churchill, as cited in Fischer, *Gandhi*, pp. 103, 135.

102. Société des Nations, Document A.25.1924.VI, *La Question de l'esclavage*, p. 3.

103. See Britain, PRO/FO, 370/365, Despatch No. 195 from Tyrrell (Paris) to A. Henderson (London), 20 February 1931; Gertrude Bussey and Margaret Tims, *Women's International League for Peace and Freedom* (London: Allen & Unwin, 1965), pp. 73–81.

104. Raphael Lemkin, *Axis Rule in Occupied Europe* (Washington, D.C.: Carnegie Endowment, 1944), pp. xiii.

105. Convention for the Creation of an International Criminal Court, in League of Nations, *Monthly Summary* 17 (November 1937): 289–95.

106. American Jewish Committee, *Human Rights and the Peace Treaties*, p. 3.

107. Adolf Hitler, *Mein Kampf*, Ralph Manheim (trans.) (Boston: Houghton Mifflin, 1962), pp. 177–78, 338–39, 383, 403, 624, 627, 657.

108. The original petition is in Archives de la SDN, Minorities, File 4/4150/3643, "Juifs en Haute Silesie allemande," and entitled "Petition des Franz Bernheim . . . ," dated 12 May 1933; eventually reproduced as League of Nations, Document C.314.1933.I.

109. "A Jew May Thwart Hitler," *Daily Express*, 22 May 1933. See also Greg Burgess, "The Human Rights Dilemma in Anti-Nazi Protest," Contemporary Europe Research Center Working Paper 2 (2002); Burgers, "The Road to San Francisco," pp. 455–59.

110. Germany, PA/AA, Referat Völkerbund, Deutschland und der Judentum, Band 1, Telegram from Neurath (Berlin) to German Delegation (Geneva), 24 May 1933.

111. *The Times* (London), "Treatment of Jews in Upper Silesia," 22 May 1933.

112. Castillo Najera, 27 May 1933, in League of Nations, *Official Journal* (July 1933): 835.

113. The open debates can be found in League of Nations, *Official Journal* (July 1933), *Minutes of the Seventy-Third Session of the Council*, 22 May–6 June 1933. See also Archives de la SDN, Minorities, File 4/4470/3643, "Jews in Upper Silesia," Confidential.

114. See Britain, PRO/FO, 371/17384, File W 4149/120/98, Minute of 17 May 1933.

115. See Britain, PRO/FO, 371/16725 and 371/16726.

116. Germany, PA/AA, Büro des Reichsministers, Aktenzeichen 18, Völkerbund, Bände 32–35; Politische Abteilung IV/Polen, Aktenzeichen Po. Juden 1. OS, Fall Bernheim, Band 5; Referat Völkerbund, Aktenzeichen Deutschland und der Judentum, Band 1; August von Keller, 4 October 1933, in League of Nations, *Official Journal*, Special Supplement 120, *Minutes of the Sixth Committee*, pp. 22–28.

117. "Les Droits de l'homme et du citoyen," *Revue diplomatique* (31 October 1933): 6–7.

118. Antoine Frangulis, 30 September 1933, in League of Nations, *Official Journal*, Special Supplement 115, *Records of the Fourteenth Ordinary Session of the Assembly, Plenary Meetings*, pp. 50–51.

119. Antoine Frangulis, 4 October 1933, in League of Nations, *Official Journal*, Special Supplement 120, *Minutes of the Sixth Committee*, pp. 32–33.

120. Britain, PRO/FO, 371/17386, File 9391/191/98, Minute by A. Clarke, 9 August 1933.

121. Antoine Frangulis, "Droits de l'homme," *Dictionnaire diplomatique* (Paris: Hoche, 1937).

122. See Britain, PRO/FO, 371/17386, Minute by A. Clark, citing Sir Vansittart, 9 August 1933; Despatch No. 223, from Douglas Hacking (Geneva) to Sir John Simon, 11 October 1933, Confidential.

123. Ibid. Frangulis submitted this proposal again in 1934, but it met the same result.

124. Boris Pasternak, as cited by Roy Medvedev, "New Pages from the Political Biography of Stalin," in Robert C. Tucker (ed.), *Stalinism* (New York: Norton, 1977), p. 212.

125. For debates about the actual numbers, see J. Arch Getty and Oleg V. Naumov, *The Road to Terror* (New Haven, Conn.: Yale University Press, 1999), pp. 587–94; Stephen Wheatcroft, "The Scale and Nature of German and Soviet Repression and Mass Killings," *Europe-Asia Studies* 48 (December 1996): 1319–53.

126. As cited in Antonio Banzi, *Razzismo fascista* (Palermo: Agate, 1939), pp. 226–31.

127. Iris Chang, *The Rape of Nanking* (New York: Penguin, 1997), p. 6. See also James Yin and Shi Young, *The Rape of Nanking* (Chicago: Innovative Publishing, 1996).

128. Bertha Lutz, as cited in Leila Rupp, *Worlds of Women: The Making of an International Women's Movement* (Princeton, N.J.: Princeton University Press, 1997), p. 213 (my emphasis).

129. League of Nations, Document C.1611, No. 7, "Letter of Resignation of James G. McDonald," 27 December 1935. I am grateful to Barbara Metzger for this reference.

130. Nansen, as cited in Bendiner, *A Time for Angels* (New York: Knopf, 1975), p. 197.

131. *Neues Volk*, "Wie Rassenfragen entstehen Weiss und Schwarz in Amerika," 4 (1936): 9–15; "700 Jahre Rassenkampf," 5 (1937): 16–21; "Rassenmischmasch," 5 (1937): 22.

132. Adolf Hitler, 22 August 1939, in Great Britain Foreign Office, *Documents on British Foreign Policy, 1919–1939* 3rd ser., 9 vols. (London: His Majesty's Stationery Office, 1949–1955), 7:258.

Chapter 5. The Crusade of World War II

1. See, among many others, Angus Calder, *The People's War* (London: Panther, 1969).

2. "The Einsatzgruppen Case," in International Military Tribunal, *Trials of War Criminals*, 15 vols. (Washington, D.C.: Government Printing Office, 1946–1948), 4:412–13.

3. Hoover Institution, Heinrich Himmler Collection, File 286, for the notorious publication *Der Untermensch*. Also see *Das Schwarze Korps* 27 (July 1941) and various issues of *Volkischer Beobachter* from 1941.

4. Roosevelt Library, Franklin Roosevelt Papers, President's Secretary File, Safe File, Box 6, File "Welles Report, 1940, Part II."

5. Franklin Roosevelt, Address of 6 January 1941, in *The Public Papers and Addresses of Franklin D. Roosevelt*, Samuel Rosenman (ed.), 13 vols. (New York: Random House, 1938–1950), 9:672.

6. See the section below entitled "Crusaders, Visions, and Proposals."

7. League of Nations Union, *The Atlantic Charter* (London: Hodgson, 1942), p. 1.

8. Franklin Roosevelt Papers, President's Secretary's File, Safe File, Box 1, File "Atlantic Charter (1)," "Log of the President's Cruise, 3–16 August 1941."

9. Winston Churchill, *The Grand Alliance* (Boston: Houghton Mifflin, 1950), p. 432.

10. Churchill's draft and the final text are in Franklin Roosevelt Papers, President's Secretary's File, Safe File, Box 1, File "Atlantic Charter (1)."

11. Elizabeth Borgwardt, *A New Deal for the World* (Cambridge, Mass.: Belknap Press of Harvard University Press, 2005), p. 4.

12. See Holly C. Shulman, *The Voice of America* (Madison: University of Wisconsin Press, 1990), p. 72; Sumner Welles, *The Time for Decision* (New York: Harper & Brothers, 1944), p. 178.

13. NANZ, EA 1, File 101/1/3 (1), Telegram (10) R, from Peter Fraser (London) to the Cabinet in Wellington, "Most Secret," 12 August 1941; Circular from Walter Nash, 14 August 1941. During the war Nash served as deputy prime minister, minister of finance, and minister to the United States.

14. Nelson Mandela, *Long Walk to Freedom* (Boston: Little, Brown, 1994), pp. 83–84.

15. See "Japanese Scorn the Eight Points," and "Wilson Revival Seen by Berlin," in *New York Times*, 15 August 1941.

16. Declaration of the United Nations, 1 January 1942, in U.S. Department of State, *FRUS, 1942*, 1:25–26. See also Britain, PRO/FO, 371/67605, Minute from Research Department, "Human Rights," 2 June 1947; Wellington Koo Papers, Rare Book and Manuscript Library, Columbia University, Box 54, File 2. These words were inserted by Franklin Roosevelt in his own handwriting in the draft of the Declaration.

17. Franklin Roosevelt, Annual Message to Congress, 6 January 1942, as cited in Louise Holborn (ed.), *War and Peace Aims of the United Nations* (Boston: World Peace Foundation, 1943), pp. 66–67. Thomas A. Bailey, *A Diplomatic History of the American People* (New York: Appleton-Century-Crofts, 1968), p. 744, describes the Declaration as "of supreme importance."

18. Final Act, Resolution XXXV, "Support and Adherence to the Principles of the 'Atlantic Charter,'" Pan American Union, *Congress and Conference Series* 36 (Washington, D.C.: Pan American Union, 1942). They also referred to the Convention on Rights and Duties of States approved at the International Conference of American States held at Montevideo in 1933.

19. Joseph Goebbels, entry of 27 March 1942, *Diaries, 1942–1943*, Louis Lochner (trans.) (New York: Doubleday, 1948), p. 147.

20. "Dokumentation," *Vierteljahrshefte für Zeitgeschichte* 1 (1953): 190–91. See also International Military Tribunal, *Trial of Major War Criminals*, 42 vols. (Nuremberg: International Military Tribunal, 1947–1949); Germany, PA/AA, Abteilung Inland, Inland I Partei, Aktenzeichen 82–35, "Rassenfrage und Rassenfoerderung," Band 6; Primo Levi, *Survival in Auschwitz* (New York: Collier, 1993), among many others.

21. Kishlansky et al., *Civilization in the West*, p. 898. Thomas G. Paterson, *On Every Front* (New York: Norton, 1979), p. 8, uses the figure twelve million.

22. See John Dower, *War Without Mercyc* (New York: Pantheon, 1986); Paul Gordon Lauren, *Kokka to Jinshuhenken* (Tokyo: TBS-Britannica, 1995); Lauren, *Power and Prejudice*, pp. 138–40.

23. Among many others, see Murphey, *A History of Asia*, pp. 355–56.

24. See Dower, *War Without Mercy*, p. 175.

25. The Goho Report, as cited in Christopher Thorne, "Racial Aspects of the Far Eastern War," *Proceedings of the British Academy* 66 (1980): 343.

26. As cited in W. H. Elsbree, *Japan's Role in Southeast Asian Nationalist Movements, 1940–1945* (Cambridge, Mass.: Harvard University Press, 1953), p. 163.

27. Cited in Irwin Gellman, "The *St. Louis* Tragedy," *American Jewish Historical Quarterly* 61 (December 1971): 156.

28. See David Wyman, *The Abandonment of the Jews* (New York: Pantheon, 1986); Monty Penkower, *The Jews Were Expendable* (Urbana: University of Illinois Press, 1983), pp. 94–95, 120.

29. See *Sydney Morning Herald*, 27 December 1941, 2 January 1942; "The Japanese," *Fortune* 25 (February 1942): 53ff; Christopher Thorne, *Allies of a Kind* (New York: Oxford University Press, 1979), pp. 1–5.

30. As cited in Dower, *War Without Mercy*, p. 7.

31. Winston Churchill, as cited in Thorne, *Allies of a Kind*, p. xxiii.

32. Winston Churchill, 10 November 1942, as cited in Fischer, *Gandhi*, p. 135.

33. Hoover Institution Archives, Joseph Stilwell Diaries, entries of 18 and 21 February 1942.

34. U.S. Commission on Wartime Relocation and Internment of Civilians, *Personal Justice Denied* (Washington, D.C.: Government Printing Office, 1982); Roger Daniels, *Concentration Camps USA* (New York: Holt, Rinehart & Winston, 1971); Peter Irons, *Justice at War* (New York: Oxford

University Press, 1983); David R. Hughes and Evelyn Kallen, *The Anatomy of Racism* (Montreal: Harvest House, 1974).

35. John Rankin, as cited in Virginius Dabney, "Nearer and Nearer the Precipice," *Atlantic Monthly* 171 (January 1943): 95.

36. See Lauren, *Power and Prejudice*, pp. 140, 151.

37. *Negro Quarterly* (Fall 1942), as cited in Nikhil Pal Singh, "Culture/Wars: Recoding Empire in an Age of Democracy," *American Quarterly* 50 (September 1998): 482.

38. See Britain, PRO/FO, 371/27889, File F/1899/17/23.

39. Lord Moyne, 1941, as cited in Laura Tabili, *"We Ask for British Justice"* (Ithaca, N.Y.: Cornell University Press, 1994), p. 161.

40. See Brawley, *The White Peril*, pp. 174–75.

41. Jan Smuts to M. C. Gillett, 7 June 1942, in *Selections from the Smuts Papers*, Jean van der Poel (ed.), 7 vols. (Cambridge: Cambridge University Press, 1973), 6:568.

42. P. S. Gerbrandy, in "Dutch Diamonds," *Bombay Chronicle*, 14 February 1942.

43. Eleanor Roosevelt, as cited in Franklin, *From Slavery to Freedom*, p. 456.

44. His study eventually appeared as Gunnar Myrdal, *An American Dilemma*, 2 vols. (New York: Harper, 1944).

45. "Willkie Says War Liberates Negroes," *New York Times*, 20 July 1942.

46. H. G. Wells, "War Aims: The Rights of Man," *The Times* (London), 25 October 1939. See also David C. Smith, *H. G. Wells, Desperately Mortal* (New Haven, Conn.: Yale University Press, 1986), pp. 428–49; Burgers, "The Road to San Francisco," pp. 465–68.

47. Lord Ritchie Calder, *On Human Rights* (London: H. G. Wells Society, 1968), pp. 3–5.

48. Geoffrey Robertson, *Crimes Against Humanity* (New York: New Press, 2002), p. 24.

49. H. G. Wells, *The Rights of Man or What Are We Fighting For?* (Harmondsworth: Penguin, 1940), p. 127.

50. Clarence Streit, *Union Now* (New York: Harper and Brothers, 1939). I am very grateful to Clarence Streit for conversations on this subject prior to his death.

51. Catholic Association for International Peace, *American Peace Aims* (Washington, D.C.: Catholic Association for International Peace, 1941), Report of Several Committees, and Appendix C, "An International Bill of Rights."

52. World Citizens Association, *The World's Destiny and the United States* (Chicago: World Citizens Association, 1941).

53. Roosevelt Library, Sumner Welles Papers, Box 192, letter from Arnold Toynbee to B. Cohen, 17 May 1941.

54. Eduard Beneš, 10 November 1941, in Holborn (ed.), *War and Peace Aims of the United Nations*, p. 420.

55. National Conference of Christians and Jews, Statement of February 1942, in ibid., pp. 633–34; Jacques Maritain, *Les Droits de l'homme de la loi naturelle* (New York: Maison Française, 1942).

56. Franklin Roosevelt, message of 14 August 1942, in Roosevelt Library, Franklin Roosevelt Papers, President's Secretary's File, Safe File, Box 1, File: Atlantic Charter (1). A note in this file from M. J. McDermott to Joseph Barnes, 10 August 1942, makes clear that Churchill could not be persuaded to jointly sign this statement.

57. Lauren, *Power and Prejudice*, pp. 155–56; Geiss, *Panafrikanismus*, pp. 300–309.

58. Sutan Sjahrir, *Out of Exile* (New York: Greenwood Press, 1969), pp. 248–49.

59. Pearl S. Buck, *American Unity and Asia* (New York: Day, 1942), p. 25.

60. See, among many examples, NANZ, EA 1, File 101/1/3 (1), including the letter from T. T. Wetere to Peter Fraser, 21 September 1942, asking for a copy of the Atlantic Charter.

61. Institute of Pacific Relations, December 1942, as cited in Brian Urquart, *Ralph Bunche* (New York: Norton, 1993), p. 105.

62. As cited in Myrdal, *An American Dilemma*, 2:1006.

63. See Brenda Gayle Plummer, *Rising Wind* (Chapel Hill: University of North Carolina Press, 1996), p. 102.

64. Alison Bernstein, *American Indians and World War II* (Norman: University of Oklahoma Press, 1991), pp. 112ff.

65. United Nations, *Political Rights of Women*, Document 1949.I.15 (New York: United Nations, 1949), chap. 1.

66. As cited in Kazuko, *Chinese Women in a Century of Revolution*, p. 166.

67. Women's Bureau, as cited in William Chafe, *The Paradox of Change* (New York: Oxford University Press, 1991), p. 133. See also Karen Anderson, *Wartime Women* (Westport, Conn.: Greenwood, 1982); Sherna Gluck, *Rosie the Riveter Revisited* (New York: New American Library, 1988).

68. See United Nations Economic and Social Council, Document E/CN.5/44, Social Commission, Third Session, 19 February 1948, pp. 46–47.

69. Franklin D. Roosevelt, State of the Union Address, 11 January 1944, U.S. Congress, *Congressional Record*, 90, pt. 1, pp. 55–57.

70. Borgwardt, *A New Deal for the World, passim.*

71. See NANZ, Peter Fraser Papers; NANZ, Walter Nash Papers, especially Folio 142; James Thorn, *Peter Fraser* (London: Odhams, 1952); 162ff.; Keith Sinclair, *Walter Nash* (Auckland: Auckland University Press, 1976), pp. 237ff.

72. See Renu Chakravartty, *Communists in the Indian Women's Movement* (New Delhi: People's Publishing House, 1980).

73. Sir William Beveridge, *Social Insurance and Allied Services* (New York: Macmillan, 1942), p. 6

74. As cited in Calder, *The People's War*, pp. 607–14.

75. Wood, *The New Zealand People at War* (Wellington: Department of Internal Affairs, 1958), p. 349.

76. See Hoover Institution Archives, Loda Mae Davis Papers, Box 1, memorandum "UNRRA, An Experiment in International Cooperation," 1947; Thomas Paterson and J. Garry Clifford, *America Ascendant* (Lexington, Mass.: Heath, 1995), p. 34.

77. Quincy Wright, "Human Rights and the World Order," *International Conciliation*, 389 (April 1943): 238–62; Glenn Tatsuya Mitoma, "Civil Society and International Human Rights: The Commission to Study the Organization of Peace and the Origins of the UN Human Rights Regime," *Human Rights Quarterly* 30 (2008): 607–30.

78. Irving Isaacs, *The International Bill of Rights and Permanent Peace Concordance* (Boston: Twentieth Century Association, 1943); Charles Baylis, "Towards an International Bill of Rights," *Public Opinion Quarterly* 8 (Summer 1944): 244–53.

79. Hersch Lauterpacht, *An International Bill of the Rights of Man* (New York: Columbia University Press, 1945).

80. American Law Institute, *Report to the Council of the Institute and Statement of Essential Human Rights* (New York: American Law Institute, 1944), p. 5, copy on file in U.S. National Archives and Records Administration (hereafter cited NARA), RG 59, Alger Hiss Files, Box 2. The best treatment of the ALI project is Hanne Hagtvedt Vik, "The United States, the American Legal Community, and the Vision of International Human Rights Protection, 1941–1953," Ph.D. dissertation, University of Oslo. See also Louis Sohn, "How American International Lawyers Prepared for the San Francisco Bill of Rights," *American Journal of International Law* 89 (July 1995): 546–53.

81. Walter Nash, in New Zealand Parliament, *Appendix to the Journals of the House of Representatives, Session 1944* (Wellington: Government Printer, 1945), 1:A-7, pp. 2–24.

82. Brunet, *La Garantie internationale des droits de l'homme*, pp. 93–94. See also Verdoodt, *Naissance et signification de la Déclaration universelle des droits de l'homme*, pp. 40–41.

83. Commission to Study the Organization of Peace, *International Safeguard of Human Rights* (New York: Organization to Study the Organization of Peace, 1944), p. 11. See also U.S. NARA, RG 59, Alger Hiss Files, Box 2, memorandum written by Alice McDiarmid, "Proposals for an International Bill of Rights," August 1944.

84. For a compilation, see Holborn, *War and Peace Aims of the United Nations.*

85. Calder, *On Human Rights*, p. 4.

86. Inter-American Juridical Committee, 5 September 1942, in Pan American Union, *Preliminary Recommendation on Postwar Problems* (Washington, D.C.: Pan American Union, 1942), pp. 17–22.

87. United Nations Declaration on Jewish Massacres, 17 December 1942, in Great Britain, Parliament, House of Commons, *The Parliamentary Debates* 5th ser., 385: 2083. See also Penkower, *The Jews Were Expendable*, pp. 87–92.

88. Declaration of Four Nations on General Security, in U.S. Department of State, *FRUS, 1943*, 1:756.

89. Winston Churchill, as cited in League of Nations Union, *The Atlantic Charter*, p. 1. See also Lauren, *Power and Prejudice*, pp. 146–47.

90. Britain, FO/PRO, 371/24232, Telegram 95, from Lothian (Washington, D.C.) to Foreign Office (London), 8 October 1940.

91. K. Ross Toole Archives at the University of Montana, Clarence Streit Papers, Box 11, File 41, "Your Sovereignty—or Your Nation's?"

92. See Baylis, "Towards an International Bill of Rights," p. 252.

93. The archival records of this advisory committee can be found in U.S., NARA, RG 59, Records of Harley A. Notter; Roosevelt Library, Sumner Welles Papers. For a published account, see U.S. Department of State, *Postwar Foreign Policy Preparation, 1939–1945* (Washington, D.C.: Government Printing Office, 1949). The precise composition and membership varied during the course of the war.

94. Some of his many wartime speeches and writings can be found in Roosevelt Library, Sumner Welles Papers, Box 195; Roosevelt Library, President's Secretary's File, Safe File, Box 1, File "Atlantic Charter." See also Sumner Welles, *World of the Four Freedoms* (New York: Simon & Schuster, 1943); Welles, *The Time for Decision.*

95. The membership included at various times G. H. Hackworth, Hamilton Fish Armstrong, Adolf Berle, Benjamin Cohen, Brooks Emeny, and James Shotwell, assisted by Durward Sandifer, John Halderman, Alice McDiarmid, and Lawrence Preuss.

96. The various drafts and language changes can be seen in U.S. NARA, RG 59, Records of Harley A. Notter, Box 75, Advisory Commission on Postwar Foreign Policy, from "Bill of Rights. Preliminary Draft," L. Document 2, Confidential, 31 July 1942, to the final "Bill of Rights," L. Document 55, Secret, 3 December 1942.

97. Ibid., "Bill of Rights," L. Document 1, Secret, 31 July 1942.

98. Ibid., "Bill of Rights—International Implementation," L. Document 30, Secret, 4 November 1942.

99. Ibid.

100. Roosevelt Library, Sumner Welles Papers, Box 189, P-IO, Document 3, untitled, 31 July 1942. See also P-IO, Document 5, "Preliminary Memorandum on International Organization," 7 August 1942.

101. U.S., NARA, RG 59, Records of Harley A. Notter, Box 215, Advisory Commission on Postwar Foreign Policy, "Draft Commentary, First Revision," written by Alice McDiarmid, 3 September 1943.

102. Ibid.

103. See K. Smith, "Our Foreign Policy Goes Realist," *American Mercury*, December 1943.

104. Roosevelt Library, Sumner Welles Papers, Box 189, P Minutes 60, 19 June 1943, Secret.

105. Franklin Roosevelt, 20 January 1945, in *The Public Papers and Addresses of Franklin D. Roosevelt*, 13:524.

106. Robert Hilderbrand, *Dumbarton Oaks* (Chapel Hill: University of North Carolina Press, 1990), p. 67.

107. The Soviets attended only the first phase and the Chinese only the last.

108. Cordell Hull, as cited in U.S. Department of State, *Postwar Foreign Policy Preparation*, p. 280.

109. The final results are found in "[The Dumbarton Oaks] Proposals for the Establishment of a General International Organization," 7 October 1944, in ibid., pp. 611–19.

110. Roosevelt, as cited in the extract from the diary of Edward Stettinius, 27 September 1944, in U.S. Department of State, *FRUS, 1944*, 1:890.

111. T. V. Soong, in an early speech of 9 June 1942, in Document 26831-11, "Public Statements by Chinese Leaders on International Organization," from the British Foreign Office, in NANZ, EA 2, 1945/6b, File 111/8/8(1).

112. Wei Tao Ming to Cordell Hull, 3 June 1944 (transmitting a letter from Chiang Kai-shek to Franklin Roosevelt), in U.S.Department of State, *FRUS, 1944*, 1:640.

113. "Tentative Chinese Proposals for a General International Organization," 23 August 1944, in ibid., 1:718.

114. Wellington Koo Papers, Box 70, File 4, "Ancient China's 'League of Nations,'" 23 August 1944.

115. Ibid., Box 76, File 5, Speech of H. H. Kung before the U.S. Senate, 24 August 1944.

116. See the extracts from the diary of Edward Stettinius, 29 August 1944, in U.S. Department of State, *FRUS, 1944*, 1:750; U.S. Department of State, *Postwar Foreign Policy Preparation*, pp. 301–38; Ruth Russell, *A History of the United Nations Charter* (Washington, D.C.: Brookings Institution, 1958), p. 329.

117. Britain, PRO/FO, 371/40716, Telegram No. 5318 from Lord Halifax (Washington, D.C.) to Foreign Office, with addition from Alexander Cadogan, 29 September 1944.

118. See U.S., NARA, RG 59, Alger Hiss Files, Box 2, memorandum entitled "Proposals for an International Bill of Rights," August 1944.

119. See "Welles Warns," *New York Times*, 25 October 1944.

120. "Additional Paragraph Suggested . . . for Inclusion in Section II, Principles, of the Draft Proposals," in U.S. Department of State, *FRUS, 1944*, 1:791.

121. See Britain, PRO/FO, 371/40716, WR.208/126, letter from the Dominion Office to the Foreign Office, "Secret and Immediate," 30 September 1944; Simpson, *Human Rights and the End of Empire*, p. 212.

122. Andrei Gromyko, as cited in Memorandum from Edward Stettinius to Cordell Hull, "Progress Report on Dumbarton Oaks Conversations," 9 September 1944, in U.S. Department of State, *FRUS, 1944*, 1:789.

123. See U.S. Department of State, *Postwar Foreign Policy Preparation*, pp. 246–338; U.S. Department of State, *FRUS, 1944*, 1:838.

124. Wellington Koo Papers, Box 76, File 5, "Notes on the Principle of the Equality of Races"; Box 77, File 2, Notes of Conversation Between Wellington Koo and Sir Alexander Cadogan, 29 September 1944.

125. Churchill, as cited in Diane Shaver Clemens, *Yalta* (New York: Oxford University Press, 1970), p. 48.

126. Wellington Koo, in Plenary Record 3, Informal Record, Secret, 3 October 1944, File of Wellington Koo, "Washington, D.C. Conversations on International Organization" (microfilm, Columbia University School of Law).

127. Hilderbrand, *Dumbarton Oaks*, p. 246.

128. Franklin Roosevelt, as cited in NANZ, EA 2, 1945/6B, File 111/8/8 (1), Memorandum 26831-5, "Private Statements by Members of United States Administration," Most Secret.

129. Leo Pasvolsky, as cited in Joint Formulation Group, Record 3, "Secret," 6 October 1944, File of Koo, "Washington, D.C. Conversations on International Organization."

130. "Welles Warns," *New York Times*, 25 October 1944.

Chapter 6. A "People's Peace": Peace and a Charter with Human Rights

1. Cordell Hull, as cited in U.S. Department of State, *Postwar Foreign Policy Preparation*, p. 304.

2. Carl Berendsen, as cited in Wood, *The New Zealand People at War*, pp. 324–25.

3. Peter Fraser, 30 June 1944, in Canada, Parliament, House of Commons, *Debates*, Session 1944 (Ottawa: Edmond Cloutier, 1945), 5:4424.

4. This is clear from NANZ, Peter Fraser Papers, Series 1, File 7; NANZ, Walter Nash Papers; New Zealand, Parliament, *Appendix to the Journals of the House of Representatives, Session 1944* (Wellington: Government Printer, 1945), 1, A-7, "International Labor Conference," p. 2; Thorn, *Peter Fraser*, pp. 232ff.; and Sinclair, *Walter Nash*, pp. 237ff.

5. NANZ, EA 2, 1945/9B, File 111/8/6 (2), Note entitled "Mr. Berendsen's Comments."

6. Joint statement from the 1944 Wellington Conference, as cited in NANZ, EA 2, 1945/9B, File 111/8/6 (2), "Document Prepared by the Australian Minister for External Affairs on International Organization," March 1945. See also in the same file a memorandum entitled "World Organization, Note for File," Secret.

7. Secretary of State for Dominion Affairs to New Zealand Minister of External Affairs, 14 November 1944, as cited in Wood, *The New Zealand People at War*, p. 322.

8. Ibid.

9. See "The Position of the Government of Uruguay Respecting the Plans of Postwar International Organization," 28 September 1944, in United Nations Conference on International Organization, *Documents of the United Nations Conference on International Organization* (hereafter UNCIO, *Documents*), 22 vols. (London: United Nations Information Organization, 1946–1955), 3:26–33.

10. "Opinion of the Department of Foreign Relations of Mexico Concerning the Dumbarton Oaks Proposals," 31 October 1944, in ibid., pp. 55ff. See also NANZ, EA 2, 1945/6B, File 111/8/8 (1).

11. "Observations of the Government of Venezuela on the Recommendations Adopted at the Dumbarton Oaks Conferences," 31 October 1944, in ibid., pp. 189ff.

12. The words are those of Harley Notter, in U.S. Department of State, *Postwar Foreign Policy Preparation*, p. 401.

13. The U.S. delegation was willing to listen to Latin American opinion, but would not sign any binding agreement. See U.S. Department of State, *FRUS, 1945, The American Republics* (Washington, D.C.: Government Printing Office, 1969), 9:1–153.

14. See, for example, Wellington Koo Papers, Columbia University, Rare Book and Manuscript Library, Box 85, File 59, "Comments at Inter-American Conference."

15. See Political Memorandum No. 4, "Conversation Between Licenciado Alfonso García Robles . . . and Messrs. Bohan and Sanders," 6 February 1945, in U.S. Department of State, *FRUS, 1945*, 9:90–95.

16. Document No. 24, CI-PR-4, "Proposal of the Delegation of the Republic of Cuba on the Declaration of the International Duties and Rights of the Individual," 27 February 1945, in Inter-American Conference on Problems of War and Peace, Document TC-9986, No. 219, C2–V-17, "An Account of the Essential Comments Made by the Delegations to the Inter-American Conference . . . Concerning the Bases of Dumbarton Oaks. . . ."

17. Final Act of the Inter-American Conference on Problems of War and Peace, 8 March 1945, in Inter-American Conference on Problems of War and Peace, Document TC-9986, No. 219, C2–V-17, "An Account of Essential Comments."

18. Pan American Union, *Inter-American Conference on War and Peace*, Congress and Conference Series, 47 (Washington, D.C.: Pan American Union, 1945), especially the "Declaration of Mexico," "Reaffirmation of the Principles of the Atlantic Charter," "Rights of Women in the Americas," "International Protection of the Essential Rights of Man," and "Racial Discrimination," pp. 39–40, 61–62, 69–70. See also "Evolution of Human Rights," *Weekly Bulletin of the United Nations*, 12 August 1946.

19. Inman, *Inter-American Conferences*, pp. 210, 213.

20. Britain, PRO/FO, 371/50699, "Results of Inter-American Conference (Mexico City, 21 February-8 March 1945)," Confidential, 8 March 1945.

21. See Edward Stettinius, "Statement by the Secretary of State on the Conclusion of the Conference," 8 March 1945, in U.S. Department of State, *Department of State Bulletin* 12, 298 (11 March 1945): 398–400; and U.S. Department of State, *FRUS 1945*, 9:140, 143.

22. See U.S. Department of State, *Department of State Bulletin* 12, 289–313 (7 January–24 June 1945).

23. U.S. Department of State, *Postwar Foreign Policy Preparation*, pp. 378–79; the observations in NANZ, EA 2, 1945/9A, File 111/8/6 (1), Memorandum entitled "United States of America," Confidential, 30 October 1944.

24. Americans United for World Organization, *Statement of Essential Human Rights* (New York: Americans United for World Organization, 1945).

25. Commission to Study the Organization of the Peace, *International Safeguard of Human Rights*; Mitoma, "Civil Society and International Human Rights," pp. 625–30; Sohn, "How American International Lawyers Prepared for the San Francisco Bill of Rights," pp. 540–53.

26. See Jacob Robinson, *Human Rights and Fundamental Freedoms in the Charter of the United Nations: A Commentary* (New York: Institute of Jewish Affairs, 1946), pp. 32–34.

27. Commission on a Just and Durable Peace, *Christian Standards and Current International Developments*, as reproduced in *International Conciliation* 409 (March 1945): 142–49.

28. Her complaints began early and attracted international attention, as seen by NANZ, EA 2, 1945/9B, File 111/8/6 (2), memorandum from Berendsen (Washington, D.C.) to McIntosh (Wellington), 30 August 1944.

29. Ernest Johnson, "A Voice at the Peace Table?" *Crisis* (November 1944): 345.

30. Rayford W. Logan, "Dumbarton Oaks Proposals Ignore Colonial Problem," *Chicago Defender*, 9 December 1944.

31. See "Human Rights for All Minorities (1945)," in Foner, *W. E. B. Du Bois Speaks*, 2:184; Singh, "Culture/Wars," *American Quarterly* 50 (September 1998): 482–83.

32. Declaration of Philadelphia, as reproduced in U.S. Senate, 81st Congress, Committee on Foreign Relations, Document No. 1223, *A Decade of American Foreign Policy* (Washington, D.C.: Government Printing Office, 1950), pp. 25–26.

33. Commission to Study the Organization of the Peace, *International Safeguard of Human Rights*, as reproduced in *International Conciliation* 403 (September 1944): 554, 569.

34. Declaration on Liberated Europe, 11 February 1945, in U.S. Department of State, *Department of State Bulletin* 12, 295 (18 February 1945): 215.

35. The Anti-Slavery and Aborigines Protection Society, *An International Colonial Convention* (London: Anti-Slavery and Aborigines Protection Society, 1943); Geiss, *Panafrikanismus*, pp. 440ff.; Wellington Koo Papers, Box 76, File 5; Wood, *The New Zealand People at War*, pp. 327–39; Commission on a Just and Durable Peace, *Christian Standards and Current International Developments*, as reproduced in *International Conciliation* 409 (March 1945): 142–49.

36. See Chapter 5 above; Lauren, *Power and Prejudice*, pp. 145–53.

37. U.S., NARA, RG 59, Records of Harley A. Notter, Box 215, Advisory Commission on Postwar Foreign Policy, "Draft Commentary, First Revision," 3 September 1943; Roosevelt Library, Sumner Welles Papers, Boxes 189, 195; Wellington Koo Papers, Boxes 70, 76; New Zealand, Parliament, *Appendix to the Journals of the House of Representatives, Session 1944*, 1:A-7, especially p. 24, among many others.

38. American Jewish Committee, *A World Charter for Human Rights*.

39. Final Act of the Inter-American Conference on Problems of War and Peace, as cited in Britain, PRO/FO, 371/50699, "Results of Inter-American Conference," Confidential, 8 March 1945.

40. Commission to Study the Organization of the Peace, *International Safeguard of Human Rights*, as reproduced in *International Conciliation* 403 (September 1944): 554.

41. "Proposal of the Delegation of the Republic of Cuba on the Declaration of the International

Duties and Rights of the Individual," 27 February 1945, in Inter-American Conference on Problems of War and Peace, Document TC-9986, No. 219, C2–V-17; U.S. Senate, 81st Congress, 1st Session, Committee on Foreign Relations, Document No. 1223, *A Decade of American Foreign Policy*, pp. 25–26; Commission on a Just and Durable Peace, *Christian Standards and Current International Developments*; among many others.

42. Franklin D. Roosevelt, as cited in U.S. Department of State, *Postwar Foreign Policy Preparation*, p. 411.

43. Alfred Tennyson, "Locksley Hall," as cited in Stephen Schlesinger, *Act of Creation* (Boulder, Colo.: Westview Press, 2003), p. 6.

44. Jan Smuts, Verbatim Minutes of the Sixth Plenary Session, 1 May 1945, in UNCIO, *Documents*, 1:420–21.

45. Harry Truman, Verbatim Minutes, 25 April 1945, in ibid., 1:113–15.

46. See Jan Smuts, in ibid., 1:425.

47. Ramaswami Mudaliar, Verbatim Minutes, 28 April 1945, in ibid., 1:245.

48. See Roosevelt Library, President's Secretary's File, Safe File, Boxes 5 and 6, File "United Nations Conference (1)."

49. The only major changes from the Dumbarton Oaks proposals made at Yalta were the compromises on voting that allowed the Soviets to have three votes in the General Assembly and that stipulated that the veto could only apply to substantive matters.

50. Winston Churchill, as cited in Robert F. Sherwood (ed.), *The White House Papers of Harry L. Hopkins*, 2 vols. (London: Eyre & Spottiswoode, 1949), 2:854.

51. Alexander Cadogan to Theodosia Cadogan, 15 May 1945, in *The Diaries of Sir Alexander Cadogan*, David Dilks (ed.) (New York: Putnam, 1971), p. 742.

52. Vyacheslav Molotov, speech at the First Plenary Session, 26 April 1945, in UNCIO, *Documents*, 1:131–36.

53. Harry Truman, as cited in Memorandum by Charles Bohlen, 23 April 1945, in U.S. Department of State, *FRUS, 1945*, 5:253.

54. See Plummer, *The Rising Wind*, p. 142; U.S. Department of State, *Postwar Foreign Policy Preparation*, p. 416.

55. Alice McDiarmid, as cited in Kirsten Sellars, *The Rise and Rise of Human Rights* (Stroud: Sutton, 2002), p. 4.

56. Leo Pasvolsky, in Minutes of the Fifth Meeting of the U.S. Delegation, 9 April 1945, in U.S. Department of State, *FRUS, 1945*, 1:223.

57. Britain, Foreign Office, U 8657/180/70, "Some Comments on the Dumbarton Oaks Proposals by Dr. C. W. Jenks," Confidential, 12 January 1945, as on file in NANZ, EA2 1945/6B, File 111/8/8 (1).

58. Proposals submitted prior to May 1945: Doc 2, G/7 (c); Doc 2, G/7 (d); Doc 2, G/7 (f); Doc 2, G/7 (l) Doc 2, G/7 (o); Doc 2, G/7 (q); as contained in UNCIO, *Documents*, 3:54ff., 254–56, 345–47, 383, 446–48, 474.

59. Proposals submitted during the first four days of May 1945 prior to the joint amendments of the Great Powers: Doc 2, G/7 (n) (l); Doc 2, G/14 (c); Doc 2, G/14 (f); Doc 2, G/14 (g); Doc 2, G/14 (h); as contained in ibid., 3:365, 472, 486, 495–502, 527.

60. Doc 2, G/7 (q), "Suggestions of the Egyptian Government," 16 April 1945, in ibid., 3:447.

61. Britain, PRO/FO, 371/50703, "Memorandum for Submission to His Majesty's Government for Their Consideration in View of the San Francisco Conference," 12 April 1945; handwritten comment on the cover.

62. "A Declaration to the Nations of the World," issued by the Non-European United Committee, South Africa, 1945, as cited in Du Bois, *The World and Africa*, pp. 39–41.

63. See U.S. Department of State, "Designation of Consultants to the United States Delegation," *Department of State Bulletin* 12, 304 (22 April 1945): 724–25; Dorothy Robins, *Experiment in Democracy* (New York: Parkside, 1971).

64. See Carol Anderson's excellent *Eyes Off the Prize* (Cambridge: Cambridge University Press, 2003), pp. 25ff; John Nurser, *For All Peoples and All Nations* (Washington, D.C.: Georgetown University Press, 2005).

65. See William Korey, *NGOs and the Universal Declaration of Human Rights* (New York: St. Martin's, 1998), pp. 29–42; Plummer, *Rising Wind*, pp. 125–40.

66. Walter White, *A Man Called White* (Athens: University of Georgia Press, 1995), p. 295.

67. Walter Kotschnig, Transcript of Proceedings, Conference on the International Declaration of Human Rights, 31 October 1947, as cited in M. Glen Johnson, "The Contributions of Eleanor and Franklin Roosevelt to the Development of International Protection for Human Rights," *Human Rights Quarterly* 9, 1 (1987): 25.

68. See Joseph Proskauer, *A Segment of My Times* (New York: Farrar, Straus, 1950), p. 225; Sellars, *The Rise and Rise of Human Rights*, pp. 1–5.

69. "Suggestions Presented by . . . India for the Amendment of the Dumbarton Oaks Proposals," Doc 2, G/14 (h), 4 May 1945, in UNCIO, *Documents*, 3:527.

70. "Proposed Amendments to the Dumbarton Oaks Proposals Submitted by the Philippine Delegation," Doc 2, G/14 (k), 5 May 1945, in ibid., 3:535; Verbatim Minutes of the Third Meeting of Commission II, Document 1144, II/16, 21 June 1945, in ibid., 8:134.

71. "Amendments to the Dumbarton Oaks Proposals," Doc 2, G/25, 5 May 1945, in ibid., 3:602.

72. See Russell, *A History of the United Nations Charter*, p. 793.

73. "New Urguayan Proposals," Doc 2 G/7 (a) (l), 5 May 1945; "Additional Amendments Proposed by the Delegation of the Republic of Panama," Doc 2, G/7 (g)(2), 5 May 1945, in ibid., 3:35 and 269.

74. "Amendments Proposed by the French Government," 21 March 1945, in ibid., 3:383.

75. U.S., NARA, RG 59, Box 2259, 501.BD Human Rights/11–1349, UNCIO CONS, Secret, Meeting 1, 2 May 1945; U.S. Department of State, *FRUS, 1945*, 1:546, statement of Leo Pasvolsky.

76. Francis Michael Forde, 27 April 1945, as cited in NANZ, EA 1, File 111/8/7 (1).

77. See UNCIO, *Documents*, 10:434; NANZ, Peter Fraser Papers, Series 3, Official Administrative Papers, File 2a, "Papers of the UN Conference," handwritten note regarding the amendment on this subject proposed by Wellington Koo.

78. Carlos Romulo, as cited in Verbatim Minutes of the Third Meeting of Commission II, Document 1144, II/16, in UNCIO, *Documents*, 8:138–39.

79. For the long list of amendments on this single issue, see UNCIO, *Documents*, 1:704–7.

80. Fraser's many speech notes are in NANZ, EA 1, File 111/8/7 (1). I am grateful to Colin Aikman for personal interviews sharing his insights on Fraser at this time. See also Alister McIntosh, "Working with Peter Fraser in Wartime," *New Zealand Journal of History* 10, 1 (April 1976): 3–20.

81. Harold Stassen, in Minutes of the Forty-Fifth Meeting of the U. S. Delegation, 18 May 1945, in U.S., Department of State, *FRUS, 1945*, 1:791.

82. NANZ, EA 1, File 111/8/32 (1), Report of the Prime Minister, *United Nations Conference on International Organization*, 1945, p. 46. See also Fraser's own papers and notes in NANZ, Peter Fraser Papers, Series 3, Official Administrative Papers, File 2a, "Papers of the UN Conference"; UNCIO, *Documents*, 10; Russell, *A History of the United Nations Charter*, pp. 808–42.

83. See UNCIO, *Documents*, 3:648–57, especially 652–53.

84. For a listing of the many amendments proposed on this matter, see ibid., 3:690–97.

85. Leo Pasvolsky, as cited in Mitoma, "Civil Society and International Human Rights," p. 628.

86. See Minutes of the Twenty-Sixth Meeting of the U.S. Delegation, 2 May 1945; Minutes of the Twenty-Eighth Meeting of the U.S. Delegation, 3 May 1945; Minutes of Second Four-Power Consultative Meeting, 3 May 1945; in U.S. Department of State, *FRUS, 1945*, 1:532, 570, 581.

87. "Amendments Proposed by the Four Sponsoring Governments," printed on 5 May 1945, in UNCIO, *Documents*, 3:640–710; Anderson, *Eyes Off the Prize*, pp. 49–50.

88. "Atrocities," *Life*, 7 May 1945 (my emphasis).

89. Charles Webster, "Making of the Charter," *History* 32 (1947–48): 23.

90. See UNCIO, *Documents*, 3:308, 314, 448; Wood, *The New Zealand People at War*, p. 384.

91. The British attributed the change of position on human rights by the United States to pressure from these Latin American countries, as seen in Britain, PRO/FO, 371/50712, Telegram No. 374 from UK Delegation San Francisco to Foreign Office, 20 May 1945.

92. See the statements of Arthur Vandenberg in U.S. Department of State, *FRUS, 1945*, 1:228; the "domestic jurisdiction" subcommittee of the delegation in U.S. Department of State, *Postwar Foreign Policy Preparation*, pp. 443–45.

93. See the description of the ceremony in Wellington Koo Papers, Box 216, Diaries.

94. Charter of the United Nations, Preamble and Article 1. Russell, *A History of the United Nations Charter*, p. 913, notes that this text was suggested by Virginia Gildersleeve.

95. Charter of the United Nations, Articles 10, 13, 24, 34, 39. See also Robinson, *Human Rights and Fundamental Freedoms in the Charter*, pp. 65ff.

96. NANZ, EA 1, File 111/8/32 (1), Report of the Prime Minister, *United Nations Conference on International Organization*, 1945, p. 11.

97. Charter of the United Nations, Articles 55, 56, 60, 62, 68, 71.

98. Charter of the United Nations, Articles 73, 74.

99. Charter of the United Nations, Articles 75, 76, and 86–91.

100. See UNCIO, *Documents*, 5:311, 17:230–31; Russell, *History of the United Nations Charter*, pp. 806–7.

101. Charter of the United Nations, Articles 77, 82, 83.

102. UNCIO, *Documents*, 5:311 and 17:230–31; NANZ, EA 1, File 111/8/32 (1); Russell, *History of the United Nations Charter*, pp. 806–7.

103. Charter of the United Nations, Articles 10, 13, 55, 62, 76, 87.

104. Document 2 6/7 (h) (1), "Comments of the Government of Costa Rica," 4 May 1945, in UNCIO, *Documents*, 3:280.

105. Philip Jessup, as cited in Commission to Study the Organization of Peace, *International Safeguard of Human Rights*, p. 16.

106. Ibid., pp. 23–24.

107. Arthur Vandenberg, Minutes of the Sixth Meeting of the U.S. Delegation, 10 April 1945, in U.S. Department of State, *FRUS, 1945*, 1:228.

108. John Foster Dulles, Minutes of the Fifty-First Meeting of the U.S. Delegation, 23 May 1945, in U.S. Department of State, *FRUS, 1945*, 1:853–54.

109. See Britain, PRO/FO, 371/46324, "World Organization: Racial Equality and Domestic Jurisdiction," 8 June 1945; Wellington Koo Papers, Box 77, Notes of a Conversation Between Herbert Evatt and Koo, 22 June 1945; Lauren, *Power and Prejudice*, pp. 162–67; Brawley, *The White Peril*, pp. 210–21.

110. Herbert Evatt, in Document 696 I/1/39, "Amendment by the Australian Delegation to Proposed Paragraph 8 of Chapter II (Principles)," 14 June 1945, in UNCIO, *Documents*, 6:436–38.

111. Charter of the United Nations, Article 2 (7).

112. Tom Connally, in Minutes of the Fifty-First Meeting of the U.S. Delegation, 23 May 1945, in U.S. Department of State, *FRUS, 1945*, 1:854. See also Simpson, *Human Rights and the End of Empire*, pp. 258–73.

113. Among many sources, see NANZ, Personal Papers, Peter Fraser Papers, Series 1, Files 7,8, 9; Series 3, File 2a; Wellington Koo Papers, Boxes 70–72, 94–99; U.S., NARA, RG 59, Records of Harley Notter; published materials in UNCIO, *Documents*, passim.

114. Edward Stettinius, in UNCIO, *Documents*, 1:691, as well as the speeches by Wellington Koo of China, Joseph Paul-Boncour of France, Jan Masaryk of Czechoslovakia, and Ezequiel Padilla of Mexico; NANZ, Peter Fraser Papers, Series 1, File 7, letter of Edward Stettinius to Fraser, 23 June 1945; Thorn, *Peter Fraser*, p. 236.

115. *Time*, as cited in Robert Divine, *Second Chance* (New York: Atheneum, 1967), p. 297.

116. Rayford Logan, as cited in Plummer, *Rising Wind*, p. 149.

117. E. B. White, *The Wild Flag* (Boston: Houghton Mifflin, 1946), p. 81.

118. W. E. B. Du Bois, 11 July 1945, in U.S. Senate, Committee on Foreign Relations, *The Charter of the United Nations: Hearings*, 79th Congress, 1st Session (Washington, D.C.: Government Printing Office, 1945), p. 392. See also W. E. B. Du Bois, *Color and Democracy* (New York: Harcourt Brace, 1945).

119. See Britain, PRO/FO, 371/40843; U.S. Senate, Committee on Foreign Affairs, *The Charter of the United Nations: Hearings*; Brawley, *The White Peril*, pp. 220ff.

120. Lord Halifax, Verbatim Minutes, 26 June 1945, in UNCIO, *Documents*, 1:698.

121. Jan Smuts, in ibid., 1:710; NANZ, EA 1, File 111/8/32 (1), Report of the Prime Minister, UN Conference on International Organization, pp. 12–14, 49; and his own notes in EA 1, File 111/8/7 (1).

122. Harry Truman, Verbatim Minutes, 26 June 1945, in UNCIO, *Documents*, 1:715–16.

Chapter 7. The Universal Declaration of Human Rights

1. See Hersch Lauterpacht, *International Law and Human Rights* (New York: Garland, 1973), pp. 3–47, 145–65.

2. As cited in Kwame Nkrumah, *Towards Colonial Freedom* (London: Panaf, 1973), pp. 44–45. See also Geiss, *Panafrikanismus*, pp. 385ff; George Padmore, *Pan-Africanism or Communism?* (New York: Roy, 1956).

3. Walter White, *A Rising Wind* (New York: Doubleday, 1945), p. 155.

4. See the wealth of material in U.S, NARA, RG 59, Box 4650; "Shameful Act," *Morning Standard* (Bombay), 16 October 1945; "Treatment of Negroes a Blot on U.S.," *Sunday Standard* (Bombay), 8 July 1945; *Trud* (Moscow), passim; American Jewish Committee, *Human Rights in the Peace Treaties*.

5. Note from Uruguayan Minister for Foreign Affairs Eduardo Rodríquez Larreta to Chiefs of Mission of the American Republics, 21 November 1945, as reprinted in U.S. Department of State, *FRUS, 1945*, 9:190–91.

6. Argentine Minister for Foreign Affairs, 29 November 1945, in ibid., pp. 198–203.

7. Haas, *Beyond the Nation State*, pp. 163–65, 343ff.

8. UNESCO, *Conference for the Establishment of the United Nations Educational, Scientific, and Cultural Organization*, ECO/CONF./29, 16 November 1945, p. 93.

9. See Borgwardt, *A New Deal for the World*, pp. 196–247; Bradley Smith, *Reaching Judgment at Nuremberg* (New York: New American Library, 1977), pp. 14–16, 60, 66–67.

10. Robert Jackson, Opening Statement, 21 November 1945, in International Military Tribunal, *Trial of the Major War Criminals*, 2:98–99,130.

11. Hermann Goering, as cited in G. M. Gilbert, *Nuremberg Diary* (New York: New American Library, 1961), p. 39.

12. "Martin Niemöller's Famous Quotation," www.history.ucsb.edu/faculty/marcuse.niem.htm, accessed 23 April 2009.

13. See Lauren, *Power and Prejudice*, pp. 170–71.

14. United Nations, Document 1949.I.15, *Political Rights of Women*.

15. Constitution of Japan, Article 24, as cited in Fujimura-Fanselow and Kameda (eds.), *Japanese Women*, p. 354.

16. Wm. Roger Louis, *The British Empire in the Middle East, 1945–1951* (New York: Clarendon Press, 1984), p. 8.

17. See U.S., NARA, RG 59, Box 6, Project No. 126, "The Negotiation of the Human Rights Articles in the Treaties of Peace . . . ," Secret, August 1949.

18. United Nations General Assembly (hereafter UN/GA), *Official Records, Plenary Meetings of the General Assembly, Verbatim Records, 1946* (Flushing Meadows, N.Y.: United Nations, 1947), pp. 953–73.

19. Vijaya Lakshmi Pandit, 7 December 1946, in ibid., pp. 1016–19. See also Lauren, *Power and Prejudice*, pp. 179–184; U.S., NARA, RG 84, U.S. Mission to the United Nations, Box 78, File "Discrimination, Race: South Africa."

20. Ibid., pp. 1009–58; UN Resolution A/RES/44 (I), "Treatment of Indians in the Union of South Africa," 8 December 1946.

21. Robert Jackson, in International Military Tribunal, *Trial of the Major War Criminals*, 2:98–155.

22. UN Resolution A/RES/96 (I), "The Crime of Genocide," 11 December 1946. The Tokyo War Crimes Trials occurred between May 1946 and November 1948.

23. UN Resolution A/RES/95 (I), "Affirmation of the Principles of International Law Recognized by the Charter of the Nuremberg Tribunal," 11 December 1946.

24. Michael Ignatieff, *Human Rights as Politics and Idolatry* (Princeton, N.J.: Princeton University Press, 2001), pp. 5–6; Robertson, *Crimes Against Humanity*, p. 231. For a discussion of the flaws, see Sellars, *The Rise and Rise of Human Rights*, pp. 25 ff.

25. International Military Tribunal, *Trial of the Major War Criminals*, 11:941.

26. Robertson, *Crimes Against Humanity*, p. 236. See also the thoughtful discussion in Borgwardt, *A New Deal for the World*, pp. 242–44.

27. Essay of 26 November 1945, in Max Lerner, *Actions and Passions: Notes on Multiple Revolutions of Our Times* (New York: Simon & Schuster, 1949), p. 263.

28. As cited in Wood, *The New Zealand People at War*, p. 344.

29. This series of resolutions can be found in UN/GA, *Official Records, Resolutions, 1946*, pp. 122–27. The details and the intensity of the debates are revealed in UN/GA, *Official Records, Summary Records of the Fourth Committee, 1946*.

30. "Status of Women," *United Nations Weekly Bulletin*, 16 September 1946.

31. UN Resolution A/RES/56 (I), "Political Rights of Women," 11 December 1946. See also UN/GA, *Official Records, Third Committee, Summary Records, 1946*, pp. 121 ff.; NANZ, EA 2, File 108/23/1 (1), personal letter from Agnes McIntosh to Peter Fraser, 16 August 1948; U.S. National Archives, RG 84, Records of the U.S. Delegation to the United Nations, Box 94, File "Women and Women's Rights, 1946–1948."

32. Trygve Lie, as cited in "Human Rights," *United Nations Weekly Bulletin*, 4 November 1946.

33. Aase Lionaes, 14 December 1946, as cited in UN/GA, *Official Records, Verbatim Records of the General Assembly, Plenary Meetings, 1946*, p. 1377.

34. Resolution 59 (I), "Calling of an International Conference on Freedom of Information," 14 December 1946, in UN/GA, *Official Records, Resolutions, 1946*, p. 95.

35. UN Document A/C.3/10, "Statement on the Refugee Question by the Delegate of the Netherlands," 29 January 1946.

36. Constitution of the World Health Organization, 22 July 1946, as reproduced in "World Health Organization," *United Nations Weekly Bulletin*, 3 August 1946. I am grateful to Sandy Lauren Shepherd for bringing this to my attention.

37. Harry Truman, 26 June 1945, in UNCIO, *Documents*, 1:715–16.

38. Resolution 43 (I), "Draft Declaration on Fundamental Human Rights and Freedoms," 11 December 1946, in UN/GA, *Official Records, Resolutions, 1946*, p. 68. See also U.S, NARA, RG 84, Box 89, File "Rights: Human, 1946–1949," memorandum from James Hendrick, "Panamanian Declaration on Human Rights," 13 November 1946.

39. Edward Stettinius, as cited in United States, Department of State, Publication 2349, *Charter of the United Nations; Report to the President on the Results of the San Francisco Conference* (Washington, D.C.: Government Printing Office, 1945), pp. 118–19. See also Philip C. Jessup, "A Good Start," *Commentary* (January 1946): 56–58; O. Frederick Nolde, "Possible Functions of the Commission on Human Rights," *Annals of the American Academy of Political and Social Science* 243 (January 1946): 144–49.

40. Britain, PRO/FO, 371/57317, "Commission on Human Rights," A.C.U. (46), 25 March 1946.

41. See UN Archives/New York, DAG-1/2.3, Office of the Under-Secretary-General for Special Political Affairs (Urquhart Papers), Box 2, "Report of the Preparatory Commission"; U.S. NARA, RG 84, Box 103, File "IO: ECOSOC: Human Rights, 1946–1949," letter of William Fowler (Department of State) to H. T. Chu (Human Rights Division, United Nations), 29 October 1946.

42. John Humphrey, *Human Rights and the United Nations* (Dobbs Ferry, N.Y.: Transnational Publishers, 1984), p. 2. See also John Humphrey, *On the Edge of Greatness*, A. J. Hobbins (ed.) (Montreal: McGill University Libraries, 1994), vol. 1.

43. Eleanor Roosevelt, as cited in Elliott Roosevelt and James Brough, *Mother R.* (New York: Putnam, 1977), pp. 151–52. This prayer serves as the title for Mary Ann Glendon, *A World Made New* (New York: Random House, 2001).

44. For more discussion, see ibid.; Blanche Wiesen Cook, "Eleanor Roosevelt and Human Rights," in Edward Crapol (ed.), *Women and American Foreign Policy* (Wilmington, Del.: Scholarly Resources, 1992), pp. 91–117; M. Glen Johnson, "The Contributions of Eleanor and Franklin Roosevelt to the Development of International Human Rights," *Human Rights Quarterly* 11 (1987): 33–47.

45. Eleanor Roosevelt, in UN Document E/HR/10, "Commission on Human Rights, Summary Record of Meetings," 6 May 1946.

46. UN Document E/38/Rev.1, "Report of the Commission on Human Rights," 21 May 1946.

47. Britain, PRO/FO, 371/57318, Telegram No. 599 from Ward to Cadogan, 14 June 1946; Telegram No. 616 from Foreign Office to UN Delegation, 16 June 1946.

48. Resolution 5 (I), 16 February 1946; and Resolution 9 (II) 21 June 1946, in United Nations Economic and Social Council, *Official Records, 1946–1949*, pp. 163–64, 400–402.

49. "Extract from the Weekly Political Intelligence Summary," No. 379, 5 February 1947, generated in London, copy on file in NANZ, EA 2, File 108/11/1(1A).

50. These individuals could not always attend the meetings in person or were replaced by others. For a personal account, see René Cassin, "La Déclaration universelle et la mise en oeuvre des droits de l'homme," *Recueil des Cours de l'Academie de Droit International* 79 (1951): 258ff.

51. For the details of the discussion in the Human Rights Commission, see UN Documents E/HR/1–31 and then E/CN.4/1 and E/CN.4/SR.1–22; the excellent Johannes Morsink, *The Universal Declaration of Human Rights* (Philadelphia: University of Pennsylvania Press, 1999); Verdoodt, *Naissance et signification de la Déclaration universelle des droits de l'homme*; Humphrey, *Human Rights and the United Nations*, pp. 23ff.

52. Citation from UN Document 1948.I.12, *For Fundamental Human Rights*, p. 17.

53. UN Archives/Geneva, SOA 317/1/01(1), Part C, draft memorandum of 12 November 1948 recounting the history.

54. See Alison Dundes Renteln, *International Human Rights: Universalism Versus Relativism* (Newbury Park, Calif.: Sage, 1990), p. 51; Adamantia Pollis and Peter Schwab (eds.), *Human Rights: Cultural and Ideological Perspectives* (New York: Praeger, 1980), p. 14.

55. UN Archives/Geneva, SOA 317/1/01(2); UN Archives/New York, Central Registry, RAG-1, Box 73, File 605-2-1-4-1, "Representatives from Specialized Agencies."

56. UN Archives/Geneva, SOA 317/03, reveals correspondence between the Division of Human Rights and the UN War Crimes Commission and the Office of Chief of Counsel for War Crimes. The addition of Dr. Egon Schwelb, who worked on the trials as a permanent staff member of the Secretariat, made this connection even stronger.

57. UN Archives/New York, Central Registry, RAG-1, Box 73, File 605-5-1-1-1, "Human Rights. Bill of Rights. Proposed Drafts by Governments"; Great Britain, Foreign Office, *United Kingdom Draft of an International Bill of Human Rights* (London: His Majesty's Stationery Office, 1947); UN/GA, Document A/148, "Statement of Essential Human Rights Presented by the Delegation from Panama," 24 October 1946; Leo Baeck Institute, Ernst Hamburger Papers, Box 6, "Final Draft of a Commentary to the Universal Declaration of Human Rights."

58. UNESCO, Document Phil/1/1947, "Memorandum on Human Rights," 27 March 1947.

59. U.S., NARA, RG 59, Box 2257, 501.BD Human Rights/12–1747, letter from Le Zhongshu (Chung-Shu Lo) to George Marshall, 19 December 1947.

60. The responses of these philosophers received widespread attention as seen in *United Nations Weekly Bulletin*, July–December 1947. See also UNESCO, Document Phil./8, "Report of the First Meeting of the Committee of Experts Convened by UNESCO on the Philosophical Principles of the Rights of Man," 31 July 1947.

61. Letter from Mohandas Gandhi to Julian Huxley, as reproduced in "The Rights of Man," p. 521.

62. UNESCO, Document Phil./10/1947/Rev., "The Grounds of an International Declaration of Human Rights," 31 July 1947. Fifty copies were sent to Laugier, Humphrey, and the Commission on Human Rights by the Director General of UNESCO, Julian Huxley, and they asked for more, as indicated in UN Archives/Geneva, SOA 317/1/01(2), File A. Cassin and Malik both credited this report as having considerable significance, as in René Cassin, "La Déclaration universelle et la mise en oeuvre des droits de l'homme," p. 272. It was eventually published as UNESCO, *The Basis of an International Bill of Rights* (Paris: UNESCO, 1949); UNESCO, with an introduction by Jacques Maritain, *Human Rights: Comments and Interpretations* (London: Allan Wingate, 1949).

63. See U.S., NARA, RG 84, Records of the US Delegation to the United Nations, Box 103, File "IO:ECOSOC:Human Rights, 1946–1949," Telegram No. 103 to Eleanor Roosevelt, 25 May 1948.

64. Roosevelt Library, Eleanor Roosevelt Papers, Box 4561, Diary entry of 4 February 1946; Britain, PRO/FO, 371/59740, memorandum entitled "Human Rights Commission," filed on 11 September 1946.

65. Edward Lawson, who served on the Division of Human Rights during these years, uses the expression "thousands" in his *Encyclopedia of Human Rights* (New York: Taylor & Francis, 1991), p. x; as does UN Department of Public Information, Background Paper No. 25, "Commission on Human Rights," 18 November 1947, p. 10.

66. See UN Archives/Geneva, SOA, 317/1/01(4)(B); U.S., NARA, RG 59, Boxes 2257, 2258.

67. UN Archives/Geneva, SOA 317/1/01(3), File A, telegram from Wolynec Czubko Iwaniuk to Eleanor Roosevelt, 2 February 1947.

68. UN Archives/New York, Branch Registries, Series: Commission on Human Rights, RAG 2/169, Box 168–7, File 169/5/01.

69. Howard Tolley, Jr., *The U.N. Commission on Human Rights* (Boulder, Colo.: Westview, 1987), p. 16.

70. Roosevelt Library, Eleanor Roosevelt Papers, Box 3766, Walter White to Eleanor Roosevelt, 20 October 1947.

71. Copies of the petition can be found in Library of Congress, Manuscript Division, W. E. B. Du Bois Papers, Reel 86, Petitions, frames 1490–1545; Roosevelt Library, Eleanor Roosevelt Papers, Box 3766.

72. W. E. B. Du Bois Papers, Reel 60, Correspondence, frame 1079, "Statement of Dr. W. E. B. Du Bois to the Representatives of the Human Rights Commission," 23 October 1947. See also U.S., NARA, RG 84, Box 78, File "Discrimination, Race: U.S., 1947"; Plummer, *Rising Wind*, pp. 178–84; Carol Anderson, *Eyes Off the Prize*, pp. 93–112.

73. Ibid., frames 708–9, Report by H. H. Smythe of the NAACP entitled "Afro-Americans Petitioning the United Nations for Equal Rights."

74. Ibid., frames 788ff., "Press Reaction to the NAACP United Nations Petition,"; U.S., NARA, RG 59, Box 4651.

75. Paul Gordon Lauren, "The Diplomats and the Diplomacy of the United Nations," in Gordon A. Craig and Francis Lowenheim (eds.), *The Diplomats, 1939–1979* (Princeton, N.J.: Princeton University Press, 1994), pp. 459ff.

76. See Boris Ponomaryov, Andrei Gromyko, and Vladimir Khvostov, *History of Soviet Foreign Policy* (Moscow: Progress Publishers, 1974), pp. 158–59.

77. Andre Vyshinsky, as cited in Joseph Lash, *Eleanor: The Years Alone* (New York: New American Library, 1973), p. 99; G. Petrov, "The Unbecoming Role of Eleanor Roosevelt," *Literary Gazette* 85 (23 October 1948).

78. For the relationship between the Cold War and racial discrimination, see U.S., NARA, RG 59, Boxes 2256, 2257, 4650, 2651; Lauren, *Power and Prejudice*, pp. 197–208; Mary Dudziak, *Cold War Civil Rights* (Princeton: N.J.: Princeton University Press, 2000).

79. Lauterpacht, *International Law and Human Rights*, pp. 157–58.

80. United States, President's Committee on Civil Rights, *To Secure These Rights* (Washington, D.C.: Government Printing Office, 1947), pp. 147–48.

81. Among many examples, see Britain, PRO/FO, 371/59741, memorandum from the Working Party on Human Rights, Confidential, 25 October 1946; PRO/FO, 371/67606, letter from Geoffrey Wilson to Paul Gore-Booth, 18 June 1947; U.S., NARA, RG, Box 2257, 501.BD Human Rights/12–2647, Telegram A-118 from Troutman to Secretary of State, Confidential, 26 December 1947.

82. See UN Archives/Geneva, SOA 317/1/01(1), File A, Memorandum from Egon Schwelb to Henri Laugier, 15 March 1948.

83. Jan Smuts, as cited in Hugh Tinker, *Race, Conflict and the International Order* (London: Macmillan, 1977), p. 111.

84. U.S., NARA, RG 59, Box 2258, 501.BD Human Rights/9–3048, Telegram A-1069 from Caffery (Paris) to Secretary of State, Secret, 30 September 1948.

85. Dean Acheson, *Present at the Creation* (New York: Norton, 1969), pp. 111–12; Vijaya Pandit, *The Scope of Happiness* (New York: Crown, 1979), pp. 250–51; Plummer, *Rising Wind*, p. 131.

86. UN Archives/New York, Central Registry, Box 73, File 605–2–1–6, "Cooperation and Support. Human Rights Program," speech by John Humphrey.

87. See UN Archives/New York, Registry Files, RAG-1, Box 73, File 605–1, "Social Affairs, Human Rights Commission"; UN Archives/Geneva, SOA, 317/1/01(3) and 317/1/02(3); U.S., NARA, RG 84, Box 89, File "Rights: Human, 1946–1949"; "Non-Governmental Organizations," *United Nations Weekly Bulletin*, 8 April 1947; Nurser, *For All Peoples and All Nations*.

88. Humphrey, *Human Rights and the United Nations*, p. 46.

89. See Vik, "The United States, the American Legal Community, and the Vision of International Human Rights Protection," pp. 223–31; issues of the *American Bar Association Journal* from 1948; UN Archives/Geneva, SOA 317/1/01(3), File A, letter from Louis Sohn to John Humphrey, 24 February 1948.

90. For excellent discussions of the drafting, see the chronological approach of Glendon, *A World Made New*, and Simpson, *Human Rights and the End of Empire*, pp. 390–461, and the topical approach of Morsink, *The Universal Declaration of Human Rights*.

91. W. R. Hodgson, as cited in Humphrey, *Human Rights and the United Nations*, p. 27. See also NANZ, EA 2, File 108/11/13/1(1), "Report of the Australian Representative at the First Meeting of the Human Rights Commission."

92. See the report in UN Archives/Geneva, SOA 317/1/01(1), File C, memorandum from John Humphrey to Edward Lawson, 4 November 1948.

93. Ibid., p. 29.

94. UN, ECOSOC, Document E/CN.4/AC.1/3, "Draft Outline of International Bill of Rights," 4 June 1947; Document E/CN.4/AC.1/3/Add.1, "Documented Outline," 4 June 1947.

95. Vladimir Koretsky, as cited in Humphrey, *Human Rights and the United Nations*, p. 40. See also U.S., NARA, RG 59, Box 2256, 501.BD Human Rights/6–2147, Telegram 7594 from W. Austin to Department of State, Restricted, 21 June 1947.

96. Hansa Mehta, as cited in "Economic and Social Council," *United Nations Weekly Bulletin*, 25 March 1947.

97. NANZ, EA 2, File 108/11/1(1A), Memorandum "Human Rights," 13 March 1947.

98. U.S., NARA, RG 84, Box 103, File "IO: ECOSOC, Human Rights 1946–1949," instructions

from Durward Sandifer to Eleanor Roosevelt, 5 February 1947. See also Eleanor Roosevelt, "Statement Regarding Order of Work," copy on file in Britain, PRO/FO, 371/67606.

99. See UN, ECOSOC, Document E/CN.4/21, "Report of the Drafting Committee to the Commission on Human Rights," 1 July 1947; E/CN.4/57, "Report of the Working Group on the Declaration of Human Rights," 10 December 1947; E/600, "Report of the Commission on Human Rights, Second Session," 17 December 1947. This three-step strategy was first suggested by André Mandelstam during the 1920s and 1930s.

100. "First Drafts of Human Rights Bill Completed," *United Nations Weekly Bulletin*, 15 January 1948.

101. See France, Assemblée Nationale, Chambre des Députés, *Rapport fait au nom de la Commission des affaires étrangères, 26 février 1948* (Paris: Imprimerie Nationale, 1948); Britain, PRO/FO, 371/72803, Letter No. U2410/62, "The International Political Situation," from R. E. Ormerod to E. B. Boothby, 7 April 1948; U.S., NARA, RG 59, Box 2256, 501.BD Human Rights.

102. Documentation of their work and internal discussions can be found respectively in Britain, PRO/FO, 371/72800–07; U.S., NARA, RG 59, Boxes 2256, 2257, 2258, 501.BD Human Rights; NANZ, EA 2, File 108/11/13/1(1).

103. "American Declaration of the Rights and Duties of Man," as reproduced in UN Document E/CN.4/122, 10 June 1948. See also Mary Ann Glendon, "The Forgotten Crucible: The Latin American Influence on the Universal Human Rights Idea," *Harvard Human Rights Journal* 16 (Spring 2003): 27–39.

104. Britain, PRO/FO, 371/72806, Telegram No. 1523 from G. Wilson to Foreign Office, 18 May 1948.

105. UN, ECOSOC, Document E/CN.4/85, *Collation of the Comments of Governments . . .* , 1 May 1948.

106. UN Archives/Geneva, SOA 317/1/01(1), Part B, letter from the Union of South Africa to the Secretary-General, 23 April 1948.

107. UN Archives/Geneva, SOA 317/1/01(1); UN/ECOSOC, Document E/CN.4/95, "Report of the Drafting Committee to the Commission on Human Rights," 21 May 1948; Document E/800, "Report of the Third Session of the Commission on Human Rights," 28 June 1948.

108. NANZ, EA 2, File 108/11/13/1(2), Memorandum entitled "Report by the New Zealand Observer on the Third Session of the Commission on Human Rights (Colin Aikman)," 1 July 1948. I am grateful to Mr. Aikman for personal interviews on his experience.

109. Eleanor Roosevelt, as cited by Meghan Loftus, "Eleanor Roosevelt: A Profile," in United States, Department of State, *eJournal USA* 13 (November 2008), p. 9.

110. UN Document E/CN.4/102, "China: Amendments to the Draft International Declaration on Human Rights," 27 May 1948.

111. UN/GA, Document A/625, "Report of the Economic and Social Council to the General Assembly, 18–29 August 1948, pp. 34ff.

112. See Morsink, "World War Two and the Universal Declaration," *Human Rights Quarterly* 15 (1993): 357; Humphrey, *Human Rights and the United Nations*, p. 66.

113. The words are those of Humphrey, *Human Rights and the United Nations*, p. 63.

114. These included Roosevelt, Malik, Cassin, Chang, Alexei Pavlov of the Soviet Union, and Hernan Santa Cruz of Chile.

115. See Susan Waltz, "Who Wrote the Universal Declaration of Human Rights?," in U.S. Department of State, *eJournal USA*, pp. 21–22; Susan Waltz, "Universal Human Rights: The Contribution of Muslim States," *Human Rights Quarterly* 26 (2004): 799–844; Susan Waltz, "Universalizing Human Rights: The Role of Small States in the Construction of the Universal Declaration of Human Rights," *Human Rights Quarterly* 23 (2001): 44–72.

116. "Searching Study of Human Rights Declaration," *United Nations Weekly Bulletin*, 1 November 1948.

117. Vladimir Koretsky, as cited in Humphrey, *Human Rights and the United Nations*, p. 42.

118. Eleanor Roosevelt, as cited in "Searching Study of Human Rights Declaration," *United Nations Weekly Bulletin*, 1 November 1948.

119. UN/GA, Third Committee, *Summary Records of Meetings, 21 September–8 December 1948*, passim; UN/GA, Document A/C.3/400, "Report of Sub Committee 4," 4 December 1948; UN/GA, Document A/777, "Draft International Declaration of Human Rights," 7 December 1948, with Emilio St. Lot of Haiti serving as rapporteur.

120. Charles Malik, as cited in Glendon, *A World Made New*, p. 164.

121. NANZ, EA 2, File 108/11/13/1(1), Memorandum entitled "Human Rights Committee, Questions for Discussion," 12 February 1948.

122. See the discussion in Morsink, *Inherent Human Rights*.

123. The text under consideration was UN/GA, Document A/777, "Draft International Declaration of Human Rights," 7 December 1948. The final version adopted became Resolution 217 A (III), "Universal Declaration of Human Rights," 10 December 1948.

124. Universal Declaration of Human Rights, Articles 1 and 2 (my emphasis). Discussions of each of the articles can be found in Morsink, *The Universal Declaration of Human Rights*, pp. 329–36; Verdoodt, *Naissance et signification de la Déclaration universelle des droits de l'homme*, pp. 78–274.

125. Universal Declaration of Human Rights, Articles 3–14, 16–20.

126. Allan Rosas, "Article 21," in Asbjørn Eide et al. (eds.), *The Universal Declaration of Human Rights*, p. 299.

127. Universal Declaration of Human Rights, Article 21.

128. Universal Declaration of Human Rights, Articles 22–28.

129. Torkel Opsahl, "Articles 29 and 30," in Eide et al. (eds.), *The Universal Declaration of Human Rights*, p. 449.

130. Universal Declaration of Human Rights, Articles 29 and 30. See also René Cassin, "De la Place faite aux devoirs de l'individu dans la Déclaration universelle des droits de l'homme," in *Mélanges offerts à Polys Medinos* (Paris: Pedone, 1968), pp. 479–88.

131. The debates can be found in UN/GA, *Official Records, Plenary Meetings, 1948*, meetings 180–83, pp. 852–934.

132. The abstentions came from Byelorussia, Czechoslovakia, Poland, Saudi Arabia, Ukraine, Soviet Union, South Africa, and Yugoslavia.

133. UN Resolution A/RES/217 A (III), "Universal Declaration of Human Rights," 10 December 1948, which is reproduced in full following Chapter 10.

134. René Cassin, in UN/GA, *Official Records, Plenary Meetings, 1948*, pp. 864–67; René Cassin, "La Déclaration universelle et la mise en oeuvre des droits de l'homme," pp. 290–96; René Cassin, *La Pensée et l'action* (Paris: Lalou, 1972), p. 118.

135. Hernan Santa Cruz and Charles Malik, in UN/GA, *Official Records, Plenary Meetings, 1948*, pp. 857 and 863.

136. Peng-chun Chang and Herbert Evatt, in ibid., pp. 895 and 934.

137. Belarmino de Athayde and Mohammed Kahn, in ibid., pp. 878, 890.

138. See UN/GA, *Official Records of the Third Committee, 1948*, p. 35.

139. Eleanor Roosevelt, full text of speech in U.S., NARA, RG 59, Box 2258, 501.BD Human Rights/12–848.

140. UN Archives/Geneva, SOA 317/1/01(4), File B, letter from Erwin Loewenfeld (Cambridge) to John Humphrey (New York), 29 December 1948.

141. See Zdenek Augenthaler of Czechoslovakia and L. I. Kaminsky of Byelorussia, in UN/GA, *Official Records, Plenary Meetings, 1948*, pp. 882, 896–97.

142. Juliusz Katz-Suchy, in ibid., p. 904.

143. Andrei Vyshinsky, in ibid., pp. 854, 857, 924–27.

144. H. T. Andrews, in ibid., pp. 910–11.

145. See Frank Holman of the American Bar Association, as cited in *New York Times*, "U.S. Delay Urged on U.N. Human Rights Plan," 1 February 1949.

146. For more discussion on this point, see the Conclusion.

147. Humphrey, *Human Rights and the United Nations*, p. 76; Eide et al. (eds.), *The Universal Declaration of Human Rights*, p. 5; Verdoodt, *La Naissance et signification de la Déclaration universelle des droits de l'homme.*

148. Abdul Rahman Kayala, in UN, GA, *Official Records, Plenary Meetings, 1948*, p. 922.

149. See U.S., NARA, RG 59, Box 89, File "Rights: Human, 1946–1949," Memorandum from James Henrick to Louis Hyde, Jr., 24 September 1947.

Chapter 8. The First Fifty Years of the Universal Declaration

1. See the quotations in NANZ, EA 2, File 108/11/13/1(2); Simpson, *Human Rights and the End of Empire*, p. 419; Nehemiah Robinson, *The Universal Declaration of Human Rights* (New York: Institute of Jewish Affairs, 1950), p. 15.

2. As cited in Simpson, *Human Rights and the End of Empire*, p. 457.

3. See UN Archives/Geneva, SOA 373/1/01, /04, /06.

4. UN Archives/Geneva, SOA 317/1/01(1)(C), memorandum from Edward Lawson to John Humphrey, 16 November 1948.

5. On the nature of restraints, see Paul Gordon Lauren, Gordon A. Craig, and Alexander L. George, *Force and Statecraft* (New York: Oxford University Press, 2007), pp. 245 ff.

6. "Treaty of Peace with Japan," 8 September 1951, in U.S. Department of State, *United States Treaties and Other International Agreements* 3, 3 (1952): 3171.

7. UN Archives/Geneva, SOA 373/1/04, letter from K. Gordon to F. Scott, 31 May 1951.

8. UN Resolution, A/RES/260 A (III), "Convention on the Prevention and Punishment of the Crime of Genocide," 9 December 1948.

9. Raphael Lemkin Papers, Manuscripts and Archives Division, New York Public Library, especially his correspondence of May–July 1950.

10. See UN Archives/Geneva, SOA 417/2/01; Henri Coursier, "L'Évolution du droit international humanitaire," *Recueil des Cours de l'Académie de Droit International* 99 (1960): 361–465; Geoffrey Best, *Humanity in Warfare* (London: Weidenfeld and Nicolson, 1980), pp. 300–301; www.icrc.org. Additional protocols added in 1977 and 2005.

11. See UN Archives/Geneva, SO 252 and SO 261, and the texts at www.ohchr.org.

12. Council of Europe, Central Archives, Binder 286, DH [Droits de l'Homme] 1, 1949–1950, Document 108, "Recommendation to the Committee of Ministers," 8 September 1949.

13. Council of Europe, *Collected Edition of the Travaux Préparatoires: Convention for the Protection of Human Rights* H (61) 4, Confidential; "Convention for the Protection of Human Rights and Fundamental Freedoms," 4 November 1950, www.humanrights.coe.int.

14. Simpson, *Human Rights and the End of Empire*, p. 3.

15. United Nations High Commissioner for Refugees, Archives, Fonds 17.5, Protection Working Files, Binder XLV, Travaux Preparatoire: Conventions and Protocols. See also www.unhcr.org.

16. Ibid., Binder 288, undated paper entitled "UNHCR's Duty to Provide International Protection."

17. Poster from UN High Commissioner for Refugees.

18. See Humphrey, *Human Rights and the United Nations*, pp. 63ff.; Lawson, *Encyclopedia of Human Rights*, p. xii.

19. See UN Archives/Geneva, SOA 317/1/01(6), memorandum to Alva Myrdal from John Humphrey, 16 June 1949; Egon Schwelb, "The Influence of the Universal Declaration of Human Rights on International and National Law," *American Society of International Law Proceedings* (1959): 217–29.

20. See Glendon, *A World Made New*, p. 195; Lauren, "The Diplomats and Diplomacy of the United Nations," in Craig and Lowenheim, *The Diplomats, 1939–1979*, pp. 463ff.

21. These tragic letters can be found in UN Archives/Geneva.

22. UN Document 1948.I.12, *For Fundamental Human Rights*, p. 35.

23. See UN Archives/Geneva, SOA 317/9/01; Lauren, *Power and Prejudice*, pp. 199–209, 240–46.

24. John Bricker, as cited in Natalie Hevener Kaufman and David Whiteman, "Opposition to Human Rights Treaties in the United States Senate," *Human Rights Quarterly* 10 (1988): 309.

25. John Bricker, "U.N. Blueprint for Tyranny," *The Freeman* 2 (28 January 1952): 265.

26. John Bricker, in U.S. Congress, *Congressional Record, 1952*, 98, pt. 1 (Washington, D.C.: Government Printing Office, 1952), p. 912.

27. UN Archives/Geneva, SOA 317/4/01(C), speech by John Humphrey, 1 January 1952.

28. Marc Bossuyt, *Guide to the "Travaux Préparatoires" of the International Covenant on Civil and Political Rights* (Dordrecht: Nijhoff, 1987); Humphrey, *Human Rights and the United Nations*, p. 64; Tolley, *The U.N. Commission on Human Rights*, p. 29.

29. Memorandum by Foreign Secretary Herbert Morrison, as cited in Anthony Lester, "Fundamental Rights: The United Kingdom Isolated?" *Public Law* (Spring 1984): 55.

30. See U.S. Department of State, *FRUS, 1952–1954*, 3:1536–81; John Foster Dulles, "The Making of Treaties and Executive Agreements," in U.S. Department of State, *Department of State Bulletin* 28 (20 April 1953): 591–93.

31. Eleanor Roosevelt, *My Day*, 9 and 10 April 1953, as cited in Johnson, "The Contributions of Eleanor and Franklin Roosevelt," pp. 46–47. See also Roosevelt Library, Eleanor Roosevelt Papers, Boxes 3855, 4560, 4587, 4588.

32. Norman Bentwich, "Marking Time for Human Rights," *Contemporary Review* 192 (August 1957): 80–81. See also Louis Henkin, "Editorial Comments—U.S. Ratification of Human Rights Conventions," *American Journal of International Law* 89 (1995): 341–51; Natalie Hevener Kaufman, *Human Rights Treaties and the Senate* (Chapel Hill: University of North Carolina Press, 1990).

33. Universal Declaration of Human Rights, Preface, Article 2.

34. See UN Archives/Geneva, SOA 317/1/02, memorandum "Human Rights in Trusteeship Territories," 20 April 1949; SOA 317/4/01, letter from M. R. Turner to Commission on Human Rights, 24 July 1949.

35. Britain, PRO/FO, 371/78945, Circular Despatch No.25102/2/49, from A. Creech Jones (Colonial Office) to Governors of the Colonies, 28 March 1949, Secret. Similar efforts were made to insert a "colonial clause" into other international treaties to prevent application in overseas possessions.

36. As cited in Simpson, *Human Rights and the End of Empire*, p. 458.

37. Britain, PRO/FO, 371/78945, letter from Lord Listowel (Colonial Office) to C. P. Mayhew, 8 April 1949.

38. UN Trusteeship Council, Document T/1/Rev., "Rules of Procedure," 23 April 1947; Document T/44, "Provisional Questionnaire," 25 April 1947, especially questions 136–48; Brian Urquart, *Ralph Bunche* (New York: Norton, 1993).

39. UN Resolution A/RES/545 (VI), "Inclusion in the International Covenant or Covenants on Human Rights of an Article Relating to the Right of People to Self-Determination," 5 February 1952; UN Resolution A/RES/637 (VII), "The Right of Peoples and Nations to Self-Determination," 16 December 1952; UN Archives/Geneva, SO 221/9 (1–4), International Covenants on Human Rights Relating to Self-Determination.

40. UN Archives/Geneva, SOA 317/1/03, memorandum from Victor Hoo to Guillaume Georges-Picot, 12 March 1952.

41. Ibid., memorandum from Egon Schwelb to Philippe de Seynes, 24 February 1955.

42. Sukarno, as cited in Republic of Indonesia, *The Asian-African Conference, 1955* (New Delhi: Information Service of Indonesia, 1955), pp. 13–18.

43. See Roland Burke, "'The Compelling Dialogue of Freedom': Human Rights at the

Bandung Conference," *Human Rights Quarterly* 28 (2006): 947–65; Lauren, *Power and Prejudice*, pp. 223–27; Final Communiqué of 24 April 1955, in Indonesia, *The Asian-African Conference*, pp. 208–15.

44. Bernard Porter, *The Lion's Share* (London: Longmans, 1975), p. 319; C. T. Thorne, in Vernon McKay (ed.), *African Diplomacy* (New York: Praeger, 1966), p. 145.

45. W. E. B. Du Bois, *The World and Africa*, p. 310. Ill health prevented him at the last moment from delivering his speech in person.

46. Geiss, *Panafrikanismus*, pp. 328–30.

47. First published as Frantz Fanon, *Les Damnés de la terre* (Paris: Masper, 1961).

48. See Henri Alleg, *The Question* (New York: Brazillier, 1958); James Le Sueur, *Uncivil War* (Philadelphia: University of Pennsylvania Press, 2001).

49. Interview with Frank Corner, 15 April 1994, in Wellington.

50. UN High Commissioner for Refugees, Archives, Fonds 11, Series 1, File 1/1/6/1, letter from W. H. J. van Wijck to A. R. Lindt, Nr 1086, 11 July 1960, Secret.

51. René Cassin, "La Commission des Droits de l'Homme de l'ONU," in *Miscellanea W. J. Ganshof van der Meersch* (Brussels: Bruylant, 1972), p. 402.

52. United Nations, *Yearbook on Human Rights, 1960* (New York: United Nations, 1962), passim.

53. UN Resolution A/RES/1514 (XV), "Declaration on the Granting of Independence to Colonial Countries and Peoples," 14 December 1960. See also UN Archives/Geneva, File SO 227, Self-Determination, 1957–1968.

54. U Thant, *View from the UN* (New York: Doubleday, 1978), p. 441; UN Archives/New York, DAG-1/5.2.7, Papers of the Secretary-General (Thant Papers), Boxes 2, 3.

55. First known as the Special Committee of Seventeen, but expanded in 1962 and given much more authority as the Special Committee of Twenty-Four.

56. Carlo Romulo, as cited in Indonesia, *The Asian-African Conference*, pp. 125–28.

57. Hendrik Verwoerd, as cited in UN Archives/New York, DAG-1, 5.1.3, Box 4, Confidential Memorandum of Meeting on 10 January 1961 with Dag Hammarskjöld. See also Columbia University, Rare Book and Manuscript Library, Andrew Cordier Papers, Box 136.

58. Nelson Mandela, 22 October 1962, as cited in Thomas Karis and Gwendoline Carter (eds.), *From Protest to Challenge*, 4 vols. (Stanford, Calif.: Hoover Institution Press, 1977), 3:725–31.

59. See UN Resolution A/RES/1761 (XVII), "The Politics of Apartheid of the Government of the Republic of South Africa," 6 November 1962; UN Resolution A/RES/1881 (XVIII), "The Politics of Apartheid," 11 October 1963.

60. D. Telli, 20 November 1963, in UN/GA, *Official Records, Plenary Meetings, 1963*, p. 13.

61. UN Resolution A/RES/2106 A (XX), "International Convention on the Elimination of All Forms of Racial Discrimination," 21 December 1965. See also Gerda Weinberger, *Gegen Rassismus und Rassendiskriminierung* (Berlin: Staatsverlag der DDR, 1976).

62. Clara Ponce de León, 16 December 1966, in UN/GA, *Official Records, Plenary Meetings, 1966*, 1495th Meeting, p. 7.

63. UN Resolution A/RES/2200 A (XXI), "International Covenant on Civil and Political Rights," and "International Covenant on Economic, Social, and Cultural Rights," 16 December 1966; UN Archives/Geneva, SOA 317/1/01 A.

64. Comments in UN/GA, *Official Records, Plenary Meetings, 1966*, pp. 6ff.

65. UN Resolution A/RES/2200 A (XXI), "Optional Protocol to the International Covenant on Civil and Political Rights," 16 December 1966; UN Resolution A/RES/44/128, "Second Optional Protocol," 15 December 1989.

66. Tolley, *The U.N. Commission on Human Rights*, pp. 54–57. Eleven more were added in 1984.

67. Seán MacBride, as cited in Howard Tolley, Jr., *The International Commission of Jurists* (Philadelphia: University of Pennsylvania Press, 1994), p. 98.

68. UN Resolution A/RES/2391 (XXIII), "Convention on the Non-Applicability of Statutory Limitations to War Crimes and Crimes Against Humanity," 26 November 1968.

69. UN Resolution, A/RES/3068 (XXVIII), "International Convention on the Suppression and Punishment of the Crime of Apartheid," 30 November 1973.

70. UN Resolution A/RES/34/180, "Convention on the Elimination of All Forms of Discrimination Against Women," 18 December 1979. See also Rebecca J. Cook (ed.), *Human Rights of Women* (Philadelphia: University of Pennsylvania Press, 1994).

71. UN Resolution, A/RES/39/46, "Convention Against Torture and Other Cruel, Inhuman, or Degrading Treatment or Punishment," 10 December 1984. See also J. Herman Burgers and Hans Danelius, *The UN Convention Against Torture* (Dordrecht: Nijhoff, 1988).

72. UN Archives/ Geneva, SO 221/9 (1–5), Rights of the Child; UN Resolution A/RES/44/25, "Convention on the Rights of the Child," 20 November 1989; UN Resolution A/RES/45/158, "International Convention on the Protection of the Rights of All Migrant Workers and Members of Their Families," 18 December 1990.

73. E. N. Nasinovsky, 16 December 1966, in UN/GA, *Official Records, Plenary Meetings, 1966,* p. 13.

74. See Council of Europe, Central Archives, DH 1, Binders 286ff.; Dossier No. 1218, Boxes 1800ff.

75. UN Archives/Geneva, SO 237; Robertson and Merrills, *Human Rights in the World*, pp. 89–91; Karl Partsch, "The Committee on the Elimination of Racial Discrimination," in Philip Alston (ed.), *The United Nations and Human Rights* (Oxford: Clarendon Press, 1992), pp. 339–68.

76. See UN Archives/Geneva, SO 221/9 (1–6); Glendon, *A World Made New*, p. 215.

77. Dana Fischer, "Reporting Under the Covenant on Civil and Political Rights," *American Journal of International Law* 76 (January 1982): 145. See also Dominic McGoldrick, *The Human Rights Committee* (Oxford: Clarendon Press, 1991); Human Rights Committee, *Annual Reports.*

78. UN Document E/CN.4/1994/42, "Report on the Effective Functioning of the Various Mechanisms Established for Supervision, Investigation, and Monitoring of the Implementation of the Treaty Obligations Entered Into by States in Regard to Human Rights," 14 February 1994; Alston (ed.), *The United Nations and Human Rights*, pp. 444–72, 509–47; recent developments on all the treaty bodies at www.ohchr.org.

79. UN, ECOSOC Resolution 75 (V), "Communications Concerning Human Rights," 5 August 1947.

80. UN Archives/Geneva, SOA 317/06, Human Rights, Study of the Right of Petition, letter from Burton Wilson to Commission on Human Rights, 6 May 1950.

81. The petition on behalf of King can be found in UN Archives/Geneva, SO 215/1, USA, Part D, Violations and Complaints, United States, Confidential File.

82. UN Document E/CN.4/SR.332, "Commission on Human Rights, Eighth Session, Summary Record," June 1952.

83. NANZ, EA 2, File 108/11/13/1(4), memorandum entitled "Covenant of Human Rights," (1949).

84. See UN Archives/New York, Branch Registries, RAG-2/169, Box 168–7, File 169/5/01, "Commission on Human Rights," memorandum from Egon Schwelb to Oscar Schachter, 26 May 1948; UN Archives/Geneva, SOA 317/06, "Study on the Right of Petition," 4 November 1949; UN Resolution E/RES/728 F (XXVIII), "Communications Concerning Human Rights," 30 July 1959.

85. ECOSOC Resolution 1235 (XLII), "Question of the Violation of Human Rights," 6 June 1967.

86. UN Resolution E/RES/1503 (XLVIII), "Procedure for Dealing with Communications Relating to Violations of Human Rights," 27 May 1970.

87. Sub-Commission on Prevention of Discrimination and Protection of Minorities, Resolution 1 (XXIV), "Question of the Violation of Human Rights . . . in All Countries," 13 August 1971 (my emphasis). See also Thomas Buergental, *International Human Rights in a Nutshell* (St. Paul, Minn.: West, 1995), pp. 89–95.

88. The confidentiality requirement had been a part of the original 1503 resolution, but had

never been implemented until this particular meeting. I am extremely grateful to Jakob Möller, who served as the Chief of the Communications Unit of the International Instruments and Procedures Section, for several lengthy conversations on this subject.

89. Interview with Jakob Möller.

90. See UN Archives/Geneva, SO 215 series, Violations and Complaints.

91. For a complete listing see "List of Countries Referred to the Commission on Human Rights Under the 1503 Procedure Since 1974," dated 1997, from the Office of the High Commissioner for Human Rights.

92. This characterization has been provided by individuals particularly knowledgeable about the 1503 procedure, who, for reasons of confidentiality, wish to remain anonymous. See also UN Archives/Geneva, SO 215/2, Part A, Inability of Governments to Accept Communications.

93. In Argentina, the Philippines, and Uruguay, the radical change of regimes brought new governments into power anxious to cooperate with the Commission on Human Rights.

94. UN Document E/CN.4/1994/42, "Effective Functioning of the Various Mechanisms," 14 February 1994, p. 17; Helena Cook, "International Human Rights Mechanisms: The Role of Special Procedure in the Protection of Human Rights," *International Commission of Jurists Review* 50 (1993): 31–55. I am grateful to Bruna Molina-Abram for sharing her observations from extensive experience with special procedures with me.

95. John Humphrey, Preface, in Bossuyt, *Guide to the "Travaux Préparatoires"*, p. xv.

96. Council of Europe, Central Archives, Binder 285, DH 2, Doc. Addendum 2 to CM/WP1 (50) 15, Confidential, Committee of Experts on Human Rights, Reply of the Turkish Representative, 27 May 1950.

97. UN Archives/Geneva, SOA 317/4/01(C), speech of John Humphrey, 1 January 1952. See also UN Archives/Geneva, SOA 317/9/05.

98. UN Archives/Geneva, SOA 373/1/01, Publicity Policy, memorandum from G. Georges-Picot (Department of Social Affairs) to Benjamin Cohen (Department of Public Information), 14 July 1952.

99. See UN Archives/Geneva, SOA 317/4/0 and /01(C); SOA 373/1/01, /04, and /06; SO 221/9 (2); Tolley, *The UN Commission on Human Rights*, pp. 32–54.

100. UN Archives/Geneva, SO 230 and SO 234; UN Documents E/CN.4/Sub.2/307/Rev.1, *Study on Racial Discrimination*, 1971, and E/CN.4/1108/Rev.1, *The Realization of Economic, Social, and Cultural Rights*, 1975; UN Publications ST/HR/2, *United Nations Action in the Field of Human Rights*, 1974, and ST/HR/4, *Human Rights—International Instruments*, 1978.

101. Thomas Reynolds, "Highest Aspirations," *Law Library Journal* 71 (February 1978): 4.

102. Peter Benenson, "The Forgotten Prisoners," *The Observer*, 18 May 1961.

103. See www.amnesty.org.

104. UN Archives/Geneva, SOA 214 (7–1), Part A, International Conference on Human Rights, letter from Inamullah Khan (Karachi) to U Thant, 28 February 1968.

105. As cited in Korey, *NGOs and the Universal Declaration of Human Rights*, p. 85.

106. See Lauren, *Power and Prejudice*, pp. 244–48.

107. John XXIII, *Pacem in Terris*, 11 April 1963, in Claudia Carlen Ihm (ed.), *The Papal Encyclicals*, 5 vols. (Raleigh, N.C.: McGrath, 1981), 5:107–29.

108. The complete text of "I Have a Dream," delivered 28 April 1963, is widely available on the Internet, including the authoritative King Papers Project at http://mlk-kpp01.stanford.edu. I remain most grateful for a personal conversation with Martin Luther King, Jr., on 8 August 1965 in New York City.

109. Lyrics originally from a gospel hymn written by Rev. Charles Tilly in 1900 (my emphasis). See www.k-state.edu/english/nelp/american studies, accessed 20 July 2009.

110. Lyndon Johnson, 15 March 1965, in *Public Papers of the Presidents of the United States: Lyndon Johnson* (Washington, D.C.: Government Printing Office, 1965), 1:281–87.

111. UN Resolution A/RES/2081, "International Year for Human Rights," 20 December 1965.

112. UN Archives/Geneva, SOA 214 (7–1), Part A, International Conference on Human Rights, letter from Inamullah Khan (Karachi) to U Thant, 28 Feburary 1968.

113. Proclamation of Teheran on Human Rights, 13 May 1968, in UN Document A/CONF.32/41, "Final Act of the International Conference on Human Rights," pp. 2–5; UN Archives/Geneva, SO 218 (1), "International Conference on Human Rights."

114. Annex to UN Resolution A/RES/3057 (XXVIII), "Decade for Action to Combat Racism and Racial Discrimination," 2 November 1973.

115. Renewed as Second Decade from 1983–1992 and the Third Decade from 1993–2002. See Lauren, *Power and Prejudice*, pp. 251–88; UN Document A/CONF.92/40, "Report of the World Conference to Combat Racism," 1978.

116. Marcus Gee, "Assessing the Decade," *MacLean's* 29 July 1985, citing a 1980 UN report.

117. UN, *The United Nations and Human Rights, 1945–1995*, p. 86; UN, *Report of the World Conference to Review and Appraise the Achievements of the United Nations Decade for Women*, 1985 (Sales No. E.85.IV.10).

118. See http://antwrp.gsfc.nasa.gov.

119. See Finland, Ulkoasiainministerion Arkisto, Ryhma 7B, ETYK; OSCE Archives/Prague, vols. 1–17; both of which hold the complete set of documents of CESC/HC, CSCE/I, and CSCE/II.

120. OSCE Archives/Prague, Jeffrey Gaines Papers, notes from Stage II, Nos. 173, 192.

121. Vojtech Mastny, *The Helsinki Process* (New York: New York University Press, 1992), p. 4; Charles Vella, retrospective speech of 30 May 1989, Conference of the Human Dimension, in OSCE Archives/Prague, Binder: Paris Meeting 1989.

122. See the excellent Daniel Thomas, *The Helsinki Effect* (Princeton: N.J.: Princeton University Press, 2001); Lauren, Craig, and George, *Force and Statecraft*, p. 163.

123. Helsinki Final Act, 1 August 1975 (my emphasis); the original is in Finland, Ulkoasiainministerion Arkisto, ETYK Helsinki, Loppuasiakirja, Alkuperainen.

124. Yuri Orlov, as cited in Thomas, *The Helsinki Effect*, p. 189.

125. See Jeri Laber, *The Courage of Strangers* (New York: Public Affairs, 2002).

126. See Kenneth Cmiel, "The Emergence of Human Rights Politics in the United States," *Journal of American History* 86 (December 1999):1231–50.

127. Jimmy Carter, *Keeping Faith* (New York: Bantam, 1982), p. 144. I am grateful to Jimmy Carter for a personal interview on this subject.

128. See Sellars, *The Rise and Rise of Human Rights*, pp. 114ff.; A. Glenn Mower, *The United States, the United Nations, and Human Rights* (Westport, Conn.: Greenwood, 1979).

129. See Jacobo Timerman, *Prisoner Without a Name, Cell Without a Number* (New York: Knopf, 1981); Marguerite Guzman Bouvard, *Revolutionizing Motherhood* (Wilmington, Del.: SR Books, 2002); www.madres.org.

130. Adopted in 1981, entered into force in 1986. See Fatsah Ouguergouz, *La Charte africaine des droits de l'homme et des peuples* (Paris: PUF, 1993).

131. See www.ohchr.org.

132. Jan Mårtenson, as cited in *Refugees* 67 (August 1989): 35.

133. UN Publication DPI/1394/Rev.1/HR, *World Conference on Human Rights: The Vienna Declaration and Programme of Action*, June 1993, 1995, p. 2.

134. Thalif Deen, "Heavy Fire over Gag Rule," *Terra Viva*, 12 June 1993.

135. See the 1990 "Cairo Declaration of Human Rights in Islam" at www.religlaw.org; UN Document A/CONF/93, "Bangkok Declaration"; Jin Yongjian, "Asia's Major Human Rights Concerns," *Beijing Review*, 19–25 April 1993.

136. Jusuf Wanandi, as cited in Leah Makabenta, "Western Wrongs, Asian Rights," *Terra Viva*, 14 June 1993. See also Korey, *NGOs and the Universal Declaration*, pp. 469–91.

137. Asian Cultural Forum on Development, *Our Voice: Bangkok NGO Declaration on Human Rights* (Bangkok: Asian Cultural Forum on Development, 1993).

138. Aung San Suu Kyi, "Freedom, Development, and Human Worth," *Journal of Democracy* 6, 2 (April 1995): 12–19; *Freedom from Fear*, p. 175.

139. Boutros Boutros-Ghali, as cited in UN Document DPI/1394/Rev.1/HR, *World Conference on Human Rights*, p. 5.

140. Vienna Declaration and Programme of Action, pp. 25–71.

141. See UN Archives/Geneva, SO 216, Advisory Services in the Field of Human Rights; UN Archives/Geneva, SOA 317/011, Advisory Services in the Filed of Human Rights, Confidential File; UN Publication ST/HR/2, *United Nations Action in the Field of Human Rights*, 1974, pp. 87, 192–97.

142. See the discussion in Clark, *International Legitimacy and World Society*, pp. 153 ff.

143. Binders on the Paris, Copenhagen, and Moscow meetings of the Conference on the Human Dimension and "Document of the Moscow Meeting" (my emphasis) in OSCE Archives/Prague.

144. See www.osce.org.

145. ODIHR binders in OSCE Archives/Prague and, more recently, on www.osce.odihr.org.

146. See "To Avert a Bloodbath," *Time*, 14 January 1985; Jerome Segal, "Violence Inevitable in South Africa," *Los Angeles Times*, 21 April 1987; among many others.

147. De Klerk, as cited in "Nelson Mandela and F. W. De Klerk," *Time*, 3 January 1994.

148. Mandela, as cited in "Triumphant Mandela," *Times* (London), 3 May 1994.

149. UN General Assembly, RES 48/141, "Commissioner for the Promotion and Protection of All Human Rights," 20 December 1993.

150. UN Resolution A/48/141, "The Post of the United Nations High Commissioner for Human Rights," 20 December 1993; UN Archives/Geneva, SO 218, "United Nations High Commissioner for Human Rights."

151. See UN Archives/Geneva, G/SO 216/1.

152. Among others, see UN Resolution A/RES/48/267, "UN Mission for . . . Compliance with the Commitments . . . on Human Rights in Guatemala," 19 September 1994.

153. UN Document E/CN.4/1997/L.91, "Draft Resolution on the Situation of Human Rights in China," 10 April 1997; Wu Jiamin, speech of 15 April 1997 before the Commission on Human Rights, as recorded from personal notes.

154. See www.unhcr.ch; UN High Commissioner for Refugees, *The State of the World Refugees* (Oxford: Oxford University Press, 2000).

155. Interviews at the UN with Zdzislaw Kedzia and Fiona Blyth-Kubota, among others.

156. UN Resolution S/RES/827, "Creation of an International Criminal Tribunal for the Former Yugoslavia," 25 May 1993; UN Resolution S/RES/995, "Establishment of an International Criminal Tribunal for Rwanda," 8 November 1994 (my emphasis).

157. Kingsly Chiedu Moghalu, "Rwanda Panel's Legacy: They Can Run But Not Hide," *International Herald Tribune*, 31 October–1 November 1998.

158. Robin Cook, BBC Report, "New World Court to Prosecute Tyrants," 20 July 1998.

159. Kofi Annan, in UN Document SG/SM/6257 (1997).

160. For the Rome conference and Statute, see www.un.org/law/icc. Among those who voted no were China, Israel, Iraq, and the United States.

161. See Priscilla Hayner, *Unspeakable Truths* (London: Routledge, 2000).

162. UN CD-ROM, *Human Rights: Bibliographical Data and International Instruments* (UN Sales No. GV.E.97.0.7), 1997.

163. Robertson, *Crimes Against Humanity*, p. 371.

164. Mary Robinson, in UN Press Release HR/98/90 of 25 November 1998.

165. "Humanité," *Le Monde*, 27 November 1998 (my emphasis).

166. Amnesty International, EUR 45/33/98, "Pinochet Decision," 9 December 1998.

167. Among many examples, see Hurst Hannum, "The Status of the Universal Declaration of

Human Rights in National and International Law," *Georgia Journal of International and Comparative Law* 25 (1995/1996): 289ff.

168. "Our Century's Greatest Achievement," at http://news.bbc.co.uk, accessed 9 December 1998.

Chapter 9. The Continuing Evolution

1. United Nations, A/RES/55/2, "United Nations Millennium Declaration," 8 September 2000.

2. Among many, see Costas Douzinas, *The End of Human Rights* (Oxford: Hart, 2000); Michael Ignatieff, "Is the Human Rights Era Ending?" *New York Times*, 5 February 2002; David Luban, "The War on Terrorism and the End of Human Rights," *Philosophy and Public Policy Quarterly* 22 (Summer 2002): 9–14.

3. See "Human Rights Instruments," www.ohchr.org.

4. See http://echr.coe.int, and, for an assessment, Steven Greer, "What's Wrong with the European Convention on Human Rights?"' *Human Rights Quarterly* 30 (August 2008): 680–702; "European Court Seems to Rankle Kremlin," *New York Times*, 28 March 2009. I am grateful to officers of the Court for allowing me to attend and observe hearings before them in Strasbourg.

5. Simpson, *Human Rights and the End of Empire*, p. 3.

6. See www.corteidh.or.cr.

7. See www.african-court.org; for a more critical assessment by the Coalition for an Effective African Court on Human and Peoples' Rights, www.africancourtcoalition.org. See also Carolyn Shaw, "The Evolution of Regional Human Rights Mechanisms: A Focus on Africa," *Journal of Human Rights* 6 (2007): 209–32.

8. Protocol III of 2005 to the Geneva Conventions, www.icrc.org.

9. See www.unhcr.org; Elsa Mason, Guide to International Refugee Law Resources on the Web, 5 March 2009, www.llrx.com: UN High Commissioner for Refugees, *Internally Displaced People* (Geneva: UNHCR, 2007); current issues of *International Journal of Refugee Law*.

10. The Appeals Court in Chile ruled that he was medically and mentally unfit to stand trial.

11. "Trial More Likely for 'Africa's Pinochet,'" http://news.bbc.co.uk, 27 September 2001.

12. See www.ictr.org.

13. See www.un.org/icty. I wish to thank officials of the International Criminal Tribunal for the Former Yugoslavia in The Hague for the opportunity to witness some of these proceedings of the Milosevic trial, Case IT-02–54, in person.

14. Carla Del Ponte, "Transcript," as cited at http://news.bbc.co.uk , 12 February 2002.

15. "The World's Most Wanted Man," www.pbs.com, accessed 2 September 2009.

16. Robert Johansen, "The International Criminal Court," in David Forsythe (ed.), *Encyclopedia of Human Rights*, 5 vols. (New York: Oxford University Press, 2009), 3:113.

17. Richard Dicker, as cited in "Historic Day for International Justice," http://news.bbc.co.uk, 11 April 2002. For current activities of the Court, see www.icc-cpi.int.

18. Rod Grams (R-Minn.), as cited in John F. Murphy, "The Quivering Gulliver: U.S. Views on a Permanent International Criminal Court," *International Lawyer* (Spring 2000), on 34 INTLLAW 45.

19. Secretary of State Colin Powell, as cited in "U.S. to Back Out of International Court Treaty," www.cnn.com, 5 May 2002.

20. U.S. Congress, HR 4775, "American Servicemembers' Protection Act," 2002.

21. Hillary Clinton, as cited in John Bellinger III, "A Global Court Quandary for the President," *Washington Post*, 10 August 2009.

22. Kofi Annan, "Two Concepts of Sovereignty," *The Economist*, 18 September 1999. For more discussion, see Stephen Krasner, *Sovereignty* (Princeton, N.J.: Princeton University Press, 1999); Bertrand Badie, *Un monde sans souveraineté* (Paris: Fayard, 1999).

23. Václav Havel, as cited in Robertson, *Crimes Against Humanity*, p. 407.

24. As cited in *Human Rights Dialogue* (Winter 2001): 4. Opinions vary greatly over this case, as evinced by other articles in *Human Rights Dialogue* and Albrecht Schnabel and Ramesh Thakur (eds.), *Kosovo and the Challenge of Humanitarian Intervention* (Tokyo: United Nations University Press, 2000).

25. Tony Blair, "Doctrine of the International Community," British Information Services Press Release, 23 April 1999. See also Thomas Weiss, "The Humanitarian Identity Crisis," *Ethics and International Affairs* 13 (1999): 1–22 and responses.

26. African Union, Constitutive Act of 2000, www.africa-union.org.

27. International Commission on Intervention and State Sovereignty, *The Responsibility to Protect*, www.iciss-ciise.gc.ca.

28. UN, A/59/2005, "World Summit Outcome," 15 September 2005.

29. UN, S/RES/1674 (2006), "Protection of Civilians in Armed Conflict," 28 April 2006.

30. See www.responsibilitytoprotect.org.

31. UN, A/63/677, "Implementing the Responsibility to Protect," 12 January 2009. See also Alex Bellamy, *Responsibility to Protect* (Cambridge: Polity Press, 2009); Gareth Evans, *The Responsibility to Protect* (Washington, D.C.: Brookings Institution, 2009).

32. Kevin Bales, *Disposable People: New Slavery in the Global Economy* (Berkeley: University of California Press, 2004).

33. See Jeffrey Sachs, *The End of Poverty* (New York: Penguin, 2006); Amy Chua, *World on Fire* (New York: Anchor, 2004); Joseph Stiglitz, *Globalization and Its Discontents* (New York: Norton, 2003); Ishay, *The History of Human Rights*, 246ff.

34. United Nations Development Program, *Human Development Report 2000* (New York: Oxford University Press, 2000), p. 6. See also Alison Brysk (ed.), *Globalization and Human Rights* (Berkeley: University of California Press, 2002); Amartya Sen, *Development as Freedom* (New York: Anchor, 2000).

35. See David Forsythe, *Human Rights in International Relations* (Cambridge: Cambridge University Press, 2000), pp. 191–213.

36. UN, E/CN.4/Sub.2/2003/12/Rev.2, "UN Norms on the Responsibilities of Transnational Corporations . . . with Regard to Human Rights"; UN, A/HRC/11/13, "Report of the Special Representative . . . on the Issue of Human Rights and Transnational Corporations," 22 April 2009.

37. Kofi Annan, as cited in United Nations, Security Council, S/PV.4370, www.un.org, accessed 12 September 2001.

38. UN, A/RES/54/164, "Human Rights and Terrorism," 17 December 1999; UN, S/RES/1373, "International Cooperation to Combat . . . Terrorist Acts," 28 September 2001, www.un.org/terrorism; Rosemary Foot, "The United Nations, Counter Terrorism, and Human Rights," *Human Rights Quarterly* 29 (May 2007): 489–514.

39. Merkel, as cited in "Germany Hits Out at U.S. Sanctioning of Secret Prisons," 9 September 2006, Deutsche Welle, www.dw-world.de, accessed 10 September 2006.

40. "Report on Terrorism and Human Rights," OEA/Ser.L/V/II.116, Doc 5 rev. 1 corr., 22 October 2002, www.cidh.oas.org, accessed 4 January 2010.

41. See International Commission of Jurists, *Assessing Damage, Urging Action* (Geneva: ICJ, 2009); Nancy Chang, "The USA PATRIOT Act: What's So Patriotic About Trampling on the Bill of Rights?" (New York: Center for Constitutional Rights, 2002); Philip Heymann, "Civil Liberties and Human Rights in the Aftermath of September," *Harvard Journal of Law and Public Policy* 25 (Spring 2002): 441–56.

42. International Convention Against Torture and Other Cruel, Inhumane, or Degrading Treatment or Punishment, www.ohchr.org.

43. Among many, see Karen Greenberg and Joshua Dratel (eds.), *The Torture Papers* (New York: Cambridge University Press, 2005); Jane Mayer, *The Dark Side* (New York: Anchor, 2009); Darius Rejali, *Torture and Democracy* (Princeton, N.J.: Princeton University Press, 2009).

44. See Andrew Sullivan, "Dear President Bush," *Atlantic* (October 2009): 78–88; "Alleged Secret Detentions and Unlawful Inter-State Transfers," Document 10957, 7 June 2006 [The "Marty Report"], http://assembly.coe.int.

45. Central Intelligence Agency, Office of the Inspector General, "Special Review: Counterterrorism Detention and Interrogation Activities," Top Secret, 7 May 2004, p. 94, National Security Archive, www.gwu.edu/ānsarchiv/torture_archive, accessed 21 September 2009.

46. These images are readily available on the Internet. See also Mark Danner, *Torture and Truth* (New York: New York Review of Books, 2004), pp. 217–24; Susan Sontag, "Regarding the Torture of Others," *New York Times*, 23 May 2004.

47. See Scott Wilson and Michael Fletcher, "In Dueling Speeches, a National Security Debate," *Washington Post*, 22 May 2009.

48. Benjamin Franklin, *Memoirs* (London: Valpy, 1818), 1: 270.

49. See Thomas McCarthy (ed.), *Attacking the Root Causes of Torture* (Geneva: World Organization Against Torture, 2006).

50. For more detail see Paul Gordon Lauren, "'To Preserve and Build on Its Achievement and to Redress Its Shortcomings': The Journey from the Commission on Human Rights to the Human Rights Council," *Human Rights Quarterly* 29 (May 2007): 307–45.

51. Ibid., p. 330.

52. Human Rights Watch, Press Release, "UN: Annan Reforms Courageous," 21 March 2005.

53. See Loubna Freih and Joanna Weschler, "Back Annan's Call for a New Human Rights Body," *International Herald Tribune*, 9 April 2005.

54. United Nations, A/RES/60/251 (2006), "Resolution on the Human Rights Council."

55. Louise Arbour, "High Commissioner Urges Support for Human Rights Council," 23 February 2006, www.iheu.org, accessed 24 February 2006. See also Yvonne Terlingen, "The Human Rights Council," *Ethics and International Affairs* 21 (Summer 2007): 167–78.

56. See www.upr-info.org and www.ohchr.org.

57. This expression is heard frequently, based upon my personal observations of sessions of the Human Rights Council.

58. Office of the High Commissioner for Human Rights, *Survey on National Human Rights Institutions* (Geneva: OHCHR, 2009); www.nhri.net; Julie Mertus, *Human Rights Matters* (Stanford, Calif.: Stanford University Press, 2009).

59. As cited in "Establishing Administrative Justice: Key to Securing Human Rights," *OSCE Magazine* (March–April 2009): 12–13. See also www.coe.int, and Commissioner for Human Rights, Document CommDH (2009)12, Annual Activity Report 2008, 22 April 2009. I am grateful to Irene Kitsou-Milonas for insightful discussions in Strasbourg about the work of this office.

60. Ignatieff, *Human Rights as Politics and Idolatry*, p. 8.

61. Amnesty International, *Annual Report 2002*, www.amnesty.org, accessed 22 July 2002. The precise number, however, will probably never be known.

62. Robert Drinan, *The Mobilization of Shame* (New Haven, Conn.: Yale University Press, 2001).

63. See Ann Marie Clark, "Human Rights NGOs at the United Nations," in Jutta Joachim and Birgit Locher (eds.), *Transnational Activism* (London: Routledge, 2009), pp. 44–60; Claude Welch, Jr. (ed.), *NGOs and Human Rights* (Philadelphia: University of Pennsylvania Press, 2001); Keck and Sikkink, *Activists Beyond Borders*; Korey, *NGOs and the Universal Declaration*; Peter Willetts (ed.), *The Conscience of the World* (Washington, D.C.: Brookings Institution, 1996).

64. "UN Images Show Sri Lanka Damage," http://news.bbc.co.uk, accessed 1 May 2009.

65. "AAAS and Human Rights Program," http://shr.aaas.org, accessed 4 November 2009.

66. The fax number in Geneva is 41–(02)22 917 90 06. See also tb-petitions@ohchr.org, urgent-action@ohchr.org; CP@ohchr.org.

67. Jean Quataert, *Advocating Dignity* (Philadelphia: University of Pennsylvania Press, 2009), is particularly good in developing this point.

68. Steven Hick et al., *Human Rights and the Internet* (New York: St. Martin's, 2000).

69. See the Web sites listed in the Bibliography.

70. See www.upr-info.org; www.hrgoweb.org/council; www.humanrights-geneva.info; www.ishr .ch.

71. "Cell Tour," www.aiusa.org, accessed 15 May 2009.

72. Sontag, "Regarding the Torture of Others," *New York Times*, 23 May 2004.

73. Pierre Sané, as cited in Jonathan Power, *Like Water on Stone* (Boston: Northeastern University Press, 2001), p. 293.

74. Shen Guofang, as cited in *China Rights Forum* (Fall 1999): 24.

75. Greenberg and Dratel, *The Torture Papers*, passim.

76. As cited in "Mary Robinson," http://news.bbc.co.uk, accessed 28 November 2001.

77. "Israel: 'Goldstone Report Filled with Lies,'" www.imemc.org, accessed 22 October 2009.

78. See George Andreopoulos and Richard Claude (eds.), *Human Rights Education for the Twenty-First Century* (Philadelphia: University of Pennsylvania Press, 1997).

79. Graduate Institute of International Studies, Geneva, "Hommage à Sergio Vieira de Mello," *Point de Vue* 4 (2003): 1–27; Samantha Power, *Chasing the Flame* (New York: Penguin, 2008).

80. United Nations, A/RES/61/295, "Declaration on the Rights of Indigenous Peoples," 13 September 2007.

81. United Nations, S/RES/1820 (2008), "Women and Peace and Security," 19 June 2008.

82. "The World Is Watching," *Economist* (5 December 1998): 15. See also Clair Apodaca, "The Whole World Could Be Watching," *Journal of Human Rights* 6 (2007): 147–64.

83. United Nations Development Program, *Human Development Report, 2000*, p. 13.

Chapter 10. Toward the Future

1. Diderot, as cited by Hunt, *The French Revolution and Human Rights*, p. 36; Equiano, *An Interesting Narrative*, p. 101.

2. Harriet Beecher Stowe, *Uncle Tom's Cabin* (New York: Barnes and Noble, 1995), p. 52. See also Cynthia Ozick, "The Moral Necessity of Metaphor," *Harper's* (May 1986): 30.

3. For examples, see James Yin and Shi Young, *The Rape of Nanking* (Chicago: Innovative, 1996); James Allen (ed.), *Without Sanctuary* (Santa Fe, N.M.: Twin Palms, 2000). See also Sontag, "Regarding the Torture of Others"; www.witness.org.

4. See Brown, *Moral Capital*; John Kane, *The Politics of Moral Capital* (Cambridge: Cambridge University Press, 2001).

5. Among many examples, see U.S. NARA, RG 84, Box 89, File "Human Rights, 1946–1949," "Statement to the United Nations on Forced Labor"; Gladstone, *Bulgarian Horrors*; Coursier, "L'Évolution du droit international humanitaire," pp. 361–465; Jay Winter, *Dreams of Peace and Freedom* (New Haven. Conn.: Yale University Press, 2006).

6. Humphrey, *Human Rights and the United Nations*, p. 41.

7. Cited in Robinson, *The Universal Declaration of Human Rights*, p. 15.

8. John Foster Dulles, *War or Peace* (New York: Macmillan, 1950), p. 201.

9. Expressions as reported and as used in NANZ, EA 2, File 108/11/13/1(2), memorandum entitled "Human Rights Committee," 12 February 1948, and memorandum entitled "Report by the New Zealand Observer," 1 July 1948.

10. See Forsythe, *Human Rights in International Relations*, p. 168; Edward Kolodziej (ed.), *A Force Profonde* (Philadelphia: University of Pennsylvania Press, 2003).

11. Angelina Grimké, as cited in Katherine Du Pre Lumpkin, *The Emancipation of Angelina Grimké* (Chapel Hill: University of North Carolina Press, 1974), p. 84.

12. Václav Havel, as cited in Laber, *The Courage of Strangers*, p. 141.

13. Mohandas Gandhi, as cited at www.memoriable-quotes.com, accessed 10 February 2010.

14. Eglantyne Jebb, as cited in International Union for Child Welfare, *International Union for Child Welfare* (Geneva: IUCW, 1970), p. 16 (my emphasis).

15. Peter Bell, as cited in Keck and Sikkink, *Activists Beyond Borders*, p. 100.

16. Eleanor Roosevelt, as cited in Blanche Wiesen Cook, "Eleanor Roosevelt and Human Rights," in Crapol (ed.), *Women and American Foreign Policy*, p. 114. See also Kerry Kennedy Cuomo, *Speak Truth to Power* (New York: Crown, 2000); Paul Rogat Loeb, *Soul of a Citizen* (New York: St. Martin's, 1999).

17. Dom Hélder Camara, as cited widely on the Internet.

18. As cited in Jonathan Power, *Like Water on Stone*, p. xi.

19. As cited in "In the Face of Repression," *The Guardian*, 12 May 2001.

20. Morton Winston, "Assessing the Effectiveness of International Human Rights NGOs," in Welch, *NGOs and Human Rights*, p. 25. See also Ann Marie Clark, *Diplomacy of Conscience* (Princeton, N.J.: Princeton University Press, 2001).

21. Edith Balantyne, 7 April 1997, meeting of Special Committee of International NGOs on Human Rights, Palais des Nations, personal notes.

22. Interview with an official of the Office of the High Commissioner for Human Rights who wishes to remain anonymous.

23. Ignatieff, *Human Rights as Politics and Idolatry*, p. 8.

24. Humphrey, *Human Rights and the United Nations*, p. 13.

25. This expression is frequently heard among activists, as evidenced in Special Committee of International NGOs on Human Rights, meeting of 7 April 1997, Palais des Nations, personal notes.

26. "Bitterness Clouds Summit Finale," referring to the World Development Summit held in Johannesburg in August and September 2002, http://news.bbc.co.uk, 4 September 2002.

27. Kofi Annan, 9 April 1997, in UN Press Release, "Discours du Secrétaire Général."

28. See Borgwardt, *A New Deal for the World*, p. 289.

29. Boutros Boutros-Ghali, 14 June 1993, as cited in UN Publication DPI/1394/Rev.1/HR, *World Conference on Human Rights*, p. 6.

30. Ndabaningi Sithole, *African Nationalism* (London: Oxford University Press, 1959), p. 23.

31. For more discussion, see Burns H. Weston, "Human Rights," in Claude and Weston (eds.), *Human Rights in the World Community*, pp. 18–20; and Vasak Karel (ed.), *Dimensions internationales des droits de l'homme*, 2 vols. (Paris: UNESCO, 1982).

32. See, among many examples, William Ewart Gladstone, *Lessons in Massacre*, passim; Hochschild, *King Leopold's Ghost*, p. 305; NANZ, EA 2, File 108/11/13/1 (4), memorandum entitled "The Problem of Implementation," 1 December 1949; the Universal Declaration of Human Rights, Preamble; UN/GA, *Official Records, Plenary Meetings, 1966*, Meeting of 16 December 1966, p. 10; H. Gordon Skilling, *Charter 77 and Human Rights in Czechoslovakia* (London: Allen & Unwin, 1981), p. 153; Morsink, *The Universal Declaration of Human Rights*, passim; Glendon, *A World Made New*, pp. 216–17.

33. Joseph Eldridge, as cited in Keck and Sikkink, *Activists Beyond Borders*, pp. 91–92.

34. See the discussions about "realism" in William Schultz, *In Our Own Best Interest* (Boston: Beacon, 2001); Forsythe, *Human Rights in International Politics*.

35. See Sumner Twiss, "A Constructive Framework for Discussing Confucianism and Human Rights," in de Bary and Tu, *Confucianism and Human Rights*, p. 31.

36. See Clark, *International Legitimacy and World Society*; Hunt, *Inventing Human Rights*, p. 26;

37. See Brown, *Moral Capital*, pp. 25, 29.

38. Hochschild, *Bury the Chains*, pp. 5, 97.

39. Paul Gordon Lauren, "History and Human Rights: People and Forces in Paradoxical Interaction," *Journal of Human Rights* 7 (April–June 2008): 91–103; Jeffrey Wasserstrom et al. (eds.), *Human Rights and Revolutions* (Lanham, Md.: Rowman & Littlefield, 2007); Joan Wallach Scott, *Only Paradoxes to Offer* (Cambridge, Mass.: Harvard University Press, 1997).

40. Expressions from UN Document E/CN.4/1996/NGO/22, "Organisation des Travaux de la Session," 26 March 1996; "Same Old Rows Hit New Rights Body," www.bbc.co.uk, accessed 27 July 2007; many personal conversations with NGO representatives in Geneva and New York

41. Sithole, *African Nationalism*, p. 23.

42. *Christian Century*, as cited in Borgwardt, *A New Deal for the World*, p. 246.

43. See UN/GA, *Official Records, 1948*, passim; \ Robinson, *The Universal Declaration of Human Rights*, p. 15.

44. W. A. Morris, as cited by Simpson, *Human Rights and the End of Empire*, pp. 309–10.

45. Anatoly Dobrynin, *In Confidence* (New York: Random House, 1995), p. 346; Thomas, *The Helsinki Effect*.

46. Rosemary Foot, *Rights Beyond Borders* (Oxford: Oxford University Press, 2000).

47. Ernst B. Haas, "Words Can Hurt You," in Stephen Krasner (ed.), *International Regimes* (Ithaca, N.Y.: Cornell University Press, 1983), pp. 23–59.

48. See Hannah Arendt, "The Perplexities of the Rights of Man," in *The Origins of Totalitarianism* (New York: World, 1951), pp. 287–98; and Jan Klabbers, "Doing the Right Thing?" in Craig Scott (ed.), *Torture as Tort* (Oxford: Hart, 2001), pp. 553–66.

49. Humphrey, *Human Rights and the United Nations*, p. 25. See also Ignatieff, *Human Rights as Politics and Idolatry*, pp. 3–52.

50. William Butler Yeats, as cited in Richard Rorty, *Philosophy and Social Hope* (New York: Penguin, 1999), p. 7.

51. H. Lauterpacht, *International Law and Human Rights* (New York: Garland, 1973), p. 131. See also UN Archives/Geneva, SOA 317/1/01 A, memorandum from Egon Schwelb to John Humphrey, Confidential, 11 February 1950; UN Archives/Geneva, SO 218, letter from Peter Benenson to John Humphrey, Private and Confidential, 13 March 1966, and International League for the Rights of Man, "Statement on the United Nations Commissioner on Human Rights," 30 March 1966; Thomas Jefferson to James Madison, 15 March 1789, in Jefferson, *The Papers of Thomas Jefferson*, 14:660.

52. See Carretta, *Equiano, the African*, p. 252.

53. As cited in Marian Ramelson, *The Petticoat Rebellio Rights* (London: Lawrence & Wishart, 1967), p. 87.

54. Olusegun Obasanjo, as cited in Power, *Like Water on Stone*, p. 17.

55. Julio de Pena Valdez, as cited in "In the Face of Repression," *The Guardian*, 12 May 2001.

56. Participant at the London Peace Implementation Conference on Bosnia, as cited in the British Broadcasting Corporation's "World News Broadcast," 5 December 1996.

57. See Commission on Human Security, *Human Security Now* (New York: Commission on Human Security, 2003), www.humansecurity-chs.org; Dan Caldwell and Robert Williams, Jr., *Seeking Security in an Insecure World* (Lanham, Md.: Rowman & Littlefield, 2006); Lauren, Craig, and George, *Force and Statecraft*; Helsinki Final Act.

58. United Nations, A/RES/60/1, "World Summit Outcome," 24 October 2005; United Nations, *A More Secure World* (New York: United Nations, 2004).

59. See Francis Deng et al., *Sovereignty as Responsibility* (Washington, D.C.: Brookings Institution, 1996); among others.

60. Eleanor Roosevelt, as cited in Joseph Lash, *Life Was Meant To Be Lived* (New York: Norton, 1984), p. 154.

61. Sellars, *The Rise and Rise of Human Rights*, p. 197; UN Document E/CN.4/1997/98, "Follow-Up to the World Conference on Human Rights: Report of the High Commissioner," 24 February 1997; Jan Mårtenson, in Eide et al. (eds.), *The Universal Declaration of Human Rights*, p. 27; among many others.

62. This development is monitored annually, as can be seen in the *Freedom in the World 2009: Global Data*, www.freedomhouse.org. See also John Lewis Gaddis, *The Cold War* (New York: Penguin, 2007), p. 264.

63. Nelson Mandela, as cited at http://www.anc.org.za, 18 August 1997. See also Robin Cook, "Human Rights into a New Century," British Foreign Office press release, 17 July 1997; Forsythe, *The Internationalization of Human Rights*, passim; among others.

64. These can be seen in daily news reports, the sessions of the Human Rights Council, the annual reports of Amnesty International and Human Rights Watch, and the various Web sites listed in the Bibliography, among others.

65. Blanche Wiesen Cook, "Eleanor Roosevelt and Human Rights," p. 113; Jan Mårtenson, "The Preamble of the Universal Declaration of Human Rights and the UN Human Rights Program," in Eide et al. (eds.), *The Universal Declaration of Human Rights*, p. 17.

66. Aung San, *Freedom from Fear*, pp. 183–85.

67. Addams, *Peace and Bread in Time of War*, p. 149.

Selected Bibliography

Archives

China. Chinese Relief and Rehabilitation Administration. Hoover Institution, Stanford.
Commission for Relief in Belgium. Hoover Institution, Stanford.
Council of Europe. Archives. Strasbourg.
Finland. Ulkoasiainministeriön Arkisto. Helsinki.
France. Archives Diplomatiques du Ministère des Affaires Étrangères. Paris.
France. Archives Nationales. Paris.
Geneva. Archives d'État de Genève.
Germany. Politisches Archive des Auswärtiges Amt. Bonn.
Great Britain. Foreign Office Correspondence, Public Record Office. London.
Japan. Delegation to the Peace Conference. Hoover Institution, Stanford.
Japan. Ministry of Foreign Affairs, Diplomatic Record Office. Tokyo.
League of Nations. Archives de la Société des Nations. Geneva.
National Association for the Advancement of Colored People. Library of Congress, Washington, D.C.
New Zealand. Department of External Affairs, National Archives. Wellington.
Organization for Security and Cooperation in Europe. Office of the Secretariat. Prague.
Union Internationale de Secours aux Enfants. Archives d'État. Geneva.
United Nations. Archives of the United Nations. New York.
United Nations. High Commissioner for Refugees. Archives. Geneva.
United Nations Office in Geneva. Registry, Records, and Archives. Palais des Nations, Geneva.
United States. Department of State. National Archives and Records Administration. Washington, D.C. and College Park, Md.

Private Papers and Personal Collections

Cordier, Andrew (Columbia University)
Davis, Loda Mae (Hoover Institution)
Du Bois, W. E. B (Library of Congress)
Fraser, Peter (National Archives of New Zealand)
Gaines, Jeffrey (OSCE Office/Prague)
Hamburger, Ernst (Leo Baeck Institute)
Hammarskjöld, Dag (Papers of the Secretary-General, UN Archives / New York)
Himmler, Heinrich (Hoover Institution)
Koo, Wellington (Columbia University)
Lansing, Robert (Library of Congress)
Lemkin, Raphael (New York Public Library)
Lie, Trygvie (Papers of the Secretary-General, UN Archives / New York)

Miller, David Hunter (Hoover Institution)
Mitchell, Anna (Hoover Institution)
Munro, Leslie (Alexander Turnbull Library)
Nash, Walter (National Archives of New Zealand)
Notter, Harley A. (U.S. National Archives and Records Administration)
Pérez de Cuéllar, Javier (Papers of the Secretary-General, UN Archives / New York)
Roosevelt, Eleanor (Roosevelt Library and Museum)
Roosevelt, Franklin D. (Roosevelt Library and Museum)
Stilwell, Joseph (Hoover Institution)
Streit, Clarence (University of Montana Archives)
Thomas, Albert (Archives Nationales / Paris)
Urquart, Brian (UN Archives / New York)
U Thant (Papers of the Secretary-General, UN Archives / New York)
Waldheim, Kurt (Papers of the Secretary-General, UN Archives / New York)
Webster, Sir Charles (London School of Economics)
Welles, Sumner (Roosevelt Library and Museum)
Wilson, Woodrow (Library of Congress)

Published Documents

Académie Diplomatique Internationale. *Séances et Travaux.*

Canada. Parliament. House of Commons. *Official Debates.*

Commission for Relief in Belgium. *Annual Report, 1914–1916.* London: Crowther & Goodman, 1916.

Conference on Security and Cooperation in Europe. *Stage I—Helsinki, Verbatim Records, Open Sessions* and *Private Sessions.* Helsinki: Valtion painatuskeskus, 1973.

Council of Europe. *The European Convention on Human Rights: Collected Texts.* Strasbourg: Council of Europe, 1963.

———. *Yearbook of the European Convention on Human Rights.*

———. Commission Européenne des Droits de l'Homme. *Compte rendu annuel.*

France. Assemblée Nationale. Chambre des Députés. *Débats parlementaires.*

———. *Rapports fait au nom de la Commission des affaires étrangères.*

———. *Conférence de la Paix, 1919–1920. Recueil des actes de la Conférence.* Paris: Imprimerie Nationale, 1922.

Germany. Auswärtiges Amt. *Die Grosse Politik der Europäischen Kabinette, 1871–1914.* 40 vols. Berlin: Deutsche Verlagsgesellschaft für Politik, 1922–1927.

Great Britain. Foreign Office. *British and Foreign State Papers.*

———. Parliament. House of Commons. *A Commentary on the Charter of the United Nations.* London: His Majesty's Stationery Office, 1945.

———. Parliament. House of Commons. *The Parliamentary Debates* and *Sessional Papers.*

———. Parliament. House of Commons. *Substance of the Debates on a Resolution for Abolishing the Slave Trade.* London: Phillips and Fardon, 1806.

Indonesia. *The Asian-African Conference, 1955.* New Delhi: Information Service of Indonesia, 1955.

International Commission on Intervention and State Sovereignty. *The Responsibility to Protect.* Ottawa: International Development Research Center, 2001.

International Labor Organization. *The I.L.O. and Human Rights.* Geneva: International Labor Office, 1968.

———. *Official Bulletin.*

International Military Tribunal. *Trial of the Major War Criminals.* 42 vols. Nuremberg: International Military Tribunal, 1947–1949.

Inter-Parliamentary Union. *Women*. Reports and Documents. Geneva: Inter- Parliamentary Union, 1997.

League of Nations. *Official Journal*.

——. *Protection of Linguistic, Racial, and Religious Minorities*. Geneva: League of Nations, 1927.

——. *La Question de l'esclavage*. Geneva: Société des Nations, 1924.

——. *Treaty Series*.

——. Permanent Mandates Commission. *Minutes* and *Reports*.

Netherlands. Ministry of Foreign Affairs. *Human Rights and Foreign Policy*. The Hague: Ministry of Foreign Affairs and Ministry of Development Co-operation, 1979.

New Zealand. Parliament. *Appendix to the Journals of the House of Representatives*. Organization of African Unity. *Basic Documents and Resolutions*.

Organization of American States. La Comisión Interamericana de Derechos Humanos. *Actividades de la Comisión Interamericana de Derechos Humanos*. Washington, D.C.: Comisión Interamericana de Derechos Humanos, 1976.

Organization for Security and Cooperation in Europe. Office of Democratic Institutions and Human Rights. *Annual Reports*.

Pan American Union. *Congress and Conference Series*.

——. *Inter-American Conference on War and Peace*. Washington, D.C.: Pan American Union, 1945.

Permanent Court of International Justice. *Publications of the Court*.

United Nations. *The African Charter on Human and Peoples' Rights*. New York: United Nations, 1990.

——. *Official Records*.

——. *The United Nations and Human Rights, 1945–1995*. New York: United Nations, 1995.

——. *United Nations Weekly Bulletin*.

——. *World Conference on Human Rights: The Vienna Declaration and Programme of Action*. New York: United Nations, 1993.

——. *Yearbook on Human Rights*.

——. Economic and Social Council. Commission on Human Rights. *Official Records*.

——. Economic and Social Council. Commission on Human Rights. Sub-Commission on Prevention and Discrimination and Protection of Minorities. *Official Records*.

——. Economic and Social Council. Human Rights Committee. *Annual Reports*.

——. General Assembly. *Official Records, Verbatim Reports*, and *Resolutions*.

——. General Assembly. Committee on the Elimination of Racial Discrimination (CERD). *Official Records*.

——. General Assembly. Special Committee Against Apartheid. *Official Records*.

——. General Assembly. Special Committee on the Situation with Regard to the Implementation of the Declaration on the Granting of Independence to Colonial Countries and Peoples. *Official Records*.

——. General Assembly. Third Committee. *Official Records*.

——. High Commissioner for Human Rights. *The High Commissioner for Human Rights: An Introduction*. Geneva: United Nations, 1996.

——. Security Council. *Official Records, Verbatim Reports*, and *Resolutions*.

——. Trusteeship Council. *Official Records*.

United Nations Conference on International Organization. *Documents of the United Nations Conference on International Organization*. 22 vols. London: United Nations Information Organization, 1946–1955.

United Nations Educational, Scientific, and Cultural Organization. *The Basis of an International Bill of Rights*. Paris: UNESCO, 1949.

——. *The Birthright of Man*. Paris: UNESCO, 1969.

——. *Human Rights: Comments and Interpretations*. London: Wingate, 1949.

United States. *Statutes at Large*.

United States. Congress. *Congressional Record.*

————. Senate. Committee on Foreign Relations. *The Charter of the United Nations: Hearings.* Washington, D.C.: Government Printing Office, 1945.

————. Department of State. *Department of State Bulletin.*

————. *Documents on German Foreign Policy, 1918–1945.* Series D.

————. *Foreign Relations of the United States.*

————. *Postwar Foreign Policy Preparation, 1939–1945.* Washington, D.C.: Government Printing Office, 1949.

————. *Treaties and Other International Instruments of the United States.*

————. Office of the President. President's Committee on Civil Rights. *To Secure These Rights.* Washington, D.C.: Government Printing Office, 1947.

Books

Addams, Jane. *Peace and Bread in Time of War.* New York: Macmillan, 1922.

Alston, Philip (ed.). *Promoting Human Rights Through Bills of Rights: Comparative Perspectives.* Oxford: Oxford University Press, 2000.

———— (ed.). *The United Nations and Human Rights: A Critical Appraisal.* Oxford: Clarendon Press, 1992.

American Jewish Committee. *A World Charter for Human Rights.* New York: American Jewish Committee, 1945.

American Law Institute. *Report to the Council of the Institute and Statement of Essential Human Rights.* New York: American Law Institute, 1944.

Anderson, Bonnie. *Joyous Greetings: The First International Women's Movement, 1830–1860.* New York: Oxford University Press, 2000.

Anderson, Carol. *Eyes Off the Prize: The United Nations and the African American Struggle for Human Rights, 1944–1955.* New York: Cambridge University Press, 2003.

Andreopoulos, George (ed.). *Genocide: Conceptual and Historical Dimensions.* Philadelphia: University of Pennsylvania Press, 1994.

Angle, Stephen. *Human Rights and Chinese Thought.* Cambridge: Cambridge University Press, 2002.

An-Naʿim, Abdullahi Ahmed (ed.). *Human Rights in Cross-Cultural Perspectives.* Philadelphia: University of Pennsylvania Press, 1995.

Anti-Slavery and Aborigines Protection Society. *An International Colonial Convention.* London: Anti-Slavery and Aborigines Protection Society, 1943.

Arendt, Hannah. *The Origins of Totalitarianism.* New York: World, 1958.

Aulard, A., and Boris Mirkine-Guetzévitch. *Les Déclarations des droits de l'homme: textes constitutionnels concernant les droits de l'homme et les garanties des libertés individuelles dans tous les pays.* Paris: Payot, 1929.

Aung San Suu Kyi. *Freedom from Fear.* London: Penguin, 1995.

Baehr, Peter, et al. (eds.). *Innovation and Inspiration: Fifty Years of the Universal Declaration of Human Rights.* Amsterdam: Royal Netherlands Academy of Arts and Sciences, 1999.

Bales, Kevin. *Disposable People: New Slavery in the Global Economy.* Berkeley: University of California Press, 2004.

Baxi, Upendra. *Inhuman Wrongs and Human Rights: Unconventional Essays.* New Delhi: Har-Anand, 1994.

Beigbeder, Ives, and Theo van Boven, *Judging War Criminals: The Politics of International Justice.* London: Palgrave Macmillan, 1999.

Beitz, Charles. *The Idea of Human Rights.* New York: Oxford University Press, 2009.

Bellamy, Alex. *Responsibility to Protect: The Global Effort to End Mass Atrocities.* Cambridge: Policy Press, 2009.

Berting, Jan, et al. (eds.), *Human Rights in a Pluralist World.* Westport, Conn.: Meckler, 1990.

Beveridge, Sir William. *Social Insurance and Allied Services.* American ed. New York: Macmillan, 1942.

Bloom, Irene, et al. (eds.). *Religious Diversity and Human Rights.* New York: Columbia University Press, 1996.

Bodin, Jean. *Les Six livres de la République.* Paris: Fayard, 1986.

Boissier, Pierre. *Histoire du Comité International de la Croix-Rouge de Solférino à Tsoushima.* Paris: Plon, 1963.

Borgwardt, Elizabeth. *A New Deal for the World: America's Vision for Human Rights.* Cambridge, Mass.: Belknap, 2007.

Bossuyt, Marc. *Guide to the "Travaux Préparatoires" of the International Covenant on Civil and Political Rights.* Dordrecht: Nijhoff, 1987.

———. *L'Interdiction de la discrimination dans le droit international des droits de l'homme.* Brussels: Bruylant, 1976.

Brandt, Irving. *The Bill of Rights: Its Origin and Meaning.* New York: New American Library, 1967.

Brown, Christopher Leslie. *Moral Capital: Foundations of British Abolitionism.* Chapel Hill: University of North Carolina Press, 2006.

Brown, Seyom. *Human Rights in World Politics.* New York: Longman, 2000.

Brunet, René. *La Garantie internationale des droits de l'homme.* Geneva: Grasset, 1947.

Bruns, Roger (ed.). *Am I Not a Man and a Brother.* New York: Chelsea House, 1983.

Brysk, Alison (ed.). *Globalization and Human Rights.* Berkeley: University of California Press, 2002.

Buergenthal, Thomas. *International Human Rights in a Nutshell.* St. Paul, Minn.: West, 1995.

Burgers, J. Herman, and Hans Danelius. *The United Nations Convention Against Torture.* Dordrecht: Nijhoff, 1988.

Burke, Edmund. *Reflections on the Revolution in France.* Chicago: Regnery, 1955.

Burns, James MacGregor, and Stewart Burns. *A People's Charter: The Pursuit of Rights in America.* New York: Vintage, 1993.

Bussey, Gertrude, and Margaret Tims. *Women's International League for Peace and Freedom.* London: Allen & Unwin, 1965.

Calder, Angus. *The People's War.* London: Panther, 1969.

Calder, Lord Richie. *On Human Rights.* London: H. G. Wells Society, 1968.

Carter, Jimmy. *Keeping Faith: Memoirs of a President.* New York: Bantam, 1982.

Cassin, René. *La Pensée et l'action.* Paris: Lalou, 1972.

Chang, Iris. *The Rape of Nanking.* New York: Penguin, 1997.

Chua, Amy. *World on Fire: How Exporting Free Market Democracy Breeds Ethnic Hatred and Global Instability.* New York: Anchor, 2004.

Cicero, Marcus Tullius. *De Legibus.* New York: Putnam, 1928.

Clapham, Andrew. *Human Rights in the Private Sphere.* Oxford: Clarendon Press, 1998.

Clark, Ann Marie. *Diplomacy of Conscience: Amnesty International and Changing Human Rights Norms.* Princeton, N.J.: Princeton University Press, 2001.

Clark, Ian. *International Legitimacy and World Society.* Oxford: Oxford University Press, 2007.

Claude, Richard Pierre, and Burns H. Weston (eds.). *Human Rights in the World Community: Issues and Action.* 2nd ed. Philadelphia: University of Pennsylvania Press, 1992. 3rd ed. 2006.

Commission to Study the Organization of the Peace. *International Safeguard of Human Rights.* New York: Commission to Study the Organization of the Peace, 1944.

———. *The United Nations and Human Rights.* Dobbs Ferry, N.Y.: Oceana, 1968.

Conrad, Joseph. *Heart of Darkness.* New York: Penguin, 1995.

Cook, Rebecca (ed.). *Human Rights of Women: National and International Perspectives.* Philadelphia: University of Pennsylvania Press, 1994.

Cotler, Irwin, and F. Pearl Eliadis (eds.). *International Human Rights Law: Theory and Practice.* Montreal: Canadian Human Rights Foundation, 1992.

Craig, Gordon A., and Francis Lowenheim (eds.). *The Diplomats, 1939–1979*. Princeton, N.J.: Princeton University Press, 1994.

Cranston, Maurice. *What Are Human Rights?* New York: Taplinger, 1973.

Cuomo, Kerry Kennedy. *Speak Truth to Power*. New York: Crown, 2000.

Daley, Caroline (ed.). *Suffrage and Beyond: International Feminist Perspectives*. New York: New York University Press, 1994.

Danner, Mark. *Torture and Truth: America, Abu Ghraib, and the War on Terror*. New York: New York Review of Books, 2004.

Davis, David Brion. *Slavery and Human Progress*. New York: Oxford University Press, 1984.

———. *Inhuman Bondage: The Rise and Fall of Slavery in the New World*. New York: Oxford University Press, 2006.

Dawes, James. *That the World May Know: Bearing Witness to Atrocity*. Cambridge, Mass.: Harvard University Press, 2007.

De Bary, Wm. Theodore, and Tu Weiming (eds.). *Confucianism and Human Rights*. New York: Columbia University Press, 1998.

Donnan, Elizabeth. *Documents Illustrative of the History of the Slave Trade*. 4 vols. Washington, D.C.: Carnegie Institution, 1930–1935.

Donnelly, Jack. *International Human Rights: Dilemmas in World Politics*. Boulder, Colo.: Westview, 2006.

———. *Universal Human Rights in Theory and Practice*. Ithaca, N.Y.: Cornell University Press, 2002.

Dower, John. *War Without Mercy: Race and Power in the Pacific*. New York: Pantheon, 1986.

Drinan, Robert. *The Cry of the Oppressed: The History and Hope of the Human Rights Revolution*. San Francisco: Harper & Row, 1987.

Drzewicki, Krzysztof. *Social Rights as Human Rights*. Abo: Institute for Human Rights, 1994.

Du Bois, W. E. B. *Dusk of Dawn*. New York: Harcourt Brace, 1940.

———. *The World and Africa*. New York: International Publishers, 1965.

Dunant, J. Henry. *A Memory of Solferino*. Washington, D.C.: American Red Cross, 1939.

Duparc, Jacques. *La Protection des minorités de race, de langue et de religion*. Paris: Dalloz, 1922.

Dworkin, Ronald. *Taking Rights Seriously*. Cambridge, Mass.: Harvard University Press, 1977.

Eide, Asbjørn, et al. (eds.). *The Universal Declaration of Human Rights: A Commentary*. Oslo: Scandinavian University Press, 1992.

Equiano, Olaudah. *The Interesting Narrative and Other Writings*. Vincent Carretta (ed.). New York: Penguin, 2003.

Ermacora, Felix. *Menschenrechte in der sich wandelnden Welt*. Vienna: Oesterreichischen Akademie der Wissenschaften, 1974.

Falk, Richard A. *Achieving Human Rights*. New York: Routledge, 2009.

Fischer, Louis. *Gandhi: His Life and Message for the World*. New York: Mentor, 1982.

Fladeland, Betty. *Men and Brothers: Anglo-American Anti-Slavery Cooperation*. Urbana: University of Illinois Press, 1972.

Fink, Carole. *Defending the Rights of Others: The Great Powers, the Jews, and International Minority Protection, 1878–1938*. New York: Cambridge University Press, 2004.

Flexner, Eleanor. *Century of Struggle: The Woman's Rights Movement in the United States*. Cambridge, Mass.: Belknap Press of Harvard University Press, 1975.

Forsythe, David (ed.). *Encyclopedia of Human Rights*. 5 vols. New York: Oxford University Press, 2009.

———. *Humanitarian Politics: The International Committee of the Red Cross*. Baltimore: Johns Hopkins University Press, 1977.

———. *Human Rights in International Relations*. Cambridge: Cambridge University Press, 2000.

Foster, Catherine. *Women for All Seasons: The Story of the Women's International League for Peace and Freedom*. Athens: University of Georgia Press, 1989.

Franklin, John Hope. *From Slavery to Freedom: A History of Negro Americans*. New York: Knopf, 1974.

Fujimura-Fanselow, Kumiko and Atsuko Kameda (eds.). *Japanese Women*. New York: Feminist Press, 1995.

Ganji, Manouchehr. *International Protection of Human Rights*. Geneva: Droz, 1962.

Geiss, Immanuel. *Panafrikanismus: Zur Geschichte der Dekolonisation*. Frankfurt am Main: Europäische Verlagsanstalt, 1968.

Gladstone, William E. *Bulgarian Horrors and the Question of the East*. London: Murray, 1876.

Glendon, Mary Ann. *A World Made New: Eleanor Roosevelt and the International Declaration of Human Rights*. New York: Random House, 2001.

Gouges, Olympe de. *Œuvres*. Paris: Mercure de France, 1986.

Greenberg, Karen, and Joshua Dratel (eds.). *The Torture Papers: The Road to Abu Ghraib*. New York: Cambridge University Press, 2005.

Grewe, W. G. *Epochen der Völkerrechtsgeschichte*. Baden-Baden: Nomos, 1988.

Griffith, Elisabeth. *In Her Own Right: The Life of Elizabeth Cady Stanton*. New York: Oxford University Press, 1984.

Grimké, Sarah. *Letters on the Equality of the Sexes and the Condition of Woman*. Boston: Knapp, 1838.

Grotius, Hugo. *The Rights of War and Peace*. Richard Tuck (ed.). Indianapolis: Liberty Fund, 2005.

Guest, Iain. *Behind the Disappearances: Argentina's Dirty War Against Human Rights and the United Nations*. Philadelphia: University of Pennsylvania Press, 1990.

Gurvitch, Georges. *La Déclaration des droits sociaux*. Paris: Vrin, 1946.

Gyatso, Tenzin. *Ocean of Wisdom*. Santa Fe, N.M.: Clear Light, 1989.

Haas, Michael. *International Human Rights*. New York: Routledge, 2008.

Hagen, William T. *The Indian Rights Association*. Tucson: University of Arizona Press, 1985.

Henkin, Louis. *The Age of Rights*. New York: Columbia University Press, 1990.

Hertslet, Edward (ed.). *The Map of Africa by Treaty*. 3 vols. London: Harrison & Sons, 1909.

———. *The Map of Europe by Treaty*. 4 vols. London: Butterworths, 1875–1891.

Hilpert, Konrad. *Die Menschenrechte: Geschichte, Theologie, Aktualität*. Düsseldorf: Patmos, 1991.

Hobbes, Thomas. *Leviathan*. New York: Washington Square Press, 1964.

Hochschild, Adam. *Bury the Chains: Prophets and Rebels in the Fight to Free an Empire's Slaves*. Boston: Houghton Mifflin, 2005.

———. *King Leopold's Ghost: A Story of Greed, Terror, and Heroism in Colonial Africa*. Boston: Houghton Mifflin, 1998.

Hoffmann, Stanley. *Duties Beyond Borders: On the Limits and Possibilities of Ethical International Politics*. Syracuse, N.Y.: Syracuse University Press, 1981.

Holborn, Louise (ed.). *War and Peace Aims of the United Nations*. Boston: World Peace Foundation, 1943.

Horne, Thomas. *Property Rights and Poverty*. Chapel Hill: University of North Carolina Press, 1990.

Hsiung, James (ed.). *Human Rights in East Asia*. New York: Paragon, 1986.

Hufton, Olwen (ed.). *Historical Change and Human Rights*. New York: Basic Books, 1995.

Humphrey, John P. *Human Rights and the United Nations*. Dobbs Ferry, N.Y.: Transnational, 1984.

Hunt, Lynn (ed.). *The French Revolution and Human Rights*. Boston: Bedford, 1996.

———. *Inventing Human Rights: A History*. New York: Norton, 2007.

Hutchinson, John. *Champions of Charity: War and the Rise of the Red Cross*. Boulder, Colo.: Westview, 1996.

Ignatieff, Michael. *Human Rights as Politics and Idolatry*. Princeton, N.J.: Princeton University Press, 2001.

Ibsen, Henrik. *A Doll's House*. London: Penguin, 1965.

Ihm, Claudia Carlen (ed.). *The Papal Encyclicals*. 5 vols. Raleigh, N.C.: McGrath, 1981.

Inman, Samuel Guy. *Inter-American Conferences*. Washington, D.C.: University Press of America, 1965.

Ishay, Micheline R. *The History of Human Rights*. Berkeley: University of California Press, 2008.

———. *The Human Rights Reader*. New York: Routledge, 2007.

Jacobs, F. G. *The European Convention on Human Rights.* Oxford: Oxford University Press, 1975.

Jayawardena, Kumari. *Feminism and Nationalism in the Third World.* London: Zed Press, 1986.

Kant, Immanuel. *Grundegung zur Metaphysik der Sitten.* Riga: Harknoch, 1785.

Karel, Vasak (ed.). *Dimensions internationales des droits de l'homme,* 2 vols. Paris: UNESCO, 1982.

Karis, Thomas, and Gwendolen Carter (eds.). *From Protest to Challenge: A Documentary History of African Politics in South Africa.* 4 vols. Stanford, Calif.: Hoover Institution Press, 1977.

Kaufman, Natalie Hevener. *Human Rights Treaties and the Senate: A History of Opposition.* Chapel Hill: University of North Carolina Press, 1990.

Kawakami, Kiyoshi Karl (ed.). *What Japan Thinks.* New York: Macmillan, 1921.

Kazuko, Ono. *Chinese Women in a Century of Revolution.* Stanford, Calif.: Stanford University Press, 1989.

Keck, Margaret, and Kathryn Sikkink. *Activists Beyond Borders: Advocacy Networks in International Politics.* Ithaca, N.Y.: Cornell University Press, 1998.

Kelsay, John, and Sumner B. Twiss (eds.), *Religion and Human Rights.* New York: Project on Religion and Human Rights, 1994.

Kiernan. Ben. *Blood and Soil: A World History of Genocide and Extermination from Sparta to Darfur.* New Haven, Conn.: Yale University Press, 2009.

Kolodziej, Edward (ed.). *A Force Profonde: The Power, Promise, and Politics of Human Rights.* Philadelphia: University of Pennsylvania Press, 2003.

Korey, William. *NGOs and the Universal Declaration of Human Rights.* New York: St. Martin's, 1998.

Koskenneimi, Martti. *The Gentle Civilizer of Nations: The Rise and Fall of International Law, 1870–1960.* Cambridge: Cambridge University Press, 2001.

Laber, Jeri. *The Courage of Strangers: Coming of Age with the Human Rights Movement.* New York: Public Affairs Press, 2002.

Landen, Robert. *The Emergence of the Modern Middle East.* New York: Van Nostrand Reinhold, 1970.

Laqueur, Walter, and Barry Rubin (eds.). *The Human Rights Reader.* New York: Meridian, 1989.

Las Casas, Bartholomé de. *In Defense of the Indians.* Stafford Poole (trans. and ed.). DeKalb: Northern Illinois University Press, 1992.

Lauren, Paul Gordon. *Power and Prejudice: The Politics and Diplomacy of Racial Discrimination.* Boulder, Colo.: Westview/HarperCollins, 1996.

Lauterpacht, Hersch. *An International Bill of the Rights of Man.* New York: Columbia University Press, 1945.

———. *International Law and Human Rights.* New York: Garland, 1973.

Lawson, Edward (ed.), *Encyclopedia of Human Rights.* New York: Taylor & Francis, 1996.

League of Nations Union. *The Atlantic Charter.* London: Hodgson, 1942.

Lemkin, Raphael. *Axis Rule in Occupied Europe.* New York: Carnegie Foundation, 1944.

Lenin, V. I. *Collected Works.* New York: International Publishers, 1929–1945.

Leo XIII. *Rerum Novarum.* New York: Paulist Press, 1939.

Lillich, Richard. *International Human Rights: Problems of Law, Policy, and Practice.* Boston: Little, Brown, 1991.

Little, David, et al. (eds.). *Human Rights and the Conflict of Cultures: Western and Islamic Perspectives on Religious Liberty.* Columbia: University of South Carolina Press, 1988.

Livezey, Lowell. *Nongovernmental Organizations and the Ideas of Human Rights.* Princeton, N.J.: Center of International Studies, 1988.

Locke, John. *Two Treatises of Government.* New York: Hafner, 1947.

Lockwood, Bert B., Jr. (ed.). *Women's Rights.* Baltimore: Johns Hopkins University Press, 2006.

Luard, Evan (ed.). *The International Protection of Human Rights.* London: Thames & Hudson, 1967.

Malanczuk, Peter. *Humanitarian Intervention and the Legitimacy of the Use of Force.* Amsterdam: Het Spinhuis, 1993.

Mandela, Nelson. *Long Walk to Freedom.* Boston: Little, Brown, 1994.

Mandelstam, André N. *Les Droits internationaux de l'homme.* Paris: Éditions Internationales, 1931.

———. *La Protection internationale des minorités.* Paris: Sirey, 1931.

Marwick, Arthur. *Women at War, 1914–1918.* London: Fontana, 1977.

Marx, Karl, and Friedrich Engels. *Manifesto of the Communist Party.* New York: Socialist Labor Party, 1888.

Mayer, Ann Elizabeth. *Islam and Human Rights: Tradition and Politics.* Boulder, Colo.: Westview, 2006.

McDougal, Myres S., Harold Lasswell, and Lung-chu Chen. *Human Rights and World Public Order.* New Haven, Conn.: Yale University Press, 1980.

McGoldrick, Dominic. *The Human Rights Committee: Its Role in the Development of the International Covenant on Civil and Political Rights.* Oxford: Clarendon Press, 1991.

Meron, Theodor. *Human Rights Law-Making in the United Nations.* Oxford: Oxford University Press, 1986.

Mertus, Julie. *Human Rights Matters: Local Politics and National Human Rights Institutions.* Stanford, Calif.: Stanford University Press, 2009.

Miers, Suzanne. *Britain and the Ending of the Slave Trade.* New York: Africana, 1975.

Mill, John Stuart. *On Liberty.* London: Parker & Son, 1859.

———. *The Subjection of Women.* London: Longmans, 1869.

Miller, Kelly. *The World War for Human Rights.* Washington, D.C.: Jenkins, 1919.

Mitri, Tarek (ed.). *Religion and Human Rights.* Geneva: World Council of Churches, 1996.

Morsink, Johannes. *Inherent Human Rights.* Philadelphia: University of Pennsylvania Press, 2009.

———. *The Universal Declaration of Human Rights.* Philadelphia: University of Pennsylvania Press, 1999.

Mower, A. Glenn. *The United States, the United Nations, and Human Rights.* Westport, Conn.: Greenwood, 1979.

Moynier, Gustave, and Louis Appia. *La Guerre et la charité: Traité théorique et pratique de philanthropie appliquée.* Geneva: Cherbuliez, 1867.

Murphey, Rhoades. *A History of Asia.* New York: HarperCollins, 1996.

Neier, Aryeh. *War Crimes.* New York: Times Books, 1998.

Nelson, Craig. *Thomas Paine.* New York: Viking, 2006.

Newman, Frank, and David Weissbrodt (eds.). *International Human Rights: Law, Policy, and Process.* Cincinnati: Anderson, 1990.

Nkrumah, Kwame. *Towards Colonial Freedom.* London: Panaf, 1973.

Nolde, O. Frederick. *Freedom's Charter: The Universal Declaration of Human Rights.* New York: Foreign Policy Association, 1949.

Normand, Roger, and Sarah Zaidi. *Human Rights at the UN.* Bloomington: University of Indiana Press, 2007.

Odinga, Oginga. *Not Yet Uhuru: The Autobiography of Oginga Odinga.* New York: Hill & Wang, 1967.

Oliver, Roland, and Anthony Atmore. *Africa Since 1800.* Cambridge: Cambridge University Press, 1981.

Oppenheim, L. *International Law: A Treatise.* London: Longmans, 1912.

Ouguergouz, Fatsah. *La Charte africaine des droits de l'homme et des peuples.* Paris: Presses Universitaires de France, 1993.

Paine, Thomas. *The Rights of Man.* New York: Heritage Press, 1961.

Perera, L. P. N. *Buddhism and Human Rights.* Columbo: Karunaratne, 1991.

Périgord, Paul. *The International Labor Organization.* New York: Appleton, 1926.

Plummer, Brenda Gayle. *Rising Wind: Black Americans and U.S. Foreign Affairs.* Chapel Hill: University of North Carolina Press, 1996.

Power, Jonathan. *Like Water on Stone: The Story of Amnesty International.* Boston: Northeastern University Press, 2001.

Power, Samantha. *A Problem from Hell: America and the Age of Genocide*. New York: Basic Books, 2002.

Power, Samantha and Graham Allison (eds.). *Realizing Human Rights: Moving from Inspiration to Impact*. New York: Palgrave Macmillan, 2006.

Quataert, Jean. *Advocating Dignity: Human Rights Mobilizations in Global Politics*. Philadelphia: University of Pennsylvania Press, 2009.

Quirk, Joel. *Unfinished Business: A Comparative Survey of Historical and Contemporary Slavery*. Paris: UNESCO, 2006.

Rabbèn, Linda. *Fierce Legion of Friends: A History of Human Rights Campaigns and Campaigners*. Hyattsville, Md.: Quixote Center, 2002.

Ramcharan, B. G. *The Concept and Present Status of the International Protection of Human Rights*. Dordecht: Kluwer, 1989.

Rawls, John. *A Theory of Justice*. New York: Belknap, 2005.

Rejali, Darius. *Torture and Democracy*. Princeton, N.J.: Princeton University Press, 2009.

Risse, Thomas, et al. (eds.). *The Power of Human Rights*. Cambridge: Cambridge University Press, 1999.

Robertson, A. H., and J. G. Merrills. *Human Rights in the World: An Introduction to the Study of International Protection of Human Rights*. Manchester: Manchester University Press, 1992.

Robertson, Geoffrey. *Crimes Against Humanity: The Study for Global Justice*. New York: New Press, 2002.

Robinson, Jacob. *Human Rights and Fundamental Freedoms in the Charter of the United Nations*. New York: Institute of Jewish Affairs, 1946.

Robinson, Nehemiah. *The Universal Declaration of Human Rights: Its Origins, Significance, and Interpretation*. New York: Institute of Jewish Affairs, 1950.

Rosenbaum, Alan (ed.). *The Philosophy of Human Rights: International Perspectives*. Westport, Conn.: Greenwood, 1980.

Rousseau, Jean-Jacques. *Contrat social, ou principes du droit politique*. Paris: Garnier, 1900.

Rudé, George. *Ideology and Popular Protest*. New York: Pantheon, 1980.

Rupp, Leila. *Worlds of Women: The Making of an International Women's Movement*. Princeton, N.J.: Princeton University Press, 1997.

Russell, Ruth. *A History of the United Nations Charter*. Washington, D.C.: Brookings Institution, 1958.

Said, Edward. *Orientalism*. New York: Vintage, 1979.

Schabas, William. *An Introduction to the International Criminal Court*. Cambridge: Cambridge University Press, 2001.

Schulz, William. *In Our Own Best Interest: How Defending Human Rights Benefits Us All*. Boston: Beacon, 2001.

Schwelb, Egon. *Human Rights and the International Community*. Chicago: Quadrangle Books, 1964.

Sée, Henri. *Histoire de la Ligue des Droits de l'Homme*. Paris: Ligue des Droits de l'Homme, 1927.

Sellars, Kirsten. *The Rise and Rise of Human Rights*. Stroud: Sutton, 2002.

Sen, Amartya. *Development as Freedom*. New York: Anchor, 2000.

Shue, Henry. *Basic Rights*. Princeton, N.J.: Princeton University Press, 1997.

Simpson, A. W. Brian. *Human Rights and the End of Empire*. New York: Oxford University Press, 2001.

Sithole, Ndabaningi. *African Nationalism*. London: Oxford University Press, 1959.

Sjahrir, Sutan. *Out of Exile*. New York: Greenwood, 1969.

Skilling, H. Gordon. *Charter 77 and Human Rights in Czechoslovakia*. London: Allen & Unwin, 1981.

Sklar, Kathryn Kish. *Women's Rights Emerges Within the Anti-Slavery Movement, 1830–1870*. Boston: Bedford, 2000.

Slaughter, Joseph. *Human Rights, Inc.: The World Novel, Narrative Form, and International Law* New York: Fordham University Press, 2007.

Smith, Bradley. *Reaching Judgment at Nuremberg.* New York: New American Library, 1977.

Sohn, Louis, and Thomas Buergenthal. *International Protection of Human Rights.* Indianapolis: Bobbs-Merrill, 1973.

Soohoo, Cynthia, et al (eds.). *Bringing Human Rights Home.* Philadelphia: University of Pennsylvania Press, 2009.

Stanton, Elizabeth Cady, et al. (eds.). *History of Woman Suffrage.* 2 vols. New York: Charles Mann, 1881.

Steiner, Henry, and Philip Alston. *International Human Rights in Context.* Oxford: Clarendon Press, 2000.

Stewart, James B. *Holy Warriors: The Abolitionists and American Slavery.* New York: Hill & Wang, 1976.

Swidler, Arlene (ed.). *Human Rights in Religious Traditions.* New York: Pilgrim Press, 1982.

Tabandeh, Sultanhussein. *A Muslim Commentary on the Universal Declaration of Human Rights.* London: Goulding, 1970.

Taylor, Robert (ed.). *The Idea of Freedom in Asia and Africa.* Stanford, Calif.: Stanford University Press, 2002.

Tesón, Fernando. *Humanitarian Intervention: Ethical, Legal, and Political Dilemmas.* Ardsley-on-Hudson, N.Y.: Transnational, 1988.

Thomas, Daniel. *The Helsinki Effect: International Norms, Human Rights, and the Demise of Communism.* Princeton, N.J.: Princeton University Press, 2001.

Thompson, E. P. *The Making of the English Working Class.* New York: Pantheon, 1964.

Thorn, James. *Peter Fraser, New Zealand's Wartime Prime Minister.* London: Odhams, 1952.

Tolley, Howard, Jr. *The International Commission of Jurists: Global Advocates for Human Rights.* Philadelphia: University of Pennsylvania Press, 1994.

———. *The U.N. Commission on Human Rights.* Boulder, Colo.: Westview, 1987.

Troclet, Léon-Eli. *Législation sociale internationale.* 3 vols. Brussels: Librairie Encyclopédique, 1952.

Tuck, Richard. *Natural Rights Theories: Their Origin and Development.* Cambridge: Cambridge University Press, 1998.

Umozurike, U. Oji. *The African Charter on Human and Peoples' Rights.* The Hague: Nijhoff, 1997.

Urquart, Brian. *Ralph Bunche.* New York: Norton, 1993.

Van Dyke, Vernon. *Human Rights, the United States, and the World Community.* New York: Oxford University Press, 1970.

Vattel, Emerich de. *Le Droit des gens, ou principes de la loi naturelle.* Washington, D.C.: Carnegie, 1916.

Veerman, Philip. *Rights of the Child and the Changing Nature of Childhood.* Dordrecht: Nijhoff, 1992.

Verdoodt, Albert. *Naissance et signification de la Déclaration universelle des droits de l'homme.* Louvain-Paris: Nauwelaerts, 1964.

Vincent, R. J. *Human Rights and International Relations.* Cambridge: Cambridge University Press, 1986.

Vogelgesang, Sandy. *American Dream, Global Nightmare: The Dilemma of U.S. Human Rights Policy.* New York: Norton, 1980.

Walters, F. P. *A History of the League of Nations.* 2 vols. London: Oxford University Press, 1952.

Wasserstrom, Jeffrey, et al. (eds.). *Human Rights and Revolutions.* Lanham, Md.: Rowman & Littlefield, 2000.

Wei Jingsheng. *Courage to Stand Alone.* New York: Penguin, 1998.

Weinberger, Gerda. *Gegen Rassismus und Rassendiskriminierung.* Berlin: Staatsverlag der DDR, 1976.

Welch, Claude, and Virginia Leary (eds.). *Asian Perspectives on Human Rights.* Boulder, Colo.: Westview, 1990.

Welles, Sumner. *World of the Four Freedoms.* New York: Simon & Schuster, 1943.

Wells, H. G. *The Rights of Man or What Are We Fighting For?* Harmondsworth: Penguin, 1940.

Weston, Burns and Stephen Marks (eds.). *The Future of International Human Rights.* Ardsley, N.Y.: Transnational, 1999.

Wilson, Ellen Gibson. *Thomas Clarkson.* New York: St. Martin's, 1990.

Wollstonecraft, Mary. *A Vindication of the Rights of Woman.* New York: Norton, 1988.

Wronka, Joseph. *Human Rights and Social Policy in the 21st Century.* Lanham, Md.: University Press of America, 1992.

Yü-sheng, Lin. *The Crisis of Chinese Consciousness.* Madison: University of Wisconsin Press, 1979.

Zilversmit, Arthur. *The First Emancipation: The Abolition of Slavery in the North.* Chicago: University of Chicago Press, 1967.

Articles

Annan, Kofi. "Two Concepts of Sovereignty." *The Economist,* 18 September 1999.

"Atrocities." *Life,* 7 May 1945.

Aung San Suu Kyi. "Freedom, Development, and Human Worth." *Democracy* 6, 2 (1995): 12–19.

Beckerlegge, Gwilym. "Human Rights in the Ramakrishna Math and Mission," *Religion* (April 1990): 119–37.

Benenson, Peter. "The Forgotten Prisoners." *The Observer,* 18 May 1961.

Bunch, Charlotte. "Women's Rights as Human Rights: A Re-Vision of Human Rights." *Human Rights Quarterly* 12 (1990): 486–98.

Burgers, J. Herman. "The Road to San Francisco: The Revival of the Human Rights Idea in the Twentieth Century." *Human Rights Quarterly* 14 (1992): 447–77.

Carozza, Paolo. "From Conquest to Constitutions: Retrieving a Latin American Tradition of the Idea of Human Rights." *Human Rights Quarterly* 25 (2003): 281–313.

Cassin, René. "La Déclaration universelle et la mise en oeuvre des droits de l'homme." *Recueil des Cours de l'Académie de Droit International,* 79 (1951): 241–367.

Cmiel, Kenneth. "The Recent History of Human Rights." *American Historical Review* 109 (February 2004): 117–35.

Cook, Helena. "International Human Rights Mechanisms: The Role of Special Procedure in the Protection of Human Rights." *International Commission of Jurists Review* 50 (1993): 31–55.

Coursier, Henri. "L'Evolution du droit international humanitaire." *Recueil des Cours de l'Académie de Droit International* 99 (1960): 361–465.

"Les Droits de l'homme et du citoyen." *Revue Diplomatique* (31 October 1933): 6–7.

Du Bois, W. E. B. "Opinion." *Crisis,* 18 (May 1919): 7.

Duse, Mohamed. "Today: India and Africa." *African Times and Orient Review* (March 1917): 46.

Fischer, Dana. "Reporting Under the Covenant on Civil and Political Rights." *American Journal of International Law* 76 (1982): 142–53.

Fonteyne, Jean-Pierre. "The Customary International Law Doctrine of Humanitarian Intervention." *California Western International Law Journal* 4 (1974): 203–58.

Frangulis, Antoine. "Droits de l'homme." *Dictionnaire diplomatique.* Paris: Hoche, 1937.

Franck, Thomas. "Are Human Rights Universal?" *Foreign Affairs* 80 (2001): 191–204.

Fraser, Arvonne. "Becoming Human: The Origins and Development of Women's Human Rights." *Human Rights Quarterly* 21 (1999): 853–906.

"Human Rights: A Suitable Target for Foreign Policy?" *The Economist* (12–18 April 1997): 15–16, 21–25.

Jin Yongjian. "Asia's Major Human Rights Concerns." *Beijing Review* 36 (19–25 April 1993): 10–11.

Johnson, M. Glen. "The Contributions of Eleanor and Franklin Roosevelt to the Development of International Protection for Human Rights." *Human Rights Quarterly* 9 (1987): 33–47.

Kaufman, Natalie Hevener, and David Whiteman. "Opposition to Human Rights Treaties in the "United States Senate: The Legacy of the Bricker Amendment." *Human Rights Quarterly* 10 (1988): 309–37.

Kia, Mehrdad. "Mizra Fath Ali Akhundzade and the Call for Modernization of the Islamic World." *Middle Eastern Studies* 31 (1995): 422–48.

Kim, Dae Jung. "Is Culture Destiny? The Myth of Asia's Anti-Democratic Values." *Foreign Affairs* 73 (1994): 189–94.

Lauren, Paul Gordon. "History and Human Rights: People and Forces in Paradoxical Interaction." *Journal of Human Rights* 7 (April-June 2008): 91–103.

———. "'To Preserve and Build on Its Achievement and to Redress Its Shortcomings': The Journey from the Commission on Human Rights to the Human Rights Council." *Human Rights Quarterly* 29 (2007): 307–45.

Lewis, Jan. "'Of Every Age, Sex, and Condition': The Representation of Women in the Constitution." *Journal of the Early Republic* 15 (Fall 1995): 359–87.

Li Xiaorong. "'Asian Values' and the Universality of Human Rights." *China Rights Forum* (Fall, 1996): 32–35.

Mandelstam, André N. "Les Dernières phases du mouvement pour la protection internationale des droits de l'homme." *Revue de Droit International* (1933): 469–510; (1934): 61–104.

———. "Der internationale Schutz der Menschenrechte und die New-Yorker Erklärung des Instituts für Völkerrecht." *Zeitschrift für ausländisches öffentliches Recht und Völkerrecht* 2 (1931): 335–77.

———. "La Protection internationale des droits de l'homme." *Cahiers des Droits de l'Homme* 31 (10 December 1931): 724–33.

———. "La Protection internationale des droits de l'homme." *Recueil des Cours de l'Académie de Droit International* 38 (1931): 129–229.

Marks, Stephen. "From the 'Single Confused Page.'" *Human Rights Quarterly* 20 (1998): 459–514.

Mirkine-Guetzevitch, M. B. "Quelques problèmes de la mise en œuvre de la Déclaration Universelle des Droits de l'Homme." *Recueil des Cours de l'Académie de Droit International* 82 (1953): 255–376.

Modinos, P. "La Charte de la Liberté de l'Europe." *Revue des Droits de l'Homme* 8 (1975): 676–86.

Möller, Jakob. "Petitioning the United Nations." *Universal Human Rights* 1 (1979): 57–72.

Monshipouri, Mahmood. "Islamic Thinking and the Internationalization of Human Rights." *Muslim World* (July–October 1994): 217–39.

Nolde, O. Frederick. "Possible Functions of the Commission on Human Rights." *Annals of the American Academy of Political and Social Science* 243 (1946): 144–49.

Rougier, Antoine. "La Théorie de l'intervention d'humanité." *Revue Générale de Droit International Public* 17 (1910): 468–526.

Schreiber, Marc. "L'Année internationale de la lutte contre le racisme et la discrimination raciale." *Revue des Droits de l'Homme* 4 (1971): 311–40.

"700 Jahr Rassenkampf," *Neues Volk* 5 (1937): 16–21.

Shestack, Jerome. "The Philosophic Foundations of Human Rights." *Human Rights Quarterly* 20 (1998): 201–34.

Sohn, Louis B. "How American International Lawyers Prepared for the San Francisco Bill of Rights." *American Journal of International Law* 89 (July 1995): 540–53.

Solf, Waldemar. "Protection of Civilians Against the Effects of Hostilities." *American University Journal of International Law and Policy* 1 (1986): 117–35.

Waltz, Susan. "Universalizing Human Rights: The Role of Small States in the Construction of the Universal Declaration." *Human Rights Quarterly* 23 (2001): 44–72.

Weissbrodt, David. "The Role of International Organizations in the Implementation of Human Rights and Humanitarian Law in Situations of Armed Conflict." *Vanderbilt Journal of Transnational Law* 21 (1988): 313–65.

Wiseberg, Laurie. "Protecting Human Rights Activists and NGOs." *Human Rights Quarterly* 13 (1991): 525–44.

Wright, Quincy. "Human Rights and the World Order." *International Conciliation* 389 (1943): 238–62.

Newspapers

Age (Melbourne)
Bombay Chronicle
Chicago Defender
China Daily
Daily Herald
Daily Telegraph
Gegenwart
Guardian
Hindu Times
Illustrated London News
International Herald Tribune
Japan Times
Journal de Genève
Le Monde
Le Monde diplomatique
Morning Standard (Bombay)
New York Times
News Letter [of the League of Colored Peoples]
Otago Witness
Sacramento Union
The Times (London)
Tribune de Genève
Victoria Daily Colonist
Volkischer Beobachter
Washington Post
Xinhau General Overseas News Service
Die Zeit

Web Sites

African Commission on Human and Peoples' Rights. www.achpr.org
Amnesty International. www.amnesty.org
Arab Association for Human Rights. www.arabhra.org
Asia Pacific Forum of National Human Rights Institutions. www.asiapacificforum.net
Asociación Madres de Plaza de Mayo. Www.madres.org
Council of Europe. Commissioner for Human Rights. www.coe.int/t/Commissioner
Derechos Human Rights. www.derechos.org
Fédération Internationale des Droits de l'Homme. www.fidh.org
Freedom House. www.freedomhouse.org
Human Rights in China. www.hrichina.org
Human Rights Council. www.hrgoweb.org/council
Human Rights Documentation Center. www.hrdc.net
Human Rights Forum. www.humanrightspost.com
Human Rights Internet. www.hri.ca
Human Rights Library, University of Minnesota. www1.umn.edu/humanrts/
Human Rights Watch. www.hrw.org
International Criminal Court. www.icc-cpi.int
International Helsinki Federation for Human Rights. www.ihf-hr.org
International Save the Children Alliance. www.savethechildren.net

Ligue des Droits de l'Homme. www.ldh-france.asso.fr

Médecins sans Frontières. www.msf.org

Minority Rights Group International. www.minorityrights.org

The Responsibility to Protect. www.iciss-ciise.gc.ca

United Nations. www.un.org

United Nations. High Commissioner for Refugees. www.unhcr.ch

United Nations. Office of the High Commissioner for Human Rights. www.ohchr.org

Universal Periodic Review. www.upr-info.org

Witness. www.witness.org

Women's Human Rights Net. www.whrnet.org

World Vision International. www.wvi.org

Index

About the Author

Paul Gordon Lauren is the Regents Professor at the University of Montana, where he previously served at the founding director of the Mansfield Center and as the Mansfield Professor of Ethics and Public Affairs. He earned his Ph.D. from Stanford University and has received fellowships and awards for teaching, research, administrative leadership, and public service. He has published many articles, chapters, and books, including the widely acclaimed *Power and Prejudice*. His work is internationally known and has been translated into seven languages, and he has been nominated for a Pulitzer Prize. Lauren has lectured widely to a variety of audiences around the world, including students and professors, activists, analysts, lawyers and judges, diplomats, military and intelligence officers, and policy makers, and delivered invited addresses at the Smithsonian Institution, the Nobel Institute, and before the United Nations, where has been described as possibly the world's leading authority on the history of human rights.